THE SECOND PERIOD OF QUAKERISM

by
William C. Braithwaite, B.A., LL.B.
PRESIDENT OF THE WOODBROOKE SETTLEMENT, SELLY OAK,
NEAR BIRMINGHAM

with
Introduction by
Rufus M. Jones, M.A., D.Litt.
PROFESSOR OF PHILOSOPHY, HAVERFORD COLLEGE, U.S.A.

HERITAGE BOOKS
2009

HERITAGE BOOKS
AN IMPRINT OF HERITAGE BOOKS, INC.

Books, CDs, and more—Worldwide

For our listing of thousands of titles see our website
at
www.HeritageBooks.com

A Facsimile Reprint
Published 2009 by
HERITAGE BOOKS, INC.
Publishing Division
100 Railroad Ave. #104
Westminster, Maryland 21157

Originally published:
MacMillan & Co., Ltd.
St. Martin Street
London
1919

— Publisher's Notice —
In reprints such as this, it is often not possible to remove blemishes from the original. We feel the contents of this book warrant its reissue despite these blemishes and hope you will agree and read it with pleasure.

International Standard Book Numbers
Paperbound: 978-0-7884-2332-1
Clothbound: 978-0-7884-8101-7

PREFACE

THE present volume is a sequel to *The Beginnings of Quakerism*, published in 1912, and completes, after fourteen years, my contribution to the History of the Society of Friends projected by my friend, the late John Wilhelm Rowntree. The wealth of materials that had to be sifted and the pre-occupations of war-time may serve to excuse its somewhat tardy appearance; but the hour is opportune for reviving the brave story of the early Quaker movement now that all serious thought is turning to the reconstruction of the Church catholic and of the Social Order. The past is pregnant with lessons for the present, not indeed by prescribing ready-made solutions for our modern problems, but by showing the spirit of dedication and adventure in which these problems must be faced. We lose its inspiration when we think of it as some far-off age untroubled by the spiritual doubts and difficulties that beset us; closer examination shows that it was crowded with its own perplexities and fateful issues, through which those could walk most worthily who fronted the dawn in glad surrender to its light.

Besides the volume of the Rowntree Series, *Spiritual Reformers in the Sixteenth and Seventeenth Centuries*, by Rufus M. Jones (1914), some further books have been written, fragrant with the bracing air of those early days, especially *Quaker Women, 1650–1690*, by Mabel R.

Brailsford (1915), *A Book of Quaker Saints*, by L. Violet Hodgkin (1917), and *The Personality of George Fox*, by A. Neave Brayshaw (1918), the last a careful collection of the materials which throw light on the character and person of the Founder of Quakerism. Other books, I make no doubt, will be written in the coming years, for there is still much tempting country to be explored. Rufus M. Jones has in preparation the concluding volume of the Rowntree Series, covering the period from 1725 to the present day.

I am very grateful to him for the Introductory Chapter, which deserves close study in amplification of some of my later chapters. Much help has been given me by the Librarians of the Reference Library of the Society of Friends at Devonshire House, and by A. Neave Brayshaw of Scarborough, Joseph Rowntree of York, Prof. G. Lyon Turner, and Charles R. Simpson of Hartshill. Herbert G. Wood, of Woodbrooke, has kindly read the book in proof. Much other incidental assistance is acknowledged in the notes.

CASTLE HOUSE, BANBURY,
November 1918.

NOTE.—For corrections and additions to *Beginnings of Quakerism*, see references in Index under title *Beginnings of Quakerism*. I may correct here note 3, *post*, p. 277. Norman Penney informs me that the minute there referred to is in the MS. Y.M. Records.

NOTE

DATES, so far as month and year are concerned, are given according to New Style (see *Beginnings of Quakerism*, pp. vi, vii), but the day of the month is left unaltered.

Quotations are corrected as to spelling and punctuation; omitted words are indicated by . . . ; words added for completing the sense by square brackets.

The following contractions are used in the notes :—

A.R.B. Colln. A collection in Dev. Ho. of about 250 letters of early Friends. See *Beginnings of Quakerism*, Appendix B.

Besse. Sufferings. See *post*, p. 284 note.

Camb. Journ. Edition of Spence MS. Journ. of Fox, two vols. Cambridge, 1911. See *Beginnings of Quakerism*, Appendix A.

Dev. Ho. for MS. materials preserved in the Friends' Reference Library at Devonshire House, Bishopsgate, London, E.C. See *post*, p. 281.

Extracts from State Papers. Supplements to J.F.H.S.

F.P.T. "The First Publishers of Truth," being early records of the introduction of Quakerism into England and Wales. Edited for the Friends' Historical Society by Norman Penney. London, 1903.

Fleming MSS. Historical MSS. Commission, XIIth Report, Appendix, pt. vii.; "The MSS. of S. H. Le Fleming of Rydal Hall" (1890).

Inner Life. "The Inner Life of the Religious Societies of the Commonwealth," by Robert Barclay, London, 1876. See *post*, p. 543.

Itinerary Journal. Journals in MS. at Dev. Ho. of the last years of Fox. See *post*, p. 433.

J.F.H.S. Journal of the Friends' Historical Society, begun 1903. Edited from Dev. Ho.

Janney's Life. "Life of William Penn," by Samuel M. Janney, sixth edn., revised. Philadelphia, 1882.

Journ. or Ellwood Journ. Ellwood edn. of the Journal of George Fox, originally printed in 1694. References are to Bicentenary edn. in two vols., London, 1891. The text of quotations is corrected to the 1694 edn. For the Journal see *Beginnings of Quakerism*, App. A, and *post*, pp. 427, 428.

Letters of Early Friends. By Abram Rawlinson Barclay. London, 1841.

viii SECOND PERIOD OF QUAKERISM

Life (or Journal). Lives or Journals published under various titles.

MS. "Books of Extracts." See *post*, p. 377.

Sewel. "History of the Rise, Increase and Progress of the Christian people called Quakers," by William Sewel, published in Dutch, 1717, and in English, translated by the author and revised, 1722. I have used the 5th edn., London, 1811, two vols.

Short Journal. By George Fox. See *Beginnings of Quakerism*, Appendix A and *post*, p. 35 note.

Smith's Catalogue. "A Descriptive Catalogue of Friends' Books," by Joseph Smith, two vols. London, 1867.

Spence MSS. vol. iii. Described in *Beginnings of Quakerism*, App. B.

Swarthm. Colln. Swarthmore Collection of MSS. at Dev. Ho., described in *Beginnings of Quakerism*, App. B.

Tanner. Three Lectures. See *post*, p. 205.

Whiting. Persecution Exposed. See *post*, pp. 120 note, 160.

Works. Collected writings of Friends published under various titles.

CONTENTS

INTRODUCTION

(By Rufus M. Jones)

	PAGE
Spiritual Reformers of Reformation period unfriendly to organization	xxiv
The Church of their dream a fellowship, a communion	xxv
Fox began with the same ideal	xxvi
His later organizing work	xxviii
Its admirable fitness to the genius of Quakerism	xxix
Formulation of Quaker doctrine	xxx
Influence of the metaphysics of the time	xxx
Estimate of Robert Barclay	xxxi
The *Apology*, its interpretation of Quakerism	xxxi
Its metaphysical limitations	xxxiii
Quietism and Quakerism	xli
Narrowing of outlook which took place	xliv

BOOK I

THE STRUGGLE FOR RELIGIOUS LIBERTY

CHAPTER I

THE RESTORATION SETTLEMENT

Quotation from Thomas Taylor	3
Hatred of military rule the prime cause of the Restoration	3
Dependence of Charles II. on Parliament	4
The religious settlement	4
Failure of "comprehension" proposals and abortive Savoy Conference	5
Act of Uniformity, 1662, and ejectment on St. Bartholomew's Day (24th August) of "Nonconformist" ministers	5
Religious toleration found no place in Restoration settlement	6
Fear of a Puritan rising	6
Cavalier suspicions of Quakers	8
Fifth Monarchy Rising, January 1661	9

SECOND PERIOD OF QUAKERISM

	PAGE
Wholesale imprisonment of Quakers	9
Declaration against plots and fightings	12
Persecution on a *praemunire*	14
Grounds of testimony against swearing	15
Parallel with the early Christians	15
Quaker testimony opposed to much in existing social order	16
Quaker method of passive resistance and patient suffering	17
Reliance on spiritual weapons meant that the Quaker held convictions in favour of religious liberty and against persecution	18

CHAPTER II

PERSECUTION, 1662–1669

Quotation from Masson	21
Dramatic unity of persecution, 1662–1672	21
The Quaker Act of 1662, and resulting persecution	22
Hubberthorne's death in prison	25
"Signs" by Solomon Eccles and two women	25
Burrough's death in prison	26
Thomas Ellwood's experiences in Newgate	27
Declaration of Indulgence, 26th December 1662	29
Northern Plot of 1663—Kaber Rigg	29
Arrests of Howgill, Fox, and Margaret Fell, and their Trials	31
Howgill's death in Appleby gaol, 1669	37
Margaret Fell's imprisonment and release in 1668	37
Imprisonment of Fox at Scarborough, and release September 1666	37
Northern Plot of 1663—Farnley Wood	39
Fears engendered by the plot led to Conventicle Act of 1664	39
Baxter's description of its effect	41
Proof that Friends bore the brunt of the persecution	41
Hertford sentences of banishment	42
London cases tried in October 1664, etc.	44
Very few actual transportations	45
Cases of the *Mary Fortune* and the *Black Eagle*	46
The Great Plague	47
Courage of London Friends	47
William Caton's epistle to suffering Friends	49
The Conventicle Act in the country	50
No case of sentence of banishment among other Dissenters	51
Probable extent of earnest Baptist witness	51
Courage of Dissenting ministers during the Plague year in London	52
Sheldon procures the Five-Mile or "Oxford" Act	52
Lessening of persecution after the Great Fire	53
Fall of Clarendon and rise of the Cabal	53
1668 a time of religious freedom	54

CHAPTER III

THE SECOND CONVENTICLE ACT, 1670–1673

Quotation from Bishop Burnet	55
William Penn throws in his lot with Friends, 1667	55

CONTENTS

	PAGE
His earlier life	55
Death of Thomas Loe, his spiritual father	60
Penn imprisoned in Tower on account of *Sandy Foundation Shaken*	61
Writes *No Cross, No Crown*; contents of first edition	61
Preparation for a new Conventicle Act	64
Parliament passes the Act : its provisions	66
Anglican services in Quaker meeting-houses	68
Meeting in Gracechurch Street, 14th August 1670	69
Trial of Penn and Meade arising out of it	70
Bushell's case, establishing the independence of juries	73
Death of Admiral Penn	73
Penn imprisoned under Five-Mile Act	74
His *Great Case of Liberty of Conscience*	74
Destruction of Horslydown and Ratcliff meeting-houses	75
Persecution at Bristol	77
The Informers and their unpopularity	78
Dutch War and Declaration of Indulgence of 15th March 1672	81
Great Pardon of 3rd September 1672	82
Declaration cancelled, March 1673	86
Order, 3rd February 1675, for diligent execution of Penal Laws	86
The three years' breathing space the foundation of modern Nonconformity	86

CHAPTER IV

THE LATER DAYS OF PERSECUTION

Quotation from Robert Barclay	88
Embittered politics of second half of reign of Charles II.	88
The Titus Oates Plot and the Whig Parliaments	90
Chief political duty of Quakers to establish supremacy of conscience over unjust law	94
William Penn's active interest in politics	94
The second Stuart despotism, 1681-1685	98
Account of the severe persecution at Bristol, December 1681, etc.	99
How the children kept up the Friends' Meetings	103
Direct use of the Act 35 Eliz. cap. 1, with its ultimate death penalty, in the case of Richard Vickris	107
Persecution of Friends in other parts of the country	108
Political animus against the fanatics, increased by Rye House Plot in spring of 1683	112
Malice and greed of Informers and bigotry of clergy	113
Summary of Quaker sufferings	114

CHAPTER V

THE DAWN OF TOLERATION

Quotation from W. E. H. Lecky	116
Fair prospects of James II. at time of his succession	116
His short-sitting Parliament (May–November 1685)	117

xii   SECOND PERIOD OF QUAKERISM

	PAGE
His friendship for Penn and Barclay, who both believed him sincerely in favour of religious toleration	117
Relief from persecution given to Friends	119
The Monmouth Rebellion : behaviour of Friends	119
The Bloody Assizes and Macaulay's charge against Penn	123
General Pardon of March 1686, and Royal Warrant for releasing Friends	125
The suppression of Informers in London and elsewhere	125
Menaces to European Protestantism in 1685	127
Progress of James in his Roman Catholic policy	127
The dispensing power, and case of *Godden v. Hales*	127
Penn's *Perswasive to Moderation* and visit to William of Orange	128
Declaration for liberty of conscience (March 1687)	130
Explanation of the attitude towards it taken by Friends	131
Penn's entrance and interest with the King	134
Charlwood Lawton's account of his behaviour	135
Purging of corporations, and nomination as alderman in the City of the Baptist leader, William Kiffin	136
Penn's attendance on royal progress through Midlands (August 1687)	138
His efforts in the Magdalen College case	138
His endeavours to check the Jesuit influences that dominated the King	141
Quakers pressed to take offices, both in England and Ireland	143
Manifesto by Prince and Princess of Orange (November 1687)	143
Re-issue of the Declaration of Indulgence, April 1688	143
Trial of the Seven Bishops	144
Invitation to William of Orange	144
Penn a wise friend to James during these critical weeks	144
Discussion on politics at Yearly Meeting of 1688	144
Penn suspected as a Jesuit	146
Barclay also under suspicion : his "Vindication"	149
His last interview with the King	149
Gilbert Latey's prophetic words to James	150

CHAPTER VI

THE TOLERATION ACT

Extract from W. E. H. Lecky	151
Maturing of the great Revolutionary plot	151
Penn's first arrest and discharge	151
The Toleration Act	153
Loss of Comprehension Bill and revision of Tests	156
The "Non-jurors"	156
Indirect influence of Friends in securing Toleration	157
Locke, the great interpreter of the Revolution of 1688	158
The liberal working of the Toleration Act	159
Its effect on the Society of Friends	160
The Quietist Yearly Meeting Epistle of 1689	160
Penn's second arrest, June 1689, and release in November	161
Penn's third arrest, July 1690, and discharge	162
Protestant Jacobite plot of December 1690	162
Warrant for the arrest of Penn, January 1691	163

CONTENTS

	PAGE
Penn goes into hiding	163
His interview with Viscount Sidney	164
Locke's offer of intervention on his behalf	166
Withdrawal of Pennsylvania from his control, October 1691	167
His solace in literary work	168
Some Fruits of Solitude	168
Reconciliation with the King, November 1693	169
Re-grant of Pennsylvania, August 1694	171
Resumption of service in the Society	172
Disaffection towards Penn of an influential section of Friends	172
Country Quakers and his own friends of the governing class able to give him readier forgiveness	175

CHAPTER VII

THE AFTERMATH OF TOLERATION

Advice of Bristol Men's Meeting, 2nd January 1721	177
George Whitehead the leader of the Society for next twenty years: his character	177
Political instability of period 1690–1715	178
Quietist policy of the Whig Quaker leaders	179
Toleration Act gave no relief as to tithes, or the disabilities of Friends in private life	180
Partial relief as to tithes afterwards given	180
The general disabilities mainly due to the necessity of taking oaths	181
The ground of the testimony against oaths	182
Affirmation Act of 1696	183
Dissatisfaction of many Friends with form of words	184
Dissatisfied districts those most zealous in opposing the consequences of wealth and worldliness by pressing a searching discipline on the Quaker Church	189
Division between Friends of Whig and Jacobite leanings	189
Tory reaction culminating at end of Anne's reign	190
Long debates in Yearly Meetings, 1712, etc.	192
Death of Anne and triumph of Whigs	194
Affirmation Act made perpetual	194
Controversy within Society during these years	195
Strong undercurrent of feeling directed against Whitehead	198
Yearly Meetings of 1716, 1717, 1719	200
Affirmation Act of 1722, with satisfactory form	201
Lessons of the Affirmation controversy	204
External history of Friends thenceforward of secondary importance	206
Meade and Penn identified by the outside world with the two extreme parties in the Society itself	207
Death of William Meade 1713, and character	207
Closing years of Penn, 1694–1718	208
Estimate of Penn's life of heroic adventure	211

xiv SECOND PERIOD OF QUAKERISM

BOOK II

SECOND PERIOD OF QUAKERISM
THE PERIOD OF EXPRESSION

CHAPTER VIII

INTERNAL HISTORY AND PROBLEMS, 1660–1668

	PAGE
Quotation from Francis Howgill	215
Quaker Missionary zeal at its height in the Restoration year . .	215
Effect of persecution in arresting organization and checking the itinerating work of " Publishers of Truth " . . .	217
Death-roll of " Publishers of Truth "	219
Illustrations, showing difficulties of itinerating work . . .	219
But the quiet meetings remained centres of power and offered invincible resistance to the authorities	225
Cases of Colchester and Reading	225
The children keep up Reading meeting	226
History of Perrot Division	228
Impression made on many Friends, e.g. Penington, Crook, Ellwood, Richard Davies	235
Perrot's chief champions : William Salt, Charles Bayly, and Jane Stokes	237
Perrot in Barbados and Jamaica : close of his life . . .	238
Fox's trenchant handling of Perrot question	242
Dewsbury's beautiful spirit	242
Farnsworth's powerful confutation	243
Farnsworth's death, June 1666 : Controversy with Muggletonians .	244
His share in the important epistle from Ministers in May 1666 .	247
The Quaker movement narrowed into a religious society . .	248
Quakerism no negative mysticism	248
The Inward Light did not supersede ethical standards but illuminated and raised them	249
Fellowship meant a common witness to a common body of Truth .	249
Quakerism in vital touch both with righteousness of life and with historic religion	249
Development of corporate consciousness and organization were forced upon the movement	250

CHAPTER IX

THE SETTLING OF MONTHLY MEETINGS

Quotation from John Stephenson Rowntree	251
Fox released from Scarborough, September 1666 . . .	251
Fox decided to go through England to set up a system of organization which should call out the service of Friends . . .	251
His conceptions of Church government	252

CONTENTS

	PAGE
Successful meetings in London for reconciling followers of Perrot	253
Setting up of the London Monthly Meetings	253
Setting up of other M.M.'s, and establishment of schools at Waltham Abbey and Shacklewell	253
Fox's "Friends' fellowship must be in the spirit"	256
The new system could only be worked well by men of enlightened spiritual experience	259
Visit of Fox to Ireland, May–August 1669	260
Fox as a minister	261
His marriage to Margaret Fell, at Bristol, 27th October 1669	262
Fox and the Second Conventicle Act	265
Severe illness, and psychical experiences	265
Visit to America, August 1671–June 1673	267
The results illustrate again the value of the itinerant work of inspired leaders	268

CHAPTER X

WOMEN'S MEETINGS AND CENTRAL ORGANIZATION

Quotation from Wm. Penn's Preface to Fox's Journal	269
In organizing Friends, Fox might easily have aggrandized his own position	269
Equality of men and women in spiritual things one of the glories of Quakerism	270
In spring of 1671, Fox took in hand the setting up of Women's Meetings	273
The system made way slowly, advice as late as 1745	274
Success, however, of the London Six Weeks' Meeting on a joint basis	275
Development of central organization	275
Regular Meetings of men ministers decided on, Christmas 1668	276
Representative Yearly Meeting developed, 1672–1678	276
Place of the travelling ministers in any Monthly or Quarterly Meeting that they felt it right to attend	278
The "Morning Meeting"	279
The "Meeting for Sufferings"	281
Position of women unrecognized in the central bodies	286
Women's Yearly Meeting in Ireland as early as 1679	287
Notice of Ellis Hookes, the "Clerk to Friends"	288

CHAPTER XI

THE WILKINSON-STORY SEPARATION

Quotation from Steven Crisp	290
Handling of the Hat question by London Two Weeks' Meeting in 1667	292
Mucklow's *Spirit of the Hat*	292
Epistle of Yearly Meeting of 1673	293
Defection at Preston Patrick through weakness in holding meetings	294
John Story and John Wilkinson	295
Points in issue, 1675	297

xvi   SECOND PERIOD OF QUAKERISM

	PAGE
Important epistle of Yearly Meeting of 1675	300
Draw-well Meeting of April 1676	304
Issue definitely joined in summer of 1676: William Rogers, John Raunce, and Charles Harris	307
Personal animus against Fox	308
Condemnation of Wilkinson and Story after Yearly Meeting of 1677	309
Final separation in Westmorland	311
Position at Bristol	312
High-handed proceedings by Wiltshire Separatists	316
Attitude of Penington, Dewsbury, and Crook	317
Rogers prepares his *Christian-Quaker*	318
Story's last visit to Kendal meeting, October 1681	321
His death, November 1681	323
Wilkinson's last years	323

CHAPTER XII

CONCEPTIONS OF CHURCH GOVERNMENT

Quotation from Dr. John Oman	324
Need for strengthening discipline	324
Issue raised of limits of spiritual liberty and of Church government	324
Difference in atmosphere from that belonging to the self-reliant, self-controlled type of personality created by free institutions	325
Lawrence Steel's experience	325
Penington on obedience and liberty	326
Crisp's analysis of tendencies at work in the Society	327
The effect of discipline in creating a compelling tradition of well-ordered and noble life	328
Vindication of Church government engaged the pen of a young Scottish convert, Robert Barclay	328
Story of the Quaker group that arose at Aberdeen about 1663	328
Alexander Jaffray, the central figure: his experience	328
Patrick Livingstone and George Keith	333
Robert Barclay's early life and convincement in 1666	334
John Swinton's probable influence	336
Anarchy of the Ranters, 1674	340
Barclay's high doctrine of Church authority	340
Rogers' opposing individualistic view	342
True doctrine: the Church has authority, and the individual has liberty in the Life, but not out of it	346
Quaker position taken at the Draw-well meeting	347
Declaration by Yearly Meeting of Ministers in 1676	348
Barbados case, and its recommendation of implicit faith	348

CHAPTER XIII

THE WORK OF THE TRAVELLING MINISTERS

Quotation from Skipton Epistle of 1660	351
High missionary zeal at Restoration	351
Convincement in Mid-Wales	352

CONTENTS

xvii

	PAGE
Expansion in Cumberland	353
Renewed activity of itinerating ministers	356
Contributions towards support of Travelling Ministers	360
Rogers' rhymed *Second Scourge for George Whitehead*	361
Ellwood's rhymed reply in *Rogero-Mastix*	362
Extracts from Yorkshire Records showing way in which help was given	362
John Burnyeat's service	366
John Banks, his experiences	367
Fox cures his numbed arm: note on "Spiritual Healing by early Friends"	368
Leonard Fell and his encounter with a highwayman	369
John Gratton's *Journal* and his experience	370
Latent Puritanism of the Restoration period	374

CHAPTER XIV

FORMULATION OF FAITH

Quotation from statement issued with approval of London Yearly Meeting, 1917	376
Quakerism developed testimonies rather than Articles of Faith	377
The formation of the MS. "Books of Extracts"	377
Early doctrinal statements	378
Isaac Penington's writings the best clue to the theological explanation that Quakerism had to give of its Faith	380
His dualistic conception of the Incarnation	383
Robert Barclay's Scottish mentality	385
His *Catechism*, *Theses Theologicae*, and *Apology*	386
His doctrine of the Seed, or Divine Principle in the hearts of all men	388
Criticism by Keith from standpoint of current theology	391
Criticism by John Norris from idealistic standpoint	392
Our modern conception	394
The truth of Barclay's and Penington's underlying experience	396

CHAPTER XV

QUAKER COLONIZATION

Quotation from William Penn	399
Puritan colonization	399
Period of Quaker self-expression, which followed the period of persecution	401
The Jerseys the earliest field of enterprise	402
Penn receives the grant of Pennsylvania, 4th March 1681	403
The glad comradeship of the early settlers	406
The migration to the Quaker colonies stripped the Society of many of its most active spirits, and must be counted among the causes of the decline into Quietism	408
Criticism by Friends of this emigration	409
Cases of actual fleeing from persecution few	411
Summary of William Penn's work as a colonizer	411

b

xviii   SECOND PERIOD OF QUAKERISM

	PAGE
John Archdale, the other Quaker colonizer of front rank	412
The meaning of colonization to the Quaker movement	414
Greatness of spirit that was shown, in spite of limiting conditions	415

CHAPTER XVI

THE PASSING OF THE LEADERS

Quotation from William Penn	416
Quaker usage as to tombstones	417
Collected writings of Friends : particulars	417
Note as to printing of Quaker Books	418
Piety Promoted	420
Religious Journals the most distinctive form of Quaker literature	420
First printed Journals those of William Caton (1689) and John Burnyeat (1691)	421
Other Journals of special interest—Richard Davies (1710), Elizabeth Stirredge (1711), Thomas Ellwood (1714), William Edmondson (1715), John Gratton (1720), George Whitehead (1725), Christopher Story (1726), John Roberts (1746), Thomas Story (1747), Thomas Chalkley (1749), Samuel Bownas (1756), Thomas Gwin (MS.)	421
Printing of George Fox's *Journal* in 1694	427
Sketch of Fox's later life, 1673–1691	427
Journal and particulars of closing days (5th–13th January 1691)	433
The character of Fox	437
His letter to Christian Barclay on death of her husband	444
Robert Barclay's death (October 1690) and character	445
Peter Gardner's mission to Ury in 1694	447
Dewsbury's death (June 1688) and character	449
Death and character of Steven Crisp, August 1692	452
Reference to death of other leaders	454
How far would later generations imitate their faith?	454

BOOK III

POSITION AND OUTLOOK AT CLOSE OF THE CENTURY

CHAPTER XVII

THE CLOSING YEARS OF THE CENTURY

Quotation from Norfolk Petition, 1699	457
Statistics of Friends at close of century	457
Social condition of Friends	460
Reports to Yearly Meeting as to state of Society	462
An adverse description of Friends about 1700	462
Growth in Norfolk, Lincolnshire, Yorkshire, Cumberland	464
Digression narrating Thomas Story's experience	466
Further fortunes of the Separatist movements	469
Reading	470

CONTENTS

	PAGE
Hertfordshire and Buckinghamshire	474
Separations in Yorkshire	475
Wiltshire, Bristol, Westmorland	478
Separatist meeting at Harp Lane, London	481
The Keith Separation	482
Storm of controversy after the Toleration Act	487
Francis Bugg's writings	487
Leslie's *Snake in the Grass*	488
Norfolk Petition and dispute at West Dereham	490
Keith's meeting at Turner's Hall	491
The mission-work of the S.P.C.K. and S.P.G. for converting Quakers	492
Keith's later life	493
Influence on the Society of the Wilkinson-Story and Keith separations	494
Quaker examination of its own orthodoxy	495

CHAPTER XVIII

THE QUAKER WAY OF LIFE

Quotation from John Whitehead	497
The inward law by which the Quaker lived	497
Prosperity clogging the spiritual life of Friends	499
Irish Friends seek to overcome worldliness by a close discipline	502
Advices as to plainness of dress, etc., in the North of England and in Scotland	510
Tendency to substitute legalism for the control of the Spirit	516
Protest by Margaret Fox	517
Estimate of question by Samuel Bownas	519
The authentic Quaker discipline of taking up the cross	522

CHAPTER XIX

PROBLEMS OF EDUCATION AND THE MINISTRY

Quotation from John Wilhelm Rowntree	524
Difference between the 17th-century and the modern conception of life	524
Early Quaker schools, especially Latin schools	525
Educational views of Fox and Penn	528
Prosecutions for teaching school without licence from bishop	532
Quaker view that learning was no necessary qualification for the ministry	533
Advices as to training of children	535
Restricted view of education that came to prevail	536
No proper cultivation of a soil suited for growing of leaders	538
Formalism prevailing among the young	539
The inward way of growth still dynamic when followed	540
Negative advices to ministers, issued in 1702	541
Constraint exercised by institution of Elders not in the ministry	542
Within a contracted sphere, ministers still did fine work	544
Growth of district "Circular Yearly Meetings" for worship	546
Character of the Quaker ministry of the period	549
Luke Cock's Sermon at York, 1721	551

xx   SECOND PERIOD OF QUAKERISM

CHAPTER XX

THE CHURCH AND SOCIAL QUESTIONS

	PAGE
Quotation from Sir Philip Sidney's *Apologie for Poetrie*	554
Early Quaker message social as well as religious	554
Summary of its social characteristics	556
Reference to Gerrard Winstanley and the "social levellers"	556
Social views of Fox, Lawson and others at end of Commonwealth period	557
Commercial integrity and justice in social dealings	560
Care by Friends of their own poor	565
Schemes for employment of poor prisoners and for setting poor to work	568
John Bellers; his spiritual experience	571
His *Proposals for raising A Colledge of Industry*, 1695	576
Bristol and Clerkenwell Workhouses	585
His further proposals: the improvement of medicine, criminal law, party spirit in politics, purity of elections, projects for Christian unity and for Peace of Europe	587
Penn's *Essay towards the Present and Future Peace of Europe*	590
Estimate of Bellers' service as a social pioneer	593
Other philanthropic service of Friends: position on temperance and slavery	594
Quaker method of confronting conscience of world with the new light and bearing personal witness to it with undaunted patience	596
The redemptive function of the Church towards the Social Order	596

CHAPTER XXI

THE CHURCH AND THE STATE

Quotation from *Epistle to Diognetus*	598
The Christian has his paramount duty as a servant of the kingdom of God, and also his position as a member of the State	598
Threefold contribution of Early Friends :—	
(1) Their protest against invasion of conscience by the State	599
(2) Their equally clear law-abiding conscience, in all just and good commands	600
(3) Their assertion of the "prophetic" function of the Church towards the State	602
Re-verification and enlargement of this threefold position needed to-day	604
The religious spirit of self-control which lies at root of our democratic self-government	607
Application of above to position taken as to war	608
Inspiration and limitations of Quaker seventeenth-century attitude	608
Not passive and negative, but a crusade for kingdom of God through the energy of righteousness and love and the strength of dedication to the Cross	610
Problems arising from existence of world-order side by side with this higher kingdom	610
Treatment of subject by Penington, Barclay, and Thomas Story	610
John Crook's *Way to a Lasting Peace*: Smith's *Banner of Love*	613

CONTENTS

	PAGE
Official document by Friends against plots	615
Richard Seller, the Yorkshire fisherman	615
Early discipline connected with bearing arms	616
Sufferings in Barbados	618
Question of joining in patrol-work, etc.	620
Difficulties of peace-testimony where Friends in America were in seat of power	621
Early Quaker witness of permanent value where outcome of a heavenly-minded order of life	623
Story, in closing, of behaviour of Irish Friends during the war between James and William	624

CHAPTER XXII

THE CHURCH AND THE KINGDOM OF GOD

Quotation from John Wilhelm Rowntree	630
Progress depends on living elements of past, present, and future co-operating in growth	630
The Quaker movement came to be resting on its past, enjoying ease of present and losing its vision	631
Thomas Story on the Dutch Mennonites in 1715	632
Failure to nourish a first-hand experience in the new generations	632
The problem of fostering inspired leadership	633
Failure to relate fully the experience of the Inward Light to the Historic Life of Christ	635
Failure to overcome a worldly and Quietist environment	636
The validity of the experience of the Inward Light the master-clue to the problems of Quaker history	637
Herein lies the great contribution of Quakerism to the basis for a catholic Christianity	638
Universal conceptions of early Friends, quotations from Burrough, Penington, and Penn	639
Need for a universal spirit in the Church to-day	641
Bishop Lightfoot's ideal for the kingdom of God	642
Bishop Westcott's sketch of the Christian fellowships of the future	644
The Franciscan Friars, the Moravians, the Quakers	644
The Quaker Church called to fresh days of daring and dedication	645
Closing quotations from John Wilhelm Rowntree	646
INDEX	649

INTRODUCTION

By RUFUS M. JONES

IN *The Beginnings of Quakerism* we were dealing at every point with a "movement." It was creative, enthusiastic, and full of surprises. In this volume Quakerism is still a movement, but it is plainly in the stage of organization, consolidation, and congealment. When the creative leaders of the great period pass off the scene, as they do toward the end of this volume, we find that the movement is pretty well stiffened and arrested, and that a system is emerging. We are passing from dynamic to static Quakerism. So long as the world continued hostile to it, and endeavoured to suppress it or transform it, it revealed an amazing vitality and energy of endurance. The men and women who shaped the Quaker history of the creative stage were sublimely indifferent to consequences. They were possessed of a vision and dedicated to a mission which made everything else on earth secondary and more or less unimportant. That situation makes an heroic story, but the very success of the policy of uncompromising endurance makes the later epochs of Quakerism less heroic and less interesting. The work of forcing back the sea and building the dykes makes necessarily a different type of persons from those who are "born to peace in the lee of the dykes." All movements of every sort undergo some such change of type.

It would seem appropriate that this Introduction should deal in the main with the transforming effect of consolidation and organization, since this is the peculiar aspect which forms the connecting link between the preceding volume and the final succeeding volume of this series.[1]

My preliminary researches, in *Studies in Mystical Religion* and in *Spiritual Reformers of the Sixteenth and Seventeenth Centuries*, have conclusively shown that there was a long historical preparation for the Quaker movement, and that it was a legitimate outcome of this painful travail of lonely souls and persecuted groups who were striving for an adequate spiritual reformation of the Church. One of the most remarkable features of this historical preparation was the almost complete absence of organization throughout the entire period. The movement went steadily forward by the propagation and transmission of ideas, by personal inspiration and by what, for want of a better term, we call contagion of ideals. Nobody during this time appeared with a genius for organization. In fact, the aspirations of the spirit of the movement were positively unfriendly to organization. As is the case with all movements which are at heart profoundly mystical, the leaders of this movement were afraid of the hampering, contracting effects of method and system, and, as a consequence, it maintained its fluidity for more than a hundred years without ever losing its power of propagation or its contagious growth.

The Church which the spiritual reformers aimed to create was an invisible Church, rather than a visible, organized, and empirical one. They took the early unorganized stage of apostolic Christianity as their model. They no doubt somewhat idealized and glorified this apostolic Church of saints, but so, too, did all types of reformers idealize the primitive Church and set it in sharp contrast to the Church with which they were familiar. Luther himself, in his early reforming period, conceived of the true Church as a spiritual congregation, composed only of the new-born, transformed persons, possessed of faith and insight, and all together ministering to the spiritual

---

[1] To be called *The Later Stage of Quakerism*, now being written by the Editor of the Series.

life of all. "I believe," he wrote, "that there is on earth, wide as the world is, only one holy universal Christian Church, which is nothing else than the community [*Gemeinde*] of the saints."[1] This conception always remained as the ideal of the spiritual reformers. The mediaeval Church, with its creeds, its hierarchy, its magical sacraments, its compromises with the world, its external imperial authority, its ambitions, its corruptions, its multitude of nominal or titular members, seemed to these high-minded idealists "an apostate Church," incapable of being reformed. It was to them a work of misguided "Babel-builders." They utterly disapproved of the course which they saw the great reformers, Luther, Zwingli and Calvin, taking to correct and remedy the intolerable situation. The alliance with the State, which was a feature of all reformed Churches, seemed to them an unholy alliance. The survivals of untransformed theology, the preservation of ancient superstitions, the continuance in the new Churches of unspiritual, nominal members, the exaltation of the letter of Scripture, and the use of persecution as a method of forcing uniformity appeared to them to be regrettable relics of paganism and apostasy. They would have none of it.

They were determined to create, or rather to restore, a wholly different type of Church. It was to have no connection whatever with the State. It was to have no infallible creed. It was to be governed by no authoritative hierarchy. It was to have no *essential* forms, rites, ritual, or ceremonies. It was not even to be an "organization" in the strict sense of the word. It was to be a fellowship, a society, a communion. All persons in all lands and in all ages who have been born of God, who partake of Christ's spirit, who are united in the bonds of love, who are travailing for the Kingdom of God, who experience the communion of the Holy Spirit, belong to this Church. It is thus both visible and invisible. It is on the earth but at the same time a super-temporal communion. It is the bride of Christ, the organ of the

[1] *Sämmtliche Werke* (Erlangen edn.), xxii. p. 20.

Spirit, the entire congregation and assembly of the saints. It is tied and bound to no fixed and unchanging external system or order. It is the growing, expanding revelation of God through men, and its one essential mark is *life*, but always life revealing itself through love and sacrifice and service. As Sebastian Franck (1499–1542) enthusiastically declares: " It is neither prince nor peasant, food nor drink, hat nor coat, here nor there, yesterday nor to-morrow, baptism nor circumcision, nor anything whatever that is external, but peace and joy in the Holy Spirit, unalloyed love out of a pure heart and good conscience, and an unfeigned faith."[1] These men, though trained in the universities of their time, were childlike in their naïve simplicity. They assumed that religion as a living, inward experience would take care of itself in the world. It would need no external supports nor contrivances. Christ, the eternal Word, the Spirit of Truth, the Light shining immediately in the human soul, would guard, guide, protect, create, construct His own Church, if only men would let Him work unhindered. Once more as in the creative apostolic days, the Spirit would fall upon the obedient, responsive, faithful believers, endow them with gifts, endue them with power, and through them continue His revelation of Light, Life, Love, and Truth. Their Church was thus to be spontaneous, free, vital, expanding, joyous, and potentially universal, because it was to be the one body of Christ.

There can be, I think, no question that George Fox began his mission with that ideal in mind. He became convinced that all existing Churches were in " apostasy." The preface to his *Great Mistery* (1658), though actually written by Edward Burrough, clearly expresses Fox's mind and position. This remarkable document says: " As our hearts inclined to the light which shined in every one of us we came to know the perfect estate of the Church ; her estate before the apostles' days, and in the apostles' days, and since the days of the apostles. Her present state we found to be as a woman who had once

[1] *Paradoxa*, Vorrede, Sect. 45.

INTRODUCTION xxvii

been clothed with the sun and the moon under her feet, who had brought forth him that was to rule the nations; but she had fled into the wilderness and was there sitting desolate!" Again it says: "As for all Churches (so called) and professions and gatherings of people, we beheld you all in the apostasy and degeneration from the true Church, not being gathered by the Spirit of the Lord, nor anointed thereby, as the true members of Christ ever were, but to be in a form, and in forms of righteousness without the power, and in imitations without life and perfect knowledge." This preface boldly declares that no true reformation has yet taken place, and that the existing Churches lack a true worship, a real religion, and practices that have life and power.

George Fox and his early followers believed that they were called to carry out the true reformation, to restore apostolic Christianity, and to make a fresh beginning in England of the Church of Christ. They never thought of themselves as a "sect," or as one "Church" among many Protestant "Churches." They thought of themselves as forming a group, a fellowship, a society they called it, of persons who were a living part of this true Church of the ages. All saints who have ever lived and who have shaped their spiritual lives by the light of Christ were members with them and with them constituted the true "Seed of God," the one Church, with Christ as its Head and Life. They believed that this Church was as wide as the world, and they went forth with unbounded faith and enthusiasm to discover in all lands those who were true fellow-members with them in this great household of God, and who were the hidden Seed of God. It was not to be a man-made or a man-governed institution. It was to be a Christ-made and a Christ-governed society or body. It was in conception a living organism rather than an organization. It was in ideal to be the work and creation of the Spirit of Christ, operating from within: and not the work and creation of human hands, building from the outside. In theory the Society had no visible head. Nobody managed it, nobody directed it. Every step was taken, however momentous, however trivial, by the entire group acting, as it believed, under the direction and guidance of the Spirit. All ministry was, in ideal, Divinely initiated and given through unordained persons who had listened and heard and who spoke because the word of God had come to them. All the work of propagation, the efforts to reach and gather the hidden Seed of God, were undertaken by men and women who were "called" out and qualified for this Divine business.

It is a mark of the wisdom and sanity of George Fox that, mystic and idealist as he was, he faced the facts of life, he learnt from experience, he came to see that disembodied spiritual movements cannot succeed and do a permanent work in the world; and, when the hour came for it, he took the leadership in organizing the Society of Friends for its abiding, expanding mission. This was obviously a delicate and difficult undertaking. It was in some degree a surrender of the original ideal, perhaps we had better say of the primitive dream. John Wilkinson and John Story, the leaders of the opposition to the organizing work of Fox, were endeavouring to stand uncompromisingly for the "pure" primitive ideal. They were the champions of an abstract liberty, theorists who refused utterly to regard consequences or to take account of things as they are. They defied experience. Fox, on the other hand, yielded to the pressure of unescapable facts. He had been a keen observer of events and tendencies within the fellowship of which he was the leading spirit. He noted the disintegrating forces. He saw the necessity for co-operation, even though it might involve some surrender of individual privilege. He was willing to adjust to the conditions and requirements of social or group existence, though it meant a reduction of his early ideals. There was no way of going forward at all without some compromise of abstract theory. Usually "stiff as a tree," in the words of his Scarborough jailers, he bent in this crisis and thus gave his movement the possibility of a successful future. Deep-seated troubles and hampering limitations lay concealed in the system of organization that was gradually worked out for the growing Society, but *any* type of organization that might have been adopted would have brought its peculiar difficulties and its limitations to this enthusiastic, spiritual undertaking. To organize is to come under the sway of habit and custom. It more or less locks up a movement and turns it into a system. Initiative decreases. Plural possibilities are eliminated. Enthusiasm wanes. A cooling process succeeds. Conservatism and loyalty to the *status quo* become powerful forces. The very things which make life possible entail at the same time perils and dangers.

It must be said, however, that the primitive form of organization which was gradually worked out by George Fox and his helpers for the Society of Friends was admirably fitted to the genius of the movement. They gave as much scope as was possible under any system for the free, unhindered circulation of the Spirit. They got as far away as possible from the model of the state-Church, the Church as conceived and constructed by the great Protestant reformers. They kept close to the ideal of a fellowship of believers, living in obedience to the Spirit revealed within them. Their Society was in idea a complete democracy, that is to say no imposed official or head was ever to interfere with any member's individual liberty. And yet it was to be a democracy of a new type. The individuals composing the Society were no longer to be thought of as bare, isolated, self-seeking units, acting capriciously. Each member of the Society was, in their thought, an over-individual. He was to be a partaker of the life of the Spirit; he was to be an organ of the indwelling Christ; he was inwardly to be raised into new and corporate life with all the other members. It was thus in thought and purpose a Divine democracy, a real communion of saints, living here below but sharing the life and mind of the eternal, invisible Christ. It was in essence a miniature kingdom of God, a little visible part of the whole family of God, a tiny fragment of the invisible Church. It had no constitution, no creed, no sacraments, no clergy, no ordained officials, no infallibilities, except the infallibility of the guiding Spirit. With all its limitations, this Society, organized in the Restoration period, against the protests of the pure idealists, has proved to be the most impressive experiment in Christian history of a group-mysticism, a religious body practising corporate silence as the basis of worship and maintaining a fundamental faith in Spirit-guided ministry.

The formulation of Quaker doctrine was, in my judgment, not as happy, was not performed in a manner as accordant with the genius of the movement as was the form of the organization of the Society. The main difficulty with the formulation of doctrine in general is that it must always of necessity be done in terms of the prevailing metaphysics of the period. It is an obvious fact that systems of metaphysics are doomed to become out-dated and inadequate with the process of thought. Fashions in metaphysics are notoriously subject to change. The result is that the religious truth of a movement, once locked up and encased in a system of thought which dies and gets left behind, is itself in danger of crystallization and arrest. Just this common course of events has occurred with the formal declaration of the Quaker principle. In the first stage Quakerism remained experimental, vital, unformulated. George Fox was naïve, spontaneous, and unreflective. He knew no school metaphysics. He simply called men to "that of God in themselves." He took almost exactly the position of the spiritual reformers. He assumed that universal experience bore witness to a Divine light within man. He rested his entire faith upon the native testimony of the soul. Wherever man is found some moral and spiritual truths are revealed in him. How the Divine and human can be conjunct, how God and man can correspond and cooperate, did not greatly concern him. He was satisfied with the clear fact. He was ready to trust the soul. But in a world of endless debate and conflict, the problem of the Divine-human relationship was sure to arise and become urgent. Controversy was inevitable; it was the very air men breathed in this seventeenth century. There could be no continuous propaganda of the faith without a definite exposition and defence of it. That meant that sooner or later it must get into the common theological terminology of the time. This work of translating the Quaker faith into a contemporary system of thought was performed by Robert Barclay of Scotland. He was a highly endowed person, of rare natural gifts. He was broadly educated and carefully trained as a scholar. He was typically Scotch in his bent and fondness for exact logical comprehension. He bears his frequent testimony as a convinced Quaker that experience is everything and system almost nothing, and yet, in spite of that personal testimony, he goes insistently forward with the development of his elaborate logically-linked system as though —however his heart felt—his mind believed that truth could not maintain itself and prevail without the solid armour of logic. He was above everything else a good man; pure, high-minded, noble, dedicated. He does not understand the common people by native instinct as George Fox does. His blood and nurture separate him from the rank and file, without his intention of having it so. He is most at home and at his best when he is talking with Princess Elizabeth or writing to her. This Stuart princess was one of the most learned women in Europe, the intimate friend and correspondent of Descartes, a combination of philosopher and saint and, in her later life, almost persuaded to become a Friend.

Barclay possessed a beautiful inner spirit. His character was one peculiarly marked by sweetness, though at the same time not lacking in firmness and strength. His religion went all through him. His soul was reached by a real experience, and all the springs of his life were fed by his experimental discovery of God. With noble purpose and with the loftiest intentions he undertook the difficult task of expounding the truth of the inward Light, as a universal religion.

The *Apology for the True Christian Divinity, as the same is held forth and preached by the People called in scorn Quakers*, was written when Barclay was twenty-eight and is an extraordinary book. The range of Barclay's knowledge of Scripture and of the Fathers and Reformers of the Church, and the depth of his penetration, compare favourably with the same qualities in the first edition of Calvin's *Institutes*, written when Calvin was twenty-six. A primary difficulty with the Apology, however, lies in the fact that the writer of it belonged to a fundamentally different school of thought from that in which the leaders of Quakerism moved. These early Quaker founders had broken away completely from the theological doctrines which the Protestant Reformers inherited and re-formulated. They cut straight across and left on one side the whole loop of theological " notions." They proposed to leave the old behind and to make a new beginning. The theological concepts about which men preached and debated seemed to them hollow, empty, and dead. They were as opposed to restoring these outworn " notions " as they were to reviving the superstitions of the mediaeval Church. " The dead might bury the dead," their business was proclaiming a gospel of Life and Light. They plainly meant to keep religion in the warm and living currents of experience ; to have their message and their entire proclamation spring out of realities discovered within the purview of their own souls. The Calvinistic account of God and man and salvation was to them an unnecessary appendix to the eternal, living Word of God ; an unwarranted supplement to apostolic Christianity. They lived and thought in another world of ideas, they were the inheritors of the long labours of mystics, heretics, martyrs, and spiritual prophets, and it was their peculiar mission to transmit this type of inner religion, at length freed from the encasing bonds of man-made doctrines.

Barclay, on the contrary, decides to find out how Quakerism stands with Reformation doctrines, and to adjust the new as far as possible with the old. He reveals at every point an intimate and minute acquaintance with the entire history of theological doctrine. He knows, as I have said, the writings of the Fathers, the Schoolmen, and the Reformers. What he does not know, at least not

INTRODUCTION xxxiii

intimately or profoundly, is the line of spiritual predecessors who have prepared the way in the wilderness for Quakerism. He had never travelled over this highway. He had missed the little books which came out of the deep experience of the great mystics. He was not familiar with the spiritual contemporaries of Luther and Calvin and Arminius, who essayed to mark out a new path to the Kingdom. He had not read, and one can but wish he had done so, the fresh and liberating interpretations of Christianity given by the Cambridge Platonists, Benjamin Whichcote, John Smith, and their friends. Here was a way of thought kindred to the spirit and genius of the Quaker principle and ideals. But Barclay's intellectual world attached elsewhere. He undertook not to reinterpret the Quaker principle in terms of this wider, fresher, deeper movement of thought, but rather to challenge the prevailing Protestant system of thought, and to show how this system would look when adjusted to fit the principle of the Inward Light. That course, judged historically, seems to me a pity. It was done with real genius, but a wholly different type of interpretation would have been far better for the "truth." It was unfortunate to lock up this new idea in that old system.

We find ourselves in the *Apology* back again with the ancient conception of "man," so familiar in the theories of the dogmatic theologians. Friends had begun their movement with a bold challenge to this Augustinian dogma. Fox, speaking out of his own experience, says that he had gravity and stayedness of mind as a child; he was from his earliest days kept pure, and when he was eleven years old he knew pureness and righteousness.[1] His experience of God in his own soul enabled him to take a fundamental view of man very unlike that of the speculative theologians. He trusts experience for his theory of man and passes by on the other side and leaves behind the dogma about man, as his spiritual predecessors had also done. The mysticism of George Fox is characteristically affirmative. He testifies elsewhere to a first-hand consciousness of God.

[1] *Journal*, i. 2.

He knows of nothing to prevent God and man finding one another and enjoying one another. Death and darkness abound, but God still more abounds and is "over" them. There is a busy Satan at work in the world, but God is "atop" of him, and "the Seed of God" is a reigning, victorious thing. Fox emphatically belongs in the anti-Augustinian movement. Barclay, however, goes back to the accepted dogma about man, and adopts it as his basis, and then endeavours to alter it to fit his view of the Inward Light. "Man by nature, man as he is *man*," Barclay says, "is corrupt and fallen." "No real good proceedeth from his nature as he is man." "A seed of sin is transmitted to all men from Adam"; "a seed is propagated to all men which in its own nature is sinful and inclines men to iniquity." No good, he declares, should be ascribed to the natural man; he is "polluted in all his ways"; he is "void of righteousness and of the knowledge of God"; he is "out of the way and in short unprofitable"; he is "unfit to make one step toward heaven."[1] A good illustration of Barclay's argumentative method is found in his comment upon the text Genesis viii. 21, "The imagination of man's heart is evil from his youth." "From which," he proceeds, "I thus argue:

"If the thoughts of man's heart be not only evil, but always evil; then are they, as they simply proceed from his heart, neither good in part nor at any time.

"But the first is true; therefore the last.

"Again,

"If man's thoughts be always and only evil, then are they altogether useless and ineffectual to him in the things of God.

"But the first is true, therefore the last."[2]

This proposition regarding the dogma of man's sinful nature is established, after the usual manner of dogmatic theologians, by a judicious selection of Scripture texts, treated in a similar way to that employed by Calvin to prove his theories of "man." The Adamic story is taken

---

[1] These passages are found in Proposition iv. of the *Apology*.
[2] *Apology*, Prop. iv. Part I. sect. 2.

as factual history; the theory of the transmission of "a seed of sin" as taught by Calvin is accepted as though it were an essential part of the gospel.[1] No attempt is made to sound the deeps of human experience itself. It does not occur to him that this is a question to be settled by the testimony of the soul, and that first of all one ought to investigate actual human life as it is and to build the theory on facts of experience. He piles up instead a structure of texts and considers that the far-reaching conclusion has been proved.

Barclay means by "the natural man" man as he would be if he were stripped of all altruistic traits, of all spiritual potency, of every upward-striving tendency, a being who is a bundle of selfish instincts and passions. He is, for theological purposes, reduced to his lowest terms. "He differeth," Barclay says, "as he is mere man, no otherwise from beasts than by the rational property," and it quickly appears that "the rational property" is nothing but a logical faculty, a cognitive capacity to form conceptions about the external world and to argue from them to other conceptions equally external. There is nothing in this "natural man" that can in any degree appreciate or apprehend spiritual truth. In his own nature he can discern nothing of the things of God; he can do no good thing; he is utterly carnal and a continual prey to evil propensities. It needs hardly to be said at this date that there is no such being as this so-called "natural man." He is an artificial construction. He is no more real than the Jabberwock is. He is an abstract figure, existing nowhere outside of books. Real man in his native fundamental being is both altruistic and selfish, both sympathetic and egotistic. It is as "natural" for him to love others as it is to promote self-interest. It is as instinctive to be social as it is to be individualistic. Man as man carries in the very ground of his nature a self-transcending spirit. Something from beyond his finite limits is bound up in him and for ever pushes him out of

---

[1] For Calvin's account of "the Seed of Sin" see the *Institutes*, Book II. chap. i.

himself and draws him on. Every revelation of the real nature of God that has come to us has come through man. Man's spirit is a candle of the Lord and can burn with a revealing flame. God and man for ever belong together, and only by an arid and artificial metaphysics are they so sundered that man is reduced to this poor thing called "mere man." "The truths of God are connatural to the soul of man," Benjamin Whichcote was saying in the very period when Barclay was writing his *Apology*, "and the soul of man makes no more resistance to them than the air does to light."[1]

It is peculiarly tragic that the fresh discovery of spiritual truth which Friends made should so quickly have been attached to the ancient dogmatic theory of "man," because it is a sound principle that "there can be no true doctrine of God that is not based on a true doctrine of man."[2] If man is not, in his real nature, a being through whom God can reveal Himself, then our world is doomed to be a Godless world, for there is no other way for revelation to come. As soon as we turn to experience, however, we are at once reassured. Man, with all his faults and failures, with all his blunders and sins, is a being who lives by ideals which come from beyond himself, who organizes all the facts of his experience under universal forms of thought that ally him at once with a deeper universe of spiritual realities. He is always living for values and by visions that raise him out of the category of "mere man." Something not of matter nor of space and time, something drawn from a realm of Spirit, is woven into the very structure of his soul and makes him akin to God whether he chooses to be the conscious child of God or not. The presence of the eternal reality, that gives permanence to any of our facts of experience, is indissolubly joined to our consciousness of self. We never possess the whole of ourselves. We are organic with a wider inner life than we have yet consciously made our own. The margins of our souls stretch farther than we dream.

[1] Whichcote's *Aphorisms*, 444.
[2] A. Seth Pringle-Pattison's *The Idea of God* (Oxford, 1917), p. 254.

INTRODUCTION

> And though thy soul sail leagues and leagues beyond,
> Still leagues beyond those leagues, there is more sea.[1]

It is possible, no doubt, to draw a narrow boundary around an abstract self and call the poor thing " mere man," and then to demonstrate that of itself it has no spiritual powers —only in every case it is man himself who makes this mere-man creation. It is not one of God's real men!

When once this fatal reduction or truncation of man has been made, the theologian must of necessity have recourse to miracle to make such a being spiritual. Salvation can then, of course, be effected only by some form of supernatural mediation. Here one discovers the peculiar ingenuity of the particular theologian. Some *vehiculum Dei*—*i.e.* mechanism by which the remote God is miraculously brought into operation in the otherwise unspiritual soul—must be contrived. Barclay's ingenuity is here of a high order. He admits " the miserable and depraved condition " of mere man,[2] but he is confident that there is an adequate supernatural provision to meet this *impasse*. Christ by His death " purchased for man " a universal Light or Divine Seed. " Through the merits of this death" this Divine Light is conferred upon every person born into the world, and " puts all mankind into a capacity for salvation."[3] " The Lord hath been pleased," Barclay says, " to reserve the more full discovery of this glorious and evangelical dispensation to this our own age."[4] In other words, he believes that the great discovery which " the Children of the Light " have made is this provision of salvation by means of a work of Divine grace within the heart of man. It was, according to his exposition, just this *gift* of light and grace which Christ " purchased " for man on the Cross of Calvary. Only it seems passing strange that there was any necessity to " purchase " at such a price a grace which one would suppose would have spontaneously flowed out from the heart of a loving Father-God.

---

[1] D. G. Rossetti, Sonnet 37, " The Choice."
[2] *Apology*, Prop. v. and vi. sect. 1.
[3] *Ibid.* Stated in the original form of the Proposition vi. and expanded in sections 4 and 25. [4] *Ibid.* Prop. v. and vi. sect. 10.

This Light, bestowed on man, as we have seen, through the purchase of Christ's death, does not in any sense belong to man's own nature, for "the natural man is wholly excluded from having any place or portion in his own salvation, by any acting, moving, or working of his own."[1] This Light, he further says, "is not any part of man's nature, nor yet any relic of any good which Adam lost by his fall." It is a "distinct, separate thing from man's soul and all the faculties of it." "It is not only distinct, but of a different nature from the soul of man and its faculties." It is to be distinguished even from "man's natural conscience, for conscience being that in man which ariseth from the natural faculties of man's soul may be defiled and corrupted."[2]

The Divine Light is thus wholly supernatural and put into man by a miraculous act, similar to that which sacramentarians attribute to the supernatural transubstantiation of bread and wine by which these elements are changed into the Divine body and blood of Christ, and which furnish the soul with "Grace." This Seed or Light becomes, in Barclay's own words, a *vehiculum Dei*[3]—a supernatural vehicle, or device, by which a distant God can operate in a soul that of its own nature has no spiritual capacity. This Light is placed in the soul at its creation, as "a spiritual Seed," after the same manner as innate ideas were supposed by Descartes to be injected by God into the substance of the soul. The supernatural Seed lies, "as a real substance," hidden away and dormant in the natural soul, as naked grain lies in barren, stony ground.[4] The natural man can "resist" this Seed, even slay and crucify it, *or* he can "receive it in his heart," "suffer it to bring forth its natural and proper effect, until Christ be formed and raised within the soul, as the new man,"[5]—and this is salvation.

The division of natures, the dualism between God and

[1] *Apology*, Prop. v. and vi. sect. 11, Consequence 6th.
[2] *Ibid*. Prop. v. and vi. sect. 16.
[3] *Ibid*. Prop. v. and vi. sect. 15, Quest. 5.
[4] *Ibid*. Prop. v. and vi. sect. 14.
[5] *Ibid*. Prop. v. and vi. sect. 13.

man, is here stated as sharply and violently as it can be stated. His initial account of man compels Barclay to resort to a supernatural scheme by which everything that can be called "spiritual" is derived from the other world and is no part of man. Barclay is strongly opposed to the doctrine of the damnation of infants and to the election scheme of Calvin, but it is not easy to see how he logically avoids these two unpleasant conclusions. If a child has nothing "spiritual" in his own nature and can become "spiritual" only by actively and voluntarily receiving the Seed into his heart and suffering it to grow and develop within him, and he dies before he has arrived at a capacity to do this, he would appear—unless a miracle is worked somewhere else—to remain for ever unspiritual and so unsaved. Again, it is difficult to see why, when we are all alike unspiritual and depraved by nature, some of us receive and respond to this "Seed" and so become saved, while the rest of us never do respond to it but go on living as if it had not been hidden in our nature. None of us can save ourselves, and yet some are saved and some are not. The "election" is somehow a mysterious fact. Barclay implies that it is due to the fact that God visits some at favoured seasons and does not in the same way visit others. There are some persons, he positively admits, who receive Grace[1] in such a measure and with such prevailing power that they cannot resist its saving operations. "In such a special manner He worketh in some, in whom Grace so prevaileth, that they necessarily obtain salvation; neither doth God suffer them to resist." If it is true that Divine Grace does in some instances manifest itself in irresistible prevailing power, one wonders why it works more feebly in others so that they can consequently resist its saving operation. The problem of free-will is difficult in any system of thought, and all theologians have found it hard to avoid some form of "election." Barclay supposed that he had escaped the net, but it is not obvious to the modern reader that he has done so. There is, of course, no way of securing or guaranteeing

[1] *Apology*, Prop. v. and vi. sect. 18.

human freedom if it be taken for granted that the natural man is inherently and essentially unspiritual and incapable of any operations that contribute to the spiritual life. In fact, if man is wholly unspiritual by nature and can be saved in any case only by miracle, the lost would appear to be lost, not through man's conscious fault but because the miracle was not worked in their case or at least not worked sufficiently to save them.

But the graver difficulty with the entire scheme is found in the fact that we are left by this device with no criterion or test of truth. We are given in this foreign and supernatural Seed a religious principle which has no genuine ground in the nature of reason, and is incapable of correlation with reason. The Light, or Seed, is of a wholly different nature from the rational soul of man. It has no likeness or similarity to the natural faculties with which we are endowed, and by which we live our normal life. It is injected into man from another sphere, and is as foreign to our life as an archangel or seraph would be in our municipal politics. It is not commensurable with any native power of ours or with any facts or features of the world in which we are placed. It is not a product of experience. It is not the result of any known process. We possess nothing in our mental outfit by which we could ever pass judgment upon the pronouncements or the revelations of this Light. Only by miracle could the "openings" thus made to us from another sphere *fit* the scenery and circumstance of our natural world with its historical problems and its social issues. We are bound all the time to live and think and work with natural men and with societies of natural men, and we must face tasks that have grown out of natural sociological and ethical movements—and yet our only guide, beyond that of instinct and unspiritual reason, is a Light wholly distinct from and unrelated to the world where the concrete problems arise. This is as strange and as difficult to rationalize as was Descartes' double-world scheme, which absolutely sunders into two unrelated spheres the mind in man from the external world where man's life is lived.

INTRODUCTION

Descartes' scheme furnishes no basis for explaining how the mind inside can ever know any outside fact. Every act of knowledge becomes miraculous. So, too, in Barclay, every spiritual action is miraculous. Man could not do it if it were not done for him and through him. Man is thus treated as a thoroughfare through which distant mysterious forces, unlike any known forces in *this* world, supernaturally operate.

These intellectual difficulties, which have for many generations been allowed to pass unanalysed and unnoted, might well have been left still unchallenged were it not for the important fact that they have carried along through all these same generations grave historical consequences. Somewhere something happened which profoundly altered the entire character of the Quaker movement. Its mysticism shifted from the dynamic affirmation mysticism of the first period to a passive and negative type. A Quietism which nobody detects in the early days settled down upon it and utterly transformed it. It has been supposed that this Quietism came from the continent of Europe and was due to foreign influences. Friends did show great interest in continental Quietism, and were at a later time strongly influenced by it, as we shall see in the next volume of this series, but the unescapable fact remains that Friends had settled into a confirmed Quietism long before they discovered and used the writings of the great Quietists of France and Italy.

It will not do, of course, to attribute the appearance of Quietism in the Quaker movement to one sole influence. Group-attitudes and habits are subtle things and can seldom be traced to one isolated cause. But it is a plain and patent fact that Barclay's formulation is charged and loaded with the essential conditions and tendencies of Quietism. The entire basis and framework of Quietism are already there.

All forms of Quietism start with a despair of the natural man. They begin with a recognition of the spiritual bankruptcy of mere man. Every spiritual step, every act that has to do with religion and salvation,

Quietism maintains, must be done in man by some Divine power beyond him. *His* only part in the transaction is a passive part. He ceases to resist the operations of God, and waits in quiet for "visitations," and for the coming of supernatural assistance. One does not need to turn to the continental Quietists for this teaching; it is all in Barclay, and is vividly and emphatically expressed there.

As we have seen, Barclay holds that natural man is "miserable," "depraved," and "unspiritual"—"without capacity for salvation." Every spiritual act of every sort is performed in man by a Divine *vehiculum* detached from his own nature and working through him. Man's only part and sole contribution is passivity. His one single function in spiritual matters is not to resist the Divine seed, the imparted grace. "He that resists it not, it becomes his salvation: so that in him that is saved the working is of the *grace* [used for 'Seed' and 'Light'], and not of the man; and it is a passiveness rather than an act."[1] Barclay continues: "The first step is not by man's working, but by his not contrary working." At the "singular seasons of man's visitation," "man is wholly unable of himself to work with the grace [*i.e.* co-operate], neither can he move one step out of his natural condition, until the grace [the superadded power] lay hold upon him; so it is possible for him to be passive and not to resist it, as it is possible for him to resist it. So we say, the grace of God works in and upon man's nature, which *though of itself wholly corrupted and defiled and prone to evil*, yet is capable to be wrought upon by the Grace of God."[2] There is thus no co-operation between man and the superadded grace. It works in its own way, accomplishes its own end. Man's only act is a decision to lie passive and not resist it. Man of himself is powerless to bring about a "visitation"—"he must," as Barclay says, "wait for it." "He cannot move and stir [it] up when he pleaseth; but it moves, and strives with man as the Lord seeth meet." "It comes at certain times and seasons,

[1] *Apology*, Prop. v. and vi. sect. 17.   [2] *Ibid.* Prop. v. and vi. sect. 17.

and he must wait for it."¹ That is the essential basis, the distinguishing mark of Quietism. Barclay's letters, especially those to the Princess Elizabeth, and his theological writings generally, use very often the Quietistic phrase, "pure love," "pure light," "pure or naked truth," "pure motion," by which he means the "love" or "light," or "truth," or "influence" Divinely imparted to the soul without any admixture at all of the human. He does not write to Elizabeth until he has a "pure" moving to do so: "I was not willing to do anything in the forwardness of my own spirit," and he adds: "I shall be glad to hear from thee as thou finds *true freeness* to let me know how things are with thee."² His proposal of marriage to Christian Molleson contains a similar Quietistic note: "I can say in the fear of the Lord that I have received a charge from Him to love thee."³

There is, however, unfortunately, no safe and sound way on this basis of "pure truth" of discriminating between the true Divine motion and the motion which has a human and subjective origin. Reason has been ruled out as the arbiter. Experience is not admitted as the test. The Divine intimation, or pure moving, is supposed to be its own sure evidence, but we are never told by what infallible sign its Divine origin can be recognized. On a certain occasion Barclay himself felt impelled by an inward moving, which he felt to be "pure," to put on sackcloth, to cover his head with ashes, and to go through the streets of Aberdeen, crying to the people to repent. His own account of the strange incident, given in "Truth Triumphant," is as follows:

"... The Command of the Lord concerning this thing came unto me that very Morning, as I awakened, and the Burthen thereof was very great; yea, seemed almost insupportable unto me, (for such a thing, until that very Moment, had never entered me before, not in the most remote Consideration.) And some, whom I

[1] *Apology*, Prop. v. and vi. sect. 16.
[2] Letter to Princess Elizabeth, 27th of 4th mo. 1676.
[3] See M. Christabel Cadbury's *Robert Barclay* (London, 1912), p. 33.

called to declare to them this thing, can bear Witness, how great was the Agony of my Spirit, how I besought the Lord with Tears, that this Cup might pass away from me! Yea, how the Pillars of my Tabernacle were shaken, and how exceedingly my Bones trembled, until I freely gave up unto the Lord's Will."

This well illustrates the difficulty involved in this Quietistic theory. There is no test, no criterion. The moving is its own evidence. One must not question *why*, one must not ask for rational grounds. Reason is excluded. One must simply obey. But the mind of man is such a curious thing, with its subliminal suggestions, its morbid whisperings, its dreams and imaginings, its imitations and its auto-possessions, that it is never quite possible to assume that "movings" which burst with force into the sphere of the mind are on their own evidence "pure" and supernatural. Barclay admits that "the devil might form a sound of words, convey it to the outward ear and deceive the outward senses, by making things appear that are not."[1] It would seem, then, that this malicious spirit might even more easily inwardly deceive the most sincere and devout soul.

Quietism, having eliminated reason, has never told its adherents how to discriminate between the false light and the true. On its presuppositions there is no answer to the question. The Divine and the human belong to two different worlds and the higher cannot be tested and verified by anything in our lower world.

One who studies with care and insight the history of Quakerism through the two centuries succeeding Barclay's formulation will see that many of the tragedies and many of the internal difficulties have sprung out of this assumed spiritual bankruptcy of man and this Quietistic contrivance for obviating it. All the controversies of later Quaker history involve Barclay. The development of each new issue has been made in reference to his positions. He was a sort of John Brown of the entire period of Quaker struggle. He died before the internal conflicts began, but

[1] *Apology*, Prop. ii. sect. 6.

his soul went moving on through the whole of them. If he had shaped the issues differently the entire trend of Quaker history would have been another matter. No Friend appeared for two hundred years who could give, or at least who did give, a searching examination of this interpretation of the fundamental basis of Quakerism and with one consent it was accepted as the final authority. The great controversialists, Elias Hicks and his orthodox opponents; Joseph John Gurney and John Wilbur; the Beaconites and their opposers, all took Barclay's account of "the natural man" as though there were no further word to say about it. Their differences were upon the question of how God had met this existing crisis and how under prevailing conditions salvation could be accomplished. They never got beneath the ancient presuppositions. The deeper questions of the real nature of God and man and their fundamental relation to one another never got adequate treatment. We find nobody breaking loose and going down to the deeper level.

Robert Barclay is not to be blamed for the historical tragedy. The formulators of truth in any field are bound to use the psychology and metaphysics of their age. They must think, if they think at all, through the terminology of their time and in the concepts that prevail around them, and they invariably determine the line of march of human thought and even fix in advance the kind of intellectual questions that will be asked in succeeding periods.

What I regret most is that the early formulation of Quakerism should have been made as an adjustment with the Augustinian and Calvinistic system instead of following the fresh and transforming path which the spiritual reformers, the real forerunners and progenitors of "the Children of the Light," had discovered. That latter course would have meant a different history and, I believe, a greater career for the movement—a real day-dawn and day-star rising for spiritual religion.

One other adjustment to the demands of the world and external history calls for a few words of comment in this Introduction—the adjustment to the State. When Quakerism burst in upon the world, its leaders took no account of consequences. They had, they believed, received an "opening," a revelation, which had complete right of way. Everything else must stand aside for it, or at least take second place. The "truth" which possessed their souls involved a new venture of life, and they were ready to risk reputation, home, family, goods, and life in their holy experiment. They had no thought of compromising at any point, of yielding any ground or bending around any obstacles, or of ceasing the *fight*—they would have said ceasing to "bear their testimony"—

> Till [they should build] Jerusalem
> In England's green and pleasant land.

This rebel-attitude toward existing situations, this unyielding spirit, produced, as it always does, a remarkable type of person and a highly dynamic and uncalculable movement. George Whitehead and those who joined with him in the patient work of securing "tolerations" and "privileges" for Friends were, without knowing it, preparing for a different type of person and were passing over from a movement charged with potential energy to a stage of arrested development and cooling enthusiasm. Once more we cannot blame these sincere adjusters. They wanted to secure their right to life, liberties, and, if not "the pursuit of happiness," at least the privilege to worship God as their hearts dictated. Why should they go on fighting further with their spiritual weapons if kindly-minded sovereigns and tolerant parliaments were ready to grant them a large measure of the claims for which they had suffered so much?

What they hardly realized, however, was the subtle though fundamental change of ground. The "Children of the Light" in their day had not been concerned for rights and privileges for themselves and were not concerned to establish claims of their own. They were champions of a universal truth; they were the bearers of a faith for the whole human race; they were contending for a new way of life for the entire world. To secure a modicum of their "truth" and to win the privilege of practising it by themselves within the peaceful area of their own homes and meeting-houses would have seemed to them no victory at all. They were the commissioned "apostles" of a new order, and there could be no stopping-place until the new kingdom was built. George Whitehead was a good man, and he was a real success in securing happy adjustments, but he marks, nevertheless, the end of an era, and is in his own person the exhibition of a changed ideal:

History itself is a revelation of God. Its processes are sometimes stern and tragic. Its judgments are often severe. But it is always cathartic and clarifying. It arouses attention. It awakens consciousness. It drives home great realities. It demonstrates moral laws. It unveils the truth and it makes the fact of God's immanent presence as sure and certain as it can be made in a world like ours. This history deals with one small human movement, covering only a fragment of time, but, even so, it is, like all genuine history, charged with spiritual significance and will bring the patient reader an illuminating message of the way God works in the world.

BOOK I

THE STRUGGLE FOR RELIGIOUS LIBERTY

CHAPTER I

THE RESTORATION SETTLEMENT

Now we may do what we will and who shall control us? Who, who shall hinder us from filling ourselves with all manner of delights, now we are settled in our way? Now will we build our decayed houses and restore our fallen worships: now will we repair the broken fences of our parks, that we may have game to the full : now shall our horses' be well fed for the race, that they may fully please us : now let the cock-pits be looked to for that (cruel) sport, and let our bowling-alleys be well dressed for our daily recreation : now shall the stage-players for our delight have their full liberty, and all the sons of vanity have due encouragement ; for the old things we love ; and that which is new, though never so much the better, our souls loathe. We like the old ways of our fathers, because, when they had Lord Bishops, and their Minster services with matins and evensongs, with organs and singing-boys and such-like things, then there was peace and plenty ; and, when the neighbourhood could meet together and sit about a bonfire or Maypole or under a bower, and drink strong drink and tell stories and sing and roar, then there was love and agreement. And when plays and pastimes and wakes were duly frequented and observed, then was it a merry time and a joyful land. . . . And when those that said they feared the Lord and so could not join with us . . . were taken a course withal, O then was it a good day, say many, and, as it was then, so would we have it now.—THOMAS TAYLOR, *Works*, p. 122.

AMONG the causes which led to the Restoration, hatred of military rule comes first in order of importance. Cromwell's reluctant absolutism had been imposed by the exigency of the times. Under Commonwealth and Protectorate, England had borne the crushing burden of a standing army, which, for the maintenance of Puritanism, had subverted Parliamentary institutions. A minority had maintained itself in power, and, however high-principled, its rule had necessarily rested on force rather than on consent. The situation was patent, even while the master-soul of Cromwell ruled, but with his death in September 1658 a period of acute political instability and rapid disintegration began. The army itself became divided, and, when Monck marched to London and declared for a free Parliament, the era of "sword-government" gave place to an eager restoration of all that stood for civil order and authority.[1]

Monarchy and episcopacy were gladly resumed, but Charles would henceforth be dependent on Parliament, except in the closing years of his reign, to a degree that his father had never recognized. The dominant factor in the religious settlement that took place would be not the tolerant and pleasure-loving Monarch, but the temper of his Ministers and of the Commons. Chief among the royal advisers was Hyde, Earl of Clarendon, the manager of the King's business during his exile, and Gilbert Sheldon, Bishop of London and afterwards Archbishop of Canterbury, who took the lead in Church affairs.

Next to the disbanding of the army and the summoning of a free Parliament, the most pressing of all questions was that of religion. In the qualified religious freedom of the Commonwealth period, Presbyterian and Independent had been in turn triumphant, but there had been much toleration for other forms of faith, except Popery and Prelacy, which were politically dangerous. How would the restored Church and Parliament deal with the Puritan bodies, and with the "fanatics," as the Quakers and other enthusiasts now came to be called?[2]

The Presbyterians were Royalist in feeling, and the King owed his restoration largely to their influence. Their rigid system had, however, failed to establish itself in England in any effective sense, and many of the leading ministers were no longer Presbyterian in the full meaning of the term, and were prepared for an accommodation with prelacy. On the 25th October 1660 the King's Declaration was published, proposing a kind of limited episcopacy,

---

[1] *Beginnings of Quakerism*, chap. xviii.
[2] The word is found as early as 1644, but came into vogue with Monck's speech to Parliament, 6th Feb. 1660, in which he said, "Be careful neither the cavalier nor phanatique party have yet a share in our military or civil power." See *Life and Times of Anthony à Wood*, edn. 1891–1900, i. 303. John Owen had written a book called *Pro Scripturis contra Fanaticos*, and Samuel Fisher, *Works*, p. 216, suggests that the name originated with him. A fanatic, in its original Latin meaning, was a temple-devotee.

THE RESTORATION SETTLEMENT

in which the bishops would have been assisted and advised by elected presbyters. A union of the two wings of the Royalist forces seemed for the moment imminent. But the King's zeal in the matter abated when exception was taken to a proviso which gave toleration to Papists as well as to Quakers and other enthusiasts; and the Bill for enacting the provisions of the Declaration was thrown out with the approval of the King's Ministers. No such opportunity for "comprehension" presented itself again. Monarchy and episcopacy grew higher in favour every day, and the abortive Savoy Conference (25th March to 25th July 1661) showed the bishops in an unbending mood. They stood for uniformity, and the relatively slight changes which Convocation afterwards made in the Book of Common Prayer (December 1661) were not in favour of Presbyterian views.

Even before the close of the Savoy Conference, the newly elected House of Commons had shown its zeal by passing a Bill for uniformity of worship, which the Lords very properly refused to consider till January 1662, after the form of worship had been settled in the revised Book of Common Prayer. The Lords proved less hot in the matter than the Commons: they would have excepted schoolmasters and have confined the Act to beneficed clergy; they would have given the displaced non-conforming ministers a fifth of the living; they proposed, at the instance of the King, some reservation to him of a dispensing power; but the Commons insisted on the whole Bill, and it became law on 19th May 1662 as the Act of Uniformity.

Already in September 1660 an Act had passed restoring all clergy ejected since the beginning of the Civil War, and many Puritans had thus lost their livings. Deprivation was now the lot of all who failed to give public assent to the new Book of Common Prayer by St. Bartholomew's Day 1662 (24th August), "Black Bartholomew" as it came to be called, and the requirements of the Act extended to schoolmasters and "lecturers." Nearly 2000 ministers were ejected, a number which scarcely satisfied

Sheldon. "If we had thought so many of them would have conformed," he said, "we would have made it straiter." With rough hand, the State thus sought to cast out all Puritan elements from the Church, and forced into separate existence Nonconformity in the modern sense of the word.[1]

This refusal to Puritanism of comprehension within the Established Church was natural, perhaps even inevitable, and, except for the harshness used, need cause no recrimination. But Church and State not only insisted on uniformity within the Establishment, they endeavoured to drive all England into the one fold by penal laws. In other words, religious toleration failed to gain a place in the Restoration Settlement.

Here again the prospect had been bright at first. Charles, in the Declaration of Breda,[2] declared

... a liberty to tender consciences, and that no man shall be disquieted or called in question for differences of opinion in matter of religion, which do not disturb the peace of the kingdom, and that we shall be ready to consent to such an Act of Parliament as, upon mature deliberation, shall be offered to us, for the full granting that indulgence.

The King's Declaration of October 1660, already referred to, repeated the promise, and there can be no doubt that it accorded with the royal mind. But in this matter Parliament would prove itself master, and the new Parliament, which met in May 1661 and is variously known as the Cavalier Parliament, the Pension Parliament, and the Long Parliament of Charles II., soon showed its persecuting spirit. Intolerance sometimes proceeds from bigotry, but oftener from fear. During the Commonwealth period the Roman Catholic and the Anglican had been treated as dangers to the State, the enemies were now the Roman Catholic and the Puritan. The Northern Plot of 1663 shows that the fear of a Puritan rising was not altogether groundless.[3] It seemed very real to an age

---

[1] For the older sense, see *Beginnings of Quakerism*, p. 4, note 1.
[2] Gardiner's *Constitutional Documents of the Puritan Revolution*, pp. 465-467.
[3] See *post*, p. 29.

that had known the resolute military rule of Cromwell, and was unpleasantly conscious of the presence in its midst of the disbanded Puritan Ironsides. Moreover, the terrible religious wars which had devastated Europe before the Peace of Westphalia in 1648 left men keenly alive to the perils of division in matters of religion and zealous for a sternly imposed uniformity.

It is only fair to remember that political fear of this kind played a larger part than mere bigotry in shaping the persecuting laws of the Restoration that are known as the Clarendon Code. The Corporation Act of 1661, which imposed, amongst other things, the sacramental test " according to the rites of the Church of England " upon officers and members of municipal corporations, had for its object the purging out of disaffected persons, " it being too well known . . . that many evil spirits are still working." The Conventicle Acts of 1664 and '70, to be considered later, were entitled Acts to prevent and suppress seditious conventicles, and in almost identical words aimed at providing " further and more speedy remedies against the growing and dangerous practices of seditious sectaries, and other disloyal persons, who under pretence of tender consciences do at their meetings contrive insurrections, as late experience hath shewed." The Five Mile Act of 1665 was directed at Nonconformist ministers, " who have settled themselves in divers corporations in England, sometimes three or more of them in a place, thereby taking an opportunity to distil the poisonous principles of schism and rebellion into the hearts of His Majesty's subjects, to the great danger of the Church and Kingdom."

The political reasons for repression extended to all forms of Nonconformity. The Presbyterian had laid England under the yoke of the Solemn League and Covenant, the Congregational sects, whether Independent or Baptist, had been the main support of the Protectorate, while Quakers, Fifth Monarchy Men, and other " fanatics " had been regarded as dangerous even by the Puritan magistrate and would, *a fortiori*, be obnoxious to Churchman and Cavalier. On every Puritan lay the onus of proving himself loyal to the new order of things.

The Cavaliers who had followed their King into exile knew nothing of the latest spawn of Puritanism, the Quakers. This wonderful spiritual movement, which George Fox began, had sprung into being since the Flight from Worcester. Its adherents perplexed and alarmed the authorities by their concerted activities, their boldness of speech, and their refusal of the Oaths of Allegiance and Supremacy. Even before the Fifth Monarchy Rising in January 1661, the Quakers (and Baptists) of Bristol were reported to London as persons of dangerous principles, who would make advantage of the first opportunity to fly out and spurn at the Government.[1] After the rising, it became for a time almost impossible to convince the country Justice that the Quaker was no plotter. One man reports that he has seized a book with a passage full of treason; another, in Holderness, finds papers, that is, records of collections and sufferings,

. . . wherein it doth appear that they have constant meetings and intelligence all over the kingdom, and contributions for to carry on their horrid designs, though masked under the specious pretence of religion and piety. . . . They also keep registers of all the affronts and injuries that is done to any of them, when, where, and by whom. Therefore it doth appear they are an active subtle people, and it is a great mercy that their designs did produce no more mischief to this kingdom.

A third notes that they buy up the best horses the country can afford; while a fourth, from Kent, tells of a great meeting of Quakers, above a hundred and fifty, who stood quaking and trembling for two hours in silence, about a mile from Cranbrook, until a stranger came with two letters from beyond sea, but what they contained the informant could not learn.[2] The fears and prejudices of headstrong Cavaliers easily turned every strange Quaker

---

[1] *Extracts from State Papers*, p. 120. In *Beginnings of Quakerism*, p. 478, this letter and another that followed should be dated October instead of November.

[2] See *Extracts from State Papers*, pp. 126, 127, 146, 147.

THE RESTORATION SETTLEMENT

practice into a piece of disaffection, and every Quaker scruple into an act of sedition.

At the close of the year 1660, Friends fancied that they had satisfied the Government of their loyalty. But the Fifth Monarchy Rising in London served to reveal and to excuse the deep suspicion under which the sects of "fanatics" lay. Some thirty-five persons, under their leader Thomas Venner, broke forth in arms from their meeting-house in Coleman Street, and threw the city into a four days' panic with their furious behaviour and cries of "King Jesus, and their heads upon the gates." On Thursday 10th January 1661 a Proclamation was issued, prohibiting meetings of Anabaptists and Quakers and Fifth Monarchy Men, and commanding Justices to tender the Oath of Allegiance to persons brought before them for assembling at such meetings. On the following Sunday Friends met as usual and many were taken, though Fox himself escaped. The zeal of the authorities soon filled the gaols with Quakers. The country felt itself in peril till they were safely under lock and key. In a few weeks imprisonments took place to the almost incredible number of 4230.[1] The sudden storm swept many counties bare of men Friends. The numbers reached 500 in London, 400 in Yorkshire, 280 in Lancashire, 240 in Warwickshire, and 100 or more in eleven other districts. At Reading, for refusing fees, twenty-two Friends were herded into the dungeon, till, in the gaoler's words, "there was not such another bed in Berkshire." At Bristol, where they had great strength, the Mayor required sureties for good behaviour, meaning thereby to hinder them from meeting, and was met with

---

[1] See the Broadside addressed to the King and his Council, "A brief Relation of some of the Cruel and Inhumane Usage . . . of above 4230 . . . Quakers, . . ." Reprinted in (London) *Friend*, 1846 vol. p. 24. The numbers given, some of them round figures, total 4257. Fox says, *Camb. Journ.* i. 388, "And all the posts was laid to search all letters, so that none could pass; but we heard of several thousands of our Friends that were cast into prison, and Margaret Fell carried the account of them to the King and Council; and the third day after we had an account of several thousands more . . . and they wondered how we could have such intelligence, seeing they had given such strict charge for the intercepting all letters." The "wonder" no doubt fed their suspicions of Friends.

the answer, typical of the Quaker spirit, that he might as well think to hinder the sun from shining or the tide from flowing, as the Lord's people from meeting to wait upon Him, whilst but two of them were left together.[1] In Cambridge they spared none, neither widows nor fatherless children, but sent all to prison. At Plymouth the women, in spite of threats, kept up the meeting while the men lay in gaol. In Lancashire there was a general imprisonment. The pistols and fowling-pieces were taken out of Swarthmore Hall, and Bridget Fell reported to her mother in London that, if "they keep men in custody that should till the ground, the time of seeding being now, it cannot be expected that we should be able to maintain them in prison, [and] hire our tillage at home." In Somerset Ilchester gaol was thronged with 212 Friends, two of whom were put in fetters and led through the streets by the hangman. About seventy were thrown into the White Lion prison in Southwark, among the felons, who rifled them of clothes and money "to the value of £28 : 1 : 9." In Westmorland, as in some other parts, the authorities had instructions to suppress meetings of Quakers and Sectaries, even before the Fifth Monarchy Rising.[2]

The Quaker leaders had their full share of suffering; indeed, after the rank and file had been released, they were often detained for months as ringleaders and as hostages for the good behaviour of the rest.

A few cases must serve for many more that could be given. John Whitehead and the saintly Isaac Penington were companions in Aylesbury gaol, lodged with sixty or seventy more in an old malt-house, "so decayed that it was scarce fit for a dog-house," and so insecure that they

---

[1] Cf. Martin Mason, "To both Houses of Parliament," 2nd Nov. 1660, quoted in Barclay's *Inner Life*, p. 477.
[2] For these instances see Besse, *Sufferings*, i. 13 (Reading); i. 42 (Bristol); i. 89 (Cambridge); i. 152 (Plymouth); i. 307 (Lancashire); i. 587 (Somerset); i. 690 (Southwark); ii. 9 (Westmorland). For Bridget Fell's letter see Helen G. Crosfield, *Margaret Fox*, pp. 87-90. Dr. Stoughton points out, *The Church of the Restoration*, i. 143, that four days before Venner's Outbreak on 6th Jan. an Order of Council (2nd Jan.) forbade the meetings of Anabaptists, Quakers and other Sectaries, in large numbers and at unusual times. Cf. instructions, dated 2nd Jan., to Adam Martindale, given in his *Life*, Chetham Society edn. p. 144.

might have gone out at pleasure.¹ Penington addressed Friends in noble words from the cold room without a chimney in which he was confined:²

> O ye dear plants of the right hand of eternity, fear not what is to come to pass in this visible creation . . . but sanctify the Lord of Hosts, and let Him be your fear and dread, that He may compass you with the arm of His power . . . and ye may be satisfied in the openings and overflowings of the love of His heart towards you. Amen, saith my soul.

He could say, in words which would again and again express the experience of Quaker sufferers:³

> [The Lord] made my bonds pleasant to me, and my noisome prison (enough to have destroyed my weakly and tenderly-educated nature) a place of pleasure and delight, where I was comforted by my God night and day, and filled with prayers for His people, as also with love to and prayers for those who had been the means of outwardly afflicting me and others upon the Lord's account.

John Whitehead, the short, thick-set Puritan soldier, occupied his leisure with a *Small Treatise* of rare worth, which contains a description of the Quakers strikingly resembling in spirit the account of the Christians in the *Apology of Aristides*.⁴

William Dewsbury, from York Castle, wrote to Friends, "whether in bonds or out of bonds," with his triumphant faith:⁵ "Stay your minds and lift up your heads, and be strong in the name of the Lord, and fear not the wrath of man, for it is limited. . . . Glad your hearts in the unlimited power of God."

George Whitehead, with three other Friends, shared a recess in the wall of Norwich Castle, called the Vice;⁶ Joseph Fuce at Dover Castle was put "into a dungeon-like hole under the bell-tower, a place very filthy . . .

---

¹ Ellwood's *Life*, 1714 edn. p. 108.
² *Works*, 1681 edn. pt. i. p. 328.
³ "Three Queries Propounded to the King and Parliament" in *Works*, 1681 edn. pt. i. p. 406.
⁴ *Life*, by Thomas Chalk, pp. 80-101. For extract from this Treatise see *post*, heading of Chap. XVIII.
⁵ *Works*, pp. 186, 188.
⁶ *Christian Progress*, p. 245.

overrun with maggots and other insects, having no windows for light, only some holes cut through the door."[1] Francis Howgill remained for a time at liberty, and wrote from London to the prisoners at Durham:[2]

> Be content, being you are in bonds upon so clear an account and causelessly. Let none seek enlargement upon dishonourable terms, being that your case is the case of thousands, for the imprisonment of Friends lies as a weight upon the nation.

The letter was taken in the post and passed to Whitehall with the comment that, for all their pretences of conscience, the Quakers had enough of self in them to stand on punctilios of honour. Edward Burrough, who was in Ireland when the storm burst, explained this so-called punctilio in a bold plea to the King and Council,[3] in which he showed that for Friends to enter into engagements for good behaviour would be to betray their innocency and confess themselves suspicious persons. Fox and Richard Hubberthorne had been prompt to draw up a Declaration against plots and fightings, which was presented to the King on 21st January, and was cried up and down the streets and at the Exchange.[4] This important document was reissued with the approval of the "Morning Meeting" in 1684, and asserted in the most absolute terms that Friends as a body could not wage war with outward weapons. Some of its sentences now form part of the official Book of Christian Practice issued by London Yearly Meeting.

> Our principle is and our practices have always been to seek peace and ensue it; to follow after righteousness and the knowledge of God, seeking the good and welfare and doing that which tends to the peace of all. We know that wars and fightings proceed from the lusts of men, as Jas. iv. 1-3, out of which lusts the Lord hath redeemed us and so out of the

---

[1] Besse, *Sufferings*, i. 291.
[2] *Extracts from State Papers*, pp. 128-130, dated 16th February 1661.
[3] *Works*, p. 782.
[4] George Fox, *Journal*, i. 494-500, with text of Declaration from the 1684 edn. Other Declarations were also published by the Independents and Baptists. There is a similar one dated January 1663, written by Wm. Bayly on behalf of Friends, in his *Works*, pp. 167-176. See *post*, p. 29, note.

THE RESTORATION SETTLEMENT

occasion of war. . . . All bloody principles and practices we as to our own particular do utterly deny, with all outward wars and strife and fightings with outward weapons for any end or under any pretence whatsoever; and this is our testimony to the whole world. . . . That Spirit of Christ, by which we are guided, is not changeable, so as once to command us from a thing as evil and again to move unto it; and we do certainly know and so testify to the world that the Spirit of Christ, which leads us into all truth, will never move us to fight and war against any man with outward weapons, neither for the kingdom of Christ nor for the kingdoms of this world. . . . For this we can say to all the world; we have wronged no man's persons or possessions; we have used no force nor violence against any man; we have been found in no plots nor guilty of sedition. When we have been wronged, we have not sought to revenge ourselves; we have not made resistance against authority; but wherein we could not obey for conscience' sake we have suffered the most of any people in the nation. We have been counted as sheep for the slaughter, persecuted and despised, beaten, stoned, wounded, stocked, whipped, imprisoned, haled out of synagogues, cast into dungeons and noisome vaults, where many have died in bonds, shut up from our friends, denied needful sustenance for many days together, with other the like cruelties.

This noble disclaimer of plotting could not fail of effect, and together with the exoneration of the Quakers by the Fifth Monarchy Leaders, who had been hanged on the 19th January, led to an Order by the Lord Mayor, issued on the 25th,[1] which stated that it was found the Quakers had no hand in the plot, and directed their release, but with the nullifying proviso, "they the said Quakers engaging themselves henceforward to live obediently according to law." There were still 500 prisoners in London in the middle of February, but soon after many were set free. It was not, however, until the 11th May, after much effort, especially by Margaret Fell and Thomas Moore, that a full liberation was secured. All Quakers in prison for refusing the oaths or for meeting contrary to the proclamation, or for not finding sureties, were to be freed, without paying fees. The King declared "that he shall expect returns of loyalty

---

[1] Kennet, *Register*, p. 366.

and all due obedience, ... His Majesty not intending them impunity if they shall offend in the future."[1] The spasm of persecution was over and the gaols throughout England were cleared, but it was evident that the Friends would soon accumulate fresh offences.

One ready weapon already lay in the hands of the authorities. As the law stood, two Justices, and, in many cases a single Justice, could require any person of eighteen or over, under the degree of baron, to take the Oath of Allegiance and of denial of the Pope's authority. The refusal of the oath involved imprisonment till next Quarter Sessions or Assizes, when it was again to be tendered in open court, and, if refused, the penalty of *praemunire* was incurred. Married women, however, were only to be imprisoned till they took the oath.[2] The term *praemunire* was taken from the writ "*praemunire facias A. B.*," "cause A. B. to be forewarned," and denoted a punishment originally devised in the fourteenth century for use against those who acknowledged foreign jurisdiction by paying to papal process an obedience due to the King's Courts alone. The person found guilty was to be put out of the King's protection, his estate was forfeited to the crown, and he was imprisoned during life or at the royal pleasure.[3] The simplicity and severity of a *praemunire* quickly recommended it, and the rusty weapon forged for use against the pretensions of Rome was turned against the harmless Quakers. Sir William Walter, at the Quarter Sessions at Oxford, October 1660, was one of the first to use the weapon, the victims being Thomas Goodaire, of Yorkshire, one of the first followers of Fox, and Benjamin Staples, of Chadlington.[4] In later years we shall have many illustrious instances of this sovereign method for laying

[1] Printed in *Extracts from State Papers*, p. 132.
[2] St. 7 Jac. I. cap. 6. See *F.P.T.* p. 355.
[3] See word "Praemunire," in *Oxford English Dictionary*. The writ was based on the St. 16 Ric. II. cap. 5.
[4] John Whiting's *Persecution Exposed*, 1715 edn. p. 230, based on two Tracts by Goodaire, "A Cry of the just against Oppression" and "A True Relation what sentence was passed, etc." Both prisoners were freed after a time. Staples after thirty-five weeks (Oxfordshire Q.M. MS. Book of Sufferings). John Story was praemunired at Salisbury, perhaps still earlier. (*The Memory of John Story Revived*, 1683).

Quakers by the heels. It proved again and again a readier instrument of persecution than the express laws against Quakers and seditious conventicles which were passed by the Cavalier Parliament.

Isaac Penington explains the far-reaching grounds on which the oath was refused by Friends. Swearing, he says, was allowed to man in the fallen state and under the Mosaic Law; but was forbidden, by Christ's express command, to men in the redeemed state, where a greater bond was known, even Christ Himself. "That which the Law called swearing, the Gospel calls confessing, which confessing, in the life, in the truth, in the renewed principle, is the weight and substance of that whereof the oath was but a shadow." The Christian could no more go back, at the bidding of men, into swearing than into any other of the beggarly elements of the Law. To accept the bond of the oath would be to disparage the weight of the principle of truth raised up in his heart by Christ. It would indeed be a denial of Christ, "for entering into the Law-bond is a laying of the Gospel-bond by." He that abides in Christ must perform the Yea and Amen in Him.[1]

Refusal to take the Oath of Allegiance was thus an essential part of loyalty to Christ. The Friend could affirm his loyalty to the King and his denial of the Pope in as ample terms as those in the Oath but he could not swear. His position closely resembled that of a Christian under the Flavian Emperors, when the offering of wine and incense before the statue of Caesar was the proof of loyalty. The Christian, if he would live, must join in the Caesar-cult—must, in the language of the Apocalypse, "worship the image of the beast."[2] That was the searching and sufficient test. The Acts of Apollonius,[3] who was martyred at Rome A.D. 185, can be paralleled from many a Quaker trial. When urged to swear by the good

---

[1] See Isaac Penington, "The Great Question concerning . . . Swearing," in *Works*, 1681 edn. pt. i. p. 315, published in 1661.
[2] Rev. xiii. 15. See article "Caesarism" in *Encyclopaedia of Religion and Ethics*.
[3] F. C. Conybeare, *Monuments of Early Christianity*, pp. 29-48. Cf. the Martyrdom of Polycarp (*The Letter of the Smyrnaeans*, chaps. viii.-x.).

fortune of the Emperor Commodus and to offer sacrifice, he was ready to give full proof of loyalty, but refused to sacrifice to empty idols. " I will not again debase myself and cast myself down into the pit." To the Friend every oath, and to the early Christian every act acknowledging the Caesar-cult, was treachery to Christ, but Apollonius was as ready as any Friend to confess his loyalty in other ways.

It is best to swear not at all, but in all things to live in peace and truth ; for a great oath is the truth, and for this reason is it a bad and an ill thing to swear by Christ ; but because of falsehood is there disbelief, and because of disbelief there is swearing. I am willing to swear in truth by the true God that we, too, love the Emperor and offer up prayers for his Majesty.

Both early Christian and Quaker seemed seditious to the world because their first allegiance was given to an inward Sovereign whom the world did not know. The world was right in regarding them as very real enemies to much in the existing order of things. Fox, in the Restoration year, addressed an outspoken letter to both Houses of Parliament.[1] They were to dwell in righteousness and truth, which preserves governors and government and people in peace. No man who was a swearer or drunkard or heady or corrupt ought to bear office ; no one should be put to death for cattle or money or outward things, and no man should be persecuted because, for conscience' sake, he could not swear or put off his hat or pay tithe. The laws should be drawn up into a short volume that every one might know them ; prisoners should be brought to speedy trial ; none should keep gaols but sober men, and taverns but wholesome people ; all was to be done in love, " that all your dominions may be as a family," and finally there should be no persecution about Churchworship and religion. The authorities saw that Quakerism was an explosive force, which if it prevailed would shatter many cherished institutions ; and, naturally enough, they failed to understand that these heralds of a new way of

---

[1] *Doctrinals*, pp. 219-221. Cf. *post*, p. 558.

I   THE RESTORATION SETTLEMENT   17

life would only use the weapons of their Master, and had renounced all violent resistance to authority. Burrough, that "Son of Thunder and Consolation . . . and Sufferer for the Testimony of Jesus," as he is called on the title-page of his collected *Works*, stated the Quaker position with convincing sincerity in this spring of 1661.[1]

For conscience' sake to God, we are bound by His just law in our hearts to yield obedience to [Authority] in all matters and cases actively or passively; that is to say, in all just and good commands of the King and the good laws of the land relating to our outward man, we must be obedient by doing . . . but . . . if anything be commanded of us by the present Authority, which is not according to equity, justice and a good conscience towards God, . . . we must in such cases obey God only and deny active obedience for conscience' sake, and patiently suffer what is inflicted upon us for such our disobedience to men. . . . And this is our principle, and hath ever been our practice, to obey Authority by doing or suffering, not disputing whether the Authority in itself be absolute of God or not, yet being an Authority over us we are to obey it, either by doing or suffering, because it is an Authority, and not to plot, rebel or rise up with carnal weapons against it; and thus must our obedience be to the King and his Government.

Such a position implied detachment from the government of the country, and cannot be applied without re-examination to the participation in free institutions that is our lot to-day,[2] but it corresponded closely with the circumstances of persecution and proscription which then limited the civil and political life of Friends. As John Whitehead expressed it, having received a kingdom that could not be shaken, Friends were not ambitious nor strove for the kingdoms of this world nor coveted dignities that would fade away; but were content in the station in which God set them, longing that His righteousness might be revealed till His kingdom came over all.[3] This had not involved an absolute refusal of all public offices. The Balby epistle of 1656 had encouraged the acceptance of these,

[1] *Works*, p. 778, between pp. 785 and 787.
[2] See *post*, Chap. XXI.
[3] "Small Treatise," in *Life*, by Thomas Chalk, p. 93.

C

where the service was for the public wealth and good,[1] and during the Year of Anarchy, 1659, a number of Friends were chosen as Commissioners for the Militia.[2] Fox told these Friends: "You cannot well leave them, seeing ye have gone amongst them : so keep in that which presses and grinds all down to the witness, the power of God ; and therein you will have freedom and wisdom and liberty to declare yourselves over the contrary part that would rule," but he warned Friends against running into places.[3]

"The government of Christ and His kingdom," says Penington, "is not opposite to any just government of a nation or people. . . . Christ's subjects . . . are more faithful to men and more subject to any just law of government than others can be, for their fidelity and subjection is out of love, and for conscience' sake." But they could not accept laws made by men in their own will and corrupt wisdom, and often for self-ends and interests. "That which is of God cannot bow to anything which is corrupt in man ; it can lie down and suffer and bear the plowing of long and deep furrows upon its back, but it cannot act that which is against its life. It cannot be disloyal to its King, to gratify the spirit of this world ; but what practice or testimony its King calls for against the evil and corruption of this world it must obey singly and faithfully."[4]

These views, like the rest of Quakerism, sprang directly from the central experience of the Inward Light, for no prescriptions of man could invade the jurisdiction of the enlightened conscience. The Quakers were stiffly resolved to obey the higher power of God at any cost of suffering from the lower civil authority. The magistrate might inflict temporal punishments for hurtful actions, but for godliness to be crime and wickedness law was an inversion

---

[1] See *Beginnings of Quakerism*, p. 313.
[2] *Ibid.* p. 461. Besides this Bristol case, Robert Rich, in the adverse piece called *Hidden Things brought to Light* (1678), pp. 28, 29, says that he had seen, in an Act for settling the Militia of Westminster dated 28th June 1659, the names of five leading Friends : Nicholas Bond, William Woodcock, Amor Stoddart, Richard Davis, and Stephen Hart.
[3] Letter to Friends at Bristol in Swarthm. Colln. vii. 157. This letter confirms the fact that some London Friends were serving, "for they were, when I was out of town, put in commission."
[4] *Works*, 1681 edn. pt. i. p. 309, "Of the Kingdom, Laws and Government of Christ," first printed in 1660.

THE RESTORATION SETTLEMENT

of justice and would bring the nation under God's judgment.[1]

Accordingly "the Quaker held on *a priori* grounds a belief in toleration to which other parties were slowly and reluctantly approximating under the force of circumstances."[2] He stood, on principle, for the rights of conscience. It is sometimes suggested that Fox himself did not favour the toleration by the State of all forms of faith. But he expresses himself on the subject in 1661, with his usual directness and robustness, and never wavered in his opinion.[3]

> As touching religion, it is for [a king's] nobility that there be universal liberty for what people soever. Let them speak their minds; let there be places and houses set forth where every man may speak his mind and judgment and opinion forth; for the king had better let men speak it forth than let it boil in their hearts and grow to a birth. . . . And let him be Jew, or Papist, or Turk, or Heathen, or Protestant, or what sort soever, or such as worship sun or moon or stocks or stones, let them have liberty where every one may bring forth his strength, and have free liberty to speak forth his mind and judgment. For the ministers of the gospel, who have the spiritual weapons, need not fear none of them all; for they have the shield of faith, the armour of light, and the breastplate of righteousness; they are armed soldiers with spiritual weapons, and they need not cry out to the magistrates . . . Therefore, as I spake before, let there be houses and places that all may speak their judgment, and let none be persecuted; and let the magistrates keep the civil peace that people may not strike one another nor wrong one another's persons but that they shall be patient to speak one to another, and they that be spiritual-minded satisfy the contrary.

Other Quaker leaders spoke with equal clearness,[4] but their point of view, though a commonplace now, was then much in advance of English thought. The reaction in

---

[1] Howgill, *Works*, p. 468, written in 1662; Burrough, *Works*, pp. 842, 856, both written in 1661.
[2] A. A. Seaton, *Theory of Toleration* (1911), pp. 172, 173.
[3] *Doctrinals*, pp. 234, 235; cf. p. 610, written in 1677, p. 1032, written in 1689.
[4] See William Caton, *The Testimony of a Cloud of Witnesses*, written in 1662 (which cites many authorities, including the States of Holland in 1579); Burrough, *Works*, p. 814 (1661); Hubberthorne, *Works*, p. 188, at end of volume.

favour of institutions had given the law of the land, whether right or wrong, a special force in men's minds, and made the breach of it, even on conscientious grounds, appear an act of sedition. There was a real fear, supported by the experience of the past, that both Roman Catholicism and Dissent menaced the peace of the realm. A generation of cruel but intermittent persecution must pass before Parliament would take the first great step towards religious liberty by passing the Toleration Act.

CHAPTER II

PERSECUTION, 1662–1669

No denomination so amazed and perplexed the authorities by their obstinacy as the Quakers. It was their boast that their worship, from its very nature, could not be stopped "by men or devils." From a meeting of Roman Catholics, they said, you have but to take away the mass-book, or the chalice, or the priest's garments, or even but to spill the water and blow out the candles, and the meeting is over. So, in a meeting of Lutherans or Episcopalians, or in a meeting of Presbyterians or Independents, or Baptists, or Socinians, there is always some implement or set of implements upon which all depends, be it in the liturgy, the gown or surplice, the Bible, or the hour-glass; remove these and make noise enough and there can be no service. Not so with a Quaker meeting. There men and women worship with their hearts without implements, in silence as well as by speech. You may break in upon them, hoot at them, roar at them, drag them about; the meeting, if it is of any size, essentially still goes on till all the component individuals are murdered. Throw them out at the doors in twos and threes and they but re-enter at the window and quietly resume their places. Pull their meeting-house down, and they reassemble next day most punctually amid the broken walls and rafters. Shovel sand or earth down upon them, and there they sit, a sight to see, musing immovably among the rubbish. This is no description from fancy; it was the actual practice of the Quakers all over the country. They held their meetings, regularly, perseveringly, and without the least concealment, keeping the doors of their meeting-houses purposely open that all might enter, Informers, constables, or soldiers, and do whatever they chose. In fact the Quakers behaved magnificently. By their peculiar method of open violation of the law and passive resistance only, they rendered a service to the common cause of all the Nonconformist sects which has never been sufficiently acknowledged.—D. MASSON, *Life of John Milton*, vi. 587-588.

The above masses the high lights of the picture, which were not, of course, all found together in any one instance. It is mainly taken from the passage in Barclay's *Apology*, cited *post*, head of Chapter IV.

THE bitter and barren persecution of Friends for the ten years from 1662 to '72 has a dramatic unity of its own. It began with a severe but futile Act directed expressly against the Quakers: it developed into a general attempt to root out Nonconformity, with Friends bearing the brunt of the attack : it died down for a time under the stress of the Plague, the Great Fire, and the Dutch War, only to gather fresh strength with the Conventicle Act of 1670 ; and it ended with the signal triumph of the King's Declaration of Indulgence in 1672, and the Great Pardon of Friends later in the same year. The dominant notes are always the same—the fears and prejudices of the authorities and of Parliament, the tolerant worldliness of the King, the honest dislike of the average Englishman to destroy his neighbours, and the victorious heroism of the victims. Pepys accurately reflected the national temper when he remarked on one occasion, "I saw several poor creatures carried by, by constables, for being at a conventicle. They go like lambs, without any resistance. I would to God they would either conform, or be more wise, and not be catched!"[1] A war to the knife could never be waged, because none but a few bigots were prepared to inflict the penalty of death. Even less trenchant weapons, fashioned for the occasion, such as transportation and the use of Informers, broke in the persecutors' hands. But, none the less, the death-roll of martyrs was a long one, for many died in crowded and pestilential gaols. The story throughout is radiant with the thronging faces of witnesses for truth, plain men and women, aglow with the Inward Light, who felt a spirit that outlived all wrath and contention, and wearied out all exaltation and cruelty, its crown meekness, its life everlasting love unfeigned.[2]

Within a few days of the final liberation of Fifth Monarchy prisoners in May 1661, the new House of Commons, flushed with Cavalier ardour, began the preparation of an Act against the Quakers.[3] The Bill was in Committee by July, where Hubberthorne, Burrough, and George Whitehead were twice heard against it, but found the members hostile. Burrough, with his accustomed boldness, let them know that if the Bill became law he

---

[1] *Diary*, 7th Aug. 1664.
[2] Nayler's words : *Beginnings of Quakerism*, p. 275.
[3] For the proceedings see *Letters of Early Friends*, pp. 95-114, and George Whitehead, *Christian Progress*, 1725 edn. pp. 260-271. The Act is printed in Besse, *Sufferings*, i. pp. xi, xii.

should continue to meet in spite of it, and should exhort others to do the same. The three Friends, and Edward Pyott of Bristol, were also heard at the bar of the House, and Hubberthorne argued with much sense that as the Quaker meetings were public they would not be used for harbouring plots. The Bill, however, was passed by the Commons and sent up to the Lords in July. It did not come down again to the Lower House till February 1662, and only received the royal assent on the 2nd of May, after conferences between the Houses. Some of the Lords spoke against it, but Clarendon and the majority secured its passage.

Like other persecuting legislation, the Quaker Act (St. 13 & 14 Car. II. cap. 1) was based on the dangerous opinions and practices of the persons aimed at, in this case their opinion about oaths and their meeting in great numbers to the public danger, and maintaining a secret correspondence to the terror of the people. Penalties were incurred if any person, who maintained "that the taking of an oath in any case whatsoever (although before a lawful magistrate) is altogether unlawful and contrary to the word of God," should wilfully refuse an oath when tendered, or endeavour to persuade another person to refuse, or should, by printing, etc., maintain the unlawfulness of an oath. The qualifications in this clause frustrated its effect, unless the person charged gave evidence against himself. The second branch of the Act made it an offence for Quakers to leave their habitations and assemble, five or more, under pretence of worship not authorized by law. On conviction by a jury, or confession, or notorious evidence of the fact, the offender, for a first and second offence, incurred fines or imprisonments, and for a third was to abjure the realm or be transported to any of His Majesty's plantations beyond the seas.

With the passing of the Act, a storm of persecution broke over London Friends.[1] For some months, from

---

[1] The chief authorities are Besse, *Sufferings*, i. 368-392, and the contemporary tracts (see Smith's *Catalogue*, i. 662, 663) on which the account in Besse is based; *F.P.T.* pp. 159-161; Ellwood's *Life*, 1714 edn. pp. 137-200, and George Whitehead, *Christian Progress*, pp. 271-274.

May till the middle of September, the meetings were frequently raided, often with great brutality, by Sir Richard Browne, the Major-General for the City till his death in 1669. He had "carried himself very honourably"[1] as Lord Mayor in the Fifth Monarchy year, and was a high-handed man, who on occasion could clap in prison those who refused compliance with his will, law or no law.[2] His soldiers would come into the Bull and Mouth with "canes in one hand and swords drawn in the other," and would force a way up the meeting, "by beating and kicking and hurling the people on heaps, and pushing them with the ends of their muskets and weapons," swearing and threatening the while. At the end of June the trial of the prisoners began, and they were astonished to find the Quaker Act put on one side within two months of its passing, and the Oath of Allegiance tendered instead, so as to run them into a *praemunire*.[3] John Crook, the first to be tried, had been a Justice of the Peace himself, and made a sturdy defence. He urged that being there as a prisoner by force and violence, he was not legally before the Court, and the oath could not be tendered him. But the Recorder said, " A man may be brought out of Smithfield by head and shoulders, and the oath tendered to him, and may be committed without taking notice how he came here."[4] Most of the prisoners were sent back to Newgate till the next Sessions, and their sufferings, seven score crowded together in the hot summer, and disabled from following their living, caused thirty London Friends to offer substituted imprisonment for some of the poorest. At the end of August, on the first coming of the Queen to London, the King ordered the release of such as were not ringleaders or preachers,[5] and most seem to have been

[1] Pepys, *Diary*, 8th January 1661.
[2] *Ibid.*, 13th June 1665.
[3] "The Cry of the Innocent," etc., which, with some omissions, is reprinted in Besse, i. 369-379, and in Sewel (1811 edn.), ii. 23-48.
[4] Cf. Ellwood's *Life*, pp. 158, 159. Crook's case found its way into the *State Trials*.
[5] *Extracts from State Papers*, p. 150. The Order also excepted persons indicted for refusing the Oath of Allegiance. Crook and the two Friends with him were released, perhaps in error, for the two Friends were re-imprisoned next day, Crook having left London. They were finally released 18th October.

discharged. Hubberthorne, the Lancashire yeoman, had already finished his testimony. Sarah Blackbury, the friend of Nayler and one of the mothers in Israel who looked after the prisoners, was by his death-bed.[1] He said at the last, much as James Parnell had done, "Do not seek to hold me, for it is too strait for me, and out of this straitness I must go, for I am wound into largeness and am to be lifted up on high, far above all," and so left the body.

Within a few days of the King's order clearing the gaols they were filled again by a savage raid made on the Bull and Mouth meeting, till the blood ran into the streets, and a man had been so cudgelled that he died some ten days later. On the day after the raid the emotional Solomon Eccles, who had been a music-teacher, went through Bartholomew Fair at Smithfield, as a Sign, "naked, with a pan on his head full of fire and brimstone, flaming up in the sight of the people, crying repentance among them, and bade them remember Sodom."[2] The next Sunday two women Friends visited St. Paul's, one supposing herself moved to go "with her face made black, and her hair down with blood poured in it, which run down upon her sackcloth which she had on, and she poured also some blood down upon the altar and spoke some words."[3] A paper was printed, "Concerning the cruelty acted in the meeting that day the man was killed,"[4] and reached the hands of the King. A lull followed, but at the end of October there were rumours of a plot by Quakers and Baptists,[5] and on the 26th some hundreds were imprisoned, with further commitments through November.

[1] *Works*, in unnumbered prefatory pages. The Guildhall Sessions Rolls (*per* G. Lyon Turner) show that he was committed for being at a meeting at the Bull and Mouth on 22nd June. Cf. Besse, i. 369.
[2] "A Brief Relation of the Persecutions . . . since . . . 7th mo. . . . 1662," p. 5. Cf. Pepys, *Diary*, 29th July 1667: for Eccles see *Camb. Journ.* ii. 428, and Sewel, ii. 241-243.
[3] "A Brief Relation."
[4] *Ibid.* It looks as though this was Richard Crane's Broadside, "A Hue and Cry after Bloodshed."
[5] Ellis Hookes to Margt. Fell, 28th October 1662 (Swarthm. Colln. i. 44, printed in *Letters of Early Friends*, p. 114) gives a good account of the fears of the authorities: cf. Pepys, *Diary*, 26th October and succeeding days. For the imprisonments on the 26th, see "A Brief Relation . . .," p. 21.

Burrough had languished in Newgate since June,[1] having come up from Bristol to London under a sense of the imminent persecution, "to lay down my life for the gospel and suffer amongst Friends in that place." He now wrote a letter to some of his friends in the country which is instinct with spiritual greatness:[2]

> Friends here are generally well in the inward and outward man, and the presence of the Lord is manifest with us through great trials and sore afflictions and grievous persecutions which we have met withal this last half-year. . . . Many have given up their lives in faithfulness in this place; and their faithfulness in keeping meetings, and patiently enduring many cruel exercises, is a crown upon Friends in this city. Here is now near 250 of us prisoners in Newgate, Bridewell, Southwark and New Prison. In Newgate we are extremely thronged, that if the mercy of the Lord had not preserved us we could not have endured: there is near a hundred in one room on the common side amongst felons, and their sufferings are great, but the Lord supports. For about six weeks' time meetings were generally quiet in the City, but these three last weeks they have fallen out more violently than ever, and imprisoned many Friends as also many Baptists; but through all this Truth is of good report, and the nobility of it gains place in many hearts, which are opened in pity and compassion towards innocent sufferers, and many are affected with our great afflictions, and Truth is increased through all trials. Here hath lately been a great talk and noise about a plot: what truth there is in it I know not; but it revived their violence towards Friends, though we are clear and innocent from all such things, who are a people that loves truth and peace, and the good of all men, and quietness withal, and the Lord will deliver us in His season from all our afflictions, though not by the arm of flesh in such a way; for our trust is in the Lord and not in man.

The deliverance that came to him was by death. "Weakness grew upon him daily, though in much patience he was carried through all."[3] He wrote a touching letter to Fox, expressing his "perfect love, which is the love of a son to his father. . . . We are well and the Truth is

---
[1] See *post*, p. 235 note.
[2] Printed in Besse, *Sufferings*, i. 389. I have followed a more primitive text in a MS. book of Letters, etc., 1662–1794 (Lloyd Colln.), belonging to me. The letter is there dated 9th November.
[3] Howgill's Testimony in Burrough's *Works*.

precious and prosperous."¹ His bosom friend, Howgill, thus describes the last hours in February 1663:²

He spoke to Friends that were about him to live in peace and love one another. . . . And he prayed for his enemies and for his persecutors, and said, "Lord, forgive Richard Browne [if] he may be forgiven.". . . And in the morning before he departed this life, being sensible of his death, he said, "Now my soul and spirit is centred into its own being with God, and this form of person must return from whence it was taken."

Friends felt the loss deeply; one woman came to Fox with a "whimsey" that "we should all be taken away," and he wrote exhorting Friends to be settled in the changeless Seed of God, in which they might feel dear E[dward] B[urrough] still among them, and have unity with him and enjoy him in the life which is invisible.³

We have a graphic picture of this persecution from the pen of young Thomas Ellwood.⁴ He and his friends are dragged from their meeting and penned in the street, like sheep in a pound, by soldiers with pikes held lengthways from one to the other. Ellwood asks the Major in command if he thinks to massacre them and is answered, "No, but I intend to have you all hanged by the wholesome laws of the land." They are marched into Fleet Street to Old Bridewell, and lodged in Wolsey's Banqueting Room, sixty feet long, but after the Sessions are sent to Newgate, to the common side among the felons, with liberty of the Hall during the day.

But in the night we all lodged in one room, which was large and round, having in the middle of it a great pillar of oaken

---

¹ Dev. Ho. A.R.B. Colln. No. 171.
² Howgill's Testimony. Josiah Coale, in his Testimony, says he desired the Lord that if it were possible He would forgive Browne, so that probably Howgill's account should read, "if he may be forgiven." Wm. Bayly, *Works*, p. 321, repeats Burrough's prayer in the form, "The Lord forgive thee, if it be yet possible."
³ For the whimsey, see *Camb. Journ.* ii. 9, for Fox's letter, *Journ.* i. 536, and cf. account of 1500 or 2000 at Burrough's funeral in *Extracts from State Papers*, p. 170. The remains of both Hubberthorne and Burrough were laid in Bunhill Fields, the Quaker *Campo Santo*, where Fox, Geo. Whitehead, Crisp, Parker, Chas. Marshall, John Bellers, with many others, were buried.
⁴ *Life*, 1714 edn. pp. 137-200.

timber, which bore up the chapel that is over it. To this pillar we fastened our hammocks at the one end, and to the opposite wall on the other end, quite round the room, and in three degrees or three storeys high, one over the other; so that they who lay in the upper and middle row of hammocks were obliged to go to bed first, because they were to climb up to the higher by getting into the lower. And under the lower rank of hammocks, by the wall sides, were laid beds upon the floor, in which the sick and such weak persons as could not get into the hammocks lay. And indeed, though the room was large and pretty airy, yet the breath and steam that came from so many bodies . . . was enough to cause sickness amongst us and I believe did so.

We hear of the Coroner's Inquest on a Friend who died, the foreman being a grave citizen, who had been impressed out of the street to serve, much against his will. He insisted on viewing the place, and so one evening, as the prisoners were going to bed, the turnkey burst in on them saying, "Hold, hold, don't undress yourselves: here's the Coroner's Inquest coming to see you." There was scarce room for them to come in at the door, and the foreman, lifting up his hand, said there was no question further how the man came by his death, for the place was enough to breed an infection, and, if he lived to the morrow, he would find means to let the King know how his subjects were dealt with. We hear also of the shabby fellow who had come to prison with Friends, a drone among the bees, on purpose to be maintained by them, and of the prisoners' shift of quarters to Bridewell, two and two abreast, without a keeper, through the Old Bailey into Fleet Street, to the pity and wonder of the people. The autumn imprisonments had been due to rumours of a plot, and Ellwood, in Newgate, was lodged in a room near to the quartered bodies of the three men who were executed as plotters in December. He saw the heads boiled before being set up in the City as gazing-stocks.

Suspicion had at first attached to Friends, but an early release of the prisoners might have taken place, if Edward Byllinge and some others, who were summoned before the Council in November, had not perversely refused to give a written undertaking on behalf of Friends not to take up

PERSECUTION, 1662-1669

arms or plot against the King.[1] Nor can a threatening letter from George Bishop of Bristol have helped matters.[2] But the King desired toleration of Nonconformists and Roman Catholics in spite of Parliament, and at the end of the year (26th December) issued his first Declaration of Indulgence. This was followed up early in January[3] by orders to release Quakers in Newgate, Southwark, and elsewhere, though persons dangerously seditious or seducers of others were excepted, and Burrough and one or two more were in consequence continued prisoners.[4] Among all the Nonconformists, the Quakers had held their ground to the last and had smarted more than any.[5]

When Parliament met in February 1663, Charles addressed them in favour of Indulgence, and a Bill was introduced in the Lords enabling him to dispense with the Act of Uniformity. But the Commons declared against his policy by a large majority and began to prepare further repressive legislation. Persecution had, however, slackened for a time, when during the summer information of a widespread Puritan plot in the North revived the zeal and fears of the authorities.[6] The scheme began in Durham towards the end of 1662, at Muggleswick in Derwentdale, and was intended to force the carrying out of the Declaration of Breda, and to secure the abolition of excise, chimney-money, and other obnoxious taxes, and the restoration of a gospel magistracy and ministry. York and other towns in the North were to be seized and it was confidently expected that thousands would rise all over the country.

---

[1] *Extracts from State Papers*, p. 153, letter of Ellis Hookes. The Declaration on behalf of Friends dated January 1663, by Wm. Bayly, *Works*, pp. 167-176, was no doubt intended to correct these impressions.
[2] Dev. Ho. Portfolio 1, No. 35, dated 5th December 1662.
[3] For these orders see *Extracts from State Papers*, pp. 159-166.
[4] *Collectitia*, p. 43, William Caton to Steven Crisp, 7th February; also Howgill's Testimony in Burrough's *Works*.
[5] *Extracts from State Papers*, p. 169, letter from Rev. William Hooke, dated 2nd March.
[6] See Rev. Henry Gee's paper, "The Derwentdale Plot of 1663," in *Royal Hist. Socy. Trans.*, 1917, pp. 125-142. The materials are found in the *Cal. State Papers, Dom.*, the *Depositions from York Castle* (Surtees Society), and the *Fleming MSS.* They are well summarized in F. Nicholson's paper, "The Kaber Rigg Plot, 1663," in *Transactions of the Cumberland and Westmorland Antiquarian, etc., Society*, 1911, pp. 212-232.

The Westmorland contingent was to be led by Robert Atkinson of Mallerstang, an old Parliamentary Captain of horse and a former Governor of Appleby Castle. The rising was fixed for the 12th October, but already in July the authorities were on the alert, and in August the Deputy-Lieutenants of the county were warned from London of a "fanatical design in hand," and directed to prevent and punish unlawful meetings and to secure dangerous persons. Captain Atkinson seems himself to have been detained, but he escaped, and on the night appointed left his home with a few men, who had gathered up to about thirty by the time they reached Kaber Rigg, a village beyond Kirkby Stephen on the road to Durham. Here, disappointed of a reinforcement from Kendal, he dismissed his men, and the Westmorland rising was over. "The poor fellows who so ludicrously set forth to overturn a kingdom, and returned home the same night hoping that they had not been seen, will cut no great figure in history."[1] But the consequences were serious and far-reaching to Friends, for the first rumours ran that the Quakers were engaged to a man;[2] and the conspirators, when taken, accused some of them.[3] One of Atkinson's company, Reginald Fawcett of Ravenstonedale, had been a Friend, though "disowned" several years before the plot.[4] Two Quakers at Kendal, the shoemaker Robert Wharton, and the surgeon George Walker, were informed against and committed for high treason, but presumably never tried.[5]

---

[1] F. Nicholson's paper, *op. cit.* p. 232.

[2] 24th July, *Extracts from State Papers*, p. 171.

[3] *Cal. State Papers, Dom.*, 1663-1664, p. 332 (9th November); p. 346 (23rd November); p. 372 (13th December).

[4] The account of Howgill's first Trial in Besse, *Sufferings*, ii. 12, has an answer by Howgill, "Fawcett has been disowned by us these six years, nor do I believe he hath pretended to come among us these two years." This seems the earliest technical use of the word "disown," which became the term for exclusion from the Quaker community. The money accounts in Swarthm. Colln. i. 306, show a collection in 1658 by the hands of Reginald Fawcett, and in 1659 he was one of the Friends from Ravenstonedale appointed to collect names for the Petition against Tithes (Kendal Early Record Book). He seems to have fled and escaped arrest.

[5] Robert Wharton was a leading Kendal Friend, one of the first to receive Fox in 1652 (*F.P.T.* p. 245), one of the local Treasurers in 1660 (Kendal Minute Books), and a Westmorland representative to the Skipton General Meeting in October 1660 (*Extracts from State Papers*, p. 119). He was alleged to have

Westmorland men Friends thought it necessary to assure the King that they were a peaceable people and utterly denied all plots, and an address to this effect, signed by 140 names, was presented to him early in January.¹ Howgill's words from Appleby prison to Fox expressed, we may be sure, the feelings of many honest-hearted Quakers who found themselves unjustly suspected because of colourable suspicions against two or three : ²

> I have borne a great weight many months upon my back, about this plotting and the like and [about] some that were too much inclined I knew to it, whom I could not wholly reject as believing in the Truth, neither yet justify; so that I have been as upon a rack betwixt my friends and enemies.

Since the Restoration, except for a short spell in prison at the time of the Fifth Monarchy Rising, Howgill had been engaged in active itinerating work, " no more weary than the first day the sickle was put into the harvest." ³ In the winter of 1662–3 he had travelled more than ever, but when he came north from London in the following summer the plot was on foot and he was quickly arrested.⁴ Others were also proceeded against, but the Quakers continued in their " insolence " to meet, " two hundred or more in one place," and thus increased the suspicions of the authorities.⁵ After the abortive rising, Daniel Fleming of Rydal Hall, most zealous of magistrates, felt the

---

refused a commission from Atkinson (*Extracts from State Papers*, p. 178). George Walker is, I think, once mentioned in the Kendal Minute Books, and was again arrested in July 1666, when Daniel Fleming described him as "a kind of a Quaker, yet much employed by most sorts of recusants. He is a person as likely for an intelligencer as most we have in this country, and one whom we had a long time in custody upon the score of Captain Atkinson's plot, but wanted then so much evidence against him as to be sufficient to try him at Appleby with the rest that were there found guilty" (*Fleming MSS*. p. 41). Both Wharton and Walker were thought to be privy to the rising, and to have been used as agents between the different groups of plotters. They would not confess to anything considerable and were apparently never brought to trial (*Extracts from State Papers*, p. 213).

¹ Dev. Ho. Portf. 3, No. 121.
² 3rd September 1664, Dev. Ho. A.R.B. Colln. No. 93.
³ See letters 23rd August, 29th September, 20th October 1661, A.R.B. Colln. Nos. 85, 83, 84.
⁴ In January 1663 he was in Bristol (*J.F.H.S.* vii. 140) ; at the end of March in London and going on to the Eastern Counties (Letter to Margt. Fell in Swarthm. Colln. i. 377) ; in June he was again in London, and was arrested in Kendal market at the end of July (Besse, *Sufferings*, ii. 11).
⁵ *Extracts from State Papers*, p. 172.

country to be pretty secure, unless from a few unlicensed ministers,

. . . or from the Quakers of whom we have too many, this part of the country joining upon that part of Lancashire where George Fox and most of his cubs are and have been for a long time kennelled. Though at present these persons are not much regarded, yet I am confident the first real danger we shall be in will be from them; for they are persons the most numerous of any one opinion that are here against us, of the closest correspondencies (keeping constantly their meetings weekly within eight miles one of another throughout all this country, if not England also) and they are such that will do mischief the most resolutely of any, if Fox or any other of their grand speakers should but dictate it unto them, which some of them half threaten already.[1]

Holding these opinions he offered a reward of £5 for the capture of Fox,[2] who was now in the North of England, and it was at his instance that the Quaker leader was taken in January 1664, soon after his arrival at Swarthmore.[3] He heard of the Justices' intentions overnight and could have escaped, but chivalrously considered that if he went away Friends would suffer the more, while his committal might stay the persecution.[4] The magistrates had him to Holker Hall, where one of the Deputy-Lieutenants called him a rebel and a traitor, but Fox replied that he had been in Derby dungeon for six months together because he would not take up arms against the King at Worcester fight.[5] He told them that he had heard of the plot when in Yorkshire, and had put out a paper against it to clear the Truth and stop foolish spirits from running into it; but the magistrates tendered him the oath, and for refusal committed him to the Quarter Sessions to be held at Lancaster on 12th January. Fleming was there and wrote to London:[6]

---

[1] *Extracts from State Papers*, p. 177 (14th November), also printed in full in B. Nightingale's *The Ejected of 1662 in Cumberland and Westmorland*, i. 114, 115.
[2] *Camb. Journ.* ii. 37, 42, confirmed by *Fleming MSS.* p. 32 (580a).
[3] *Extracts from State Papers*, p. 185 (7th January), and *Camb. Journ.* ii. 38.
[4] *Camb. Journ.* ii. 38.
[5] For this examination and the four subsequent trials see the various papers in *Camb. Journ.* ii. 39-89. The paper against plots is given in *Journal*, 1694 edn. p. 267.
[6] *Extracts from State Papers*, p. 186, also reporting action at Kendal and

PERSECUTION, 1662-1669

We proceeded smartly against the Quakers: we praemunired one, committed to close gaol George Fox and half a score more, for refusing of the Oath of Allegiance, and we fined near three-score upon the new Act for unlawful meetings, notwithstanding Mrs. Fell used her utmost endeavours with many of the Justices to prevent it. . . . I doubt not but this . . . will break their meetings and other designs in a short time, if they procure not somewhat by way of favour from you at Whitehall.

In a later letter Fleming reported that Margaret Fell held a greater meeting than ever at her house on the following Sunday, " on purpose, as 'tis generally thought, to affront our authority," and, if he received any encouragement from London, he proposed to tender her the oath and have her praemunired, as she was the chief maintainer of Quakers in the district.[1] He had a reply from the Government, with the help of which he persuaded the reluctant Justices to send for Margaret Fell,[2] who had recently returned home after a long religious journey through the West of England and the Northern Counties.[3] As she would not engage to keep no more meetings at her house the oath was tendered her, and, for refusal, she was committed for trial at Lancaster. The Assizes were held in March, and Fleming writes that as the charge to the Grand Jury was not so home to the fanatics as the county Justices expected, they waited on the Judge, Sir Thomas Twisden, and found that he had intended to leave the Quaker cases over to be dealt with by the county magistrates at Quarter Sessions, but, after seeing the letter from London, he consented to proceed against Fox and Margaret Fell.[4] Twisden was an upright but quick-tempered man, who met Fox's loud protests by threatening

---
Appleby. John Stubbs, lately returned from Egypt, and William Wilson of Langdale, who had travelled to Hamburg, were two of the other prisoners (*Cumb. Journ.* ii. 49, 50). Wilson wrote to Fleming from Lancaster Castle on 9th December (*Fleming MSS.* p. 31 and *Collection of Letters of William Wilson*, 1685, p. 41), reproving him for boasting that he had "holed the Fox and stayed his Hamburg Quaker from travelling."

[1] *Extracts from State Papers*, p. 188.
[2] *Ibid.* p. 189, Fleming to Williamson, 19th February, from which it appears that Margaret Fell was committed on 18th February.
[3] Margaret Fell, *Works*, pp. 4-7.
[4] *Extracts from State Papers*, p. 191. For Margaret Fell's two trials see *Works*, pp. 276-290.

D

to send for three or four criers to drown his voice, and abusively called him "Sirrah";[1] but had previously treated Margaret Fell courteously, having her four daughters by him on the bench, and brushing aside a whispered suggestion from the Sheriff that she should be tried under the St. 35 Eliz. cap. 1 with the words, "I could tell you of a law, but it is too penal for you, for it might cost you your life," to which the intrepid woman replied, "I must offer and tender my life and all for my testimony, if it be required of me."[2] Both prisoners were continued to the next Assizes, having claimed their right to "traverse" or postpone the trial. The same course was taken with Howgill at Appleby a few days later. During the next months the possible connection of the Quaker leaders with the plot was engaging the attention of the authorities, and a certain Richard Fletcher, who mixed with Friends but had conformed, was "sifted very much" by Sir Philip Musgrave to see if he would discover anything against Fox or Howgill. All he could say was that they were much esteemed among the Quakers, but he had nothing against them for they were altogether for peace.[3] George Whitehead, in London, was also suspected because Westmorland born, but he cleared himself by a letter to the Secretary of State.[4] When the summer Assizes came at the end of August,[5] Howgill and Margaret Fell were praemunired, but the errors in Fox's indictment were so grave that he was acquitted, though at once tendered the oath again

---

[1] After the trial Fox addressed a curious piece to the judges rebuking their use of evil words. See *Ellwood Journ.* ii. 36.

[2] For Act see *post*, p. 106. A Friend could not "abjure," and so ran himself into a felony. There was a Surrey case under this Act in 1662 affecting twenty-seven Friends (Besse, *Sufferings*, i. 690, 691, Sewel, ii. 19-22), and the sentence passed would have ultimately led to the death penalty, but the prisoners seem to have been released. Cf. case of Richard Vickris, *post*, p. 107.

[3] Howgill to Fox, 3rd September 1664, Dev. Ho. A.R.B. Colln. No. 93. For Fletcher cf. *Camb. Journ.* ii. 36.

[4] *Christian Progress*, p. 282; and *Extracts from State Papers*, p. 198.

[5] In Margaret Fell, *Works*, p. 284, the date is given as 20th September, which conflicts with the date for the trials of both Margaret Fell and Fox given in *Camb. Journ.* ii. 72-79, namely, 29th, 30th August. The September date is also shown to be wrong by a letter of Fleming's on 1st October (*Extracts from State Papers*, p. 221), which says that the Quakers have held meetings at Swarthmore for *several* Sundays since Margaret Fell was praemunired.

and recommitted for trial. Before the Assizes two of Margaret Fell's daughters had been to the King, who told them that there were Quakers in the last plot, whose names he had, but promised that if their mother were praemunired, her estate should not be taken away.[1] When sentence was pronounced she said, "Although I am out of the King's protection, yet I am not out of the protection of Almighty God."[2]

Fox rose to the full height of his personality during the trial. The key-note of his experience in this year 1664, as he revolved in mind the victories of heroes of faith in the past and thought of his own former sufferings and of the flood of trial that was swelling round Friends, may be given in his own words, which in substance recur over and over again:

> In the Seed sit down, in Whom ye have life and peace; and He remaineth and changeth not, Who now reigneth and is over all; and in Him live, that hath been slain from the foundation of the world and prisoned and pressed as a cart with sheaves, and yet gave His back and cheeks to the smiter and His hairs to the pluckers of them off. And so, in Him the second Adam you will not be weary, nor faint, nor think the time long of your sufferings; for all the weariness and faintings is in Adam in the Fall.[3]

On the second day of the Assizes, before he came to the bar, he was moved to pray that the Lord would confound the wickedness and envy of his persecutors, and would set His Truth over all and exalt His Seed, and the answer came in an uprush of power which filled him with an overcoming life such as he had known in Nottingham fifteen years before.[4]

The thundering voice said, "I have glorified thee and will glorify thee again": and I was so filled full of glory that my

---

[1] Mary Fell to Margaret Fell, 27th June, in *Letters of Early Friends*, p. 129.
[2] Margaret Fell, *Works*, p. 8.
[3] We know the thoughts that occupied Fox's mind from the fact that the collection of his sufferings which goes under the name of the *Short Journal* (see *Beginnings of Quakerism*, pp. 535, 536) was made during his Lancaster imprisonment, and from Fox, *Epistles*, pp. 202-225. My quotation is from p. 213.
[4] *Camb. Journ.* ii. 76, and for Nottingham episode, *Beginnings of Quakerism*, p. 52, cf. pp. 53, 54.

head and ears was filled full of glory; and then, when the trumpets and Judges came up again, they all appeared as dead men under me.

He induced the court to throw out the indictment for its errors, and, seeing that the Judge designed to tender him the oath again, looked him in the face with his piercing gaze, "and the witness started up in him and made him blush." In refusing this second tender, he held up the Bible as the book which forbad swearing and said he wondered it was at liberty, how did it chance that they did not imprison the book, a saying which went round the country as a byword. Then he cried out, "I am a Christian, and shall show forth Christianity this day; and it is for Christ's sake I stand; for it is *Lo-tishshab'un bekŏl-dabar*; and," he adds, "they all gazed, and there was a great calm, and then they took me away."[1] He had used the Hebrew for "Ye shall not swear by anything," and it is not surprising that the strange words amazed the Lancaster folk that August day. He had till the next Assizes for his trial, the Judge saying at the last, "I would the laws were otherways."

So I was put up in a smoky tower, where the smoke of the other rooms came up and stood as a dew upon the walls, where it rained in also upon my bed: and the smoke was so thick as I could hardly see a candle sometimes, and many times locked under three locks ... and so starved with cold and rain that my body was almost numbed, and my body swelled with the cold. And many times, when I went to stop out the rain off me in the cold winter season, my shift would be as wet as muck with rain that came in upon me: and as fast as I stopped it the wind being high and fierce would blow it out again: and in this manner did I lie all that long cold winter till the next Assizes.[2]

At the Assizes in March 1665,[3] the errors in the new indictment were found to be as grave as in the former one, so the Judge had the jury find Fox guilty, and he was treated as a praemunired person, though he had not

---

[1] *Camb. Journ.* ii. 78, cf. *Beginnings of Quakerism*, p. 302.
[2] *Camb. Journ.* ii. 83.
[3] *Ellwood Journ.* ii. 53, wrongly states that Margaret Fell was praemunired at these Assizes.

been sentenced in open court. Fourteen months had passed since he was first committed to Lancaster Castle.

The three Quaker leaders who had thus been put away suffered diverse fates. Howgill lay in the prison on the old bridge at Appleby till his death in January 1669,[1] stuffed up for want of air, and at the mercy of a tyrannous gaoler.[2] He behaved himself as "a man wholly given up into the will of God," and won the affection of the town,[3] and the rhymed elegies of his intimate friends,

> Sure Appleby may now its loss bewail;
> It hath no more such to detain in gaol,
> No man so fit your differences to end:
> 'Mongst lawyers now your money you may spend.[4]

He could write from prison to his fellow-sufferers,[5]

God by His Holy Spirit gives daily hints of His love in the inward man unto all stayed minds, and assurance of the victory, which makes me often overlook present suffering and forget the afflictions that are passed and little to heed present things though they seem to frown; because the light of God's countenance is lifted up, and His favour and love and strengthening power felt in the inward man, which balances all and weighs down the scale of present trouble and affliction.

Margaret Fell was not released till the summer of 1668, when Fleming complains that "her discharge from her easy imprisonment doth not a little encourage that rabble of fanatics and discourage all magistrates from acting against them."[6] Fox had a shorter but harsher confinement, the rigour of which seems to have been chiefly due to the Kirkbys of Furness,[7] Colonel Richard Kirkby, a member of the Cavalier Parliament, and his brother William. They had been active during the earlier stages of the matter, and now found that Fox was

---

[1] *Works*, early page.
[2] Howgill to Margaret Fell, 18th July 1665, Dev. Ho. A.R.B. Colln. No. 78.
[3] Richard Pinder's Testimony in *Works*.
[4] Rhymed Testimony by Thos. Langhorne and Thos. Carleton in *Works*.
[5] *Works*, p. 734 (22nd August 1668).
[6] 21st August 1668, *Extracts from State Papers*, p. 277. Dr. Richard Lower, brother of Margaret Fell's future son-in-law, Thomas Lower, seems to have used his influence for her release. (Thomas Salthouse to Margaret Fell, 19th May 1668, in *Letters of Early Friends*, p. 164, from Swarthm. Colln. i. 103.)
[7] For the Kirkbys see *Camb. Journ.* ii. 390, 391.

shaking the country, even from his prison-cell. A special order was procured for removing him to Scarborough.[1] Weak with his long durance in Lancaster, he was hurried across the country under military escort, and for the next sixteen months was, in his own phrase, "as a man buried alive,"[2] shut off from his friends, and the butt and gazing-stock of curious visitors at Scarborough Spa. Howgill says,[3] "I wrote once to him the last summer; but I heard my letter was lying still in Scarborough town so I forbore to write any more." The Deputy-Governor of the Castle seems to have told Fox that he was in custody there, in order that if there was any stir in the nation he might be hung over the walls,[4] to which he replied that he was ready, not fearing death and being innocent of all plots. Kept close prisoner, he had to hire a soldier to fetch him bread and water and firing; he became numbed and swollen in his limbs from the cold; a threepenny loaf served him three weeks or more, and his life was pining away on Scarborough rock. He could scarcely have lasted another winter. The Governor, however, had become his friend, and urged his case in London, where Richard Marche, one of the King's bedchamber, and an old friend of Fox, for whose liberty he would have gone a hundred miles barefoot,[5] procured an order for his release, as a man found to be against all plots and fightings and ready to discover rather than to make them. John Whitehead carried the order down, and it must have given the old soldier rare pleasure to revisit on this glad errand the Castle where he had been garrisoned at the time of his convincement.[6] Fox was

---

[1] *Camb. Journ.* ii. 92, confirmed by Ellis Hookes to Margaret Fell, 22nd May 1665, in *Letters of Early Friends*, p. 146, from Swarthm. Colln. i. 49.
[2] *Camb. Journ.* ii. 101, also in *Epistles*, No. 244 (1666).
[3] Howgill to Margaret Fell, 18th December (I think) 1665, Dev. Ho. A.R.B. Colln. No. 90.
[4] *Camb. Journ.* ii. 101.
[5] See J. J. Green's careful article on "Esquire Marsh" in *J.F.H.S.* iii., 147-156.
[6] For the release see *Camb. Journ.* ii. 101-104, especially the letter at p. 102 from Ellis Hookes to Margaret Fell, 14th August, which shows that the chief danger lay in the affair coming to the ears of Colonel Kirkby. There is an earlier letter from Hookes in *J.F.H.S.* ix. 96, from the Thirnbeck Colln.

freed on the 1st September 1666, with this testimony from the officers and soldiers, " He is as stiff as a tree and as pure as a bell, for we could never stir him."[1] Fleming, opening Friends' letters, found them jubilant over the release, and feared it would much discourage the Lancashire and Westmorland Justices from acting anything against the Quakers.[2]

The direct results of the Northern Plot of 1663 have now been shown in the case of the great Quaker leaders. The Westmorland rising at Kaber Rigg was, however, only one part of the affair. Its ramifications extended to London and the South, but the heart of the scheme lay in Yorkshire, where armed insurgents assembled at Farnley Wood, near Leeds, and threw up entrenchments, though they did not hold out after daylight. For complicity in this some twenty-one prisoners were sentenced to death at York in January 1664. In Yorkshire, however, no proof of serious intermeddling could be brought home to any of the leading Quakers, indeed they had given the authorities some assistance in the discovery.[3] But all the Puritan sects in the North of England came under suspicion of sedition. The plan was believed to have been hatched at their conventicles, and the authorities, with trainbands only, in most districts, at their command, were prodigiously alarmed at the thought of disbanded officers and soldiers of Cromwell's army roving the country and devising mischief to Church and State. Accordingly, when Parliament met in March 1664, the King discoursed largely of the plots, and petitions and letters came up

[1] *Camb. Journ.* ii. 104.
[2] 15th September 1666, *Extracts from State Papers*, p. 256.
[3] The *Extracts from State Papers* show that in August 1663 the Quakers told the High Sheriff, Sir Thomas Gower, at York, that they had been solicited but refused all use of carnal weapons (p. 171 ; see also p. 179, which may refer to same interview). Joseph Helling, a Quaker prisoner in Durham, who had fallen under the Ranter influence of Blanche Pope, and was out of unity with Friends, is stated (p. 178) to have sent a letter to Richardson, one of the plotters, in which he regarded " the favourable conjunction of the stars as hopeful for action." (For Helling see *Camb. Journ.* i. 463.) Richard Robinson, of Countersett (see *Beginnings of Quakerism*, pp. 148-150) admitted knowledge of one of the arch-plotters, John Atkinson of Askrigg, the stockinger, who seems to have been something of a Quaker, as Robinson and he had been in prison at York together (p. 177), and both names occur in the Fifth Monarchy imprisonments in Besse, *Sufferings*, ii. 101, 102. Robinson himself seems to have been quite clear.

like that from Westmorland, "desiring them to press home proper remedies ... for the future prevention of all danger from the Quakers and other fanatics."[1] A Bill was prepared to put down meetings where insurrections might be contrived, as late experience had shown. The Conventicle Act of 1664 (St. 16 Car. II. cap. 4), which resulted, was the Quaker Act stiffened and extended to all Nonconformists. It began by declaring the St. 35 Eliz. cap. 1 to be still in force, in order, I suppose, to allow the ultimate death penalty under that Act to be used. Any person sixteen years old committed an offence under the new Act who was present at a conventicle, or meeting under colour of religion in other manner than allowed by the Liturgy, at which there were five or more persons beyond the household. The Quaker Act had required a jury, but now two Justices could convict and imprison on a first and second offence for three and six months, unless fines not exceeding £5 and £10 were paid down—the Quaker Act had allowed a week for payment. For a third offence elaborate provisions for banishment were devised. After conviction at Quarter Sessions or Assizes a sentence was to be passed of seven years' transportation to any plantation except Virginia and New England, unless £100 fine were paid, but married women, whose husbands were not under sentence, were liable instead to twelve months' imprisonment. The Act also dealt with Quakers refusing oaths, in terms more effectual than the abortive clauses of the Quaker Act. The mere refusal of a judicial oath was to be recorded as a conviction, incurring the punishment of transportation, though, generally speaking, only after committal to the Assizes and refusal there. The law was to come into force 1st July 1664 and to continue for three years from the end of the session, and to the end of the next session after such three years—a clause which brought it to a close on 2nd March 1669.[2]

---

[1] *Extracts from State Papers*, p. 213; cf. speech of Speaker in presenting Conventicle Bill for royal assent (Masson, *Life of Milton*, vi. 249).

[2] See *post*, p. 53 note. The Act is printed in Besse, *Sufferings*, i. pp. xiii-xx.

Baxter well describes the effect of this oppressive measure.[1] After pointing out the vagueness of the reference to the Liturgy and the arbitrary power given to Justices without a jury, he says that the mass of the Nonconformists was now put to the test as well as the ministers. While the Nonconformist minister alone had suffered, the people had been very courageous and had exhorted him to stand it out, and preach till he went to prison; but now that it was their own case they would go to prison once, but then their judgments altered, and they agreed that it was better to preach often to a few than once or twice in public to many. Some durst scarce crave a blessing on their meat if above four persons came in to dine with them. In London, where the houses joined, some thought the law would not be broken if they heard one another through the wall.[2] Others were of opinion that they might venture if they withdrew into another room and left the strangers by themselves. But, adds Baxter,

... here the fanatics called Quakers did greatly relieve the sober people for a time: for they were so resolute, and gloried in their constancy and sufferings, that they assembled openly, at the Bull and Mouth near Aldersgate, and were dragged away daily to the Common Gaol, and yet desisted not, but the rest came the next day nevertheless, so that the Gaol at Newgate was filled with them. Abundance of them died in prison, and yet they continued their assemblies still! And the poor deluded souls would sometimes meet only to sit still in silence, when, as they said, the Spirit did not speak, and it was a great question whether this silence was a religious exercise not allowed by the Liturgy, &c. ... Yea, many turned Quakers, because the Quakers kept their meetings openly and went to prison for it cheerfully.

The records prove that Baxter is right, and that the Friends bore the brunt of the persecution. There is a bundle of forty-eight certificates, containing convictions in Middlesex, outside the City, from 24th July 1664 to 31st December 1665.[3] Of the 909 convictions, affecting

[1] *Reliquiae Baxterianae*, pt. ii. 435-437. Cf. *infra*, p. 51.
[2] Cf. *Extracts from State Papers*, p. 287.
[3] See *Middlesex County Records*, edited by J. C. Jeaffreson, vol. iii. pp. 340-

782 persons, no less than 859 or 94½ per cent are certainly for attendance at Quaker meetings, held, with one exception, at William Beane's house in Mile-end, at Wheeler Street, Spitalfields, or at John Elson's house at the sign of the Peel in Clerkenwell. In the City itself, the meeting at the Bull and Mouth was the centre of persecution, and, on the Surrey side, within two days of the coming into force of the Act, Friends were taken from their meeting-house at Horslydown. Within a year, there had been over 2100 imprisonments on account of attendance at these five meetings—the other Quaker meetings in London having been apparently unmolested. The sentences on the first and second offence were commonly light, not in mercy to the prisoners, but at the instance of the authorities, so as to lead more rapidly to transportation.[1] At Hertford Assizes, six weeks after the Act came into force, there were nine cases ripe for banishment. The Grand Jury was persuaded to find a true bill, after having first ignored it, and the witnesses gave evidence that the prisoners at the bar had met together, but they neither saw anything they did, nor heard anything they spoke. The Judge was Sir Orlando Bridgeman, a man of moderation and integrity, but timorous and unable to free himself from the disordered imaginations of the time. To his eyes, as to those of Parliament, a silent Friends' meeting was a very babel of

---

349, and Preface, pp. xxiii-xxvii. Neither the editor nor Frank Bate, *The Declaration of Indulgence, 1672*, is aware that these certificates relate almost entirely to Quakers, but the fact is clear from the close comparison which I have made with the independent accounts in Besse, *Sufferings*, i. pp. 393-395, 398-400, 402-408. The dates and the numbers taken closely correspond; and the names of the first case, which Jeaffreson gives in full, are Quaker names. His particulars name the houses of Beane and Elson, but the Spitalfields house is disguised as a "building or room in the possession of an unknown man in Stepney," no doubt because it was in the name of Gilbert Latey (see *post*, p. 77). I have deposited in the Dev. Ho. Library a copy of my notes on this and the further question of the Friends sentenced to banishment, under title "London Friends sentenced to Transportation, 1664-1665."

[1] George Whitehead suggests this, *Christian Progress*, p. 286, and John Lawrence, of Wramplingham, writing at the end of July (*Extracts from State Papers*, p. 214), says that the Judge at Norwich Assizes, acting, no doubt, on his instructions from Whitehall, had advised the Justices "to send none to prison for more than three or four days at a time that so they might proceed to banishment the sooner." Cf. *F.P.T.* p. 164 and *post*, pp. 51, 52.

secret and presumably seditious intercourse. He charged the jury as follows :

My masters, you are not to expect a plain, punctual evidence against them for anything they said or did at their meeting ; for they may speak to one another, though not with or by auricular sound, but by a cast of the eye, or a motion of the head or foot, or gesture of the body ; for dumb men may speak to one another so as they may understand each other by signs. And they themselves say that the worship of God is inward, in the Spirit, and that they can discern spirits and know one another in spirit. So that, if you find or believe in your hearts that they were in the meeting under colour of religion in their way, though they sat still only and looked upon each other, seeing they cannot say what they did there, it was an unlawful meeting and their use and practice not according to the Liturgy of the Church of England, for it allows and commands when people meet together in the church that Divine service shall be read, etc. And you must find the Bill, for you must have respect to the meaning and intent of the Law, which the King and Parliament have in wisdom and policy made not only against conventicles, but the words "assembly" and "meeting" was added ; for we have had late experience of the danger of such meetings under colour of religion, and it is an easy matter at such meetings to conspire and consult mischief. . . . It doth not touch conscience at all, as I confess some other Laws do . . . but this Law leaves men's consciences free so they do not meet.[1]

Eight of the nine were sentenced to banishment, four to Barbados and four to Jamaica, and seven were put on the *Ann*, of London, but the master having contracted for their passage on the footing that they were free men, and being baffled by the wind for nearly two months between London and Deal, put them ashore to go whither they pleased, with a certificate declaring that he perceived that the hand of the Lord was against him, and

[1] George Whitehead, in July, had strongly argued that a Friends' meeting was not disallowed by the Liturgy (*Christian Progress*, p. 279). See also Farnsworth's Tract, beginning of June, called "Christian Religious Meetings Allowed by the Liturgie Are no Seditious Conventicles, etc." Cf. Baxter, *ante*, p. 41. A letter in *Extracts from State Papers*, p. 219, dated in September, says that Sir Matthew Hale ruled at Exeter that if no sedition appeared under the exercise of religion the Act did not apply. This, if acted on, would have cleared the Quakers. Cf. case of Fox, *post*, p. 220, under the Quaker Act.

that his men refused to go the voyage if he carried the Quakers. So they returned to London, and calmly notified the King of the facts. As was to be expected, an Order in Council was made directing them to be secured until means of transportation could be found, and under this order they continued in prison until the Great Pardon of 1672. They found twenty-one other Friends under like sentence, and five more followed. The Quaker group in Hertfordshire had been caught up into a common heroism which expressed itself in the words of Lewis Laundy, in refusing to pay the £100 fine: "It is for the testimony of my conscience towards God that I am sentenced, and, if I had an hundred lives, and could redeem them all with an hundred pence, I should not give them in this case."[1]

The London cases were not brought to trial till October, although Sir John Kelyng, an able but high-handed judge, had made a violent attack on the Quakers in a charge to the Grand Jury in September. Their leaders, he said, taught the unlawfulness of oaths because their end was rebellion and blood. He had served the King at York in the Farnley Wood trials, and had found that the plot was hatched and carried on at conventicles. If he could catch the culprits, he would try them by a law which if executed would take away their lives.[2]

From October to March the Middlesex and City Sessions, at Hick's Hall and the Old Bailey, were busy

---

[1] For the Hertford cases see Besse, *Sufferings*, i. 244-249 and 250, based on "A True, Short, Impartial Relation . . . of the Proceedings . . . at the Town of Hertford, etc.," by W[illiam] S[tout], 1664, "A Second Relation from Hertford, etc.," by W[illiam] S[tout], 1664, and "A True and Impartial Naration of the Remarkable Providences . . . for us his Oppressed Servants . . . sentenced to be Transported, etc.," 1664. Cf. *Friends' Quarterly Examiner*, 1916, pp. 358-370, article by Samuel Graveson on "The Hertford Quaker Trials of 1664," who states that Wm. Stout, of Hertford, edited the two first pamphlets. Besse does not specify the sentence on the last five cases, but the *Herts Sessions Rolls, J.F.H.S.* vii. 98, show that it was transportation to Barbados, which was evidently not carried out, as the names appear in the Pardon of 1672. Edward Maning published "The Masked Devil or Quaker," 1664, attacking the seven sent to be transported, and Sewel, ii. 137-143, narrates the facts but supposes that the seven escaped further punishment.

[2] Besse, *Sufferings*, i. 396. His aspersions were replied to by W[illiam] S[tout] in "The Innocency and Conscientiousness of the Quakers Asserted and Cleared from The Evil Surmises . . . of Judge Keeling."

with the Quakers. The proceedings were chronicled at the time in four pamphlets, called "The Cry of the Innocent and Oppressed for Justice," "Another Cry . . . or A Second Relation," "Another Cry . . . or a Third Relation," and "One Cry more . . . Being a Fourth Relation."[1] In all some 109 men Friends and 44 women were condemned to banishment. None but Quakers received this sentence in Middlesex,[2] nor, so far as I can learn, in the City: it was the Quakers alone who braved the Act, openly and repeatedly, even to the third offence. Public opinion ran strongly in their favour. A first batch of sixteen Friends was found by the jury guilty of meeting at the Bull and Mouth, but not guilty of meeting contrary to the Liturgy of the Church of England. They were, however, continued in prison.[3] In spite of browbeating, six of the jury stood to their verdict, and, in violation of constitutional law, were bound over in a hundred pounds apiece to answer at the King's Bench, as a warning which might serve to make later juries more pliant.[4] On another occasion a juryman became so conscience-stricken for what he had done that he published a paper under the title of "The Wounded Heart, or the Juryman's Offences declared."[5] Very few London Friends were actually transported to the colonies. Three were put on the *Jamaica Merchant* in March 1665, one dying soon after, and two being carried to Jamaica—Edward Brush, an elderly Friend, who lived to return to England in 1669, and James Harding, a much younger man, who married

---

[1] Summarized in Besse, *Sufferings*, i. 399-406. See also "God's Holy Name magnified . . . by the Testimony of his Faithful Servants who have suffered . . . Banishment," by Richard Crane, 1665.

[2] The Middlesex cases can be checked from *Middlesex County Records*, vol. iii.

[3] Guildhall Sessions Rolls, *per* G. Lyon Turner.

[4] Besse, *Sufferings*, i. 401, and references by George Whitehead and Ellis Hookes in *Letters of Early Friends*, pp. 140, 141 (from Swarthm. Colln. iv. 61, and i. 47), and by Esther Biddle and H. P. in *Extracts from State Papers*, pp. 220, 222. The case against the Jury was not prosecuted. See "Truth Rescued from Imposture" in Penn's *Works*, 1726 edn. i. 513, 514. The action of the Jury in one of the Quaker cases led to *Rex* v. *Wagstaffe*, 1 Keble, 934, 938, and 1 Siderfin, 272, which was overruled in *Bushell's Case*, see *post*, p. 73, and had been one of the grounds on which in December 1667 the Commons voted that fining juries was an innovation of dangerous consequence to the lives and liberties of the people.

[5] Besse, *Sufferings*, i. 403.

and settled in the island.¹ Seven were transported in April, and reached Nevis,² and one other Friend, being sent to Bridewell as a vagabond, was shipped with three criminals to Virginia, not under the Conventicle Act, to be sold as a slave for seven years.³ Eight more, sentenced to Barbados, were embarked at the end of May.⁴ But it was found almost impossible to procure passages. Seamen were being pressed for the Dutch War, which made the narrow seas dangerous, and the shipmasters had got the salutary notion into their heads that no Englishman should be carried out of his country against his will.⁵ The Hertford experience had been repeated at Bristol.⁶ There a persecuting mayor had hoped to banish 400 Quakers before he went out of office, but, in spite of 350 Quaker convictions under the Act, had only procured the sentence upon three. After three weeks on the *Mary Fortune*, the Friends were put ashore on the ground that it was contrary to the laws of England and Barbados to transport them out of England or bring them into Barbados against their will, and because the master had no indemnity against possible penalties.⁷ In May there was an idea of sending the accumulation of London Quakers

---

¹ Besse, *Sufferings*, i. 405. Crouch, *Posthuma Christiana*, chap. iv., gives the warrant to the Governor of Jamaica, and in Dev. Ho. Portf. 23, No. 137, the "Lamentation over London" of the exiles may be read. On reaching Jamaica they had much liberty from the Governor, see Esther Biddle to John Smith, 29th Nov. 1665, in Dev. Ho. A.R.B. Colln. No. 94, and John Taylor's *Journal*, 1830 edn. p. 38. In 1695, when more than 90, Brush published "The Invisible Power of God Known in Weakness," relating his sufferings. Harding visited London in July 1685 (Fox, *Itinerary Journal*, at Dev. Ho. Cf. *Camb. Journ.* ii. 408).

² Esther Biddle's letter says, "We have heard from Mevis, from Thomas Gibson, and the other seven, that the Lord struck the master of the ship dumb, and about a fortnight after he died, and was thrown overboard about four days before they came to land." ³ Besse, *Sufferings*, i. 404.

⁴ *Ibid.* i. 405 : the John Raunce mentioned was not the well-known High Wycombe doctor, as we find him imprisoned in Buckinghamshire five weeks later (*ibid.* i. 77), but a blacksmith of Horslydown (Guildhall Sessions Rolls, *per* G. Lyon Turner). Elizabeth Hooton (see *F.H.S. Supplement*, No. xii. p. 54) speaks of three ships having carried sentenced Friends, in addition to the *Black Eagle*, which confirms my conclusions.

⁵ Besse, *Sufferings*, i. 51, 246.

⁶ *Ibid.* i. 51-52 ; Crouch, *Posthuma Christiana*, chap. iv. ; and *Extracts from State Papers*, p. 230.

⁷ The succeeding Bristol Mayors were more moderate, but the gaols for a time were thronged with Quakers (Besse, i. 52); and George Bishop, the leading Bristol Friend, was sentenced to banishment (see his "Manifesto," printed in 1665).

in a prize ship.¹ At length² the Sheriffs found a man to their purpose, named Fudge, nicknamed "lying Fudge," master of the *Black Eagle*, who boasted that he would not stick to transport even his nearest relations. Five-and-fifty Quakers were taken out of Newgate towards the end of July, and carried down the river to Fudge's ship, which lay below Greenwich in Bugby's Hole. How neatly the names fit the transaction. The sailors refused to lend a hand and the Quakers passively resisted, so only four were put on board, and the turnkeys returned the rest to Newgate. A fortnight later some soldiers from the Tower finished the sorry business: they dragged some, kicked and punched others, hove up many by legs and arms, and so in an hour's time tumbled them into the ship, thirty-seven men and eighteen women in all. Bugby's Hole in mid-August of the year of pestilence 1665 was not a pleasant spot. The Plague had come to London from Amsterdam and was now at its height, though at first the river was immune. It had broken out shortly after the first Friends had been transported, in the house next to that of Edward Brush, in Bearbinder Lane.³ George Whitehead had not felt free to leave the city, but diligently visited Friends in prison and at their houses, even when many lay sick of the contagion, and on First-days would take his night-caps in his pocket when he went to meetings, expecting imprisonment and resigned either to live or die. Gilbert Latey, the former court-tailor, was equally courageous, and became the almoner of country Quakers, who sent up money for the Plague-victims, especially for poor people confined to their own houses, many of whom had running sores upon them. In October, when the sickness was abating, he caught the infection,

---

¹ *Extracts from State Papers*, p. 240.
² Besse, *Sufferings*, i. 406; Crouch, *Posthuma Christiana*, chap. iv. for letters of two of the banished Friends, Degory Marshall and Lawrence Fullove; George Whitehead, *Christian Progress*, pp. 291-295, 299-301; *Life of Gilbert Latey*, pp. 62-65, Sewel, ii. 172, 173, 195. At Amsterdam in 1664, Friends had behaved with great constancy, visiting the sick and watching with them and maintaining the meeting in a plague-stricken house. (William Caton to Friends, 8th September 1665, in *Collectitia*, p. 139.)
³ Sewel, ii. 171. Cf. George Whitehead, *Christian Progress*, p. 300.

"but the Lord was good unto him, and, having further service for him to do, raised him up again." Ellis Hookes, the Clerk to Friends, a man of delicate health but high heart, also kept his post, and writes :[1]

As a brand is plucked out of the fire, so has the Lord delivered me; for I have often laid down my head in sorrow, and rose as I went to bed, and not slept a wink for the groans of them that lay a-dying; and every morning I counted it a great mercy that the Lord gave me another day.

The *Black Eagle* lay seven weeks in the river, before she made the Downs, during which time half the prisoners died, many being buried in the marshes below Gravesend. George Whitehead visited the infected ship and had a meeting on board. Fudge, the master, was arrested for debt and had trouble with his crew, some deserting, and the mate and boatswain telling him that they would not go the voyage, for if they did they would be destroyed, as they saw that the Lord was against them.[2] Red-coat soldiers from the Tower kept guard over the prisoners: another master was found, but the ship was still in the Downs in January 1666, and did not reach Plymouth till the latter part of February, where we hear of local Friends going to the vessel's side with fresh provisions.[3] A few hours later she was taken as a prize by a Dutch privateer. The two ships, each freighted with Friends, were parted in a storm. The prize sailed round Ireland and Scotland to Norway and lay in Bergen harbour for twenty days, the Quakers distributing books to curious visitors. At length about the end of April she reached Horn in North Holland, some time after the privateer. The Quakers on both ships were soon set at liberty and were hospitably received by Amsterdam Friends, returning with their help to England, except one Dutchman, John Claus, who remained in Holland. "Thus," says Sewel, "the banished were delivered, and the design of their

---

[1] *J.F.H.S.* i. 20, from letter of 7th November 1665, to Margaret Fell, in Swarthm. Colln. iv. 121.
[2] Letter, Mary Booth to Edmond Crosse, no date, in Dev. Ho. Crosse Colln. p. 105.   [3] *Camb. Journ.* ii. 91.

persecutors was brought to nought by an Almighty hand."

Amid perils of pestilence, perils of exile, and perils of prison, London Friends nobly maintained their meetings, though by small numbers who were at liberty and with frequent interruption from soldiers.[1] They were kept out of the Bull and Mouth, which was boarded up, but met in the street.[2] By the end of 1665, meetings were very large " of strange faces and good honest countenances, who with exceeding hungerings receive the Truth."[3] The suffering of Christians had once again proved a fruitful seed.

Out of many enheartening epistles addressed to the stricken flock in London and elsewhere, one quotation must suffice. It comes from a letter written by Caton from Amsterdam in September of the Plague year,[4] and gives fine expression to the faith which outlasts all trials.

> The righteous are at rest and truly content in whatsoever the Lord suffers to pass. If bonds and imprisonments attend them for the gospel's sake, they are content. If losses and crosses happen daily to them, they bear them with patience. If they are tried with confiscation of their goods and transportation of their persons, this they also bear with patience. If they or their families be visited with the plague or any other sickness, they are quiet in their minds, submitting themselves to the hand of the Lord, being assured in themselves [that] none of these things come to pass without the Lord's permission; and in all these conditions they are in much less danger of being exalted, of forgetting the Lord and of sinning against Him, than otherwise they should be in the day of prosperity. . . . Let now bowels of mercy and compassion be shown, not only though especially to them of the household of faith, but to all that are in distress, to all that are helpless, poor and needy, . . . and let it now be manifest to the world that your love and faith and confidence in the Lord do transcend others, and that you are freed from that slavish fear, with which many thousands are possessed . . . and know that you are in the hand of the Lord, and that whether you live or die you are the Lord's.

---

[1] Crouch, *Posthuma Christiana*, chap. v. The letter of Ellis Hookes, already referred to, names the Friends who died on the ship, and 52 others who died of the plague in Newgate.
[2] See *Letters of Early Friends*, pp. 149, 153, 156.
[3] Morgan Watkins in *Letters of Early Friends*, p. 156.
[4] *Collectitia*, pp. 136-139, from the Colchester Colln.

The Quakers, almost single-handed, had fought and vanquished the Conventicle Act in London. In the country its impotence, so far as Friends were concerned, was quickly realized, and the sentences of banishment on the third offence were relatively few. Outside London and Hertford there were, I think, forty-five cases, and in these actual banishment was only attempted in the three from Bristol, already mentioned.[1] In the summer of 1665 Sir John Lowther was lamenting from Cumberland that through "the want of the executive part, transportation, our good intentions stand us in little stead."[2] The weapon had broken in the hands of the persecutors. Friends everywhere continued to hold their meetings as though no persecuting Act were in being. They braved the storm and weathered it triumphantly. It is worth while to summarize the results. About 230 Friends seem to have been sentenced to banishment, but I have failed to discover a single case under the Act in other dissenting bodies. Of these 230 less than a score were actually transported, but most of those sentenced in the country were held prisoners till the Pardon of 1672.

The fortunes of the one hundred and fifty-three sentenced in London can be traced with great minuteness.[3] For

[1] Besse, *Sufferings*, gives four cases in Berkshire, and Christopher Cheesman must be added, nine in Durham, four in Norfolk, sixteen in Northants, seven in Yorkshire, a total with the three Bristol cases and George Bishop of forty-five. There may have been a few others, in spite of the care taken in recording sufferings. The Berkshire cases, with much other persecution, are told in "Persecution appearing With its own Open Face in Wiliam Armorer," 1667, the Norfolk in "The Norffs President of Persecution (unto Banishment), &c.," 1666, and the Northants in "The Voice of the Innocent uttered forth," 1665, and "Another Out-Cry of the Innocent and Oppressed," 1665. The four Bristol Friends seem to have escaped imprisonment; of the remaining forty-one sentenced persons most were included in the Pardon of 1672, and some others are known to have died or been released beforehand. For example, in the Yorkshire Q.M. Accounts, 14th Mar. 1667, we find £3 given "to George Ellis, of Burton [near Barnsley], to buy a horse to help to get a livelihood, whose poverty, occasioned by his sore suffering, is much, being one of the sentenced Friends." On the whole there is no reason to think that any of these forty-one were actually transported.

[2] *Extracts from State Papers*, p. 241.

[3] It looks as though we had now full particulars of the London cases in the *Middlesex County Records* and in the elaborate extracts from the Guildhall Sessions Rolls made by G. Lyon Turner, and deposited by him at Dev. Ho., which are a mine of information. With the help of these and of the material in Besse, I have carefully analysed the sentences of banishment (with names and particulars) in my notes on "London Friends sentenced to Transportation, 1664–1665," also deposited at Dev. Ho.

one, after seven months' imprisonment, the £100 fine was paid.¹ Eighteen were actually transported, one died on shipboard on the *Jamaica Merchant* and twenty-eight on the *Black Eagle*, twenty-seven failed to be transported through the capture of the *Black Eagle*, thirty-seven died in prison, nine are said to have "escaped" at the time of the Great Fire, which included Newgate, thirty-one disappear from notice, one only remained in prison until the Pardon of 1672.

I have said that I find no evidence that any other Dissenters were sentenced to banishment.² This is almost certainly the case in London, and I think holds good equally of the rest of the country. Their point of view did not push them to the same extreme of heroic witness. Many of the ministers, like Adam Martindale,³ felt it right to conform to the law and preached their sermon over four or five times, dividing their flock into as many parts. Others, like Thomas Ewins, the imprisoned pastor of the Broadmead Baptist Church at Bristol, urged a bolder though still a prudent course. His judicious letter on the matter merits quotation:⁴

> I have thought and do still think that it would have been much better for you to have continued the public meetings in the usual place, till you had been some of you taken up. . . . I conceive your testimony is not to the full or it is not finished. . . . When you have suffered the first penalty, either by fine or imprisonment, then, I conceive, you have borne your testimony, and then you might come to family meetings, as Paul did at Corinth, Acts xviii. 4; xix. 8, 9. Why should any fear or draw back, upon the account of the first penalty of this Act? It is not worth the mentioning. You may redeem yourselves out for a shilling; if not, they will turn you out in a week or two. But some will say, They will do that but in policy, that they may take us again, and hasten our banishment. I answer, let their

---

¹ This was John Peachey, an ejected Presbyterian minister, who for a time gained his living as a scrivener, and seems to have thrown in his lot with Friends. In 1672 he secured a licence to preach as a Presbyterian at his own house. *Per* G. Lyon Turner. Cf. *Original Records of Nonconformity*, ii. 978; iii. 380.

² Neither in the *Middlesex County Records* nor in G. Lyon Turner's extracts is there any non-Quaker sentence of transportation under the Act.

³ *Life*, Chetham Society edn. p. 176.

⁴ *Broadmead Baptist Records*, pp. 80, 81. Cf. *ante*, p. 41.

ends be what they will; if you be out, you may then confine yourselves to private family meetings and so escape banishment —having borne your testimony so fully, you may comfortably rest and leave the work to those that have not yet been taken.

This was probably the extent to which earnest Baptist witness went; and, among Nonconformists generally, except Friends, private meetings were for a time the rule.

Baxter tells us that after the Act of Uniformity many silenced ministers, anxious to conform to the law as far as possible, at first did their work very privately; but when the Plague grew hot, and many of the clergy fled, they resolved to go into the forsaken pulpits and preach to the poor people before they died, feeling that no law could justify them for neglecting men's souls and bodies in such an extremity. Their fervent preaching reached many, and "religion took that hold on the people's hearts as could never afterward be loosed."[1] Sheldon himself stanchly remained in London at his post of duty; but, when Parliament met at Oxford in the autumn, he and Clarendon procured the passage of the harsh Five Mile Act (17 Car. II. cap. 2), which excluded ministers from teaching school or living within five miles of any corporate or Parliamentary borough or of any place where they had preached, unless they took an oath never to endeavour any alteration of government in Church or State.[2] The temper of the Commons was shown in a proposal to extend this oath to the whole nation, which was only defeated by six votes. A few ministers took the oath, others withdrew to the country or to unincorporated towns like Birmingham and Manchester, whose Nonconformity and prosperity profited by the fact that they were outside the Act; many, under great privations, heroically braved the law and preached till they went to prison.[3]

Though the Conventicle Act did not technically expire

---

[1] *Reliquiae Baxterianae*, pt. iii. 2.
[2] Printed in Grant Robertson, *Select Statutes, etc.*, 2nd edn. pp. 67-70, and Besse, *Sufferings*, i. pp. xx-xxii.
[3] *Reliquiae Baxterianae*, pt. iii. 2-15.

till 2nd March 1669,[1] it had been in little use for some time before. Baxter notes that after the Fire of London in September 1666, which destroyed many City churches, the Nonconformists were more than ever resolved to preach till they were imprisoned, and several kept their meetings very openly and even furnished rooms and chapels with pulpits, seats, and galleries. The City, like many other parts of England, had retained much of its Puritan seriousness and sobriety, in spite of the moral corruption of the Court, and welcomed the freer conditions.[2]

The year 1667 saw the Dutch fleet in the Medway and the fall of Clarendon. His services to Charles had been great. But the King wanted men of easier morals and more tolerant opinions, and was not sorry to offer him up as the sacrifice which the public demanded to atone for the humiliation from the Dutch. He would now be advised by the so-called Cabal—which was composed partly of liberal-minded Protestants and partly of secret Roman Catholics, and had to deal with a suspicious and often hostile Cavalier Parliament. Violent perturbations of policy resulted as circumstances gave dominance to one or other factor of influence.

At first Buckingham and the Liberals had a chief hand in guiding affairs. Buckingham was a man " of no religion but notoriously and professedly lustful ; and yet of greater wit and parts and sounder principles as to the interest of humanity and the common good than most lords in the Court."[3] In January 1668 negotiations were on foot for a possible comprehension and toleration,[4] and in February Charles recommended a toleration to Parliament. But the Commons were as stoutly hostile as ever, and desired the King to order the strict enforcement of the

---

[1] *Cal. State Papers, Dom.*, 1668–9, p. 256 ; cf. proclamations, *ibid.* p. 108, and *ibid.*, 1667–8, p. 591. The Act was to continue till end of next session after 17th May 1667. The session began in October and sat with recesses till May 1668, when it adjourned till August, and again till November, and till 1st March 1669, being prorogued from that date. Pepys, 11th August 1668, was told that the Act was then out, to the great joy of Nonconformists ; and *Reliquiae Baxterianae*, pt. iii. 50, speaks of it, in June 1669, as "long ago expired."
[2] *Reliquiae Baxterianae*, pt. iii. 17, 22. The Bull and Mouth meeting-house was among the places burnt. Occupation was resumed five years later.
[3] *Ibid.* p. 21.
[4] *Ibid.* pp. 22–36.

Penal Laws against Papists and Nonconformists.[1] They passed a severe Bill for the continuance of the expiring Conventicle Act, but were adjourned in May, before it had passed the Lords, and did not meet again for business till October 1669. A few extracts from the *Journal* of a Cumberland travelling Friend, John Banks, will show the freedom generally enjoyed in this year 1668. At Bradford, Yorkshire, "they flock to our meetings like doves to the windows." "Great openness," he says, "and tenderness there was in those days among Friends and many other people where we came and the witness of God was soon reached." Of Bristol he writes, "meetings are very large, peaceable and quiet almost everywhere; and a great calm there now is, whatever will be the end thereof the Lord knoweth."[2]

---

[1] A Proclamation was issued on 10th March, *Cal. State Papers, Dom.*, 1667-8, p. 276. Thomas Salthouse wrote to Margaret Fell from Somerset (*Letters of Early Friends*, p. 245, from Swarthm. Colln. i. 102) that they were resolved to meet in spite of the Proclamation and were preparing their minds for prisons.

[2] *Journ.* 1712 edn. pp. 20, 27, 31. Cf. p. 24 (Somerset).

CHAPTER III

THE SECOND CONVENTICLE ACT, 1670–1673

This Act [the Second Conventicle Act] was executed in the City very severely in Starling's mayoralty, and put things in such disorder that many of the trading men of the City began to talk of removing with their stock over to Holland; but the king ordered a stop to be put to further severities. Many of the sects either discontinued their meetings, or held them very secretly with small numbers, and not in the hours of the public worship; yet Informers were encouraged and were everywhere at work. The behaviour of the Quakers was more particular, and had something in it that looked bold. They met at the same place and at the same hour as before, and when they were seized none of them would go out of the way; they went all together to prison; they stayed there till they were dismissed, for they would not petition to be set at liberty, nor would they pay the fines set on them, nor so much as the gaol fees, calling these the wages of unrighteousness. And, as soon as they were let out, they went to their meeting-houses again; and, when they found these were shut up by order, they held their meetings on the streets before the doors of those houses. They said they would not disown or be ashamed of their meeting together to worship God, but, in imitation of Daniel, they would do it the more publicly because they were forbidden doing it. Some called this obstinacy, while others called it firmness. But by it they carried their point; for the Government grew weary of dealing with so much perverseness, and so began with letting them alone.—GILBERT BURNET, *History of my own Time*, vol. i. p. 491 (Osmund Airy's edn.).

At the end of 1667, during the lull in persecution, William Penn, the foremost champion in England of religious liberty during the next twenty years, threw in his lot with Friends. We turn aside for a time from the annals of Quaker sufferings to recall the early career of this extraordinary man, whose imperishable name belongs equally to England and America. Born in London in the year of Marston Moor and Milton's *Areopagitica*, he was at this time an accomplished young gentleman of twenty-three, and his father, Admiral Sir William Penn, stood high in favour at Court. Eleven years earlier, when a lad of twelve, he had first heard

Thomas Loe, the Oxford Quaker, at his father's house in County Cork, where the Admiral owned important property. On this occasion, a black servant of the family could not contain himself from weeping aloud, and even the Admiral was in tears. Young Penn was persuaded in his heart, and thought to himself, "What, if they would all be Quakers."[1] From this time the knowledge of God, inwardly witnessed, was dear to him; indeed, he never had any other religion, except some degree of religious profession that came with his education at Chigwell Grammar School. None of his relations inclined to so solitary and spiritual a way: he was as a child alone; yet was confirmed and comforted in his experience by the heavenly opening of the scriptures to his understanding and by more immediate inspirations.[2] At sixteen he went to Oxford, but, for writing a piece which offended the college authorities, was sent down from Christ Church in disgrace a year later in the autumn of 1661, much to the Admiral's chagrin. He had come under the influence of the late Dean, the great Puritan divine John Owen, who had been ejected from the College at the Restoration, and Penn and other religiously-minded students continued to hold prayer-meetings among themselves, and were fined for their nonconformity.[3] "Bitter usage," he says, "I underwent when I returned to my father, whipping, beating, and turning out of doors in 1662."[4] Sir William had thoughts of sending him to Cambridge, but finally dispatched the youth to France to finish his education in company with some persons

---

[1] The best clue to the religious development of Penn's mind is found in his letter to Mary Pennyman, 22nd Nov. 1673, *Works*, 1726 edn. i. 159, and in an autobiographical passage in his "Travels in Holland and Germany," 1677, when visiting the Labadists. See also the Account of his convincement given to Thomas Harvey by Penn about 1697, and printed in Maria Webb, *Penns and Peningtons*, from which the detail in the text is taken. The old *Life*, by Joseph Besse, prefixed to Penn's *Works*, is authentic, so far as it goes, being "chiefly extracted out of his own private memoirs."

[2] Letter to Mary Pennyman.

[3] For his college life, see Pepys, *Diary*, 28th April 1662, Besse's *Life*, and Harvey's account. For his being fined, see "An Answer by an Anabaptist to the Three Considerations proposed to Mr. William Penn by a Pretended Baptist," 1688, p. 10.

[4] Penn's Address to the Labadists.

III SECOND CONVENTICLE ACT, 1670–1673   57

of quality who were making the Grand Tour of Europe. In Paris he proved his skill as a swordsman,[1] and became a modish gentleman, who wore pantaloon breeches, and had acquired a good deal of the vanity of the French garb and affected manner of speech and gait.[2] But he kept unstained the purity of his nature,[3] and spent some time at Saumur, where he made good progress with his studies under Moyse Amyraut, a famous theologian of the French Reformed Church.[4] He had gone forward to Italy, but was recalled home from Turin, in the summer of 1664, upon prospect of the Dutch War. He now added to his various knowledge a grounding in law as student in Lincoln's Inn, and a taste of the sea at the sailing of the fleet in April 1665.[5] The later experiences of the terrible Plague Year revived his sense of "the vanity of this world ; [and] of the irreligiousness of the religions of it."[6] He was earnest in seeking a way of salvation, and was resolved to follow it through reproach and suffering, but as yet he had found no primitive spirit and Church on the earth, and became ready to faint with disappointed hope. His father sent him in the spring of 1666 to the brilliant Court of the Duke of Ormonde in Ireland, and for a time his soul abandoned its weary and unrewarded quest. In his own words, "the glory of the world overtook me and I was even ready to give up myself unto it."[7] He acquitted himself bravely with the Duke's son, Lord Arran, in quelling a mutiny at Carrickfergus, and his fine portrait in armour, of this date, helps us to understand how the pride of life would allure his noble and uncorrupted youth.[8] He was put in charge of his

---

[1] *No Cross, No Crown*, edn. 1682, pt. i. chap. 9.
[2] Pepys, *Diary*, 26th, 30th August 1664, and note in *J.F.H.S.* iv. 141.
[3] See his answer to Sir John Robinson, February 1671, in Besse's *Life*, "I make this bold challenge to all men . . . justly to accuse me with ever having seen me drunk, heard me swear, utter a curse, or speak one obscene word . . . I speak this to God's glory, that has ever preserved me from the power of those pollutions, and that from a child begot an hatred in me towards them."   [4] Sewel, ii. 220.
[5] Lincoln's Inn Register shows that he was admitted a student 7th February 1665. For his taste of the sea, see Granville Penn, *Memorials of Sir William Penn*, ii. 318, and Pepys, *Diary*, 25th April 1665.
[6] Address to the Labadists.   [7] *Ibid.*
[8] The portrait is dated 14th Oct. 1666, *aetatis* 22, with Oliver Cromwell's

father's Irish estate, and there, in the following year, 1667, he renewed his acquaintance with Friends. By a strange providence Thomas Loe was again at Cork, and the young courtier heard from him the sermon that revealed the state of spiritual defeat under which he lay, and pointed out the way to victory if he would choose "rather to suffer affliction with the people of God, than to enjoy the pleasures of sin for a season." Loe began with the words, "There is a faith that overcomes the world; and there is a faith that is overcome by the world," and enlarged on his subject with much clearness and energy.[1] We seem to have an echo of the sermon in a letter written by Penn nine years later to the Princess Elizabeth and her companion, two high-born women whose experience resembled his own. In the case of Abraham, he writes, faith was a righteous act of obedience in his soul, "and blessed are his spiritual offspring for ever, whose faith overcomes and is not overcome of the world. For those are false faiths, forced and imaginary conceits, that cleanse not, which true faith doth—[true faith] that works by that love which conquers the world and loves God above all."[2]

Penn was exceedingly reached by this sermon even to tears,[3] though his full "convincement" as a Friend was gradual. One day at the beginning of November a soldier disturbed the meeting, and the new convert, taking him by the collar, would have thrown him down the stairs had Friends allowed him.[4] Penn, with others, was

---

motto, "Pax quaeritur bello," which, by a happy irony, his later life did so much to disprove. The face shows no trace of the smallpox which he had when three years old. "When but three years old, [he] so lost his hair by the smallpox that he wore them [*i.e.* wigs] then long; and about six years before his convincement he wore one; and after that he endeavoured to go in his own hair, but when kept a close prisoner in the Tower, next the lead, nine month, and no barber suffered to come at him, his hair shed away; and since he has worn a very short civil thing, and he has been in danger of his life after violent heats in meetings and riding after them; and he wears them to keep his head and ears warm and not for pride, which is manifest in that his periwigs cost him many pounds apiece, formerly when of the world, and now his border but a five shillings." Geo. Fox to Henry Sidon, of Baddesley, 25th May 1677, in *J.F.H.S.* vi. 187.
[1] Besse's *Life*.
[2] *Works*, 1726 edn. i. 179.   [3] Harvey's account.
[4] *Ibid.* Besse, *Sufferings*, ii. 475, calls him Wm. Paine.

taken before the mayor and imprisoned, whereupon he addressed a spirited letter, not yet Quakerized in language, to the Earl of Orrery, Lord President of Munster,[1] in which he urged the enlightened views as to liberty of conscience that he already held. But the Earl, while releasing him, wrote to the Admiral with such effect that the son was forthwith ordered home. We find him in London by the beginning of December 1667, and it is reported to Pepys that he "is a Quaker again or some very melancholy thing; that he cares for no company, nor comes into any, which is a pleasant thing, after his being abroad so long, and his father such a hypocritical rogue, and at this time an atheist."[2] He had come by Bristol and had travelled to London with Josiah Coale, one of the most ardent Quaker Publishers of Truth.[3]

"In the eternal light I knew him," says Penn, "and had often and sweet fellowship with him therein to my great refreshment, even in the gloomy and dark day of my early and deep exercises; and, though he was a man free in his disposition and ready to help all, through the tenderness of his spirit, yet was he . . . dreadful in his testimony against the life, glory and customs of the world."[4]

When Penn came home, the angry Admiral spoke his mind plainly. In learning and courtly accomplishments, his son was fit to be an ambassador or one of the King's Ministers, what then did he mean by consorting with Quakers? The son answered that he believed he was obeying the will of God, but that it was a cross to his own nature. He told his father that he had been convinced at first hearing Loe, eleven years before, but could not then give up the grandeur of the world. The plain sailor, who was by no means the hypocrite drawn by the jealous pen of Pepys, had his son into a private room, looked earnestly at him, and, laying his hands on the table, solemnly told him that he was going to pray to

---

[1] Besse's *Life*; Maria Webb, *Penns and Peningtons*, p. 160, alters the name to the Earl of Ossory, who was the eldest son of the Duke of Ormonde. But Roger Boyle, Earl of Orrery, was Lord President of Munster at this time.
[2] Pepys, *Diary*, 5th and 29th December 1667.
[3] Harvey's account.   [4] Coale's *Works*, pt. i. p. 15.

Almighty God that he might not become a Quaker, nor ever again go to a Quaker meeting. The son averted the threatened prayer by opening the window and declaring that rather than listen to it he would leap out into the street. Both in fact behaved with a noble directness and simplicity. Penn remained for some time under his father's roof, only gradually adopting Quaker dress and ways, but he had at once refused his father's offer that he might "thee and thou" any one he pleased except the King, the Duke of York, and himself.[1] Janney, though only on tradition, tells how he came to leave off wearing a sword, a fashion in vogue after the Restoration. He asked Fox's advice on the matter, who is said to have answered, "Wear it as long as thou canst," but the sword was gone when next they met. "William, where is thy sword?" said George. "Oh," answered Penn, "I have taken thy advice: I wore it as long as I could."[2]

A few months later, when he had begun to preach and to do itinerating work, his father felt it hopeless to recover him, and for a time forbade him his house.[3] He must have been in some straits for money, but his mother is thought to have helped him, and the Admiral's resentment gradually wore off. There was little persecution in 1668, with the reins of government in the hands of the tolerant Buckingham, and Penn had free service, besides going once or twice to Court in the summer on behalf of suffering Friends.[4] Thomas Loe, who was a man of weak constitution, passed away in October, after giving his spiritual son the dying message which a few months later inspired the writing of *No Cross, No Crown*.

"Taking me by the hand," says Penn, "he spake thus, 'Dear heart, bear thy cross: stand faithful for God and bear thy testimony in thy day and generation, and God will give thee an eternal crown of glory, that none shall ever take from thee.

---

[1] Harvey's account.
[2] Samuel M. Janney, *Life of William Penn*, 6th ed. p. 50.
[3] Harvey's account.
[4] Fragment of Apology given by Janney, p. 60, from "Memoirs of the Historical Society of Pennsylvania," iii.

III SECOND CONVENTICLE ACT, 1670–1673

There is not another way. This is the way the holy men of old walked in, and it shall prosper.'"[1]

The eager convert soon became an author, and in his third piece, occasioned by a public dispute with the Presbyterian Thomas Vincent and published towards the end of the year, zeal outran discretion. *The Sandy Foundation Shaken* challenged "those so generally believed and applauded doctrines of one God, subsisting in three distinct and separate persons, the impossibility of God's pardoning sinners without a plenary satisfaction, the justification of impure persons by an imputative righteousness." The book was at once stigmatized as a "horrid and abominable piece against the Holy Trinity,"[2] and the author was committed to the Tower,[3] the familiar building of his boyhood, for he was born on Tower Hill. Pepys, weak in the eyes but curious after novelties, procured a copy which his wife read to him, and he reports much as Beza had done, when he sent the Codex Bezae to Cambridge, "I find it so well writ as I think it is too good for him ever to have writ it; and it is a serious sort of book, and not fit for everybody to read."[4] The tract has the onesidedness that belongs to controversy; it is a powerful criticism of the scholastic terms of theology and the forensic view of the atonement, but it leaves Penn's positive faith uncertain, and needed the explanation which followed in *Innocency with her open Face*. He was visited by his father and, with a view to his reformation, by Dr. Stillingfleet, afterwards Bishop of Worcester, and occupied his ample leisure in writing *No Cross, No Crown*[5]—a worthy contribution to the world's immortal prison-literature.[6] It is best known in the

---

[1] Dated 17th Oct. 1668 and printed in *Penns and Peningtons*, p. 181. I follow text in Dev. Ho. Penington MS. Colln. iv. 6.
[2] Newsletter in *Fleming MSS*. p. 61.
[3] *Extracts from State Papers*, p. 279.
[4] *Diary*, 12th February 1668-9.   [5] See Preface to 1682 edn.
[6] *No Cross, No Crown* is printed in Penn's Collected Works and elsewhere from the 2nd edn. of 1682, which is stated on the title-page to be "corrected and much enlarged." The "Morning Meeting," which, *inter alia*, revised Friends' books, had its say in the matter: Minute, 20th December 1675, directed it to be reprinted: Minute 23rd February 1680, "Wm. Penn, in pursuance of an ancient order of this meeting to have *No Cross, No Crown*,

matured second edition of 1682. As first published, it was directly addressed with great moral courage to the group of intimate friends whom he had left when he became a Quaker, and consisted of "several sober reasons against hat-honour, titular respects, you to a single person, with the apparel and recreations of the times." A few pages are given to the question of Hat-honour and the use of Thou instead of You, but the substance of the treatise consists of Penn's uncompromising testimony, often tersely and wittily expressed, against luxury of dress and against frivolity and viciousness of amusement, as things utterly opposed to true religion. We may smile at his extravagances and controvert his instances, yet we must feel that the great message of this little book, if restated in terms of modern luxury, rings out in insistent

---

reprinted, in order thereunto brought several sheets of addition, part of which was read and approved," and an appointment was made "to hear the rest, for the better dispatch thereof." But the book was still being touched up two years later, see reference in Part ii. to the Princess Elizabeth, who died in 1680, "about two years since." The "ancient" friends for whose benefit it was primarily written are indicated by initials : F. S., E. B., H. S., J. C., I. N., A. L., M. L., T. C. In several cases these can be filled out. F. S. seems to stand for Fleetwood Shepherd, his old acquaintance and friend (see Apology in Janney's *Life*, p. 110). H. S. is surely Henry Sidney (1641-1704), created Earl of Romney, 1694, brother of Algernon Sidney, and a lifelong friend of Penn. A. L. and M. L. are Anthony Lowther of Marske, Yorkshire, and his wife Margaret, who was Penn's only sister (See *J.F.H.S.* iv. 143). I. N. may be Isaac Newton (1642-1727). "By whatsoever is dear," writes Penn, "I would beseech you to relinquish that very vanity of vanities—I mean those fashions, pleasures, and that whole variety of conversation, which make up the life and satisfaction of the age and are those earthly impediments that clog your souls' flight to more sublime and heavenly contemplations." A collation of the 1669 edn. with the 1682 edn. shows that the first eight chapters of the 1682 edn. and chapters xi.-xiii. were added—these containing the ripe experience of several years' discipleship, which had led him to see that "the great work and business of the cross of Christ in man is self-denial." (See beginning of chap. iv.) The original contents of the book were, Introduction to the reader, 1682 edn., chap. x. sect. 11 ;—Sixteen reasons against cap-honour and titular respects, corresponding with 1682 edn. chap. ix. sect. 4-37, which is much more elaborate, and incorporates little of the original wording ;—Testimonies of ancient and modern writers on the same subject, 1682 edn. chap. ix. sect. 38-40 ;—Twelve reasons for use of Thou, with testimonies, 1682 edn. chap. x ;—Reasons against luxury in apparel and idle recreations, 1682 edn. chap. xiv. sect. 4. to chap. xviii. ;—Testimonies to the foregoing, included with many enlargements in 1682 edn. pt. ii. Everywhere the text of the 1669 edn. is freely revised, sometimes to its hurt. A critical edn. of *No Cross, No Crown*, will, no doubt, be included in the exhaustive edition of Penn's Works upon which Albert Cook Myers of Moylan, Pennsylvania, has been for some years engaged. An exaggerated impression of Penn's early religious maturity has been caused by the 1682 edn. being used as though it had been composed in 1669.

III SECOND CONVENTICLE ACT, 1670–1673

challenge to the complacent self-righteousness of our Christianity. Penn, moreover, anticipated John Woolman in his clear perception of the connection between misused wealth and social oppression.

When people have first learned to fear and obey their Creator, to pay their numerous debts . . . to alleviate and abate their oppressed tenants; but, above all outward regard, when the pale faces are more commiserated, the griped bellies relieved, and naked backs clothed; when the famished poor, the distressed widow and helpless orphan—God's works and your fellow-creatures—are provided for; then I say, if then, it will be early enough for you to plead the indifferency of your pleasures. But that the sweat and tedious labour of the husbandman, be it early or late, cold or hot, wet or dry, should be converted into the pleasure, ease, and pastime of a small number of men; that the cart, the plough, the thrash, should be in that continual severity laid upon nineteen parts of the land to feed the inordinate lusts and delicious appetites of the twentieth, is so far from the appointment of the great Governor of the world and God of the spirits of all men, that to imagine such horrible injustice as the effect of His determinations and not the intemperance of men were wretched and blasphemous. . . . Wherefore this we offer and address to the serious consideration as well of magistrates as others, that if the money which is expended in every parish, there being near 10,000 in the land, in those unnecessary, vain, nay sinful fashions and entertainments, as laces, jewels, embroideries, ribbons, presents, plays, treats, balls, taverns, unnecessary provisions and attendants of servants, horses, coaches, gaudy furnitures . . were collected into a public stock, which would indubitably amount to several hundred thousand pounds a year, there might be reparations to the broken tenant, workhouses erected where the able might at easy labour procure a plentiful subsistence; and the unable and aged might have such an annuity as would free the land from beggars . . . nay the Exchequer's needs, on just emergencies, might be supplied.[1]

In another place he says, "'Tis the vanity of the few great ones that makes so much toil for the many small; and the great excess of the one occasions the great labour of the other."[2]

Penn kept a stout heart throughout his imprisonment,

[1] 1669 edn. pp. 61, 62.   [2] *Ibid.* p. 50.

even when told that the Bishop of London was resolved that he should either recant or die a prisoner.[1] When Dr. Stillingfleet would persuade him out of his errors he retorted that the Tower was the worst argument in the world,[2] and his letter in June to Lord Arlington, while affirming his faith in "the eternal Deity of Jesus Christ and substantial unity of Father, Word and Spirit," is no apology for his conduct but rather a bold plea for religious liberty,[3] ending with the wish that Englishmen, in the phrase of Tacitus,[4] might enjoy the rare felicity of being allowed to think what they would and to say what they thought. On his release in August 1669, it was generally believed that he was to be delivered to his father to be transported.[5] In fact he went to Ireland for a time to look after the family property, and, as it fell out, to busy himself on behalf of persecuted Friends. He found "those of the city of Cork almost all in prison, and the gaol by that means became a meeting-house and a workhouse, for they would not be idle anywhere."[6] It was not till the summer of 1670 that he returned to London, to play a memorable part in the orgy of persecution that followed the passing of the Second Conventicle Act.

The Cavalier Parliament, after refusing the King's recommendation of a toleration, had pushed forward a severe Bill for the continuance of the Conventicle Act, but was adjourned in May 1668 and did not meet again for business till October of the following year. Meanwhile, the conduct of affairs was, as we have seen, in the hands of the Cabal, who were men with few scruples and many varying political ambitions.

Clifford was passionately Roman Catholic. Anthony Ashley Cooper, afterwards first Earl of Shaftesbury, was a sceptic who believed in civil liberty and religious toleration for all Protestants, through all changes of Government, through

---

[1] Besse's *Life*.   [2] Fragment of Apology in Janney, p. 61.
[3] *Extracts from State Papers*, pp. 279-286.   [4] See *Hist.* i. 1.
[5] Newsletter in *Fleming MSS.* p. 65.
[6] Fragment of Apology in Janney, p. 63.

III SECOND CONVENTICLE ACT, 1670–1673

all the shifting arts of his criminal career. . . . Buckingham, who slew in duel the man whose wife he had seduced, was the friend and patron of the Independents, whose religious views he sometimes embraced. Arlington inclined to Catholicism. Scottish Lauderdale had no principle; he was a Covenanter at heart, a Prelatist and persecutor in act. Thus there was not one sound Anglican in all the Cabal.[1]

The King himself, freed from Clarendon, was already secretly intriguing with France in pursuance of his covert designs for Roman Catholicism and absolute rule. The toleration of Dissent consorted with his own temperament but was chiefly useful as an aid to these ulterior aims. Baxter, as early as the autumn of 1668, had become suspicious when, on a semi-official hint, the Presbyterians had been induced to address the King and had received a gracious though non-committal reply.[2] There was a growing opinion in the country in favour of toleration, largely on secular grounds. Ashley, for example, in a memorial to the King, urged that the granting of it would check emigration and attract immigrants, land would rise in value, and industry and commerce would prosper.[3] If the question could have been freed on the one hand from the memories of Puritanism in power and on the other from the fears of Jesuit domination, twenty years of struggle and suffering might have been spared. As it was, the quick growth of conventicles and the alarm of Church and magistracy forced the Government out of its apathy, and in the summer of 1669 the King assured Archbishop Sheldon of his support, and desired that inquiries should be set on foot as to Dissenting meetings and the numbers attending them.[4] A little later a proclamation charged Justices to execute the laws for

---

[1] G. M. Trevelyan, *England under the Stuarts*, p. 364.
[2] *Reliquiae Baxterianae*, pt. iii. 36-37.
[3] Christie, *Life of the First Earl of Shaftesbury*, ii. App. i.
[4] *Fleming MSS*. p. 64, Letter from Sheldon to the Archbishop of York, 8th June 1669. The returns, so far as preserved in vol. 639 of the Codices Tenisoniani in the Lambeth Palace Library, are given by G. Lyon Turner in his monumental work, *Original Records of Early Nonconformity*, vol. i. pp. 3-191, and for Oxfordshire, vol. iii. pp. 823-836.

F

suppressing conventicles, which it stated were held in greater number than formerly and endangered the public peace.[1] Prior to the meeting of Parliament in October, it was reported that the Bishops intended to have a new Act.[2] Sheldon had been collecting his information, the detailed statistics of which we shall notice later.[3] One of his questions had been: Upon what hope the conventiclers looked for impunity? and he no doubt made great play with such returns as the following:

From St. Asaph diocese, they "build their impunity upon the example of London and other places in the kingdom"; from a parish in Ely Deanery, "indulgence, remissness of the magistrate, rumour of comprehension, the King's connivance, grandees at Court, are their encouragement and hopes"; from one in Cambridge Deanery, "the conventicle near Whitehall, in a house fitted for it, is their especial encouragement"; from Derbyshire, "the expiration of the Act of Parliament, the hopes of its [Parliament's] being dissolved, the King's allowance and friends at Court"; from Stepney Parish, "these meetings have increased since the rigour of the Oxford Act was suspended: whilst the magistrates were active they were rarely heard of, except Quakers, and those not a quarter the number they now are: many of these meeting-people, especially Presbyterians and Independents, did, till of late, frequent the Church, and will easily be reconciled again, if they see the Government resolute"; from Andover Deanery, "the authority they all pretend is His Majesty's connivance, and that they have some friends that, if occasion be, will interpose between them and the punishment of the laws."

In view of such answers it was evident to Sheldon that any new law required special provisions encouraging prosecution and penalizing remissness on the part of magistrates. He failed to see that such forced and reluctant execution would hurt the Church of England without destroying Dissent. Parliament, after a short session in the late autumn, had been prorogued till February 1670, when the financial needs of the King obliged him to consent to the new and stringent Con-

---

[1] *Cal. State Papers, Dom.*, 1668–9, p. 412, dated 16th July.
[2] Ellis Hookes to Fox, 10th October 1669, in Swarthm. Colln. i. 385 (*Letters of Early Friends*, p. 168). [3] *Post*, Chap. XVII.

venticle Act which Sheldon had been framing. In the Commons the weight of the speeches was in favour of toleration, but the votes went for persecution by 138 to 78 ; and the Bill, with some small alleviations introduced by the Lords, was rapidly passed into law. The King tried without success to secure a dispensing power.[1] The Act, in Marvell's phrase, was "the quintessence of arbitrary malice,"[2] and was to be enforced without the safeguard of a jury. A single Justice could convict, and fines of five and ten shillings were imposed for a first and any further offence. Two new offences were created,—a person preaching at a conventicle was to be fined £20 for a first and £40 for any further offence, and a person harbouring a conventicle was to be fined £20. Fines were recoverable by distress, and were directed to go in thirds to the King, the poor, and the Informer. Where the offenders were strangers or poor their fines could be distrained for up to ten pounds on any other person convicted of being present. Transportation was dropped, and the policy of the Act was to ruin rather than imprison the offenders. Petty officers refusing to enforce the law incurred a penalty of £5 ; Justices were to forfeit £100, half of which went to the Informer. Justices could break into suspected houses, and the militia was at their disposal "to dissolve, dissipate, or prevent all such unlawful meetings." Prosecution, however, could only be within three months of the offence, and conviction was a bar to conviction for the same offence under any other Act. On the other hand, the Act, unlike that of 1664, had no time-limit, and all its clauses were to be "construed most largely and beneficially for the suppressing of conventicles and for the justification and encouragement of all persons to be employed in the execution thereof." On the whole, a workmanlike tool seemed to have been added to the armoury of persecution.

[1] The Parliamentary history of the Act is well told in Bate, *The Declaration of Indulgence, 1672*, pp. 65-67.
[2] 22 Car. II. cap. 1. Printed in Grant Robertson, *Select Statutes, etc.*, pp. 70-74, and Besse, *Sufferings*, i. pp. xxii-xxvii. For Marvell's phrase, see *Works*, edn. Grosart, ii. 316.

Sheldon indulged sanguine hopes in a circular letter which he addressed to the Bishops on the 7th May, three days before the Act came into operation.[1]

And now, what the success will be, we must leave to God Almighty. Yet I have this confidence under God, that, if we do our parts now at first diligently, by God's help and the assistance of the civil power—considering the abundant care and provisions this Act contains for our advantages—we shall within a few months see so great an alteration in the distractions of these times, as that the seduced people returning from their seditious and self-serving teachers to the unity of the Church and uniformity in God's service, it will be [to] the glory of God, the welfare of the Church, the praise of His Majesty's Government, and the happiness of the whole kingdom.

The course of events in London can be readily traced.[2] At first there was open, and as the authorities thought, concerted defiance of the law. Drastic measures were taken in June. Two disaffected aldermen were committed to Newgate; old Cromwellian soldiers were banished from the city for six months; and an order was made for pulling down the seats and pulpits in all the meeting-houses in London, Bristol, and other places.[3] On the 19th June the Governor of the Tower could report, with some exaggeration, "there was no Quaker nor any sect else had any preaching in their public places in the City this day."[4]

Friends from the first found their meeting-houses occupied by guards of watchmen, but met outside in the court or the open street. The Bishop of London, Humphrey Henchman, in his zeal for religion, decided in mid-June forcibly to feed the Nonconformists with the pure milk of the word.[5] He began by sending his clergy

---

[1] Printed, *e.g.*, in Neal, *History of the Puritans*, 1796 edn. iv. 448. I have followed the text in Staley, *Life and Times of Gilbert Sheldon*, pp. 127-131.

[2] See especially the series of reports from Sir John Robinson, the Governor of the Tower, to Williamson in *Cal. State Papers, Dom.*, 1670, and Newsletter, 14th June 1670, in *Fleming MSS.*

[3] Newsletter in *Fleming MSS.*

[4] *Extracts from State Papers*, p. 312. Besse, however, *Sufferings*, i. 410, reports meetings at Whitchart Court, and outside the City at Westminster and Ratcliff.

[5] See Besse, *Sufferings*, i. 410-415; George Whitehead, *Christian Progress*,

to the two chief Presbyterian meetings, but a week later included the new Quaker meeting-house at Whitehart Court in Gracechurch Street, which had been seized for the King, marked with the broad arrow and padlocked against Friends. Here, for five or six weeks, the unedifying spectacle might be seen of a clergyman, guarded by soldiers, reading the common-prayer and preaching from the gallery, while drums drowned the Quaker ministry outside. When Friends spoke at these Anglican services they were at once turned, as the magistrates held, into unlawful conventicles: the officiating clergyman, on the first Sunday, exhorted to love and charity, while the soldiers around him were abusing Friends, but upon George Whitehead improving the same theme it was straightway sedition. The following week the priest's courage failed him, and he slunk away amid the derision of the people. After this the soldiers kept Friends in the street, where, alas, they could gain no spiritual benefit from either liturgy or sermon. The clergyman at last was attended only by a rude rabble, for few persons of credit cared to countenance his sorry travesty of worship.

In mid-August, the methods of exclusion came to a head. On the 14th, owing to the soldiers, the meeting was being held in Gracechurch Street. Says John Rous:[1]

> As near as I could judge, several thousands [were] at it, but by reason of the multitude of rude people who came mostly to gaze it was more like a tumult than a solid assembly, which was no small grief to me to see. William Penn was there, and spoke most that was spoken; there were some watchmen with halberds and musketeers came to take him down while he was speaking; but the multitude crowded so close about him that they could not come to him; but, to prevent further disturbance, he promised when the meeting was done to come to them; and so he and one Meade, who is lately convinced, went to them: they carried them before the [Lord] Mayor, and he committed them for a riot.

330-333 and 617; William Crouch, *Posthuma Christiana*, chap. v.; and *Cal. State Papers, Dom.*, 1670, pp. 240, 283, 300, 314, the last printed in *Extracts from State Papers*, p. 314. See also "The Second Part of the People's Ancient and Just Liberties Asserted," 1670, p. 12.

[1] Rous to Sarah Fell, 15th August 1670, printed in *Letters of Early Friends*, p. 177, and in *Fells of Swarthmoor Hall*, p. 268, from W. F. Miller Colln.

William Meade was a prosperous linen-draper, who afterwards married Margaret Fell's daughter Sarah. The two Quakers were brought to trial in September at the Old Bailey, and as they were indicted for a riot and not under the Conventicle Act they had the benefit of a jury.[1] An astonishing thing happened. A prejudiced Bench, which began by fining Penn and Meade forty marks apiece for keeping on their hats, failed either to overbear the spirit of the prisoners or to browbeat their jury. Invincible Quakers might indeed be expected, but an undaunted jury was a welcome novelty in those servile times. The happy conjunction of the two made the trial an epoch in the history of the liberty of the subject, to which the opposers of arbitrary government, cloaked under the forms of law, can still turn for inspiration. The witnesses gave their evidence honestly enough; they knew little of Meade but had seen Penn speaking, though they could not hear what he said because of the noise. Penn, in his defence, declared that all the powers upon earth should not divert him from worshipping God, and demanded production of the law he was alleged to have broken, whereupon he was rudely haled into the bail-dock, a small room at a distance from the Bench, taken from one of the corners of the Court and left open at the top. The Recorder, Sir John Howell, cried, "Take him away," and then said to the Lord Mayor, Sir Samuel Starling, "My Lord, if you take not some course with this pestilent fellow, to stop his mouth, we shall not be able to do anything to-night." On this the Lord Mayor called out, "Take him away, take him away, turn him into the bail-dock," and Penn rejoined:

These are but so many vain exclamations. Is this justice or true judgment? Must I therefore be taken away because I plead for the fundamental laws of England? However this I

---

[1] For the Trial see "The People's Ancient and Just Liberties Asserted," 1670 (reprinted in Besse, *Sufferings*, i. 416-426); "The Second Part of the People's Ancient and Just Liberties Asserted," 1670; "An Answer to the Seditious and Scandalous Pamphlet, entituled The Tryal of W. Penn and W. Mead," by S[amuel] S[tarling] 1670 (reprinted in *The Harleian Miscellany*); William Penn, "Truth Rescued from Imposture, or a Brief Reply," 1670 (*Works*, i. 486-521).

leave upon your consciences who are of the jury, and my sole judges, that if these ancient fundamental laws which relate to liberty and property, and are not limited to particular persuasions in matters of religion, must not be indispensably maintained and observed, who can say he hath right to the coat upon his back? Certainly our liberties are openly to be invaded, our wives to be ravished, our children slaved, our families ruined and our estates led away in triumph, by every sturdy beggar and malicious Informer, as their trophies but our pretended forfeits for conscience' sake. The Lord of heaven and earth will be judge between us in this matter.

Meade, in his turn, was put in the bail-dock for explaining to the jury the Common Law definition of a riot, which the Recorder had refused to give. Then, in the absence of the prisoners, the case was summed up, Penn and Meade protesting in the distance. After some division of opinion, the jury found Penn "Guilty of speaking in Gracious Street," and on the Court refusing the verdict, for street talk was no crime, even in Restoration days, repeated it in writing, and found Meade Not Guilty. There was an adjournment till seven next morning, a Sunday, the Recorder saying, "Gentlemen, you shall not be dismissed till we have a verdict that the Court will accept; and you shall be locked up, without meat, drink, fire, and tobacco; you shall not think thus to abuse the Court; we will have a verdict by the help of God or you shall starve for it." Penn, as the Court broke up, looked his jury in the face and said, "You are Englishmen; mind your privilege; give not away your right," and Edward Bushell,[1] the man who had nerved them to the sticking-point, replied, "Nor will we ever do it." Sunday found the jury still resolute, and the Bench passionate. Take the following piece of browbeating:

> *Recorder* [to Bushell]. You are a factious fellow; I will set a mark upon you, and whilst I have anything to do in the City I will have an eye upon you.
> *Lord Mayor* [to the jury]. Have you no more wit than to be led by such a pitiful fellow? I will cut his nose.

---

[1] 1620–1694, a member of the family of Bushell, of Frodsham, Cheshire, see *Transactions Cong. Hist. Society*, vi. 379 (1915).

Penn. It is intolerable that my jury should be thus menaced. Is this according to the fundamental laws? Are not they my proper judges by the Great Charter of England? What hope is there of ever having justice done, when juries are threatened and their verdicts rejected? . . .

Recorder [to the Lord Mayor]. My Lord, you must take a course with that same fellow.

Lord Mayor. Stop his mouth, gaoler; bring fetters and stake him to the ground.

Penn [his mind carried over the heads of all his judges]. Do your pleasure; I matter not your fetters.

Recorder [beside himself with passion]. Till now I never understood the reason of the policy and prudence of the Spaniards, in suffering the Inquisition among them. And certainly it will never be well with us, till something like the Spanish Inquisition be in England.

Jury [to the Bench]. We ought not to be returned, having all agreed and set our hands to the verdict.

Recorder. Your verdict is nothing; you play upon the Court. I say you shall go together and bring in another verdict, or you shall starve, and I will have you carted about the City as in Edward the Third's time.

Foreman. We have given in our verdict, and all agreed to it; and, if we give in another, it will be a force upon us to save our lives.

So the case stood over till Monday, when the jury, spent with their privations but undefeated, tendered the same written verdict, but, as it was still refused, they found both the prisoners Not Guilty, "upon which the Bench were amazed and the whole Court so satisfied that they made a kind of hymn."[1] Thereupon English liberties were further outraged by a fine on the jury of forty marks a head, and imprisonment till paid, the Recorder adding the words which of all others could least be said of twelve such men, "God keep my life out of your hands." A layman might suppose that, on acquittal, the prisoners would at once have been released; but, in spite of another appeal by Penn to the Great Charter, they were kept in custody because fined for their hats, and the trial ended with Penn's biting words to his judges,

---

[1] Wm. Penn to his father, 5th September 1670, in Janney's *Life*, p. 81.

with which London must have rung for days, "I can never urge the fundamental laws of England, but you cry, Take him away, take him away. But 'tis no wonder, since the Spanish Inquisition hath so great a place in the Recorder's heart."

The jurymen chafed under their imprisonment: by advice of Counsel they began by demanding their freedom every six hours, and in November were brought before the Court of Common Pleas and admitted to bail.[1] After much argument and a year's suspense, the whole body of judges decided that, in spite of *Wagstaffe's Case* already referred to,[2] no jury could be fined for its verdict.[3] The decision in *Bushell's Case*, as it is styled, became one of the impregnable bulwarks of English liberty. Baxter describes the effect of the judgment delivered by the Lord Chief Justice, Sir John Vaughan:[4]—"when he had in a speech of two or three hours long spoke vehemently to that purpose, never thing since the King's return was received with greater joy and applause by the people, and the judges still taken for the pillars of law and liberty."[5]

"If the judge from the evidence," said Vaughan, "shall by his own judgment first resolve upon any trial what the fact is; and so knowing the fact shall then resolve what the law is; and order the jury penally to find accordingly, what either necessary or convenient use can be fancied of juries, or to continue trials by them at all?"[6]

At the time of the trial, Penn's father was lying dangerously ill; but the son, though eager to see him,

[1] Penn to his father, 6th September 1670, in Janney's *Life*, p. 82; and *Extracts from State Papers*, pp. 322, 323.
[2] *Supra*, p. 45 note.
[3] For *Bushell's Case* see Vaughan's *Reports*, pp. 135-158; and Grant Robertson, *Select Statutes, Cases, and Documents*, pp. 362-367; also text-books on Constitutional History.
[4] Lord Chief Justice Vaughan (1603-1674) was no friend to Nonconformity and Puritans (*Reliquiae Baxterianae*, pt. iii. 59), and must be distinguished from another Sir John Vaughan (1640-1713), afterwards third Earl of Carbery, who attended Friends' meetings as a young man, was imprisoned for this under the first Conventicle Act, and always retained a kindness to Friends. (See George Whitehead, *Christian Progress*, p. 270, authenticated as to the imprisonment, 17th July 1664, by *Middlesex County Records*, iii. 340).
[5] *Reliquiae Baxterianae*, pt. iii. 87.
[6] Vaughan's *Reports*, p. 143.

could in conscience neither pay the fine put upon him, nor suffer it to be paid.[1] Some settlement of the matter was made without his knowledge, and his presence cheered the Admiral's last days.[2] The dying man bade farewell in a sailor's bluff way, "Son William, if you and your Friends keep to your plain way of preaching and keep to your plain way of living, you will make an end of the priests to the end of the world."

Penn, though now a wealthy man, soon found himself in prison again, this time for six months under the Five Mile Act, which on any fair construction did not include Quaker preachers.[3] At the Old Bailey the authorities had been foiled in their attempt to imprison him on a trial by jury, they were now able to gain their end under an Act directed solely against persons pretending to holy orders: on neither occasion had they used the express but milder remedy provided by the Conventicle Act.

Penn's courage, his vigorous writings, and his high station, no doubt made him a man specially aimed at. Before the Old Bailey trial he had published the first edition of "The Great Case of Liberty of Conscience once more briefly Debated and Defended," which has been called "the completest exposition of the theory of toleration" in the Restoration period.[4] The piece contains some of the pithy sayings of which he was a master: " The Christian religion entreats all but compels none "; " Force may make an hypocrite, 'tis faith grounded upon knowledge and consent that makes a Christian "; " Force never yet made either a good Christian or a good subject." Shortly after his release, twenty-one years of

---

[1] Letters in Janney's *Life*, p. 82.
[2] In *No Cross, No Crown*, 2nd edn. chap. xxi. sect. 37, Penn gives his father's dying expressions.
[3] For the Act see *ante*, p. 52. For Penn's trial, see Besse, *Sufferings*, i. 432-435 (5th February 1671).
[4] Seaton, *Theory of Toleration*, p. 172. The pamphlet is usually stated to have been written during the six months' imprisonment under the Five Mile Act, although the preface to the *second* edn. is dated from Newgate 7th February 1671, *two* days after that imprisonment began. The first edn., which is briefer and contains a dedication to the King, bears on the title-page the initials "W.P.j.," and is thus earlier than Admiral Penn's death 16th Sept. 1670. The letter to the King shows that it was written, "before the late Act has made too great a progress."

SECOND CONVENTICLE ACT, 1670-1673

happy wedded life opened before him with his marriage to Gulielma Springett, the daughter of Mary Penington by her first husband the gallant Sir William Springett. We must henceforth think of all his high adventure and achievement with this glad domestic background in mind. She was his "entire and constant friend, of a more than common capacity and greater modesty and humility, yet most equal and undaunted in danger."[1] She became his companion and second self, bearing her equal share in all his toils and troubles, nothing ruling between them but love.[2]

Penn's courage was characteristic of Friends. Fox tells a story of the Governor of Dover Castle in 1671.

When the King asked him, if he had dispersed all the sectaries' meetings, he said that he had, but the Quakers the devil could not. For if that he did imprison them and break them up, they would meet again; and, if he should beat them and knock them down or kill some of them, all was one, they would meet, and not resist again.[3]

It was in this spirit that the London Quakers met the master-stroke which the authorities devised against Dissenters in the summer of 1670. Conventicles were seized in the King's name and in several cases "disfurnished," but, as Friends proved intractable, orders were obtained for pulling down their meeting-houses in London. The Lord Mayor's Court thought of demolishing Gracechurch Street meeting-house as an irregular building under the Act for rebuilding the City after the Fire; but do not seem to have pursued the matter.[4] At the end of July an Order in Council directed the King's Surveyor, the famous Christopher Wren, to pull down the meeting-house at Horslydown.[5] Three weeks later, on a Saturday,

---

[1] From Penn's tribute to her memory in Janney's *Life*, p. 389, written after her death, 23rd February 1694.
[2] I apply the phrases in Penn's *Some Fruits of Solitude*, Nos. 92, 100.
[3] *Epistles*, p. 5.
[4] Besse, *Sufferings*, i. 429.
[5] *Ibid.* i. 695-698, containing a reprint of "The Cry of Innocent Blood . . . being a short Relation of the Barbarous Cruelties inflicted lately upon . . . Quakers at their Meeting in Horslydown," 1670. For Horslydown see *Beginnings of Quakerism*, p. 380.

"a party of soldiers came with carpenters and others and pulled down the meeting-house and carried away the boards, windows, benches, and forms, and sold them." The destruction was probably only partial,[1] but in any case Friends met next day upon the rubbish, until dragged off by the soldiers. Week by week, they continued to meet, though outrageously abused. The record runs for four of these weeks to the following effect: "The number of those that were wounded and sorely bruised and had their blood spilt this day was above twenty, thirty, fifty, twenty persons." It was not until February 1671 that the meeting was unmolested, "from the constant attending of which, it was sufficiently proved, no human power nor any penalties could deter them."

Ratcliff meeting, which is held on the old site to the present day, has a like heroic chapter in its story.[2] Sir John Robinson, the Governor of the Tower, was determined to purge the Tower Hamlets of Dissent. In the middle of August he took away the tables and sixty-one forms, but the meeting went on. By the end of the month he had suppressed the other conventicles and decided to pull down the Quakers' house. A company of soldiers did the work in a day and night, carrying off twelve cartloads of doors and other plunder and selling the rest on the spot for money or drink. Friends met on the ruins or as near to them as the constables allowed, and in November of the following year, when persecution had slackened, were rebuilding their meeting-house. After the "disfurnishing" in August, Sir John had come himself to disperse the meeting, and the Quakers had continued covered in his presence. His men snatched off the offending hats and threw them over the wall to the rabble, but one of the trainband, Benjamin Bangs, was so convinced by this instance of passive resistance that he became a Friend himself.

---

[1] See Monthly Meeting Minutes in Beck and Ball, *London Friends' Meetings*, p. 218; cf. *Life of Gilbert Latey*, p. 70.
[2] Besse, *Sufferings*, i. 416, 428, 429, 431; *Extracts from State Papers*, pp. 318, 333, 334; and *Life* of Benjamin Bangs (1652-1741), who became a leading minister in the Society.

III SECOND CONVENTICLE ACT, 1670–1673

The shrewdness of the former court-tailor, Gilbert Latey, rescued the Wheeler Street meeting-house from a like fate.[1] News of Sir John's intentions came to him while travelling in the West of England; and as the title to the house was in his name, he wrote to London, and Friends obtained a respite till his return. Meanwhile he put in a poor Friend as the occupying tenant under a lease, so that the house became a dwelling-house, used for other purposes than meetings. This stopped Sir John's design and became the recognized way of preventing the mischief for the future.[2]

With respect to meeting-houses and the violent breaking up of meetings, the persecution that followed the Conventicle Act was hottest in London. There were not elsewhere many buildings used only for meetings, though in several places, often quite illegally, private houses were padlocked by the authorities, and Friends were forced to meet in the streets. At Bristol, three meeting-houses had been used, one at the lower end of Broadmead, afterwards occupied by the Baptists,[3] and two newly built, the first on the other side of Bristol Bridge in Temple Street, and the second near Broadmead at the Friars, on a site chosen by lot, to secure full unity on a much debated question.[4] After the Conventicle Act, the houses were seized for the King, there being no known proprietors, and Friends met in the street often in silence. In September they broke into one of their houses and several were imprisoned; but it is clear that they behaved with less resolution than their London brethren, for Fox wrote to them from his sick-bed in January 1671, to go into their meeting-places as at other times; and, on receipt of this letter, "Friends with one voice concluded that 'tis our duty as Christians to enter into one of our meeting-houses, and that our neglect thereof hath been a weakening to our neighbouring

---

[1] *Life of Gilbert Latey*, pp. 70–77.
[2] *Ibid.* See also, on the King's alleged rights, "The Second Part of the People's Ancient and Just Liberties Asserted," 1670, p. 36. Cf. a Minute of the Y.M. of 1684 as to a Warwickshire meeting-house.
[3] They first met in it 20th August 1671 (*Broadmead Baptist Records*, p. 164).
[4] Tanner, *Three Lectures on . . . Friends in Bristol and Somersetshire*, pp. 73, 74.

Friends." Arrangements were made for opening first the old Broadmead house, then the Friars, and then the one over the bridge, and a committee was appointed to consider whether the doors should be opened without " owning the houses, or whether they shall be owned by any particular person or persons," who would thereupon become exposed to the heavy fine of £20 a meeting laid upon owners.[1]

It was no doubt the dread of Informers that weakened for a time the witness of Bristol Friends. London had suffered little from these mercenaries of persecution. One of them haled Fox before the Lord Mayor on the Sunday after the Act came into force but was discovered for a Papist and barely escaped lynching by the mob. "And this Informer," adds Fox, "was so frightened that there durst hardly any Informer appear in London for several years after."[2] In the country, however, the Act became virulent chiefly through their poisonous evidence. Archbishop Sancroft tried to excuse their perjuries, a few years later, by pleading that a ship could not be built without some crooked timber;[3] but the whole tribe stank in the nostrils of honest Englishmen.

"An Informer of the baser sort," says one tract, "is one of the devil's nut-hooks, a privileged trepan or a common barrator under pretence of authority, a pettifogging caterpillar . . . he ferrets a conventicle just as a polecat does rabbits in their burrows; and the rich men there skulk down in their pews when they see him come in, dreading him more than a partridge does a hawk, or a city crack a marshal's man."[4]

---

[1] See Besse, *Sufferings*, i. 52, 53; *Extracts from State Papers*, pp. 298, 320; Fox, *Epistles*, No. 283; and Minutes of Bristol Men's Meeting, 17th October 1670 and 11th January (cited in text), and 6th February 1671. The following Men's Meetings arranged the apprenticing of two sons of a Friend in prison, Thomas Parsons of Portishead, who had lost nearly everything through allowing Friends to meet at his house. See also Dev. Ho. Dix Colln. No. 4B, and Tanner, *op. cit.* pp. 41-43.

[2] *Camb. Journ.* ii. 162. Sir John Robinson, writing 12th June 1670 (*Cal. State Papers, Dom.*, 1670, p. 270) says that in the Tower Hamlets he had to send out his own agents to discover what conventicles were held, as neither constable, officer, nor head-borough would come with information to him or the Justices.

[3] Crouch, *Posthuma Christiana*, chap. vii.

[4] Cited from *Camb. Journ.* ii. 417. A nut-hook, used in nutting to pull down the branches, was a slang term for a constable, etc.

Ellwood[1] gives a lively account of two Informers who worked in his district and were known as the trepan and the cow-stealer. He rid the county of the rascal crew by obtaining a verdict of wilful perjury against the cow-stealer and a third comrade of the craft, who had sworn that two Friends, Thomas Zachary and his wife, were at a meeting, when they were in fact in London, twenty miles away. In Somerset, distraints to the value of about £1000 were made on Friends in 1670,[2] often on false informations. Suffolk escaped with half this amount. At Guildford £180 in distresses were taken for meetings held in the street, when Friends were kept out of the meeting-house. In the North Riding a Richmond innkeeper named William Thornaby kept a minute record, unique among rogues' diaries, of the services done by him and his agents during fourteen months. The booty in fines from seventy-nine meetings was £2000, often excessively levied. From Nottinghamshire came a protest, signed by above two hundred Quakers, men and women, which stated clearly the public mischief of the Act.[3]

Whereas we have been capable of doing good unto others, and have relieved many in their outward wants, and paid our taxes to the King, and our rents unto whom they were due, and maintained considerable families in a comfortable manner, we are now made altogether uncapable of doing such things through the violence of some men against us that pretend your Act for what they do.

London Friends, in their relative immunity, raised a generous fund for the victims of cruelty, amounting, I conjecture, to about a thousand pounds, to which in several cases the county Friends added contributions of their own.[4] But the help fell far short of the loss that had been suffered. Yorkshire, to take a case that can be followed in detail, received eighty pounds from London

[1] *Life*, pp. 276-291.
[2] For this and succeeding cases, see Besse, *Sufferings*, i. 609, 674-677, 699; ii. 120-129.
[3] *Extracts from State Papers*, p. 338.
[4] See Yorkshire Q.M. Minutes, 23rd March 1671, with letters from London and reply made, also references in Records of Bristol, Westmorland, Oxfordshire, Berkshire, etc.

and added thirty more, dividing the whole among its fourteen Monthly Meetings. York Monthly Meeting had £8 : 13 : 9, towards losses of £164 : 1s., receiving therefore about 1s. 1d. in the pound.[1]

The steady goodwill of neighbours often defeated the rapacity of Informers. John Gratton, of Derbyshire, had been fined twenty pounds for preaching and a reluctant constable was ordered to levy the distress.[2] Some of the neighbours came to the Quaker's house and took the best of his goods away into their own safe custody; and the shamefaced officer of the law gladly arranged with Gratton to take an inventory of the remainder and proclaim them for sale at the market-cross and in the church, leaving them in the house till purchasers appeared. "When people heard them proclaimed they wished sad things to such as bought any of them; so that none were sold." The constable reported his ill-success to the Justices. One said, "If you cannot sell them in Derbyshire, you must carry them into Yorkshire." "No," said another, who loved honest Friends, but hated hypocrites, "thou hast executed thy warrant and hast done thy office; if thou canst not sell them, thou canst but go thy ways home, and let it be as it is." So the goods on this and like occasions rested unsold in Gratton's house.

At Welshpool a weaver boasted that he would enrich himself by informing against Richard Davies, the Quaker hatter, for preaching at meetings in the gaol, where he and other Friends lay prisoners. An enraged relative vowed to cut off one of the rogue's ears, and the man was boycotted by the townsmen and snubbed by the Justices. It was ill enough to have their peaceable neighbours in prison without ruining them for the benefit of scoundrels.[3]

Colchester, we are told, "would afford no Informers, but two came out of Norfolk and informed against one meeting; but the rabble stoned them so much that they desired to know of the mayor where they might lodge

---

[1] York M.M. Minute 6th April 1671.
[2] *Journ.* 1779 edn. pp. 104-115.   [3] *Life*, 1771 edn. pp. 141-146.

safe. He told them he knew nowhere safer than in the town gaol, so thither they went and got away very early in the morning and never came more to disturb Friends."[1]

Persecution raged fiercely through the land while Parliament sat. The House of Commons was busy with a Bill to strengthen the Act when the prorogation came in April 1671. Charles meanwhile, behind the back of Parliament, had become a secret Roman Catholic and the pensioner of Louis XIV., pledged with France to destroy the Dutch Republic. The nation did not gauge the depth of his perfidy, but was gravely disturbed at the unnatural alliance with Catholic France against Protestant Holland. The King had, in fact, sold himself to Louis, and the country in a vague way seemed to know it. Its temper was not improved by the arbitrary proceedings of the Government. The Exchequer stopped payment, to the ruin of the London goldsmiths; and a few weeks later, on 15th March 1672, the King exercised his pretended dispensing power in matters ecclesiastical by issuing a proclamation to suspend the Penal Laws against Nonconformists and Popish recusants.[2]

The Declaration of Indulgence marks an era in the history of toleration. Issued on the eve of the war with Holland, it was intended, in Arlington's words, to "keep all quiet at home whilst we are busiest abroad." James, who was now a declared Roman Catholic, claimed that he had been the prime mover in the matter;[3] but the whole of the Cabal made themselves responsible for it, and the wording suggests the pen of Shaftesbury. After confessing the failure of the policy of persecution and confirming the position of the Church of England, it suspended the execution of all the Penal Laws, and authorized meetings of Nonconformists, but not of Papists, in allowed places and with approved teachers, if open and

[1] *F.P.T.* p. 95.
[2] For the Declaration of Indulgence see Bate, *The Declaration of Indulgence*, 1672, and authorities there cited.
[3] George Whitehead, *Christian Progress*, p. 577, in an interview with James II. in 1685.

free to all persons. Roman Catholics shared the relief, but were granted the exercise of worship in their private houses only.

The Declaration startled the country and alarmed the Established Church. A zealous country Justice like Fleming could write to Whitehall with latent criticism that it was great news, and he heartily wished all Nonconformists might be content with it and not demand an ell when they had been given an inch.[1] But to his intimates he would vent his dislike freely: " Nor find I any pleased therewith, after such a rate as the Papists run. . . . It's looked upon as great a prerogative act as hath been done this good while. It's said to have been shot out of our grand minister's quiver." [2] The Chancellor of the Duchy of Lancaster prayed God that the Nonconformists made no ill return for the Declaration, which he was highly satisfied with, as it was the King's pleasure, though nothing else could have made him relish it.[3] The clergy openly preached against Popery, headed by Sheldon and Henchman, the Bishop of London.[4] Baxter was suspicious, though he finally procured a licence for preaching, and other Nonconformists shared his hesitation. Naturally enough, however, they availed themselves of the readily granted licences. Adam Martindale gives us an insight into the feelings of many of the Presbyterian ministers.[5] He doubted the exercise of the prerogative, and liked a universal toleration so little that he would have refused religious liberty for himself if it had meant that he gave his consent that Papists, Quakers, and all other wicked sects should have theirs also.

The Quakers, in common with others, felt the relief. But they solicited no licences either for preacher or place, not admitting the need of any. They took advantage, however, of the new policy to urge the case of imprisoned Friends. George Whitehead and Thomas Moore of

---

[1] *Cal. State Papers, Dom.*, 1671–2, p. 311.
[2] *Fleming MSS.* p. 90. (The grand minister was Shaftesbury.)
[3] *Cal. State Papers, Dom.*, 1671–2, p. 215.
[4] Burnet, *History*, Airy's edn. i. 555.
[5] *Life*, Chetham Society edn. p. 198.

Reigate devoted themselves to the matter.[1] Moore got speech with Charles II., and afterwards he and Whitehead and Thomas Green were allowed to plead their case before the King in Council. They furnished themselves with a list, including 125 praemunired persons, besides sixty under sentence of banishment, and the King said, "I'll pardon them," the Lord Keeper and Lauderdale explaining that the persons and estates of those praemunired could only be legally discharged by a Pardon under the Great Seal. Returns of prisoners were called for from the various gaols, and reported on by the Lord Keeper early in May, whereupon the Council directed a Pardon to be prepared. The affair was most exacting, especially to Whitehead and Ellis Hookes, the Clerk to Friends. Hookes writes in August:

The weakness of my body is such that it makes the exercises I meet with much more hard: I am often ready to fall under by reason thereof. G. W. and myself have been much employed this summer in the business of the prisoners' liberty; and it is such a troublesome business to go through as I have not met with the like. It lies now in the Secretary's hands, ready signed by the King, and wants only dating: I have engrossed it once already and it contains six of the largest skins of parchment I could get; and I must engross it once more for the Signet Office, and from thence it is to go to the Crown Office or Patent Office, and to be engrossed in Chancery hand, when I suppose it will make at least twelve skins. If we could once get it past the Signet and Privy Seal, I hope it would soon be done: in the meantime we must attend in patience.

The document under the sign-manual of the King, and the Letters Patent of 3rd September, on eleven skins of

---

[1] George Whitehead, *Christian Progress*, pp. 350-366, is the chief authority for the Pardon. For the first list furnished to the Council see *Extracts from State Papers*, p. 350, which bases the plea for release upon the Declaration of Indulgence. The returns were ordered on the 29th March (*Letters of Early Friends*, p. 185, gives the document, issued the day before the letter on p. 184, which should be dated 30th, not 3rd March). For the Order of Council, 8th May, with list of names to be included in the Pardon, see *Extracts from State Papers*, pp. 342-347, and for warrant to Attorney-General to draw up Pardon, *Christian Progress*, p. 355. The Pardon itself is printed, *Christian Progress*, pp. 696-712, with an index of the names. Letters respecting the matter from Ellis Hookes to Margt. Fox are given in *Letters of Early Friends*, pp. 185-191; also 8th July 1672, in Swarthm. Colln. i. 60; Edward Man to Margt. Fox, 13th April 1672, in Swarthm. Colln. i. 133; and 20th July 1672, in *Camb. Journ.* ii. 215.

vellum, with the Great Seal attached, are both preserved in the Friends' Reference Library at Devonshire House. The 491 names included in the Patent were repeated eleven times over, hence its length, but the King directed that it should pass and pay as one Pardon, and the Lord Keeper remitted his fees,—thereby making some amends for his harsh proceedings when trying the Quakers at Hertford.[1] It was no easy matter to get the Patent carried into effect. George Whitehead had two duplicates made and these went on circuit. He himself, with Edward Man and William Gosnell, took the original through the Eastern Counties. They went on horseback, Man carrying the bulky Patent tied across the saddle behind him in its leather case, with the tin box for the Great Seal hanging from it. Some Quaker artist should paint us the three Friends carrying it down in the autumn and drawing rein on their welcome errand at the Inn by Chelmsford prison.

For the more remote counties it was found sufficient to show the Patent to the under-sheriffs, when they came up to London to the Michaelmas law-term, and to prepare for their use a *liberate*, covering the prisoners in each gaol. By the end of the year the great work was complete, though Ellis Hookes had a list of some fifty Friends left in prison through the oversight of the authorities in making their returns.

The names in the Great Pardon deserve examination. Reading easily comes first with 75, the spoil of Armorer's persecuting zeal.[2] Courtier-like, he procured a warrant for their discharge on the very day when the Privy Council set the proceedings for the Pardon in hand. He came down from London at the beginning of April, telling people on the road that he was going to free the Quakers. He had the men-prisoners to his house and told

---

[1] See *ante*, p. 42. A letter was sent down by London Friends, dated 5th June, asking prisoners to contribute their proportion of charges, which in Yorkshire (see Q.M. Minutes) worked out at 13s. 6d. apiece. This was paid in all or part by the Q.M. in several cases, including the two non-Friends of the county whose names were in the Pardon.

[2] For the Reading persecution, see *post*, Chap. VIII.

III SECOND CONVENTICLE ACT, 1670–1673

them that he had an order to release them all, which he was as willing to do as ever he had been to put them in, "for," said he, "what I did then was to execute the King's laws, and seeing now it is the King's pleasure to release you I do it with all my heart, hoping you will live peaceable."[1] The Reading Friends had been close prisoners, but in some cases those now released had been treated less strictly. Yorkshire Friends paid £30 to the Castle gaoler for indictments preferred against him for giving liberty to his prisoners.[2] A group of Hampshire Friends suffered strait confinement for half a year, but afterwards the gaoler allowed them to be at large.[3]

A number of the itinerating Publishers of Truth were now freed, worn and enfeebled by bondage but with spirits unbroken. Ambrose Rigge established himself as a schoolmaster, and, in the opinion of the parish priest, "being a man of parts and learning, doth a great deal of mischief in seducing others."[4] Dewsbury went forth to a few years of liberty which were filled with unwearied service. Thomas Taylor also travelled largely, with Stafford as his centre of residence.

The Pardon included some who were not Quakers, Whitehead generously advising the friends of these to petition the King to insert their names, "for when we had made way," he says, "and beaten the path, 'twas easy for them to follow." The names occur chiefly in the lists for Bedfordshire, Kent, and Wiltshire, and John Bunyan, whose first book had been directed against the Quakers, now owed his liberty to their assistance.[5]

The King had acted within his prerogative of mercy in pardoning individuals, however numerous, but the Declaration suspending the execution of the Penal Laws was another matter. Need of money obliged him to call

---

[1] See MS. Q.M. Sufferings; Edward Man to Margt. Fox, 13th April 1672, in Swarthm. Colln. i. 133; and Warrant 29th March in *Cal. State Papers, Dom.*, 1671–2, p. 252.
[2] Q.M. Minutes and Accounts, 12th June, 11th Sept. 1673, 9th Dec. 1675.
[3] Besse, *Sufferings*, i. 234. See *post*, p. 220 for this case.
[4] T. W. Marsh, *Early Friends in Surrey and Sussex*, p. 68.
[5] George Whitehead, *Christian Progress*, p. 358. John Brown, *John Bunyan*, p. 187, *J.F.H.S.* x. 290.

Parliament together at the beginning of February 1673; and he found it resolved to have no tampering with its legislative power in the interests, as it believed, of Roman Catholic domination. After a month of acute constitutional crisis, the King gave way, cancelled the Declaration, and broke the seal with his own hand.[1]

Nonconformity had enjoyed precarious recognition for less than a year. Yet so well had it improved its freedom that licences had been issued for some 1500 preachers and for a much larger number of preaching-places. The Yorkshire Tory magnate, Sir John Reresby, says[2] that the Declaration "was the greatest blow that ever was given, since the King's restoration, to the Church of England; all Sectaries by this means repairing publicly to their meetings and conventicles, insomuch that all the laws and care of their execution against these Separatists afterwards could never bring them back to due conformity." The ground won could not be wholly lost even as the result of a fresh outburst of persecution. A Bill giving some degree of toleration passed the Commons but was wrecked in the Lords. It would not have reached to the Quakers, but shows the dying down of a violent persecuting spirit in the Cavalier Parliament. The licences granted were not immediately revoked, and continued to give an uncertain protection to their holders. The Justices as a rule waited for clear directions before putting the laws in execution. It was, in fact, only when Charles in 1674 shifted from reliance on France to the natural alliance between Anglicanism and the royal prerogative, that persecution became again an active policy. An Order in Council, dated 3rd February 1675, directed the more diligent execution of the Penal Laws, and declared that all licences had been long since recalled. The period of royal indulgence was over, and the era of Parliamentary toleration had not yet dawned.

For Friends as for other Dissenters there had been an

---

[1] The withdrawal of the Declaration and the subsequent history are carefully told in Bate, *The Declaration of Indulgence, 1672*, chaps. vi. vii.

[2] *Memoirs*, edn. 1875, p. 86.

invaluable breathing space of three years. There would be in the future much sporadic harrying by Informers and one terrible spell of persecution, but it was no longer possible to root out Dissent, the only practical question was how to find a legal place for it in the national life.

CHAPTER IV

LATER DAYS OF PERSECUTION

Of this excellent patience and sufferings, the witnesses of God, in scorn called Quakers, have given a manifest proof; for . . . they went up and down, as they were moved of the Lord, preaching and propagating the Truth in market-places, highways, streets and public temples, though daily beaten, whipped, bruised, haled and imprisoned therefor. And, when there was anywhere a Church or assembly gathered, they taught them to keep their meetings openly; and not to shut the door nor do it by stealth, that all might know it and who would might enter. And as hereby all just occasion of fear of plotting against the Government was fully removed, so this their courage and faithfulness . . . did so weary out the malice of their adversaries that often-times they were forced to leave their work undone. For when they came to break up a meeting, they were forced to take every individual out by force, they not being free to give up their liberty by dissolving at their command: and when they were haled out, unless they were kept forth by violence, they presently returned peaceably to their place. Yea, when sometimes the magistrates have pulled down their meeting-houses, they have met the next day openly upon the rubbish, and so by innocency kept their possession and ground, being properly their own, and their right to meet and worship God being not forfeited to any. So that, when armed men have come to dissolve them, it was impossible for them to do it, unless they had killed every one, for they stood so close together that no force could move anyone to stir until violently pulled down, so that, when the malice of their opposers stirred them to take shovels and throw the rubbish upon them, there they stood unmoved, being willing, if the Lord should so permit, to have been there buried alive witnessing for Him. As this patient but yet courageous way of suffering made the persecutors' work very heavy and wearisome unto them, so the courage and patience of the sufferers using no resistance nor bringing any weapons to defend themselves nor seeking anyways revenge upon such occasions did secretly smite the hearts of the persecutors and make their chariot-wheels go on heavily. Thus after much and many kind of sufferings thus patiently borne, . . . a kind of negative liberty has been obtained; so that at present for the most part we meet together without disturbance from the magistrate. — ROBERT BARCLAY, *Apology* (1st English edn., 1678), Prop. xiv. sect. 6.

THE second half of the reign of Charles II. was a period of embittered politics, inspired by fear of the Catholics and centring round the succession to the throne. The issues that were to triumph in the Revolution of 1688 came into prominence, and England more than once trembled on the verge of Civil War. But, though this was averted, the war of factions was scarcely less ruthless, and our modern party system sprang to birth amid the delations by Titus Oates and the trials of Russell and Sidney. Then, with the King and the Church wielding despotic power, Charles died. Thenceforward the crisis matured rapidly. Absolutism, supported by the Tories and the Church, had succeeded under Charles ; but the menace of Roman Catholic despotism under James alienated this support and carried the defeated Whig cause to its crowning victories of 1689—a Protestant sovereign, a limited monarchy, and religious toleration.

The passing of the Test Act of 1673 against Catholics in office under the Crown broke up the Cabal and drove the Duke of York (afterwards James II.) from the Admiralty. In the following winter the refusal of supplies forced peace with Holland. Charles was now alive to the miscarriage of his Catholic aims and left their further pursuit in the hands of his more bigoted and less politic brother. But he found it possible to manage Parliament for his own ends, with the help of his new minister, Sir Thomas Osborne, made Earl of Danby. Danby created the Tory party to stand for Church and King and rallied many good Englishmen by avowed hostility to France and by carrying through the marriage of the Duke of York's daughter Mary to William of Orange, the champion of Protestant Europe against Louis XIV. Charles and his Minister aimed at absolute rule, and but for a quarrel between the two Houses would have provided for a permanently Tory Parliament by a law disabling any one from sitting until he had sworn to alter nothing in Church or State.

The Commons had now continued without a dissolution since 1661. The membership was greatly altered. George Whitehead says :[1] " Many or most of our old adversaries and rigid persecutors therein were removed by

[1] *Christian Progress*, p. 490.

death; and new ones of better spirits and tempers chosen in their rooms." In these last years of life Parliament developed a powerful opposition, under the dangerous leadership of Shaftesbury, who had turned against the King and was bent on forcing a dissolution. As early as the spring of 1675 this was in the air; and the Morning Meeting advised Friends as follows:[1]

That Friends in the several counties seriously consider together and be unanimous about giving their voice in election of Parliament-men to appear or not appear therein as in the wisdom of God they see convenient and safe.

That such moderate and indifferent [*i.e.* impartial] men, as they are free to give their voice for, first be advised to sign to Friends this or the like engagement, viz. :—

1. To be for a general Liberty of Conscience for all to worship God according to their persuasions.
2. To endeavour, to the utmost of his power, to remove all oppressive and Popish laws that are for coercion or persecution about religion.

Parliament, however, was prorogued till October; and did not meet again for fifteen months. On reassembling in February 1677, Shaftesbury, eager to force the issue, moved in the Lords that the long prorogation made it an unlawful assembly. His legal grounds were weak, and the Peers committed him to the Tower, where he had leisure for a year to reproach himself for playing into the King's hands. Meanwhile Danby was lavish in the arts of political corruption, and a majority of the Pensionary Parliament, as it was now called, enjoyed the spoils of office which he provided and obediently played his tune. The Whigs suspected the intrigue of Charles with France and the Papist danger, but nothing was certainly known. They were "mad with the rage of a baffled and ill-used faction ... but a liar came to their deliverance. In the autumn of 1678, Titus Oates deposed that the Jesuit congregation had met on the 24th April in the White Horse Tavern and taken counsel to murder the King."[2] The random charges received some countenance

---

[1] Minutes of 31st May 1675.
[2] G. M. Trevelyan, *England under the Stuarts*, p. 382.

with the arrest of Coleman, the Duke of York's Secretary; whose papers showed that a treasonable correspondence had been on foot with the Papal Nuncio and Père La Chaise, the French King's Confessor. This discovery was followed by the murder of Sir Edmund Berry Godfrey, the magistrate to whom Oates had first confided his precious information, and thereupon frenzy and panic took possession of Protestant London. When Parliament met on 21st October, a resolution was passed *nemine contradicente* that "there has been, and still is, a damnable and hellish Plot contrived and carried on by Popish recusants, for the assassinating and murdering the King; and for subverting the Government and rooting out and destroying the Protestant religion."

Charles, who alone of Englishmen was in a position to avow his disbelief in the plot against his own life, was compelled by the addresses of Parliament to call out the militia, enforce the Penal Laws, fill the prisons with hundreds of Catholics, plant cannon round Whitehall, and issue a proclamation commanding all Popish recusants to depart ten miles from London. . . . The Test Act of 1673 had excluded Catholics from service under the Crown; this winter they were excluded from sitting in either House of Parliament, by an Act which remained in force till the days of O'Connell and Wellington.[1]

Coleman's letters implicated the King's brother, and the Whig leaders attacked James and hinted at his exclusion from the Crown. Had their choice of a successor fallen on the next heirs, Mary and William of Orange, they might have antedated the Revolution by ten years. But they schemed for one who would be the puppet of their own faction—either the bastard Duke of Monmouth or some infant child of Charles after he had been divorced from his barren wife and married to a Protestant. The French King, whose interest lay in a weak and distracted England, provided them with their deadliest weapon. He furnished proof of a secret treaty procured from Charles in March 1678, in return for a yearly pension of £300,000 in French gold. Danby

---

[1] G. M. Trevelyan, *England under the Stuarts*, p. 387.

had reluctantly agreed to this base compact in order to retain office, and the King had written on the instructions, "I approve this letter, C.R." When the documents were read out to the House in December, the Whig triumph seemed assured.

A pretence was made in public speaking to shield the real traitor, Charles, in order to crush the instrument, Danby, under the full weight of the charge. The responsibility of Ministers was established at Danby's expense; and his Tory plea that it had been his duty to obey the King was rejected. His impeachment was voted; and his head was in great danger, if the Houses sat another month. He therefore persuaded Charles to dissolve the Cavalier Parliament, nearly eighteen years after it had first met. At last the Whigs had forced the King's hand.[1]

The new Parliament met in March 1679, with the Whigs in power. It introduced a Bill for the exclusion of James from the throne; and was prorogued in May and dissolved in July. Its one achievement was the passing of the Habeas Corpus Act, which effectually advanced the liberty of the subject by securing the early trial of prisoners. In the summer the King's dangerous illness brought Civil War very near, for Monmouth was at the height of his popularity and was in command of the armies that two months earlier had conquered the Scottish rebels at Bothwell Brig. James was hastily summoned from Brussels, where he had been living in politic exile, to find his brother out of danger and feigning surprise at his return. Charles ordered both claimants out of England, James to Scotland and Monmouth to Holland, and in October prorogued the newly-elected Second Whig Parliament. During the next twelve months the country seethed with agitation. Monmouth returned to London amid lines of bonfires, and made interest with the Whigs and the West of England.

A reference by young John Whiting, then a prisoner at Ilchester, with some thirty other Friends,[2] shows this dangerous political campaign at its height:

---
[1] G. M. Trevelyan, *England under the Stuarts*, p. 396.
[2] *Persecution Exposed*, p. 32.

In the Sixth-month this year [August 1680], came down the Duke of Monmouth, in his Progress in the West, and came through Ivelchester with some thousands on horseback attending him; the country flocking to him and after him, the eyes of the nation being upon him and towards him as the hopes and head of the Protestant interest at that time in opposition to the Duke of York and Popish party; so that the affections of the people run exceedingly after him. We stood in the Friary-gate as he rode through the town; and as he passed by, taking notice of so many Quakers together with their hats on, he stopped and put off his hat to us; and our Friend, John Anderdon, had a mind to speak to him and tell him that we were prisoners for conscience' sake; but had a stop in his mind, lest there should be an ill use made of it, in applying to him and making him too popular—the Court having a watchful eye over him. However, we could not but have a respect to him for his affability; and therefore were the more concerned for him when his fall came.

Whigs and Tories during these months became transformed into Petitioners and Abhorrers,—those who petitioned for the calling of the newly-elected Parliament; and those who "abhorred" any restraint upon the King's free discretion. In June Shaftesbury had dared to present James to the Grand Jury at Westminster Hall, as a Popish recusant, and to indict the King's Popish mistress, Madam Carwell (De Querouaille), the Duchess of Portsmouth, as a "common nuisance." At last the Houses met in October 1680, and through the superb debating skill of Halifax the Exclusion Bill was thrown out by the Lords. The Commons raged, and in January 1681 Parliament was again dissolved. For a third time the Whigs were returned. They thought that the King was now at their mercy; for the Exchequer was empty and no supplies would be granted without the Exclusion Bill. Charles, however, had secretly obtained from the French King the promise of a three years' supply and remained master of the event. He called the Houses together in March in Cavalier Oxford; and, while the Bill was being hurried through, suddenly dissolved them. The Whigs were thrown into a panic; and the King's last Parliament fled in confusion.

The Quakers, as a body, were outside the clash of party strife. The Cavalier Parliament, tyrannous because of its fears, had made their conscience a crime and had only treated them as faithful subjects if they were unfaithful Christians. The chief political duty left them was to establish, by steadfast witness and patient suffering, the supremacy of conscience over unjust law. If England to-day recognizes that a nation is committing moral suicide when it sets the State above men's souls, the lesson has been learnt through the ineffectual stoning of prophets and imprisonment of saints which went on in the merry days of the Restoration. It was a difficult witness, but it was maintained to the end — without concealment, without plotting, without violence. Robert Barclay's *Apology* is prefaced by a noble letter to the King, dated 25th November 1675, which illustrates the Quaker attitude. After pointing out that in all the plots no Friend had been found guilty; and that in the hottest persecution they had shown their constancy by boldly keeping up their meetings without creeping into holes and corners, he urges that they had never sought to render the King and his Government odious by nameless and scandalous pamphlets and libels, but had always discharged their consciences towards him without flattering words. He knew "their faithfulness towards their God, their patience in suffering, their peaceableness towards the King, their honesty, plainness and integrity in their faithful warnings and testimonies."

While agreeing with his Friends in their negative patriotism of standing clear from plots and their positive witness for a Christian order of society, one Friend, William Penn, was a man of still more universal spirit, who could not, even under the oppression of the time, withdraw himself from the political interests of his country. By education and position a member of the governing class, he had the accomplishments of a man of affairs, and added an eagerness and reach of spirit in all that concerned the public welfare. Amid the first unrest of the Popish plot, he had warned Friends against the danger of allowing their spirits to be caught by the panic-fears of the crowd and its clamour for some arm of flesh to work deliverance.[1] "Yet," he adds, "can we not be insensible of their infirmities, as well as we shall not be free from some of their sufferings; we must make their case as our own, and travail alike in spirit for them as for ourselves." His own generous nature threw him with zest into the election on the dissolution of the Pension Parliament; and he gave active support to his friend, Algernon Sidney, the Whig candidate for Guildford. Sidney was Penn's senior by twenty-two years, a man of independent opinions and great influence, who had fought against Charles I. and served in the Council of State during the early years of the Commonwealth; but had disputed the validity of the King's trial and held aloof from Cromwell's Protectorate. He had lived abroad after the Restoration, nursing republican designs, but returned to England in 1677 to look after his family affairs. To Penn he must have seemed the type of man the country needed; but the Court knew him to be one of its most dangerous opponents, and, though Guildford elected him by a large majority, the Sheriff returned the other candidate, on the plea that Sidney was not a freeman of the borough.[2] Penn's proceedings did not find favour with Friends, if we may take the following Minute of the Meeting for Sufferings as referring to the matter:[3]

Friends being sensible of the great scandal cast on William Penn, and that his absence adds to the same; it's the desire of Friends that Thomas Zachary write to him this post.

A month later, however, we find the meeting approving a letter which he had drawn up for Friends to send to their Members of Parliament asking for redress of their grievances and sufferings.[4] When the first Whig Parliament was dissolved in July 1679, Penn resumed his

---

[1] Epistle to the Children of Light, 4th November 1678, in *Works*.
[2] See letter from Penn to Sidney in Janney's *Life*, p. 154.
[3] Minute of 20th February 1679.
[4] Minute of 20th March 1679; a later meeting reported many letters from counties to Members of Parliament.

activities. Under the *nom de plume* of "Philanglus," he issued addresses to the electors and to the new legislature.[1] The first is a finely worded appeal to refuse bribes, vote against all reputed pensioners and officers at Court, and choose men of industry and courage, sincere Protestants who will maintain civil rights and favour liberty of conscience. Frequent Parliaments, he says, are the only check on arbitrary ministers. Voters need to be jealous of their political rights for their well-being depends on their preservation. In the spirit of this address he used all his influence, though without success, to bring in Sidney as member for the Sussex borough of Bramber, not far from his own seat at Worminghurst.[2] The second is a project for the good of England, based on the position that civil safety depended on civil union, and civil union on toleration, "witness the careful government of Holland, where the preservation of their civil interest from fracture hath secured them against the growth of Popery, though it be almost tolerated by them; so powerful are the effects of an united civil interest in government." He urged with great wisdom that the nature of things was a better guide in statesmanship than the prejudices of men; and that bigotry in civil government could only thin the people, lessen trade, create jealousies, and endanger the peace and wealth of the whole. Have regard, he says, to the true national interests; let superstition mutter what it will.

A third more considerable piece, called *An Address to Protestants*, was published in the same year, 1679, over his own name. It seems earlier than the other two,[3] and is one of Penn's best writings; but is chiefly

[1] "England's Great Interest in the Choice of this New Parliament; dedicated to all her Freeholders and Electors," dated by internal evidence prior to the second Whig Parliament; and "One Project for the Good of England . . . humbly dedicated to . . . Parliament," placed after the first in Penn's *Works*.
[2] See letter to Sidney in Janney's *Life*, p. 155; and Gilbert Spencer to Henry Sidney, 1st Sept. 1679, R. W. Blencowe, *Diary of the Times of Charles II. by Henry Sidney* (1843), i. 114-120.
[3] Printed from 2nd edn. 1692, in Penn's *Works*. A reference in pt. ii. sect. 6 to the seventeen years' duration of "the late Parliament" fixes date. The greater part of argument as to province of Caesar and of Christ had been printed by Penn in appendix to his "Continued Cry of the Oppressed for Justice," 1675.

noteworthy, so far as his political position is concerned, for its careful attempt to determine the province of Church and State. In a fine passage he says:

> But this way of proceeding ... is of an ill consequence upon this account, that heaven is barred, as much as in men lies, from all farther illuminations. Let God send what light He pleases into the world, it must not be received by Caesar's people, without Caesar's licence; and, if it happen that Caesar be not presently [*i.e.* immediately] convinced, as well as I, that it is of God, I must either renounce my convictions and lose my soul to please Caesar, or profess and persevere in my persuasion and so lose my life, liberty or estate to please God. Therefore I would entreat Caesar to consider the sad consequence of imposition, and remember both that God did never ask man leave to introduce truth or make farther discoveries of His mind to the world, and that it hath been a woeful snare to those Governments that have been drawn to employ their power against His work and people. This way of procedure endeavours to stifle or else to punish sincerity; for fear or hopes, frowns or favour, prevail only with base minds — souls degenerated from true nobleness. Every spark of integrity must be extinguished where conscience is sacrificed to worldly safety and preferment. This net holds no temporizers; honest men are all the fish it catches. . . . There is not so ready a way to atheism as this of extinguishing the sense of conscience for worldly ends: destroy that internal rule of faith, worship and practice towards God, and the reason of my religion will be civil injunctions and not Divine convictions; consequently I am to be of as many religions as the civil authority shall impose, however untrue or contradictory.

The Whig Parliaments largely shared Penn's views; and the Second introduced a Bill in December 1680, for "Ease to all Protestant Dissenters," which was in several of its clauses the model upon which the Toleration Act was afterwards framed.[1] Moreover, the Commons resolved on 10th January 1681,[2] in their last expiring days:—
"That the prosecution of Protestant Dissenters upon the Penal Laws is at this time grievous to the subject, a weakening of the Protestant interest, an encouragement to Popery and dangerous to the peace of the kingdom."

---
[1] George Whitehead, *Christian Progress*, pp. 492-497, see *post*, p. 153.
[2] *Ibid.* p. 497.

The attitude of Friends during these years of bitter political struggle naturally inclined to the Whigs, and is expressed though without any party spirit in the letter issued by the Meeting for Sufferings after the dissolution of the Second Whig Parliament:[1]

> As we ought not to be discouraged in our endeavours for the relief of the oppressed by any present disappointments, so we desire that all Friends who are in capacity, as they have freedom and clearness, may appear and make what good interest they can in this election of Parliament-men, for sober, discreet and moderate men, such as live in love with their neighbours, that are against persecution and Popery, and that deport themselves tenderly towards our Friends. Be very cautious of giving any just cause of offence. We desire God's wisdom may be with you in the discharge of your duty and conscience in these things.

Persecution though in general much abated was still grievous in certain directions, and the Conventicle Act was being enforced with severity in several counties " in a way of revenge, since our Friends have appeared in the late elections for such members of Parliament as they believed would most approve themselves just men for the general good of their country."[2] The party in power was beginning to avail itself of persecuting laws as ready weapons against its supposed enemies.

The independence of the electors, made possible by the number of borough seats and the yeoman franchise in the counties, had resulted in the return of three successive Whig majorities, and had thrown the Tories into a blind support of absolute rule. Even before despotism had triumphed with the Whig flight from Oxford in March 1681, great changes had been made in the magistracy and the militia. A bitter and relentless spirit was abroad, which struck at the beaten party and for the time crushed it. Shaftesbury, in the character of

---

[1] *Letters of Early Friends*, p. 203.
[2] Document, printed in John Whiting, *Persecution Exposed*, p. 33, "The Case of . . . Quakers . . . especially upon old Statutes made against Popish Recusants." At the end was a summary of sufferings 1660–1680, showing 243 deaths, 276 in prison, October 1680, total number of imprisonments, 10,778. This includes 624 Friends excommunicated and imprisoned for not conforming to the Church-service and 198 sentenced to banishment—a figure which should be raised to about 230, see *ante*, p. 50.

Ahithophel, became the butt of Dryden's terrible satire; and his acquittal in November 1681 by a London jury was the last Whig success. In the following year the Government procured the election of Tory Sheriffs in the City by a mixture of fraud and force, and twelve months after his acquittal Ahithophel fled the realm. The Whig cause was driven into underground channels which issued in the Rye House plot of April 1683 to assassinate Charles, and in the consequent trial and execution of Lord Russell and Algernon Sidney. Then came a root-and-branch forfeiture of borough-charters, and by the year 1684 free local government, like Parliament, was a thing of the past.

The King had become absolute with the help of French gold and through alliance with the Tories and the Church. As part of the price for this alliance persecution was unleashed for the hunting of Dissent. When William Penn returned to England in October 1684, after his first stay of two years in Pennsylvania, he writes:[1]

> I found things in general with another face than I left them, sour and stern; and [saw that the Government was] resolved to hold the reins of power with a stiffer hand than heretofore, especially over those that were observed to be State or Church Dissenters, conceiving that the opposition which made the Government uneasy came from that sort of people; and therefore they should either bow or break.

We must now record the culminating outburst of intolerant rage, mainly as it affected Friends. It fell with greatest severity on the large towns, where the Tories were bent on crushing all opponents in order to confirm their own precarious power.

Bristol, the second city in the kingdom and the capital of the disaffected West that welcomed Monmouth, was naturally enough a chief centre of anxiety to the Government and of persecuting rigour by its instruments. Two-thirds of the leading inhabitants were said to be Presbyterians, Independents, Baptists, or Quakers.[2] Friends

---

[1] See his Apology, as printed in Janney's *Life*, p. 261.
[2] Richard Ellsworth to Williamson, 27th Oct. 1677, in *Cal. State Papers, Dom.*, 1677-8, p. 426.

had already suffered two persecutions in the city, one in 1655, the other in 1663 and '4; this third period, "like the third blast of wind or wave of the sea, was the most violent of all."[1] The chief agent was one of the Sheriffs, John Knight,[2] who was knighted in reward for his activities and was dubbed "the pillar of Bristol." The King seems to have given him his instructions, urging him to zeal with the words, "Have but a good mind to it and the business will be done."[3] All Dissenters were to be harried, and their meeting-houses closed as nests of Puritanical and plotting Whigs; and this was to be done by overbearing the Mayor and the other Sheriff and the moderate magistrates.[4]

A new form of persecution, peculiarly destructive in its effects, had been developed in the preceding years under the stimulus of the Papist terror. In February 1676, an Order in Council[5] had directed the strict enforcement of the laws against conventicles and Popish recusants. Under the Acts against recusants[6] any person over sixteen not attending church could be sentenced to forfeit Twenty Pounds to the Exchequer for every month of non-attendance, or the King could take two-thirds of the offender's lands into his own hands until he came to church, leaving him one-third for his maintenance. As with the process of *praemunire*, the law was perverted into a scourge for the Quakers. A list, which was presented to the Privy Council about the year 1677, already shows eight hundred cases, mostly from Westmorland, Cambridgeshire, Lancashire, and Norfolk.[7] The newly

---

[1] Whiting, *Persecution Exposed*, p. 59.
[2] *Ibid.* p. 62, formerly a factor at Nevis (Besse, *Sufferings*, i. 59) and to be distinguished from "old Sir John Knight," who had been zealous in the second Bristol persecution; see *ibid.* p. 59, and from another John Knight, Mayor of Bristol, 1670. [3] *Broadmead Baptist Records*, p. 441.
[4] A paper from Bristol, dated 25th Aug. 1680, and endorsed as a "seditious presentment," is among the State Papers, justifying the Churchmen in the Corporation who were moderate towards dissenting Protestants and in favour of uniting all Protestants against the Papists (*Cal. State Papers, Dom.*, 1679-1680, p. 619).
[5] *Fleming MSS.* p. 125.
[6] St. 23 Eliz. cap. 1, sect. 5, 29 Eliz. cap. 6, sections 3, 4, and 3 Jac. I. cap. 4, regulated the matter; and were all directed against the Papists.
[7] See *J.F.H.S.* xi. 135. I now think the date must be about 1677. The

established Meeting for Sufferings was active in seeking redress from King and Parliament, but without success.[1] The King admitted the hardship of Friends suffering for the Papists' faults as well as for their own; the expiring Pension Parliament and the Whig Parliaments designed relief but were prorogued before it could be effected.[2] When the hour of Tory vengeance struck, this ready means for ruining Dissent still disgraced the Statute Book.

The blow fell at Bristol at the end of 1681.[3] There were at this time six Dissenting meeting-houses in the city, two being Baptist, two Quaker, and one of the others Presbyterian. Under colour of fining the houses for not sending a soldier to the trainbands, three of these, including the Quaker house at the Friars, were pillaged in mid-December, and the others in the following weeks. A month later all the Dissenting congregations were

---

Meeting for Sufferings of 21st June 1677, inquired about preparing the list; and on 12th July directed it to be sent to the Treasurer (the Earl of Danby). Westmorland Q.M. on 6th July paid 15s. for two copies "of the rolls of convictions upon the statute of recusancy."

[1] The Meeting for Sufferings on 24th Aug. 1676 had Westmorland cases reported to it, and directed inquiry "whether it be the King's mind that this course should be taken against Dissent." The subject was constantly under consideration.

[2] Wm. Penn reported to the Meeting for Sufferings that on 16th Jan. 1678 the King in Council said it was very unreasonable that Friends should be prosecuted on Statutes against Papists; but it had been answered that relief must come from Parliament, to whom application was accordingly made. Algernon Sidney, writing on 13th April, says that Friends had good success with the Committee of the Commons, "and it is hoped that if the House sit long enough to perfect that business they will find means of exempting them . . . nevertheless I find many Parliament-men very bitter upon them in private conversation" (*J.F.H.S.* xi. 68). A Bill was prepared for the first Whig Parliament, and after its prorogation in May 1679, a deputation to the Council was arranged, see George Whitehead, *Christian Progress*, pp. 374-376.

[3] The main sources for the persecution at Bristol are the *Broadmead Baptist Records*, pp. 431-494, and Besse, *Sufferings*, i. 54-74. The account in Besse is based on a series of pamphlets published in 1682: "The Distressed Case of the . . . Quakers in the City of Bristol," "The Sad and Lamentable Cry," "More Sad and Lamentable News from Bristol," "The Devouring Informers of Bristol," "The New and Strange Imprisonment of the . . . Quakers in the City of Bristol," "A Farther Account from several Letters," "A Narrative of the Cruelties and Abuses Acted by Isaac Dennis, Keeper, his Wife and Servants." (See full titles in Smith, *Catalogue*, ii. 678-681.) The last pamphlet is later in date than the others, 6th February 1684. Besse also uses references in John Whiting, *Persecution Exposed*. See also George Whitehead, *Christian Progress*, pp. 504-512. For MS. materials consult especially Minutes of Meeting for Sufferings, containing abstracts of letters from Bristol, and Bristol Meeting MS. Records, *e.g.* Bristol MSS. v. Nos. 136-155. For a modern account see Tanner, *Three Lectures*, pp. 30-36.

meeting privately except the Quakers, who met at Temple Street and in the long entry and court by the Friars, the meeting-house being at the time nailed up and seized for the King.[1] The Baptists suffered severely but decided to meet privately; and their records contain graphic accounts of their meetings in Kingswood and other places, the risks they ran, and the constancy they showed. The Quakers, however, with their open defiance, drew on themselves as usual the chief fury of the persecutors. They were crowded into Newgate almost to suffocation; till the Bridewell had to be added for their accommodation; they were barbarously handled at their meetings and then indicted for a riot; and excessive distraints were made on their goods. The pack of Informers behaved in the most arbitrary fashion:

> Their manner of levying . . . distress is as follows: viz., when they enter a shop, albeit there is abundance of goods in view, yet they break open chests, counters, etc., and thence take away the money; if no money to be had, then they take either shop or household goods, and of them generally to double their value. If any durst speak to them by way of reproof for these unreasonable proceedings, then they huff and threaten to send them to prison, which power they assume to themselves commonly when they go to disturb the Quakers' meetings, thinking no doubt but they are privileged to it by the office of constable and the example of their grand abettor and brother Informer, Sheriff Knight . . . It's generally believed, by the long date of the warrants, these distresses have been levied for convictions made clandestinely in a tavern.[2]

By June 1682 the number of Friends in prison had reached about one hundred and fifty; but the meeting continued to be kept up, chiefly by children.[3] On the 18th June six boys were taken from the Temple Street meeting and put for an hour in the stocks, and some thirty children were imprisoned for a time. In July the meetings consisted of hardly any but children. On the 23rd the boys' hats were taken away and cast into a neighbour's yard, and eight lads were put in the stocks

---

[1] *Broadmead Baptist Records*, p. 445.
[2] Besse, *Sufferings*, i. 61.   [3] Cf. Reading case, *post*, p. 226.

for two hours, who behaved themselves soberly and cheerfully. On the 30th, in the afternoon outside the Friars, the meeting was held by seven women and about fifty children. The children were now frequently imprisoned, contrary to all law, showing themselves very bold for the Truth. John Whiting says:

> Now after the men and women were mostly taken up and imprisoned, the meetings were mostly kept up by children . . . whom they abused very much . . . putting them in the stocks several times, Helliar beating the children with a twisted whalebone stick . . . but Truth taught them to forgive. Another time, Tilly, inhuman wretch, beat them with a faggot-stick, which they bore patiently, the Lord no doubt supporting them and accepting the kindness of their youth. . . . He sent several to Bridewell; and when discharged, threatened them if they did so any more they should be whipped in Bridewell . . . endeavouring to make them promise to go no more to meeting, but in vain. . . . Thomas Lugg, at one meeting, calling for a pot of holy water, by force crossed several boys and girls in the forehead, and sent nineteen to Bridewell; and when discharged threatened to whip them if they came again.[1]

Through the hottest days of persecution the children "remained steadfast; and thus showed, in spite of their enemies, that God would not suffer that the Quakers' meeting should be altogether suppressed, as it was intended."[2] But the difficulties increased throughout the autumn; and, in October, a solemn meeting was arranged at Widow Dowell's house to wait on the Lord for increase of strength, and to endeavour to stir up one another in the discharge of the duty of keeping up the public meeting.[3] A fortnight later, Friends are discouraged from inviting great numbers to funerals, "reproach [being] brought upon the Truth by the great resort of Friends at buryings at this juncture, whiles our public meetings for the worship of God are so thinly supplied." At the same meeting,

---

[1] *Persecution Exposed*, pp. 76, 77; cf. Besse, and Minutes of Meeting for Sufferings.
[2] Sewel, ii. 392.
[3] Draft Minute of Men's Meeting, 16th October. There was an Elizabeth Dowell, widow, who in the following year was heavily fined for non-attendance at church.

"a great concern for the honour of God . . . came upon Friends, being grieved that our said meetings are reduced to so low a condition and mean appearance"; and another solemn meeting was arranged for stirring up to faithfulness, and in order to wait on God for strength.[1] The Deeds of the Friars were with William Rogers, one of the Trustees, who was now disaffected to Friends as the leader of the Wilkinson-Story party, and had not been at meeting for forty weeks; but had recently been reading his *Christian-Quaker* at the meeting-house door and threatening for burglary any Friend who should open it, and expose him to the fine of £20 under the Conventicle Act.[2] Charles Harford, a leading Bristol Friend, in business as a soap-maker,[3] was willing to own the house; but Rogers refused to part with the writings unless his subscriptions towards building the meeting-houses were repaid.[4] Friends felt strongly "the public dishonour to the Truth in suffering our meeting-house at the Friars to be so long in the unjust and illegal possession of its public and open adversaries without being owned by Friends,"[5] and sought advice from London. They did not, however, resume full possession till July 1686, when persecution was entirely abated.

In this autumn of 1682, Bristol Dissenters were threatened with heavier sufferings than any they had undergone;[6] and these took the form of enormous fines under the Statutes against Recusancy. Some 1200 persons were indicted: "When they are convicted and the sum collected, 'tis said it will amount to above £100,000."[7] The list included 500 Friends; and

---

[1] Draft Minutes of 30th October.
[2] Minutes of Meeting for Sufferings, 6th October.
[3] See *J.F.H.S.* ix. 102. He already owned the Temple Street house on behalf of Friends.
[4] Thos. Robertson to Sarah Meade, Bristol, Newgate, 29th Sept. 1682, in Dev. Ho. A.R.B. Colln. No. 112. In another letter to the Yearly Meeting, in the Y.M. Minutes of 1682, he speaks of the "Christian-Quakers" "flinching in their testimonies."
[5] Minutes of Men's Meeting, 16th and 30th October, and for the resumption of possession, 7th and 21st June, 19th July, 16th Aug. 1686.
[6] Letter of Thos. Robertson to Sarah Meade cited above.
[7] For the 1200, see Minutes of Meeting for Sufferings, 22nd December 1682; for the total estimated amount, Luttrell's *Brief Relation*, i. 216, Aug. 1682.

warrants were in the officers' hands for distresses on 191, amounting to £16,440. It is, I think, clear that many were never executed: John Whiting says, "several were seized, but how many or how much I cannot give account."¹ From the *Broadmead Baptist Records* we learn² that the writs only came down in December 1683, and the Sheriff at once went into the Dissenters' shops and seized all the goods, releasing them on payment of the fines. Such as brought certificates of having conformed had to pay the town-clerk £20 apiece for the charge of reversing the sentence.

As to meetings the fury of persecution was now somewhat lessened; and John Whiting tells of a pretty full week-day afternoon meeting at the Friars, where he heard William Bingley, a leading London minister—the galleries all broken down and unrepaired, but the meeting quiet.³ From 1682 to '85, however, the gaol and the Bridewell had been crowded with Quakers; and it became customary for intentions of marriage to be notified to Friends in prison before being passed.⁴ The leading Bristol Quakers were in Newgate, and twice wrote to London Yearly Meeting of their earthly trials and spiritual triumphs.

In these things they have no conquest nor glory, thus to oppress the innocent, even in their prison, where they have thus thrust us in heaps. But in this is our rejoicing that they cannot keep God from us.

God enable us to love Him above all, and to cleave to Him through the loss of all. We are but worms and of no might, and have none . . . but Him alone. . . . Praise God with us for His wonderful goodness in preserving our health—a work to a wonder. Oh, that we may ever be thankful for it, and also that He has thus made us worthy to suffer for His name's sake only. We are not quite an hundred; are well, and in good content, peace and love, and want nothing. We pray God keep you and crown your assemblies with His ancient glory.⁵

---

¹ *Persecution Exposed*, p. 95; Besse, *Sufferings*, i. 68-70, gives lists.
² P. 483.
³ *Persecution Exposed*, pp. 91, 92. For Bingley, see *Camb. Journ.* ii. 496.
⁴ See Bristol Men's Meeting, 20th Feb. 1682, and later Minutes. Cf. documents in *J.F.H.S.* ii. 15. ⁵ Besse, *Sufferings*, i. 73, 74.

How, we ask, were these wholesale imprisonments made, since the Second Conventicle Act had punished with fines, and had provided that no person fined should suffer for the same offence under any other law? The answer is that the authorities found scope for their persecuting zeal by making a new use of the Act 35 Eliz. cap. 1, which was a temporary measure passed for the purpose of driving into exile the Separatists of Elizabeth's reign, but had been declared still in force by the First Conventicle Act.[1] It provided that any person, over sixteen, present at an unlawful conventicle should on conviction conform within three months or forfeit his estate and abjure the realm. If he refused to abjure he should suffer death as a felon without benefit of clergy. The Dissenting meeting was accordingly treated as unlawful under the Act of Elizabeth, and thus became a riot or rout or unlawful assembly under the Common Law, entailing fine or imprisonment on conviction by a jury.

The use of this old Act was the more tyrannical because the Second Whig Parliament had passed a Bill for its repeal, which failed to receive the royal assent, being withheld, it was alleged, by the King's particular order.[2] He or his creature would have been held to account had the short-lived Oxford Parliament survived.

Under this Act then, which should no longer have been an Act, the peaceable worshipping of God was deemed a riot. The riotous behaviour was indeed often supplied by the Informers, so that a Quaker woman could say to the Bristol Sheriff, "Though we cannot be suffered to serve God, these shall to serve the Devil."[3] The days of persecution at Bristol became saturnalia of intoxicated malice. The meetings were disturbed with drums and fiddles. Lewd fellows of the baser sort had licence to commit all kinds of insolency, and, once, Friends were nailed up in their meeting-house for six hours. After one raid the women were driven along the streets

[1] See *F.P.T.* pp. 359-361.
[2] Whitehead, *Christian Progress*, p. 498; Burnet, *Hist. of Our Own Times*, Airy's edn. ii. 278-279. The law, says Burnet, had only once been put in execution.   [3] Besse, *Sufferings*, i. 60.

like cattle, the Informer Helliar crying, "P'throw, p'throw," to make himself sport.

The Act of Elizabeth, with its ultimate death penalty, was also itself used at Bristol against two prominent citizens by way of a salutary threat to Dissent.[1] One of the victims was Dr. Ichabod Chauncey, a Nonconformist physician, who at the Restoration had been Chaplain to Sir Edward Harley, the Governor of Dunkirk. After conviction he abjured the realm and thus escaped the capital sentence.[2] The other was Richard Vickris, a leading Quaker merchant, "in his day an honest Friend and a gentleman of good sense and reputation."[3] When told that he must conform or abjure, he replied that he presumed the Recorder did not desire him to conform unless he could do so conscientiously; for to play the hypocrite was hateful to man and much more to God. Abjuring involved an oath, and accordingly he lay in the Newgate at Bristol awaiting execution; but was removed to London by *habeas corpus* for trial on errors in the indictment.[4] A letter from two of his fellow-prisoners in Bristol, dated 4th November 1684, says:[5]

> He is well and in fine content; but not yet come to his trial at the King's Bench. It's a great case: let all our hearts be in prayer to the Lord, in Whom alone all our help stands.

Penn had used his influence with the Duke of York, assuring him that Vickris would live peaceably under the Government, and the Duke had intervened, although the King was grown very harsh and irritable on the subject of any indulgence to Dissent. The notorious Jeffreys was Lord Chief Justice, and when the case came on in November had no difficulty in quashing the indictment.

---

[1] Penn's Apology in Janney's *Life*, p. 262 ; but Penn calls Chauncey "Cheny."
[2] *Broadmead Baptist Records*, pp. 486, 489; cf. 191 *n*. In March 1682, he, with three other physicians, certified that the Quakers were crowded together in Newgate, to the danger of their lives (Besse, *Sufferings*, i. 58).
[3] Thos. Story, *Life*, p. 624.
[4] For the proceedings against Vickris see Whiting, *Persecution Exposed*, pp. 89-91, 119-120, abstracted in Besse, *Sufferings*, i. 71, 72 ; and Penn's Apology, *ubi supra*.
[5] Letter to Dorset Friends in Dorset Q.M. Minutes, 1st April 1685.

In 1662, there were Quaker cases under the Act,[1] and a little later one non-Quaker case in which the death penalty was actually pronounced. At Aylesbury in 1664 the country Justices had sought to distinguish themselves by their persecuting zeal. Ten men and two women, all Baptists, on refusing to conform or abjure the realm, were declared guilty of felony and sentenced to death. This "struck the whole town with great horror and surprise." The son of one of the condemned "felons" immediately took horse for London, and applied himself to the great Baptist leader, William Kiffin, who knew Clarendon, and thus was given access to the King. "The King seemed very much surprised that any of his subjects should be put to death for their religion only; and inquired whether there was any law in force that justified such proceedings." A reprieve was promptly granted and a full pardon followed.[2]

Englishmen in general had a healthy repugnance to making conscience felony; and in the middle of the persecuting Restoration period an Act had been passed (St. 29 Car. II. cap. 9), abolishing the obsolescent writ for burning heretics, "and all punishment by death in pursuance of any ecclesiastical censures."[3]

Intolerance had free licence through England during these closing years of Charles II.—the years of the second Stuart despotism. Again the Quakers were the bulwark of Dissent.

---

[1] See *ante*, p. 34 note; cf. p. 44. When George Whitehead of London and Thomas Burr of Ware were imprisoned at Norwich, March-July 1680, the Recorder threatened to have them hanged under the Act, if they would not abjure the realm, "if the King should give order to have it put in execution" (Whitehead's *Christian Progress*, pp. 383, 389). In 1682, Nathaniel Vincent, a Nonconformist minister in Southwark, ejected in 1662, was sentenced under the Act, and lay in prison many months, "but was at last released by the intercession of some great men" (Neal's *History of the Puritans*, 1796 edn. iv. 601; Stoughton, *Eccl. Hist.*, *The Church of the Restoration*, ii. 54-57). York M.M. Minutes, 1st March 1683, include a letter from the Meeting for Sufferings, stating that Counsel advised Friends indicted on 35 Eliz. cap. 1 to stand mute and refuse to plead or traverse. This shows a fear that Vickris's case would be followed by others.

[2] Crosby, *Hist. of the English Baptists*, ii. 180.

[3] For the Act see Robertson, *Select Statutes*, etc., p. 85, and Traill, *Social England*, illustrated edn. iv. 506, 507. Welsh Friends and their legal adviser, Counsellor Thomas Corbet, seem to have been instrumental in securing this reform. See Richard Davies, *Life*, p. 163.

All other Protestant Dissenters were now suppressed; . . . and some there were, who, in their nocturnal meetings, would pray God that it might please Him to keep the Quakers steadfast, that so they might be as a wall about them, in order that other Dissenters might not be rooted out.[1]

The hydra-headed character of the persecution is well shown by the Petition addressed to King James and Parliament at the beginning of the new reign.[2] There were then 1383 Friends in prison, under some dozen statutes, including about 200 women. One hundred had died in prison since 1680, especially during the terribly severe winters of '83 and '84; and enormous fines had been levied at the instance of devouring Informers. The list appended showed 103 prisoners in Bristol, 104 in Devonshire, where serge-makers, who employed 500 workpeople, were disabled by imprisonment, 66 in Gloucestershire, and the same number in London and Middlesex, 73 in Lancashire, over 50 in Norfolk and in Northampton, 79 in Suffolk, one being a woollen manufacturer who employed 200 people, and no less than 279 in Yorkshire. "A company of idle, extravagant, and merciless Informers" had made the Quakers their prey, "many being convicted and fined, unsummoned and unheard in their own defence." Several of the Informers were "impudent women, who swear for their profit in part of the fines and seizures, their husbands being prisoners for debt through their own extravagances."

The Yearly Meeting held in June 1682 aptly styles itself "A Yearly Meeting for Sufferings," and was mainly occupied with the persecution.[3] County Meetings for Sufferings were recommended; also regular attendance at assizes and quarter-sessions; and Divine judgments on persecutors were to be recorded. Two advices were given which show the fine spirit of Friends in these days of peril to property and person. Those threatened with

---

[1] Sewel, ii. 394.
[2] *Ibid.* 406-415. The Suffolk Friend was either Samuel Cooper or Daniel Groom, who were both in prison on a *praemunire*. See Besse, *Sufferings*, ii. 686.
[3] See the printed Y.M. Epistles, and in illustration of the action taken in the Q.M.'s, the Kendal Early Record Book, p. 118, also Yorkshire Q.M. Minutes.

the heavy fines for recusancy were counselled "before conviction and distresses taken, to clear their accounts, and secure or satisfy for their debts which they owe to all persons; and suffer for their testimony with no other estate but their own."[1] Friends who owned meeting-houses in trust were advised to stand by their trust in time of persecution, but where any had not strength for this, other Friends should take up the trusts in faith.

The position in London during these years of despotism is well summarized by George Whitehead:[2]

Our being shut out of our meeting-houses for divers years . . . and our meetings kept in the streets in all sorts of weather, winter and summer, was a trial and hardship upon us. . . . But that trial was not so great as to have our estates and livelihoods exposed to ruin by a pack of ravenous Informers; although 'twas no small hardship to our persons to be kept out of doors in the streets, in the great, severe, and long frost and snow in the year 1683, for about three months together, when the river Thames was so frozen up that horses, coaches, and carts could pass to and fro upon it, and a street also be erected and [a] stand over it. And yet in all that hard season when we were so long kept out in the streets, in the bitter cold air, I do not remember that I got any harm or injury thereby. . . . We had in those days some opportunities, and were permitted to publish the Truth openly in the streets, and also to make public supplication to God; but more frequently not permitted but pulled away by force, by the trained bands or officers, and either sent to prison or turned into the meeting-house, and there detained under guard until the meeting was ended in the street . . . and scarce suffered many times to declare two or three sentences, without being haled away.

The detailed account of the sufferings in London at this time[3] closes with a list of sixty-five men and twenty-

[1] See also Fox's full letter (*Journ.* ii. 379), sent down with Y.M. Epistle of 1683; and Minute of Leinster Province Meeting at Castledermot, 5th April 1689, during the troublous times in Ireland, advising "all Friends not only against going into debt, but also to use all utmost endeavours to pay off what debts they owe; that in these calamitous times Friends may only run the hazard of their own substance" (Swarthm. Colln. v. No. 115). Steven Crisp gives similar advice to the Norwich prisoners in 1682 (*Works*, p. 466). Cf. John Gratton's behaviour, *post*, p. 422.

[2] *Christian Progress*, pp. 543, 544.

[3] Besse, *Sufferings*, i. 449-484; the list is at p. 484. There is a further account of one case of suffering in *F.P.T.* pp. 153-157; and see p. 361. For George Fox's experiences see his *Journal*.

one women Ministers—many of them Friends from the country—who were worthy of special honour for their stanchness in preaching in the city; "esteeming no worldly interest too near or dear to part with, that they might be found in a faithful discharge of their duty." A newsletter of the period illustrates the constancy of these ministers :[1]

> The Quakers are extreme stubborn. Their meeting-house in Gracechurch Street being kept shut, they in great numbers resorted thither in the street, bringing forms, chairs, etc.; and one beginning to speak, he was taken away either by the constables or soldiers, but immediately his room was supplied by another, and so successively; and some were committed.

At Norwich, where there had lately been a Quaker revival, persecution was especially severe.[2] Steven Crisp, in 1681, had "beheld the work of the Lord arising again in that great city"; and a year later found the Friends there "as soldiers, with their armour on, well-prepared for the approaching conflict."[3] George Whitehead and Thomas Burr, a maltster of Ware in Hertfordshire, had suffered sixteen weeks' imprisonment for refusing the Oath of Allegiance; and now, in the autumn of 1682, some sixty Friends were thrown into prison at the Guildhall, for keeping their meeting in the street, having been kept out of their meeting-house. An affidavit shows their loathsome usage at the hands of a merciless gaoler:

> In one room, called the Hole, which is the place wherein felons are usually imprisoned (which is a room 12 steps into ground) and in the house of office belonging to the said room, there are 16 beds and a hammock . . . in which beds do constantly 29 persons lay every night . . . the said room, if it were empty, containing not much above 16 foot in breadth and 37 foot in length. . . . They have likewise viewed another room . . . called the Chuck, which is a room without a chimney, 11

---

[1] Lady Newdigate-Newdegate, *Cavalier and Puritan*, p. 96. Cf. Thos. Wilson, *Life*, 1728 edn. p. 19.
[2] For Norwich see *F.P.T.* pp. 169-193 and p. 361; also Whitehead's *Christian Progress*, pp. 524-536 (to which, I think, Besse adds nothing); and *Life of Gilbert Latey*, pp. 89-97. For the case of Whitehead and Burr, see *Christian Progress*, pp. 377-489.
[3] Steven Crisp, *Works*, pp. 52, 54.

steps within ground, containing about 18 foot in length and 13 foot in breadth. In which room there are . . . 9 persons called Quakers confined.

It was only after much labour and repeated applications to the King that the prisoners were discharged in the summer of 1683.

At the end of the King's reign, Yorkshire had the largest number of prisoners. Many were from the West Riding, amongst others twelve who were lying at the King's mercy, under sentence of banishment on the Quaker Act, and one hundred and nineteen who were committed for refusing the Oath of Allegiance.[1] The Quaker Act had been out of use; but *praemunire* for refusing the oath had always been the readiest instrument of oppression.

The sufferings of Friends were part of the general spoliation of Dissent. When set on foot by the authorities, political motives were paramount. At Court it was said underhand that if Mr. Penn or Mr. Whitehead would undertake for the Quakers not to vote at elections of Parliament-men they should be freed from further persecution.[2] The Secretary of State, Sir Lionel Jenkins, a high-prerogative man, told his fellow-Welshman, Richard Davies, that he was not against Friends, but, said he, they " gave their votes for the election of Parliament-men that were against the King's interest."[3] The Rye House Plot of the spring of 1683, which was the result of driving the Whig cause into underground channels, was generally called the " fanatical plot," and inflamed the position. In an address to the King, presented in August of the same year, Friends declared themselves " clear in the sight of God, angels and men, from all hellish plots, . . . against the King, his brother, or any person on earth whatsoever." They went on to declare their obedience to magistracy, save in matters of conscience, and in such matters their willingness patiently to suffer and not to rebel, nor seek

---

[1] Besse, *Sufferings*, ii. 154, 155, and Case, pp. 160-162, which summarizes the sufferings. The Quaker Act seems to have been threatened in the Norwich cases, see *F.P.T.* pp. 178, 357, and Meeting for Sufferings, 28th Dec. 1683.

[2] Sewel, ii. 389.   [3] Davies, *Life*, p. 184.

revenge.[1] Meanwhile, we are told,[2] "since the discovery of this fanatic conspiracy, the pulpits for the most part have been busied with nothing but discourses against the Dissenters, preaching up loyalty and passive obedience." In the autumn of 1684, when persecution was hot in London, Friends reprinted the Declaration against plots issued at the time of the Fifth Monarchy rising,[3] adding, "This was our testimony above twenty years ago, and since then we have not been found acting contrary to it, nor ever shall; for the Truth that is our guide is unchangeable. And this is now reprinted to the men of this age, many of whom were then children, and doth stand as our certain testimony against all plotting and fighting with carnal weapons."

But while much of the persecution was political in character, a vast amount was due to the malice and greed of Informers and the bigotry of the clergy. The Informer had been encouraged under the Penal Statutes, because the ordinary Englishman, even when "dressed in a little brief authority," was averse to harrying his honest neighbours. But now the Bench, the magistracy, and the corporations were packed with the creatures of tyranny; and he became the master of men's liberties and estates. He could invoke the Penal Laws against the Justice who had the temerity or the independence to disregard his trumped-up charges: he throve on perjury and excessive distraints: if he pressed for fines rather than imprisonments, it was not from mercy but from greed: a bribe was the only passport to his indulgence; and he feared nothing but the raking up of his own past. He preyed upon the industry of the country; though with small profit to the King's Exchequer:[4] his only talent was the

---

[1] Sewel, ii. 402-404. [2] Luttrell's *Brief Relation*, i. 278.
[3] Fox, *Journal*, i. 494-500 and Minute of Morning Meeting, 6th October 1684, see *ante*, p. 12.
[4] Richard Davies was told by a leading Catholic nobleman that of £8000 exacted from Catholics of Lancashire practically nothing reached the Exchequer (*Life*, p. 198). John Whiting, *Persecution Exposed*, p. 125, says: "The Justices and Informers, being often poor themselves, as a Justice said he was poor, commonly kept the poor's part, and King's too ... so that the King and poor got little by it."

art by which he exploited the tyranny of the times. Church and State had demanded a passive obedience which was a euphemism for servility; and the second Stuart tyranny, built upon this doctrine, had crushed liberty and oppressed conscience for the sake of a vicious king and a carrion tribe of Informers.

We may here summarize the persecution of the Restoration days as it affected Friends. The statements compiled at various times show the following:

    Fifth Monarchy imprisonments (1661) . . 4257.[1]
    In prison, October 1662, after the Quaker Act, about 1300.[2]
    In prison at time of Great Pardon, 1672, about 500.[3]
    In prison, August 1683 . . . about 1000.[4]
    In prison, March 1685 . . . . 1460.[5]

As Friends bore the brunt of persecution, it seems unlikely that Penn is correct in saying with respect to the sufferings of all Dissenters:[6] "There have been ruined, since the late King's Restoration, above 15,000 families, and more than 5000 persons dead under bonds for matters of mere conscience to God." He has previously said of the whole period of Church of England dominance from the time of Queen Elizabeth, "Some have been hanged, many banished, more imprisoned, and some to death, and abundance impoverished," a sentence which does not support his high figures. Jeremy White (1629–1707), who had been chaplain to Oliver Cromwell, estimated the number of sufferers during the two reigns at 60,000, of whom 5000 had died through their hardships in prison;[7] and Oldmixon adds a story that James pressed him for the list, in order to expose

---

[1] See *ante*, p. 9.
[2] "A Brief Relation of the Persecutions . . . in and about the City of London, since the beginning of the 7th Month last" (1662).
[3] See *ante*, p. 84.
[4] "Petition of above a Thousand Prisoners," in Besse, *Sufferings*, i. xxxv.
[5] See *ante*, p. 109; 1460 is the number in the Petition to the King.
[6] "Conclusion" of "Good Advice to the Church-of-England, Roman Catholick, and Protestant Dissenter" (1687), in Penn's *Works*, 1726 edn. ii. 749-773; Jeremy White may be conjectured to have been his authority.
[7] Oldmixon, *History of England under the Royal House of Stuart*, p. 715. The estimate is not known to be extant. (*Dict. Nat. Biog.*)

the Church, but that White declined to furnish it. The indexes in Besse's *Sufferings* contain 12,406 names for England and Wales, several occurring in more than one index. These cover both the Commonwealth and Restoration periods ; and over 3000 Friends had suffered during the Commonwealth,[1] though most of these, if surviving, would be fresh sufferers during the Restoration. As the indexes in Besse are imperfect and the accounts are incomplete, especially as regards the Fifth Monarchy and London imprisonments, it is quite likely that the total number of Quaker sufferers by imprisonment and otherwise in England and Wales during the Restoration period considerably exceeded 15,000.[2] A special index in Besse gives the names of 366 who died under their sufferings, say 320 in England and Wales during the Restoration,[3] a figure which should probably be raised to at least 450. With these data to guide us, it looks as though White's estimate of deaths was far wide of the mark; and we suspect that his gross total of sufferers, though more credible, is a mere conjecture.

[1] See *Beginnings of Quakerism*, p. 464.
[2] Cf. return in 1680, *ante*, p. 98 note, which states that the imprisonments alone numbered over 10,000 for the period from 1660 to 1680.
[3] Petition to Parliament, 1685 (Sewel, ii. 407), gives this figure. The accurate Quaker genealogist, Joseph J. Green, found the names of 20,721 sufferers enumerated in Besse for England and Wales, say 15,000 for the Restoration period ; and has satisfied himself that deaths during or resulting from imprisonment were at least 450.

CHAPTER V

THE DAWN OF TOLERATION

Had the old dynasty adhered to the national faith, its position would have been impregnable ; and in the existing disposition of men's minds it was neither impossible nor improbable that the free institutions of England would have shared the fate of those of Spain, of Italy, and of France. Most happily for the country, a bigoted Catholic, singularly destitute both of the tact and sagacity of a statesman, and of the qualities that win the affection of a people, mounted the throne, devoted all the energies of his nature and all the resources of his position to extending the religion most hateful to his people, attacked with a strange fatuity the very Church on whose teaching the monarchical enthusiasm mainly rested, and thus drove the most loyal of his subjects into violent opposition. . . . The overtures of the King to the Nonconformists, whom the Church regarded as her bitterest enemies, his manifest intention to displace Protestants by Catholics in the leading posts of the Government, the violation of the constitution of an Oxford college which assailed the clergy in the very citadel of their power, and, finally, the prosecution of the seven bishops, at last forced the advocates of passive obedience into reluctant opposition to their sovereign.—W. E. H. LECKY, *History of England in the Eighteenth Century*, edn. 1913, i. 12, 13.

JAMES II., a sincere but bigoted Roman Catholic, and the friend and benefactor of Penn, succeeded to the despotic powers wielded by Charles during the closing years of his reign. Master of the corporations and the country Justices, able to change Judges at his will, and to control elections to Parliament, possessed of a standing army, and blindly supported by the Church and the Tories, he seemed well-secured against the disaffected but defeated Whigs, many of whom were fugitives in Holland. His declaration that he would defend Church and State as by law established gave general satisfaction ; and it was believed that he would continue to treat his creed as a thing of private concern, which would not affect his public policy. But he had already risked for his religion his prospect of

THE DAWN OF TOLERATION

succeeding to the Crown; and Charles had been right in saying,[1] "You know my brother long ago, that he is as stiff as a mulet." He no doubt counted on the passive obedience to which the Church stood committed; but in any case was of a temper to push his faith with little regard to consequences.

The King went publicly to Mass; but when the newly elected Tory Parliament met in May 1685 he renewed his assurances to support the Church of England; and it readily voted him the same revenue as had been granted to his brother. News now came of the Argyll insurrection in Scotland and of the Duke of Monmouth's landing at Lyme Regis. The latter proved a serious though short-lived menace to the throne; for the Duke showed himself a skilful captain, and any success might have been followed by a rising in London and elsewhere. Sedgemoor and the capture and execution of Monmouth removed the danger, while leaving the Prince and Princess of Orange the hope of the disaffected Whigs. Parliament had been adjourned during the crisis, but met again in November. The King had increased his standing army, and had appointed a number of Popish officers, contrary to law. The matter became the subject of hot debates; and after a few days Parliament was prorogued and did not meet again for business.

During these first months the persecution of Dissent continued with unabated fury, except in the case of the Quakers, who had powerful friends at Court. Penn was the King's intimate companion and was satisfied that he was against persecution.

"And in his honour, as well as in my own defence," he writes, "I am obliged in conscience to say that he has ever declared to me it was his opinion; and on all occasions, when Duke, he never refused me the repeated proofs of it, as often as I had any poor sufferers for conscience' sake to solicit his help for."[2]

James was regarded, even by the Whig Burnet, as

---

[1] Burnet, *History*, ii. 5 (Airy's edn.).
[2] Penn's Letter to Popple, 24th October 1688, in *Works*, 1726 edn. i. 135, 136.

"naturally candid and sincere and a firm friend,"[1] and, while his leaning to toleration[2] was more due than Penn appreciated to his desire to free Catholics from the Penal Laws, there is no reason to question the great Quaker's absolute good faith in the matter. His gratitude to the King and firm belief in his sincerity on this point were the ground of all his intercourse, and give the key to any fair judgment upon the equivocal positions into which the champion of religious liberty was led.

Robert Barclay, distantly related to the Royal Family, had become another of the King's friends. The bent of Barclay's mind was Tory, or, more properly, Conservative in the best sense of the word ; for it was without trace of faction. In a *Vindication*,[3] written in 1689 after the Revolution, he gives a candid account of his relations with James :

It was the 1676 before I ever spoke to him [the Duke of York], or saw him that I mind of ; and then it was of no design of becoming a courtier, but, being at London and employed by my Friends to obtain a liberty for them out of their imprisonment at Aberdeen[4] . . . and not being able to gain any ground upon the Duke of Lauderdale . . . I was advised by a friend to try the Duke of York, who was said to be the only man whom Lauderdale would bear to meddle in his province or was like to do it with any success. And . . . I found him inclinable to interpose in it, he having then and always since to me professed himself to be for liberty of conscience. And, though not for several years yet at last his interposing proved very helpful in that matter, and, to do him right, I never found reason to doubt his sincerity in the matter of liberty of conscience, which his granting so universally after he came to the Crown hath to me much confirmed. After, his happening to be in Scotland, giving me opportunity of more frequent access, and that begetting an opinion of interest, I acknowledge freely that I was ready to use

---

[1] Burnet, *History*, i. 295 (Airy's edn.).
[2] James claimed to have suggested the Declaration of Indulgence of 1672, see *ante*, p. 81, and George Whitehead (*Christian Progress*, p. 622) recognized in 1686 that the King had been for liberty of conscience for twenty years past. Reresby (*Memoirs*, p. 81) records an instance in 1670, which he imputes to policy rather than conviction.
[3] From a MS. formerly at Ury, given in *Reliquiae Barclaianae*.
[4] For the Aberdeen imprisonments see Barclay, *Diary of Alexander Jaffray*, pp. 325-427, who gives abundant details of their excessive rigour.

it to the advantage of my friends and acquaintances—what I esteemed just and reasonable for me to meddle in . . . I must own nor will I decline to avow that I love King James, that I wish him well, that I have been and am sensibly touched with a feeling of his misfortunes, and that I cannot excuse myself from the duty of praying for him that God may bless him and sanctify his afflictions to him. And, if so be His will to take from him an earthly crown, He may prepare his heart and direct his steps so that he may obtain through mercy an heavenly one, which all good Christians judge the most preferable.

Within a month of the late King's death, Friends presented James with their Petition[1] showing 1460 Quaker prisoners. In May, they saw him again, on the day when the Tory Commons voted "that the laws be put in execution against all Dissenters whatsoever."[2] Barclay accompanied George Whitehead; and the King told them that he had designed a general Coronation Pardon, but deferred it to prevent certain obnoxious Whigs from sitting in the Parliament. He intended, however, to discharge Friends out of prison; and promised to stop the ravages of Informers.[3] The writs for seizing Friends' estates for £20 a month, under the Acts against Recusants, had already been suspended till the next Law Term.[4]

Meanwhile the Monmouth rising had occurred. The strong groups of Friends in Somerset had suffered their full share of persecution. At the time of the Fifth Monarchy rising, 212 Friends had been thrown into prison at Ilchester,[5] which continued during the reign of Charles the compulsory headquarters of the Quaker community.[6] There were a hundred in prison in 1663; and after the Second Conventicle Act the county was harried by Informers. Thirty-nine Friends were released by the Great Pardon; but when John Whiting, of Nailsea, then a young man of twenty-three, was committed to

---

[1] See *ante*, p. 109.   [2] Reresby, *Memoirs*, p. 328.
[3] Whitehead, *Christian Progress*, pp. 570-587. Fox conferred with Penn, Barclay, and Whitehead over the matter on the day before the interview with the King (MS. *Itinerary Journal* of Fox at Dev. Ho. under date 25th May).
[4] *Life of Gilbert Latey*, p. 111. George Whitehead, *Christian Progress*, pp. 609-614, a section which is placed out of chronological order. Cf. Richard Davies, *Life*, pp. 196-199.
[5] See *ante*, p. 10.   [6] For Somerset sufferings see Besse.

Ilchester in 1679 for tithes,[1] he found thirty-three Friends in prison, several in the Sheriff's ward, formerly a nunnery, by the river's side over against the common gaol, but most in the Friary at the other end of the town, where Roger Bacon is said to have been born.[2] Meetings were kept in the great hall at the Friary, which had a walled orchard of four acres, where Friends used to walk ; and in the Friary the Quarterly Meetings for the county were often held. In 1682 the persecution that was rife in Bristol spread to Somerset, and crowded Ilchester with fresh prisoners, amongst others Christopher Holder, whose ears had been cropped by the Puritans of Massachusetts.[3] There were a hundred and forty in gaol in January 1684, but eighty-three were discharged,

"which has gratified the country so much," writes Whiting, "in the freeing Friends, that it is thought if Sir Edward Phillips who was Judge of the Sessions did put in to be Parliament-man the cry of the country would be for him, almost on that account, especially Taunton ; for there was a sad cry in the country before, about sending so many Friends to prison, which kept so many at work that the poor were like to be starved for the lack of it."[4]

On the accession of James it was generally expected that Friends would be released ; but when relief was delayed the proverb ran, that "liberty of conscience was in the press," it was so long coming out.[5] Some thought that if it had been granted there might have been no rebellion in the West ; for the generality of the nation was weary and sick of persecution.[6] No such rapid conversion of the dominant Church and Tory party took

---

[1] John Whiting, *Persecution Exposed*, p. 18. This important source, largely written in prison, contains a full narrative of events from 1679-1696, with many biographical notices of Friends, chiefly compilations from printed material. In 1699 Whiting removed to London, and is the first of our Quaker bibliographers, issuing his *Catalogue of Friends' Books* in 1708. He died in 1722. The further details given are taken from *Persecution Exposed*.
[2] Tanner, *Three Lectures*, p. 69 n.
[3] See *Quakers in the American Colonies*, p. 75, and other references.
[4] *Persecution Exposed*, p. 103.   [5] *Ibid.* p. 140.
[6] *Ibid.* giving as authority the "Third Letter from a Gentleman in the Country," referred to *infra*, p. 131, and supposed to be by Penn. This says (p. 9), "'tis certain, that had he [James] declared for Liberty of Conscience, when he told us of his religion, there had been no rebellion in the West."

place; and Somerset and Dorset, as well as other parts of England, were in a gravely disaffected state when Monmouth landed, and many rallied to his banner.

We have already noted the prudent behaviour of the Ilchester prisoners at the time of Monmouth's Progress through the West in 1680.[1] They now acted with equal loyalty.[2]

On the 18th day of June last past, a party of the late Duke of Monmouth's horsemen rid thither, and turned out of prison several that were detained on his account; and also, forcing out one of our Friends, left him in the market-place; but he immediately returned to prison again. And, though they strictly charged the keeper no more to detain our Friends, yet they took no advantage of that authority, nor accept[ed] of their liberty in such an indirect way.[3]

John Whiting's adventures are worth recording.[4] He had liberty from the keeper at the time; and was at Nailsea when he heard of Monmouth's landing. On the 22nd June he set out to return to prison, but, riding through Wrington, was stopped by the Watch. They were secretly for the Duke, and let him pass, on learning that he was going south to Somerton. In this neighbourhood he stayed till the 25th, and attended the Quarterly Meeting held that day at Stoke St. Gregory, half-way between Somerton and Taunton, when Friends testified[5] that "whatever our sufferings were, we must not expect deliverance by the arm of flesh, but look unto the Lord, from Whom our salvation comes, and Who will not save us by sword nor spear, but by His own Spirit. And therefore our Friends were warned not to concern themselves in this war; and all unanimously consented thereunto." Whiting was engaged to Sarah Hurd, of Long Sutton,[6] and after the meeting found her sister in great

---

[1] See *ante*, p. 93.
[2] The best general account is in Tanner, *Three Lectures*, pp. 105-110, based on the documents hereinafter cited.
[3] Testimony of the peaceable Quakers, signed by thirty Friends from Somerset, Devon, and Dorset, in Bristol MSS. ii. No. 68; printed in Joseph Wyeth's *A Switch for the Snake*, 1699, pp. 368-372; cf. *Persecution Exposed*, p. 141.
[4] *Persecution Exposed*, pp. 140-144.
[5] Document above cited in Bristol MSS. ii. No. 68.
[6] For this courtship, see article in *J.F.H.S.* xii. 89-94, by M. Ethel Crawshaw.

trouble, for her husband, a Friend named Francis Scott, was gone to the Duke to sell him horses for his army. They found the man next day at Taunton; "but he had appeared to the Duke, and involved himself so with his horses, that we could not get him home with us." The sister saw Monmouth, who told her that he did not desire any to appear with him against their consciences. Going out of the town, Whiting exchanged a few words with him, and notes that he looked "very thoughtful and dejected" and thinner than at Ilchester five years before. Whiting spent the next days at Long Sutton, amid the turmoil made by the King's troops; and on the 7th July, the morrow of Sedgemoor, saw the soldiers hunting for rebels and sending them to prison by droves. Scott was taken in the battle, and put into Weston Zoyland church for the night with many more, in order to be hanged next day; but he got out at the little north door while the Watch slept, and hid in the growing corn till night, when he made good his escape. Some years later, in 1692, after long dealing by the Monthly Meeting,[1] he was brought to condemn his action and to acknowledge that, whatever his end was, he went out of the way of Truth "and caused reproach thereunto and grieved the hearts of faithful Friends." Sir Edward Phillips, the moderate-spirited Chairman of Quarter Sessions, established his headquarters at Sarah Hurd's house, sitting and sleeping in her chair, while young John Whiting, as he says, "lay innocently out in the garden . . . being unwilling to be seen, because I was a prisoner; but wished after I had appeared." He soon returned to his prison, judging it "the safest place, as things were," but met for a time with the savagest treatment from an embittered gaoler.

---

[1] See Minutes of West Somerset M.M., 12th April 1686 and 14th March 1692, in *J.F.H.S.* xii. 35. One of the first recorded Minutes of Somerset Q.M., held at Ilchester 24th September 1668, deals with Francis Scott "for his disorderly walking and fighting and abusing his brother"; but he was fined £10 for a meeting in 1680, and imprisoned for tithes in 1683 (Besse, *Sufferings*, i. 615, 635). Elias Osborne, of Chillington, near Chard, who "had an eminent testimony, till he died in 1720" (*F.P.T.* 228) narrowly escaped imprisonment on a false charge of supplying horses, see his *Life* (1723), p. 43. For Osborne, see Tanner *Three Lectures*, p. 97.

THE DAWN OF TOLERATION

London Friends were prejudiced in their efforts at Court by the suspicions under which Friends in the West of England lay.[1] They procured, however, in August a satisfactory testimony of clearness from Somerset, Dorset, and Devon Friends,[2] together with certificates granted them by the churchwardens and others in their home-parishes; and these were to be laid before the King by Penn. George Whitehead says that the unfavourable impression at Court was wearing off, and recommends Friends to clear themselves to the magistrates, but to be careful not to charge particular persons by name, as concerned in the rebellion, even "though they be apostates."

There were one or two cases of complicity besides that of Francis Scott. A certain John Hellier, of Mark, near Highbridge, was dealt with for taking up arms.[3] Of more moment was the case of Thomas Plaice, of Edington, who had been released from a two-years' imprisonment by the Great Pardon. From the testimony of disownment issued against him,[4] it appears that he was "very active and conversant" in the rebellion, though not in arms. I suppose this to be the man whose name appears in the Newgate Calendar of December 1686, as committed the previous month on his own confession of having been in Monmouth's army.[5]

The cruel vengeance which followed the rebellion was not confined to ringleaders, and disgraced the King and Judge Jeffreys, who returned from the "Bloody Assizes" to be made Lord Chancellor. About three hundred rebels were hanged and a thousand sentenced to be transported. Many of these were given to the courtiers; and Penn

---

[1] The proceedings can be traced in various papers:—Bristol MSS. i. Nos. 45, 46, ii. Nos. 48-50, 53, 57, No. 68, already cited; Dev. Ho. Dix Colln. H. No. 2s, and Mtg. for Sufferings Minutes, 31st July and 28th August 1685. On 22nd August, Fox was at a conference on the subject; see his *Itinerary Journal*. At Bristol money was raised for expenses due to the Rebellion by appointing various Friends to municipal offices and fining them for not taking the Tests. *Per* A. Neave Brayshaw, who has consulted the Corporation Records. Cf. *J.F.H.S.* xv. 111.

[2] Printed, with a specimen churchwarden's certificate, in Joseph Wyeth's *A Switch for the Snake*, 1699, pp. 368-373.

[3] Minutes of West Somerset M.M., 12th April 1686, in *J.F.H.S.* xii. 35.

[4] Minutes of Somerset Q.M., 24th Sept. 1685, in Tanner, *Three Lectures*, p. 109.

[5] *Middlesex County Records*, iv. 312.

writes that he begged twenty of the King, presumably to go to Pennsylvania.¹ Macaulay, in the first and most odious of his biased charges against Penn, alleges that he acted as agent for the Queen's Maids of Honour to arrange the fines to be paid to them by the "Maids of Taunton," who were to be pardoned. In proof he cites a letter from Lord Sunderland, dated Whitehall, 13th February 1686, to a "Mr. Penne," asking him and a Mr. Walden to make the most advantageous composition they can. But it seems clear that these were the local agents employed ; and it is certain that Penn was not in Somerset at the time.² He had been present at two executions in London in the autumn of 1685—the hanging of Cornish, for alleged complicity in the Rye House Plot, and the burning on the same day of Elizabeth

[1] Letter to James Harrison, 2nd October 1685, cited in Janney's *Life*, p. 268. It would be interesting to trace their further history.

[2] According to Oldmixon (*History*, ii. 708), the chief agent of the Maids of Honour in the matter was the Popish lawyer Brent, who had an under-agent, one Crane of Bridgwater. But the good offices were solicited of Sir Francis Warre, Colonel of the Taunton regiment, who lived near that town, and he was asked to nominate some one who could do the bargaining on the spot. The letter cited by Macaulay seems to be the authority given to the men he named. The "Mr. Penne" was most probably a George Penne, Esq., who had been concerned during the previous August in arranging a ransom for Azariah Pinney, and lived in Dorset. He is known to have acquired 99 convicts given to Jeremiah Nepho, one of whom, Henry Pitman, Monmouth's surgeon, has preserved an account of his experiences at the hands of this "needy Papist" (Arber's *English Garner*, vii. 333-378, and letter of C. E. Doble, reprinted from *The Academy* in (London) *Friend*, 1893, p. 294). In *Cal. State Papers, Dom.*, 1675-6, pp. 410, 433, 459, 517, is a series of papers concerning the grant of a Fair to George Penne the younger, at the Hoarstone, on Toller Whelme Downs, near Beaminster ; and in 1687 the Books of the Privy Council refer to a Petition by him for a lottery in America. John Whiting, *Persecution Exposed*, pp. 172, 173, says that July 1687 was the first time, as he remembers, that Penn was ever in Somerset. During the early months of 1686, Penn was chiefly in London. See letters to Tillotson, 22nd Jan., 29th Jan., 27th April, in *Life*, in *Works*, 1726 edn. i. 126-129. Prior to the last of these, he had spent a short time in Yorkshire, visiting Anthony and Margaret Lowther, Penn's sister, in Cleveland (Letter of John Rous to Margaret Fox, 20th March 1686, in Helen G. Crosfield's *Margaret Fox*, p. 208, from the Abraham Colln.). His intimacy with Lord Sunderland would have made a letter superfluous. To suppose that a man of Penn's standing at Court, occupied with important affairs concerning his province, would have been asked to arrange the details of this pettifogging business, shows a strange lack of historical perspective on Macaulay's part. Macaulay's various charges against Penn are refuted by William Edward Forster in his preface to a new edition of Clarkson's *Life* of Penn, 1849 ; by Hepworth Dixon, and by Janney in their *Lives*, and by John Paget, in *An Inquiry into . . . the Charges*, 1858, and *Paradoxes and Puzzles*, 1874. In the last edition of Macaulay, 1907, edited by T. F. Henderson, with notes, the editor says, "There is really no evidence that William Penn the Quaker was the person referred to."

Gaunt, for harbouring a rebel. He told the historian Burnet[1] that "there appeared nothing in Cornish's conduct at the place of execution but a just indignation that innocence might very naturally give"; and expressed his opinion of Jeffreys' proceedings in plain terms:

If the King's own inclinations had not been biased that way; and if his priests had not thought it the interest of their party to let that butcher loose, by whom so many men that were like to oppose them were put out of the way, it was not to be imagined that there would have been such a run of barbarous cruelty, and that in so many instances.

Of Elizabeth Gaunt he wrote: "She died composedly and fearless, interpreting the cause of her death God's cause."[2]

During this year 1685, Friends were earnestly promoting the release of Quaker prisoners for conscience. The King's General Pardon to his subjects came out in March '86; and in the middle of the month a Royal Warrant was issued, directing the release of scheduled lists of Friends, and the discharge of all fines charged on any of them for not coming to church.[3] Under this Pardon, William Dewsbury was probably released from his last long imprisonment in Warwick.

The suppression of Informers was now taken in hand. Friends determined that London at least should be freed from the scourge.[4] On their Petition the King appointed two Commissioners to examine into the matter, Richard Graham and Philip Burton, "the two famous solicitors for the King."[5] Graham was the Principal of Clifford's Inn,[6]

---

[1] *Hist.* ii. 61. In Penn's indulgent view "the King was much to be pitied, who was hurried into this effusion of blood by Jeffreys' impetuous and cruel temper."

[2] Letter to Harrison, Oct. 1685, cited in Janney's *Life*, p. 269. Cf. Burnet, *Hist.* i. 648-650 (fol. edn.). Again Macaulay sneers at Penn, on which Henderson remarks: "There are no adequate grounds for Macaulay's insinuation against Penn's humanity. There is, on the contrary, evidence, even in Burnet, that Penn strongly sympathised with the sufferers." Elizabeth Gaunt was a Fothergill of Ravenstonedale. (See Rev. W. Nicholls, *History and Traditions of Ravenstonedale*, ii. 102.)

[3] George Whitehead, *Christian Progress*, pp. 587-591, and Minutes of Meeting for Sufferings.

[4] For this account, see George Whitehead, *Christian Progress*, pp. 591-609, and *Life of Gilbert Latey*, pp. 118-120.

[5] Luttrell, *Brief Relation*, i. 450.   [6] *Ibid.* 185.

and held the inquiry there in June. George Whitehead managed the case for Friends, and notes with relish the rage of the Informers when they saw the strong array of Quakers ready to prove their misdoings. "Here comes all the devils in hell," they cried; and then, on catching sight of Whitehead, "And there comes the old devil of all." He began with cases where the Informers had sworn falsely in fact, as, for example, that a Friend had been at a meeting when he was not there, or that a meeting had been held where it had not been held. The arch-culprit, Captain John Hilton, when called to answer, was not allowed by the rest of the gang to appear, being drunk; and Whitehead in his rôle of prosecuting Counsel, armed with six broadsides of brief, seems to have proved his case up to the hilt, though without reaching his second count of illegal breaking open of houses and shops for levying distress. In fact he wearied out the Commissioners with damaging instances, the room being thronged and the season hot and the Informers in great shame and confusion. At a second hearing they were represented by Counsel, and the shrewd Quaker, who had learnt his Conventicle Act in the school of persecution, down to its least proviso, had the satisfaction of refuting and silencing all his arguments. With but half the charges heard, the Commissioners thought they had enough for their purpose; though Whitehead was allowed to show them the second part of his case, and also to see their Draft Report, which he induced them to strengthen. In the result, the magistrates were encouraged to put a stop to the Informing trade; several of the practitioners were convicted of perjury,[1] some absconded, others were reduced to beggary, and the plague abated through the land. Hilton himself came to beg clothes to fit him for entering into some great man's service, and Whitehead gave him something, glad to find the case so altered that the poor wretches who had made spoil of Friends were now fain to ask their charity. Hilton, for his part, thought, no doubt, that he had a good claim to compensation for disturbance.

[1] See *e.g.* Luttrell, *Brief Relation*, i. 387 (Nov. 1686).

THE DAWN OF TOLERATION

It has been remarked that the year 1685 witnessed a gathering of dark clouds round the Protestant cause in Europe, and may be pronounced the most fatal in all its annals.

In February an English King declared himself a Papist. In June, Charles, the Elector Palatine, dying without issue, the electoral dignity passed to the bigoted Popish House of Neuburg. In October, Louis XIV. revoked the Edict of Nantes, and began that ferocious persecution which completed the work of St. Bartholomew in France. In December the Duke of Savoy was induced by French persuasion to put an end to the toleration of the Vaudois.[1]

It is not therefore surprising that the King's Tory Parliament was alarmed by the appointment of Popish officers in the army, and that the nation looked with jealousy upon every step which James took in his Roman Catholic policy. But the arbitrary government which had developed at the close of the last reign enabled him to proceed far in his dangerous designs without a check. Judges could be put in and out at pleasure, and the Bench was repacked with men favourable to prerogative. Then in June 1686 came the collusive action of *Godden* v. *Hales*,[2] in which Sir Edward Hales was sued for neglecting to take the oaths required by the Test Act, and successfully pleaded a dispensation from the King. Eleven out of the twelve Judges held that it was the King's inseparable prerogative to dispense with penal laws in particular cases and upon particular reasons, and of these reasons he himself was sole judge. We are told that, after this case, the Judges on circuit had not the same respect as formerly;[3] and another contemporary diarist says: "This judgment was very surprising, and occasioned much discourse in the kingdom."[4] The adherents of James regarded it as a natural corollary to the King's undoubted power to pardon; but to many others it

---

[1] Lecky, *Hist. of England in the Eighteenth Century*, 1913 edn. i. 24, 25; from Burnet.
[2] 2 Shower, p. 475; 11 State Trials, p. 1165; Robertson, *Select Statutes*, etc., pp. 384-388.
[3] Luttrell, *Brief Relation*, i. 384.   [4] Reresby, *Memoirs*, p. 364.

seemed a thing of most perilous consequence, and had Parliament met would undoubtedly have led to hot debates. It was, however, " by no means evident that the decision . . . was against law ";[1] and for the time it afforded a legal foundation for the exercise of the dispensing prerogative by which James tampered with the Tests and the Penal Laws against Catholics and Dissenters. He had now a Jesuit for his adviser, Father Edward Petre, and " went on faster than formerly in promoting the Roman Catholic religion."[2]

Penn had issued in the spring of 1686 his *Persuasive to Moderation*,[3] by which he meant " liberty to Church Dissenters." It was addressed to King and Council, and developed his great argument that " it is the union of interests and not of opinions that gives peace to kingdoms." Holland, as before, was his most illustrious instance,

Holland, that bog of the world, neither sea nor dry land, now the rival of tallest monarchs, not by conquests, marriages or accession of royal blood, the usual ways to empire, but by her own superlative clemency and industry—for the one was the effect of the other. She cherished her people, whatsoever were their opinions, as the reasonable stock of the country, the heads and hands of her trade and wealth; and making them easy in the main point, their conscience, she became great by them: this made her fill with people; and they filled her with riches and strength.

In the summer he visited Holland and Germany, and was asked by the King to see the Prince of Orange, and secure his support to a general toleration and the abolition of the Tests. Burnet was with William at the time,[4] and wrote that Penn,

. . . who is a man of many words and much vanity in his discourse, had a long conversation with the Prince, who answered

---

[1] This is the cautious conclusion of Hallam, *Constitutional History* (7th edn.), ii. 62, as against the more partisan statements of Campbell and Macaulay.
[2] Reresby, *Memoirs*, p. 363.
[3] The date is fixed by a reference in a letter this spring to James Harrison: "My *Persuasive* works much among all sorts, and is divers spoken of" (Janney's *Life*, p. 282).
[4] Burnet, *Hist.* i. 693, 694 (fol. edn.). I cite from the " Original Memoirs," as given in H. C. Foxcroft, *Supplement to Burnet* (Airy's edn.) p. 227.

him very frankly that he himself was as great an enemy to persecution upon the account of religion as any man could possibly be; and therefore he should be very glad to see such methods taken that none should be disturbed for his conscience; but at the same time he showed as great an aversion to the admitting of Papists into any share of the government; and all that Penn could say did not carry him further.

Burnet and Penn found themselves in opposite camps; and the historian etches the great Quaker's character in his usual acid way:[1]

> He is a man of good parts, but extremely vain; he loves mightily to hear himself talk; he has a flourishing of learning, and with it a copious fancy; and his head is much turned to the notion of government. He has been long and much in the King's confidence, which has brought great suspicion as if he were secretly a Papist; but I have known him long, and I think myself bound to acquit him, as far as one man can judge of another. . . . Penn has been likewise a zealous promoter of liberty of conscience, which was all that the Popish party thought fit to pretend to at first; and . . . the King made great use of him and seemed to depend much on his advice.

Burnet, it will be seen, vindicates Penn's honesty of purpose at the expense of his penetration. His appreciation of the King's friendship and his own sanguine temperament undoubtedly led him to put an over-indulgent interpretation upon the course that James was taking, and the Prince of Orange showed a sound political judgment in preferring Burnet's advice.[2] But Penn was not blind to the more sinister influences that surrounded the King, and did his utmost to counter them.

James was now making free use of his power to dispense with the Tests in particular cases, and many Roman Catholics were advanced to office. Parliament was kept in being by successive prorogations, but did not meet for business. Meanwhile its members were sounded as to their attitude towards the Tests and the Penal

---

[1] "Original Memoirs," p. 218; cf. *Hist.* i. 702 (fol. edn.).
[2] Penn returned to England prior to the 23rd September (see letter of this date to James Harrison in Janney's *Life*, p. 284). Cf. extract from Van Citter's Letters in the Dutch Archives, 26th Nov., cited in W. E. Forster's Preface to Clarkson's *Life*, p. liii.

Laws ; and, if their answers were unfavourable or evasive, they risked the loss of any office they might hold.[1] Little resulted to the King's purpose ; and, accordingly, James thought it not safe to call the Parliament ; and on 18th March 1687[2] prorogued it till November, and in July dissolved it, " which startled many." At the Council in March he took a new step. He declared that none of his four predecessors had succeeded in effecting a uniformity in religion, and that the attempts to do so had rather proved prejudicial to the kingdom. He had now resolved on a declaration for toleration or liberty of conscience to all Dissenters, hoping that it would contribute to the peace of the kingdom, and to the increase of people and of trade. About three weeks later the Declaration appeared.[3] It was put forth " by virtue of our royal prerogative . . . making no doubt of the concurrence of our two Houses of Parliament, when we shall think it convenient for them to meet." While expressing his wish that all his subjects were Catholics, he stated his settled conviction that conscience ought not to be forced, and declared that he would maintain the Church of England, but that all Penal Laws should be immediately suspended. His subjects should have free leave to meet in private houses or in meeting-houses, provided nothing was preached to alienate people from the King, the meetings were held openly, with free admission of all persons, and notice of the places set apart for meetings was given to the Justices. The Declaration also purported to remove all religious tests for any civil or military office.

This Indulgence went far beyond the particular dispensing power secured by the judgment in *Godden* v.

[1] *Fleming MSS.* p. 203, letter of 24th Feb. ; cf. Luttrell, *Brief Relation*, i. 394 (March), and the full account in Reresby, *Memoirs*, pp. 370, 371. The Judges on Circuit were used for this solicitation. Penn, after his return from Holland, had visited his sister Lowther and Friends in the North of England (see letter to James Harrison, from Worminghurst, 28th Jan. 1687, in Janney's *Life*, p. 285) ; but I find no evidence that he was employed. He returned to London by 6th November, and had used his influence to prevent persecution under the Conventicle Act (*Fleming MSS.* pp. 201, 202).

[2] Reresby, *Memoirs*, pp. 371, 374.

[3] 4th April 1687. For the text see Robertson, *Select Statutes*, etc., p. 388.

Hales; and was more sweeping than the Indulgence of 1672, which had brought Charles into disastrous collision with the Cavalier Parliament. It was a high-handed act of authority which, in the issue, strained the prerogative to the breaking-point; and undoubtedly violated the whole spirit of English Institutions. The writer of " A Third Letter From a Gentleman in the Country To His Friends in London," licensed 16th May,[1] could only say by way of excuse, " This Declaration seems to me no more than a Royal Bill without doors, informing the kingdom of His Majesty's mind, and preparing both Houses to make it the subject of their next session."

But to many of the Dissenters, and especially to the Quakers, harried by persecution for twenty-five years, the Declaration necessarily bore a benign complexion. They had suffered long and cruelly at the hands of an intolerant Parliament, acting in the interests of a narrow-minded Church ascendancy. The Commons of England, who should have been the custodians of liberty, had added weapon after weapon to the arsenal of tyranny; till the persons and estates of Friends lay at the mercy of a horde of Informers. Any lenitives had been due to the Lords or to the uncertain indulgence of the Crown. Their conventicles had been treated as seditious, when there was no sedition; they had been fined and imprisoned as Popish recusants, when they were no Papists; their peaceable meetings had been indicted as riots; they had rotted in prison with no legal charge against them; and been acquitted in Court only to find themselves trapped with the tender of an oath on pain of a *praemunire.* No legal chicanery, no arbitrary proceeding had been too gross if it had served the turn of their oppressors. In a word, they had been treated for a generation as outlaws, living and worshipping on sufferance, and only living and worshipping at all because cruelty is capricious and their honest neighbours refused

---

[1] This with the " Letter from a Gentleman in the Country," and the " Second Letter," licensed 11th April 1687, are given in Smith's *Catalogue* as " supposed by W[illiam] P[enn]."

to aid in their destruction. The law denied the Quaker the common rights of an Englishman. If strictly administered, his marriage was no marriage; he was disabled from giving legal evidence [1] or taking up his freedom in the town where he traded; and, in common with other Nonconformists, public offices were closed to him. It had even been held that Quaker burying-grounds seized by the King should have the bodies taken out and buried at the cross-ways.[2] While preserving the shadow of freedom, a persecuting Parliament had been incessantly destroying its substance. Can we wonder that Quakers feared the despotism of the majority in the Commons, more than the prerogative of the King? The tyranny of a majority is as dangerous as the Divine right of kings, and in the long run has always proved equally repugnant to the tolerant spirit of the English nation.

Burrough, in 1659,[3] had admirably expressed the political standpoint of the early Friends in a passage which has found its place in the current edition of the Society's *Christian Practice*.[4]

We are not for names, nor men, nor titles of Government; but we are for justice and mercy and truth and peace and true freedom, that these may be exalted in our nation; and that goodness, righteousness, meekness, temperance, peace, and unity with God and with one another, that these things may abound.

Friends therefore regarded chiefly the substance of the Declaration. The form was obviously precarious and provisional, inasmuch as it depended upon the royal pleasure and had nothing of the stability that would attach to an Act of Parliament; but the substance was satisfactory. They stood for a general liberty of

---

[1] As the Address to the King in June 1688 says (Sewel ii. 445), the question of oaths disabled Friends "in reference to freedoms in corporations, probates of wills and testaments, and administrations, answers in chancery and exchequer, trials of our just titles and debts, proceeding in our trade at the custom-house, serving the office of constables, etc." James dispensed with the oaths in certain cases (*e.g.* in the case of Southwark constables, Sewel, ii. 440; and of Norwich freemen, Sewel, ii. 447), but these indulgences were open to the same objection as other exercises of his alleged dispensing power.
[2] See Minutes of Meeting for Sufferings, 20th March 1686.
[3] *Works*, p. 604. See further *Beginnings of Quakerism*, pp. 466, 467.
[4] Edn. 1911, p. 124.

conscience, freed from all penal laws and tests, and no fear of Roman Catholic domination could make them recede from this principle. Macaulay says with truth[1] that upon the Declaration "followed an auction, the strangest that history has recorded. On one side the King, on the other the Church, began to bid eagerly against each other for the favour of those [the Dissenters] whom up to that time King and Church had combined to oppose." The Church, in fear of the Jesuits and to secure its domination, saw that it could only preserve the Tests by uniting the Protestants with the help of a toleration. Friends could trust neither Church nor Parliament; they had ground for trusting the King; and they believed that the application of so good a principle as liberty of conscience must work out good results.

The first Address of Thanks came from the Baptists;[2] but it was soon followed by one from London Friends,[3] and when the Yearly Meeting met in May, a further Address was prepared, read three times over to the meeting, and unanimously passed,[4] which was presented at Windsor by a deputation, with Penn for spokesman.[5] It expressed the warm thanks of Friends and their assurance that the Indulgence was well received in the country. Echoing the phraseology of the Declaration itself, it added: "We hope the good effects thereof, for the peace, trade and prosperity of the kingdom, will produce such a concurrence from the Parliament as may secure it to our posterity in after times," to which the

---

[1] *Hist.*, 1907 edn. p. 228.
[2] Luttrell, *Brief Relation*, i. 400; *Transactions Baptist Hist. Soc.* v. No. 2, pp. 83-89.
[3] Luttrell, *Brief Relation*, i. 402, Bishop Cartwright, *Diary*, p. 51, and Minute of Meeting for Sufferings, 29th April 1687, which says, "The King looked very pleasant and smilingly upon Friends; and seemed very much contented with it." The Address is given in Sewel, ii. 435.
[4] *Yearly Meeting Epistles, 1681-1857*, i. 33.
[5] Sewel, i. 436-439. Sewel shrewdly adds: "Here we see what the king declared to be his intention; but perhaps that prince did not consider that if such a general liberty had been procured, he should not have been able to make it continue longer than the Popish clergy would have thought it convenient." Amongst the further Addresses noted in Luttrell are the following, "From the Quakers in Scotland," "the West of Scotland," "Ireland," "the North-west parts of England and Wales," and "Bristol."

King replied : " What I have promised . . . I will continue to perform as long as I live ; and I hope before I die to settle it so that after ages shall have no reason to alter it."

Robert Barclay was in London, and suggested an Address from Aberdeen Friends.[1] They took exception to the word " humble " used in that from England, but were ready to suppose it a mistake of the printer of the *Gazette*. Humble thanks they judged only proper to God, " Who is the alone fountain of all goodness, even as it streams through man as an instrument." With this caution, a commission was signed by sixty Friends authorizing Barclay to draw up and present an Address in their name. The document therefore is from his pen, and throws light on his own feelings. It reminds James that when Charles ordered him off to Scotland in 1679,[2] his own prospects began to improve, and his influence in Scotland had opened the prison-doors to Friends, " where many of us had lien several years in most noisome holes." As they then praised God for the prosperous turn given to the King's affairs, so they had acknowledged the royal favour and kindness in having procured for them what they call " our peaceable fruition of the exercise of our consciences." The King's Declaration was therefore no surprise,

[we] having been so long by a sensible experience convinced both of his principle and inclination in that matter, which as it prevented the evil contagion of jealousy from taking place in our hearts, so we hope it will root it out of all those where the malice of ill men hath sowed it.

Penn had now " great entrance and interest with the King," and devoted himself to the work of seeing " poor England fixed [and] the Penal Laws repealed that are now suspended."[3] He did his best to root out the widespread " contagion of jealousy " in the nation, especially at this juncture by his " Good Advice to the Church-

---

[1] See Records of Aberdeen Monthly Meeting, given in *J.F.H.S.* viii. 62-64. Luttrell dates the Address about 15th June.
[2] *Ante*, p. 32.
[3] These expressions are in a Letter to James Harrison in Janney's *Life*, p. 298.

of-England, Roman Catholick, and Protestant Dissenter," [1] licensed 30th June, which urged the repeal of the Penal Laws and Tests. The piece was convincing to any who disregarded the Papist menace. Penn estimates the number of Roman Catholics as thirty thousand out of a population of eight millions, and these much divided in opinion. He makes light of the King's standing army, and of danger from France, treating such fears as mere bogeys to frighten children. He admits, however, that there "may be some poor silly bigots that hope bigger and talk farther," but is satisfied that moderation will be so clearly in the interests of the Roman Catholics that they will not run into extremes. His political sagacity was at fault; but this piece and his other efforts were endeavours on entirely constitutional lines to persuade the country to follow up the King's Indulgence by an Act of Parliament—a new and glorious Magna Carta.

Penn was now living at Holland House, and his good offices at Court were in great request. Gerard Croese gives a lively and probable account of his position, which may deserve insertion, though he is not a first-rate authority: [2]

William Penn had great intimacy with the King, who confided nearly all his counsels to him. He would frequently talk with him in private for hours at a time, while others were waiting for audience. One of them remarking on this, the King told him that Penn always talked cleverly and was worth listening to. . . . His house and vestibules were daily thronged by clients and petitioners, desiring his good offices with the King. Sometimes there were not less than two hundred in attendance.

One of his acquaintances at this time was Charlwood Lawton, a young man who moved in Whig circles.[3] The account he gives of Penn's service in procuring pardons for disaffected Whigs and in giving the King frank advice

---

[1] Reprinted in *Works*, 1726 edn. ii. 749-773.
[2] *Historia Quakeriana*, edn. 1695, pp. 369, 370; English edn., 1696, pp. 106, 107.
[3] *Dict. Nat. Biography*. Lawton (1660–1721) designed a volume of Memoirs. He wrote a fragment relating his early intercourse with Penn, printed in *Memoirs of the Hist. Society of Pennsylvania*, vol. iii. pt. ii. pp. 213-232, and in Janney's *Life*, pp. 299-307.

is very favourable, but was written many years later after Penn's death. It seems, however, based on papers collected to serve as materials for his Memoirs; and may be accepted as in the main correct. Lawton calls Penn "this best-natured man" with "an inexhaustible spring of benevolence toward all his fellow-creatures, without any narrow or stingy regard to either civil or religious parties." We find ourselves walking with the two from Eton to Windsor, the young Whig inveighing against the putting out of the Declaration of Indulgence upon the dispensing power, to which Penn makes no answer, the reason being, as Lawton found out years after, that Penn himself had been against the use of so unpopular a prerogative. We join them on the terrace at Windsor, enjoying the fine prospect and contriving pardons for Whig exiles. We come into the garden of Holland House, and then into the King's own closet, where Lawton urges the need of securing the national Church and the liberties of England if liberty of conscience is established; and the King calmly replies, "I assure you I have no design on either." Then we hear of anonymous letters written for Penn to show the King, and of another royal interview in which James lays stress on the Church of England's belief in passive obedience, and Lawton agrees that this is the honest belief of most Churchmen, but it does not follow that they will live up to it in times of provocation, any more than their honest belief that swearing and drunkenness are sins will ensure that they never swear or get drunk. The writer, like other diarists, has himself for hero, but was greatly charmed by the easy way in which Penn forwarded his Whig designs. He is no doubt right in thinking that Penn was anxious through him and others to counteract the Jesuits that surrounded the King, and to bring about an accommodation of the position which should satisfy the nation while securing religious freedom for Catholics and Dissenters.

Much purging of corporations was now taking place; and in the City Tory aldermen were dismissed and Dissenters put in. Amongst others, the great Baptist leader William Kiffin, a prosperous City merchant, found his name set down. Two of his grandsons had been executed for their share in the Monmouth rebellion, and the old man naturally disclaimed the dubious honour thrust upon him.

"As soon as I heard it," he says,[1] "I used all the means I could to be excused, both by some lords near the King, and also by Sir Nicholas Butler and Mr. Penn. But it was all in vain; I was told that they knew I had an interest that might serve the King, and although they knew my sufferings were great, in cutting off my two grandchildren and losing their estates, yet it should be made up to me both in their estates, and also in what honour or advantage I could reasonably desire for myself."

He was obliged to serve, but after holding office for a few months obtained a discharge.[2]

In July Penn paid a visit to the West of England, and was at Bristol Fair, "where were mighty meetings," says John Whiting,[3] "notwithstanding the late persecution in that city: I never knew greater . . . people flocked to them like doves to the windows." With Francis Stamper, a London Friend, he held a great meeting at the house of Richard Vickris, at Chew, under the big oak in his close;[4] and on his journey home

. . . he had a meeting at the Devizes, in the great market-house, where many thousands of people were to hear him: wonderful sober the people were, of all sorts and greatly satisfied. From thence he came to Marlborough, had a large meeting . . . hundreds of people stood to hear him in the street. The rooms

---

[1] Orme, *Life of Kiffin*, p. 85. Macaulay, edn. 1907, p. 231, says wrongly, "Penn was employed in the work of seduction but to no purpose." It is clear from the passage cited that Kiffin applied to Penn. On his error being pointed out, Macaulay tried to evade the charge by alleging that the word "they" in the phrase "they knew I had an interest," meant Nicholas and Penn, when the true interpretation, as Henderson points out, is, "I was told by the lords to whom I applied or by Nicholas or Penn that the Government knew." Kiffin pleaded with the King to release him, saying, "The death of my grandsons gave a wound to my heart, which is still bleeding and never will close, but in the grave." James replied, with his characteristic misreading of human nature, "I shall find a balsam for that sore."

[2] Luttrell, *Brief Relation*, i. 411, mentions Kiffin as a new alderman in August. Cf. Orme, *Life of Kiffin*. pp. 86-88.

[3] *Persecution Exposed*, p. 172; William Hitchcock to John and Amy Harding, Marlborough, 28th September 1687, in *J.F.H.S.* iv. 72-76.

[4] Whiting, as above.

being full, the glass of the windows being taken down, Friends stood in the pent-house and spoke to the people to their great satisfaction.[1]

He returned home in time to accompany the King in his royal progress in the latter part of August to Bath, Shrewsbury, and Chester, and so back by Oxford.[2] On Sunday the 28th, at Chester, says Bishop Cartwright,[3] the King "went to his devotions in the Shire Hall, and Mr. Penn held forth in the Tennis Court, and I preached in the Cathedral." At Oxford he became concerned in the Magdalen College case. This was the most notorious of a long series of encroachments by James upon the privileges of the English Church. In the previous July he had set up, in violation of the law, a Court of High Commission for ecclesiastical affairs. One of its first acts had been to suspend Dr. Henry Compton, the Bishop of London, who had strongly opposed his Catholic designs. The Master and two Fellows of University College, Oxford, became Papists, and retained office by royal dispensation. A layman, in the same way, was made Dean of Christ Church. At Cambridge, the Vice-Chancellor was commanded by royal letter to confer the degree of M.A. upon a Benedictine, Alban Francis. The senate protested, not "from any principle of disobedience and stubbornness, but from a conscientious sense of our obligations to laws and oaths." The Court deprived the Vice-Chancellor of his office; but the degree was not conferred. James now enjoined the Fellows of Magdalen College, Oxford, to elect a Roman Catholic convert of bad character to their vacant Presidency. The Fellows refused to violate their statutes, and made choice of Dr. Hough. The King had the election annulled by the High Commission Court, and directed them to choose Dr. Samuel Parker, who had been made Bishop of Oxford in 1686 for his Erastian views. They replied that there was no vacancy to fill, as they had already elected Hough.

---

[1] Hitchcock's letter, as above.
[2] Penn to James Harrison, 8th September 1687, in Janney's *Life*, pp. 298, 299.
[3] *Diary*, p. 74, and Penn to Harrison, as above. Barclay was also at Chester (see Barclay, *Diary of Alexander Jaffray*, pp. 445, 446).

James accordingly, when he came to the University, called them before him, and rated them soundly.

> You have been a stubborn and turbulent College. . . . Is this your Church of England loyalty? . . . Get ye gone; know I am your King, and command you to be gone; go, and admit the Bishop of Oxford. . . . Let him know that refuses it. Look to't; they shall find the weight of their sovereign's displeasure.[1]

In Chapel afterwards they adhered to their resolution; and awaited the consequences of the royal anger. Penn, dining with Thomas Creech, talked over the matter, and on the next day heard their case from the Fellows, and wrote the King on their behalf, "intimating that such mandates were a force on conscience, and not very agreeable to his other gracious indulgences."[2] A month after this frank letter, which only a privileged Mentor like Penn would have been willing to write, Hough and others attended him at Windsor and had a long talk, for the tenor of which the superseded President of Magdalen is our only authority.[3] After explaining his friendship with James and his own position as a Dissenting Protestant, Penn said he desired to serve the College, though he was afraid it was too late, but any ill-success would be due to

---

[1] For the documents concerning Penn's intervention, see J. R. Bloxam, *Magdalen College and King James II.*, Oxford Historical Society, 1886, pp. 88-106, Paget's *Inquiry*, pp. 44-73, and Janney's *Life*, 317-330. Macaulay, 1907 edn. pp. 249, 250, perverts the facts to suit his own prejudice, and makes Penn the King's agent to seduce the College, when it is clear, as Henderson points out, that "Penn intervened, at the instance not of the King, but of the Fellows."

[2] Creech to Charlett, 6th September, cited in Bloxam, p. 93, Paget, p. 55, with other confirmatory letters. Macaulay adduces an anonymous letter to Dr. Thomas Bailey, one of the Senior Fellows, which Bailey supposed came from Penn, from its charitable purpose and his knowledge of Penn's good offices with the King on behalf of his conscientious subjects (see letters in Bloxam, pp. 98-101, Janney, pp. 321-323). The letter counselled compliance on various prudential grounds, but is not in the plain language nor in Penn's style. Hepworth Dixon, *Life of Penn*, 1856 edn. p. xxvii, says: "The contemporary account of these transactions, preserved at Magdalen (Hunt MS. fol. 45) has this remark on the margin of the letter: 'This letter Mr. Penn disowned.'" Bloxam, p. 99, says the note is by George Hunt, one of the Fellows, and on the deputation to Penn at Windsor.

[3] Letter of 9th October, printed in Bloxam, pp. 104-106, Paget, pp. 64-70, Janney, pp. 324-328. Macaulay seizes on Penn's jocular remark, and charges him with becoming "a broker in simony" and using "a bishopric as a bait to tempt a divine to perjury." Henderson comments: "All that Penn did was to let them know his opinion as to possibilities; he certainly did not offer any proposal by way of accommodation; though it must be remembered that he did not approve of the monopoly of the Universities to the Church of England."

want of power not of goodwill. He promised to read every word of their papers to the King, "unless he was peremptorily commanded to forbear." He cleared Sunderland of the business, and threw the blame on Jeffreys. Hough continues:

I thank God that he did not so much as offer at any proposal by way of accommodation, which was the thing I most dreaded; only once, upon the mention of the Bishop of Oxford's indisposition, he said smiling, "If the Bishop of Oxford should die, Dr. Hough may be made bishop; what think you of that, gentlemen?" Mr. Cradock answered, They should be heartily glad of it, for it would do very well with the presidentship.

Hough was in no mood for banter; and disclaimed all ambition for any post but the Presidency, saying that being conscious of no disloyalty, he could not understand why he was judged incapable. Penn replied, Majesty did not love to be thwarted; and, after so long a dispute, they could not expect to be restored to the King's favour without making some concessions. He naturally felt that his task with James would be easier if he were the bearer of some offer, but made no suggestion of his own. Hough told him that they were ready to make all concessions that were consistent with honesty and conscience.

"However," he said, "Mr. Penn, in this I will be plain with you; we have our statutes and oaths to justify us in all we have done hitherto; but, setting this aside, we have a religion to defend; and I suppose that you yourself would think us knaves if we should tamely give it up. The Papists have already got Christ Church and University College, the present struggle is for Magdalen; and they threaten that in a short time they will have the rest. He replied with vehemence, 'That they shall never have, assure yourselves. If once they proceed so far, they will quickly find themselves destitute of their present assistance. For my part, I have always declared my opinion that the preferments of the Church should not be put into any other hands but such as they at present are in; but I hope that you would not have the two Universities such invincible bulwarks for the Church of England that none but they must be capable of giving their children a learned education. I suppose two or three colleges will content the Papists. Christ Church is a noble structure;

University College is a pleasant place; and Magdalen College is a comely building. The walks are pleasant; and it is conveniently situated, just at the entrance of the town, etc.'"

The good Churchman had found it distasteful enough to appeal to a Quaker at all; but when Penn took the opportunity for pointing out the grievance under which Catholics and Dissenters lay in being debarred from the Universities — an injustice only remedied in the last century — Hough felt he was being trifled with, and regarded it as settled that Magdalen would go to the Papists. All the Fellows could do was to see that it was taken and not given.

We cannot doubt that Penn, for his part, faithfully kept his promise. It was too late, however, to turn the King's purpose. Four days after the interview he directed a visitation of Magdalen by Bishop Cartwright and others,[1] and on the 22nd October the Bishop of Oxford, despite Hough's public protest, was installed as President. The Fellows, excepting two, were expelled, and at the Bishop's death a few months later a Roman Catholic succeeded to Magdalen. The King's arbitrary and rash obstinacy had gained its end at the cost of rousing against him a resentful Church.

Penn was at this time eagerly seeking to check the influences that dominated the King. In July he had a long interview, and thought he had convinced James that he would never get a Parliament to his mind until he acted with more moderation and refused to listen to the counsels of the intemperate Jesuits.[2] So far from altering his policy, the King now devoted himself to procuring a subservient Parliament. In October he announced in Council his intention of having the Penal Laws and Tests repealed, and engaged its members to use their interest for that purpose.[3] During the following month—Penn being in Cleveland with his sister[4]—an inquiry was set

---

[1] See Bishop Cartwright's *Diary*, pp. 83-93.
[2] Van Citters to Prince of Orange, 19th July 1687, in Dutch Archives, cited in W. E. Forster's Preface to Clarkson's *Life of Penn*, 1849 edn. p. liv.
[3] Luttrell, *Brief Relation*, i. 415.
[4] Lawton's Account in Janney, *Life of Penn*, p. 303.

on foot in the counties, and a general regulation of corporations was taken in hand, by turning out those who were against the King's policy and putting in others who favoured it.¹ The inquiry asked three questions of the country gentry:²

> 1. In case the King should call a Parliament, and they should be chosen of it, would they give their votes to take away the Test and Penal Laws?
> 2. Would they give their votes for the choosing of such members as they believed would be for the taking them away?
> 3. Would they live peaceably with such as dissented from them in religion, as good Christians ought to do?

Refractory Deputy-Lieutenants and Justices were generally displaced. The regulation answer of Churchmen was that if chosen members they would vote as the reasons of the debate directed them, and at elections for such as would act in this way. As to the third question, they would live quietly with all men as good Christians and loyal subjects. Penn—and it is a blemish on his character—countenanced these proceedings in his zeal for a new Magna Carta of religious liberty. He told his friend Lawton that the King desired to make him a Justice, and would find a corporation where some honest gentlemen would bring him in as their member of Parliament. Lawton replied with spirit that he should be glad if a regulated Parliament did any good; but, by the help of God, he would never make one of them.³ In March 1688⁴ an anonymous pamphlet by Penn appeared, in which he urged that it should not be thought a crime in the King that he desired a repeal by Parliament,

> ... or that he takes the next and plainest ways to discriminate persons for that end; for, if the consequence of his endeavours

---

¹ Luttrell, *Brief Relation*, i. 419, 420.
² Reresby, *Memoirs*, pp. 387-389.
³ Lawton's Account in Janney's *Life*, p. 305.
⁴ The piece is stated to be by Penn in the *Life* prefixed to his *Works*. It is called "The Great and Popular Objection Against the Repeal of the Penal Laws and Tests briefly Stated and Consider'd," and was licensed 4th Feb. 1688. My citation is from p. 14.

were to ruin others for a party, it might be thought packing indeed; but, when it is to open enclosures and level interests, and by law to secure them from the ambition of one another, it seems to me to be unpacking for the good of the whole that which hath been so long packed for the sole good of a party.

In other words, the methods by which Parliament had been made a Tory preserve might be used in order to make one of a better complexion; and the end justified the means.

At the end of 1687, Friends began to be asked to take offices, both in England and Ireland, but generally declined.[1] Steven Crisp, of Colchester, was asked to be a Justice, but, says Sewel,[2] "was too circumspect to be caught thus."

The country was now thoroughly alive to the King's designs, and, under stress of the Roman Catholic menace, a great education of opinion was going on. When the Prince and Princess of Orange, in a famous manifesto, dated 4th November, allowed the Grand Pensionary Fagel to declare that they were against all persecution and freely consented to cover Papists from the severity of the Penal Laws, and to grant full liberty to Dissenters; but that they could not consent to remove the Test or other laws that secured the Protestant religion,[3] the declaration was received in England with much satisfaction, and corresponded closely with the weight of English opinion. Had James possessed his brother's sure sense of political values, he would have recognized the extreme danger of advancing farther in his campaign.

The bloodless Revolution which would seat William and Mary on the throne was already in process of incubation when the King, at the end of April 1688, reissued his Declaration of Indulgence with an addendum which

---

[1] See Dublin Half-Year's Meeting, Nov. 1687, and letter sent by Fox to Wm. Edmondson, printed in Rutty, *History of Friends in Ireland*, 2nd edn. p. 142. Sewel, ii. 440, gives a letter excusing three Quaker constables at Southwark from the oath. William Stout, of Lancaster, *Autobiography*, p. 23, says, "Even the Quakers were encouraged to undertake to be Justices of Peace and Magistrates in corporations, but generally declined." See *post*, Chap. XXI.

[2] ii. 443.

[3] Seaton, *Theory of Toleration*, pp. 231, 232.

explained that he could only employ those who concurred in his design, and appealed to his subjects to choose apt members for a Parliament to be held in the following November. A week later he took the fatal step of directing the reading of the Declaration on two successive Sundays in all churches and chapels. There followed an outspoken petition to the King by the "Seven Bishops," a general refusal by the clergy, the committal of the Bishops to the Tower[1] on the 8th June, and their acquittal for seditious libel on the 30th. On the same night the invitation to William was signed.

Penn played the part of a wise friend to James throughout these critical weeks. He advised against the order directing the reading of the Declaration;[2] he opposed the commitment of the Bishops to the Tower; and on the birth of a son to the King on 10th June went to James and pressed for their release in honour of the event.[3] This birth, which again confused the whole future, elated the Catholics, but depressed the country and hurried it forward to revolutionary courses.

The Society of Friends, as a whole, continued to support the repeal both of Penal Laws and Tests. But there are indications of some difference of opinion. We are told that with respect to the three questions the Quakers beyond Morecambe Sands, presumably at the instance of Thomas Lower and Margaret Fox, were for the negative, that is, against the King.[4] At the Yearly Meeting in June the following debate took place:

> *Bray Doily*, of Adderbury, proposes about choosing Parliament-men; and about accepting offices as Justices of Peace.
>
> *Steven Crisp*, 1. [*i.e.* choosing M.P.'s]. As to making use of their right, 'tis left to freedom: not expected that all must be alike in that use of privilege.
>
> 2. [*i.e.* accepting offices]. Men capable and way made

---

[1] Barclay saw them in the Tower (Sewel, ii. 44) and Richard Davies visited the Bishop of St. Asaph (*Life*, pp. 199-201).
[2] Johnstone, *Correspondence*, 23rd May 1688.
[3] Lawton's Account in Janney's *Life*, p. 307. Lord Clarendon, *Diary*, 23rd June 1688, notices Penn's attempts to thwart Jesuit influences.
[4] *Fleming MSS.* p. 207.

> open, with a clear conscience in their testimony, may be employed. But that is not yet.
>
> *George Fox.* Not safe to conclude such things in a Yearly Meeting. But keep to the power of God, and discourse of such things among themselves that are concerned in them.
>
> *William Penn.* Some to be appointed with whom to advise thereof. Nothing to be a bond of unity but the Truth: but circumstances differ, which needs advice and help.
>
> *George Fox.* It was not in the wisdom of God to propound such things here. Serve all men in the Truth and righteousness.
>
> *Steven Crisp.* We all have liberty to give advice one to another in straits.
>
> *William Penn.* They to come to the Testimony, the Testimony not to them.[1]

It is in the light of this discussion that we must read the careful words of the Address adopted for presenting to the King.[2] After thanking James for the blessed effects of the liberty granted, Friends urge their hardships in respect of tithes and oaths; and, referring to the late Declaration and the King's " gracious assurance to pursue the establishment of this Christian liberty and property upon an unalterable foundation "—a phrase parallel to William Penn's hope of a new Magna Carta—they conclude with the words:

> We think ourselves deeply engaged to renew our assurances of fidelity and affection; and with God's help intend to do our parts for the perfecting so blessed and glorious a work; that so it may be out of the power of any one party to hurt another upon the account of conscience: and, as we firmly believe that God will never desert this just and righteous cause of liberty, nor the King in maintaining of it, so we hope by God's grace to let the world see we can honestly and heartily appear for liberty of conscience, and be inviolably true to our own religion, whatever the folly or malice of some men on that account may suggest to the contrary.

---

[1] J. B. Braithwaite, *Bi-centenary of the Death of George Fox*, pp. 47, 48. Penn's words at the end meant that Friends were to form convictions of their own and not accept them ready-made from others. Cf. Geo. Bishop, *post*, p. 312.

[2] Sewel, ii. 444, 445.

Sewel says that some regarded these words as concerned with the office of magistrate; but they seem to me rather intended to encourage Friends not to shrink from supporting liberty of conscience because of the misconstructions that would be placed on their actions. It was in this sense that Yorkshire Quarterly Meeting [1] encouraged Friends to vote at the election and also paid for the supply of some of the current literature printed in London.[2]

Misconstructions of the position taken by Friends were naturally rife at this critical time.[3] Penn was the object of continual suspicion as a Jesuit. After the late King's death, he had to defend himself to his fellow-members against being the author of some sorry "condoling and congratulating verses" on Charles and James, which had been issued by a "penny-poet" over the initials "W. P."[4] At the beginning of 1686 there was an exchange of letters between him and Dr. Tillotson, whom Penn highly esteemed for his "moderation, simplicity, and integrity," which fully satisfied the Doctor that his suspicions of a correspondence between Penn and the Jesuits were ungrounded.[5] Now, in October 1688, his friend William Popple, secretary to the Plantation Office, wrote a delightfully worded letter, urging Penn to vindicate his good name from the imputation of Popery. The charge was a cumulative one: whoever had any

---

[1] Yorkshire Q.M. Minutes, 26th, 27th September 1688. The Y.M. Address was presented on 9th June. See Luttrell, *Brief Relation*, i. 443.

[2] In October they procured 50 of the "Three Letters tending to demonstrate how the Security of this Nation against al Future Persecution for Religion lys in the Abolishment of the Present Penal Laws and Tests, and in the Establishment of A New Law for universal Liberty of Conscience," supposed to be by Penn; and a little later, 100 copies of Popple's letter to Penn and his answer (see below), and 50 copies of a paper called "The Quakers' Caveats," which I have not identified.

[3] The Minutes of the Morning Meeting, 17th October 1687, refer to a paper by George Whitehead to Peter Acklam, of Hornsea, which Friends signed, "to clear William Penn from aspersions cast on him." Acklam probably simply reported rumours which in his opinion required an answer.

[4] *Life of Penn*, prefixed to *Works*, 1726 edn. i. 125.

[5] *Ibid.* i. 126-129. The tale Tillotson had heard seems to be the one recounted by Francis Bugg in his *Great Mystery of the Little Whore*, 1712, pt. iv. sect. 18 (first given by Bugg in print in 1700). The alleged correspondence was in 1677, see pp. 295, 296, where the charge that "Father" Penn said Mass several times is also made.

part in the King's counsels must be popishly affected; whoever took a great part in them must be an absolute Papist. Indeed, so the talk went, Penn must be a Jesuit, bred, men said, in the Jesuits' College at St. Omer, with orders taken at Rome and a dispensation to marry, moreover frequently officiating as a priest in the celebration of Mass at Whitehall, St. James's, and other places.

"Thus," wrote Popple, "the charge of Popery draws after it a tail like the *et cetera* oath, and by endless innuendoes prejudicates you as guilty of whatever malice can invent or folly believe: but that charge being removed the inferences that are drawn from it will vanish, and your reputation will return to its former brightness."[1]

Penn's answer is the fullest reply to his critics that we possess. He says, that so far from being bred at St. Omer and receiving orders from Rome, he was never at either place, nor knew or corresponded with anybody there, nor was ever a priest or officiated as such, nor ever so much as looked into any Romish chapel, but was a true Protestant Dissenter, whose religious opinions the King had always respected. The student of the stories in the Apocryphal Gospels is aware that just as a raindrop is formed round some minute nucleus of solid matter, so the most grotesque of these tales has been developed from some Logion of Jesus or out of some Old Testament saying which was supposed to require fulfilment in His life. So it is here. We find the necessary nucleus in the fact that Penn had studied at Saumur, not St. Omer, under the great Universalist theologian, Moyse Amyraut.[2] He had followed these studies by a visit to Italy, but had been recalled to England before he had gone farther than Turin. Credulous gossip had con-

---

[1] *Life*, prefixed to *Works*, 1726 edn. i. 131-139, printed separately with Penn's answer, 1688, and twice reprinted. Cf. the story of Penn being a Jesuit, bred at St. Omer, which was inquired into by York Monthly Meeting, Minutes of 3rd October 1690 (with report) and 3rd July 1691.

[2] Hepworth Dixon, *Life*, 1856 edn. p. 266, gives a story of a question put to Penn in a coach, Why he and Barclay and Keith had so much learning, when the Quakers despised letters? "I suppose," said Penn, "it comes of my having been educated at Saumur." This went the round of the coffee-houses as St. Omer. The story is in *Gentleman's Magazine*, 1737.

structed the rest of the allegations in the prejudiced atmosphere created by his suspicious intimacy with the King, careless or ignorant of the quasi-guardianship which his father, the Admiral, had asked James to discharge. For the rest, Penn declared that he had held no office from the King,[1] nor was ever a member of any council, cabinet, or committee, where the affairs of the kingdom were transacted.

And, unless calling at Whitehall once a day, upon many occasions, . . . be the evidence of my complying in disagreeable things, I know not what else can with any truth be alleged against me. However, one thing I know, that I have everywhere most religiously observed and endeavoured in conversation with persons of all ranks and opinions to allay heats and moderate extremities, even in the politics.

His action for liberty of conscience had indeed been against his own interest as proprietor of a plantation wanting immigrants:

Would I have made my market of the fears and jealousies of the people, when this King came to the Crown, I had put £20,000 into my pocket, and 100,000 into my province; for mighty numbers of people were then upon the wing: but I waived it all; hoped for better times; expected the effects of the King's word for liberty of conscience, and happiness by it; and, till I saw my friends with the kingdom delivered from the legal bondage which penal laws for religion had subjected them to, I could with no satisfaction think of leaving England; though much to my prejudice beyond sea and at my great expense here—having in all this time never had either office or pension, and always refusing the rewards or gratuities of those I have been able to oblige.

Penn thus shows the main charge to be baseless, which we who have followed his career needed not to be told, and his intimacy with the King is fully explained by gratitude and personal friendship, and by zeal for liberty of conscience. Penn's influence, we feel, was a salutary one; and was honestly even when mistakenly used;

---

[1] Luttrell, *Brief Relation*, i. 453, 461 (August-September 1688), says that Penn was made supervisor of the revenue of the excise and hearth money. But this was merely a piece of unreliable coffee-house gossip. (See *Ellis Corr*. ii. 211.)

though James adopted his advice only partially, and then from mixed and partly bigoted motives. Barclay, who frequented the Court in the summer of 1688, also fell "under the lash of envy, malice, and slandering tongues,"[1] as a reputed Papist and Jesuit and a caballer with Father Petre, to whom he had never spoken. His *Vindication* is convincing, except for his share in the first rough draft of a paper which seems to have contained political proposals. The paper, he says, had been spread without his knowledge and would never have had his consent. Holding strong convictions of the duty of non-resistance and passive obedience, Barclay was the least likely man in Scotland to engage himself in any Jacobite plot. He disliked the Revolution, but it was against his principles to be active in any attempt to undo it.

Of Barclay's last interview with James, we have an interesting account.[2] It belongs to the weeks of nervous apprehension, when the purpose of William's array of ships and men was apparent, but it was not known where he would strike. The King, at last alive to the danger, was engaged in reversing many of his most foolish actions —the Bishop of London and the Magdalen Fellows were re-instated; corporations and magisterial benches were restored to their former complexion; the High Commission Court was dissolved. Barclay's grandson says:

At this time he took his last leave of the King, for whose apparent misfortunes he was much concerned; having, as my grandmother informed me, several times discoursed with him upon the posture of affairs at that juncture, about settling the differences like to arise; and sometimes agreeable resolutions were taken, but one way or other prevented from being executed. At their parting, being in a window with the King, where none other was present, who looking out said, The wind was now fair for the Prince of Orange coming over; upon which my grandfather took occasion to say, It was hard that no expedient could be found out to satisfy the people: to which the King replied, That he would do anything becoming a gentleman except to part with liberty of conscience, which he never would while he lived.

---
[1] See his "Vindication" (1689) in *Reliquiae Barclaianae*.
[2] Cited from Barclay, *Diary of Alexander Jaffray*, p. 447.

Gilbert Latey, earlier in the year, before William's invasion was expected, had seen the King with Penn and Whitehead ; and after their business on behalf of Friends was done had thanked him for his royal kindness in their time of exercise and sore distress ; and had added, as the words sprang in his heart, " and I truly desire that God may show the King mercy and favour in the time of his trouble and sore distress." James remembered this afterwards in his extremity in Ireland, and said to a Friend, " I shall never forget," adding that the trouble was now upon him and he prayed that the favour might also come to pass, upon which Gilbert sent word that the Lord had given the King his life.[1]

[1] *Life*, pp. 121-123.

CHAPTER VI

THE TOLERATION ACT

The English Revolution . . . was a movement essentially aristocratic. The whole course of its policy was shaped by a few men who were far in advance of the general sentiments of the nation. The King, in spite of his great abilities, was profoundly unpopular; and his cold and unsympathetic manners, and his manifest dislike to the island over which he reigned, checked all real enthusiasm even among the Whigs. The Church was sullen and discontented, exasperated by the Act of Toleration, which the clergy were anxious to repeal, implacably hostile to the scheme of comprehension, by which William wished to unite the Protestant bodies, and to the purely secular theory of government which triumphed at the Revolution. . . . The moral feelings of the community were scandalized by the spectacle of a child making war upon her father, by the base treachery of many whom the dethroned sovereign had loaded with benefits, by the tergiversation of multitudes, who, in taking the oaths to a revolutionary government, were belying the principles which for years they had most strenuously maintained. . . . A great and by no means successful war was entailed upon the nation, and thousands of Englishmen had been mown down by the sword or by disease in Flanders and in Ireland.—W. E. H. LECKY, *History of England in the Eighteenth Century*, edn. 1913, i. 19, 20.

WITHIN a fortnight of Penn's answer to Popple, William landed at Torbay (5th November 1688), and the great revolutionary plot matured. In the fateful weeks that followed, the King found his military and political support in England crumbling away, and the nation was thrown into a great hurry and confusion. James sought refuge in France, Sunderland and Father Petre fled the realm, Jeffreys was taken at Wapping disguised as a sailor. Penn, as a royal favourite, was, naturally, under suspicion. Conscious of innocence, he made no attempt at flight; but was walking in Whitehall when the Lords of the Council sent for him on 10th December.[1] While at liberty under

[1] *Life*, prefixed to *Works*, 1726 edn. i. 139.

heavy bail,[1] a warrant (27th February) was issued for his arrest, but, on his writing to Lord Shrewsbury, disclaiming all plotting, he was allowed by William to go to his house in the country,[2] and at the end of the Easter Term was cleared, for the time being, in open court.

It is not within my design to trace the concurrence of favouring circumstances which allowed the Whig leaders to plant William and Mary jointly upon the throne and to secure the one course out of several possible ones, which broke with the popular doctrine of the Divine right of kings and inaugurated a new form of English Government, well in advance of the national conceptions. It is difficult to determine whether England owes most to the folly of James, the blindness of the Tories, the high purpose and statesmanship of William, or the dexterity of the Whigs. It is certain, however, that William, with his large ambition of withstanding the French attempt to dominate Europe, was the man of most inflexible mind, who succeeded in the main in making Tory principles and Whig revenge bend to the urgent necessities of the times. But it belongs to our subject to inquire how it came to pass that the Revolution Settlement carried the principle of religious

[1] *Ellis Corr.* ii. 356.
[2] Janney's *Life*, pp. 353, 354; Paget, *Inquiry*, pp. 76-78. Macaulay, *Hist.*, 1907 edn. pp. 494, 495, on the strength of a dispatch from Avaux to Louis XIV., dated 5th June 1689, charges Penn with doing "everything in his power to bring a foreign army into the heart of his own country." "It was hardly possible to be at once a consistent Quaker and a consistent courtier; but it was utterly impossible to be at once a consistent Quaker and a conspirator." Avaux, writing from Dublin, where James was then holding his Court, communicates news from England and Scotland received through James, and says, "The beginning of the news dated from England is the copy of a letter from Mr. Pen, of which I have seen the original." The accompanying Memoir accordingly begins: "The Prince of Orange begins to be much disgusted with the temper of the English; and the appearance of things is changing quickly, according to the nature of insular people; and his health is very bad. A cloud is beginning to arise in the North of the two kingdoms, where the King has many friends, which gives much uneasiness to the chief friends of the Prince of Orange. . . . They fear an invasion from Ireland and from France; and in this case the King will have more friends than ever." This falls far short of Macaulay's charge; and the later sentences may probably be from the Scottish rather than the English letter. It is also not unlikely that the Mr. Pen was Nevill Penn or Payne, whom Macaulay calls (p. 519) "one of the most adroit and resolute agents of the exiled family." (See Paget, *Inquiry*, pp. 78-83; *Paradoxes and Puzzles*, pp. 175-177, and Hepworth Dixon, *Life of Penn*, 1856 edn. pp. xxxv-xliv.) Payne and Penn were names easily confused; see *e.g. ante*, p. 58 note.

liberty to its great though qualified victory in the Toleration Act of 1689.

William himself, on much the same grounds as Penn, regarded Toleration as a political necessity of the country. Bred a Calvinist, and by conviction a Latitudinarian, he aimed at three things—Toleration, Comprehension, and a revision of the Tests. The first would unite the interests of a divided nation, the second he hoped would bring many Nonconformists into the Church, the third would enable capable Dissenters to serve the State. He was only able to secure the first. His Whig allies approved it, and the promises made by the Church in its hour of peril could not be honourably repudiated, while the nation as a whole was weary with fifty years of religious strife. Model Bills for Toleration and Comprehension already existed in those prepared nine years before at the time of the short Whig Parliaments.[1] The Earl of Nottingham, as Daniel Finch, had then been in charge of the Bills, and now reintroduced them in the Lords. Macaulay says:[2]

Of all the ministers of the new Sovereigns, he had the largest share of the confidence of the clergy. Shrewsbury was certainly a Whig, and probably a free-thinker: he had lost one religion; and it did not very clearly appear that he had found another. Halifax had been during many years accused of scepticism, deism, atheism. Danby's attachment to episcopacy and the liturgy was rather political than religious. But Nottingham was such a son as the Church was proud to own.

He sincerely favoured Toleration; but desired Comprehension so as to bring in Dissenters, and prevent any effort to alter the Test Act in their favour. Macaulay thinks it probable that he gave his aid on condition that the Whigs dropped the revision of the Tests.

The Toleration Bill had a smooth passage through Parliament and became law 24th May 1689. A dangerous amendment to make it a temporary measure in order to put Dissenters on their good behaviour was, happily, lost.

---

[1] *Ante*, p. 97.   [2] *Hist.*, 1907 edn. p. 364.

Its provisions well illustrate the pedestrian pace of English progress.[1]

Bagehot wittily says of Englishmen :[2]

> The way to lead them—the best and acknowledged way—is to affect a studied and illogical moderation. You may hear men say, "Without committing myself to the tenet that $3 + 2$ make 5, though I am free to admit that the honourable member for Bradford has advanced very grave arguments in behalf of it, I think I may, with the permission of the Committee, assume that $2 + 3$ do not make 4, which will be a sufficient basis for the important propositions which I shall venture to submit on the present occasion."

It was highly dangerous to urge that liberty of conscience was an inherent right of the peaceable subject, for the menace of Roman Catholicism and the experience of Puritan domination were too near; it was not even necessary to press for a direct repeal of the Penal Laws in the case of Protestant Dissenters; it was enough for practical purposes to suspend their operation; and so this line of least resistance was taken. The Act, like much else of our legislation, is formless and devoid of principle, a mere invertebrate *modus vivendi* made to pass the two Houses and to do its work of easing the nation.

The Preamble confessed the modesty of the design :[3] "Forasmuch as some ease to scrupulous consciences in the exercise of religion, may be an effectual means to unite Their Majesties' Protestant subjects in interest and affection." It excluded from its benefits all Papist recusants and persons denying the doctrine of the Trinity as set out in the formularies of the Church of England. Tithes and prosecutions for tithes were preserved. Subject to these exceptions, the armoury of persecuting laws was to rust unused on certain prescribed conditions. The Oaths

---

[1] Macaulay's development of this point (*Hist.*, 1907 edn. p. 365) is one of his strongest pieces of political writing.
[2] *English Constitution*, 1896 edn. p. 143.
[3] 1 W. & M. st. 1., cap. 18, printed in Robertson, *Select Statutes* etc., p. 123, etc., and in Besse, *Sufferings*, i. xlvi-lii. Though known from the first as the Act of Toleration, its true title is "An Act for exempting Their Majesties' Protestant subjects, dissenting from the Church of England, from the penalties of certain laws."

of Allegiance and Supremacy must be taken and the Declaration against Transubstantiation be subscribed at Quarter Sessions. The Dissenting clergy were also to subscribe the Thirty-nine Articles, except those declaring that the Church has power to regulate ceremonies, that the doctrines in the Book of Homilies are sound, and that there is nothing superstitious in the ordination service. Any minister scrupling the baptizing of infants was also excused from affirming that infant baptism is a laudable practice. Meeting-places were to be certified and registered in the Bishop's or Archdeacon's Court or at Quarter Sessions, and no religious meetings were to be held with locked doors. It was made penal, however, to enter a meeting-place for the purpose of disturbing the congregation.

A larger exemption was necessary in the case of Quakers. It was accordingly provided that persons who scrupled the taking of any oath should subscribe the Declaration against Transubstantiation and also the two following Declarations:

I, A. B., do sincerely promise and solemnly declare before God and the world that I will be true and faithful to King William and Queen Mary. And I do solemnly profess and declare that I do from my heart abhor . . . that damnable doctrine and position, that Princes excommunicated or deprived by the Pope . . . may be deposed or murdered by their subjects or any other whatsoever. And I do declare that no Foreign Prince, Person, Prelate, State or Potentate, hath or ought to have any Power, . . . ecclesiastical or spiritual, within this realm.

I, A. B., profess faith in God the Father, and in Jesus Christ, His eternal Son, the true God, and in the Holy Spirit, one God blessed for evermore: and do acknowledge the Holy Scriptures of the Old and New Testament to be given by Divine Inspiration.

The final form of the second Declaration had been offered by Friends.[1] It had originally stood:

I, A. B., profess faith in God the Father, and in Jesus Christ, His eternal Son, the true God, and in the Holy Spirit, *co-equal with the Father, and the Son*, one God blessed for ever: and do

---

[1] Whitehead, *Christian Progress*, pp. 634-636.

acknowledge the Holy Scriptures of the Old and New Testaments to be *the revealed Will and Word of God.*

Sir Thomas Clarges, who sat for Oxford University, had urged Friends to propose words to clear them from the imputation of not being Christians, which had been made in the House. His friendly offices show the change which had taken place since the days when he cried out against Nayler, in the Protector's Second Parliament, "Let us all stop our ears and stone him."[1] Friends, at the risk of finding themselves excluded from the Bill, were put under the necessity, says George Whitehead, of offering some form of confession. The words were confined to scripture terms, though Whitehead bases his willingness to accept the Trinitarian formula, except the unscriptural phrase, "co-equal with the Father and the Son," upon the spurious insertion in 1 John v. 7, 8, which Erasmus had admitted into his third edition of the Greek Testament, in redemption of a rash promise. It is tempting to speculate on what might have happened to Friends under the Toleration Act if this proof-text for the Trinity, on which they relied in many another doctrinal difficulty, had been absent from the Authorized Version.

Representative Friends were called before the Committee, and answered it clearly as to their owning the Deity and accepting the scriptures as given by Divine inspiration. The latter was the point most in doubt, and rightly so, for there was, as appears from a comparison of the original with the amended form of the Declaration, a substantial difference between the position taken by Friends and the current orthodox view.

The Comprehension Bill, to which the Quakers were indifferent, had less favourable treatment, and was assailed both by Churchmen jealous of interference with their ritual and Dissenters jealous of defection to the Church. The Whigs were divided: one part desired to drop the Bill and relieve the Dissenters from the Tests; the other was for passing the Bill and adjourning the revision of the

---

[1] *Beginnings of Quakerism*, p. 260.

Tests. A further question complicated the matter. All political parties were agreed that, having regard to the change of Government, holders of civil and military offices must take a new oath of allegiance, or lose office. But was the same drastic course to be taken with Churchmen holding ecclesiastical or academic positions? The King thought he could secure a compromise. He addressed both Houses in person, urging the revision of the Tests, and letting it be understood that in that event he would dispense with the Oath in the case of clergymen already beneficed. But the Whigs would not waive their revenge on the Church, nor the Tories the integrity of their Tests. William's wisdom would be afterwards vindicated but his political sagacity was at fault. In the result, the Comprehension Bill and the revision of the Tests were lost, but the new Oath was insisted on.

Six of the "Seven Bishops" honourably adhered to their old doctrines of non-resistance and hereditary right, refused to swear allegiance to the usurper, and, together with four hundred of the most advanced High Churchmen, were deprived by Act of Parliament. These "Non-Jurors" long maintained a private Church dear to the Anglican Jacobites. Their exodus left the field open for the elevation of men like Tillotson and Burnet, as overseers of a flock that hated them. The appointment of Latitudinarian Bishops was the chief grievance of the Tories against William. But it was only thus that the religious peace could be kept in England against the outcries of the country parsons and the intrigues of the High Church party, which was in that age distinguished, not by ritualistic practices, but by the desire to go back on the Act of Toleration.[1]

Friends, it will be seen, had little direct share in the passing of the Toleration Act. Penn, the persistent champion of religious liberty and their only English Leader belonging to the governing class, was under a cloud of suspicion. Barclay was suffering a like eclipse. The Society was too self-contained and aloof from the passions and strife of parties to have either power or wish to shape the course of public affairs. But its indirect influence had been great and has been too little regarded.

[1] G. M. Trevelyan, *England under the Stuarts*, p. 451.

More than once in the long struggle, as I have shown, the stiffness and the endurance of Friends had opposed an impregnable obstruction to the annihilation of Dissent. The great company of unresisting martyrs had not suffered and died in vain. They had forfeited their liberties and their estates, but every forfeit hastened the downfall of unjust law. The very inconsequence of the Act shows only the more clearly that it was no clever conception of statesmen, but the grudging recognition of unwelcome but inevitable facts. The law might ruin and imprison; it might, in its bigoted folly, raze meeting-houses to the ground and outlaw men of upright and sober life; it had been shown to have no further power over Christians who were determined through endurance to win their souls. The more it was used, the more was its injustice exposed. In thirty years the intolerance of Church and State had effected a greater advance in the rights of conscience than was gained by the next hundred years of toleration. For from each stroke of persecution an appeal rang to something greater than the law, the conscience of England. The country felt the shame of the cruelty and heeded the cry of the oppressed. Once delivered from the panic fears of Puritan plots, it had left persecution to predatory prelates and the black tribe of Informers. It was content enough, for its part, to live and let live. It did not express itself, for the Englishman expects his rulers to understand him without speech; but it had made up its own irrevocable mind. When Toleration came, it heard with satisfaction but without undue surprise that the powers that be had at last come round to its own way of thinking; and, feeling that there might be some sense in the Government after all, went on somewhat less discontentedly with its hard round of daily toil.

John Locke became the great interpreter of the Revolution of 1688. In his famous (first) *Letter concerning Toleration* he enunciated the Whig principles which found imperfect expression in the Act. Written in 1685, it was published in Latin in the spring of 1689, and in the autumn appeared in an English translation, made by Penn's friend, William Popple. Locke separates the business of Civil Government from that of religion; the State is only concerned with civil interests, such as life, liberty, health, and the possession of property. The weapon of the magistrate is outward force; but true religion consists in the inward persuasion of the mind, which is so made that it cannot be compelled to the belief of anything. Even if penalties could produce conviction, their use would not help in the salvation of souls, for only one country would be in the right, and men would owe their eternal happiness or misery to the places of their nativity. Sincerity is of the essence of true religion. "I cannot be saved by a religion that I distrust, and by a worship that I abhor." A Church, in his view, is a voluntary society of men, united for worshipping God in the way they judge acceptable to Him and effectual for their salvation. No outside body can prescribe its laws, nor can one Church have jurisdiction over another. The real remedy for mistaken opinions lies in serious and friendly discourse by those whose profession is the care of souls. "Truth certainly would do well enough, if she were once left to shift for herself." But Locke, though he would extend toleration to idolaters, excepts Roman Catholics as politically dangerous, and atheists as denying the being of God, and therefore persons on whom the bonds of human society—promises, covenants, and oaths—have no hold. His toleration, boundless in theory, is in fact limited by the supposed overriding necessities of the State, though not as stringently as was the Act itself which excluded Unitarians. His philosophy, unconsciously to himself, was vitiated by his political fears, and moved within the horizons of its own age.

In practice the working of Toleration was more liberal than the clauses of the Act or the provisos of Locke.

Mass was said regularly in private houses; there were many well-known Catholic chapels and some monasteries; the priests conciliated opinion by passing about in disguise, but were seldom hunted and imprisoned. Periodic outbursts of Protestant zeal took the form of fresh Penal Laws that were not enforced Thus Catholics and Unitarians, though denied the exercise of public worship, were saved from cruel persecution, owing to William's temperament, England's European alliances [with Catholic States and the Pope], and the spirit of humanitarianism, rationalism, and indifferentism now pervading high places and infecting public opinion.[1]

The Toleration Act began a new era for Friends and other Nonconformists. Besse concludes his great *Collection of Sufferings* at this point; and here John Whiting thought at first to shut up his discourse on *Persecution Expos'd*, being arrived at the mark he aimed at. A "seditious conventicle" was now a meeting protected by law; the Quaker could not again be snared into a *praemunire*, or ravaged by an Informer. He no longer held life and property at the mercy of prejudiced zeal or legalized greed. He had passed from persecution into peace. His weather-beaten Ark, which had stoutly ridden out the storm, found itself, as by a miracle, in calm waters. It seemed a time for refitting the ship; not for the fresh heroic adventure of launching forth into the deep.

In this spirit, so consistent with long years of passive resistance and yet so perilous for days of ease, the Yearly Meeting that met in May 1689 issued the advice that would prove the keynote of the Society's policy through the next generation:

Walk wisely and circumspectly towards all men, in the peaceable spirit of Christ Jesus, giving no offence nor occasions to those in outward government, nor way to any controversies, heats or distractions of this world, about the kingdoms thereof. But pray for the good of all; and submit all to that Divine power and wisdom which rules over the kingdoms of men. That, as the Lord's hidden ones, that are always quiet in the land, and as those prudent ones and wise in heart, who know when and where to keep silent, you may all approve your hearts to God; keeping out of all airy discourses and words, that may anyways become snares, or hurtful to Truth or Friends, as being sensible

---

[1] G. M. Trevelyan, *England under the Stuarts*, p. 450, based on Lecky, *Hist. of England in the Eighteenth Century* (1913 edn.), i. 349-363.

that any personal occasion of reproach causes a reflection upon the body.¹

A month later, William Penn was arrested for the second time, on suspicion of High Treason,² during the anxious weeks when the Irish Protestants were standing at bay behind the walls of Derry. James had written letters to a number of his friends, which were taken in a cave on the shore of Flintshire, with the carriers of the dispatches and a key to the cipher in which some were penned. Upon this discovery, one man was committed to the Tower and warrants were issued against others.³ We may conclude that it was one of these letters that appeared to incriminate Penn. Croese gives the substance of his examination,⁴ which seems to have taken place before the King and to have lasted for two hours.⁵ The letter had asked for assistance, in return for past favours. Penn said that he could not prevent it from having been written; and

---

¹ *Yearly Meeting Epistles*, 1681–1857, i. pp. 44, 45. Part of this paragraph, with a similar one from the Epistle of the following year, was included in the MS. "Books of Extracts," which were the standard discipline of the Society in the eighteenth century, and has been continued in the later printed editions down to the present *Christian Practice*, 1911 edn. p. 124. The extract so incorporated now ends with "kingdoms of men," and the 1690 extract is omitted.
² The warrant is dated 22nd June 1689, see *Cal. State Papers, Dom.*, 1689–1690, p. 163. Besse, *Life* prefixed to Penn's *Works*, 1726 edn. i. 140, wrongly places the affair in 1690, which has misled Penn's biographers and Macaulay, *Hist.* 1907 edn. p. 498; and has caused Paget, *Inquiry*, pp. 87-89, to conclude that the examination, probably before William III., never took place, because he was in Ireland in that year. We have confirmatory evidence of Penn's detention, however, in the Minutes of the Morning Meeting, which show that between 3rd June and 8th July Penn failed to keep an appointment; and, "he not coming nor hearing from him," the matter had to be proceeded with in his absence. Fox's MS. *Itinerary Journal* at Dev. Ho. records that on 27th September he visited Penn, who was then in the custody of the King's Messenger in Piccadilly. Luttrell, *Brief Relation*, i. 553 (June), speaks of his arrest, and, i. 610, of his being discharged by the King's Bench, 28th November, at the end of Michaelmas Term, not Trinity, as Besse has it.
³ Luttrell, *Brief Relation*, i. 551, 552; *Fleming MSS.* p. 247.
⁴ Latin edn., 1695, pp. 378, 379; Engl. edn., 1696, pp. 112, 113. Clarkson, *Life of Penn*, 1849 edn. p. 212, also cites a reference to Penn's examination in Picart's *Religious Customs and Ceremonies*.
⁵ Besse, *Life* prefixed to *Works*, 1726 edn. i. 140, says, "In the year 1690 [correct this to 1689] he was again brought before the Lords of the Council,". . . and . . . appealed to King William himself, who, after a conference of near two hours, inclined to acquit him, but, to please some of the Council, he was held upon bail for a while and in Trinity [Mich.] Term the same year again discharged." Cf. *post*, p. 165.

... supposed King James would have him to endeavour his restitution; and that, though he could not decline the suspicion, yet he could avoid the guilt. And, since he had loved King James in his prosperity, he should not hate him in his adversity; yea, he loved him still for many favours he had conferred on him, though he would not join with him in what concerned the state of the kingdom.

He added, that he would reward the kindness of James in any private way in his power, but only so far as was consistent with his inviolable duty to the Government. His candour and generous spirit allayed suspicion, and after a light confinement he was set free in November.

In the following summer William went in person to Ireland, leaving Mary as Queen-regnant. During these critical months, when a French invasion was expected, a Proclamation was issued, on 14th July 1690, for the arrest, amongst others, of Penn,[1] on a charge of conspiracy. He desired bail, being indisposed, which was allowed him; and he and others were cleared at the end of the Michaelmas Term.[2] He now hoped that he was through his troubles, and planned an early return to America, where affairs in Pennsylvania urgently needed him. But at this very juncture a serious Jacobite plot was hatching. William was impatient to attend a Congress at the Hague of the Powers in league against France, and his absence would give the conspirators their opportunity. A meeting of Protestant Jacobites was held in December, which advised James, who was now again at St. Germain, to prelude a new attempt on England by securing toleration for the Protestant exiles in France; and, when he came in the spring, to keep any accompanying French force in the background, and to declare his resolve to protect the Church and to govern according to law and through Parliament.

Viscount Preston, who towards the end of the late

---

[1] For a facsimile of the Proclamation see *J.F.H.S.* vi. 5.
[2] See *Fleming MSS.* pp. 280, 285; and Luttrell, *Brief Relation*, ii. 77, 121, 135. Henry Gouldney, writing to Sir John Rodes, 10th December, says, "As to our friend W. P., he was fully cleared, without any objection, the last Term" (*Quaker Post-bag*, p. 49).

reign had succeeded Sunderland as President of the Council, was chosen as the agent who should go to St. Germain with the proposals, but he and his papers were seized in the Thames on the 31st December. Two letters from Penn were among the documents, and a brief note made by Preston for his own use: " A commission given to me from Mr. P——, two vessels of £150 price for Pennsylvania for 13 or 14 months."[1] Clearly Penn was for a fourth time under grave suspicion, and his safety for the moment lay in concealment. Preston and others were committed to the Tower on the 3rd January, and there was a warrant out against Penn.[2] He ran the risk of attending and speaking at the funeral of the great Quaker leader, George Fox, who died on the 13th, and says :[3]

> I was with him [when he died]; he earnestly recommended to me his love to you all [in Pennsylvania], and said, "William, mind poor Friends in America." He died triumphantly over death; very easily foresaw his change. He was buried on the 6th day—like a General Meeting—2000 people at his burial, Friends and others. I was never more public than that day; I felt myself easy; he was got into his inn, before the storm that is coming overtook him; and that night, very providentially, I escaped the [King's] Messenger's hands.

On the following day, Preston was brought to trial for High Treason, and was found guilty, on the eve of the King's departure for Holland. The Secretary of State, Henry, Viscount Sidney, afterwards Earl of Romney, was an old friend of Penn, one of those to whom *No Cross, No Crown* had been addressed in 1669. Yet in his report to William, on the 20th, of Preston's trial he has to write :[4]

---

[1] Macaulay, *Hist.* 1907 edn. p. 531 note, cites this memorandum, with an interlined addition about the French Fleet hindering the English and Dutch from joining, which, candidly enough, he thinks was jotted down by Preston at another time on a place left vacant between the first and second lines of the note as to the commission entrusted to him by Penn. But the interlineation may have prejudiced the Government against Penn, though he would be unaware of its existence.

[2] See Luttrell, *Brief Relation*, ii. 153, "and several warrants are out to take up divers persons." Cf. *ibid.* 162 (20th January).

[3] Letter to Thos. Lloyd, 14th June 1691, in Janney's *Life*, p. 370.

[4] *Cal. State Papers, Dom.*, 1690-91, p. 228.

[Lord Preston] will, if he obtain his pardon, be a good evidence, and what he can say against Lord Clarendon, the Bishop of Ely and Mr. Penn, which he will be ready to do, is of great importance. We cannot find the Bishop, nor Mr. Penn; and, it being all over the town that Lord Preston has confessed or intends confession, will make them use all endeavours to hide. Mr. Penn is as much in this business as anybody; and two of the letters are certainly of his writing; and, if we can catch him, it will so appear.

A fortnight later, Caermarthen, the discoverer of the plot, advised the reprieve of Preston, as the only witness against Lord Clarendon, the Bishop, and Penn.[1] As the last two were in hiding, a Proclamation for their finding and apprehension was issued on 5th February;[2] but no great efforts to arrest Penn seem to have been made.

Through his brother-in-law, Anthony Lowther, he had offered to see Sidney, if he had a promise that he might return without being molested. Sidney gave this, with the Queen's permission, and saw Penn on 25th February. He reported the interview to the King:[3]

[I] found him just as he used to be, not at all disguised, but in the same clothes and same humour I have formerly seen him in. It would be too long for you to read a full account of our discourse, but in short it was this; that he was a true and faithful servant to King William and Queen Mary; and, if he knew anything that was prejudicial to them or their Government, he would readily discover it. He protested in the presence of God that he knew of no plot; nor did he believe there was any in Europe, but what King Louis had said; and he was of opinion that King James knew the bottom of this plot as little as other people. . . . To the letters that were found with my Lord Preston and the papers of the conference, he would not give any positive answer; but said, If he could have the honour to see the King, and, if the King would be pleased to believe the sincerity of what he said and pardon the ingenuity [*i.e.* ingenuousness] of what he confessed, he would freely tell everything he knew of himself, and other things which would be important for His Majesty's service and interest to know. But,

---

[1] *Cal. State Papers, Dom.*, 1690–91, p. 244.
[2] *Ibid.* p. 246, facsimile in *J.F.H.S.* vi. 5.
[3] *Ibid.* p. 282, dispatch dated 27th February; also in *J.F.H.S.* vi. 56, 57, and Paget, *Inquiry*, pp. 96–98.

if he cannot obtain this favour, he will be obliged to quit the kingdom, which he is very unwilling to do. He also said, He might have gone away twenty times, if he had pleased, but he is so confident of giving you satisfaction, if you would hear him, that he is resolved to wait your return, before he took any sort of measures. What he intends to do is all he can do for your service; for he cannot be a witness if he would, it being, as he says, "against his conscience and his principles to take an oath." This is the sum of our conference, and I am sure you will judge it as you ought to do.

The King came to England for a few weeks in April, and Sidney returned with him to the Continent. Two letters to Sidney during these weeks throw some further light on Penn's position.[1] In the first he offers the security of the Society of Friends for his peaceful living; and adds,[2] "Pray him [the King] to reflect on what passed the last time I saw him; and, whatever anybody tells him, I am neither more culpable nor less sincere and candid than he was pleased to think me at that time." The answer was, "The King took it so, as I should not have been displeased to have heard it." The second letter disclaimed emphatically all knowledge of invasions or insurrections,

... or any junto or consult for advice or correspondency in order to it. Nor have I ever met with those named as the members of this conspiracy; or prepared any measures with them or any[one] else for the Lord [Preston] to carry with him as one sense or judgment. Nor did I know of his being sent for up for any such voyage. If I saw him a few days before by his great importunity, as some say, I am able to defend [myself] from the imputations cast upon me, and that with great truth and sincerity, though in rigour, perhaps, it may incur the censure of a misdemeanour; and therefore I have no reason to own it, without an assurance that no hurt should ensue to me. ... Let me go to America, or be protected here.

The answer to this was that the King's hurry was so great that nothing could be done in it at the moment;

---

[1] 22nd April, and one undated, but earlier than 2nd May, when the King sailed, printed in Janney's *Life*, pp. 367-369.
[2] This seems to refer to the interview in the summer of 1689, and accordingly confirms Besse's account, *ante*, p. 161, note.

but on the voyage and in Holland, where Penn had fewer ill-wishers, Sidney would move him in it. The correspondence looks as though it had been carried on through a third person, presumably Anthony Lowther, who no doubt waited on Sidney for his verbal answers.

I have detailed the evidence, so that the reader may form his own opinion on Penn's conduct. Sidney was a man of defective morals; but was probably William's stanchest English friend, and would not have used his good offices, if he had thought Penn seriously implicated. It looks to me as though Penn had no hand in any plot; but had met Preston, and had indiscreetly entrusted him with a commission about ships for Pennsylvania, and with a letter or letters to James containing expressions of personal friendship. This was no doubt "comforting the enemy," and corresponding with him, but did not involve any intentional disloyalty to William and Mary.

If the evidence supplied by the discovery of the Preston plot had been all, Penn, no doubt, would have surrendered himself and been cleared, as on the three former occasions. But, in the background, on the King's part, lay certain questions of policy; and, on Penn's part, fear of random charges by unscrupulous witnesses. William, who was managing a great War against French domination in Europe, felt the Quaker proprietorship of Pennsylvania a weakness: Penn was already being ruined in his Irish estates by proceedings in that kingdom, on the evidence of a wretch named Fuller;[1] and did not know what trumped-up charges his enemies might make against him if he gave himself up. He felt it best to seclude himself in London till the clouds lifted.

Locke was one of those who visited him in his retirement. Their friendship had begun at the University; and they were men of kindred tastes and both friends of the learned Benjamin Furly, of Rotterdam, who had helped Fox with the *Battle-Door* and collected a wonder-

---

[1] Letter early in 1692, in Janney's *Life*, p. 378; and Letter to Rochester, *ibid.* p. 380. Fuller brought charges of High Treason against a number of persons, but his evidence was suspected by Parliament by the beginning of 1692, and in February he was voted an impostor.

ful library of mystical theology.[1] Penn in 1685 had been anxious to obtain a pardon for Locke, then a Whig exile in Holland, but Locke refused it, saying "he had no occasion for a pardon, having been guilty of no crime."[2] The case was now altered. Locke desired to procure a pardon from William for Penn; and it was the Quaker who declined a way of relief which would have implied his guilt.[3]

Penn wrote to the Yearly Meeting at the end of May that his privacy was not because men had sworn truly, but falsely, against him,[4] and in June, in what seems his first letter on the subject to Thomas Lloyd, the head of the Council in Pennsylvania,[5] he calls himself the victim of "the jealousies of some and unworthy dealing of others." In August he addressed his friend Tillotson, the newly-appointed Archbishop of Canterbury, complaining that he was still under suspicion, while many men were pardoned who had actually rebelled.[6] Early in 1692 he speaks of the harshness of his treatment, which looked to him like intentional persecution by the Government.[7] In October of the same year, at the time when the arrogance of Louis had reached its highest point with the fall of Namur, Penn received the heaviest of his blows, and Pennsylvania was withdrawn from his control and placed in the hands of Colonel Benjamin Fletcher, the Governor of New York, who did not however assume the reins of government till the following spring.[8]

He was now, to all seeming, a broken man, his financial position embarrassed, his "Holy Experiment" in peril, and his wife sinking in health under her anxieties. But

---

[1] Articles on "Benjamin Furly, Quaker Merchant, and his Statesmen Friends," and "Benjamin Furly and his Library," both by Charles R. Simpson, in *J.F.H.S.* xi. 62-73.
[2] *Ibid.* p. 66.
[3] Clarkson's *Life of Penn*, 1849 edn. pp. 217, 218.
[4] Janney's *Life*, p. 367. [5] *Ibid.* p. 369.
[6] Letter of 30th August 1691, in Sudeley Colln. of Penn MSS., cited in *Athenaeum*, 5th January 1901. Macaulay, *Hist.* 1907 edn. p. 540, speaks of Penn lying hid in London for some months and then stealing down to the coast of Sussex and escaping to France. This escape to France is based on Luttrell, *Brief Relation*, ii. 286 (Sept.), and is quite unreliable.
[7] Janney's *Life*, p. 378.
[8] *Ibid.* pp. 390, 391.

his high courage and inward spiritual experience gave him heart amid the oppression of outward circumstance. He had been sailing against wind and tide all his life.[1] Literary work became the solace of his retirement, a short preface to John Burnyeat's *Works*, a much fuller one, written about August 1691,[2] to those of Robert Barclay, in November an Epistle called *Just Measures*,[3] in October 1692, a *Key*, or summary statement of Friends' Principles,[4] and in the same year answers to some adverse remarks on Friends in the *Athenian Mercury*; while in 1693 he wrote the remarkable *Essay towards the Present and Future Peace of Europe*,[5] and, before July, the fine Preface to the *Journal* of Fox.[6] Of greater interest for our present purpose is the series of pithy reflections on life, published anonymously the same year, called *Some Fruits of Solitude*.[7]

"Reader," says Penn, "this Enchiridion I present thee with is the Fruit of Solitude—a school few care to learn in, though none instructs us better. . . . The author blesseth God for his retirement; and kisses that gentle hand which led him into it. For, though it should prove barren to the world, it can never do so to him. He has now had some time he could call his own— a property he was never so much master of before—in which he has taken a view of himself and the world; and observed wherein he hath hit and missed the mark, what might have been done, what mended and what avoided in his human conduct, together with the omissions and excesses of others, as well societies and governments as private families and persons. And he verily thinks, were he to live over his life again, he could not only, with God's grace, serve Him but his neighbour and himself

---

[1] Penn's own expression, cited from Fiske, *The Dutch and Quaker Colonies in America*, ii. 307.
[2] Minutes of Morning Meeting, 14th September 1691.
[3] *Ibid.* 9th November.   [4] *Ibid.* 7th, 14th November 1692.
[5] See *post*, Chap. XX. This did not go to the Morning Meeting, but was afterwards included in his *Works*, 1726 edn. ii. pp. 838-848.
[6] Minutes of Morning Meeting, 24th July 1693.
[7] The book was licensed 24th May 1693 (see Gosse's edn.) and ran into many editions. In 1718, the year of his death, it was printed, apparently from a revised and enlarged MS. of the author's, together with *More Fruits of Solitude*, first printed in 1702, and this has become the standard text. (See Gosse's edn.) Penn's authorship is stated explicitly in Besse's *Life* prefixed to *Works*, 1726 edn. i. 141, cf. *Quaker Post-bag*, p. 27, and both parts of the *Fruits* are printed in *Works*, 1726 edn. i. 818-858. See now the convenient edition, London, 1900, Freemantle, with preface by Edmund Gosse.

better than he hath done, and have seven years of his time to spare. And yet perhaps he hath not been the worst or the idlest man in the world, nor is he the oldest."

The book is in Penn's most finished style, modelled on the *Maximes* of La Rochefoucauld, the *Pensées* of Pascal, and the *Caractères* of La Bruyère, which by their example had done much to break up the heavy periods of English prose into short sentences. But the urbanity is Penn's own; and is all the more striking when we remember that for four years he had been "hunted up and down, and could never be allowed to live quietly in city or country."[1] The solitude was passed in outward gloom; but an inward sun had made its fruits mellow. Dr. Edmund Gosse says of the book:

Life was not bitter to Penn. ... His heart is on his sleeve. ... Nothing is more amusing than Penn's rooted dislike to reserve :— "They are next to unnatural," he says, "that are not communicable." Nor has he any foible for political prudence; ... "A cunning man is a kind of lurcher in politics." ... We see Penn revealed as a man of no great subtlety or *finesse d'esprit*, but as an honest and shrewd observer of life, Quakerish, utilitarian, optimistic.

In December 1879, when Robert Louis Stevenson was wandering in weary convalescence about the streets of San Francisco, this "sweet, dignified and wholesome book," retrieved from a chance bookstall, brought him refreshment and new heart. "I found it," he says, "in all times and places a peaceful and sweet companion. ... There is not the man living—no, nor recently dead—that could put, with so lovely a spirit, so much honest, kind wisdom into words."[2]

His fortunes were now mending. His friends at Court, on the King's return from the French War in the autumn of 1693, took occasion to reopen his case.[3] The

[1] Letter, beginning of 1692, in Janney's *Life*, p. 378.
[2] See Gosse's Preface.
[3] The Letter to Thomas Lloyd, cited below, dated 11th December, from Hoddesdon where his wife lay dying (Janney's *Life*, pp. 386, 387), is our most reliable authority. Besse, *Life* prefixed to *Works*, 1726 edn. i. 141, says: "In the latter end of the year 1693, through the mediation of his friends, the Lord Ranelagh, Lord Somers, Duke of Buckingham and Sir John Trenchard,

evidence against him had been already discredited by the character of the witnesses; his friends were satisfied that he had stayed in England because he would not leave in defiance of the Government;[1] and Rochester, Ranelagh, and Sidney, the three Lords who saw the King in the matter, were able to assure him that they had long known Penn, some of them for thirty years, and had never known him to do an ill thing, but many good offices, to which, writes Penn, "King William answered, That I was his old acquaintance, as well as theirs, and that I might follow my business as freely as ever; and that he had nothing to say to me." On this they procured the King's leave to tell his mind to the Secretary of State, Sir John Trenchard, who was seen by Sidney as Penn's greatest acquaintance. Penn adds:

And the Secretary, after speaking himself and having it from King William's own mouth, appointed me a time to meet him at home; and did with the Marquis of Winchester; and told me I was as free as ever; and as he doubted not my prudence about my quiet living; for he assured me I should not be molested or injured in any of my affairs, at least while he held that post. The Secretary is my old friend, and one I served after the Duke of Monmouth and Lord Russell's business; I carried him in my coach to Windsor, and presented him to King James; and, when the Revolution came, he bought my four horses that carried us. It was about three or four months before the Revolution. The Lords spoke the 25th of November and he discharged me on the 30th.[2]

---

or some of them, he was admitted to appear before the King and Council, where he so pleaded his innocency that he was acquitted." Penn's letter seems a complete account of the transaction, while Besse's use of the expression, "or some of them," suggests imperfect information. It is not therefore safe to conclude that he appeared before the King and Council during the six days.

[1] This makes it likely that the Letter to Rochester in Janney's *Life*, pp. 380, 381, belongs here, and was sent him for use with the King. Penn there states his intention of going to Pennsylvania, but cannot accept liberty on condition of going, and so be looked on as exiled.

[2] In this extract, the words "and as he doubted not my prudence" are obscure, unless we take "as" in its vernacular use of "that." Macaulay, *Hist.* 1907 edn. p. 540, throws a last poisoned shaft at Penn, saying: "The return which he made for the lenity with which he had been treated does not much raise his character. Scarcely had he again begun to harangue in public about the unlawfulness of war, when he sent a message earnestly exhorting James to make an immediate descent on England with thirty thousand men." This is

It is pleasant, amid the selfishness of the times, to find this case of gratitude in high places.

Penn's friends continued active on his behalf, and with their help he secured in August 1694 a re-grant of Pennsylvania from the Crown, on conditions.[1] The military weakness of a Quaker settlement was the chief preoccupation of the Government, and before the Committee of Trade and Plantations Penn stated his intention of going to the colony to attend to its affairs and to provide for its safety; and to that end undertook to transmit all orders received from the Home Government; and went on to say, in words which he would find it difficult to make good, that he doubted not the compliance of the colony with such orders and with any directions that might be sent "for the supplying such quota of men, or the defraying their part of such charges, as Their Majesties shall think necessary for the safety and preservation of Their Majesties' dominions in that part of America." He further undertook to retain Governor Fletcher's deputy-governor, Penn's cousin, Colonel William Markham, and engaged that if the colony should fail to comply with the orders that the Home Government might send, he would then submit the direction of military affairs to Their Majesties' pleasure.[2]

Penn was fully alive to the stringency of these conditions. He wrote to Pennsylvania in November,[3] explaining to Friends that if the position was not entirely satisfactory, they must not take it amiss, for neither the straitness of the times—that is, I suppose, the War with France — nor his engagements to the Lords of the Plantations allowed another method at that time. He would make them entirely easy as soon as he could. "We must creep," he wrote, "where we cannot go; and it is as necessary for us, in the things of this life, to be

---

based on a Paper of Information from England, collected by a fourth-rate spy, whose evidence is quite untrustworthy. For the good offices to Trenchard, cf. Lawton's account in Janney's *Life*, pp. 301, 302.

[1] *Cal. State Papers, Dom.*, 1694-95, p. 261, dated 11th August 1694.

[2] See the important Minutes of the Committee of Trade and Plantations on 1st and 3rd August 1694, given in Janney's *Life*, pp. 395, 396.

[3] Letter from Bristol, 24th November 1694, in Janney's *Life*, pp. 396, 397.

wise as to be innocent." By December[1] he was arranging that the Lords of the Plantations should allow the civil affairs of the colony to be in Quaker hands, and treat the retention of military power by Markham as answering their intention and the substance of his engagement. Matters were adjusted on this basis, but the military question was bound to create chronic difficulty, since Pennsylvania was a province of the Crown as well as a settlement of peace-loving Quakers. We praise the Christian statesmanship and daring faith which adventured the " Holy Experiment "; and in common justice must make allowance for the defects in realization which were inherent in the scheme whose inception we applaud. Penn held from the Crown, and its sovereign power and policy were liable on occasion to override his own. If this be understood, we shall admire his large measure of success, within the limitations of his grant.[2]

He now resumed service in the Society ; but found that his conduct during the recent troubles was censured by an influential section of Friends, headed by two of the sons-in-law of Margaret Fox—William Meade, who had stood with him in the dock at the famous trial, and Thomas Lower. Writing to Margaret Fox on the 2nd December, immediately after Penn's discharge, Lower says :[3]

Yesterday, at Bull and Mouth Meeting, appeared William Penn. . . . Friends thought he would first have appeared

---

[1] Janney's *Life*, p. 396.
[2] For a further discussion of the question, see *post*, Chap. XXI. President Isaac Sharpless, in *A Quaker Experiment in Government*, p. 194, thinks Penn disingenuous in assuring the Committee of Plantations that he "doubts not ' the compliance of his colony with orders from the Home Government, "He must have known that these Quaker bodies would do nothing of the kind. . . . It looks as if he intended to promise a course of action for the future, and then to unload this promise upon a body which would not redeem it." Cf. his similar criticism in *Quakers in the American Colonies*, p. 426. But it is fair to say that Penn had also agreed that if compliance was not forthcoming he would then submit the direction of military affairs to the Crown's pleasure, which shows that the Committee was aware of the practical difficulties that surrounded the question. J. W. Graham, *William Penn*, p. 223, surmises that the Minute of the Committee may have overstated the undertaking given. President Sharpless's estimate of the weaknesses and strength of Penn's character in *Quakers in the American Colonies*, pp. 422-436, is an eminently fair and candid piece of work.
[3] Thirnbeck MSS., printed in *J.F.H.S.* ix. 176.

amongst them and have given them some satisfaction privately touching the scandal brought upon Truth and Friends by his long absconding and the matters laid to his charge; and not to have appeared in the offering of his gift, before he had been reconciled to them he had given offence unto. But his appearing first to preach in a public meeting before reconciliation looks too triumphant and high; and is not well resented amongst some Friends here.

In the following month Lower sends his mother-in-law the draft of "what was upon my mind to offer, and which I have since offered, to W. P. as an expedient for a reconciliation betwixt him and Friends." [1]

First, for W. P. to write a tender, reconciling epistle unto all Friends, as in the love and wisdom of God it shall be opened unto him:

Secondly, in the closure thereof to insert as followeth, or to the following effect:—"And if in any things during these late revolutions I have concerned myself, either by words or writings (in love, pity or goodwill to any in distress), further than consisted with Truth's honour or the Church's peace, I am sorry for it; and the Government having passed it by, I desire it may be by you also. That so we may be all kept and preserved in the holy tie and bond of love and peace to serve God and His Truth in our generation, to the honour of His holy Name and Truth, which will render us acceptable to God and more precious one unto another and finally bring us, through Jesus Christ our Lord, to the participation of that immortal crown, which is prepared for all that continue faithful in well-doing unto the end."

William Meade felt so strongly about Penn that he objected to his writing the Preface to Fox's *Journal*. In this same January the perusal by Friends of the *Journal*, as revised by Thomas Ellwood, had been completed, and Meade was prepared to advance the money for setting the press to work. The Preface had also been passed; but the Morning Meeting, which dealt with these matters, offered to re-read it with Meade and Lower present, and

---

[1] Letter from London, 22nd January 1694, printed in Clarkson's *Life*, 1849 edn. p. 225, without a date. I have supplied date and followed text of Letter, as preserved among my late father's papers. The reference to "any in distress" will refer primarily to Penn's letters to James.

to print it, either with the *Journal*, or with the *Epistles* of Fox, as the relations might prefer. The attempt at conference failed; and it was reported in April that Meade refused to hear the Preface, "being resolved it shall not be printed with the *Journal*, if he can help it." Upon this it was handed back to Penn, with liberty to print on his own account.[1] Accordingly it is lacking from many copies of the first folio edition.[2]

The Fell circle and a number of other Friends, including in some degree the veteran Quaker leader, George Whitehead, long remained dissatisfied; and the question was raised in the Yearly Meeting of 1698, not, I imagine, because Penn was absent in Ireland, but because Margaret Fox, then in her eighty-fourth year, was in London.[3] Thomas Gwin, of Falmouth, says:[4]

Being present when a paper was given in by some one, as a charge against a Friend then out of the nation, which occasioned great noise and was like to make parties, I was one of those nominated with many elder Friends for to examine and return our judgment to the meeting. In this I appeared for pacification and not for parties; and was troubled to see the peace of the Churches like to be rent on these occasions.

John Tomkins, the collector of the first three parts of the obituary notices of Friends, known as *Piety Promoted*, and a warm partisan of Penn, writes:[5]

Friends [at the Yearly Meeting] have not been without some exercise, particularly by the means of M[argaret] F[ox], whose extreme age some few did impose upon to her dishonour, and the grief of many faithful brethren. But Friends would not admit of anything of that kind and all ended well. . . . W. P.'s

---

[1] Minutes of 15th January, 19th and 28th March, and 9th April 1694.

[2] The copy I have used is one of these, and also has the original p. 309, to the alteration of which Meade also objected. (See Smith's *Catalogue*, i. 691.)

[3] For references to this dissatisfaction, in addition to those quoted in the notes, see *Quaker Post-bag*, pp. 58, 121, 134, and *Quakers in the American Colonies*, p. 429, text and note; also Thomas Story, *Journal*, pp. 134-137. Story calls them a "shameless and implacable party," and their work the "fruits of emulation and envy." We have already noted that Furness Friends, presumably under Lower's influence, had returned a negative answer to the questions administered by James (see *ante*, p. 144), and there was no doubt a strong political aversion to Penn on the part of Lower and others. Cf. *post*, pp. 207, 208.

[4] MS. Journal.

[5] Letter to Sir John Rodes, 18th July 1698, in *Quaker Post-bag*, pp. 139-142.

service [in Ireland] has been unspeakably to the honour of Truth and his own reputation therein . . . so that what his adversaries can do amounts to no more than the striking a lighted torch against a post, which occasions its light to burn the brighter.

In the following year, Margaret Rous, another of the Fell family, writes to her mother that they hope that if Penn condemn his misdoings, though but in part, things will grow better among Friends, and Truth will come up in its ancient purity over the false wrong spirit that has hurt it.[1] Whitehead, when he saw the King in April 1695, on William remarking that some Friends were disaffected to the Government, confessed that they had been lately aspersed " with such nicknames as Meadites and Pennites, as if we set up sect-masters among us, yet own no such thing." [2]

Penn's friendship for James had brought odium upon Friends who had no Jacobite leanings. England, for years after the Revolution, was in a perilously unstable state, with a rival Court at St. Germain and the French menace an imminent danger. It seemed intolerable to many in the Society that their most prominent member, by station and capacity, should be branded as a dangerous Jacobite. They failed to see that, in becoming a Friend, Penn had not ceased to belong, by birth and breeding, to the governing class, and had lived out his Quakerism in that difficult sphere with perfect sincerity, though not without an admixture of censurable actions, due for the most part to his over-trusting and sanguine nature. To us the Founder of Pennsylvania, the vindicator of justice to native races, the framer of laws which presaged the Constitution of the United States, and the champion of liberty of conscience, shines in his true greatness; and we agree that a statesman may also be a spiritually-minded Christian. The more simple-minded Friends of his own day were of the same opinion. They could not understand his greatness, but rejoiced in his service for the Church, and were content to feel

---

[1] Helen G. Crosfield, *Margaret Fox*, p. 231 (Letter of 13th June 1699); cf. p. 230. [2] *Christian Progress*, p. 639.

his spiritual power and to love him for himself. But it is not surprising that others, of less simplicity, especially those who resented his politics and gave ear to the suspicions that had gathered round him, magnified his weaknesses and judged him harshly. In this matter, indeed, the men of his own governing class could do him better justice and give his faults readier forgiveness.

CHAPTER VII

THE AFTERMATH OF TOLERATION

We take the liberty further to acquaint you that, though in the beginning and some time afterwards, our Friends in this city [of Bristol] were exposed to great hardships and sufferings, yet we have at this time great cause to be truly thankful to God, who has in His good providence so ordered it that we enjoy great tranquillity in that respect ; and the magistrates now, and for a long time past, have been very favourable to us ; so that we have free access to 'em, and a candid treatment in all cases reasonable. And therefore, as we do not perfectly know the reason of your desiring these accounts [of the first ministering Friends who travelled to this city and what sufferings ensued], so we doubt not but you will think it necessary to act with that caution in a thing of this nature as may give no occasion either to the Government in general, under whom we enjoy so many favours, or the magistrates of this city in particular.—From the Men's Meeting at Bristol, 2nd January 1721, in answer to the request of the Meeting for Sufferings. (See *F.P.T.* p. 11.)

No single life has done more than Penn's to raise the name and establish the ideals of the Society of Friends. The historian would be unworthy of his office who did not give it a full place in his narrative, in its changing light and shade. But we must now return to the more commonplace task of showing the way in which Quakerism sought to profit by its newly-granted toleration. We leave the larger air in which Penn so adventurously moved, and follow the cautious and pedestrian guidance of George Whitehead.

Still on the right side of sixty, and a man who had borne hard persecution and never spared himself in efforts on behalf of suffering Friends, he was now the leading survivor of the First Publishers of Truth, and would guide the policy of the Society for the next quarter of a century. He was the embodiment of worthy and drab respectability, devoid of genius, and of little humour, but industrious and politic, one who had achieved so much for Quakerism that he no longer sought fresh adventures or inspired new enthusiasms. There was little mercury in his composition; but he was a personable man, and could manage a royal interview or a sitting of the Yearly Meeting with the deferential persuasiveness born of long experience and an intimate knowledge of his subject. The repository of the Quaker tradition of the past, he had persuaded himself, and was often able to satisfy others, that Friends had always behaved and believed after the pattern of his own orthodoxy. Such men seem born to become the pillars of the Church that is privileged to count them as its members. He might serve as an efficient and eminent example of the Nonconformist office-bearer, once familiar to us all, who was jealously devoted to his beloved Society, and drudged without stint in its service, but was somewhat withheld by its set horizons from larger vision of the Kingdom of God. With it all, Whitehead was at heart a man of deep spiritual experience, and I like to think of him, in the Bull and Mouth meeting, in 1713, when an old man of seventy-seven, reviving the well-known story of John, the beloved disciple :-

. . . that when he was grown old and forced to be led to the assembly of God's people, in that day his sermon was short; "Little children" or "Dear children, love one another"; and, as it's said, being asked why he always used that exhortation, his answer was: That, if they abode in the true faith and loved one another, it was the substance of all religion; for, without charity and true love, all is as nothing.[1]

The Revolution of 1688 had been the resultant of many forces, dexterously managed by a governing class that had no illusions, but great practical patriotism. But a settlement that subverted the Divine right of kings, gave tolerance to Dissent, and committed England to the

---

[1] Peter Briggin's Diary, 2nd October 1713, in *Eliot Papers*, No. II. p. 55. Whitehead survived till 1723, and was buried in Bunhill Fields. The story is found in Jerome (*Comm. in Galat.* vi. 10).

arduous European struggle against French domination, was essentially precarious. The rival claims of James and afterwards of the Pretender, the anxieties as to the succession through the failure of issue to Mary and Anne, and a sequence of bad harvests from 1693 to '99, aggravated the position. The reign of Anne ended with the Tory party in full power. Had the Queen survived only a few months a Jacobite succession would probably have been secured. As events fell, the House of Hanover came in and the Whigs were established in their long rule.

During this period of bitter and unstable politics, the defence of toleration became more and more identified with the Whig cause. Instead of Jacobites like Penn and Barclay accepting indulgences for the Society from James, we now find the leading Friends who supported the Revolution making favour with the Whigs, in both cases at some sacrifice of consistency. The Quaker Church, effectively organized as a state within the State, was now mainly concerned with preserving its own quiet way of life; and, driven in on itself by storms of persecution and by the growth of a narrowing discipline, was no longer aflame with a mission to the world. But no religious community can rightly live *in vacuo*; its members, unless disabled by the State, have to reconcile their responsibilities and common life as citizens with their duties as Christians. The Society, indeed, yearned for quiet; but when the Georgian years of ease came, they would be years of outward respectability and inward spiritual decline.

The yearning expressed itself in a letter, issued by Steven Crisp and George Whitehead with the Printed Epistle from the Yearly Meeting in 1692:

Away with those upbraiding characters of Jacobites and Williamites, Jemmites and Billites, &c., so used by the world's people one against another. . . . Let us have no such upbraiding distinctions in God's camp, nor anything tending to strife, sedition or discord; no more than of Whig and Tory, long since judged out and testified against.
And show forth your affection to Christ, to His kingdom and

government, by a quiet life and peaceable subjection unto the higher powers that God is pleased to set over us; which are at His disposing and not ours; it being our Christian duty to desire their good, and to persuade them to what good we can, for their safety and our ease and relief. . . .

O Friends, truth and innocency will live and work through all; and our ancient testimony and life therein will stand and continue the same through all revolutions and interchanges that God is pleased to bring or suffer among men, for causes best known to Himself; which therefore must not be the subjects of dispute or controversy among any of His people, His judgments being unsearchable and His ways past finding out. Wherefore let all study to be quiet and mind their own business, in God's holy fear, and none to be meddling or exercising themselves in things too high for them.

The Toleration Act had only given ease with respect to public worship and the Oaths of Allegiance. Its requirements as to the registration of meeting-places and the subscription of the Declarations were, during William's reign, generally observed.[1] But tithes had been excepted from the Act, and the personal disabilities of Friends in their private life remained.

In the matter of tithes and other ecclesiastical demands,[2] Acts were passed in 1696 and later, which afforded substantial relief by enabling two Justices to ascertain

---

[1] See reports from the counties in the Yearly Meeting Minutes. Yorkshire Q.M. in September 1689 made careful arrangements for registration; cf. J. W. Rowntree, *Essays and Addresses*, pp. 36-39. Wiltshire Q.M. arranged for this in August, Bristol Men's Meeting in December. Westmorland Q.M. had acted in July 1687, in connection with the Declaration of Indulgence by James II.; see *ante*, p. 130. *The Fleming MSS.* p. 267, 16th February and 3rd March 1690, speak of the Declarations being made at Ulverston by sixty Quakers and at Rydal by thirty-six. An entry in the *Middlesex County Records* (Sessions Books, 1689-1709, p. 341) records their taking by Richard Claridge in 1709, and calls them "the long test." To save complicating a sufficiently involved subject, I have not discussed the objection, taken chiefly in Ireland, to the reference to God in the various Declarations of Fidelity in force in this and subsequent reigns.

[2] A general Act for the more easy recovery of small tithes, etc., not exceeding the yearly value of 40s., was passed 7 & 8 Will. III. cap. 6, made perpetual 3 & 4 Ann. cap. 18, and extended to a yearly value of £10 by 53 Geo. III. cap. 127. The special Quaker Act was passed at the instance of the clergy (Besse, *Sufferings*, ii. 535), and was contained in clauses of the Affirmation Act of 1696, 7 & 8 Will. III. cap. 34. It covered a yearly value of £10, and was continued by 13 & 14 Will. III. cap. 4, and was made perpetual, and extended to church-rates, etc., by 1 Geo. I. cap. 6, and the yearly value was increased to £50 by 53 Geo. III. cap. 127. There is a full account of the matter, with references to the literature printed, in Gough, *History of the Quakers*, iv. 278-307. Under the Tithe Commutation Act, 6 & 7 Will. IV. cap. 71, tithe has now become a rent-charge, recoverable by distress.

VII THE AFTERMATH OF TOLERATION

what was due, and levy the amount by distress. But the Acts did not compel the adoption of this cheap and summary process; and the clergy could still carry their tithe cases before the Exchequer or the Ecclesiastical Courts. Relief from this superfluous persecution was attempted in the Georgian days of Whig domination. It was shown that in the forty years prior to 1736 above 1100 Friends had been prosecuted before these Courts, of whom 302 had been imprisoned and nine had died in prison. In ten selected cases, £800 had been taken in respect of original demands amounting altogether to £15. Walpole in his elections had been brought into much contact with Friends, and easily passed through the Commons a Bill making compulsory the summary method for levying tithe. Much to his chagrin, it was lost in the Lords through the opposition of the Bishops.[1] As late as 1795 seven Friends of Lothersdale in Yorkshire were imprisoned for tithe in York Castle for over two years, and were only freed under a special clause inserted in an Act of Parliament. One of the seven died a prisoner.[2]

The general disabilities of Friends after the Toleration Act were, however, mainly due to the necessity for taking oaths. Without these, they could not sue for their debts, nor carry through their transactions with the customs and the excise, nor defend their titles, nor give evidence: they were, in strict law, unable to prove wills or be admitted to copyholds, or take up their freedom in corporations, and in some places they were kept from voting at elections. Nor could they answer prosecutions in ecclesiastical courts for tithes and church-rates.[3] By the end of 1690 a Bill on the subject had passed the Lords, but fell through with the adjournment and subsequent prorogation.[4] The attempt showed the difficulties of the question, which became during the next thirty years a thing of sharp controversy among Friends.

[1] Lecky, *Hist. of England in the Eighteenth Century*, 1913 edn. i. 325, 326.
[2] See *The Yorkshireman*, iv. 332-340; George Baker, *Unhistoric Acts*, pp. 84-88.
[3] Whitehead, *Christian Progress*, pp. 644, 641.
[4] See letters of Henry Gouldney to Sir John Rodes, 22nd November and 10th December 1690, in *Quaker Post-bag*, pp. 47-51, and George Fox, MS. *Itinerary Journal* at Dev. Ho. 29th October 1690.

In Dryden's curious religious bestiary in favour of Roman Catholicism, called *The Hind and Panther*, we are told that

> Among the timorous kind the quaking Hare
> Professed neutrality, but would not swear;

but, though the best known of Quaker testimonies, this was the one least intelligible to the outside world. It was a branch of the witness for a single standard of life, in speech, dress, and intercourse. Oaths had been allowed in Old Testament times; but Christ Himself, who had said "Swear not at all," was now the true bond of society.[1] Disciples who possessed His Spirit would speak the truth in love on all occasions, and would be disloyal to Him if they allowed the outward form and ritual of the oath to constitute the sanction for their truth-speaking. Friends objected to the substitution of this unreal and magical sanction for the genuine one provided by the fear of God and the love of Christ in the heart; they could not accept the kissing of the book or the lifting up of the hand, nor the imprecatory words which said, "So help me God [in the Day of Doom]." At the same time, they often stated in their own language on solemn occasions the substance of the oath, by acknowledging that God, the Searcher of hearts, was present, and that the truth was being spoken in His fear.[2] Any rigid formula to this effect, however, unless of the simplest and least formal kind, would offend the conscience of many, as substituting some other sanction than that furnished by their allegiance to Christ. As regards the civil effect of the oath, the matter was much easier, for Friends were always willing that the penalties for perjury should equally attach to any false Affirmation.

In the first abortive Bill, the Affirmation was to be said bareheaded; and the form prescribed included the words: "I call God to witness, and appeal to Him as Judge of the truth of what I shall say." Many Friends

---

[1] *Ante*, p. 15. Cf. Howgill's *Works*, p. 427, and *Treatise of Oaths*, by Penn and Richard Richardson (1675), in Penn's *Works*, 1726 edn. i. 612-672.
[2] See Barclay, *Apology*, 1678 edn. p. 376.

could not adopt this; though some would have accepted it with reluctance. Others, besides Friends, considered with reason that such an Affirmation was an oath.

The question, What expressions Friends could accept, was debated for several days in the Yearly Meeting of 1692; and the representatives from the counties were asked their opinions one by one. With only five or six exceptions they approved such terms as "before God"—the phrase in the Declaration of Fidelity provided for the Quakers by the Toleration Act[1]—"in the sight of God," "in the presence of God," or "in the fear of God," and this was recorded as the agreement of the Society.[2] The Meeting for Sufferings was encouraged to pursue the matter,[3] and made further efforts at relief.[4] Little progress, however, resulted until April 1695, when Whitehead, soliciting the King for the release of some Quakers still in prison, asked him to stand their friend when the question was reintroduced, and referred him to the case of the Mennonites, who, a hundred years before, had been allowed by the then Prince of Orange to have their word accepted instead of an oath. The King plied him with questions; he did not understand the position of Quaker ministers, nor the divisions in the Society, and thought some Friends disaffected to the Government. But the politic Quaker evidently satisfied him on these points; for William promised his good offices, and proved as good as his word.[5] After careful canvassing of members, a Bill was brought in in December, and became law in the following May. It was passed for seven years; and the Affirmation finally inserted ran as follows:

---

[1] But with the addition of the words, "and the world," which softened the meaning. See *ante*, p. 155.

[2] *A Letter From a Satisfied To a Dissatisfied Friend concerning The Solemn Affirmation* (1713), p. 14, and Yearly Meeting Minutes.

[3] *Yearly Meeting Epistles*, 1681-1857, i. 66.

[4] Thos. Lower to Margt. Fox, 2nd December 1693, in *J.F.H.S.* ix. 177, from the Thirnbeck Colln.; and Sewel, ii. 510-516. There are frequent Minutes of the Meeting for Sufferings on the subject.

[5] Whitehead, *Christian Progress*, pp. 637-640, and for the Mennonite precedent, *ibid.* pp. 638, 651-652. Cf. *Life of Gilbert Latey*, pp. 133-141; John Taylor's *Journal*, 1830 edn. pp. 85, 92, 93. In January 1694, the Meeting for Sufferings had procured from Holland abstracts of the "placates" in favour of the Mennonites.

I, A. B., do declare in the presence of Almighty God, the Witness of the truth of what I say.[1]

This wording was only accepted by Friends under pressure. They were advised that it was useless to propose a bare affirmation without reference to God; and accordingly, pursuant to the agreement of the Yearly Meeting, accepted the expression "in the presence of Almighty God," "which," says Whitehead, "we durst not gainsay, lest we should be deemed atheistical, it being our principle that God is omnipresent and omniscient also." In this form the Bill, after full debate, passed the Commons by large majorities; but, in the Lords, the Bishops urged the addition of other words, such as, "I call God to witness and judge," or "as Witness and Judge," or "I call God to record upon my soul and appeal to God as Judge." Whitehead explained in the lobby to several peers that any such words invoking God as Judge would be tantamount to an oath; but they urged that to save the Bill, some expression at least should be added which without direct invocation of God should acknowledge Him as the Witness of what was said. Whitehead accepted this, "forasmuch as God is really Witness to the truth sincerely declared, He being omniscient as well as omnipresent"; and on this over-subtle compromise the Bill was carried. Dr. Tillotson, six years earlier, had preached a sermon on the lawfulness of oaths, in which he said that an oath was a solemn appeal to God, as a Witness of the truth of what was said. It was this definition, improved by calling God "the" Witness, that the Bishops had accepted, and they at least considered it a solemn oath.[2]

To agree to words which could be regarded as an oath by the civil authority that administered the Affirma-

---

[1] For the proceedings on the Bill, see Whitehead, *Christian Progress*, pp. 646-655, and Minutes of Meeting for Sufferings. The Act (7 & 8 Will. III. cap. 34) is printed in Sewel, ii. 523-526, and did not extend to evidence in criminal cases, nor to service on a jury or in any office or place of profit in the Government. In order to influence the Peers, the Meeting for Sufferings had three hundred copies of the Paper against Plotting printed, and a hundred copies of Barclay's *Works* bound in calf-leather for distribution.

[2] Thomas Story, *Life*, pp. 761, 762.

tion, but as less than an oath by those that took it, did not provide an honest solution of the question. Moreover, some Friends were already uneasy at the phrase "in the presence of Almighty God," although approved by the Yearly Meeting. John Fisher of Hoddesdon, who in 1682 had suffered long imprisonment on a *praemunire* for refusing the Oath of Allegiance,[1] had published in 1692 *A Position and Testimony against All Swearing*,[2] in which he cautioned Friends against "the danger of venturing to use, instead of an oath, any higher form or manner of speech than Christ hath prescribed and allowed them, lest they be drawn into an oath unawares." Many others were unable to satisfy themselves that the further words which Whitehead had accepted naturally bore the refined general sense that he was pleased to put upon them. To their minds their plain meaning was to invoke God as Witness, and this was made the sanction for the truth of the evidence given. The prescribed formula, accordingly, was felt by them to partake of the nature of an oath, though stripped of the accessories and the imprecation; and constituted a sanction for truth-speaking, which obscured that provided by allegiance to Christ.

These views had already found expression. In January 1694, the Wiltshire Quarterly Meeting wrote desiring that the matter "be no otherwise solicited than that Friends be left to their Yea and Nay, free from a set form of speech."[3] Irish Friends had written to the same effect. The Meeting for Sufferings was alive to the adverse feeling; for it issued at the beginning of May 1696 an Epistle to Friends, mainly directed to satisfying any who had doubts.[4] This contains a careful *catena*

---

[1] Besse, *Sufferings*, i. 252.
[2] Published anonymously under the name "Philothrenes." Richard Claridge, *The Novelty and Nullity of Dissatisfaction*, 1714 edn. p. 163, attributes the piece to him, partly on the ground that, if you allow Ph to stand for F, the author's surname is contained in the word Philothrenes. I suspect Penn to be the writer of the Postscript, which closes with "*Vale*," quite in his style.
[3] Q.M. Minutes, The Devizes, 1st Jan. 1694.
[4] Printed Epistle from Meeting for Sufferings, "by their order 17th 2nd. mo. and 1st 3rd. mo. 1696." I add the *catena* of passages cited, in case any readers desire to pursue the subject further: George Fox, 1655, *Beginnings of Quakerism*, p. 179; 1674, *Journ.* 1694 edn. p. 399; Richard Farnsworth, 1655, at Banbury,

of passages, showing that leading Friends, on solemn occasions, had felt free to use such phrases as "in the presence of God," "the Lord is Witness," "God is my Record," and the like. Charles II. had asked Richard Hubberthorne at the time of the Restoration :

> But can you not promise as before the Lord, which is the substance of the oath?
>
> *R. H.*—Yes, what we do affirm, we can promise before the Lord, and take Him to our Witness in it ; but our so promising hath not been accepted ; but the ceremony of an oath they have stood for, without which all other things were accounted of no effect.[1]

And when the Quaker Act of 1662 was under discussion, the paper of objections, prepared by Friends, had said :

> We are willing at all times, and upon every good occasion, to affirm or deny in Yea or Yes, in Nay or No, and that as in the presence of God, or, God is our Witness, or, We speak the truth in Christ, &c. ; we are ready to give testimony in all lawful cases on this wise.[2]

In 1679, '80, and '88, Friends had offered to subscribe Tests beginning, "I, A. B., do solemnly in the presence of God, and in my conscience, profess."[3]

The Epistle must have reassured many by its ample show of authority for the course taken ; but conscientious objections, developed at a time when the question has been faced as a living practical issue, cannot be overborne by any array of precedents, however imposing, drawn from a period when there was no prospect of relief on any terms. It is the living issue itself that reveals to men the real extent and grounds of their duty, and brings them to the moment of decisive judgment. In this case

---

The Saints' Testimony, p. 2 ; William Smith's *Works*, p. 125 ; Penington's *Works*, 1681 edn. pt. i. p. 319 ; Francis Howgill's *Works*, pp. 677, 679, 680 ; Samuel Fisher's *Works*, pp. 803-805, and Answer to Bishop Gauden, pp. 70, 91 ; Edward Burrough's *Works*, pp. 773, 774 ; Thos. Ellwood's *Truth Prevailing*, pp. 155-160 ; Robert Barclay's *Apology*, 1678 edn. p. 376, cf. *Works*, 1692 edn. p. 238 ; George Whitehead, *Case of the Quakers concerning Oaths*, 1675 ; William Penn, *Works*, 1726 edn. i. 464, ii. 794 ; and references given in text.

[1] Hubberthorne's *Works*, p. 269.
[2] Epistle from Meeting for Sufferings, pp. 6, 7.
[3] *Ibid.* pp. 21-23.

VII THE AFTERMATH OF TOLERATION 187

the swift education left many honestly satisfied and others honestly dissatisfied; though there was naturally a great mass of Friends of less independent mind, content to accept the accomplished and officially approved fact, with gratitude to the leaders whose efforts had secured it. At the Yearly Meeting in June, the ease obtained was gratefully accepted by most Friends; but out of forty-four districts that reported, fifteen were silent, and eleven used qualifying expressions. Friends of Worcestershire, for example, "are thankful to God for this little ease; and hopes the Lord will make way for more; and Friends' care [of the Meeting for Sufferings] they greatly esteem and acknowledge."

Westmorland Friends referred guardedly to the matter; and at the end of the year addressed the Meeting for Sufferings, desiring a further improvement which might be easier for some tender spirits.[1] The Yearly Meeting itself acknowledged the great favour shown, and added:

> Inasmuch as 'tis evident that the words ... are not alike easy and satisfactory unto all Friends, it is the sense and desire of this meeting that all Friends ... will walk charitably and tenderly one towards another and not judge or think hardly one of another, for either using or not using the liberty granted by the Act.[2]

Irish Friends, who at this time were conspicuous for their zeal, took no benefit under the English Act, and looked on the words with disfavour. At their Half-Year's Meeting in May all the representatives answered, man by man after the English precedent, that they would rather suffer than subscribe any such thing, one Friend only asking for time to consider. The same method was pursued in the subordinate Meetings with a like result. Strong representations were made to England, and at a select meeting chosen by the London Yearly Meeting of 1697, and held in May, it was agreed that endeavours should be used to procure further relief to the general ease and satisfaction of all; and that when way should

---

[1] Q.M. Minute, 1st January 1697.
[2] See Yearly Meeting Minutes and Minute as printed in *A Letter From a Satisfied To a Dissatisfied Friend*, pp. 15, 16.

be made for this, " a fair and friendly correspondence shall be held with Friends in Ireland, as of other parts, to have things of that nature carried by a general consent." Irish Friends accordingly appointed representatives, who should be ready to go to London when called on.[1]

At the beginning of 1702 the Affirmation Act was renewed for a further term of years by 13 & 14 Will. III. cap. 4; but the Meeting for Sufferings failed to give the Irish Friends adequate notice.[2] They came up to Dublin, ready to cross by the first ship, only to hear that the Bill was in Committee, and likely to pass speedily. Is not this, they wrote, " a violation of the agreement in the year 1697, and, if so, may be of bad consequence and a very ill precedent to others?" Westmorland Friends reached London in time, and met with "hard exercise and travail," but bore their testimony against the Solemn Affirmation and the spirit that tended to a breach of unity.[3] Ten years later, when this second Act was running out, Westmorland consulted all its meetings, and found Friends unanimous for soliciting an Affirmation easy for all, and failing this, did not wish any attempt made to continue the Act.[4] Friends in the North of Scotland, to whom the Act did not extend, were also in strong opposition, as appears from a frank correspondence between Robert Barclay, the son of the Apologist, and George

---

[1] See London Yearly Meeting Minutes of select meeting held 26th, 27th May 1697, and the Minutes of the Half-Year's Meetings, May and November 1696, and May 1698, and of Leinster Province Meeting, 26th Sept. 1696. The Half-Year's Meeting and Leinster Province Meeting Records are preserved at the meeting-house, Eustace Street, Dublin, and there are copies of many of the Minutes in Dev. Ho. Swarthm. Colln. v. No. 115. The Recording Clerk, Edith Webb, has also furnished me with the substance of the correspondence that passed between Dublin and London.

[2] The urgency of the political situation was no doubt the reason. See *post*, p. 191, and cf. Letter from John Tomkins to Sir John Rodes, 10th March 1702, in *Quaker Post-bag*, p. 178. The letter of the Meeting for Sufferings was dated 12th December 1701; the Bill was read a second time in the Commons before the end of January, and passed the Lords by the end of February.

[3] Q.M. Minutes, 2nd January, 3rd April 1702. In July the Q.M. accepted the conclusion of the Yearly Meeting held in May that when opportunity offered for an alteration representatives from the counties should go up to London in the matter.

[4] The proceedings can be traced in Minutes of the Q.M. 2nd January and 3rd April 1713, in a letter to the Yearly Meeting approved at an adjourned Q.M. 17th April, and in Minutes of Kendal M.M. 26th March and Kendal Preparative Meeting 4th March 1713: cf. Minute of Sedbergh M.M. 31st March.

VII THE AFTERMATH OF TOLERATION 189

Whitehead.¹ In a fruitless solicitation made to Parliament by dissatisfied Friends, after the Union with Scotland in 1707,² it was stated that they had the support of Scottish Friends and of many in the Northern Counties and divers other parts of England.³

It is worthy of remark that the dissatisfied districts were those which, during the same period, were most zealously opposing the consequences of the growth of wealth and worldliness among Friends by pressing a searching discipline on the Church.⁴ The "worldly" Friends who had prospered in trade and were anxious for the ease afforded by the Affirmation of 1696 were mostly Whig in their sympathies, and, accordingly, the division of feeling already existing between them and Friends of Jacobite leanings inflamed the situation.

The political bias which prejudiced the deeper issues is indicated in a paper by Margaret Fox, written in December 1697 from the house of her son-in-law William Meade, the leading Whig Friend. It roundly asserts that

... the rise and beginning of all this contest and differences was that Friends might not seek to this Power and Government for anything, which God hath now placed over the powers of darkness, praises to His holy name.⁵

---

[1] See *Reliquiae Barclaianae*, pp. 127, etc., containing letters from Barclay to Whitehead, 1711, and to the Aberdeen Q.M. correspondents in London; Whitehead's reply, 4th March 1712; further letter from Barclay in April; letter from Whitehead, 15th October 1713, and Barclay's reply in November; apparently Barclay's letter in April 1712 was not actually sent.

[2] See preface to Richard Claridge, *The Novelty and Nullity of Dissatisfaction*; cf. letter, Henry Gouldney to Barclay, 21st February 1708, in *Reliquiae Barclaianae*, p. 117.

[3] In 1714, at the height of the controversy, the Minutes of London Yearly Meeting show that, excepting Northumberland, all the Northern Q.M.'s were against renewing the old Affirmation, also Scotland and Ireland. In other parts, most Q.M.'s were satisfied, some were divided, Dorset was "mostly dissatisfied," and Somerset was against renewal. London was for renewal, but one M.M. in Middlesex was "partly dissatisfied." A Yearly Meeting Committee summarized the results as follows: 21 for renewal and 10 more for renewal than against, 2 equally divided, 6 against renewal and 4 more against than for, the nation of Ireland also against. Somerset was the chief centre of dissatisfaction in the South, and in 1715 (see Meeting for Sufferings Minutes, 15th April 1715) asked that no form of Affirmation be accepted, "but such as may be taken and complied with by the least child of God amongst us."

[4] See *post*, Chap. XVIII.

[5] W. F. Miller Colln. No. 14; cf. Richard Claridge, *The Novelty and Nullity of Dissatisfaction*, p. 4, marginal note.

William Penn, the leading Jacobite, on the other hand, had provided his Colony with a simple form of Affirmation for all.[1] A clause of the first "Great Law" of 1682 enacted that all witnesses should give evidence "by solemnly promising to speak the truth, the whole truth and nothing but the truth to the matter or thing in question." In 1696, when many non-Quakers had immigrated, the Affirmation was confined to those whose consciences did not permit them to swear. Seven years later, however, an order from Queen Anne brought into use the form prescribed by the English Act. Penn, who was now in England, after his second residence in Pennsylvania, strongly objected, and wrote in 1704:[2]

I do abhor the new Affirmation, carried here [in England] and then there [in Pennsylvania] by absolute faction; and, if I can, I will waive it. For I would rather Friends were never in power, so our old Affirmation were confirmed for Friends and others scrupulous, and oaths for the rest: unless a short way of bond's penalty for truth of what is said were made practicable and acceptable, as I have often thought it might be.

The Affirmation controversy was, as we have now shown, embittered both by party bias and by the crusade for discipline, and an atmosphere was created which hindered reconciliation on the direct issue involved. But, even had the Society been agreed, it would have been unable for some years to have secured further redress from Parliament.[3]

Toleration had been conceded by the Church and the Tories as a nauseous necessity. The Tests which excluded Dissenters from office had, however, been preserved against the wishes of the Whigs and the King. They were evaded

---

[1] See President Sharpless, *A Quaker Experiment in Government*, pp. 138-150, and *Quakers in the American Colonies*, pp. 471, 472. The question as to the form of Affirmation, which was settled in 1725, after its settlement in England, was complicated with the question of a Quaker magistrate administering an oath, which was only ended by the gradual abdication of judicial functions by Pennsylvanian Friends. It should perhaps be added that in affirming a jury a somewhat fuller form was used in Pennsylvania, bringing in the name of God, in much the same manner as in the Declaration under the Toleration Act: "In the presence of Almighty God and this Court, you shall promise well and truly to try, etc." (See *A Letter From a Satisfied To a Dissatisfied Friend*, p. 3.)

[2] Janney's *Life of Penn*, 1882 edn. p. 476.

[3] Cf. Thomas Story, Interview with Earl of Sunderland, *Life*, p. 754.

by some Nonconformists by what was called "occasional conformity"; and from 1697 onwards the High Church party made the suppression of this a main object of their policy. William had curbed this party by appointing Low Churchmen and Latitudinarians to the chief places in the Church, but extremists dominated the Lower House of Convocation, who "were only half loyal to the reigning sovereigns and were wild with hatred of Dissent."[1] The Parliament of January 1701 was strongly Tory; but in the face of the dangerous French aggression on Spain the King dissolved it, and the Whigs were in power when William died. Whitehead had skilfully taken advantage of the moment to secure, as we have seen, the continuance of the Affirmation Act. Anne was Tory and High Church, but the Whigs held a majority in the Lords. The Commons were at first Tory, but afterwards Whig, till the ill-advised persecution of the High Church parson, Dr. Sacheverell, for a sermon in 1710 against the doctrines of the Revolution, created a strong Tory reaction and left the Whigs in a hopeless minority during the last two Parliaments of the reign. The Occasional Conformity Bill was passed on a compromise with the Lords; and then by a *coup d'état* a Tory majority was secured in the Upper House by the creation of twelve new peers. In order to crush Dissent, the Schism Act was passed in 1714, confining all secondary education to Anglican teachers licensed by the Bishops; and, as Lecky says,[2]

There can be little doubt that, had the Tory ascendancy been but a little prolonged, the Toleration Act would have been repealed; and it is more than doubtful whether the purely political conquests of the Revolution would have survived.

It was during these years of Tory reaction that the question of continuing or amending the Affirmation Act had again to be faced, for it would expire in 1715.[3] Early in 1712 the dissatisfied Friends printed a *Solicita-*

---

[1] G. M. Trevelyan, *England under the Stuarts*, p. 451.
[2] Lecky, *Hist. of England in the Eighteenth Century*, 1913 edn. i. 120.
[3] It expired at the end of the next session, after eleven years from the end of the session after 22nd Nov. 1702. This session ended 3rd April 1704, so that the Act would have expired at the end of the session after 3rd April 1715.

tion, grounding their scruple on the mention of the name of God in the Affirmation;[1] and Whitehead wrote:[2]

> This late bustle in public solicitation against the name of God in the Solemn Affirmation has rendered us very little as a people very weak and inconsistent in the eye of the Government; and opened the mouths of many against Friends. It has greatly offended our friends in the Government and caused our adversaries to rejoice over us.

Long and inconclusive debates took place in the Yearly Meeting, both this and the following year, on the general subject, and on the question whether sufferings for refusing the Affirmation should be recorded with the other sufferings.[3] It was a trying time for the Friends who disliked faction. The account given by Thomas Gwin, of Falmouth, shows the contentious spirit that prevailed in the Yearly Meeting of 1712:[4]

> First-day the 8th [June], I was at Gracechurch Street Meeting, but . . . there were so many Friends and such different apprehensions in respect of the Affirmation that it appeared in public preaching; so I was silent that day. The week following we were daily at the Yearly Meeting, where we wanted not contests. The first dispute was in relation to entering the sufferings of such as refused to affirm on their entries of leather, which was refused by some, but, after a day's and a half's contention, was agreed to be entered, "for not making their entries as the law directs. . . ." After many days' debate, in which we came to no end, it [the question of continuing the Affirmation] was committed to eight Friends, four of each party, to viz., George Whitehead, Thomas Ellwood, Benjamin Coole, Joseph Wyeth, *pro*, and William Penn, Joseph Pike, Robert Haydock, Roderick Forbes, *contra*,[5] who agreed on the following Minute: That the dissatisfied should proceed to solicit next session, and, in case they obtained not, no endeavours should be used to destroy the

---

[1] Preface to Richard Claridge, *The Novelty and Nullity of Dissatisfaction*.
[2] Letter to Robert Barclay, 4th March 1712, in *Reliquiae Barclaianae*, p. 131. The Petition was rejected by the Commons in February 1712 (see Luttrell's *Brief Relation*, vi. 724).
[3] Diary of Peter Briggins, a Whig Quaker merchant in London, in *Eliot Papers*, No. II. p. 50.   [4] MS. *Journal*.
[5] Most of these Friends are referred to elsewhere: Robert Haydock was a brother of Roger Haydock of Penketh, near Warrington; Roderick Forbes represented the dissatisfied Friends in the North of Scotland (see *Reliquiae Barclaianae*, p. 128).

present Affirmation, and the satisfied to concur in such solicitations.¹ This took, they being wearied with disputes; and so it was quieted for the present. During all this controversy, I was as a fool or a child; I said almost nothing of either side, being altogether unwilling to promote faction . . . though those quarrels struck deep on my spirit, and I went in a bowed-down sense from day to day. . . . Other matters were soon finished; but this dispute made it hold eleven days, that might otherwise end in less than half the time. The parting meeting was not attended with usual freshness; and at least they seemed to strive who should have the last word. . . . [At the meetings for worship] the dissatisfied seemed to be the most living ministers, yet I still wanted what I found formerly in those meetings, that I mourned in secret and was ready to wish myself at home.

In 1713 the Yearly Meeting continued for two weeks:

". . . occasioned," says William Stout, the Lancaster grocer and ironmonger, whose *Autobiography* gives a good picture of the life of a Quaker country tradesman, "by reason the Act . . . was near expiring, and to consider how to solicit to have it renewed to the satisfaction of the whole of our Society. But, as now the High [Church] party, who was not all well-affected to us, had the ascendant with Parliament and with the Queen, it was by most Friends thought most proper to let it expire and wait for an opportunity to get it renewed to the satisfaction of all. But Friends in London and thereaway were for the present solicitation; which was condescended to, and a solicitation made to the Parliament, to the cost of many hundred pounds, but to no effect—being that most of our Friends in the late elections for Members of Parliament had voted against the now prevailing party in Parliament, which was not acceptable."²

It appears³ that the dissatisfied Friends stoutly resisted a Minute stating that the Meeting did not regard the form of the Affirmation as an oath, nor allowed reflections contrary to the advice given in 1692; and that Whitehead suggested two expedients, one that Friends should not repeat the words themselves, but should answer Yes

---

¹ For the full Minute see Yearly Meeting MS. Minutes.
² *Autobiography*, edited by J. Harland, 1851, p. 87. As to the MSS. of the *Autobiography* see *J.F.H.S.* xi. 142.
³ For these proceedings see Peter Briggins in *Eliot Papers*, No. II. pp. 50, 51. Reading this we should suppose the Minute rejected, but it was passed and sent down to the counties; see *Novelty and Nullity of Dissatisfaction*, p. 5. The Minutes of the Y.M.'s of 1713 and 1714 show the tension that existed.

or No when they were put to them by the Clerk to the Court, the other that the closing words should be omitted, "the Witness of the truth of what I say." He also proposed a free conference on the subject; and evidently did his best from his "satisfied" point of view to obtain an accommodation. The Printed Epistle, as we should expect, laid stress on the need for a reconciling spirit.

The Yearly Meeting of the following year, held after the failure to secure the Bill, with or without amendment, when the Queen was dying and the Schism Act was being hurried through Parliament, lasted for ten days.

"There seems at present," said the Printed Epistle, "to hang over us a cloud threatening a storm. Let us all watch and pray, and retire to our munition and stronghold in our spiritual rock and foundation, which standeth sure; that our God may defend, help and bless us, as His peculiar people, to the end of our days. . . . The God of Peace bruise Satan, the author of strife and confusion, under our feet; that primitive love and concord may be renewed and fully restored among His people."

The Queen died on the day that the Schism Act came into force. The alertness of the Whigs secured the undisturbed succession of the Hanoverian Prince whose Protestantism was his one qualification for the Crown, but whose defects of personality agreed well with the Whig principle of a limited monarchy. Six months later, aided by the unscrupulous use of Court influence, the Whigs were returned by an immense majority to the new Parliament, which met for business at the end of March 1715. The Dissenters, who had given them strong support, were roughly handled by mobs in many provincial towns; and at Oxford, the nursery of budding Tories, the Quaker meeting-house was wrecked.[1] At the Yearly Meeting in June, in spite of extremists on both sides, it was agreed, in the first place, to solicit for a plain Affirmation, without the sacred name. As this could not be obtained, a Bill was promoted and passed (1 Geo. I. cap. 6), making the

---

[1] See account in Thomas Story. *Life*, pp. 474-476. The damage, amounting to £55 : 13 : 7, was defrayed by the Meeting for Sufferings (Oxfordshire Q.M. Minute, 26th June 1716).

old Act perpetual and extending it to Scotland, and for five years to the Plantations; but the Meeting for Sufferings was directed to press for further ease at a fit season.[1] Thomas Story, a Friend of great practical sagacity as well as deep spiritual experience, who had returned the previous autumn from a long residence in America on service for Penn, and had been foremost in counsels of moderation, thus describes the position in the Society:[2]

> I find things pretty quiet about the Affirmation, the point long desired by some being gained; and I think the more tender sort that are for it [are] fully desirous of a further solicitation, the stiffest of all being about London and Bristol. And I believe not half the number they have boasted of in the world are in their own judgments really for it; but many have been misled by practice and management, whose eyes the Lord will open in His own time, and make all conclude to His own glory.

He adds that many were still burdened, but this was better than an open division, which would have been a great stumbling-block to people, the eyes of many being still on Friends.

During these critical years the burning controversy within the Society flamed into print. In 1713 *A Letter From a Satisfied To a Dissatisfied Friend* appeared. The writer, whose initials G. H. give no certain clue to the authorship, is anxious that the dissatisfied should be careful of condemning a reverent using of God's name, and should "maintain a perfect charity and concord, though we should not exactly think alike." The guidance of the Spirit, he says, does not mean an identity of view in all circumstantial matters; for it is not bestowed "to gratify our curiosities, and give a sanction to our nice conceptions, but to lead us into all necessary truth." He cites the views of ancient Friends, and pleads for liberty on the basis of the Yearly Meeting's Minute of 1696, already quoted. He concludes by saying that after ages will scarcely believe that these publishers of a new doctrine

---

[1] Thomas Story, *Life*, pp. 476, 477; and Minutes of Meeting for Sufferings.
[2] Letter to James Dickinson, 25th July 1715, in *Life*, p. 489. As to the attitude of Bristol Friends cf. William Tanner, *Three Lectures*, pp. 111, 112.

against using the Name of God should carry their mistaken scruple so high as to oppose the renewal of the Affirmation, if they fail to get one on their own terms. This seems unreasonably stiff, and a forcing of their consciences upon the Friends who are satisfied with the words. Later in the year, though not in direct answer to the above, an anonymous *Essay upon the Vth of Matthew, From Verse 33d to 37th* came out. This was written by Joseph Skidmore, a Rickmansworth Friend, who helped in the preparation of Penn's Collected Works in 1725.[1] The piece was an elaborate vindication of the general position taken by the dissatisfied; but went to the point of laying down that, in giving evidence, a man should use no more words than are necessary, and especially should "use neither form nor ceremony wholly extrinsic to the matter as a medium either to oblige [him] to speak the truth, or others to believe it."[2] While objecting to extrinsic media, he did not explicitly assert that all such were oaths. The Meeting for Sufferings, however, in a printed paper to Friends,[3] laid hold of these and similar expressions to argue that they would exclude such a phrase as "I solemnly and sincerely declare," and seemed to render both satisfied and dissatisfied Friends guilty of swearing. So easy was it for both parties to refine their conscientious position into logical extremes. As is often the case, the most important part of Skidmore's piece is the postscript. When man, he says, lost his first state of purity, he also lost that sanction in himself which made his speech pure and veracious, and multiplied divers inventions to give credit to his words. These fruits of the Fall were prohibited by Christ, who gave the Holy Spirit, whereby the inward sanction, the holy veracity, is restored. He forbade not only imprecations or invocations, but also solemn asseverations, saying that whatsoever is more than Yea and Nay cometh of evil. Skidmore does not judge ancient Friends, but he cannot limit himself to their mind-mark. Truth is revealed

---

[1] Letter from Henry Gouldney to Sir John Rodes, 19th August 1725, in *Quaker Post-bag*, p. 109.
[2] *Ibid.* p. 35.   [3] Epistle dated 16th April 1714.

gradually, and a man should stand open to further advances. Expedients last for a while, Truth only will stand last on the earth, in its plainness and simplicity as it was first, "before all oaths, vows, inventions, or expedients was either needed or used to ascertain the truth."

The *Essay upon the Vth of Matthew* was answered by Richard Claridge, the clergyman turned Baptist and Baptist turned Quaker, who seventeen years before, when a man of about fifty, had dedicated his ripe learning to the controversial service of Friends. His *Novelty and Nullity of Dissatisfaction* appeared by April 1714,[1] and ran to 184 pages. He regards[2] the mentioning the Name of God, instead of swearing, as one of the testimonies set up by ancient Friends as stones of memorial for the Church in future ages, and, on this question-begging assumption, controverts the *Essay* with some acerbity and ample research, section by section. Skidmore replied, at still greater length, in *Primitive Simplicity Demonstrated*, published at the end of the year.[3] A private letter from a dissatisfied "Pennite" Friend says that "it will stir the old man so," meaning, I think, Claridge, "that for all he will scarcely be able to help himself."[4] The Preface reflected on the Meeting for Sufferings for its printed paper, adopted against a strong minority and sent down to the counties "to amuse weak though well-minded people," and noted that "to their no small mortification, the Yearly Meeting, whose deputy the Meeting for Sufferings is, instead of confirming it, as was desired, refused to approve it or to suffer the account thereof to be entered amongst their written Minutes." This drew from the Meeting for Sufferings a further printed paper, emphasizing its view that the *Essay* regarded all extrinsic media as oaths.[5] Skidmore, however, may be allowed to have the last word as to his own meaning.[6] Oaths being prohibited by Christ,

---

[1] Henry Gouldney to Sir John Rodes, 6th April 1714, in *Quaker Post-bag*, pp. 97-99.   [2] P. 3.
[3] Henry Gouldney to Sir John Rodes, 21st Dec. 1714, *Quaker Post-bag*, p. 101.   [4] *Ibid.*   [5] Dated 11th March 1715.
[6] *Primitive Simplicity Demonstrated*, p. 161.

... it cannot be consistent with the gospel dispensation, in which signs, figures, &c., have no place, to institute or substitute another medium. ... For, if it be wholly extrinsic, what is it used for? If it be said to awe to truth-speaking, that was its property in an oath. If it be said to add a sanction or credit to the speech, that likewise was its property in an oath. So that, it having this general and common property of an oath :—viz. being extrinsic—and those two other particular properties last recited also, and, being used in the place and stead of one upon the very same occasion, it can be no more consistent with the gospel dispensation than baptism or rantism, *i.e.* sprinkling with water, is, which some folks tell us is come in stead or place of circumcision.

Skidmore, in fact, regarded any form of words, which was treated as the sanction for truth-speaking, not indeed as always an oath, but as always forbidden by Christ, and contrary to the spirit of the gospel. It was this feeling that made any practical agreement on the question so difficult. Whitehead complained to Barclay that it was impossible to find out whether the dissatisfied agreed to any form, and, if so, what form. They had three times changed the form; from "sincerely and solemnly declare and affirm" to "sincerely declare and affirm," and then to "sincerely declare," and some would have no form at all.[1]

The main controversial pieces[2] above referred to are almost free from personal reflections, but a strong undercurrent of feeling was directed against Whitehead himself. There was "a factious circular letter, signed by James Hoskins, Thomas Busby,[3] and thirteen more, clandestinely sent to the Quarterly Meetings against the Meeting for Sufferings, and an ancient member thereof."[4] Aberdeen Friends wrote an Epistle to the Yearly Meeting of 1713, of which Whitehead complains for its "severe censures, smiting and prophesying,"[5] to which Barclay returns that

[1] Letter of 15th Oct. 1713, *Reliquiae Barclaianae*, pp. 138-141.
[2] John Lamb, of Croydon, published in 1714 "Friendly Advice, or A Circumcising Knife to cut off that superfluous Branch, the Affirmation; Because the Old Subtil Serpent, I think, is very plainly Proved to be the Author of it."
[3] James Hoskins, a Cumberland Friend, living at Westminster, was disowned in 1725, after appealing to the Y.M. Thomas Busby, a London woollen-draper, died at Banbury, 1726. (*Per* M. Ethel Crawshaw.)
[4] *The Affirmation Vindicated* (1713), p. 3 of the Letter to the Publisher.
[5] Letter of 15th October 1713, cited above.

they would not have acted their part faithfully, if they had not borne their testimony against the disturbers of Zion's peace. They had named no one ; they never meant the innocent, but always meant the guilty ; and, if there were any so notoriously guilty of having acted the cunning or worldly-wise man as to draw the eyes of the whole meeting upon them, it could not be the fault of the writers of the epistle but of these criminals themselves that they should be so publicly exposed.[1]

Why should thou be so suspicious of our meaning thee? This cannot, in my apprehension, proceed but from one of those two causes, either somebody has told thee we meant thee, or then a consciousness of thy own guilt makes thee imagine so.

Joseph Pike, a zealous Friend of Cork, who had circulated a manuscript letter against the Solemn Affirmation,[2] wrote in 1714 of the flood of liberty and ungodliness which had made too large a progress in the Church.[3]

And what is very grievous to consider is that some would be accounted as elders, who do greatly strengthen the hands of such libertines, even such as I believe were at first rightly called into the Lord's service . . . but have now in old age grown lukewarm or cold, having lost their first love and zeal for the Lord and His Truth.

Henry Gouldney, of London, who had been an ardent partisan of Penn against all his detractors, and was now a dissatisfied Friend, gives a sarcastic account of the presentation at Court of the Whiggish address from the Yearly Meeting to George I., in 1716, after the suppression of the Pretender's rebellion.[4]

[1] Reply, dated Nov. 1713, in *Reliquiae Barclaianae*, pp. 141-149.
[2] *The Affirmation Vindicated*, pp. 4, 12, of " A Distinction, etc."
[3] Letter to James Wilson (of Kendal), 26th March 1714, in Appendix to *Life*, first published by John Barclay from the original MS., in 1837.
[4] Letter to Sir John Rodes, 31st May 1716, in *Quaker Post-bag*, p. 101. A facsimile of the Printed Address is also given, which speaks of the King's just and mild administration, and of God signally appearing to confound that Black Conspiracy, and prays " that when it shall please the Almighty to remove from us so precious a life, by taking it to Himself, there may not want a branch of thy royal family, endowed with wisdom and virtue, to fill the throne, till time shall be no more." Whitehead assured the King that, after this great deliverance, he might well be addressed as George, by the Grace of God King of Great Britain, and desired that, as men carried this stamped on the money in their pockets, it might also be imprinted in their hearts. (Sewel, ii. 617.) This apt little speech scarcely deserves Gouldney's comment.

This afternoon we were admitted to the King's presence, attending him with our address. G. W. had the usual honour to present it with an introductory discourse. Though not very long, yet considering it was not lively, was too long in the occasions. Upon presenting it, it was returned by the King to him for reading, and he, by a previous agreement, delivered it to B[enjamin] Coole [of Bristol], who read it with an air usual to his eloquence, and made humble curtseys at the end of every paragraph. At the end he concluded with, "Amen, saith the reader"; and G. W. as wittily added, "And so we say all." The King seemed pleased with our appearance, and I suppose might have been favoured to kiss his hand, which some seemed willing enough of, had we not before declared our "Dissatisfaction", in introducing a "Novelty"; and, if they would, we would either not go, or at least signify to him our strait in the case.

The Yearly Meeting of 1716 was a trying time to the dissatisfied Friends:

. . . chiefly owing to some rude and forward spirits, who [took] boldness from the connivance and indulgence they had met with from such as had . . . contended to force the Affirmation upon all; but, though the comfort of our meeting was greatly lessened and hindered by that means, yet the imposing designs of these were frustrated, and the Body preserved together and entire, by establishing a just liberty.[1]

In the following year, things were better:

. . . for those Friends . . . having obtained their end, were now quiet on that side; and those who could not for conscience' sake receive it, continuing in Christian patience, bore the yoke willingly, though alone and more heavy than before; [and] upon that bottom were quiet. And, besides, many satisfied Friends sympathizing with them, and the intention of solicitation for further ease to the whole being kept on foot, things were quiet.[2]

The disposition on the part of satisfied Friends to help the dissatisfied asserted itself strongly in the Yearly Meeting of 1719. One of these Friends, John Gurney,

---

[1] Thomas Story, *Life*, p. 529. Cf. Westmorland Q.M. Minute, 6th July 1716, speaking of "hard exercises"; and Henry Gouldney to Sir John Rodes, 31st May 1716, in *Quaker Post-bag*, p. 102, "We had rough work at our meeting sometimes, but at last concluded pretty easy."

[2] Thomas Story, *Life*, p. 578. Cf. Westmorland Q.M. Minute, 5th July 1717, matters "managed in much coolness."

THE AFTERMATH OF TOLERATION

jun., of Norwich, proposed a further solicitation for ease to the dissatisfied, and was supported by two others, John Eccleston of London, and Richard Ashby of Norfolk:

> ... and, while things run in that channel, there was a considerable glory over the meeting; and the peaceable and Divine Truth comforted many, and His peaceable wisdom prevailed with most of the meeting to assent and acquiesce. But, as there were some particular persons there, who ... (designing to set the Affirmation as it then was over all, and not at all in any other terms) in their usual subtlety raised several objections, and [brought] a palpable cloud of darkness over the meeting ... which, after some time, being dispelled, and that spirit made manifest and repulsed, the meeting concluded for a fresh solicitation the next session.[1]

In 1721 a similar decision was unanimously taken,[2] which took effect at the end of the year. The Whigs had protected Dissent after a somewhat uncertain fashion. They had continued the Test Act, while promoting its lax administration. But in 1718 they repealed the Schism Act and the Occasional Conformity Act; and in the following year they passed a liberal Toleration Act in Ireland. The solicitation of the Quakers found the Ministry predisposed to help. The sufferings of dissatisfied Friends had been considerable,[3] by imprisonment in a few cases but oftener by loss of property. William Richardson, of Ayton in Yorkshire, for example, was fined, until a third of his little property was sacrificed, because he could not take the Affirmation in excise matters, required in his business as a tanner.[4] In 1720 and '21, Thomas Story was a prisoner in the Fleet a year and a half, for refusing the Affirmation.[5]

The Bill had now the support of all Friends. One of the "satisfied," Joseph Wyeth, of London, had written

[1] Thomas Story, *Life*, p. 617.
[2] Westmorland Q.M. Minute, 7th July 1721.
[3] See the Petition to Parliament, in Gough's *History*, iv. 181, 182.
[4] J. S. Rowntree, Paper at Scarborough Summer School, 1897.
[5] Thomas Story, *Life*, p. 634. See the case of *Wood v. Story and Bell*, 1. P. Williams, 781, where Lord Chancellor Macclesfield said the process of a Court of Justice should not be made a means of oppression, and discharged Story from custody. A like order had been made in the case of Dr. Heathcote, presumably the Quaker, Gilbert Heathcote, the brother-in-law of Sir John Rodes.

to the King about it;[1] another, Andrew Pitt, of Hampstead, the friend of Voltaire, in spite of censures that had been passed upon him by the "dissatisfied," gave ready help,[2] and the old bitterness on both sides disappeared. Henry Gouldney writes:[3]

Our Friends satisfied with the old Affirmation, in a most hearty and prudent manner, assisted to set the solicitation on foot; spared no pain to press it on; and never left it until it was crowned with success. The chief of them were John Gurney [Jr.], Joseph Wyeth, Andrew Pitt, Joshua Gee [of London]; and John Eccleston, though mentioned last, was not the least in his zealous endeavours. Many more contributed thereto; so that we went on in a general harmony; and a good disposition seems to be cultivated among us.

The Bill passed the Lower House easily, but met with strong opposition in the Lords.[4] Atterbury, the Jacobite Bishop of Rochester, and leader of the High Church party, denounced the Quakers as "a set of people who were hardly Christians," and a hostile petition was presented from some of the London clergy, but rejected as a seditious libel. Thomas Story understood that many of them were threepenny curates, unbeneficed, who said "prayers for the richer sort for threepence a time, which is paid, twopence in farthings and a dish of coffee."[5] An amendment to exclude the Affirmation in cases of tithe was voted down by a large majority, and the Bill passed on 19th January 1722.[6]

The Act[7] handsomely acknowledged the loyalty of Friends, reciting

---

[1] Thomas Story, *Life*, pp. 755, 756. The Appendix to Story's *Life* contains a full account of his efforts at this time. [2] *Ibid.* For Pitt see *J.F.H.S.* xiii. 27.
[3] Letter to Sir John Rodes, 20th January 1722, in *Quaker Post-bag*, pp. 104-107, which also contains particulars of the "strong debates" in the Lords.
[4] *Ibid.*; and Gough's *History*, iv. 185-190.
[5] Thomas Story, *Life*, p. 757.
[6] Gouldney's letter, *ubi supra*.
[7] 8 Geo. I. cap. 6, not extended to all cases until 3 & 4 Will. IV. cap. 49. It was decided in the Lincoln case of *King v. Maurice* (1698) Carth. 448, 5 Mod. 402, 12 Mod. 190, that taking up the freedom of a city was not a place of profit within the exception to the Affirmation Act. I may here summarize the corresponding legislation in Ireland. An Affirmation Act, on the English lines, was passed in 1722, though only for three years (Rutty, *Hist. of Friends in Ireland*, 2nd edn. p. 295). This was extended from time to time, but was not made perpetual until 1746 (*ibid.* p. 339; and Gough's *History*, iv. 260, note).

... that it was evident that the ... Quakers had not abused the liberty and indulgence allowed to them by law, and that they had given testimony of their fidelity and affection to His Majesty and the settlement of the Crown in the Protestant line.

It extended to the Declaration of Fidelity, as well as to the civil occasions when an oath was required; but kept alive the proviso of the Affirmation Act, which disabled Friends from giving evidence in criminal cases or serving on a jury or in any office or place of profit in the Government. The form of words omitted all reference to God, and was of the simplest kind: "I, A. B., do solemnly, sincerely, and truly declare and affirm." Westmorland Friends were able to record "that this meeting is entirely easy and well-satisfied with the present form in which it's now obtained."[1] It will be noted, however, that there was still a solemn form of words. It would have been open for Skidmore to say that this introduced an extrinsic medium, which replaced the true gospel sanction for truth-speaking, although he would have agreed that it was no oath. Lord Mansfield, in the case of *Atcheson v. Everit*,[2] gave it as his opinion that "the affirmation of a Quaker ought to be admitted in all cases, as well as the oath of a Jew or a Gentoo, or of any other person who thinks himself really bound by the mode and form in which he attests." Even in this liberal opinion, however, which as regards non-Christians was already[3] English law, the form is regarded as the sanction of which the law takes cognizance; and it is clear that a process of education had been going forward among some of the dissatisfied Friends. They had receded somewhat from the extreme position, and been brought to see that in an imperfect world, where legal institutions are still needed, it was right to accept a form which correctly expressed the inward spirit out of which truthful evidence was given.

The Yearly Meeting of 1722 was "managed in great

---

[1] Minute of 7th July 1721. The Minute also contains an acknowledgment of the readiness and willingness of Friends in and about London to "assist our dissatisfied brethren in obtaining ease." [2] Cowp. 382.
[3] Leach's Cases 52; 1 Atk. 21.

love and peace," and the Printed Epistle states that from accounts received " we find [the Affirmation] very satisfactory to all the brethren, for which we are truly thankful to God and those in authority." The meeting approved an Epistle of caution sent down by the Meeting for Sufferings, which exhorted Friends to be worthy of their high profession, and discouraged them from litigation among themselves or with others.[1]

The tedious tale of the Affirmation is now told. Its pregnant lessons made it worth the telling. Beneath the placid exterior of Georgian Quakerism there were divergences of temperament and conviction no less difficult of reconciliation than those which have threatened the unity of the Church in later days. Political principles, then as now, played their part in the formation of a man's conscientious convictions, not always without an admixture of prejudice, which confused the moral issue, and caused a biased judgment upon the action of others. The world, with its benumbing prosperity, was leading many to forsake the way of the cross. The tradition of the fathers and the strength of the Society's central organization were at times used to overbear the scruples of tender consciences. In the other party there had been much bitterness of judgment and over-refinement of argument, and on both sides the beginnings of a dividing spirit.[2] We see forces at work which bear a close resemblance to those that perplex the solution of our modern problems. But we see also much to admire, especially the long patience which allowed the question to remain open through the years of heated feeling until it could be settled with a cool and united

---

[1] The Epistle is printed in Gough's *History*, iv. 191-197.
[2] Robert Barclay, in his Letter to Whitehead, November 1713 (*Reliquiae Barclaianae*, p. 148), says that Aberdeen Friends do not propose to disquiet themselves further in the matter, " the rather that our correspondents, by what influence I shall not determine, have solemnly under their hands, to our last Quarterly Meeting here, laid down their office as correspondents, and that without either our desire or knowledge ; and thereby have discontinued, broke off and liberate[d] us from any relation we had to the Meeting for Sufferings." He adds that this leaves them free to act for themselves, without shadow of offence to their brethren in England. They have all along remonstrated both against the Affirmation and against meddling in elections.

judgment in a way easy to all. The dissatisfied could have denounced as swearers and apostates those who secured and used the old form of Affirmation, and the satisfied have reviled as atheists the Friends who scrupled all reference to the Name of God. But there was very little of this wilful misreading of motives. This is the more remarkable, as the restraint of speech which is common to-day is one of the consequences of the self-controlled freedom that we enjoy, and was not the character of Englishmen two hundred years ago. Passion was nearer the surface than it is now; and it was not without reason that John Bellers, the Quaker Social pioneer, addressed to his friends in 1702 a pithily-worded "Caution Against All Perturbations of the Mind; But more particularly against (the Passion of) Anger, as an Enemy to the Soul, By making of it Unfit for The Presence of God, And Unable to Enter The Kingdom of Heaven." To be angry, he says, and let the sun of righteousness and peace set in your soul, is to part with a kingdom for a cockle, for "the mind is much less capable to help itself or others, or know what is right, or to do what is just, than if it were kept cool and sedate." There is no greater enemy to a religious meeting than the passion of anger, which oppresses the meeting and excludes the guilty from a sense of the love of God, though it is only in a sense of this love that they can have the Divine counsel to guide them. His Life "cannot be enjoyed but in a serene and still mind, bound up as in the bundle of life; whereas passion hurries the mind, as a stone slung out of a sling." It was in the sabbath-calm of this higher air, breathed by such men as Thomas Story and John Gurney, jun., that the light shone which showed the Church the way of peace, and set the jostling arguments and prejudices which had perplexed the question in their true order.

William Tanner, whose *Three Lectures on the Early History of the Society of Friends in Bristol and Somersetshire*, published in 1858, is one of the first books to handle Quaker records with historical discrimination and insight, recalls [1] the powerful reference made to the subject by Samuel Tuke, in the Yearly Meeting of 1848, that heated year of European revolutions.

The grounds of Christian unity were laid down by him on that occasion in a most truly catholic manner. He showed, among other things, that, whilst that unity does not always bring men to see eye to eye, it prepares them to bear with one another in their differences; and he illustrated this position by a reference to the differences of opinion which arose among the Apostles themselves, and to the difficulty under which our early Friends laboured for nearly forty years in determining what constituted an oath. I do not know that I ever listened to a discourse of which I should be so glad to possess a verbatim report.

In this matter, as in others, the Church won her soul through patience; but we must not forget that in 1722 the times were changed from the troubled days of 1714 or 1701. The Revolution Settlement was now secure; and in the Society political animosities had died away. There was no longer a Jacobite body of Friends, who feared the Government and all its favours, nor Whig extremists who shivered under the nightmare of imminent Tory reaction. The great national issues had been settled; and candid consideration could be given to the case of conscience, both by Parliament and by the Quaker Church, during the serene years of undisputed Whiggery.

With the accommodation of the Affirmation question, the external history of Friends becomes of secondary importance. They had passed from being the outlaws of the State into a position of privileged security. They were rapidly acquiring that savour of respectability [2] which attaches to estimable characters, known to be free from disturbing enthusiasms. The State had learnt how to silence their obstinate witness by prudent concessions; and Quakerism, mute in its quiet and sheltered ways of life, would need a new vision of its great social responsibilities before it could ring out again to the world its insistent message, as in the days which had been resonant with service and eloquent through suffering.

---

[1] P. 112.   [2] See extract at head of chapter, and *post*, p. 636.

VII   THE AFTERMATH OF TOLERATION

It is fitting that this chapter should close with a reference to the last years of William Meade and William Penn, the two names identified by the outside world with the extreme parties in the Society itself. William Meade was the senior by sixteen years, and died in 1713 in his eighty-sixth year. He is singled out from other London Friends, in an adverse notice of 1672,[1] as "Captain Meade, now a Quaker, a person of great estate and great trade; he hath been a Presbyterian and Independent and what not." He did good service in the affairs of the Society in London; and in 1677 undertook for a year the management of a stock set on foot for employing poor Friends in spinning.[2] His second marriage, in 1681, was to Margaret Fox's fourth daughter Sarah, a woman of unusual business ability. Two years later we find him bringing forward in the Meeting for Sufferings "the unruliness upon the day called Christmas," and instantly offering himself to go to speak to the Lord Mayor about it,[3] and on more than one occasion he assisted George Whitehead in his solicitations on behalf of suffering Friends. Fox during the last years of his life often made his home at Meade's country house at Gooses near Romford in Essex, part of which is still standing.[4] Meade was a man of strong opinions and quick decisions, downright in speech and behaviour. When Fox told him he was complained against for wearing a wig, "he bid me," says George, "put my hand upon his head and feel it, and said he never wore periwig in his life, and wondered at it."[5] He showed little charity towards Penn, and was probably

---

[1] Stowe MSS. vol. 186, cited from *J.F.H.S.* iv. 122.
[2] Six Weeks' Meeting Minutes; see *J.F.H.S.* xii. 122, and *post*, Chap. XX.
[3] Minute of 21st December 1683.
[4] See Cambridge edn. of Fox's *Journal*, ii. 420. The suggestion there made, on the hint contained in a note by Morris Birkbeck in an adverse book which he wrongly attributes to Meade (see Smith's *Catalogue*, ii. 162), that Meade lost his love to Friends, is, I think, to be rejected. Birkbeck's note seems to be based on the friction with Penn. Meade, only a year before his death, was collaborating with Whitehead in a vindication of Friends from High Church aspersions (see Smith's *Catalogue*, ii. 171). He was buried in the Friends' Burial Ground at Barking: he left legacies to poor Friends (see his Will, etc., in *J.F.H.S.* iii. 42-45), and his son, Nathaniel Meade, who afterwards left Friends and was knighted, was treasurer of Barking Monthly Meeting for some time, closing in 1732 (*Camb. Journ.* ii. 491).
[5] *J.F.H.S.* vi. 187.

at the back of the attack made upon him at the Yearly Meeting of 1698,[1] but his support of the Whig principles of the Revolution increases our regard for the man whose name, linked with that of the great Quaker whose politics he detested, will live as long as our English race values a fair trial and the independence of juries.

The closing years of Penn's life were harassed by colonial difficulties and financial embarrassments. These belong primarily to the American side of Quaker history and need not be elaborated here.[2] He only spent a second period of not quite two years in Pennsylvania (1st December 1699–3rd November 1701), being called to England by proposals in Parliament for annexing to the Crown the proprietary colonial governments. His financial difficulties were due to the drain of the colony on his resources, and to his own lack of business efficiency, which resulted in his man of affairs, a Friend of the name of Philip Ford, running an account against him, which charged unreasonable commissions and high interest and made Penn his debtor to the tune of £10,500, secured by a charge on the province. After Ford's death Penn was obliged in 1707 to take refuge in the Fleet, pending measures for an adjudication of the claim. In the following year it was settled for £7600, which his friends lent him on mortgage of the province, and he was again a free man. The friction between him and certain English Friends, especially George Whitehead, Lower, and Meade, who were in correspondence with the opposition party in America, added to his trials.[3] But his friend, Isaac Norris, could write of him:

---

[1] John Tomkins, in a letter to Sir John Rodes, 11th February 1698 (*Quaker Post-bag*, pp. 133-135), says: "Our ancient Friend M[argaret] Fox is here about town. I wish she had stayed in Lancashire, or returned back soon after she came. I fear, by reason of her age, that she will be led by her son William into something or other, which may not be of the best consequence to Truth, nor the quiet of the Church, nor her own honour."

[2] See *Quakers in the American Colonies*, pp. 423-436.

[3] The best available account of these various embarrassments is in Janney's *Life*. In Thomas Gwin's MS. *Journal*, there is a reference to Penn in the Fleet, dated May, June 1708. "Afterwards visited our Friend Wm. Penn in the place of his confinement, who was very kind and told me no man loved me better than he. . . . The Sixth-day I was at Bull, where sundry besides John Gratton spoke.

THE AFTERMATH OF TOLERATION

After all, I think the fable of the palm good in him: "The more he is pressed, the more he rises." He seems of a spirit to bear and rub through difficulties; and, as thou observes, his foundation remains. I have been at some meetings with him, and have been much comforted in them.[1]

After 1710 his prospects brightened, but he was arranging terms for selling the province to the Crown, when in 1712 a paralytic seizure deprived him of his mental power, though leaving his spiritual faculties unimpaired. It was not, however, till 30th July 1718 that he passed away, and was buried a few days later at Jordans.

We have many accounts of these last six years of second childhood.[2] That of his close friend Thomas Story is the most discriminating. Penn was living during these years at Ruscombe, near Twyford in Berkshire, under the care of his admirable second wife, Hannah, daughter of Thomas Callowhill of Bristol, delighting in walking and taking the air, or in diverting himself from room to room in the house, and when able driving in to Reading meeting. Story, just back from Pennsylvania, visited him in December 1714, and says:[3]

His memory was almost quite lost, and the use of his understanding suspended; so that he was not so conversable as formerly; and yet as near the Truth, in the love of it, as before. Wherein appeared the great mercy and favour of God, who looks not as man looks. . . .

When I went to the house, I thought myself strong enough to see him in that condition; but, when I entered the room, and perceived the great defect of his expressions for want of memory, it greatly bowed my spirit, under a consideration of the uncertainty of all human qualifications; and what the finest of men are soon reduced to by a disorder of the organs of that body with which the soul is connected and acts during this present mode of being. When these are but a little obstructed in their various functions, a man of the clearest parts and finest expression becomes scarce

---

Wm. Penn was there, the Term then beginning he had liberty, which was the last time I then saw him."

[1] Janney's *Life*, p. 516.
[2] See passages cited in *J.F.H.S.* iv. 133-139, from Story, Hannah Penn, and Diary of Rebecca Butterfield; letters of Hannah Penn, in Janney's *Life*, pp. 540-546, and account of Lydia Lancaster's visit to Penn, in *Quaker Post-bag*, p. 98; also *Life* at beginning of Penn's *Works*. [3] *Life*, pp. 463, 464.

intelligible. Nevertheless, no insanity or lunacy at all appeared in his actions, and his mind was in an innocent state, as appeared by his very loving deportment to all that came near him. And that he had still a good sense of Truth was plain by some very clear sentences he spoke in the life and power of Truth in an evening meeting we had together there; wherein we were greatly comforted; so that I was ready to think this was a sort of sequestration of him from all the concerns of this life which so much oppressed him, not in judgment, but in mercy, that he might have rest and not be oppressed thereby to the end.

When their honoured friend Onas died, the Indians, after their fashion of poetic action, sent his widow "materials to form a garment of skins, suitable for travelling through a thorny wilderness,"[1] and, through the last six years of oblivion into which her husband had been translated, it had been her solace to know that the thorns which still beset their lives no longer troubled his mind.

Reading Monthly Meeting summarized his character in an ably-written testimony:

He was a man of great abilities, of an excellent sweetness of disposition, quick of thought and [of] ready utterance, full of the qualification of true discipleship, even love without dissimulation, as extensive in charity as comprehensive in knowledge; and to whom malice or ingratitude were utter strangers, so ready to forgive enemies that the ungrateful were not excepted.

Had not the management of his temporal affairs been attended with some difficulties, envy itself would be to seek for matter of accusation; and yet in charity even that part of his conduct may be ascribed to a peculiar sublimity of mind.

Notwithstanding which, he may, without straining his character, be ranked among the learned, good and great, whose abilities are sufficiently manifested through his elaborate writings, which are so many lasting monuments of his admired qualifications, and are the esteem of learned and judicious men among all persuasions.

And, though in old age, by reason of some shocks of a violent distemper, his intellects were much impaired, yet his sweetness and loving disposition surmounted its utmost efforts and remained when reason almost failed.

In fine, he was learned without vanity, facetious in conversation yet weighty and serious, apt without forwardness, of an extraordinary greatness of mind yet void of the stain of ambition,

---

[1] Janney's *Life*, pp. 548, 549.

VII THE AFTERMATH OF TOLERATION

as free from rigid gravity as he was clear of unseemly levity, a man, a scholar, a friend, a minister surpassing in superlative endowments, whose memorial will be valued by the wise and blessed with the just.[1]

Life to Penn was an arena for adventurous service. His eagerness of mind and universal spirit made him leap from the seats of the spectators with which so many are content into the thick of action. Rapt in great designs and careless of self, he was often buffeted and baffled, deceived or mistaken, but his courage was never defeated, nor the fineness of his temper marred. It was courage begotten of a good cause, nerved by faith in justice, and in his fellow-man and in the Kingdom of God. Splendidly equipped for the service of the hour, both in natural parts and noble education, and in the strength that comes from daily intimacy with the Divine, he was prompt in all generous action and high achievement, glad to possess powers that he could spend. If Browning is right in saying,[2]

> And the sin I impute to each frustrate ghost
> Is the unlit lamp and the ungirt loin,

the Churches and many of their members have a heavy guilt to bear for their unused opportunities, and may learn from Penn that lavish and ready championship of Truth is a greater thing than the sedulous conservation of spiritual energy.

This daring spirit was matched, as it may be to-day, with a sweetness and gaiety of heart, free from all envy, which reflected the candour of his soul, making him a man who delighted in friendship, as well as a great voyager through unfurrowed oceans of Truth. We go to others for flawless thought and deeds of massive patience, but for the kindled vision compacted into glowing act, out of which the famous deeds of history are wrought, what other Englishman of that age can rank with the hero of our religious freedom, and of the Holy Experiment of Pennsylvania?

[1] Dated 31st March 1719. I have followed a copy that differs slightly from that printed in Janney's *Life*, p. 570. The preface to Penn's *Works* begins with an echo of this Minute. [2] "The Statue and the Bust."

BOOK II

SECOND PERIOD OF QUAKERISM
THE PERIOD OF EXPRESSION

CHAPTER VIII

INTERNAL HISTORY AND PROBLEMS, 1660–1668

> Dear Friends everywhere . . . keep your first love; and let not the threats of men, neither the frowns of the world, affright you from that which you have prized more than all the world, now the sun is up and a time of scorching is come. . . . Let it teach you all more diligence to be as those that press after glory, immortality and everlasting life. The way of God was ever hated by the world and the powers thereof. Never heed the rough spirit nor the heavy; for their bound is set and their limit known; but mind the Seed, which hath dominion over all: and forsake not the assembling of yourselves together, in which you have found God and His promise and power amongst you—and blessing, your understandings opened. Oh rather suffer all things than let go that which you have believed . . . The Lord God preserve you all unto the end faithful.—FRANCIS HOWGILL, Epistle from Appleby Gaol, 10th May 1664 (*Works*, p. 536).

WE now turn to the inner story of the Quaker movement during the early years of the Restoration period. How did these men and women who were companions " in the tribulation and kingdom and patience which are in Jesus " prevail to maintain their fellowship and proclaim their message? How did they behave themselves when liberty and estate lay always at the mercy of cruel men? How far was the Church disabled by persecution; and how far did its sufferings baptize it into more heroic and abundant life?

At the eve of the Restoration the Quaker leaders were high of heart and purpose and full of missionary enterprise. Indeed, some of the most notable attacks on the outer world were launched in 1660 and the following years, especially that second mission to the East[1] which was provided with spiritual ammunition in the form of epistles from Fox to the King of Spain, the Emperor and

---

[1] See *Beginnings of Quakerism*, pp. 429-433.

the House of Austria, the King of France, the Pope, the magistrates of Malta, the Turk, the Emperor of China, Prester John, and, lest any should be missed, "all the nations under the whole heavens."

A letter from Fox to Friends, in August 1661,[1] shows missionary activity at its highest at the moment when the Cavalier House of Commons had just forged its first weapon of persecution.

Things beyond seas are pretty well and Truth is spreading: and Truth spread[s] in the Barbados, as we have heard and letters from thence; and spreads in New England; and there is love and unity amongst Friends, though there is one lately put to death and several in prison by the rage of the rulers who drink the blood of the saints. And, in Holland and Germany and other parts that way, Truth spreads and hath a good report. And several more Friends are gone for Barbados and New England; and in Bermudas and Virginia and Maryland and other places Truth spreads; and Friends in Ireland are most of them out of prison; but Friends in the Isle of Man are under sufferings. Charles Bayly, who had been prisoner in Rome and came

---

[1] Swarthm. Colln. vii. 111. For details of most of these visits see *Beginnings of Quakerism* or *Quakers in the American Colonies*. The last of these missionary adventures, in 1662, may be here narrated. John Philley was a Dover Friend, of enthusiastic temperament, who rode before Elizabeth Adams through Canterbury, when she stirred the city to uproar in the autumn of 1660, by riding up and down the streets at midday with a burning torch in her hand (Caton to Fox, 16th Nov. 1660, in Swarthm. Colln. iv. 272; for Elizth. Adams cf. M. R. Brailsford, *Quaker Women*, p. 265). In the latter part of 1661 he was eager to go to Venice (Letter to Fox, Swarthm. Colln. iv. 158), and shortly after went to Holland, where he found a companion in a Scottish Friend, William Moore, who knew languages (Letter to Fox from Vienna, 13th April 1662, Swarthm. Colln. iii. 103). Their adventurous journey to the war zone between Austrians and Turks round Pressburg and Komorn is told in Besse, *Sufferings*, ii. 420-432, and shows how the cruel mercies of Inquisitors racked their bodies but spared their lives. On his return to Holland in 1664, Philley published "The Arraignment of Christendom, etc.," signed after the Perrot fashion with his name John, written in prison near Vienna, and spread among the nations in 1000 copies, in English and German. (See Smith's *Catalogue*, ii. 410.) Philley had been a husbandman and "maltman," but in 1670 was imprisoned at Maidstone for teaching school without licence (Besse, *Sufferings*, i. 295). Crisp censured him in 1669 for the disservice he had done to Truth: was not his dreams and falsehoods enough, whereby he had stopped the progress of Truth in Germany, but he must now scribble to the Duke of Buckingham? (Letter, 23rd Nov. 1669, in *Steven Crisp and his Correspondents*, p. 46). As was the case with others of the Quaker enthusiasts who carried the message to the Continent, his sufferings and emotional nature had impaired his judgment. For Philley, see also Letter, Joseph Fuce to Crisp, 30th Mar. 1664, *ibid.* p. 42, and Caton to Crisp, 1st July 1664, *Collectitia*, p. 122. I have found no further information of Wm. Moore. His account of the mission, printed in Besse, was first published in 1664 under title "Newes out of the East," etc., with preface by Caton.

VIII   INTERNAL HISTORY AND PROBLEMS   217

along with John Perrot is now prisoner in France for crying against their idol priests and their idols; one pretty Friend who is a Frenchman is lately gone over into France. Robert Malins is gone for Jamaica, and many others are preparing to go after him. John Stubbs and Henry Fell are gone towards the East Indies, who lost Daniel Baker and Richard Scosthrop about Smyrna. Here is a Friend who hath been three years out in the East Indies; who hath done much service and brings a good report of many that received his testimony, who hath travelled to many nations and islands.

The movement was thus occupied with great projects for the conversion of stubborn humanity, when the storm of persecution arrested organization at home and paralysed the life-giving itinerating service of the Publishers of Truth.

Baxter, in a shrewd passage,[1] points out how the Penal Laws obliged the Presbyterians to become Congregationalist in their practice though not in their principles, and Quakerism was also forced, for a time, though with injury to itself, to find its main strength in congregational life. Cut off from wider fellowship and larger vision, it began to take a domestic character and to lose something of its universal outlook. The later years of the Commonwealth had seen the growth of County meetings, with less frequent General Meetings for groups of counties and even one for the whole country at Skipton in April 1660.[2] This incipient organization was beginning to bring a sense of corporate unity, and in spite of Penal Laws some parts of it survived the years of persecution. We do not hear of any General Meeting of the Northern Counties after 1661, nor could the Skipton meeting be repeated. A national collection for the service of Truth beyond seas was taken up about 1662[3] but not again till seven years later, the charge being borne by London Friends in the interim.[4] County meetings, however, were kept up

[1] *Reliquiae Baxterianae*, pt. iii. pp. 42, 43.
[2] *Beginnings of Quakerism*, chap. xiii.
[3] *Ibid.* p. 338. Somerset sent £30. See Jno. Anderdon's letter, 11th Nov. 1663, in (London) *Friend*, vol. ii. p. 170, excusing the smallness of the sum because of sufferings.
[4] The Y.M. MS. Records at Dev. Ho. vol. i. begin with a letter from Friends in the Ministry, 16th Jan. 1669, which says that five or six years previously a

wherever possible, which prevented the organization from being reduced to a merely congregational basis. This was the case in Somerset,[1] and the Westmorland accounts, which are extant for the whole period, show that a common fund was maintained for the "Churches" of that district.[2] In Yorkshire, at the beginning of 1666, we find a Quarterly Meeting and five Monthly Meetings,[3] and Friends kept a methodical record of their sufferings from 1652 onwards in a thick folio which unhappily fell into the hands of the authorities.[4] Such books of sufferings are often the earliest Quaker records for the district.[5]

But, as we have seen, the correspondence between the Quaker groups on this and other matters greatly disturbed the authorities,[6] and, in the state of feeling that existed, it would in some cases be almost impossible to maintain even the simple organization enjoined in the advice by Fox to the counties in April 1661 :[7]

Be valiant for the Truth upon the earth, and of a noble mind, and keep your men's meetings in every county concerning the poor, and see that nothing be lacking : then all is well, and they being refreshed then you are refreshed : and see that all your sufferings be gathered up and that none of them be lost of any sort, that they may be sent up, as they have been formerly to London . . . that the sufferings may be laid on their heads that are to rectify things.

Side by side with the obstruction of organization was the still more serious interference with itinerating work.

The Publishers of Truth had been like rich life-blood circulating through the body and had preserved its health by the vitalizing influence of their inspiring presences. Through them, far more than through organization, the

---

paper had been drawn up for a collection but not sent ; and that a year or two ago the matter had been again considered, and it was now left to country Friends to do as the Lord should move their hearts and to send the collection to any of the five Friends appointed at Skipton.

[1] John Whiting, in John Banks, *Journal*, p. 140.
[2] Kendal MSS., "Book of Account for Westmorland."
[3] York MSS., "Treasurer's Account Book, 1665-1677." The M.M.'s were East Riding, Kirby Moorside, Pontefract, Skipton and Richmond. Fox, *Camb. Journ.* ii. 134, speaks of seven but this seems a mistake.
[4] *Extracts from State Papers*, p. 316 ; cf. *ibid.* p. 127, cited *ante*, p. 8.
[5] See *Beginnings of Quakerism*, p. 315, etc.
[6] *Ante*, p. 8.   [7] Swarthm. Colln. vii. No. 168.

Quaker groups had become one living fellowship. Now the prisons hindered many from their work, and untimely death was taking others who could ill be spared. Howgill, himself held fast in Appleby gaol, writes to Margaret Fell at the end of 1665,[1] on hearing of the death at twenty-nine of William Caton, the "very pillar" of Quakerism in Holland:

> Truly, when I consider of the taking away of so many faithful men which could and would have done most service for the Lord in our generation, [it] makes my heart sad; and also it is often in me that God intends great evil and judgment to the nation, though as for them I cannot so much be sorry, for they are at rest with and in the Lord, and it's only their personal presence that we want in the body, for their life and spirit we enjoy. Well, let us rest in the will of God and be content, and love and strengthen and comfort one another that God would preserve His people faithful in the midst of trials.

The Camp of the Lord, which in the first years of Quakerism had issued forth two and two from the North, was by this time sadly reduced. John Camm[2] had passed away after less than three years of lavish labour at Bristol. His yokefellow, John Audland, died in March 1664, worn out with service at thirty-four. Burrough and Hubberthorne had been persecuted to death; Caton and Ames were gone, and Howgill was ending his days in Appleby. The gloom and glory of James Nayler's life were over, and leaders from the South of England had been taken, like Humphrey Smith, George Fox the younger, and the learned Samuel Fisher.

The difficulties of itinerating service at this time may be illustrated from a few cases. George Fox travelled diligently prior to his Lancaster imprisonment. At Bristol in July 1662, at the Fair time, he narrowly escaped arrest. The trainbands were out to take him in the meeting: he came in, an hour late, at a side door, and passed through to the usual place of standing, where Margaret Thomas was speaking, who at once stopped, and Fox spoke and prayed and then spoke again. Just

---

[1] Dev. Ho. A.R.B. Colln. No. 90, to be dated, I think, 18th Dec. 1665.
[2] *Beginnings of Quakerism*, p. 356.

as he had finished, the report came that the soldiers were coming, but he got away safely and the meeting of some two thousand persons dispersed without disturbance.[1] A few weeks later he was seized at a Friend's house at Swannington and taken to Leicester prison.

So as we went we passed through the people in the fields at their harvest and in the towns; and we declared the Truth to them with our open Bibles in our hands, and the two women they carried wheels on their laps to spin in prison. So we rid through the country to Leicester in that manner, five of us, and declared how we were the prisoners of the Lord Jesus Christ for His name, and His truth' sake; and the people was mightily affected.[2]

He was tendered the Oath of Allegiance and convicted at the Quarter Sessions, though soon after released. At Tenterden in Kent in the following spring he was taken on the Quaker Act, but persuaded the magistrates that it only reached such as met to plot against the King. Not long after, at the end of May 1663, a large meeting arranged in a barn near Poulner, a mile and a half from Ringwood in Hampshire, put him in further peril.[3] The meeting was to gather at eleven, and between eight and nine Fox heard that the trainbands were out to break it up. He walked out of an orchard into a close, and when he had turned up by the hedge he looked and saw soldiers all about the house and heard them inquiring for him. They took two or three men Friends and returned to Ringwood. At eleven "a large glorious meeting we had,"

---

[1] I follow letter written by John Stubbs to Margaret Fell at the time, in *Camb. Journ.* ii. 20. During the Wilkinson-Story controversy, William Rogers charged Fox with fleeing from persecution down the backstairs (*Christian-Quaker*, pt. v.), but the letter of Stubbs shows that Dennis Hollister had been trying to dissuade Fox from going into the very mouth of the destroyer, and that he was behaving with the blend of courage and prudence which he showed on other occasions.

[2] *Camb. Journ.* ii. 14, before Bristol incident, though mention of harvest shows it must be later. The *Camb. Journ.* wrongly places a visit to the Eastern Counties earlier still at p. 9, though a reference to Burrough's death fixes it to beginning of 1663, and Fox, *Epistles*, No. 222 is dated from Essex, Jan. 1663. The order is right in the so-called "Short Journal," and in *Ellwood Journal*, which has a short visit to Essex in 1661, besides this second one in 1663; see vol. i. p. 518 and parallel passage in *Camb. Journ.* ii. 10.

[3] The facts are not seriously in dispute and are given in *Camb. Journ.* ii. 24. Rogers (*Christian-Quaker*, pt. v.) turns them against Fox. For Poulner see *J.F.H.S.* vii. p. 76. The fate of the persecutors is told in Fox's *Itinerary Journal* at Dev. Ho. under date May 1683.

but between one and two a gaily dressed man looked in at the door and hurried off. Fox saw that he was gone for the military, who were a mile and a half away, and, after the meeting had broken up about three, took his leave of Friends, walked a furlong leading his horse, and then, hearing that the soldiers were coming, rode away twenty miles that night into Wiltshire. The officers were greatly angered at having missed their prey and took some men Friends to Winchester prison. In Somerset a few weeks later, he was knocked up at two in the night by a man with a sword at his side, who stared at him and saying, "You are not the man I look for," went his way.[1] Other hairbreadth escapes are recorded; though it was only when he reached the district affected by the Northern plot that he was made a prisoner.[2]

William Dewsbury, whose name ranks only second to Fox in Quaker annals, may be described as passing his life in prison with brief intervals of freedom.

"When Sion's enemies," he wrote on one occasion, "puts [the Lord's servants] in holes and dungeons, God makes a prison more comfortable than a pleasant palace, and fetters of iron far surpassing chains of gold: yea, He causeth them to sing in tribulation as Paul and Silas did in the stocks."[3]

Dewsbury had been released in June 1661 from his imprisonment in York Castle at the time of the Fifth Monarchy Rising.[4] He visited Friends in Yorkshire and then went through several of the Midland counties to London, intending to go on to the West of England. He was, however, taken at a meeting at Acton, and thrown into Newgate in October for refusing the Oath of Allegiance,[5] where he lay till the spring. He wrote a glowing letter to Margaret Fell, rejoicing in his opportunity of fellowship with dear brethren who had travelled in the heat of the

---

[1] *Camb. Journ.* ii. 33. [2] *Ante*, p. 32.
[3] From epistle to Bristol Friends, Warwick, April 1678, "copied by J. W.," Bristol MSS. vol. i. No. 17, evidently the one which he gave John Whiting to carry to Friends, when the young man visited him and thought him "an extraordinary man many ways, and as exact a pattern of a perfect man as ever I knew" (*Persecution Exposed*, p. 12). Cf. Dewsbury's dying words, *post*, p. 450.
[4] Letter to Margaret Fell, 10th June 1661, in Swarthm. Colln. iv. 147.
[5] Letter to Margaret Fell, 14th Oct. 1661, in Swarthm. Colln. iv. 148.

days past, "Oh, the refreshings which we have in one another melts my heart in the flame of eternal love." Fox, Burrough, Howgill, and Hubberthorne were all in London and comforted him greatly in his bonds.[1] After a few brief weeks of freedom, he was again arrested at his home at Dirtcar, near Wakefield, as a Quaker ringleader, and taken to his old quarters in York.[2] He was not released till the spring of 1663, and at the close of the same year began a long imprisonment in Warwick which lasted till the Great Pardon.[3] He and his friends were praemunired without legal trial. One of them, Henry Jackson, a prominent man from Wooldale in Yorkshire, gives a vivid glimpse of their privations,[4]

. . . thronged up in stinking rooms, and sometimes in one room, above twenty of us, where we could not all lie down at once and no straw allowed us to lie upon, except we would pay 2s. 6d. for one bolting, which was sold to the felons for 2d., and no manner of victuals allowed to be brought to us, except we would pay 6d. for one penny loaf of bread, and as much for a quart of milk, and 3d. for a quart of water, etc. . . . And this was continued for four or five days together at one time, insomuch that moderate people in the town, although not of our judgment, hearing of this cruelty inflicted upon us, was stirred up in tenderness to throw bread over a housetop into the dungeon court for our present relief to the frustrating of the expectation of our cruel oppressors.

The old gaol in Northgate Street is still standing and contains an underground dungeon, which was perhaps the room in question. The philanthropist John Howard calls it "an octagonal dungeon about twenty-one feet in diameter, down thirty-one steps, damp and offensive; the gaoler on going down always took a preservative."[5] Edward Bourn, the Quaker physician of Worcester, en-

---

[1] Letter to Margaret Fell, 26th April [1662], in Swarthm. Colln. iv. 151.
[2] Besse, *Sufferings*, ii. 106.
[3] The first dated letter from Warwick is 8th Jan. 1664 (*Works*, p. 238). This agrees with the "above two years and nine months" of Henry Jackson (*Extracts from State Papers*, p. 255, 17th Nov. 1666). Besse (*Sufferings*, i. 764) wrongly puts the imprisonment in 1661, though as to three of the party, two of them Banbury Friends, the entry under Oxfordshire (*ibid.* 569) is 1663.
[4] *Extracts from State Papers*, pp. 248-255, the passage quoted is at p. 250.
[5] White, *Friends in Warwickshire*, 3rd edn. p. 30, with an illustration.

dured its horrors with seventeen others at the time of the Fifth Monarchy imprisonments.[1] On one occasion as many as fifty-nine Friends are said to have been crowded together in this dark close hole, so that they had not even room to lie by one another.[2] Such are the sacred places of Quakerism, hallowed by the heroic witness of men of faith. Dewsbury, held fast in Warwick during the persecution of 1664, visited his fellow-sufferers elsewhere with a fine series of letters from prison, addressed, for example, "To all the faithful and suffering members in all holes, prisons and gaols," "This for dear Friends in London and them that are aboard the ship in order to transportation," "For the dear daughters of Sion, whom the Lord hath or shall suffer their dear and tender husbands to be separated from them beyond the seas, or elsewhere, for the testimony of the Lord Jesus Christ."[3] His words ring in triumph as he writes to the Friends under sentence of banishment:

O happy men that ever you were born, and blessed be the day that ever the Lord called you in His power to stand faithful in what the Lord requires of you; in which living testimony you stream through the whole body, as a river of oil and virtuous refreshings, whose memorial shall never perish but preach to ages and generations, to the glory of the name of our God for ever.[4]

He was kept close prisoner about four years,[5] but afterwards had more liberty, and was married in May 1667 to his second wife, Alice Meades, of Warwick.[6]

There is hardly a Publisher of Truth whose itinerating work was not hampered or cut short by imprisonment. Dewsbury's old friend Thomas Goodaire was his fellow-prisoner at Warwick; Thomas Taylor, the minister to the Westmorland Seekers who joined Fox, lay at Stafford for ten years and a half under a *praemunire*, and spent his time in teaching school and in witnessing against the vices round him. Heathenish practices at Christmas, lotteries,

---

[1] Besse, *Sufferings*, i. 766, and letter in Dev. Ho. A.R.B. Colln. No. 81, printed in part in *Friends in Warwickshire*, p. 29.
[2] Besse, *Sufferings*, i. 764.   [3] *Works*, pp. 247-271.
[4] *Works*, p. 261.   [5] *Works*, p. 376.
[6] For the marriage certificate see Dev. Ho. Fox Colln. No. 10.

cock-pits, bowling alleys and playhouses, debauchery, fencing, bull and bear baiting, all came under his criticism. Sometimes he was suffered to be with his wife and family at their hired house in the town, but could not travel, though in the habit of preaching out of the prison window to the passers-by.[1] Ambrose Rigge, the Grayrigg school-teacher, had a like term of bondage at Horsham, again on a *praemunire*, made doubly oppressive by the cruelty of his gaolers, egged on by a persecuting priest.[2]

A travelling minister was commonly regarded as engaged in sinister designs. Thus, the Langdale tailor and old royalist soldier, William Wilson,[3] on his release from Lancaster after the Kaber Rigg Plot, wrote:

As for going to visit Friends in Scotland, I am something stopped in my mind at this time . . . because of stirs and fears that seems to be in people's mind by their diligent inquiry about any that passes or repasses up and down the country; that it stands much with me at present to labour my vocation at home. I, being a clear man, desires not that jealousies or suspicious fears should in the least be occasioned by me or my going out of the country so soon after my imprisonment, but I shall wait in the guidance of God, that I may do His will and keep my holy peace with Him above all other things.[4]

In 1665, when the storm was fiercest, James Parke, an untiring itinerant,[5] wrote from Berkshire that everywhere he had found the blind, halt, and lame of all professions coming among Friends; but faithful labourers were few, "so many being snared in prison-houses . . . and some places hath not been tried by any of the brethren . . . this twelvemonth."[6]

Richard Davies, the Welshpool hatter, about the same

---

[1] Particulars taken from his *Works*.

[2] Besse, *Sufferings*, i. 713; Postscript by R. T. to Rigge's "The Good old Way," 1669; and *Extracts from State Papers*, p. 166.

[3] For Wm. Wilson, see *ante*, p. 33, note, *Beginnings of Quakerism*, p. 415, and the careful account in *Records of Colthouse Burial Ground*, by Elizth. J. Satterthwaite, pp. 46-48.

[4] Letter to Fox, 3rd May 1664, Swarthm. Colln. iv. 175.

[5] James Parke came, I think, from Lancashire, and had been in fellowship with the Independents of Wrexham and Welshpool (see Richard Davies, *Life*, pp. 83-101, and *Answer to John Wiggan's Book*, 1665, p. 7). He afterwards lived in London and died in 1696. (See Smith's *Catalogue*.)

[6] Letter to John Lawson, 7th Jan. 1665; Swarthm. Colln. iv. 128.

year writes, "this was a time when most travelling Friends were taken up prisoners,"[1] and gives a racy account of a visit he paid to Bristol and South Wales with the reluctant leave of a friendly gaoler, who said, " I warrant you will go to preach somewhere or other, and then you will be taken to prison, and what shall I do then?" He returned, however, safe and sound, much to the good man's relief.

On every side persecution hampered the work of Friends. It acted like the winter snow by cutting off the local groups from the outside world, and in consequence they often hibernated, through lack of illuminating intercourse with others and of opportunities for expansive service.

Mystical movements, with their emphasis on inward experience, have seldom had much institutional stability. It would not have been surprising if Quakerism, with leadership and organization weakened by persecution, had languished and declined. But the quiet meetings, resolutely maintained up and down the land, remained centres of power, and offered an almost invincible resistance to the persecutors. They did not hatch sedition, as the authorities feared, but they were undeniably places where the local groups were continually renewing their strength and finding themselves, in the stress of suffering, touched with the life of God. The Quaker stiffness on points of conscience, which in some things magnified trifles and fostered extravagances, here magnificently justified itself. By holding meetings through storms of persecution with unflinching tenacity, publicly and with open doors, Friends not only secured the continuance of their own Society, but greatly contributed to the preservation of Nonconformity as a whole. Two typical cases may be given, those of Colchester and Reading. Throughout the winter of 1663–4, a determined effort was made to suppress the Colchester meeting. Forms, seats, and windows were broken, and the congregation was forced to gather in the street. Then, for several weeks in succession,

[1] *Life*, p. 114.

a troop of horse violently assaulted Friends, who, at all hazards, continued to meet.[1]

These troopers at last went away, and others came that were more moderate but would turn Friends away, who then met in their burying-ground, their time being out in their hired house. So that it came in Friends' heart, in the midst and greatest of their fury and abusing Friends, and when about sixty of the richest Friends had been first cast in the town prison before these fighting troopers came, to build a very large meeting-house, which was an amazement both to the troopers and to the town in general.

Steven Crisp, one of the prisoners, wrote to the mayor that he was dealing with a people whose God and worship were dearer to them than life, and even if they died, yet the thing he struck at would still flourish more and more and their assemblies would yet daily increase.[2] At Reading, a few months before the First Conventicle Act, the meeting, held at Thomas Curtis's house, began to be harried systematically by Sir William Armorer,[3] an equerry to the King and one of his boon-companions, "the Reading knight-arrant and always in armour for the devil."[4] In March 1664 he took thirty-four Friends from meeting to prison on the Quaker Act, and others, chiefly women, on the next two Sundays. Two weeks later, he came again in great fury, but found only a few children and young maidens, whom he pulled out and struck at with his staff, threatening to gaol them. The women were released in June, but during the summer and autumn the meeting was again stripped of nearly all its adult members. Yet the Quaker witness was nobly maintained, and Curtis could write to Fox:

Our little children kept the meetings up, when we were all in

---

[1] Besse, *Sufferings*, i. pp. 199-201, drawn from "A True and Faithful Relation from . . . Colchester," Jan. 1664; cf. Sewel, ii. 68, and *F.P.T.* pp. 98-101, from which I quote. The oldest graveyard was in Moor Elms Lane.
[2] *Works*, p. 112.
[3] For Armorer see Pepys, *Diary*, 23rd Sept. 1667, and *Cal. State Papers, Dom.*, 1671-72, pp. 96, 328. The Reading persecutions are in Besse, *Sufferings*, i. pp. 14-28, drawn from "Persecution appearing With its own Open Face in Wiliam Armorer," 1667; cf. Berks Q.M. Books of Sufferings, and *Extracts from State Papers*, pp. 194-199. Curtis's letter to Fox, 15th Jan. 1665, is in *Letters of Early Friends*, p. 240, from Swarthm. Colln. iii. 88, with a letter from Fox.
[4] Penn, *Works*, 1726 edn. i. 463, with a summary of his proceedings.

prison, notwithstanding their wicked Justice, when he came and found them there, with a staff that he had with a spear in it would pull them out of the meeting and punch them in the back, till some of them have been black in the face : I cannot much enlarge ; his fellow I believe is not to be found in England—a Justice of the Peace.[1]

The men were never brought up on the Quaker Act, but after forty weeks in gaol were tried on the Oath of Allegiance and acquitted ; but many were soon taken again, and for some years the principal Friends were in prison, and the meeting at Thomas Curtis's was kept up by young people and a few stray adults, mostly women. Armorer came one morning in January 1666, and found only four young maids. A servant brought him water, which he threw again and again in their faces, and turned them out. After the Second Conventicle Act, which came into force in May 1670, he illegally padlocked two doors, for it was Curtis's private house ; but Friends met in another room, which he also nailed up. The meeting, however, met next First-day as usual, the door having been broken open. The men were in prison and it consisted entirely of women and maids, into whose faces he caused bucketfuls of water to be thrown, repeating this hydropathic treatment a week later. He threatened them with scalding water if they met again, and had the seats chopped up and the door nailed fast,—a pretty piece of " sabbath-day " work. Friends resolutely kept on meeting, till most of the women were imprisoned in January 1671. The company was now reduced to four women and three children, about seventy Friends being in gaol. The constable took the women to prison, and in this extremity one of the four, the widow Margaret Whithart, gave fine utterance to the Quaker witness :

This is the place we met in in the beginning, and have ever since. . . . We do not meet here in wilfulness or stubbornness, God is our witness, but we cannot run into corners to meet as some do, but must bear our testimony publicly in this thing, whatever we suffer . . . to us it's a weighty matter, and our case is the same as it was with Daniel in days past.

---

[1] Cf. the Bristol case, *ante*, p. 102.

The town had its Quaker martyr in Joseph Coale. In order to take this young and ardent Publisher of Truth, Armorer had broken into Curtis's house in July 1664, and the innocent victim of his cruelty died in gaol after six years' imprisonment, when only thirty-four. His triumphant words show how the Reading Friends were caught up into a life and testimony beyond themselves : [1]

> I am well, blessed be the Lord, with my dear companions and fellow-sufferers, and neither prison-walls and locks nor the cruelty of man can obstruct the issues of the Lord's love, nor the manifestation of His presence, which is our joy and comfort and carries above all sufferings, and makes days and hours and years pleasant unto us, which pass away as a moment because of the enjoyment of and seeing Him. . . . And if the rage and cruelty of wicked men do extend so far as to wear out and consume these bodies in holes and dens of the earth, yet will our testimony stand in ages to come, and, though dying, yet shall [we] live in the remembrance of the faithful for evermore.

In the stanch maintenance of their meetings, Friends not only found the rallying-point against their enemies; they were also consolidating their own ranks and preserving themselves from the internal disintegration which threatened the Church. Resistance to the forces without could only be sustained by a group-witness to Truth, enriching and gathering together the witness of the individual units. It was equally necessary that the centrifugal tendencies which were bound to show themselves where each unit had an individual inward illumination should have the restraint of a strong group-witness and group-illumination. Unless Friends were to become shattered into fragments, this group-witness was bound to be maintained so as to control the aberrations of guidance in the individual. The vital nature of the problem will be seen as we proceed to study the character and history of the Perrot division.

John Perrot had taken part in the amazing Quaker mission to the East in 1657.[2] Baffled in the attempt to

---

[1] *Works*, pp. 146-148, epistle, 25th Aug. 1666, to Friends in Devon and Cornwall, where he had travelled.

[2] See *Beginnings of Quakerism*, pp. 420-426; and Mabel R. Brailsford, *Quaker Women* (1915), chap. vi.

reach Jerusalem, he had returned from Smyrna to Venice, and with his friend John Luffe had fallen into the hands of the Inquisition at Rome in the following spring. Luffe was hanged,[1] but Perrot was put into the madhouse and three years later was released. It looks as though his emotional and imaginative temperament saved his life, by inclining the Inquisitors to treat him as a man of disordered mind. He had already, on his way to the East, written in an affected style to his Friends in Ireland, beginning with the phrase, " I, John, a servant and disciple of Immanuel, God with us,"[2] and his epistles from Rome followed the same apostolic mode. I know nothing like them in early Quaker literature. They glow with the fires of a mystical love which unites him in his prison of madmen to his absent Friends. Thus he writes:

Ye the born of God . . . mine endless love reacheth you and with the sweet arms of the grace and peace of my Heavenly Father I embrace you. I greet, salute and kiss you, one by one, yea, all as one (in the One only, in whom is no variation or changing), with the undefiled lips of sincerity. . . . Feel and know me as near you as the flesh which cleaveth to your bones, as purely and perfectly in you as the blood of life in your hearts.

He breaks into verse of some merit:[3]

> My soul is planted in your holy ground,
> And here your flames of love do me surround;
> And on your substance, which distils as drops
> Of heavenly dew, I feed like honey sops.
>
> . . . .
>
> My life in Sion would be always found
> Among the Seed, a salve to every wound,
> And perfect medicine to every grief,
> And to the oppressed an arm of good relief.
> Let not my love's heart languish under sorrow,
> For lo, thy joy approacheth with the morrow:
> The yoke to self, and cross to flesh fly never,
> That death may die and life may live for ever.
>
> . . . .

---

[1] *Beginnings of Quakerism*, pp. 424, 425. Add reference in *Camb. Journ.* i. 183.
[2] Letter from Zante, 7th Sept. 1657, in Swarthm. Colln. v. 25.
[3] Both quotations are from a tract dated 1660, " J. P., The follower of the Lamb, to the Shepheards Flock, Salutation." This and other verses are also in " A Sea of the Seed's Sufferings, Through which Runs A River of Rich Rejoycing," 1661.

> Whenas the woods in summer time are green,
> The throstle's tune is heard, though she not seen
> By any mortal, yet there is an Eye
> Which sees how she from tree to tree doth fly,
> And doth perceive whence her sweet notes aspire,
> And what's the thing her life doth most desire—
> Which is the book wherein I read your race,
> Beyond wide lands, seas, time and utmost space :
> And here with you I rest, I live and dwell,
> Like silkworms hid in one wrought case and shell.

One other quotation must be allowed, if we are to understand the charm of Perrot's personality to many Friends. The prisoner in far-off Rome, held fast in that seat of cruelty, writes to the "suffering Seed of royalty," who under the Fifth Monarchy imprisonment are "shut up in dens and holes, in crowds and clusters."[1]

> Though your dens are noisome and your dungeons darkness, yet the breath of your God is a precious perfume continually in the midst of your dwelling . . . and now more than ever you know Him to be God indeed, and very gracious and good indeed, a sure shelter and a safe refuge indeed, which will never fail you as you never fail trusting in Him, but stand to the utmost and say . . . as my tender soul hath said, What is liberty without God, and what is more pleasant than a prison with my God? . . . Blessed be the day, yea, thrice blessed be the hour wherein I was born for proof and trial in the sharpness and severity of bonds, and yet you know not the weight thereof, neither can I tell you a tenth part thereof. . . . I have been driven in the deeps with whales and hunted in the earth by foxes, wolves and lions, and been subtilly wept and lamented for by cruel crocodiles, yea, cockatrices have spit venom in my face and serpents have followed hard after me . . . in all which I had no safety but in the secret clift of the rock, making fear my bread and trembling my cup of wine : and so I bolted my doors with trust, and double-barred them with confidence, and made my bed of patience and pillow of peace, and covered myself with the clothing of content.

The saintly Isaac Penington only uttered the hearts of many Friends when he wrote that the great sufferings of Perrot, his signal deliverance from the Inquisition and "the precious sparklings of life which brake forth from

---

[1] "To the Suffering Seed of Royalty," 1661.

him while he was in prison," had been very wonderful to him, and the impression had been deepened by the way in which Perrot, after his arrival in London in August 1661,[1] had reached, raised and refreshed the life in many, "insomuch as the meetings where he was ordered to be were much fresher than lately had been known."[2]

Two remarkable letters had preceded Perrot's arrival.[3] The first, from Rome, laid emphasis on the Humility of God: he cannot describe how infinitely the tender and merciful Father stands below us and round about us, waiting and watching in grace and in loving-kindness to serve us; the day is come which is to show if Friends bear the image of His holy spirit of humility as Jesus did: there they may know the bosom of love, from which all pure service proceeds—service to God, service to man, service to beasts, service to fowls, service to fishes, and service to worms, "all in the love, in which they were by the humble Spirit created, according to all their respective kinds." The Lord God requires of His people "rent souls, broken spirits, contrite hearts, breathing minds, fervent prayers," thus shall they enter into the deeps of the Spirit of God. He is ravished and overcome in the sense of the glory to come among Friends.

Truly the glory is such that for glory I cannot behold, but I cry, but I cry, O the depths of love which will wound enmity, O the weight of mercy which will kill cruelty, O the pleasantness of patience which will extinguish persecution, O the depth of wisdom which will work over stratagems, O the worth of virtue which will crown with diadems, O the dread of life and power of supremacy which will wear the glory of an everlasting dominion! This will be the sting, the woe and the torment unto every unclean spirit upon the face of the earth until she shall bear that spirit no more upon her face; but all things shall be as they were in the beginning, and God in more infinite measure gloriously known and enjoyed than ever in any age that is past, since the days that Adam was made a true and living soul.

The second letter, "concerning judgment," from Lyons on the way home, was fantastically signed, "I am your

---

[1] Fox to Friends, London, 22nd Aug. 1661, in Swarthm. Colln. vii. 111.
[2] Paper in Dev. Ho. Crosse Colln. p. 6.   [3] "Two Epistles, etc.," 1661.

Sister in our Spouse, John," and was addressed to his beloved sisters and brethren. He began with the same thought of the Humility of God, Who is not rigorous, rash, nor cruel, but tender, pitiful, forgiving, long-suffering and merciful. The children of Light must grow into His likeness, and in cases of evil will utterly deny the sin but tenderly admonish the offender to forsake and repent of it, not cutting him off except after admonition upon admonition, reproof upon reproof, for hastiness is out of the nature of the Father, Who wooeth sinners and correcteth gently. Trespass between brother and brother will be dealt with in the same way, for the brethren in such cases must mind forgiveness more than judgment. He adds, in words which would later apply to his own case:

> The merciful Lamb of God, which taketh away the sin of the world, said, Judge not, lest ye be judged, because every tittle out of His Spirit is to be judged by His Spirit, since in all judgment besides it there is a secret seed of prejudice and enmity in the heart which stirreth up prejudice in the hearts of the persons judged : and such judged souls, by shyness and strangeness kept at sword's point and at severe distance from Friends, hardens their hearts from God, which [thing] saves not but destroys the soul, which is a sore weight to fall upon any spirit—viz. not to be an instrument of salvation but rather of damnation : which for ten thousand times ten thousand the price of all the treasures of the earth I would not should fall justly upon my back through an act of the spirit of rashness.

Perrot, on reaching England, had acted in the spirit of these letters. He had borne himself with a great show of humility ; he had deprecated a judging spirit, and he had excited an expectation that a more glorious day of the Lord was dawning. But the spiritual raptures he had indulged at Rome had led him into a negative mysticism which denied even the simplest forms in use in public worship. He issued a paper in manuscript against putting off the hat in prayer :[1]

I would not that the true Israel of God should be ignorant how that the purpose of God is to bring to naught all the

---

[1] Paper undated in Swarthm. Colln. v. 17. He had issued either this or some similar paper prior to 8th Nov. 1661 ; see Crosse Colln. p. 98.

VIII INTERNAL HISTORY AND PROBLEMS

customary, traditional ways of worship of the sons of men, which have entered into the world and stand unto this day in the curse and state of apostasy from the true power of the living worship. For which cause I preach the cross of our Lord Jesus Christ unto that reasoning part in all which seems to stand in opposition to that which I have received by express commandment from the Lord God of heaven in the day of my captivity in Rome, viz., to bear a sure testimony against the custom and tradition of taking off the hat by men when they go to pray to God, which they never had by commandment from God, and therefore unto them may be righteously said, Who hath required this thing at your hands?

In the meetings of Friends a "comely order," as Fox styles it, had quite naturally grown up with respect to such matters as putting off the hat in time of prayer, shaking hands (which Perrot also condemned), and the like.[1] If Perrot was right in his action, previous Quaker practice under the guidance of the apostles of the movement had been wrong; or, assuming them to have acted up to their lights, then it followed that Perrot with his mystical experiences at Rome had received a new and higher illumination on the subject. If he were wrong, his supposed revelation came from a spirit of delusion. The issue thus raised was a serious one and sharply divided Friends in the South of England. The Perrot position, as events showed, led to the denial of all human arrangements, even for meeting at stated times and places, and, had it been adopted, would have meant the rapid disintegration of the movement. Travelling ministers when in London used to resort to Gerrard Roberts' house for conference and worship together, and here [2] Perrot had at once been taken to task by Fox and others for the extravagances in his letters, one of which was highly objectionable in its wording, and, with perhaps less reason, for the cost of his travels and for placing money at the disposal of the women Friends who were prisoners of the Inquisition at

---

[1] Hand and Hat are connected together in Fox, *Epistles*, No. 214 (1662); R. W. (probably the printer Robert Wilson) in Crosse Colln. p. 28, and Patrick Livingstone, "Plain and Downright-Dealing, etc.," 1667.

[2] There are full particulars in the Paper from Perrot to Fox printed in Robert Rich, *Hidden Things brought to Light*, 1678, pp. 2 ff. On the first night after his arrival Fox kept Perrot up till 2 A.M.

Malta.[1] He had explained to Fox, with respect to the Hat, that he did not oppose any man who was moved by the word of the Living God to take it off in prayer, but this of course could not put the matter on a satisfactory footing while he continued publicly to promulgate his own view. He tried to get a general meeting with ministers, but Fox and Burrough did not encourage it, and after a few weeks in London Perrot went into the Eastern Counties, where he soon gained a following, which included Robert and Ann Duncon, of Mendlesham, and two Colchester Friends, Benjamin Furly, part-author of the *Battle-Door*, and Edmund Crosse, whose collection of letters is a chief source of information.[2] He proposed a meeting at the Bull and Mouth on 19th November with all dissatisfied Friends, which passed off much to his comfort:

"The savour of my spirit in that meeting," he writes, "will stand I believe to the end of this age. . . . And all was silenced and hushed, though I named neither hat nor cap in the meeting, for the counsel of God's uniting Spirit was with me; and all the lambs in the meeting were sweetly refreshed therein."[3]

At the end of December, before leaving the city, he had a great farewell meeting with Friends, and two others with the Quaker leaders, whose love and unity he desired should go along with him.[4] Fox, Howgill, Hubberthorne, and George Whitehead were there and some of Perrot's own followers. Fox was anxious there should be no further writing of papers, and he and Howgill embraced Perrot on parting. But by this time John, as he still styled himself, had become to many Friends the prophet of a more spiritual manifestation, and neither the Leaders nor Perrot himself could check his influence. He went by way of Isaac Penington's to Bristol, and on to Ireland, no doubt to his home near Waterford, returning to Minehead and visiting Cornwall before he came back to London

---

[1] *Beginnings of Quakerism*, pp. 428-432.
[2] Dev. Ho. Crosse Colln. added to Friends' Reference Library in 1897.
[3] John to R[obert] D[uncon], London, 28th Nov. 1661, in Crosse Colln. p. 99.
[4] Isabel Hacker to A[nn] D[uncon], 1st Jan. 1662, in Crosse Colln. p. 100, and acct. in Robt. Rich, *Hidden Things brought to Light*, pp. 9-11.

in the spring of 1662. In June he was carried before Sir Richard Browne under the Quaker Act,[1] and committed to Newgate. According to John Whiting, the earliest Quaker bibliographer, he accepted liberty on condition of going into voluntary exile, "and never prospered after."[2] He sailed for Barbados in the autumn, reaching the island in October.[3]

Perrot had spent only a year in England and would never return. But his sufferings, his imaginative gifts, his freshness of speech, and, more than these, his personal charm with its show of affection, humility, and spirituality, had brought him into high esteem with many Friends, and had prepared them to think that his innovation with regard to the hat might be the beginning of a new revelation. We cannot sweep aside as a mere apostate a man who deeply impressed Penington and affected for a time John Crook and young Ellwood. It did not seem unlikely to Penington that there might be a further appearance of the Lord, for "who can say that the Lord hath put forth His utmost skill in manifesting His life, either for the gathering of them after Him who stand ready to follow Him in spirit, or for the leaving of them behind who may stick in the letter of this dispensation?" To prejudge such a question meant that the soul would stand ready to resist and oppose any further appearance of Christ.[4] As to Perrot, he would neither admire nor lift him up on the one hand nor throw him down on the other. He had often felt the uprightness of his heart to the Lord, and seen sparklings of true glory break forth through him.[5] Penington also published a paper, "Many deep Considerations," omitted from the first edition of his *Works*, which supported the idea that some of the eminent Quaker leaders might decline and fall.[6] Howgill, in

[1] Sewel, ii. 8. The Guildhall Sessions Rolls (*per* G. Lyon Turner) show that he was committed with Burrough and William Bayly for being at a meeting at the Bull and Mouth on June 1st. Cf. Besse, *Sufferings*, i. 368.
[2] *Persecution Exposed*, p. 83, in the letter to J[ohn] M[oone] of Bristol, who in like fashion accepted liberty in order to go to Pennsylvania in 1683. See *post*, p. 411. Cf. *ibid.* p. 88.
[3] Joseph Nicholson to Margaret Fell, Barbados, 14th Oct. 1662, in Swarthm. Colln. iv. 104.   [4] Crosse Colln. p. 4.
[5] Crosse Colln. p. 6.   [6] *Works*, 1761 edn. i. 629; 1784 edn. ii. 455.

June 1663,[1] wrote him a letter of wise but loving counsel:

> It is a dangerous word to speak of a further dispensation than that whereby eternal life comes to be witnessed unto the creature. And, while many have talked of this, they have neglected and undervalued that which they have attained unto, and so gaze and wonder at they know not what, and so lose that which they did already enjoy : but a growth and increase in life and power and glory we have always spoken of; but still it's the same and not another. And them that have spoken of another dispensation have grown weary, as Israel did of manna, and so have undervalued heavenly food, and last of all fed on husks. And them that have spoken of those things unto us would have had their necks out of the yoke, and so run into trifles.

Helped perhaps by this piece of sure analysis, Penington came to see that he was mistaken and that his papers had weakened the action of the Quaker leaders and had strengthened the spirit that was ensnaring Friends.[2] Crook was influenced in much the same way for a time,[3] while John Whitehead refused to take sides, but felt that a man might pray covered or uncovered in the motion of life.[4] Ellwood had been led astray under the idea that Perrot was bringing in a greater spirituality.[5] Richard Davies, the Welshpool hatter, when in London about 1663, fell into the same snare which also affected the group of newly-convinced Friends in Mid-Wales.[6] He says :

> The tendency of that spirit was to speak evil of Friends that bore the burden and heat of the day and so to cry out against Friends as dead and formal. They expected a more glorious

---

[1] Dev. Ho. Penington Colln. iv. p. 4, also in Dev. Ho. Portf. 3, No. 83 (p).

[2] See paper in Penn, *Judas and the Jews*, p. 69, paper to Friends, 14th July 1666, in Penington's *Works*, 1681 edn., pt. i. pp. 436-441, and letter to Virginia Friends, dated 29th May 1675, in Dev. Ho. Penington Colln. i. 143, and also in MS. Records of Virginia Y.M. (*per* Thomas, *Hist. of Friends in America*, 4th edn. p. 49 *n*., with similar letter from John Crook).

[3] See last-mentioned letter, also Joseph Fuce to Crisp, 30th March 1664, in *Steven Crisp and his Correspondents*, p. 43, and Crook's paper, in *Judas and the Jews*, p. 71, referring to a paper circulated by him at the time of the controversy.

[4] Letter 7th Jan. 1663 in Dev. Ho. Penington Colln. iv. 20, and *Judas and the Jews*, pp. 67, 113.   [5] *Life*, pp. 241-247.

[6] See *post*, Chap. XIII. A letter of warning against the Perrot spirit from Thos. Jackson to Charles Lloyd, dated Shrewsbury 8th Feb. 1664, in a MS. Colln. of Lloyd documents in my possession, has the appended note, "This I received after that the Lord recovered me out of that spirit."

VIII INTERNAL HISTORY AND PROBLEMS 237

dispensation than had been yet known among Friends. . . . But it pleased the Lord to rend that veil of darkness and cause the light of His countenance to shine again upon me, whereby I was led to see the doleful place I was led into, by a spirit that tended to nothing else but exaltation.[1]

The strong groups of Friends in the North were almost untouched by the controversy :[2] it chiefly affected London, and the Eastern Counties and the West of England, where Perrot had visited ; but, with Quaker organization not yet developed, it led to disaffection rather than to open separation. A few persons became zealous champions of Perrot, especially Benjamin Furly of Colchester, who afterwards recanted,[3] John Whitehouse of Staffordshire,[4] and three chief followers, William Salt, Charles Bayly and Jane Stokes. Salt had been in Launceston gaol with Fox and had afterwards been imprisoned in France.[5] As late as October 1660 he was an ardent disciple of the great Quaker leader.[6] He carried the Perrot position to the extreme point of discouraging the holding of a meeting " without the immediate leadings of the Spirit of the Lord ; and as it stands in the man's day, time or will, which is wholly to be ceased from for ever."[7] He recommended the Church to stand still till the flood of persecution abated. " As there was a time of bringing all home, so let there be a time of keeping at home, and so every one to sit down under his own vine, and quietly to enjoy the fruit of his labour."[8] After visiting Barbados he returned to England and is spoken of in 1665 as " a bad spirit and creeper in darkness," who was spreading Perrot's papers abroad, but was denied by Friends.[9] Charles Bayly and

---

[1] *Life*, pp. 112, 113.
[2] Penn states this explicitly in *Judas and the Jews*, p. 24.
[3] His paper against George Fox is in Crosse Colln. pp. 22-25 : Fox's reply in Swarthm. Colln. vii. 107, and Furly's letter of self-condemnation, 1669, in *Collectitia*, p. 149, from Colchester Colln.
[4] Richard Davies, *Life*, pp. 120-124, also referring to another "Hat-man," Cadwallader Edwards. There are references to John Whitehouse, a "Hat-man," in the Horslydown M.M. Minutes, 1667, at Dev. Ho.
[5] *Beginnings of Quakerism*, pp. 232, 417. [6] *Camb. Journ.* i. 381.
[7] Letter in Crosse Colln. p. 44 : cf. his printed tract, "Some Breathings of Life from a Naked Heart," 1663, with Perrot's paper attached, which is referred to in a letter from George Whitehead to Fox, Stoke, 9th Nov. 1663, in Swarthm. Colln. iv. 95. [8] "Some Breathings, etc."
[9] James Parke to Fox, 7th Jan. 1665, in Swarthm. Colln. iv. 128.

Jane Stokes had both helped in securing Perrot's release, and had been imprisoned at Rome by the authorities.[1] We find Bayly behaving extravagantly at Dover, imprisoned at Bristol " for witnessing against the idol priests against whom the anger of the Lord is kindled, Who hath decreed that not one of them shall remain in the land," and later confined in the Tower, for alleged seditious practices.[2] Fox says, " he came to nought,"[3] but he stoutly believed in Perrot to the last. Jane Stokes helped to spread the schism in America,[4] although by 1672 she had settled with her husband in Jamaica, and says Fox, " is come in finely and hath given a paper of condemnation."[5] Perrot himself, on reaching Barbados, was warmly welcomed by the large Quaker communities in the island, and Penington speaks of " the freshness and power which was reported to break forth through him in Barbados, contrary to the expectations and predictions of some."[6] He went on to Jamaica with his old friend John Browne, and they were in Virginia and Maryland in the autumn of 1663, returning in the winter to Barbados.[7] Perrot had left England " sorely smitten and wounded with hard dealing " from Friends,[8] though they looked after his wife till she could join her husband. Their disavowal of him had removed all restraints upon the development of his individualistic mysticism, and he became a desolating influence. One Friend writes from Barbados in February 1664, " Here is sad work and mad work . . . all upon

[1] *Beginnings of Quakerism*, p. 426, and Fox to Friends, London, 22nd Aug. 1661, in Swarthm. Colln. vii. 111, cited *ante*, p. 216.
[2] See Luke Howard's *Works*, p. 103, etc., *Extracts from State Papers*, pp. 173, 263, and letter, Fuce to Crisp, London, 30th Mar. 1664, in *Steven Crisp and his Correspondents*, p. 42. See also Bayly's " The Causes of God's Wrath against England," 1665, which contains the outspoken advice to the King to avoid rioting and excess, chambering and wantonness. In 1667 he was prisoner in the Tower upon charity, *Cal. State Papers, Dom.*, 1666-67, p. 530 ; " an old Quaker with a long beard," *J.F.H.S.* xiii. 67.
[3] *Camb. Journ.* ii. 314. [4] *Ibid.* ii. 434. [5] *Ibid.* ii. 207.
[6] Paper in Crosse Colln. p. 6.
[7] The Crosse Colln. supplies the facts, and contains, p. 57, a curious account of John Browne coming specially from Barbados to London, for the purpose of testifying by a Sign, at the Bull and Mouth meeting, 20th July 1664, the woes that would come on England for its persecuting spirit, *e.g.* he explains one of his actions thus : " The cutting off the hair is the cutting off the seeming glory of all flesh, not only C[harles] and J[ames] and others of that rank, etc."
[8] Crosse Colln. p. 36. (Mary Booth to Edmund Crosse.)

heaps; the like I never saw: they are not like the people they were . . . truly they are full of confusion . . . this people will hear nothing against Perrot, although they are much condemned within themselves."[1] Another, at the end of the year,[2] found many who had been hurt by him and carried away with his imaginations out of the cross into fleshly liberty, pretending to be against forms, and so slighting meeting together and waiting on the Lord, counting that to be a form. Next year, going to Virginia, the same Friend writes that the greater part of the Quaker community had been led aside by Perrot, not meeting together once in the year. Many had abandoned the plain language, and were become loose and careless, and one with the world in many things, so that the cross of Christ was shunned and sufferings were escaped.

Perrot himself had relaxed much of his Quakerism, and strange tales of his doings reached England. Jamaica, which Admiral Penn had taken from Spain, was in sore need of immigrants and of trading relations with the Spanish possessions which encircled it. Sir Thomas Modyford, taking up the Governorship in 1664, came across Perrot in Barbados and intrigued him in his plans. He reported home that he was employing Perrot, an eminent preaching Quaker, who was content for his Majesty's service to appear in a black satin suit with sword and belt and be called Captain. He judged him a man of good temper and capacity, who was likely to influence Friends to come to Jamaica. Modyford was sending him and another to treat on commercial relations with the President-General of San Domingo, and had instructed them how to approach the Spaniards. After magnifying his Majesty's power, his great love of peace, and how much friendly proceedings would be to the advantage of both nations, they were to get discourse with the inhabitants and very warily treat with them for a trade at Jamaica, especially for blacks, and if possible were to induce some Spaniards to come to Jamaica to see Modyford.[3] The strange

---

[1] Joseph Nicholson to Fox, 10th Feb. 1664, in Swarthm. Colln. iv. 155.
[2] John Burnyeat's *Journal*, 1664, 1665.
[3] *Cal. State Papers, Amer. and W. Indies*, 1661–1668, p. 739.

embassy was courteously received and promised all kindness imaginable, though we are told, with a side-reference to buccaneering, " it is improbable Jamaica will be advantaged by it, . . . for we and they have used too many mutual barbarisms to have a sudden correspondence."[1]

Perrot had been reproached for extravagance when travelling to the East, and his closing years were clouded with financial embarrassments due to his unbalanced temperament.[2] He had emigrated from England on borrowed money, and was fitted up with a well-freighted trading sloop by Barbados Friends. On the strength of this he settled in Jamaica, where his wife joined him; engaged in some disastrous tobacco dealings, and built himself a house, which was burnt down. He became Clerk to one of the petty Courts, administered oaths, and mixed with the loose-living planters of the island.

He lost his credit and repute among men, and the very world spewed him out; and so he ended his days miserably. For soon after he was dead and buried, in an old Popish mass-house, all that he had left, which was not much, was seized on for debt; yea, the very bed that was under his wife, when she lay sick upon it.

When sterilized of its bias, this does not necessarily mean more than that Perrot, as we should suppose, had no head for business and slipped back into the ways of the world round him, while retaining his mystical Quakerism to the end. His own letters are not those of a vicious man. After his visit to San Domingo he says:

I have yet had success in all things, amongst English and Spaniards. . . . If I live to see a day open for travel and service and feel a power engaging, the earth is not birdlime to my spirit that the wings of my mind may not fly to do the Lord of the whole earth a service.[3]

---

[1] *Cal. State Papers, Amer. and W. Indies*, 1661–1668, pp. 744, 767. Cf. Rich, *Hidden Things brought to Light*, p. 26; and *Loving and Friendly Invitation*, 1683, p. 13.

[2] I take these facts from *Loving and Friendly Invitation*, 1683, a reply to Robert Rich, with an account of Perrot's latter end, by John Taylor of York, then in Jamaica. Perrot's "Vision . . . wherein is contained the Future State of Europe, . . . As it was Shewed him in the Island of Jamaica, a little before his Death," shows him an emotional rhapsodist to the last.

[3] Letter to Mary Booth, 25th June 1664, Crosse Colln. p. 59. He uses the "heathen name" of the month for the first time.

At the end of 1664 he is expecting to entertain the Friends banished from England.[1] A month or two later his wife has arrived and he writes to his sympathizer, Mary Booth, to be still and quiet, and to keep love and mercy for all.[2] His friend Robert Rich, who had been Nayler's stanch defender, has preserved us one of Perrot's last letters, written shortly before his death about the end of 1665.[3] It is the letter of one who still deserves a place in the hearts of his friends.

Why is there contention about the righteousness of an unworthy man? ... Pacify my adversaries, bearing them this message from me, I am viler and worse before the Lord than they have represented me in the eyes of men by evil and wrong reports. ... Finally, dear babes, let me beg you with the present drops of mine eyes not to look upon me as you have done, setting me where you should not do, nor look for voices from me, but as the Lamb Himself spake ... and, if the work of my day is wrought and over, yet murmur ye not that another must work farther. For I have served God in my generation and discharged an honest conscience amongst you all; and yet the next generation in a purer glory shall shine in that life which by more than words I have exemplified to Israel—yea, amongst my brethren in a good measure—and I boast not, but give the evidence of God's goodness and mercy to me therein, to Whom be glory for ever. Let none receive me but those that see my soul.—JOHN PERROT.

Rich gives another letter written from Jamaica to Fox, which looks forward to a day when all misunderstandings shall be cleared up:

My love in simplicity is to thee and all the holy Seed everywhere ... I breathe for the birth of all in a clearer day of amity and unity, which will be when we all shall cease our beings in these earthly tabernacles. ... I live to love thee in the Lord and can die to serve thee.

---

[1] Letter to Mary Booth, 6th Dec. 1664, Crosse Colln. p. 71. The banished Friends would be some of those sentenced at Hertford, see *ante*, p. 43, but never in fact transported. Two Friends, Edward Brush and James Harding, were transported later, see *ante*, p. 45.

[2] Letter to Mary Booth, 27th Feb. 1664-5, Crosse Colln. p. 71.

[3] *Hidden Things brought to Light*, p. 19. For date of his death, see Henry Fell to Margt. Fell, Barbados, 20th June 1666, Thirnbeck Colln. in *J.F.H.S.* ix. 94, and reference to him as dead in Wm. Bayly's *Works*, p. 598 (before p. 569), in a Testimony dated Sept. 1667.

We have now to inquire how the Quaker leaders dealt with the situation, especially the three men of greatest weight, Fox, Dewsbury, and Farnsworth. Fox handled the question trenchantly. To him it was an unsavoury turning from fellowship and union in the power of God into outward things, which imperilled the Quaker movement by leading Friends out of the power into strife and jangling and vain disputes. The spirit that kept on the hat was in his judgment a dark, subtle and sophistical spirit, carrying Friends into a false love and liberty which the power and Spirit of God could not own. The Ranters and Nayler in his hour of darkness had kept on their hats in prayer: to make such a practice a basis of fellowship was to sink back into the world and to foster prejudice and envy.

Fox himself with his passion for reality was far removed from the imaginative mysticism of Perrot, whose poetic ardours left him cold. He could neither understand nor tolerate a spirituality that invaded the austere standards of Quaker conduct. With him tenderness to the individual must be subordinated to the welfare of the Church. On Perrot's departure from England he wrote him a letter filled with reproaches, and said that he could not own his going anywhere except back to his wife.[1] He was henceforth to Fox a lost soul, who "turned a swearer and drunkard and so died."[2] In this and other cases the great Quaker prophet showed himself a man of sure but unsympathetic judgment.

With Dewsbury the case was different. He saw the hurt that had been done no less clearly than Fox, but felt less the outrage than the need for healing and restoration, and could write in the words which had been taught his heart by a merciful God:

Oh, how did my bowels yearn for the preservation of J[ohn] P[errot], in what I could to have drawn and separated him from

---

[1] See Fox's various papers on the subject in *Ellwood Journ.* i. 519 (1661), *Epistles*, Nos. 199, 214 (1661), and epistle to Friends beyond sea, from Lancaster prison, 5th May 1664, in Swarthm. Colln. vii. 122. The letter to Perrot on his departure is in *Hidden Things brought to Light*, p. 17.

[2] *Camb. Journ.* ii. 314.

that spirit which gave forth the paper that propagated the keeping on the hat in prayer and reflected judgment upon those that called upon the name of the Lord with their heads uncovered. But after much counselling of him in tender love to have stopped that paper from going abroad, but he would not be separated from that spirit that gave it forth, then I cleared my conscience in the word of the Lord, which now, in my freedom in God, I declare to the children of Sion—what the eternal judgment was that did arise in my heart, in words to this purpose : John, if thou propagate what thou hast written in this paper, thou wilt wound more hearts and cause more trouble of spirit amongst the tender-hearted people of the Lord than when the temptation entered dear J[ames] N[ayler], who deeply suffered but the Lord restored him again by true repentance. And, as to my particular [self], it is not my nature to be found striving with thee or any upon the earth ; but, having declared the truth to thee, I will return to my rest in the Lord, and let every birth live the length of its day ; and time manifest what is born of God, for that spirit that stands up in self-striving will weary itself and die and end in the earth.[1]

Farnsworth again, with his strong reasoning powers, had his own line of service. He had done little work that brought him into prominence during the last years of the Commonwealth period.[2] But in October 1661 Dewsbury wrote to Margaret Fell,[3] " Richard Farnsworth is raised up in great power and hath been abroad among Friends : the sweet presence of the Lord hath gone along with him." In the summer of 1663 [4] he wrote a confutation of the Perrot position which shows us the underlying issues better than any other contemporary piece that I have seen. He is chiefly concerned with the argument, natural to the current dualism, that the inward man was the seat of religion, and outward forms could only be a bodily exercise that profited little. He pointed out that, though the outward was subordinate to the inward, the two were necessary to each other ; and the man who would separate them was dividing the human outward man from the Divine inward man, and excluding the human from action and worship ; and was so making it

---

[1] " To all the Faithfull in Christ," 1663, also in *Works*, p. 219.
[2] *Beginnings of Quakerism*, p. 360.   [3] Swarthm. Colln. iv. 148.
[4] Dev. Ho. Penington Colln. iv. 40.

useless in the creation both towards God and man. Most dangerous consequences would follow. For it would be held that the inward man was subject to spiritual laws, government, and worship, and no outward law could extend to it: it was subject to the inward teachings of God and should rest satisfied in Him.

But, as for the outward man, might not the enemy tell them it is useless and unprofitable and may do what it will, as it is visible amongst men and conversant with them: it may be subject to outward laws, worships and governments of men, as outward, useless and unserviceable things, and needs not be liable to any persecutions of suffering for righteousness' sake.

The true position to take is that God commands both the inward and outward man to do Him service, and true and faithful service in both kinds, in obedience to His requirings, is accepted of Him.

Farnsworth came to London in April 1664,[1] and was a good deal in the city till his death there from a fever at the end of June two years later.[2] With Josiah Coale and others he continued to combat the Perrot spirit, and had also engaged himself against the Muggletonians.[3] This strange sect[4] based its claims on supposed outward voices of God which came to John Reeve in February 1652,[5] and in consequence scorned the Quaker doctrine of the Inward Light. Reeve, the Moses of the sect, died in '58, but left Lodowick Muggleton as his Aaron, and the two claimed to be the two witnesses of Revelation xi., who should seal the elect and the reprobate before the coming of Christ. They had points of contact with Quakerism, calling their adherents "Friends," and opposing war and persecution for conscience' sake, but held an obscurantist doctrine that God was one and eternal, with a material body rather larger than human, clear as crystal, Who came

---

[1] *Letters of Early Friends*, pp. 128, 131.   [2] Smith's *Catalogue*.
[3] *Truth Ascended*, 1663.
[4] See *Beginnings of Quakerism*, pp. 19-21; Muggleton's *Acts of the Witnesses of the Spirit*, printed in 1699, after his death in 1698, and Article "Muggletonians," by W. T. Whitley, in Hastings' *Encyclopaedia of Religion and Ethics*; also Alexander Gordon, *The Origin of the Muggletonians*, Liverpool, 1869, and *Ancient and Modern Muggletonians*, Liverpool, 1870, referred to in Barclay, *Inner Life*, pp. 420, 421.   [5] *Acts of the Witnesses*, p. 39.

to earth as Jesus, leaving the universe in charge of Elijah. They held that the soul was mortal, rising with the body at the resurrection, and that the world contained two races, cursed and blessed, owing to the fallen angel having entered bodily into Eve. They did not practise prayer or preaching, but Muggleton believed that he possessed a commission of the Spirit to curse or bless to all eternity. His copious controversy [1] with Friends brought him into violent collision with many of their leaders, who underwent impartial and dispassionate damnation at his hands. In *The Answer to William Penn*, published in 1673, he sketches these encounters, calling his adversaries "serpents," as belonging to the brood of the Serpent that tempted Eve. The graphic personal touches deserve reproduction:

As he was journeying in the spiritual wilderness of the North Midlands, "there came many serpents and put forth their stings, thinking to have stinged me by the feet . . . the serpents were five or six Quakers at Nottingham and Mansfield. . . . And there came forth another serpent, he was not speckled but more like the colour of an old adder and something brown : . . . this serpent-adder was Edward Bourn [the Quaker physician of Worcester]. . . . After this . . . there came forth out of the fern and mossy ground two fiery serpents . . . William Smith [of Besthorpe, near Newark] and Samuel Hooton. . . . After this . . . a great red dragon, very fierce and fell: he was exceeding fat and full of fury: he has two great wings on the sides of his breasts, and his tongue was, as it were, all in a fire with the poison that was in it . . . and there this dragon died about a year and a little more after he was wounded—this great red dragon it was Richard Farnsworth. . . . [In 1667] there came out of the wood a great old fat fox: the fox had no horns, but, however, he had ears; and they stood both upright, as stiff as if his ears had been horns; also this fox had two teeth before, as sharp as needles . . . it was old George Fox. . . . [In 1668 there was] a wild bull . . . died in less than three weeks after . . . Thomas Loe, speaker of the Quakers. . . . [The same year came] a wild boar, his bristles were all off his back, and he was so besmeared and daubed with his own dung that his flesh could hardly be seen; also he stank that a man might have smelt him at a great distance before he came near: he was very giddy

---

[1] The bibliography in Smith's *Bibliotheca Anti-Quakeriana*, pp. 300-318, excuses me from enumerating these pieces.

in the head, as if he were frenzy in the brain; for he could live with less food than any of the wild beasts in the wilderness, being much given to fasting, which made his head to totter or joggle, and his eyes dazzle and his brains to hang loose . . . one Solomon Eccles [the emotional music-teacher turned Quaker]. . . . [In the same year came] George Whitehead and Josiah Coale . . . and since, Josiah Coale is gone out of the body, as they do vainly imagine. . . . [Then] a young spruce serpent: he was very quick and nimble, he was hardly a year and a half old . . . William Penn the younger. . . . [Then] an old she-speckled serpent . . . Elizabeth Hooton, the mother of Samuel Hooton."

In this extraordinary catalogue it will be noticed that Muggleton claims to have hastened by his damnation the death of three Quakers, Farnsworth, Loe, and Josiah Coale. This, of course, Friends flatly denied. As regards Farnsworth, the lapse of time admitted by Muggleton makes the case obviously weak; Loe died a few weeks after he had rebuked the prophet and been damned for his pains,[1] but Penn told Muggleton[2] that he was known to be an infirm man for sixteen years before his death and was about his usual service when he fell sick. In Coale's case, the illness began within a few days of the damnation and he died three months later.[3] He heard that Muggleton was boasting against him, and testified on his death-bed that he had no fear of the consequences but had "peace with the Lord; and His majesty is with me, and His crown of life upon me."[4]

On one occasion, in 1674, about which Muggleton keeps politic silence, John Gratton, of Derbyshire, neatly exposed the prophet's fallibility.[5] He visited him with Barclay and Patrick Livingstone, and Muggleton at first refused to have any dealings with Scotsmen. But when Gratton told him he was English they fell into talk, in the course of which the prophet said he had no power to bless after he had once cursed, but was drawn into telling

[1] *Acts of the Witnesses*, pp. 114-116.
[2] Penn's "The New Witnesses Prov'd Old Hereticks," 1672, printed in *Works*, 1726 edn. ii. 169.
[3] *Acts of the Witnesses*, pp. 116-122. He was damned 17th Oct. 1668 and died 15th Jan. 1669.
[4] Coale's *Works*, pp. 343, 344.   [5] *Journ.* 1779 edn. pp. 99-103.

Gratton that, if he was careful, it would be well with him in the end. Now he had already associated for a time with Muggletonians, and had himself been duly cursed for convincing the wife of one of their members.[1] On learning the facts, says Gratton, Muggleton "was sadly confounded and made no further reply to me. So we left him and went away."

Farnsworth's death was regarded by some of the Perrot party as a judgment upon his strong action against them. As to this, he bore a dying testimony against those who wore what he called "linsey-woolsey garments," and said:

God hath been mightily with me, and hath stood by me at this time; and His power and presence hath accompanied me all along, though some think that I am under a cloud for something; but God hath appeared for the owning of our testimony, and hath broken in upon me as a flood, and I am filled with His love more than I am able to express; and God is really appeared for us."[2]

In May 1666, only a month before his death, he took a leading part in a specially convened meeting of ministers in London, which issued an important epistle from his pen.[3]

The epistle addressed itself to those who under pretence of crying down man and forms were in effect crying down ministry and meetings, and so destroying the work of God and laying waste His heritage. It declared that that spirit should not be allowed office or rule in the Church of Christ, and that those who were joined to it had no true spiritual right to be judges in the Church, "for of right the elders and members of the Church which keep their habitation in the Truth ought to judge matters and things that differ." It dealt with persons claiming to be Friends who would not submit to be judged by the Church, "by the Spirit of Truth in the elders and members," though it was "according to Truth and consistent with the doctrine of such good ancient

---

[1] *Post*, p. 374.
[2] Testimony in Josiah Coale's *Works*, pt. ii. p. 125.
[3] *Letters of Early Friends*, p. 318. Farnsworth's authorship is stated by Ellis Hookes in a letter to Margt. Fell, 14th Aug. 1666, in *Camb. Journ.* ii. 102. For other anti-Perrot work by Farnsworth see Testimony by Josiah Coale in Coale's *Works*, pt. ii. p. 223, after p. 122, and " Truth Vindicated, or an Answer to a Letter sent from John Perrot," 1665, by Farnsworth and others. John Story was invited and gave them his good wishes (see Dev. Ho. A.R.B. Colln. No. 119).

Friends as have been and are sound in the faith, and agreeable to the witness of God in His people." Such persons were to be rejected as having erred from the Truth. Another clause related to travelling ministers. Wherever these either in life or doctrine grieved "good Friends that are steadfast in the Truth and sound in the faith" then they ought to forbear going abroad until reconciled. Friends were warned against having any hand in printing or spreading books tending to scandal or division, and it was recommended that faithful and sound Friends should have the view of books before they went to the press, as had formerly been the case,[1] "that nothing but what is sound and savoury, that will answer the witness of God in all people, even in our adversaries, may be exposed to public view." Finally, those who were overseers of the flock were advised against admitting to their number persons of weak faith, for none should order public business in the Church "but such as are felt in a measure of the universal Spirit of Truth."

This letter had behind it the full weight of the ministers.[2] Fox, however, was at the time in Scarborough Castle, "as a man buried alive," and can have had no hand in it. It obviously marks an important stage in Quaker history. Individual guidance is subordinated to the corporate sense of the Church, which is treated as finding authoritative expression through the elders who are sound in the faith. The fellowship is still grounded in a common experience of spiritual life; but agreement with the approved practices and principles which have sprung from that experience is also essential. In other words, Quakerism has narrowed itself into a religious Society.

The change was bound to come, and had in fact begun long before the letter, though it was then brought to a head by the need for a clear witness in times of persecution and for combating spiritual vagaries that were disintegrating in tendency. Quakerism had never been merely subjective. A living inward experience had produced righteousness of life; and if this fruit did not follow, the experience had either been a delusion or had been departed from. The Children of the Light must be walking

---

[1] See *Beginnings of Quakerism*, p. 304.
[2] The signatories are Farnsworth, Parker, George Whitehead, Loe, Josiah Coale, John Whitehead, Crisp, Thomas Green, John Moone, Thomas Briggs, and James Parke. Fox, Howgill, Dewsbury, and Thos. Taylor were in prison.

in the Light. Perrot's way of voluntary humility was one of those ways of a negative mysticism, which, by utterly abasing man, tend to disorganize personality rather than to co-ordinate and enrich it. True Quakerism had been very different. The great leaders were men of an intense sincerity, hungering and thirsting after the fuller life whose prize is righteousness.[1] The quest had heightened and compacted their natures and filled life with higher moral values. The Inward Light did not supersede ethical standards but illuminated and raised them. It had led the first Friends out from the world into a definite body of testimonies, which had been the natural expression in life of the great indwelling experience which they enjoyed, and from the first years fellowship had meant this common witness to a common body of Truth.[2]

Further, it is important to note that neither Fox nor the companies of Seekers who came to share his spiritual experience had developed Quakerism in isolation from historic Christianity. There had been, in their view, a long night of apostasy since the apostles' days, but now the Day of the Lord was come, and Christ would reign again in the hearts of His people. This view cut them off, it is true, from the later stream of Catholic tradition, but it united them the more closely both to primitive Christianity and to prophetic religion; and in both these rich periods of first-hand spiritual experience they found authoritative precedents for their principles and practice. Fox calls his accessions of fresh truth "openings," "the pure openings of the Light," but he was continually verifying them from the scriptures, and throughout his life his doctrinal treatises were in the main *catenae* of more or less relevant scripture passages and instances. His friends, according to Croese, averred that, though the Bible were lost, it might be had from the mouth of George Fox.[3] In

---

[1] As is well known, the Greek in Matt. v. 6 is emphatic, the verbs directly govern the word "righteousness," without any preposition. So also Tindale and the Vulgate.
[2] Cf. *Beginnings of Quakerism*, pp. 47-50, 277, 278, 137, 138.
[3] *Hist. of the Quakers*, 1696, English edn. p. 14.

speaking of his openings, he says that he found "they answered one another, and answered the scriptures"[1]—a significant statement, which shows that his own faculties of judgment were actively at work, co-ordinating the revelations that came to him into a harmony of truth, and comparing them with the experiences that had come to prophets and apostles. The Quaker scheme of thought, though imperfect, was essentially sane because the Light Within was continually being tested by the witness of the prophets and of primitive Christianity.

Quakerism then had always kept in vital touch both with righteousness of life and with historic religion. It had also, especially after Nayler's Fall,[2] abated its high language about personal infallibility, and been increasingly conscious of the special dangers that attended enthusiasm. But it had relied hitherto almost entirely upon the personal influence exercised by itinerating ministers and local elders, whose living witness for the Truth had been its most potent defence. The cohesive forces had been weakened by the storm of persecution, and it had become a pressing need to provide the body with means for dealing with those who had definitely ceased to maintain the Quaker witness. The 1666 epistle was a first attempt to strengthen government in the Church. The rapid developments that followed will be told in the next chapter.

[1] *Ellwood Journ.* i. 9.
[2] *Beginnings of Quakerism*, chap. xi. I may add some further elucidations of this chap. xi. that have come to light. It seems clear from Robert Rich, *Hidden Things brought to Light*, p. 37, that the phrase used by Fox (p. 248), "it was my foot," means "it was my foot he should kiss." With Margaret Fell's letter to Nayler (p. 249) may be compared a letter that she wrote to Thos. Ayrey, (Swarthm. Colln. vii. No. 98), who had evidently charged her with making a god of Fox. Robert Crab, mentioned p. 269, was like Samuel Cater from Littleport and died in 1656, presumably from the effects of an imprisonment (*per* J. J. Green and see Besse, *Sufferings*, i. 86). Rich (*op. cit.* p. 13) gives the names of the women who disturbed London meetings (p. 269) as "Mildred and Judah Crouch and Mary Powel." For a later reference to Hannah Salter, in Delaware, 1679-80, see *Quakers in the American Colonies*, p. 419, note.

CHAPTER IX

THE SETTLING OF MONTHLY MEETINGS

Beginning his ministry as an iconoclast—the apostle of a singularly individualistic faith—George Fox preserved that saving sense of the proportion of things, which qualified him to become the architect of a system of Church-organization suitable for the present needs of a great religious democracy. . . . In the main, experience has vindicated the wisdom of George Fox's ecclesiastical legislation. Some of it has been tested in two continents, through the lifetime of eight generations, with singularly successful results, whilst parts which have been neglected or forgotten might have prevented the development of much denominational weakness.—JOHN S. ROWNTREE in *Present Day Papers*, vol. iii. pp. 179, 180. Cf. the paragraphs on the organization of the Society of Friends, by Rufus M. Jones, *supra*, Introduction.

AT the beginning of September 1666, three months after the letter issued by the ministers, Fox was released from Scarborough Castle. He visited meetings in Yorkshire, and then came gently south to London, which he reached by the middle of November, his body so benumbed that he could hardly mount his horse, nor could he well bend his knees nor easily endure fire or warm meat, he had been kept so long from them.[1] He found the City in ashes, and the body of Friends bruised by persecution without and weakened by the dividing Perrot spirit within. The first need was to reinvigorate the desolated Church. The movement was suffering from arrested organization and poverty of leadership. Fox decided to go through England to reanimate and consolidate Quakerism, and to set up a system which should allow every man and woman with spiritual gifts to have an office and be serviceable. In order to reinforce the influence of the itinerating Publishers of Truth, he called into being the corporate

[1] *Camb. Journ.* ii. 110.

service of the Friends in each district who were grown in the Truth.

It is quite clear that with Fox this organization of Friends into Monthly Meetings, as the district meetings were called, had for its object the release of energy for the service of the Church. It was not in his view a step back into earthly things, but a step up into the life and order of the gospel. This is shown by reiterated phrases in his *Journal*, which for convenience I may be allowed to summarize in modern language. In the first place, he saw that true authority in the Church was not of man but of God. The sovereign power was the power of God. Then it came to him that all the heirs of the gospel, both men and women, inherited its authority, and ought to be entering into their inheritance. It followed naturally that there was a true gospel order in Church affairs—to be exercised by all spiritually-minded Friends met together to wait upon the Lord.

So they come to inherit and possess the joyful order of the joyful gospel, the comfortable order of the comfortable gospel, and the glorious order of the glorious gospel, and the everlasting order of the everlasting gospel—the power of God which will last for ever and outlast all the orders of the devil and that which is of men or by men.[1]

There is a simple directness about the arguments and the conclusions of Fox which may well amaze us. Theories of government in Church and State were the burning issues of the age. But it is most unlikely that he had read or would have cared to read the *Ecclesiastical Polity* of Hooker, or the *Leviathan* of Hobbes. His statesmanship, like that of other prophets, depended upon revelation and moral insight. He felt the lack of authority in the Church, and came to see that it was there all the time, in the highest form, if only those who should be using it rose to their responsibilities. Scarcely able to mount his horse, he rode through England, in spite of bodily weakness, with the fervour of an evangelist, because he felt himself to be calling Friends to exercise a glorious order

[1] *Camb. Journ.* ii. 128 and previous pp. Cf. ii. 343.

SETTLING OF MONTHLY MEETINGS

of the gospel which was among the highest of their spiritual prerogatives.

The work had begun in London in the spring of 1667, and was preceded by an earnest and in the main a successful attempt to restore the unity which had been impaired by the Perrot division. A "solemn meeting was appointed ... for a travail in spirit on behalf of those who had thus gone out,"[1] which held several days, on account of the number who wished, personally or by letter, to condemn their actions. Perrot was now dead, and many whom he had influenced had already forsaken the special practices which he favoured; so that the meetings were chiefly for confession and reinstatement. They afforded a good illustration of the way in which the gathered Church, using the authority residing in it, would be able to act in matters of discipline. Five Monthly Meetings were now set up in London, in addition to the old Two Weeks' Meeting begun about 1656, whose jurisdiction now became confined on most matters to the area within the City walls.[2] The early records are only extant in the case of Horslydown, where almost at once cases of discipline occur—marriage by the priest, drunkenness, keeping on the hat in prayer, "going to dig at Banbury for money," running into imaginations and studying astrology, using false measures, playing at ninepins—the medicine for these varied ills consisting in visits even to the fourth and fifth time, and in papers of denial from the parties, which were brought into the meeting, or, in case of marriages, carried to the priest. At this stage of the discipline and for years after, there was much long-suffering on the part of Friends, and it was only after persistent wrong-doing that "disownment" took place.

In the late summer of 1667, Fox began his missionary

---

[1] Thomas Ellwood, *Life*, pp. 243, 244; cf. *Camb. Journ.* ii. 111.
[2] *Camb. Journ.* ii. 111, and Beck and Ball, *London Friends' Meetings*, p. 88, who show that the old Two Weeks' Meeting (see for this, *Beginnings of Quakerism*, pp. 339, 340) continued for some years, and gave rise to Gracechurch Street M.M., after which it was maintained for nearly 120 years longer as a meeting having special charge of all marriages in the London M.M.'s. The six M.M.'s were Gracechurch Street, Devonshire House, Horslydown or Southwark, Peel, Ratcliff, and Westminster.

tour through the country, by the Eastern Counties to Lincoln, which he reached at Christmas; then through the North Midlands to South Lancashire, whence he sent papers into the Northern Counties and Scotland; then south through the West Midlands and the borders of Wales to Bristol, where we find him at the end of March 1668. Here the word of the Lord came to him to go back to London; and on his arrival he took steps to strengthen the marriage procedure of Friends, and also secured the establishment of two schools, one for children at Waltham Abbey, and one at Shacklewell, "set up to instruct young lasses and maidens in whatsoever things was civil and useful in the creation."[1]

Both these important developments were germane to the work in hand. It was inevitable that the fresh sense of authority in the Church should assert itself to bring marriages under the direct care of the Monthly Meetings, nor could group-consciousness be better promoted than by the institution of schools for Friends' children, where the atmosphere and ethical standards would foster the Quaker way of life.

Fox resumed his travels early in May, and before the end of the year had visited the remaining counties in the South and West of England. In one naïve passage he tells us how the settlement of meetings in which all might take care of God's glory and admonish those who walked contrary to it, made the very Justices say that "never such a man came into their country, that had reconciled neighbour to neighbour and husband to wife and turned many people from their loose lives." "And indeed," he adds, "these meetings did make a great reformation amongst people."[2]

There was opposition in some places to the new arrangements, and at Minehead in June he had forebodings one night that a dark spirit was abroad, striving to get up to disturb the Church.[3] Fox, however, had force of

---

[1] *Camb. Journ.* ii. 119. A fragment of rules of discipline for school-children in Fox's handwriting is given in *J.F.H.S.* v. 2, and may belong here. It is cited *post*, p. 441.
[2] *Camb. Journ.* ii. 120.   [3] *Ellwood Journ.* ii. 93.

personality to carry through his great work, and, though some must have disliked it from the first, the immediate benefits of the system disarmed for a time the hostility which afterwards asserted itself in what is known as the Wilkinson-Story separation. The crown of his labours was found in meetings held in London at the end of the year, first, for setting up again the annual meeting of ministers, which we last heard of in 1661,[1] and, secondly, for recovering Friends led astray by the Perrot spirit. A letter to the counties, asking for a collection, says, "Here hath been several blessed meetings which hath restored many that have been long out";[2] and John Rous, the Barbados planter who had an ear cropped at Boston and married young Margaret Fell, tells us that power and glory broke forth so irresistibly that the testimonies against the Perrot spirit came spontaneously from the Friends affected by it, and further meetings were to be held, as long as any honest-hearted among them were left ungathered.[3] Some not at the meetings, like Benjamin Furly and Penington, added their testimonies, and for the time Friends felt themselves again united into one soul and one mind. Even John Pennyman, the eccentric London merchant-draper, in an interval of clear-sightedness, confessed that Friends who had opposed the Perrot spirit were right, and is reported as saying, "If you had not stood, we had perished."[4]

Fox had made good use of the lull in persecution which preceded the passing of the Second Conventicle Act. The Society of Friends, for so we may henceforth call it, was

---

[1] See *Beginnings of Quakerism*, p. 337, and *J.F.H.S.* ii. 62. The 1666 meeting and the one held in April 1668 according to *Yearly Meeting Epistles, 1681-1857*, i. p. xiv, seem to have been specially summoned. The April 1668 meeting was presumably the occasion on which Fox promulgated his marriage regulations. The meeting at Christmas 1668 decided on annual meetings, the first to be at Easter 1670. (See epistle in *Letters of Early Friends*, p. 324, and a second in MS. Y.M. Minutes, beginning of vol. i.)

[2] See last-named epistle.

[3] *Letters of Early Friends*, p. 166, from Swarthm. Colln. i. 108.

[4] See Penn's *Judas and the Jews* (1673) in *Works*, 1726 edn. ii. 205. Furly's testimony is in *Collectitia*, p. 149, with another striking one from John Lodge of Amsterdam. Several testimonies, including those from John Whitehead, Penington, Crook, James Claypole, John Osgood, and William Gosnell, are given in Penn's *Judas and the Jews*, 1673; see also Dev. Ho. Penington MSS. i. 61, by Penington, dated 26th Oct. 1671.

now provided with an organization which would outstand all shocks, and has continued to the present day. We have ample evidence of the thoroughness with which the foundation work was done. In many districts the Minute Books date back to this period and include records of the first establishment of the Monthly Meetings.[1] Where this is the case, we may expect to find a paper containing a list of the meetings in the county, divided up into Monthly Meetings, with the place and time of their holding and a list of the principal Friends of each particular meeting. Sometimes the presence of Fox is mentioned, as in the Dorset entry: "Note that at this meeting was our dear friend and elder brother in the Truth, George Fox, who was then travelling through the nation, being moved of the Lord thereunto, in order to the settling of both Monthly and Quarterly Meetings amongst Friends in their respective counties, which work the Lord blessed and prospered in his hands."[2] The objects in view may be found briefly recorded, as "for the supply of the poor and other affairs of the Church," and in many cases a paper is added, written by Fox about January 1669, and presumably approved by the Yearly Meeting of ministers that was then sitting, beginning, "Friends' fellowship must be in the Spirit."[3] Its nineteen sections contain a body of discipline for the use of the new meetings, and within a few months of its promulgation it was printed by adverse hands as "Canons and institutions drawn up and agreed upon by the . . . Quakers from all parts of the kingdom at their new theatre in Gracechurch Street in or about

---

[1] Data are probably extant for a Book of Meetings of Friends, at the time of setting up the Monthly Meetings : see for Yorkshire, *J.F.H.S.* ii. 32, 73, 101, and map at end of J. W. Rowntree, *Essays and Addresses*; for Ely, Cambs. and Hunts, *J.F.H.S.* vi. 12; for Dorset, reference in *J.F.H.S.* v. 39; for Lincoln, the Q.M. Minutes; for Somerset, Bristol MSS. ii. No. 10; for Sussex, Frontispiece to T. W. Marsh, *Early Friends in Surrey and Sussex*; besides much other information in *F.P.T.* and other printed books. In 1691 there were 151 Monthly Meetings in England and Wales. (See Y.M. printed epistle and MS. Minutes.)

[2] *J.F.H.S.* v. 40.

[3] Printed, with an omission, in Beck and Ball, *London Friends' Meetings*, pp. 47-52, who say that they have found record of its being periodically read in business meetings as late as 1776. Cf. Barclay, *Inner Life*, pp. 394-399, who seems to have been the first to point out the significance of the document. I have used a MS. Copy in the Kendal Early Record Book.

January 1668/9, George Fox being their president." A summary rearranged as to order will show what Church government meant to Fox when he established it. Church meetings, he says, began with relief of the poor. The law had ordained that there was not to be a beggar in Israel,[1] "and amongst the Christians' meetings in the first age, there was a man's meeting to be set up at Jerusalem to see that nothing was lacking, which was the gospel's order according to the law of Jesus." But the apostasy came, and the true Church was in the wilderness for 1260 days, but now was come up out of it, and "the everlasting gospel shall be preached again, as [it] was among the apostles, and the gospel order shall be set up, as [it] was amongst them, and a man's meeting, as [it] was at the first conversion, to see that nothing be lacking in the Church: then all is well." Fox, as was his wont, rooted his new system firmly in apostolic precedent.

In recommending subjects for consideration, he makes no distinction between the Monthly and Quarterly Meetings, nor was any clear difference drawn in the earlier years, though gradually the Monthly Meetings took full control of much local work. The meetings are to visit and reprove persons of disorderly life and those who have gone from the Truth, or been married by the priest, or wear their hats when Friends pray "and are gotten into the old rotten principles of the Ranters." There is a good deal about marriage, including a paragraph advising that if a widow marries, the question of settling the estate of her first husband upon his children by her should be attended to, and another condemning those whose affections run now after one person and now after another. Fox also condemns slanderers, railers, and such as go "up and down to cheat by borrowing and getting money of Friends in by-places." Prisoners and the poor are to be relieved, and differences are to be settled by the arbitration of other Friends. Inquiry is to be made as to any who pay tithes, and so make void "the testimony and sufferings of all our brethren who have suffered many of them to death." Sufferings are to be carefully reported to the Quarterly Meetings and so to London, "that nothing of the memorial of the blood and cruel sufferings of the brethren be lost." Children are to be trained in the fear of the Lord, and burying-grounds provided,

---

[1] See Deut. xv. 4, and *post*, p. 559.

also books for registering births, marriages, and burials. The paper closes with a beautiful paragraph, which expresses the spirit of the discipline in these early days :

"Dear Friends, be faithful in the service of God, and mind the Lord's business, and be diligent, and bring the power of the Lord over all those that have gainsaid it : and all you that be faithful go to visit them all that have been convinced from house to house, that if it be possible you may not leave a hoof in Egypt : and so every one go seek the lost sheep and bring him home on your back to the fold, and there will be more joy of that one sheep than ninety-nine in the fold."

The new meetings naturally took over the Church work which had previously been done in a less systematic way ; the fresh departure consisting in the corporate action that was henceforth regularly taken in cases of delinquency. This had not been entirely neglected : we shall remember the advice in the Balby letter of 1656 [1] that persons who walked disorderly should be spoken to in private, then before two or three witnesses, then, if necessary, before the Church, with a final resort to some of the Quaker leaders ; and similar advice had been given at the meetings at Horsham, Cerne, and Glastonbury in 1659.[2] In Somerset, Friends from 1660 onwards had administered discipline in their meetings,[3] though there was evidently a development in '68, for one of the first Minutes deals with a Friend who had said that a Bishop's Court was being set up. There was a Two Weeks' Meeting at London, and five Monthly Meetings had existed, as we have seen, in Yorkshire prior to the division into fourteen Monthly Meetings made with the help of Fox in March 1669.[4] My impression is that these meetings, and others like them, confined disciplinary action mainly to warnings and exhortations, but, with the establishment of Monthly Meetings, Fox seems to have laid down a more specific procedure.[5] Where delinquents had been admonished four or five times, without result, Friends were advised to

---

[1] *Beginnings of Quakerism*, pp. 310-314.   [2] *Ibid.* pp. 314-317.
[3] John Whiting, in John Banks, *Journal*, p. 140.
[4] *Camb. Journ.* ii. 134, and *ante*, p. 218.
[5] The document is in Kendal Early Record Book among other papers of 1669. Cf. Fox, *Epistles*, No. 220, last para., under date 1662, which may be wrong.

draw up a paper against them at their Quarterly Meeting, showing that they had no unity with such workers of darkness, who had cast out themselves by going from the life and power of God in which the fellowship of Friends consisted. In September 1669, the Bristol Friends set up a Monthly Meeting for cases of discipline, in relief of their Two Weeks' Meeting, the opening Minute of which shows that it was to proceed upon the lines of Fox's advice. Many cases at once came forward for treatment, amongst others John Foster was to be spoken to for going to the Baptist Meeting. After four visits the entry is made: "Disowned, for that he is wholly departed from Truth."[1] This became the usual term for the final step in cases of discipline. There was no formal membership till a much later date,[2] and therefore all that could be done was to refuse to recognize the delinquent as a true Friend.

Fox was copious in counsel at this time. The so-called Canons were very early published with additions.[3] Other advice ranges from counsel as to sleeping in meetings and keeping meetings "civil and quiet," free from "rude boys and unruly spirits," to far-sighted proposals for the poor and the infirm in mind or body.[4] In a notable sentence he expresses the view of personal responsibility which marks off Quakerism definitely from priestly forms of religion. "The least member in the Church hath an office and is serviceable, and every member hath need one of another."[5]

As we make our way through the mass of wholesome though tedious advice, we feel the excellence of much that was laid upon the new meetings, but wonder if those who were to give corporate expression to the spiritual judgment of a county or a district would always rise to their responsibilities. The system could only be worked well by men of enlightened spiritual experience.

Fox himself was emphatic on this point, though he

---

[1] *J.F.H.S.* v. 2. There is a Bristol Minute of 16th Dec. 1667 "disowning" a marriage. [2] See *post*, p. 459.
[3] The edn. bears date 1668, *i.e.* before 25th March 1669. The reprint in Fox, *Epistles*, p. 276, is dated 1669.
[4] Fox, *Epistles*, pp. 257, 276, 287. See *post*, pp. 570, 571.
[5] Fox, *Epistles*, p. 290.

failed to see that in the long run the level of character could not be much higher than the general level of each Quaker group.

The Quarterly Meeting should be made up of weighty, seasoned, and substantial Friends that understands the business of the Church; for no unruly and unseasoned persons should come there, nor indeed into the Monthly Meetings, but [those] who are single-hearted, seasoned and honest.[1]

In May 1669 Fox went to Ireland in company with four other able ministers, James Lancaster, John Stubbs, Thomas Briggs, and Robert Lodge, all of whom except Briggs had already visited the country. "When we came on shore," says George, with his abnormal spiritual scent, "the earth and the very air smelt with the corruption of the nation, and gave another smell than England to me, with the corruption and the blood and the massacres and the foulness that ascended."[2] Friends, however, had suffered little persecution except for tithes and other ecclesiastical demands. They had increased in numbers, and there were about thirty settled meetings in Leinster, Ulster, and Munster, mostly, as in England, held in private houses. The Perrot spirit had found small entrance,[3] and the Quaker communities were full of vigour and zeal. William Edmondson, the apostle of Irish Quakerism—an old Ironside who named one of his daughters Hindrance and his youngest son Trial[4]—had long felt the need for discipline in the Church. As early as 1661 the sense of this came weightily upon him, and, says he,

. . . I was made a thrashing instrument in the hand of the Lord to thrash sharply, reprove and rebuke such as walked loosely, in the liberty of their wills and flesh, and held the profession of Truth in unrighteousness: I could not get from under this burden, till it pleased God to send His servant George Fox to set up Men's and Women's Meetings, and then I was eased.[5]

He promoted the new system with joy, since "this gave every faithful Friend a share of the burden."[6] Pro-

---

[1] Fox, *Epistles*, p. 290. Cf. advice given by Fox when setting up Dorset M.M.'s, *J.F.H.S.* v. 39.   [2] *Camb. Journ.* ii. 137.
[3] *Ibid.* 148.   [4] *J.F.H.S.* iii. 14.   [5] *Journ.*   [6] *Ibid.*

SETTLING OF MONTHLY MEETINGS

vincial Meetings every six weeks were set up in 1668, and, when Fox came, district Monthly Meetings were added and soon after a National Half-Year's Meeting, which was at first chiefly occupied with sufferings, and began in May 1670 at the lodgings of the young convert, William Penn, who was paying a visit to Dublin.[1]

The visit to Ireland was carried through with the glad courage that Fox had shown in the Commonwealth days. There were warrants out against him, which we should like to have seen, describing his hair, his hat, his clothes, his person, and his horse; but he escaped them all, and made "a gallant visitation" to persons of "a gallant spirit," "worthy to be visited," to use his own phrases. At Cork,

... the power of the Lord was so great that Friends, in the power and Spirit of the Lord, brake out into singing many together with an audible voice, making melody in their hearts.[2]

Fox himself had a rhythmic message beating in his soul for Friends in the ministry, by which he would stir them to a fresh sense of the urgency and power of the gospel entrusted to them. They were the trumpets of the Lord to sound abroad His voice, and his address had for its reiterated refrain the word "Sound."[3]

Sound, sound abroad, you faithful servants of the Lord and witnesses in His name, ... and prophets of the Highest, and angels of the Lord! Sound ye all abroad in the world, to the awakening and raising of the dead, that they may be awakened, and raised up out of the grave, to hear the voice that is living. For the dead have long heard the dead, and the blind have long wandered among the blind, and the deaf amongst the deaf. Therefore sound, sound, ye servants and prophets and angels of the Lord, ye trumpets of the Lord, that you may awaken the dead, and awaken them that be asleep in their graves of sin, death and hell, and sepulchres and sea and earth, and who lie in the tombs. Sound, sound abroad, ye trumpets, and raise up the dead, that the dead may hear the voice of the Son of God,

---

[1] Rutty, *Hist. of Friends in Ireland*, 1800 edn. pp. 115-118.
[2] *Camb. Journ.* ii. 141.
[3] *Ellwood Journ.* ii. 111. The passage is used in current (1912) edn. of *Christian Practice of the Society of Friends*, p. 40.

the voice of the second Adam that never fell; the voice of the Light, and the voice of the Life; the voice of the Power, and the voice of the Truth; the voice of the Righteous, and the voice of the Just. Sound, sound the pleasant and melodious sound; sound, sound ye the trumpets, the melodious sound abroad, that all the deaf ears may be opened to hear the pleasant sound of the trumpet to judgment and Life, to condemnation and Light.

Such a passage, if pondered, helps us to understand Penn's description of Fox's ministry, that though his expression

... might sound uncouth and unfashionable to nice ears, his matter was nevertheless very profound; and would not only bear to be often considered, but, the more it was so, the more weighty and instructing it appeared. And, as abruptly and brokenly as sometimes his sentences would seem to fall from him about Divine things, it is well known they were often as texts to many fairer declarations.[1]

Fox was now a man of forty-five, and his strenuous service and heavy sufferings had already left their mark. There can have been little to choose between him and Margaret Fell, who was ten years his senior but would survive him eleven years. It seems probable that the idea of marriage had been formed while both were prisoners at Lancaster in 1664 and '5. Margaret Fell was not released till the summer of '68, but had liberty the previous winter to see Fox in Cheshire, and saw him again in London the following winter, when he told her that the time was drawing on for their marriage but he must first visit Ireland.[2] He landed in England on the 13th August, "much wearied with his hard service,"[3] and met Margaret Fell at Bristol in October. In his mind the union seems to have had a mystical fitness at a time when the Church, through the Quaker movement, was come up out of the wilderness, and the gospel order had been again set up. He wrote a paper on the subject to all the Church meetings of Friends, which is said to have

---

[1] Preface to Fox's *Journal*.
[2] See *Camb. Journ.* ii. 114, 133, 154, and Margt. Fell, Testimony in Fox's *Journal*.
[3] John Rous to Margt. Fell, London, 24th Aug. 1669, in Dev. Ho. Gibson MSS. ii. p. 11.

been so "ill resented, and so much disliked that it was called in again, and a rare thing it was to get a sight thereof."[1] Forty years later it was printed in the envenomed writings of Francis Bugg, from a copy given him by an "ancient Quaker," which seems genuine, as it agrees with what we know of the contents from other sources.[2] Fox wrote that the marriage was commanded him as a figure or testimony of the Church coming out of the wilderness and of the marriage of the Lamb before the world was. He witnessed this marriage of the Lamb in the restoration which had come to him out of the Fall and in the Seed of Life. Its nature had been seen by him for many years past, but the command from God to fulfil the thing had only come of late. He explained his reasons to one of his old Leicestershire neighbours in the same way: "as a testimony that all might come up into the marriage as was in the beginning; and as a testimony that all might come up out of the wilderness to the marriage of the Lamb" (Rev. xix. 7).[3] In his mind the living spiritual experience which had come to Friends and redeemed them up out of the Fall made them partakers of this heavenly order of marriage.

Margaret Fell had one son, hostile to her and Fox for their Quakerism, and six surviving daughters, three married and three unmarried. The daughters had shared their mother's religious convictions from the first, and the marriage had their approval.[4] It was passed by Bristol Friends, first at their Two Weeks' Meeting, three days later at a meeting of both men and women, and on the following day at the Friday public meeting for worship.[5]

[1] *The Spirit of the Hat* (1673), p. 42, which gives purport of paper, no doubt the one referred to in *Camb. Journ.* ii. 153 (correct note, ii. 416, accordingly). Mucklow's criticism is enlarged in *The Snake in the Grass*, 3rd edn. 1698, p. 191.
[2] *Great Mystery of the Little Whore*, pt. iv. p. 268, letter dated 2nd Oct. 1669.
[3] *Camb. Journ.* ii. 154: for Fox's reasons cf. *Epistles*, pp. 278-281, and Marriage Certificate, *infra*.
[4] The daughters' testimonies of approval are in Helen G. Crosfield's *Margaret Fox*, p. 140, from the MS. in Dev. Ho. referred to in *Camb. Journ.* ii. 416. The seventh daughter, Bridget Draper, may have died before 1669. But consider Helen G. Crosfield, pp. 95, 96.
[5] The particulars are in the Marriage Certificate, printed in Helen G. Crosfield's *Margaret Fox*, p. 254, from Thirnbeck Colln., but without the

Fox was also careful not to take any benefit in his wife's property.[1] The marriage took place at the Broadmead meeting-house on the 27th October, and the certificate is signed by the six daughters and three sons-in-law of Margaret Fell as well as by many other Friends. The paramount claims of service soon separated husband and wife, and during their twenty-one years of married life they seem only to have spent about five or six together. Margaret Fox says :

> And though the Lord had provided an outward habitation for him, yet he was not willing to stay at it, because it was so remote and far from London, where his service most lay. And my concern for God and His holy, eternal Truth was then in the North, where God had placed and set me, and likewise for the ordering and governing of my children and family; so that we were very willing, both of us, to live apart some years upon God's account and His Truth's service, and to deny ourselves of that comfort which we might have had in being together.[2]

After his marriage Fox resumed the important work of consolidating the Quaker Church. One of the finest of his epistles bears date this winter,[3] and exhorts Friends not to quench the motions of the Spirit in themselves nor its movings in others.

Many, he says, have gone beyond their measures, but more have quenched the Spirit and so become dead and dull or subject to a false fear. War should be made with the Philistine who would stop up the wells and springs, for in the Light every one should have something to offer. "What can the ploughman say for God with his spiritual plough? Is the fallow ground ploughed up? Has he abundance of the heavenly seed of life? So what can the heavenly husbandman say? Has he abundance of spiritual fruit in store? What can the thresher say? Has he gotten the wheat out of the sheaf—the heavenly wheat, with his heavenly flail?" All have their place in God's vineyard, "yet none are to find fault one with another, but every one labouring in their places, praising the Lord, looking to Him for their wages,

---

signatures, which are in *J.F.H.S.* ix. 99. For the Minutes see *J.F.H.S.* viii. 136. For the wording cf. Fox, *Epistles*, pp. 278, 279.

[1] *Camb. Journ.* ii. 153; cf. *Ellwood Journ.* ii. 357.

[2] Testimony in *Ellwood Journ.*

[3] Fox, *Epistles*, No. 275, original dated 6th Jan. 1670, in Swarthm. Colln. vii. No. 44, with somewhat cruder wording.

their heavenly penny of life from the Lord of Life." "Come fishermen, what have you catched with your nets? What can you say for God? Your brethren Peter and John, fishermen, could say much for God. Read in the Acts and you may see it: I would not have you degenerate from their spirit."

Fox, it is clear, felt strongly that the future of the Society depended upon a widespread and eager individual faithfulness.

The year 1670 was full of peril to Nonconformity. Intolerance was once more in the saddle, and the new Conventicle Act seemed fitted to satisfy the policy of prelates and the avarice of Informers. Margaret Fox had been thrown into prison again upon her old *praemunire*,[1] and a little later, when the new Act came into force, Fox had braved its first dangers and only narrowly escaped.[2] He discerned the ecclesiastical subtlety behind it, which sought to enforce conformity by seizing the goods rather than the person of the offender, and urged Friends to set their affections above earthly things:[3]

If so be that the Lord do suffer you to be tried, let all be given up; and look at the Lord and His power, which is over the whole world, and will be when the world is gone. . . . Friends, the Lord hath blessed you in outward things; and now the Lord may try you, whether your minds be in the outward things or with the Lord that gave you them. Therefore keep in the Seed, by which all outward things were made and which is over them all. What? Shall not I pray and speak to God, with my face towards heavenly Jerusalem, according to my wonted time? And let not anyone's Delilah shave his head, lest such lose their strength: neither rest in its lap, lest the Philistines be upon you; for your rest is in Christ Jesus; therefore rest not in anything else.

The persecuting spirit behind the Act burdened him sorely, and in the late summer, while returning towards London from a visit through the South, he was struck down with severe illness[4]—outwardly a fever and ague,

---

[1] *Camb. Journ.* ii. 155. [2] *Ante*, p. 78; *Camb. Journ.* ii. 155-162.
[3] *Ellwood Journ.* ii. 123.
[4] For this illness see *Camb. Journ.* ii. 165-176, letters of Margt. Rous, John Rous, and John Stubbs, of 14th Oct., 4th Nov., and 25th Oct., in Helen G. Crosfield's *Margaret Fox*, pp. 146-149, from the Swarthm., Abraham, and

but inwardly a profound psychical disturbance, which showed that body and spirit had been grievously overstrained under the oppression of the age. Lying, as was thought, at the point of death, with sight and hearing gone, he removed himself from Stratford to Gerrard Roberts' house at Edmonton, and three weeks later, though he could hardly stand, he visited his dying friend Amor Stoddart at Enfield. He lay there that winter at a widow Friend's named Elizabeth Dry, lovingly tended amongst others by his wife's daughter Margaret Rous, and by his old friend John Stubbs. He says:

> I lay . . . all that winter warring with the evil spirits, and could not endure the smell of any flesh-meat; and saw all the religions and people that lived in them : and the priests that held them up a company of men-eaters, and how they eat up the people like bread and gnawing the flesh off their bones. And great sufferings I was under at this time, beyond words to declare, for I was come into the deep and the men-eaters was about me, and I warred with their spirits.[1]

"And so," he adds, with a side glance at the Puritan persecutors of Massachusetts Bay,[2] "the Church was but a company of men-eaters, men of cruel visages and of long teeth, that had cried against the men-eaters in New England ; but I saw they was in the same natures." This was the great incubus that oppressed him ; but other experiences also came : he saw a black coffin but passed over it : hypocrisy sickened him in the form of an ugly slobbering hound, and he had a vision of the stones and earth which had been piled up over man since he went from the image of God. Under the stones and earth was a vault "topfull of people," whom he set free : and below this a second, and, if I understand him aright, a third :

> . . . and I went down and went along the vault, and there sat a woman in white looking at time how it passed away : and there followed me a woman down in the vault, in which vault was the treasure, and so she laid her hand on the treasure on my left

---

Shackleton Collns., and especially comments of Rufus M. Jones in *Beginnings of Quakerism*, p. xxx.

[1] *Camb. Journ.* ii. 167. [2] *Ibid.* p. 168.

hand, and then time whisked on apace; but I clapped my hand upon her and said, Touch not the treasure : and then time passed not so swift.[1]

More intelligible is his opening about the New Jerusalem. With the help of his two learned friends, Richard Richardson and John Stubbs, and of the text of Rev. xxi. 16 in the Antwerp Polyglot,[2] Fox satisfied himself that the heavenly city of Apocalyptic vision was ten times the compass of the earth, and reached by tortuous mathematics the sound conclusion that the whole world was within its light and within the spiritual reign of Christ. This we may suppose was a meditation of his convalescence, for as the persecution ceased so he came from under his travail and suffering. By April he was in London, his wife's pardon procured, and his mind already turned to further labours for developing the corporate life of Friends.[3] A man of less indomitable heart would have shrunk from beginning, spent with illness, the most arduous journey of his life. The visit to America, from 11th August 1671 to 28th June 1673, does not fall within the scope of this history,[4] except as it illustrates the character and policy of Fox and his companions. It is clear that their primary object was to bring the transatlantic Quaker communities into line with the Society at home, both in practice and Church government. At the time of settling the Men's Monthly Meeting system in England, Fox had written to Barbados and America for Friends there to do the same,[5] and Burnyeat, crossing the seas in 1670, had done a good deal of preparatory work. Vigorous Church life throughout the colonies dates from this period, though not without opposition from some. But the group of Friends from the mother-country, labouring now together

---

[1] *Camb. Journ.* ii. 175.
[2] *Ibid.* pp. 170-175. The new reading was "twelve twelve thousand furlongs" for the length, which they multiplied by 12 instead of by 4 to get the circuit, adding a fresh circuit for each of the dimensions, because the height and length and breadth were all equal. By this strange spiritual arithmetic a total of 1,728,000 furlongs was obtained, *i.e.* 216,000 miles or ten times the compass of the earth.
[3] John Rous to Margaret Fox, 4th April 1671, Swarthm. Colln. i. 83.
[4] *Camb. Journ.* ii. 176-255, and *Quakers in the American Colonies*, pp. 111-121 (New England), 229-231 (New York), 280-288 (Southern Colonies), 359-362 (New Jersey). [5] *Camb. Journ.* ii. 126.

and now in twos and threes, besides their work of consolidation, did a great piece of Quaker extension, adding many to the meetings and breaking much fresh ground. They had eager audiences and a freedom of speech which more than compensated for the hardships of American travel. Fox was at his best; at one place he writes, "they said that if they had money enough that they would hire me . . . and I said, Then it was time for me to go away; . . . for that, viz. hiring, had spoiled them and many, for not improving their own talents; for we brought every one to their own Teacher."[1] He had for helpers Stubbs, "learned in the Hebrew and Greek," Burnyeat, a man "of a moderate spirit and an able speaker," and Edmondson, the old Ironside, " a stout portly man of a great voice."[2] James Lancaster, his former travelling companion, and Robert Widders, "a valiant man for God and His Truth,"[3] were also with him, as well as other less-known Friends. The deep impression made and the lasting results show again the supreme value to the Quaker movement of the itinerant work of inspired leaders. The dynamic lives of these men, who counted nothing too hard in the service of Christ, corrected disorder more surely than any system of Church government, and declared Truth more vitally than any creed.

[1] *Camb. Journ.* ii. 224.
[2] See Roger Williams' descriptions in *Quakers in the American Colonies*, p. 116 *n*.
[3] John Whiting, *Persecution Exposed*, p. 171.

CHAPTER X

WOMEN'S MEETINGS AND CENTRAL ORGANIZATION

> And truly I must say that though God had visibly clothed him [George Fox] with a Divine preference and authority—and indeed his very presence expressed a religious majesty—yet he never abused it; but held his place in the Church of God with great meekness and a most engaging humility and moderation. For, upon all occasions, like his blessed Master, he was a servant to all, holding and exercising his eldership in the invisible power that had gathered them, with reverence to the Head and care over the body; and was received only in that spirit and power of Christ as the first and chief elder in this age. Who, as he was therefore worthy of double honour, so for the same reason it was given by the faithful of this day, because his authority was inward and not outward; and that he got it and kept it by the love of God and power of an endless life. I write my knowledge and not report; and my witness is true, having been with him for weeks and months together on divers occasions, and those of the nearest and most exercising nature, and that by night and by day, by sea and by land, in this and in foreign countries; and I can say, I never saw him out of his place, or not a match for every service or occasion.—WILLIAM PENN, Preface to Fox's *Journal*.

I HAVE already pointed out that the setting-up of Men's Monthly Meetings was designed to reinforce the leadership which had been given by the ardent Publishers of Truth. The object of Fox was to strengthen government in the Church by laying it, both as a privilege and a responsibility, upon the whole body of honest-hearted Friends. He had established the system with the help of numerous letters of advice, and it would have been easy for an ambitious man to have continued to act as the central authority of the Society, with the help of a few others chosen by himself. Church history would have furnished abundant precedents. But Fox had no thought of self: what seemed to unsympathetic critics his boundless self-confidence was rather his bold reliance on the Truth, and Truth was a living experience open to all, not the monopoly of an individual. Accordingly, while letters of counsel would continue to be issued, government in the Church would be freely developed on the same broad lines upon which Fox had founded it. Meetings would be set up, which would give women their place of service, and the central control of the Society would be spread over a number of important bodies which met in London—in particular, the Yearly Meeting, the Morning Meeting, and the Meeting for Sufferings. We must describe these developments before we tell the story of the great controversy upon Church government which arose in the Society and marred its fellowship.

The equality of men and women in spiritual privilege and responsibility has always been one of the glories of Quakerism. Fox, in his years of wandering, had met with a strange sort of people who held that "women have no souls, no more than a goose." He had aptly reproved them with the case of Mary, as shown by the opening words of the Magnificat, "My soul doth magnify the Lord,"[1] and, a little later, had interfered in a public religious debate to defend the right of a woman to ask a question.[2] His early epistles contain sentences such as the following: "The Lamb of God, the Son of God, is but one in all His males and females, sons and daughters, and they all are one in Christ, and Christ one in them all."[3] We recognize to-day that in the freedom of the gospel "there can be neither Jew nor Greek; there can be neither bond nor free; there can be no male and female; for ye are all one man in Christ Jesus." Friends accepted to the full these great words to the Galatian Churches, and refused to adopt the narrower and somewhat contradictory attitude towards women which Paul sometimes took, especially in writing to the Church at Corinth.[4]

---

[1] *Ellwood Journal*, i. 8.   [2] *Ibid.* i. 25.
[3] Fox, *Epistles*, No. 27; cf. Nos. 25, 29, 35, and his piece, "The Woman learning in Silence" (1656), in *Doctrinals*, pp. 77-82.
[4] Gal. iii. 28; and for women keeping silence in the Church, 1 Cor. xiv. 34-36, and 1 Tim. ii. 11, but cf. 1 Cor. xi. 5. Tischendorf and Von Soden, followed by Dr. James Moffatt, in his New Testament translation of 1913, read the latter part of 1 Cor. xiv. 33 with v. 34, "As in all the Churches of the saints, let the women keep silence in the Churches." But the fact that an important group of authorities places vv. 34, 35, beginning "Let the women keep silence in the

They found abundant evidence of women sharing in the gift of prophecy, as, for example, in the Old Testament, in Peter's quotation from Joel on the day of Pentecost, and in the experience of the primitive Church.[1] It was clear to them that neither a separated clergy nor a privileged sex was to monopolize any of the gifts of the Spirit.

From the first, women took a large part in the publishing of the Quaker message. Many were stirred by Fox to an enthusiastic devotion — not without its extravagances—which suggested to the scoffing world the credulous explanation that he had bewitched them into following him by tying ribbons about their arms.[2] Almost his first convert was a woman, Elizabeth Hooton of Skegby in Nottinghamshire, and her name heads the noble roll of women-ministers. Her motherly solicitude for the prophet of Quakerism led her, at the age of seventy, to join the party to America, "to do the best that is required for him," though in Jamaica, almost at the outset of the service, a sudden illness seized her, and in Fox's words she died "in peace like a lamb."[3] Another woman, Margaret Fell, made her home at Swarthmore Hall the centre of the Quaker movement during its years of most rapid expansion. Women began the work in London and at the Universities, and were the first to reach Massachusetts, while the efforts to carry the message to Mediterranean lands will always be linked with the names of Mary Fisher and Katharine Evans.[4]

Churches," after v. 40 favours the view that the clause "as in all the Churches of the saints" belongs, as in R.V. and A.V., to vv. 32, 33. Nor does it seem likely that the word "Churches" would be used in the same sentence in two different meanings, first "Churches," secondly "Church-meetings." Indeed, it is very doubtful whether Paul would have been justified in so sweeping a statement, in view of the service of women at Philippi and the work of such a leader as Priscilla. On the other hand, the direction to keep silent might be warranted if confined to the Church at Corinth under the circumstances of the time.

[1] Barclay, *Apology*, Prop. x. sect. 27, deals briefly with the question.
[2] *Beginnings of Quakerism*, p. 181; cf. pp. 67, 102, 110.
[3] *Ibid.* p. 44, letter to Margt. Fox, 1670, in Swarthm. Colln. i. 152, letter from John Stubbs to Elizabeth Hooton, Enfield, 5th Dec. 1670, in Dev. Ho. A.R.B. Colln. No. 97, and *Camb. Journ.* ii. 213, and note at p. 463. An adequate account of Elizabeth Hooton has now been written by Emily Manners and published (1914) as *J.F.H.S.* Supplement No. 12; cf. *J.F.H.S.* xii. 86-89.
[4] *Beginnings of Quakerism*, pp. 98-110, 134-136, 157-159, 402, 420-431. The age of Mary Fisher should be given (p. 423) as thirty-five.

The early business meetings of Friends in the North had been made up of men only, but, after the institution of the Two Weeks' Men's Meeting in London, about 1656, two Women's Meetings developed in the city, the Box Meeting and the Two Weeks' Meeting.[1] The Box Meeting gathered moneys for poor relief in a box, and seems to have begun soon after the Men's Meeting, on direct encouragement from Fox. It met once a week, and was not accountable to any other body. A little later, if I interpret our sources aright, the other meeting was set on foot by the Men's Meeting in order to help them in visiting the sick and the prisoners and in looking after the poor, the widows and the fatherless, its poor relief being provided largely by the Men's Meeting and being administered on lines agreed with them. It was this meeting, growing up in co-ordination with the Men's Meeting, which became a model of other Women's Meetings begun later. In addition to the services I have named, it came to concern itself with the orderly conversation of women Friends, endeavouring to reclaim any who had gone astray and to stop false reports and things tending to division. It took in hand the finding of places for maid-servants who were Friends and, where necessary, regulated the relations between them and their mistresses. It also dealt with women who married non-Friends or were married at church.

A similar meeting, for the care of the poor, was

[1] Cf. *Beginnings of Quakerism*, pp. 340-342. Our sources of information are the following: (*a*) 1662, Burrough's account in *Letters of Early Friends*, pp. 308, 309; (*b*) 1675, Epistle from London Women Friends in *Letters of Early Friends*, pp. 343-346; (*c*) 1676, Fox's account in *Epistles*, p. 6, *Camb. Journ.* ii. 342; (*d*) 1680, *An Epistle for True Love*, etc., by Ann Whitehead and Mary Elson; (*e*) 1707, *Life of Gilbert Latey*, pp. 145-149. Mary Elson's account is the most precise: she speaks of origin of meeting some twenty-three years earlier, say 1657, as due to Fox, cf. account (*c*), and tells how they established a "conveniency" for receiving offerings, and that after some time there came two of the brethren from the Men's Meeting to them, cf. account (*e*), expressing their unity and offering pecuniary help. This looks as though the "Box" Meeting were earlier than the other. Beck and Ball, *London Friends' Meetings*, pp. 348, 349, think it somewhat the later. In none of the sources are two meetings spoken of, and the distinction between the two was, I think, one rather of function than of membership. For use made of contents of Box, women Friends were accountable to no one; the other meeting was in direct association with the Men's Two Weeks' Meeting. Sewel, ii. 194, refers origin of meeting to needs of Plague-year, 1665, but this is certainly several years too late.

established at Bristol,[1] and there were perhaps others; but it was only, I think, in the spring of 1671, after recovery from his illness, that Fox took the settling of Women's Meetings seriously in hand. His circular letter of 16th June,[2] after referring to their existence in other places, urges their establishment, "that so the women may come into the practice of pure religion, which is to visit the widows and fatherless and to see that all be kept from the spots of the world." Christ has redeemed Friends out of the old Adam in the Fall into the higher life of righteousness before the Fall, in which women are "all helpsmeet to the men in righteousness and truth and holiness and justice and the wisdom of God." A passage in a somewhat later epistle [3] puts the view of Fox quite clearly:

Friends, keep your women's meetings in the power of God, which the devil is out of: and take your possession of that which you are heirs of; and keep the gospel-order. For man and woman were helpsmeet, in the image of God and in righteousness and holiness, in the dominion before they fell: but, after the Fall, in the transgression, the man was to rule over his wife. But, in the restoration by Christ, into the image of God and His righteousness and holiness again, in that they are helpsmeet, man and woman, as they were in before the Fall.

It has been sometimes thought, by hasty students of Quaker history, that the separate Women's Meetings were designed to give women some share in Church government but not an equal share with the men. That was indeed the effect of their institution, but it is clear from this and many other passages in the epistles of Fox that the question whether the women should be given less or more authority was not in his mind. What he was concerned with was to give them their place, their right place, and to stir them up to take it. His prime motive, as in the case of the Men's Meetings, was to liberate for the service

[1] *Camb. Journ.* ii. 116. Rogers, *Christian-Quaker*, pt. i. p. 64, says there was a Women's Meeting in Bristol many years before 1669. In Aug. 1675 they had leave to invite the younger women to meet with them once a quarter so that they might have an opportunity of contributing to the poor and of being trained in the service of the meeting.
[2] Kendal Early Record Book, p. 47; also in inferior text, but with date, in Marsh, *Early Friends in Surrey and Sussex*, p. 40, from Guildford Minute Book.
[3] Ep. No. 291; cf. *Beginnings of Quakerism*, p. 39, and *Epistles*, p. 349.

of the Church the gifts of government which lay dormant and barren both in men and women, though the need of the time called for their use. The venture, in the case of the Women's Meetings, was a daring one, and taxed seventeenth-century feminine capacity to the utmost, but this only adds to its significance as a landmark in the movement for giving woman her true place of equal partnership with man.

The difficulty of starting these meetings may be illustrated from Buckinghamshire.[1] Here, with the approval of the men, a meeting was begun in September 1671, met again the next month, and for a third time two months later, and then, for lack of business, was discontinued till the men or women should see cause to resume it, which was not the case for some four years.

The system of Women's Meetings became widely established, but with much holding back in some districts. The Yearly Meeting encouraged their settlement in 1675, 1691, and 1707, and returned to the subject as late as 1744 and '45, seventy years after the first advice had been issued.[2] In London, with the exception of Ratcliff, the Women's Monthly Meetings only date from this period, though it should be remembered that there were the two Women's Meetings for the whole of London to which I have already referred. The men and women[3] met together, as is now again the practice in the Society, but, under the limited conceptions of the age, such joint Monthly Meetings do not seem to have given women their freedom in the affairs of the Church.[4]

---

[1] *J.F.H.S.* vii. 63. For the business of a well-conducted Women's Q.M. see Sarah Fell's instructions, 1681, in *J.F.H.S.* ix. 135-137.

[2] See MS. "Books of Extracts," heading "Meetings for Discipline."

[3] Beck and Ball, *London Friends' Meetings*, p. 353 (Y.M. Report, 1755).

[4] See Marsh, *Early Friends in Surrey and Sussex*, p. 41, for joint meetings in Capel M.M. The opponents of Women's Meetings were willing for them to meet with the men; cf. Fox's Letter, 30th Jan. 1675 (in Kendal Early Record Book, p. 59, and imperfectly in Fox, *Epistles*, No. 313), "there is some dark spirits that would have no women's meetings, but as men should meet with them, which women cannot for civility and modesty' sake speak amongst men of women's matters, neither can modest men desire it, and none but Ranters will desire to look into women's matters." In Oct. 1674 Berkshire Q.M. concluded "that all faithful women . . . ought to meet together with the men, or apart as they in the wisdom of God shall see meet when met together, to endeavour

One select meeting of London Friends, the Six Weeks' Meeting begun in 1671, seems to have worked well as a joint body. It consisted at first of thirty-four men and the same number of women, besides such Friends in the ministry as cared to attend. Instituted for considering matters not suitable for discussion in the Two Weeks' Meeting, it became for a time the prime meeting in the city, to which all the Monthly Meetings could appeal; and its minutes cover a wide range of important subjects. By the end of the century it had been put on a representative basis, the Monthly Meetings sending an equal number of men and women, though ministers still retained their right of attendance. Fox, it is interesting to note, favoured direct representation, while insisting on the importance of choosing men and women of character, who would not be drawn away into sects and parties.[1] Made up of picked persons, originally perhaps chosen by Fox before he left for America, it was no doubt exceptionally strong in the capacity of its women members, and could be held as a joint meeting without hurt.[2]

We now turn to the development of central organization. In the Commonwealth period there had been a series of three annual meetings for ministers from all parts of the country in the springs of 1658 and following years. A fourth meeting, no doubt of the same kind, was held in London about May 1661.[3] There had also been one business meeting of Friends from all parts of the country at Skipton in April 1660.[4] Further meetings of the kind had been impossible in the succeeding years of persecution. Fox in the spring of '63 considered

---

and be helpful unanimously for the prosperity of Truth." The whole subject had an important place in the Wilkinson-Story controversy. See *post*, Chap. XI.

[1] The Minutes, with names of members of meeting, are at Dev. Ho., beginning 28th Oct. 1671. See also Beck and Ball, *London Friends' Meetings*, pp. 91-102, giving extracts and printing *in extenso* a summary of papers by Fox on the constitution and functions, which is entered on the Minutes in 1691. Beck and Ball suggest that it belongs to 1683, but Fox attended several Six Weeks' Meetings during the last months of his life, and may have issued advice at various times. The representative basis was not finally adopted till 1696.

[2] Beck and Ball, *London Friends' Meetings*, p. 92, suggest that Fox picked the first list. At Bristol the Men's Meeting for Cases of Discipline became a joint meeting of men and women in 1673 and seems to have answered.

[3] *Beginnings of Quakerism*, p. 337.   [4] *Ibid.* pp. 335-337.

holding a meeting of ministers, but the matter was not proceeded with,[1] and I find no evidence of any such meeting until the one in May '66, already described. This and another in April '68 seem to have been summoned for special purposes; and a regular annual Meeting of Ministers such as we last heard of in 1661 does not reappear till the one held at Christmas '68, when, in the words of the epistle then issued,[2]

... we did conclude among ourselves to settle a meeting, to see one another's faces and open our hearts one to another in the Truth of God, once a year as formerly it used to be.

This meeting, held after the settling of the Monthly Meeting system, set on foot again a general collection for books and the expenses of work beyond seas,[3] and laid a foundation for the series of Ministers' Meetings which finally led up to the central body known as London Yearly Meeting. It fixed its next meeting for Easter 1670, a few weeks before the Second Conventicle Act came into force, and we know, from one brief reference, that this was held.[4] In June 1671 there was a "mighty meeting" to which many came up from all parts,[5] and a year later a large amount of important business was done, and it was decided to form a central body, by representation from the counties, which should meet annually in London in Whitsun week, "to advise about the managing of the public affairs of Friends throughout the nation." Ministering Friends were entitled to be present, but no others, except the representatives, without special leave. Each county was to send two Friends, besides six from the City of London, three from Bristol, and two from Colchester, an interesting indication of the strength of Quakerism in these places.[6] The 1672 meeting cannot,

[1] Howgill to Margt. Fell, 26th March 1663, in Swarthm. Colln. i. 377.
[2] *Letters of Early Friends*, p. 324. See also *ante*, p. 217, note. The letter is dated 16th Jan. 1669, and the meeting seems to have lasted into this month.
[3] The letter for a collection is in MS. Y.M. Minutes at Dev. Ho.
[4] Burnyeat attended it; see *J.F.H.S.* iii. 79, citing his *Works*, p. 38.
[5] *Camb. Journ.* ii. 176. The Minutes are in *Yearly Meeting Epistles, 1681–1857*, i. p. xvii, from the Register Book of Longford M.M., and there is also a copy in Minutes of Berkshire Q.M.
[6] The proceedings are detailed in MS. Yearly Meeting Minutes. See also epistles in *Letters of Early Friends*, pp. 326, 327, 328. The second directed a

I think, have been confined to ministers, and seems to have included Friends from the different counties. The Minutes suggest that a General Meeting of all Friends took place on the first day of the gathering; on the second a large committee of nine London Friends and one from each county dealt in detail with the dispersal of books, and later in the day the General Meeting met, approved their proposals, and ordered a collection; while on the third day the Meeting of Ministers seems to have met. In any case the 1673 meeting was representative in character, but, curiously enough, decided that, whilst the Yearly Meeting of Ministers was to continue, the representative Yearly Meeting should be laid down, " till Friends in God's wisdom shall see a further occasion." [1] Accordingly, during the next four years the meeting was one of ministers only; but in 1677 the Meeting of Ministers set up the representative meeting again on the basis agreed to five years before, and this met in 1678, and thenceforth continued year by year side by side with the Meeting of Ministers.[2] The Minute to the Quarterly Meetings shows that its powers were at first advisory, depending upon its ability to express the general mind of the Society upon the matters in hand, rather than upon any control delegated to it by the Quarterly Meetings.[3]

It is the desire of this meeting that you would nominate one or two Friends to come up the next year at the usual time for the service of Truth, and that they bring with them the total of the sufferings of the foregoing year not before sent up: and, whatsoever else you desire information or assistance in, let it be written and subscribed by some of your meeting in the name of the rest, the end of this meeting not being limited to the case of sufferings, but intended for the more general service of the

---

collection; the third was addressed to ministers and overseers, and contains much wise advice in discouragement of extravagances. We see how inevitably a central body cast its influence on the side of sobriety.

[1] See MS. Y.M. Minutes, and, for epistle, *Letters of Early Friends*, p. 336.
[2] The Minutes of these meetings are in MS. Y.M. Minutes, in part, and others in the old MS. "Books of Extracts."
[3] This Minute is in the old MS. "Books of Extracts," but not in the MS. Y.M. Records. The Minutes for this year were entered in the Meeting for Sufferings Minute Book, where it duly appears.

Truth and body of Friends in all those things wherein we may be capable to serve one another in love.

The settlement of the Yearly Meeting thus occupied nearly ten years. Such a central body was a novelty in that age and roused much adverse criticism. It was not established swiftly and surely, under strong religious concern, as had been the case with the setting up of the Monthly Meetings; it was superadded to an existing system, and was due, at first, to the practical convenience of calling in representatives to bring in reports of sufferings, control collections, and settle the proportions in which the counties should receive Quaker books. Its higher value lay in training and consolidating the membership. To bring together from all parts of the country the men of most weight in the movement, for conference and fellowship and the re-kindling of vision, was a true way of developing a corporate life which should carry the Society forward in one common service.

We note that the spiritual leaders were the chief factor in the organized Society of Friends, as they had been in the earlier stages of the movement. It is not easy to define the position of the Quaker minister: his authority was great, but it was not derived from human appointment; it depended from meeting to meeting upon the call of the Lord and upon the message which He might give raising up the witness to its truth in the hearts of Friends. Such illuminative leadership could not be restricted to one kind of meeting, nor to the particular district to which the minister belonged. Every business meeting was concerned with knowing the mind of the Lord, and sought to guide its action by the weight of spiritual judgment, rather than by the mechanical counting of heads, or the rhetorical and argumentative skill of the speakers. " Friends," wrote Fox, "are not to meet like a company of people about town or parish business, neither in their men's nor women's meetings, but to wait upon the Lord." [1] The position is clearly stated in answers returned by York-

---

[1] *Epistles*, p. 349, written from Worcester prison, 30th Jan. 1675.

shire Quarterly Meeting to Pontefract Monthly Meeting in March 1686:[1].

Question.—Of what members doth the Quarterly Meeting simply and strictly consist: of representatives only; or of representatives and other Friends who may be there from the Quarterly Meeting; or of representatives, other Quarterly Meeting Friends and Friends from other parts of the nation?

Answer.—The Quarterly Meeting doth consist of such faithful Friends in the Truth as may be appointed and allowed ot by the several Monthly Meetings to attend the service there, not excluding others who may be there assembled with them in the name of our Lord Jesus Christ to serve God and one another in love.

Question.—Is the deciding power in the Quarterly Meeting with the representatives only; or in all members of the Quarterly Meeting present; or in all Friends present?

Answer.—The decisive power of ordering as well as judging and determining principally resteth in the Divine Spirit; and those persons gathered together as aforesaid, by the help and counsel thereof, may order, judge, and determine such matters as be within their cognizance and are regularly brought before them.

The leadership and the organization through which it acted were both, during this period, live things. If corporate judgment was claiming to regulate in some degree individual concern, the judgment was mainly the vital group-experience of the leaders, and was as yet only beginning to be the creature of tradition and precedent. The action of the body known as the Morning Meeting shows it at work on the whole successfully in matters of much difficulty and delicacy.

Travelling ministers, when in London, with Gerrard Roberts' house as their headquarters, had been accustomed to keep in close touch with one another.[2] At least as early as 1670 they were in the practice of meeting together on the First-day morning for the purpose of declaring the meeting which each was moved to attend.[3] Another subject fell peculiarly within their province, since the written word may be even more potent than the spoken.

---

[1] Q.M. Minutes. [2] See *Beginnings of Quakerism*, p. 342, and *ante*, p. 233.
[3] *Camb. Journ.* ii. 155, and note at p. 418. See further, *post*, p. 544.

In the Commonwealth days Friends had been in the habit of consulting Fox or other leaders before printing, but the practice had of necessity fallen into disuse in days when the chief leaders were in prison. The important letter of May 1666 had urged its revival, and in 1672 the Yearly Meeting took up the matter and appointed ten Friends to see that books were carefully corrected and that no new book or new edition of an old one should be printed without order.[1] This small executive committee confined itself to seeing the books through the press, but a year later, when in London after his return from America, Fox set up the "Second-day's Morning Meeting" of men ministers, meeting every week, chiefly for supervising books and for distributing the ministry in the London area.[2] We have a characteristic account of its functions from the pen of the great Quaker leader, coloured by his chagrin at its temerity in refusing circulation at a critical moment to a strongly-worded paper of his on the matters in debate in the Wilkinson-Story controversy:[3]

> I was not moved to set up that meeting to make orders against the reading of my papers; but to gather up bad books that was scandalous against Friends; and to see that young Friends' books that was sent to be printed might be stood by; and to see where every one had their motion to the meeting that they might not go in heaps; and not for them to have an authority over the Monthly and Quarterly and other Meetings or for them to stop things to the nation which I was moved of the Lord to give forth to them.

The minutes begin on 15th September 1673 and reflect

---

[1] MS. Y.M. Minutes.

[2] Fox to London Women Friends, 28th April 1676, Swarthm. Colln. v. p. 9. I find no trace of the meeting before 1673. Beck and Ball, *London Friends' Meetings*, p. 336, follow a report of 1794, which cites a reference in William Crouch to the Two Weeks' Meeting as though it related to the Morning Meeting. Cf. *Beginnings of Quakerism*, pp. 340, 341. The adverse criticism of the "Second-day's Meeting at Devonshire House" in *The Spirit of the Hat*, 1673, also refers to the Two Weeks' Meeting, which met on the Second-day. In the 1794 Report, as cited in Beck and Ball, 1661 is to be corrected to 1681.

[3] Fox to London Women Friends, *ubi supra*. The rejected paper is, I think, *Epistles*, No. 317, dated from Swarthmore, 12th Feb. 1676. There is a copy in Bristol MSS. vol. v. No. 8, with a covering letter, No. 11, telling Dennis Hollister to have it read at Bristol, and to send copies into neighbouring counties. In the Swarthm. Colln. it immediately precedes the letter to London Women Friends. Yorkshire Q.M., 9th Mar. 1676, orders that "John Hall send copies of George's paper, that came last from Swarthmore, to every M.M."

Fox's description. Two of a sort of all books written by Friends are to be procured and kept together, "that, if any book be perverted by our adversaries, we may know where to find it," and a copy is to be got of every book "written against the Truth from the beginning." Here we have the origin of the unique collection of Quaker and anti-Quaker literature preserved in the Friends' Reference Library at Devonshire House, London, and, though the Morning Meeting ceased to meet in 1901, its archives remain as the unexhausted quarry from which the historian builds again the fabric of the past. The meeting also acted occasionally for the Society in matters of urgency, and had an important voice in the settling of new meetings in London and the neighbourhood. Moreover, it prohibited ministers charged with moral lapses from preaching until they had cleared themselves.

It is evident that with respect to the message of Friends, whether spoken or written, the Morning Meeting was a body of the first importance. It fostered controversial polemic overmuch, according to our ways of thinking. Its criticism, on the other hand, seems usually to have been moderate and sensible. But, in any case, controversy and criticism alike were an intellectual education to those who attended, and did much to keep the flame of learning alive. Ministers from all parts had the right of entry, and, when in London, took a large share in the business. This kept them in touch with the thought of Quakerism; and also helped to vary and freshen the thought of the Morning Meeting.

A little later a second central body developed, under the significant name of the Meeting for Sufferings. It still meets, under the same title, on the first Friday in every month in London, and is now the general executive body of the Society of Friends. Organization had not been developed as a defence against persecution, but it was natural that the new corporate consciousness should be used in this way, and that the experience and skill of the London leaders, who had long laboured in the matter, should be placed at the service of Friends throughout the country. Fox, with his keen moral insight, saw, as modern social reformers are beginning to see, that oppression often prevails because of a dulled or an unawakened conscience. He had strong faith in the redemptive workings of an aroused public opinion. The Friend could not resist evil by evil, but neither could he propitiate arrogance and cruelty by craven silence: it was his duty to expose the oppression and set the judgment of righteousness upon the heart of the persecutor and the heart of the nation.[1] Evil must be confronted with the light, which would reach the witness in the heart of the oppressor, and would either bring repentance or hardening—and in the latter case the judgment of God.[2] Friends must record and publish their sufferings, and by reiterated letter and interview pour the stream of facts into the unwilling ears of their persecutors; then only would they be clear. It is safe to say that the Recording Angel has no better kept documents on his shelves than the forty-four folio volumes of sufferings at Devonshire House. The myriad acts of oppression there detailed were resolutely dragged into the light, to the confusion of priestcraft and statecraft: the Judgment Day upon the issue of Liberty of Conscience took place in England and at least that increment of the Kingdom of God came to men.

In 1660 and onwards Ellis Hookes, the Clerk to Friends, was busy digesting the sufferings that came up from the counties into the first two of the forty-four volumes.[3] He was a man of brave spirit, but weak constitution, over-weighted with work, and, as befitted his office, a jealous custodian of the books in his keeping.[4] In 1672 the Yearly Meeting assisted him by urging country Friends to be exact and brief in drawing up

---

[1] See *Beginnings of Quakerism*, pp. 315, 316.
[2] Friends acted in the spirit of Rom. xii. 17-21, and, we may now add, of *Testaments of the Twelve Patriarchs*, Gad vi. 3-7, which urges long-suffering forgiveness of the wrong-doer, and concludes, "but, if he be shameless and persisteth in his wrong-doing, even so forgive him from the heart, and leave to God the avenging." As thus understood, the "Judgment of God on persecutors" had a distinct place in their scheme of thought; see note in *Camb. Journ.* i. 394, and references in its Index, "Judgments."
[3] *J.F.H.S.* i. p. 15.
[4] See *Extracts from State Papers*, p. 154.

their sufferings and diligent in reporting them.[1] But business-like returns were hard to get. In May 1675 a circular letter to the counties shows that many were received in an imperfect form, on loose pieces of paper, sometimes only directed on the outside, without clue to the sender or attesting signature, so that they seemed to have been simply passed on, without having been recorded locally. Sometimes the same matters were returned two or three times, making much unnecessary work. Hookes urged the county registrars to mark their books in the margin when they made the returns, and to draw them out according to a regular method and send them up properly attested yearly or oftener.[2] When the Yearly Meeting met, it advised the counties on these lines, and arranged for a representative conference on the subject in the autumn.[3] The invitation to this seems to have been prepared by the Morning Meeting,[4] who included "a tender caution . . . that none discourage such as are free to lay the sufferings upon the powers or to endeavour to prevent and stop the persecutors." The Conference took place on 18th October and reached some important conclusions.[5] Conscientious resistance to authority takes many forms in modern times, and the Quaker standpoint of the year 1675 is by no means out of date. How far, it was debated, could force or methods of legal redress be invoked? There seems to have been no need to confirm the well-understood non-militant attitude of Friends, except with respect to tithes, as to which the advice was given that "though innocent endeavours may be used to save them from being taken away, yet that Friends be careful of violent struggling to retain them, when the adversary comes to take them by force." But, with respect to legal remedies, the case was more difficult.

---

[1] MS. Y.M. Records. Correspondents were appointed in the counties who were to indemnify London Friends for expenses incurred. (See Q.M. Minutes, Berkshire, 7th May 1669; Somerset, 18th March 1669.)
[2] I take this from the Berkshire Q.M. Records.
[3] *Y.M. Epistles*, 1675–1759, folio edn. p. 1.
[4] Morning Meeting Minutes, 31st May 1675.
[5] Given in MS. Y.M. Records and, differently arranged, in Meeting for Sufferings Minutes.

Saintly men like Dewsbury and Penington refused to set the law in motion for their own relief, assured that their persecutors could hold them in prison no longer than the determined time appointed by God,[1] but this extreme of passivity went beyond the views of Fox and most Friends. Accordingly, the Conference advised "that Friends do not judge nor reflect upon one another in these cases, a freedom being left upon urgent occasions to take such course for relief and ease to the oppressed as may not be prejudicial to Truth's testimony."[2] The matter was gone into again at the Yearly Meeting in 1676, which advised against the use of anything that savoured of legal chicanery, but gave latitude to pursue straightforward methods of legal redress.[3] London Friends were assiduous in helping on these lines, but the Conference on Sufferings felt the need of advising sufferers "not to let out their minds into too much expectation of outward relief by Friends here in point of law; but that they patiently and principally depend upon the Lord and His power to plead their cause."

There was hesitation as to the use of the law; but there was none upon the third question which occupied the Conference, the bringing the oppression home to the persecutors. An appointment was made to draw up instances of gross suffering to lay before Parliament, also to prepare the Book of Sufferings at large and to print those which occurred "before the King came in," with leave to add warnings given to rulers, "and to insert what eminent judgments did fall upon the persecutors in those days."[4] It was unanimously agreed that the

---

[1] Dewsbury's *Works*, an early unnumbered page. See also his vindication of his own position in epistle of April 1678 in Bristol MSS. i. No. 17.

[2] The MS. "Books of Extracts" contained the bulk of these paragraphs under the title "Law."

[3] Epistle in *Y.M. Epistles*, 1675–1759, fol. edn. p. 5.

[4] Numerous pieces relating to particular sufferings had been printed from time to time; see Smith's *Catalogue*, title "Sufferings of Friends," which contains 66 prior to the Restoration, 89 for 1660–1670, 32 for 1671–1680, and 37 for 1681–1689, or 224 items in all, and the MS. Records were written up from year to year, but this is the first decision to print a general collection. References to its preparation seem to occur in Yorkshire Q.M. Minutes, 14th Sept. 1676, Berkshire Q.M., 5th Oct. 1676, but it was not proceeded with. Cf. Wm. Penn to Fox, 1st Dec. 1674, in *Letters of Early Friends*, p. 199. Many years later, in

sufferings should be "laid upon those in power," and it was felt that Friends should in all cases be assisted in understanding the law and its administration.

A scheme was drawn up for a standing vigilance Committee, which, as modified in detail after the Yearly Meeting of 1676,[1] took the following shape. A full Meeting for Sufferings was to be held before each Law Term, consisting of London Friends appointed to correspond with the several counties, together with members of the Morning Meeting, and at least one Friend from each county prepared to attend when required. In the intervals a weekly meeting was constituted of one-fourth of the full London list, the service shifting each term. It is probably the practical representation for the whole country secured by these arrangements which led to the Meeting acquiring wider executive functions. The county correspondents could attend or could instruct their London representatives upon the matter in hand. In 1679 the Yearly Meeting directed that the expense attending waiting upon King and Council, Courts and Parliament in and about the national sufferings should be paid out of the general collection from the counties, the charges to be "such only as shall be agreed and directed by the weekly Meeting for Sufferings in London and not any other."[2] In the Minutes this direction seems confined to the expenses specified, but it came to be treated as conferring control over all expenditure.[3] The same Yearly

---

1726, James Dickinson agitated in the matter, see *Journ.* 1847 edn. pp. 215-216, and, as a result, Joseph Besse, of Colchester, took up the work of digesting the ample MS. and printed materials. His *Abstract* appeared in three parts in 8vo, 1733-1738, and his *Collection of the Sufferings of the People called Quakers*, 1650-1689, in 2 vols. fol. in 1753. In this great book his materials took final shape. The work is conscientiously done, and may be generally relied on, but the sources behind it often yield fuller and sometimes more accurate information. A complete and critical collection of our *Acta Martyrum* would be a vast undertaking, but of great service to the local historian and to the Quaker genealogist.

[1] The modifying documents, dated 12th June 1676, are in *Letters of Early Friends*, pp. 346-353, and Bristol MSS. iii. No. 25. Yorkshire Q.M. appointed four local Friends, 9th March 1676. The Minutes of the Meeting for Sufferings begin 22nd June 1676, and the business of the weekly meeting was often transacted by eight or ten Friends.

[2] MS. Y.M. Records.

[3] The sentence quoted is given without any limiting context in the old MS. "Books of Extracts," under title "Stock National."

Meeting put the printing of books in charge of the Meeting for Sufferings, and in 1680 this was extended to their distribution.[1] This did not affect the revising functions of the Morning Meeting.

The position of women with respect to the central meetings must be briefly referred to. Their want of business training no doubt precluded their admission to important executive bodies such as the Morning Meeting and the Meeting for Sufferings. In rare cases, a woman capable of serving might have been found, as, for example, Sarah Fell, who managed her Quarterly Meeting Books as admirably as her household accounts, and, when she came to London as the wife of William Meade in 1681, effected a swift reform in the methods of the Box Meeting.[2] Their absence from the business sittings of the Yearly Meeting resulted from its being a select meeting made up of men ministers and representatives from the men's Quarterly Meetings. They had a share in the ministry at the public meetings held at the time of the Yearly Meeting, though not a large one. We may take the practice of Ann Camm, formerly Ann Audland, who, alike by courageous service and spiritual force, was the leading woman Friend in Westmorland, as typical of the way in which the women of ripe experience behaved.

She had wisdom to know the time and season of her service, in which she was a good example to her sex; for without extraordinary impulse and concern it was rare for her to preach in large meetings, where she knew there were brethren qualified for the service of such meetings; and she was grieved when any, especially of her sex, should be too hasty, forward, or unseasonable in their appearing in such meetings.[3]

It is not until the close of the century that we hear of attempts to give women a somewhat fuller scope in connection with the Morning Meeting and the Yearly

---

[1] MS. Y.M. Records. The Six Weeks' Meeting, see Minutes, 20th May 1679, sent forward recommendations, both as to finance and books, which were adopted. The arrangements for printing replaced those come to in 1672, see *ante*, p. 280. Fox had been writing on the subject.

[2] See *J.F.H.S.* ix. 135; *Margaret Fox*, by Helen G. Crosfield, pp. 241-253; and Box Meeting documents at Dev. Ho.

[3] *Piety Promoted*, pt. iii. p. 208. She was a stanch opponent of tithes.

Meeting. At the Yearly Meeting of Ministers in 1697 leave was given for women ministers to have a meeting by themselves on the following day,[1] and the same year the Yearly Meeting gave them liberty to sit with their brethren in future at the Yearly Meeting of Ministers.[2] This considerable advance was followed in the autumn of 1698 by the Morning Meeting holding some general monthly meetings of men and women ministers.[3] I cannot find that these became regularly established, and at the beginning of 1701 the Morning Meeting suppressed an incipient meeting of women ministers, and cautioned women against overmuch speaking.[4] The Minutes reveal somewhat crudely the attitude of the men.

> There being several women Friends in and about this city that have a public testimony for the Truth and have sometimes met on the Seventh-day, this meeting, having considered the same, do declare that they do not understand that ever this meeting gave direction for the setting up the said meeting; neither do they judge there is any necessity for it or service in the continuance thereof: and therefore do advise that when any public approved women Friends have a concern of service upon them to go to any particular public meeting in or about this city, they may leave their names at the Chamber, that Friends may have notice thereof; and such may as much as may be have an opportunity to clear themselves, and yet be careful not to interfere with their brethren in their public mixed meetings.

And again:

> This meeting finding that it is a hurt to Truth for women Friends to take up too much time, as some do, in our public meetings, when several public and serviceable men Friends are present and are by them prevented in their serving, it's therefore advised that the women Friends should be tenderly cautioned against taking up too much time in our mixed public meetings.

It should be added that although English Friends did not fully establish a Women's Yearly Meeting until 1784, Ireland had one as early as 1679, and they were in general

---

[1] Morning Meeting Minutes, 24th May 1697.
[2] MS. Y.M. Minutes, also in MS. "Books of Extracts," title "Yearly Meeting."
[3] Morning Meeting Minutes, 3rd Oct., 7th Nov. 1698.
[4] J. S. Rowntree, *Meetings on Ministry and Oversight*, No. 2, p. 16.

use in the American colonies, though I think in all cases their powers as meetings of discipline were strictly limited. The conception of women taking part in Church government was so novel that we should take note of the advanced position of early Quakerism even though it was not and probably could not have been fully worked out in practice.

Before leaving the question of central organization, we may fitly dedicate a few closing sentences to the faithful servant of the Society, Ellis Hookes, upon whom much more than the clerical work of the whole system depended. Happy is the Church that can command such devotion.[1] His twenty-four years of service (1657–1681) began, we may conjecture, with the setting up of the Men's Two Weeks' Meeting in London, and covered the whole transition period of developing organization, till, at his death, he found himself clerk to the Morning Meeting, the Meeting for Sufferings, the Six Weeks' Meeting and its Cash Committee of Twelve Friends, as well as Executive Officer of the Yearly Meeting. He had a "Chamber" to work in and one man to assist. A great tenacity of spirit triumphed over his frailty of body and he steadily discharged his manifold duties through persecution and plague, through the press of obtaining the Great Pardon and the constant fret of changing organization and exacting masters, always high of heart for the Truth, but accounting himself one of the poorest and least among the brethren. His literary hack-work was prodigious. He found time, omitting lesser pieces, to edit in folio the works of his friends Burrough and Howgill, the apostles of London Quakerism, and those of Samuel Fisher and William Smith, and to write an elaborate history of martyrs, under the title *The Spirit of the Martyrs Revived*, besides making his great manuscript collection of Quaker Sufferings. He placed his learning at the disposal of Fox, who published in joint-authorship with him an historical *Arraignment of Popery*, and, stranger still, to

---

[1] The best account of Ellis Hookes is by Norman Penney in *J.F.H.S.* i. 12-22. Cf. references in *Camb. Journ.* ii. 402, and *Beginnings of Quakerism*, pp. 488, 489. See also Index to present volume.

us who know the Quaker leader's manifold sins against orthography, *An Instruction for Right Spelling*. Hookes spent himself in affectionate loyalty to his leaders and unstinting fidelity to duty. To use his own words, he conceived it his business to be

> . . . willing and desirous to serve in that true love which stands in the life and truth of our God, Who requires faithfulness of us all, that we may remain living witnesses in our several places this short time of our pilgrimage; and in the end lay down our heads in peace and assurance of a crown of life and glory as our everlasting reward; for this is the end that crowns all the diligence and works of the faithful.[1]

This blessed hope made his ceaseless drudgery a round of happy toil, and, when his life flickered out in a consumption at the age of fifty, he could go forth gladly into the joy of his Lord, knowing that in all faithful use of talents "the end crowns the work."

[1] Epistle dedicatory to Burrough's *Works*.

CHAPTER XI

THE WILKINSON-STORY SEPARATION

> I have often with deep sorrow lamented the state of some . . . when I have seen what a good beginning they have made in the way of God . . . and yet, after some good progress . . . for want of a diligent watchfulness and keeping close to the daily cross, and the self-denial, have laid themselves open to the spoilers, who have cunningly got an entrance into them, some in the affectionate part, some in the wise reasoning part, some thorough sowing the seeds of prejudice, and some one way and some another, and have beguiled them of the simplicity and drawn them from the sincerity that is in the Truth ; and so they have both lost their first love and their first work also. . . . Dear hearts, sink down, sink down, while yet an Arm of love is reached out to you to receive you, and wait in lowliness to be brought into that heavenly house where there is meat indeed and drink indeed. . . . How is fleshly reasoning gotten up to shun the cross and the sufferings that attend the gospel ? . . . It is indeed impossible that the love to God and His Truth should remain in its former strength when the love to the brethren decays. They came together and they will go together. . . . Therefore Friends, wait to feel the daily renewings by the Holy Spirit in yourselves ; and that will renew your love to God and to His Truth and the testimonies of it, and to the brethren . . . and to all the faithful followers of the Lamb of God everywhere . . . and then you will see that the service of all that is given you is but to serve the Lord in His Truth.—STEVEN CRISP, " A Faithful Warning and Exhortation to Friends to beware of Seducing Spirits " (1684), *Works*, pp. 473-497.

EVERY crisis, whether in the life of a nation or of a movement, is, as the word implies, a time of criticism and judging, during which tendencies are vivified into vital issues, and their meaning is made clear to masses of men by a swift and intense process of education which leads rapidly to far-reaching decisions. Accordingly the historian may do great injustice if he reads back into the events which led up to the crisis the enlightenment which developed during its progress, or the judgment by which it was ended. Men act according to their lights and discover the consequences later. To judge them fairly, we must chiefly consider their motives and intentions rather than the results of their actions. I leave therefore to a future chapter, as far as possible, the conception of Church government to which the Society of Friends was brought as a result of internal controversy; and shall tell the perplexed story in the first instance as though we had not decided what its outcome would be.

The Quaker movement under the necessity for self-expression and at the touch of one man's insistent conviction had crystallized into a religious Society controlled by the corporate spiritual authority of its leaders. The central and local organizations arose without any full understanding by Friends of the consequences of introducing them; and we have no reason for supposing that any man, even Fox himself, saw the lengths to which disciplinary powers would reach in the coming years. The introducer of the chisel could not foresee the developments of ecclesiastical architecture made possible by his new tool. In the Minute Books the Quarterly Meetings are commonly stated to have been set up " for and concerning the poor and other affairs of Truth,"[1] while the Monthly Meeting functions, at their origin, are, I think, fairly given in this Minute of Berkshire Quarterly Meeting,

to consider of outward business, [and] to see if there be any such as have been convinced and walks disorderly.[2]

The use and the nature of the disciplinary powers were at first left quite vague; nor was there any clear division of functions between Monthly and Quarterly Meetings, nor any definite linking together of the Quarterly Meetings. Everything depended, quite naturally from the Quaker point of view, on the corporate spiritual guidance which controlled the meetings, and it was assumed by Fox that this must conform with the lines of discipline which he had formulated. It is a remarkable tribute both to his personality and his statesmanship that he carried

[1] Dorset Q.M. in *J.F.H.S.* v. 40; cf. similar entries in Minutes of Berks Q.M., 24th April 1668; Somerset Q.M., 24th Sept. 1668; Sussex Q.M., 9th Sept. 1668 (in frontispiece to Marsh, *Early Friends in Surrey and Sussex*).
[2] Minute of 16th Oct. 1668.

the main body of Friends with him ; but the adjustment of the new group-authority to the older conception of individual spiritual guidance, was bound to cause serious and long-continued strains in the Quaker Church.

Fox, as we have seen, had set up these meetings in conference with local Friends ; and had travelled the length and breadth of England for the purpose. Though there was opposition in some places,[1] we have ample evidence that the spiritual judgment of the leading Friends in each district united with his own strong " concern " in the matter ; and the fresh departure began well. But everything would depend upon the Christian consideration and wise judgment with which the new bodies used their powers. The first difficulty was a sequel to the handling of the Hat question in London in 1667 and onwards.[2] A piece was published anonymously in 1673, whose diffuse title summarizes its contents :

The Spirit of the Hat, or the Government of the Quakers Among Themselves, As it hath been Exercised of late years by George Fox, and other Leading-Men, in their Monday, or Second-dayes Meeting at Devonshire-House,[3] brought to Light. In a Bemoaning Letter of a certain ingenious Quaker to another his Friend ; Wherein their Tyrannical and Persecuting Practises are detected and redargued.

It deserves attention for its powerful presentation of the case that could be made against Fox. The writer argued that the spiritual man must wait until God revealed the truth : he could not yield subjection to an order of the Church, when he had no manifestation of its truth within him. The new view, which he styled " Foxonian-unity," treated the dissenting Friend as thereby opposing God and His Truth. This made the body the touchstone by which to judge the Spirit of the Lord and had two consequences—" to deprive us of the law of the Spirit and to bring in a tyrannical government : it would lead us from the rule within to subject us to a rule without." He criticized the Letter issued by the Quaker leaders in

---

[1] See *Camb. Journ.* ii. 112, 114, 124.   [2] *Ante*, p. 253.
[3] This was the Men's Two Weeks' Meeting, not the " Morning Meeting."

May 1666 for taking this position, whereas Christ Himself is the immediate Lawgiver and Judge in this day of His power. The Church was not to be kept in peace by suppressing error but by preserving its members in faith and love. " In the true Church unity stands in diversities; but in the false unity will not stand without uniformity." Where the emphasis was laid on uniformity there was sure to be a limiting of the Spirit. Certain Friends, he complained, with the London method of distributing the ministry in mind, were already appointed to spend the whole time in speaking in every meeting, " and all the rest to come as hearers, neglecting the gift in themselves, only waiting upon their lips."

Such arbitrary courses have an ill operation upon the spirits of men: it weakens their hearts and cools their courage and begets in them a slavish temper and disposition; and where this arbitrary and unlimited power is set up a way is open not only for the security but for the advancement and encouragement of evil and a means to increase flatterers. Such men are aptest to cry up the Body in all respects and are the only good Friends; but others, though exemplary in their conversations, who cannot yield and comply against the Light in their consciences to some of their proceedings, are subject to their jealousy, censure, if not an ejection.[1]

The epistle of the Yearly Meeting of 1673 is chiefly addressed to this spirit of disaffection, and was signed, amongst others, by William Rogers and several more who afterwards supported Wilkinson and Story.[2] The enemy, it said, was secretly at work to make rents, and beget a

[1] The piece was sold for sixpence, see Arber's *Term Catalogues*, Trinity, 1673, and is attributed, with its sequels, to William Mucklow, a London Friend (1631–1713), whose love, in later life, "was renewed toward Friends"; see note in *Camb. Journ.* ii. 448. He had befriended Ellwood in 1662 when in Bridewell (Ellwood, *Life*, p. 149). Penn replied in "The Spirit of Alexander the Coppersmith . . . Justly Rebuk'd," 1673, which was answered the same year by "Tyranny and Hypocrisy detected," leading to a further rejoinder by Penn, "Judas and the Jews." Penn's pamphlets are in his *Works*, 1726 edn., but without the important testimonies by Penington and others as to the Perrot spirit. Mucklow also wrote in 1673 on "Liberty of Conscience," to which George Whitehead replied in "The Apostate Incendiary Rebuked"; cf. *Camb. Journ.* ii. 273.
[2] *Letters of Early Friends*, pp. 336-342. Fox was in America. *An Exalted Diotrephes*, 1681, by Richard Snead and other Bristol Friends, p. 19, treats the epistle as directed against the Wilkinson-Story spirit, but no such claim is made in the reference in *The Accuser of our Brethren cast down*, p. 84.

disesteem and slight of the faithful labourers in the Lord's work. Friends were exhorted to keep out of all roughness and harshness towards one another, and out of all self-rule and dominion, which was not in the Life but in the will of the flesh.

And though a general care be not laid upon every member, touching the good order and government in the Church's affairs, nor have many travailed therein; yet the Lord hath laid it more upon some in whom He hath opened counsel for that end—and particularly in our dear brother and God's faithful labourer George Fox, for the help of many.

This epistle was generally accepted by Friends, for the new order of Church government seemed justified rather than condemned by its success in diminishing the number of the "hat-men," as the followers of Perrot were called, and in checking the disintegrating tendencies of his negative mysticism. The forcible arguments of *The Spirit of the Hat* had little effect when used to support this discredited point of view: but would soon be tested under less equivocal conditions.

The Second Conventicle Act, as we shall remember, imposed heavy fines on the preachers at conventicles and on the owners of the houses where the meetings were held; and it is not surprising that Nonconformists should seek to evade the arbitrary malice of their destroyers. Friends generally maintained their public meetings at all cost, but there was some weakness for a time at Bristol, and in other places,[1] and a serious defection showed itself at Preston Patrick in Westmorland, the mother-church of the Seekers who joined Fox in 1652. Through fear of Informers, the congregation met in ghylls, woods, and unaccustomed places, instead of gathering openly at the houses of Friends; and, when their conduct brought them under the censure of the reorganized business meetings and of visiting ministers, alienation resulted, and a party was formed in Westmorland which developed a general

---

[1] *Ante*, pp. 77, 78. At Looe, in Cornwall, it was reported that they met on the rocks and sand, to avoid being fined for the house (*Extracts from State Papers*, p. 314); cf. *post*, pp. 374, 375, and the practice of the Baptists during the persecution at Bristol, *ante*, p. 102.

opposition to the new system of Church government and became separated from the main body, first in its business meetings, and later in its worship. The leaders were John Story and John Wilkinson, two of the early Publishers of Truth, Westmorland men both, one from Preston Patrick and the other from Hutton, who for many years had laboured together in Wiltshire and the West of England. Story at this time was about forty and an able disputant, " being well-read in Holy Scripture and had a large understanding and memory and a grave carriage,"[1] but, according to information given to Penington,[2] was " never thoroughly gathered and cleansed from the professing spirit and wisdom ; but always held the knowledge of the Truth partly therein." Wilkinson, though the older man, took a subordinate part, and did not associate himself with the disaffected party till after Story's return at the end of 1672 from a visit to the South.[3]

The course of events at first is somewhat obscure.[4] In October 1671 Wilkinson had approved the setting up of a Women's Meeting, and a year later he joined in a remonstrance to Preston Patrick Friends for their neglect in coming to the meetings for Church affairs.[5] The friction chiefly developed during the two and a half years prior to the setting up of a separate business meeting in May 1675. Preston Patrick Friends were perhaps overmuch reproved for their backsliding in time of persecution. Friends from a distance, we are told, were moved " to clear their consciences in God's sight, to the comfort and heartbreaking gladness of the upright amongst us, but to the grief and vexation of the other sort ; whereupon they cried out against imposition, over-driving and urging things with severity."[6] Margaret Fox, who was not on

[1] F.P.T. p. 256 ; cf. *Beginnings of Quakerism*, pp. 85, 92.
[2] Dev. Ho. Penington MSS. iv. p. 143 (letter to Thos. Curtis, 24th Dec. 1677).
[3] F.P.T. p. 267.
[4] Our chief authorities are the Kendal M.M. and Q.M. Minutes ; William Rogers, *The Christian-Quaker*, 1680 ; and *Anti-Christian Treachery Discovered*, pt. ii., by John Blaykling and others (1683). The two books are from opposite standpoints ; their statements of bare matter-of-fact are usually accurate, but their inferences are prejudiced. Both are confused in arrangement.
[5] Minutes of 6th Oct. 1671 and 4th Oct. 1672.
[6] *Anti-Christian Treachery*, p. 29.

good terms with Story, intervened at the beginning of 1673 during her husband's absence in America,[1] but Fox, on his return, did everything in his power to get the difficulty composed without the assertion of his own authority.[2] But the personal element was bound to be mixed up with the general questions under debate. Story and Wilkinson had begun by chafing under the admonition of the other leaders in the North; and as these naturally prayed in aid the corporate authority of the Church, acting through the business meetings, opposition developed to the new system, and almost inevitably to Fox as its founder and upholder. As late, however, as the close of his Worcester imprisonment, January 1675,[3] there was no personal breach. Thomas Lower gives a lively but biased account[4] of a long discussion in the Castle Garden between Fox and the two Johns, with himself and Thomas and Ann Curtis of Reading as seconds of the respective protagonists, but kept at arm's-length. He says plaintively:

My father once or twice bid me walk away, when I drew near to hearken to their discourse. . . . I walked five hours upon the gravel walk expecting when to be called; and often took occasion to mind my father of going in lest he took cold; and A. C. was as careful of dear John Story, as she called him. . . . I hear [my

---

[1] *Anti-Christian Treachery*, pp. 29, 87-89; *Christian-Quaker*, pt. iv. pp. 7-14.

[2] Fox, from Worcester prison, seems to have encouraged the Q.M. to inquire into the weakness of Preston Patrick Friends, see Q.M. Minute, 3rd April 1674, but cf. letter to his wife, 4th May, in Dev. Ho. Gibson Colln. i. p. 122, and he obtained answers from Story and Wilkinson on specific points, see *Christian-Quaker*, pt. iv. pp. 7-14. Nor did he fail, as we shall see, to write on the main points in controversy. But letters to Penn, 28th Aug. 1674 and 30th Sept. 1675 (*J.F.H.S.* x. 143, 146), and Parker to Fox, 5th Oct. 1675 (Dev. Ho. Gibson MSS. ii. 11), show clearly that he was careful to leave the responsibility to the bodies concerned. In the first, extant in a corrupt text, he welcomes the suggested arbitration of the difference by Alexander Parker and George Whitehead, and wishes that they had acted earlier while he was in America; in the second he explains that he has not been concerned in the meetings that have taken place and could not himself propose a meeting without bringing the previous proceedings into question; in the third Parker writes, "What yet may be done I know not, unless thou step in and stand in the gap. I know thou hast power: I wish thou had faith in it." George Whitehead had been at a Q.M., 4th July 1673, and had approved a Minute against going behind the back of a Friend to whisper and backbite, which must have been designed to stop the growing bitterness of feeling on both sides.

[3] For this imprisonment see *post* p. 427. Lower had married Mary Fell.

[4] Spence MSS. vol. iii. fol. 165, letter to Margt. Fox, 11th Feb. 1675.

father] cut and hewed them to pieces and kept them at sword's point still; and told them if they continued in that spirit they were in he must bear as great a testimony against them as ever he did against the priests . . . and my father stood in the authority of God over them.

Lower says:

They went forth at Worcester a day and a half before me; and yet at Wigan I overtook them, J[ohn] St[ory] pretending he was not able to travel fast—half day's journey in a day. Their great friends have sent them home well-mounted and well-clothed; and J[ohn] St[ory] with his extraordinary broad-brimmed beaver hat and his periwig and broad belt with silver buckles and great hose &c. hath great obeisance rendered to him in the country where he comes by those that know him not.

They must have travelled north with little hopes of avoiding a breach with Fox, and confirmed in their opinions by the strong backing received from their friends in the West of England. Accordingly, events now moved forward rapidly to an overt separation.

The following points were by this time in issue:[1]

1st. They saw no service in Women's Meetings, except in cities, like London and Bristol, for dealing with the poor, and especially objected to marriages being submitted to them, a practice introduced in Westmorland at the beginning of 1673.[2] The Women's Meetings were often principally times of worship, and John Story called a separate meeting for this purpose monstrous and ridiculous.

2nd. They objected to the recording of papers of condemnation, except at the instance of the party himself. The Quarterly Meeting Book of condemnations had been begun as early as 1669, with a copy of the one given against himself by Christopher Atkinson fourteen years earlier,[3] but the practice was much in debate in 1672 and following years.[4]

3rd. While opposed to tithes, they would have no other force used but "the word of life" to stir Friends up to the maintenance of their testimony. Here again the Quarterly Meeting had been urgent with Friends to give their testimonies in writing, and at

---

[1] I draw these, mainly, from their own replies in *Christian-Quaker*, pt. iv. pp. 7-14, 37-40; cf. *Anti-Christian Treachery*, p. 45.
[2] There is a striking Minute on the first marriage passed, see Women's Minute Book, 3rd Jan. 1673.   [3] *Beginnings of Quakerism*, pp. 164-165.
[4] See especially Minute, 1st Nov. 1672.

one meeting in 1674 seems to have insisted on this before a Friend was judged fit to take part in the business.¹

4th. They disliked Friends "groaning, singing, or sounding," whilst another was speaking or praying, and, on one occasion, Story had publicly protested, not being able to distinguish Margaret Fox's words at prayer, "because of the noise of deceit."

5th. Story would not directly admit that he had encouraged Friends to flee persecution; but he no doubt took the position afterwards stated by William Rogers:² "We have been made willing, praises be to our God, to continue the assembling of ourselves together, waiting upon the Lord in the day of persecution . . . for that we believe 'tis the duty of every Christian to think nothing too dear to offer up for the Lord, when He commands or calls for it. Mark, we do not say, at every time that any Informer, that thirsteth after our ruin and estates thorough malice, especially when not prompted thereto by such as are ministers of the law, calls for it; but we say, when the Lord commands or calls for it. And if, peradventure, any should be so overcome as through disobedience, fear or weakness not to stand steadfast . . . even in that manner that the Lord willeth, it is then the duty of those that are strong to deal gently with such and . . . endeavour to convince them of such their weakness, that so their faith and strength in the Truth may come to increase; and not be so remote from bearing the infirmities of the weak . . . as instead thereof to publish such their weakness, by way of recrimination, through the nation—especially whilst such weakness might truly be termed want of sight or clear conviction."

In April 1671, when the Quarterly Meeting received £30 from London for sufferers from the Conventicle Act and added a like collection of its own, the four centres that received help were Strickland Head £29, Sedbergh £11, Underbarrow £13, and Poolbank £7. The other meetings, including Preston Patrick, seem to have escaped or evaded the ravages of Informers.

6th. They spoke slightingly of the Church meetings and desired them to consist of appointed delegates, no other Friends from the county or from a distance having a voice in them, "but if they had anything to offer there, they might declare their message and withdraw."³ Story explained later that in the Monthly Meeting for the service of the poor &c. he did not wish to

---

¹ 3rd April 1674, but we find action respecting tithes as early as 6th Oct. 1671. There was a good deal of weakness at Preston Patrick and Underbarrow.
² *Christian-Quaker*, pt. i. p. 28.
³ See *Anti-Christian Treachery*, pp. 33, 34. Cf. Kendal M.M. Minutes, 25th Dec. 1673, 2nd Jan. 1674. Cf. *ante*, p. 279.

exclude any who would accompany Friends in a spirit of love and unity and had a concern to add a helping hand.[1]

By April 1675 matters had come to a head and we find the Quarterly Meeting reading over four papers from Fox, George Whitehead, Parker, and Penn, and resolving that they should be recorded and be read in every particular meeting.[2] The papers had been received at various stages of the discussion. Fox wrote from Worcester prison in favour of Women's Meetings and against dark spirits that called the separate worship at these times monstrous and ridiculous, while Penn sent an elaborate paper showing the necessity of condemning miscarriages and the service of recording them.

He raised the whole issue of Church discipline, contending that if the Church were silent it would be overrun with lukewarm hypocrites and loose walkers, for it was not like a flock without a shepherd or feeding on a wild common. Every member had an interest in it and the Church a kind of property in every member. Church order was no doubt a new thing, which had come through Fox, but it came in its due season, for there must be people convinced of the Truth before you could have a fellowship, and the fellowship must develop in some degree before it could become a Church. The heavenly discipline put itself forth as the Church became able to receive it. Fox was as much a servant of God when he brought the message of holy order for Church communion as when he brought the glad tidings of salvation at the rise of Quakerism. To withstand this was the ready way to let in an apostasy and to frustrate the glorious work of God that had been begun.

It must have been at this Quarterly Meeting that Friends declined proposals made in a paper signed by eighty-seven of the Wilkinson-Story party, which demanded that the business meetings should be put on the closed representative basis already referred to.[3] There-

---

[1] Letter, 30th Sept. 1677, in *The Memory of John Story Revived*, p. 40.

[2] Minute, 2nd April 1675. The papers are accordingly transcribed in Kendal Early Record Book. Fox's paper is dated 30th Jan. 1675, and is printed, with omissions, in *Epistles*, No. 313.

[3] See *Anti-Christian Treachery*, pp. 33-35, and the particulars of the signatories in a paper dated 12th Sept. 1678 by Thos. Langhorne, and Thos. and Ann Camm, in Bristol MSS. ii. No. 19, when about eighteen had already withdrawn from the separation. Fox, writing to Penn, 30th Sept. 1675 (*J.F.H.S.* x. 146), calls some of them " such as were married by priests and such as have not come amongst Friends for several years past and some boys." Cf. *post*, p. 310.

upon, at the beginning of May, the opposers set up a distinct business meeting,[1] and the breach became an open one, which almost at once came under the notice of the Yearly Meeting of Ministers, gathered in London at the end of the month. An important letter, the foundation of the official discipline, was issued under twelve heads, seven of which were addressed to the matters in controversy in Westmorland.[2]

It affirmed that the establishment of Men's and Women's Meetings had been done in the leading of the Spirit, and if any "resist counsel and persist in that work of division, we can't but look upon them as therein not in unity with the Church of Christ and order of the gospel : and therefore let Friends go on in the power of God and in that work for Him, His Truth and people ; and not be swayed or hindered by them or their oppositions." They also approved "serious sighing, sensible groaning and reverent singing . . . in blessed unity with the brethren while they are in the public labour and service of the gospel, whether by preaching, praying or praising God"—an approval not of congregational singing [3] as we understand it, but of words or sounds breaking forth from others during ministry or prayer, as still happens among fervent simple-hearted folk at a Methodist Camp Meeting.[4] They urged strict maintenance of the testimony against tithes, and declared the duty of open public worship in times of persecution in words which are still preserved, as a precious memorial, in the modern Church-discipline of the Society of Friends : "As it hath been our care and practice from the

---

[1] The Kendal Books contain Minutes of first two meetings followed by a Q.M. Minute of 2nd July 1675, appointing two Friends to "go to those Friends above mentioned to know their reason wherefore they did meet by themselves to dispose of money forth of the general stock, without the consent of the M.M."

[2] See MS. Y.M. Records and Kendal Early Record Book. Many of the paragraphs were transferred to the MS. "Books of Extracts."

[3] Congregational singing was only gradually introduced in the Nonconformist churches, not till 1690 by the Baptists (Barclay, *Inner Life*, pp. 453-461).

[4] At end of Thirsk M.M. Men's Minute Book there is an unwisely worded paper by Fox, from Worcester Gaol, 22nd Jan. 1674, which claims that, when some one is speaking out of the life, the life breathes itself forth for its liberty through groans, sighs, or sounds in others and stops him. Cf. epistle to Westmorland Friends by Fox in Swarthm. Colln. ii. 13. The remarkable account of the last meeting attended by John Story at Kendal, *post*, p. 321, shows the disorder that might result. The M.M.'s had sometimes to deal with individual cases, *e.g.* York Two Weeks' Meeting, 4th April 1677, "Christopher Gilburne, being this day here as desired, did acknowledge his being drawn out, by the power of God, as he saith, to express himself by that singing noise in the meetings, and that he endeavoured to suppress it several times, but could not : yet for the future, rather than be offensive, he will labour to refrain from it."

beginning that an open testimony for the Lord should be borne and a public standard for truth and righteousness upheld in the power and Spirit of God by our open and known meetings . . . so it is our advice and judgment that all Friends gathered in the name of Jesus keep up those public testimonies in their respective places, and [do] not decline, forsake or remove their public assemblies, because of times of sufferings, as worldly, fearful and politic professors have done, because of Informers and the like persecutors; for such practices are not consistent with the nobility of the Truth and therefore not to be owned in the Church of Christ."

They approved the recording of condemnations in a distinct book for the clearing of Truth, to be published however only so far as might be needful. But after a Friend had been restored to unity, let "none among you so remember his transgression as to cast it at him, or upbraid him with it; for that is not according to the mercies of God." They condemned those who styled Men's and Women's Meetings courts, sessions, or synods, and papers from faithful Friends edicts and canons, or spoke of such Friends as popes or bishops; and they confirmed the rule that marriages should be propounded both to the Men's and Women's Meetings. They did not, however, assume any binding authority for their conclusions, which they were content to "recommend to the evidence of God's holy witness in the hearts of His people."

The paper, as a whole, though with some qualifications, condemned the position taken by the Wilkinson-Story party and was supported by a separate epistle from Fox, covering the same ground.[1] Westmorland Friends, confronted with the separation which had taken place and acting on advice from London, arranged a conference with Story and some of his followers, who refused discussion because the charges against them were not in writing.[2] Another meeting was convened in July at Poolbank, to which nine leading Friends from a distance were invited, and meanwhile the Quarterly Meeting took action regarding the separate business meeting, and issued its paper censuring the weakness of Preston Patrick Friends.[3] Story and Wilkinson announced that they would not attend

[1] In Kendal Early Record Book.
[2] *Anti-Christian Treachery*, pp. 42-59, becomes the main printed authority. The meeting was held at Draw-well and must not be confused with the later more important meeting at the same place.
[3] Q.M. Minutes, 2nd July 1675, and Book of Condemnations under same date.

before persons who chose the judges and were both accusers and witnesses. The meeting adjourned for a day to Milnthorpe but they still refused to appear, though they seem to have offered to refer the hearing to two Friends, one chosen by each side. In their absence the charges were heard, and a paper was given forth against them by the Friends from a distance who had met apart from Westmorland Friends to consider their judgment.[1] The spirit of Story and Wilkinson was condemned, because

> ... it expressly strikes against us in the ground, in our godly order and proceedings, which is for no other end but for the putting forward and keeping up of righteousness. ... The holy God doth own us with His presence to our great refreshment and confirmation in this our holy practice and heavenly order; and therefore we cannot but in the power of God place judgment upon the head of that spirit ... that would put stumbling-blocks in the way.

This sense of satisfaction with the new system carried with it an adverse verdict on the various points in debate.

These proceedings may have been excusable, especially in view of the overt act of separation; but they were ill-calculated for healing the breach, and a request by Fox that the two leaders should attend him at Swarthmore was resented and did not help the position. The two Johns, as we have seen, were in high esteem in the West of England, and the report that they had been judged without a hearing caused a widespread feeling that they had received hard measure.

The establishment of business meetings had taken a

---

[1] John Burnyeat's *Journal* describes their proceedings, and shows that six of them had spent some hours with Story and Wilkinson in the morning, trying to persuade them to come to the Milnthorpe meeting. The nine judges were leading Cumberland and Yorkshire Friends:—John Burnyeat; John Grave, of Isell Meeting, another tireless itinerant, who died a few months later; John Tiffin, of Pardshaw, who paid nine visits to Irish Friends, "a sweet, tender-spirited man, sound in judgment, and had a living testimony" (*F.P.T.* p. 38); Hugh Tickell, of Portinscales, who had travelled in Scotland and in the West of England; and Thomas Laythes, also of Portinscales, "well-beloved by most of men for his honesty and true-heartedness ... a lowly, meek, and sweet-spirited man ... sound in judgment, serviceable in the Church for discipline" (*F.P.T.* p. 45), but not a preacher. The Yorkshire Friends included Robert Lodge, of Richmond M.M., who travelled widely, often in company with Burnyeat; and Richard Robinson, another veteran Publisher of Truth (see *Beginnings of Quakerism*, pp. 148-150). The men chosen were evidently all leaders of ripe experience.

weight of responsibility off the shoulders of Fox,[1] and he now made no attempt to control their action. He was himself content with the Milnthorpe verdict and declined to suggest its revision, but wrote that if Friends in the South, who had already intermeddled from a distance, " think others has not judged equally, they may come and mend the matter if they can."[2] The important meeting about sufferings referred to in the last chapter,[3] had been arranged for 18th October, and advantage was taken of the occasion, with the consent of Friends from the North, to ask George Whitehead, John Whitehead, William Gibson, Alexander Parker, and two Friends to be chosen from Bristol to go into the North and meet with Westmorland Friends and Wilkinson and Story "for the assisting the Church and Friends there to hear and determine the said difference, as in the wisdom and counsel of God they shall be directed, for peace and unity in the Church." The proposal showed the lengths to which Friends were prepared to go in order to secure a reconciliation, and was eminently fair, for George Whitehead and Parker were friendly with the two Johns[4] and room was left for two Friends from Bristol, where feeling ran high in their favour. The Morning Meeting, who had the carriage of the arrangements, stood neutral even to the point of suspending the reading of a paper submitted by Westmorland Friends, "till such time that Friends find no hope and likelihood of a meeting to end that difference which is the ground thereof,"[5] and also directed that a controversial letter by Fox should not be read in London.[6] Fox vented his disgust in a hotly worded letter:

> These doings ... is an evil savour in the nation; and had they been brotherly they might have written down to me about

---

[1] In a letter to the 1676 Y.M., dated 28th April (*Journ.* ii. 244), Fox says, "It eased me when those meetings were set up; for men and women, that are heirs of the gospel, have right to the gospel-order and it belongs to them."

[2] Fox to Penn, 30th Sept. 1675, in *J.F.H.S.* x. 146-148. The letter shows the shrewd common sense of Fox at its best.

[3] *Ante*, p. 283. The Minute is in Morning Meeting Minutes and in *Anti-Christian Treachery*, p. 50.

[4] See *e.g. J.F.H.S.* x. 143.   [5] Minute, 7th Feb. 1676.

[6] Fox to Rebecca Travers and others, 28th April 1676, Swarthm. Colln. v. 9, also cited *ante*, p. 280.

it, before they had made an order; for it was time to write, when Men and Women's Meetings was lying waste and altering. . . . For I was constrained and moved of the Lord to write for His Truth's sake and people's sake, when I saw a wilful, heady spirit was going up and down to lay God's heritage waste, and so many taking their parts which neither they nor them had concerned themselves in the settling and establishing the meetings in the power of God—and hath taken more pains to unsettle Friends and disquiet them when they were settled than ever they did for Truth.

On the other hand, the Morning Meeting printed a reconciling epistle from Dewsbury to Friends, in which he touched the live issues, such as the endurance of persecution, maintaining meetings, administering discipline, "singing" in meetings, and loyalty to Quaker leaders, out of a spiritual experience which had learnt that "in peace are we to conquer and in quietness to prevail."[1]

But in spite of the confidence that these proceedings might have inspired, it was only with much ado and through the personal influence of George Whitehead, that the two Johns were persuaded to give Friends the desired meeting.[2] They were now in the West of England, in close intercourse with William Rogers, who would represent Bristol Friends. He was a leading merchant, a man of fixed and narrow opinions, whose capacity and persistence made him a commanding figure in the strong but self-centred Quakerism of the city. A second Bristol Friend had been designed, but, as none was available, another sympathizer, Gervase Benson, one of the old Westmorland Seekers, took his place.[3] The Friends concerned in the Milnthorpe judgment and some other leaders from the North of England were also present, but not George Fox. The meeting took place at the beginning of April 1676, and lasted four days. It was held at Draw-well, near Sedbergh, at John Blaykling's

---

[1] Minute, 17th Jan. 1676, and Dewsbury's *Works*, pp. 331-342, dated from London three days earlier.
[2] Morning Meeting, 7th Feb. 1676, and *Anti-Christian Treachery*, p. 52.
[3] *F.P.T.* p. 252, "He came to see the wrongness of their spirit . . . and deserted them and kept to Friends' meetings and in love and unity with them to the end of his days." He died in 1679, buried 5th May.

house, still standing on its sunny slope above the Lune, a place for peace and open-hearted fellowship.

An honest attempt was made to reach an understanding. At the beginning of the meeting Wilkinson and Story asked Friends to say whether in matters of faith, and of discipline which might become matter of faith, all God's people ought not to be left to the manifestation of His Spirit and Truth in their own hearts, and whether, since there were diversities of gifts, a judgment given forth by a part of the members of Christ's body could be a bond upon any other part further than their understandings were illuminated thereby. The answer ran:

> To the first Question we say Yea, and Nay to the second Question, with that true and simple sense that the words import and Friends have been used to understand them; but not to strengthen prejudiced spirits, who have made that their plea for their separation, and against Truth's authority in our Monthly and Quarterly Meetings, nor yet to justify any that are ignorant, through their own sloth and unfaithfulness, or to excuse them that would not be accounted weak, but strong, wise and as pillars.[1]

This largely satisfied the two Johns, who told the meeting that they had no desire to encourage apostates and bad spirits, who argued from such principles in favour of fleshly liberty and so opposed the power of God itself and the practice of God's people in the power. Both sides, therefore, rejected any outwardly imposed authority and only claimed that which came from the illumination of the Spirit in the heart, provided the heart were open to the light and resolute to obey it. The real difficulty lay in this last proviso. The events that had already taken place made each party regard the other as acting from a wrong spirit—the spirit of outward authority in the one case and of fleshly liberty in the other. At Draw-well itself a visitation of spiritual power was known, which at last led Wilkinson and Story, while retaining their own convictions on the general questions, to accept the view

---

[1] Printed in *The Memory of John Story Revived*, 1683, p. 37, and the comments of Wilkinson and Story in *ibid.*, and in *Christian-Quaker*, pt. iv. p. 40.

of the meeting that they had been wrong in opposing other faithful Friends in the practice of things which they believed to be their duty.[1] Their paper to this effect played so important a part in the succeeding controversy that it must be set out, though I would gladly spare the reader the perusal of its confused English.

We are sensible that in the hour of temptation that hath appeared through us—which hath given an occasion of offence to the Churches of God unto whom the knowledge of the northern differences hath come—and since the inward sense of our brethren (who we are sensible have a travail on their spirits for preservation of peace and unity in the Church of God) concerning us is such;
> That jealousies have entered us, and that we have been at some times exercised in things, tending to oppose Friends in the practice of those things that they testify are commendable in the Church of God;

We are sorry that any weakness should appear in us to give occasion for such offence; and, as satisfaction to our brethren and the Church of God in general, we do from the very bottom of our hearts condemn that spirit, whether it hath appeared in us or any that hath given offence to the Church of God in general, or that oppose the order of the gospel, or any faithful brethren in the practice of those things they believe are their duty.

Story said that he would give further satisfaction, as the Lord gave him understanding; and Friends parted in the hope that the separate business meeting would be given up. Story and Wilkinson visited Fox at Swarthmore, who "was very loving to them, and tender on their behalf, letting them see the danger they were in, if they did not return to the ancient power—in it to become one with God's people again in the service and labour of the Truth—and for that end desired them to break up the

---

[1] See their answers to the charges against them, in *Christian-Quaker*, pt. iv. pp. 37-40, and their so-called paper of Condemnation, in *Anti-Christian Treachery*, p. 55, and *An Exalted Diotrephes*, p. 12, the text of which I have followed. For the meaning of this paper cf. *post*, p. 320. The Draw-well meeting is described in *Anti-Christian Treachery*, pp. 52-59; cf. *Christian-Quaker*, pt. iv. pp. 36-37, and *An Exalted Diotrephes*, pp. 10, 11. For John Steele's striking testimony at this meeting, see Dev. Ho. Penington Colln. iv. 132 and Portf. 23, No. 145, printed in *Irish Friend*, ii. p. 27, with a wrong reference to Barclay, who was not present.

separate meeting."[1] Any hopes that had been raised would be soon shattered.

Rogers had objected to the meeting coming to any judgment of its own as it included others besides the six Friends appointed, but, after he had left, the Friends present drew up a narrative of the proceedings, which declared Story and Wilkinson "faulty in the most material things exhibited in charge against them," and referred to their paper of regret, but without giving it at length, as a condemnation against themselves and their spirit of division. This embittered Rogers, who had drawn up the document in question, and now urged, with equal inexactitude, that "there was nothing in it"; that "the most innocent man might own it, and never hurt himself"; and "that it was no better than a rattle to please children."[2] Several of the Draw-well meeting were at the Yearly Meeting of Ministers in London in May, and addressed an urgent but fruitless letter to Story and Wilkinson, signed by many other ministers, beseeching them to end the separation.[3] The issue became definitely joined during this summer of 1676. Story went South to rally supporters, and Rogers moved about with his narrative of the Draw-well meeting, while Wilkinson and some eleven others subscribed a manuscript which was sent up and down the country by way of remonstrance.[4] John Raunce and Charles Harris, the two leading Friends of High Wycombe, supported the Separatists, under cover of disinterestedness. Penn, however, stigmatized them as partisans in a strongly-worded letter, which states the standpoint taken by the majority of Friends with less obscurity than usual.

Where doth our apostasy lie? In not suffering loose and libertine spirits to tread down our hedge, under the specious pretence of being left to the Light within? As if the Light were inconsistent with itself, or admitted of unity under not only different but contrary practices in the one family and flock of God.[5]

---

[1] *Anti-Christian Treachery*, p. 59. Cf. Fox's letter to Wilkinson, 16th Dec. 1676, in *Christian-Quaker*, pt. iv. p. 44, at p. 59.
[2] *An Exalted Diotrephes*, p. 13.   [3] *Anti-Christian Treachery*, p. 60.
[4] *Ibid.* p. 62.   [5] 11th Sept. 1676, in Dev. Ho. Penington Colln. iv. 133.

Penington wrote to Story about the same time [1] under the sense that he was nourishing hard thoughts against "dear George Fox, whom the Lord hath honoured and is with," and, as time passed, this personal side of the difference became more prominent. The jealous mind of Rogers satisfied itself that Fox was playing the part of an inspired law-giver to Friends, so that with many their faith stood in him, when it ought to stand "in none but the Power of God."[2] The two Johns, to his thinking, were persecuted saints, against whom was ranged the official party in the Society, who, instead of following Christ's Light in the conscience, accepted submissively the orders of the Quaker Moses.

Fox, during his Worcester imprisonment, had answered such criticism beforehand in a noble vindication of himself, framed after the Pauline model:[3]

> It concerns all, that profess themselves to be ministers, to be humble, else they are no learners of Christ . . . not to be lords over God's inheritance, but let Him be Lord Whose right it is. And you have known the manner of my life the best part of thirty years, since I went forth and forsook all things. I sought not myself; I sought you and His glory that sent me; and, when I turned you to Him that is able to save you, I left you to Him. And my travails hath been great, in hungers and colds, when there was few [Friends], for the first six or seven years—that I often lay in woods and commons in the night, that many times it was as a byword that I would not come into houses and lie in their beds; and the prisons have been made my home a great part of my time, and in danger of my life and in jeopardy daily. And amongst you I have made myself of no reputation to keep the Truth up in reputation, as you all very well know it that be in the fear of God. With the low I made myself low; and with the weak and feeble I was as one with them, and condescended to all conditions, for the Lord had fitted me so before He sent me forth; and so I passed through great sufferings in my body as you have been sensible.

This fine *Apologia* was the utterance of a man who

---

[1] 21st Sept. 1676, in Dev. Ho. Penington Colln. iv. 141. Cf. a later letter, 26th April 1677, in Dev. Ho. Penington Colln. iv. 142.
[2] Letter to Fox, 27th March 1677, in *Christian-Quaker*, pt. iv. pp. 81-89. Cf. Thos. Lower's letter, *post*, p. 428, and Penn's letter, *post*, p. 474.
[3] *Epistles*, No. 308.

knew that his best work was done and was well content that the care of the Churches, which had rested so heavily on his own shoulders, should be taken by others. It has nothing in it of the spirit of the hierarch. His long rest at Swarthmore left him still weak, and when he resumed active service in the spring of 1677 it was only by slow stages that he gained London before the Yearly Meeting of Ministers at the beginning of June, conferring with Dewsbury on the way. A strong condemnation of Story and Wilkinson was issued, after some of the ministers had left, and without the approval of others. The sixty-six names, for example, do not include George Whitehead's, who said that his service would be hurt by his putting his hand to it.[1] Fox was in London but kept in the background. The paper [2] says:

We do hereby reprove and judge that jealous, rending and separating spirit—and them and their separate company, as being in that spirit of separation; and that by the power and Spirit of our God. And we do warn all to whom this comes to beware of the said J. S. and J. W., whose way at present is not the way of peace and Christian concord, for if it were they would not offer their gift till reconciled to their brethren. Therefore brethren everywhere . . . where they come, warn them in the name of the Lord to go home and be reconciled to their brethren, and not go thus up and down to offer up their gift. . . . But, forasmuch as the way of the working of this subtle enemy has been to suggest that it is the design of some to make themselves

---

[1] See Rogers' "A Second Scourge for George Whitehead," 1685, p. 10. After saying that the number 66 was the tail of the Beast whose number was 666, and so was without power to kill, he goes on, in the prosy rhymes for which he seems to have fancied himself:

  And, tho' a BULL was sign'd by th' Sixty-Six,
  Yet Whitehead to 't refus'd His Name to Fix:
  And why? 'Twas said that Warn'd He was by God
  Not to Sign it. . . .
  . . . .
  . . . My Hand, said He,
  Would hurt the Service of My Ministry,
  Or Words to that Effect.

[2] Printed in *Anti-Christian Treachery*, pp. 74-78, and in *Y.M. Printed Epistles*, vol. i. (1681–1769) pp. li-lvi. In *Christian-Quaker*, pt. ii. pp. 72-84, certain Bristol Friends criticize the document, and challenge it as issued from no regular meeting. It bears date 12th June 1677, a Tuesday, the day of the Six Weeks' Meeting, but the names of only a few members of that meeting are in the list so that the criticism holds good.

lords over God's heritage, and to set up a worldly and arbitrary power in the Church of Christ, and then to run out into severe exclamations against imposition, crying up liberty of conscience, . . . this we feel ourselves constrained in the love of the Lord, for the good of all, to declare . . . that we deny and abhor any such thing; for we have one Lord, Judge, King and Lawgiver in the Church. . . . And though it is far from us to bruise or hurt the poorest or least member in the Church of Christ, who may not have that clearness of sight or strength of faith which the Lord has brought us to, but that they may be cherished, yet by that salt which we have in ourselves from the Lord are we enabled to savour between the transformations of the enemy and the scruples of the innocent, and, as to be tender of the one, so to give judgment against the other.

Let their own paper[1] . . . be read and weighed . . . and therein we well suppose will be found the true nature of imposition, in that none of their own county are allowed to be of the Monthly or Quarterly Meetings, but such as are appointed and chosen by the particular meetings; next, that none of other counties, though public labourers of the gospel, are to be admitted to be at their meetings, unless it be to tell their message and immediately to depart: and these with such-like things eighty-seven subscribed as the reasons of their separation and foundation of a new government among themselves, which is a plain independency from the life and practice of the Church of Christ throughout the world.

The strong lead thus given by the Quaker ministers may have steadied the main body of Friends, but stirred to fresh action the persons directly concerned on both sides. Hitherto actual separation had only taken place in Westmorland, and had been confined to business meetings, all Friends worshipping together. The Quarterly Meeting now decided to withdraw meetings for worship from the houses of disaffected Friends, and thus itself took the step of bringing about a complete schism, or, as the Wilkinson-Story party styled it, an excommunication. Story was at the time in Wiltshire, but sent his Northern supporters a paper endorsed by his adherents in the West of England, which he desired should serve as a basis for a reconciling conference. In lieu of this the Westmorland Friends appointed a

[1] *Ante*, p. 299.

meeting "in order to receive any tender confession or condemnation of their weakness who have been in the separation, as also in order to hear John Story's paper, if they bring it there to be read," and, upon this leading to nothing, they finally, at the beginning of March 1678, subscribed a paper to the separate party, "wherein their separation is denied, and they, in the condition they stands in, are discharged from meddling or being concerned in the affairs of the Church of Christ."[1] The schism chiefly affected three of the Westmorland meetings, and Robert Barrow of Kendal gives a vivid though prejudiced account of the position in a letter to Penn about this time.[2]

The party, he says, grows insolent, though they are scattering. Now and then one comes back to the fold, looking like a man frighted with death. Some, however, that came in before the Yearly Meeting are now pretty well restored. Separate meetings for worship are held at Underbarrow and Preston Patrick, and at Hutton, where Wilkinson has drawn off the whole meeting, some half-dozen families, all of them tithe-payers. Preston Patrick will be a fine meeting again, for the ancient standard of righteousness set up in the days of Camm and Audland is again raised up in Thomas and Ann Camm. Thomas Camm had been led astray by Story in the time of the Informers; but had afterwards suffered a two years' imprisonment for tithes, and during this time had seen his error and came forth clear. At Underbarrow also the greater part will be preserved, "though those among them who are rich in wit and wealth are of the separation." Indeed there is no true Friend left in Underbarrow itself, where "dear Edward Burrough was born, and also

---

[1] The above statement summarizes much scattered material, which should be consulted by the curious student (if any) in the following order : Q.M. proceedings of 6th July 1677, in Westmorland Minutes, and in *Anti-Christian Treachery*, pp. 78-81, and the paper from the Q.M. in Dev. Ho. Penington Colln. iv. 166. Reply to Q.M. action by Story and others in the South, see *Christian-Quaker*, pt. iv. p. 107, and Story's paper in *Memory of John Story Revived*, p. 40, dated 30th Sept. Answer to proposals re this paper by the M.M. 2nd Nov., see paper in Dev. Ho. Portf. 2, No. 41. Further Minutes of M.M. 7th Dec., and Q.M. 1st March in Westmorland Minutes. See also *Anti-Christian Treachery*, pp. 108 and following page, numbered 105.

[2] Dev. Ho. Penington Colln. iv. 164, and in Dev. Ho. Portf. 31, No. 116. Thomas Camm was son to John Camm, and married Ann, widow of John Audland. His testimony against himself, dated 4th Oct. 1677, and also one a few months later from twenty-nine Friends of Preston Patrick, are in the M.M. Minute Book at Kendal.

received the Truth, as also Miles Halhead and Miles Hubbersty," and it must now be called Crook. "In some respects," he adds, in allusion to the discontinuance of joint meetings for worship, "we are greatly eased, for the weight of the dark spirit and the enmity which proceeded from it did often burden us."

The storm-centre now shifted to the South. Bristol, with its strong body of Friends, was, as we have seen, a somewhat independent meeting, jealous of outside interference. Its veteran leader, George Bishop, had protested before his death against the 1666 letter, which was a first attempt to strengthen government in the Quaker Church:[1]

In the apostles' days were pastors, teachers, elders, etc., but in this day the Spirit itself is the pastor, teacher, elder, etc. . . . That which would be otherwise than this, leads into the apostasy and will seek to bring dark night in again; and so will place the thing to the person and not the person to the thing. And for my part, if that day should prevail or those things which your paper seems to hold forth and enforce, I have no other expectation but that the same exercise we shall receive at your hands as we received at the hands of those who would have held us in captivity in the day that the Lord first visited us.

A Women's Meeting for the care of the poor had existed in the city for some years,[2] and when the question of Women's Monthly Meetings was first in agitation in 1671, the Men's Meeting concluded[3] that the best expedient for preserving peace was to desire the women to forbear setting up a Monthly Meeting till they were agreed among themselves, and had the unity of the men. The matter was settled in 1673, by including women in another business meeting held at Bristol called the Meeting for Cases of Discipline.[4] The tendencies to independency in Bristol, and personal affection for the two Johns, combined to prejudice several Friends in their favour, and feeling ran high after the London letter

---

[1] Bishop's comments are in Thomas Crisp's "First Part of Babel's-Builders Unmasking Themselves," an adverse piece printed in 1682.
[2] *Ante*, pp. 272, 273.
[3] See Minutes of Men's Two Weeks' Meeting, 27th Nov., 11th and 25th Dec. 1671. The first of these is in Rogers' own handwriting and is initialled by him.
[4] Minute of Men's Meeting, 11th Aug. 1673, and of Meeting for Discipline and resulting Conference of men and women, 7th and 17th July. Cf. the Six Weeks' Meeting, *ante*, p. 275.

of June 1677, which had been signed by four Bristol Friends. When this was read in the Men's Meeting, certain Friends drew up a paper of protest and the same course was taken in Wiltshire.[1] In October the reading of a letter[2] from Penn in the joint Meeting for Discipline caused the partisans of Wilkinson and Story to say that the charges made could not be proved. Thus challenged, Friends gave notice of a meeting to make them good—styled a separate meeting by Rogers, because he did not consider it properly appointed. John Burnyeat of Cumberland and Jasper Batt of Somerset were present, and a dreary *dossier* of documents was read amid interruptions and protests from Rogers. They chiefly related to the Draw-well meeting but included a Vision which Fox had lately written to Richard Vickris from Amsterdam, describing the spirit of strife and separation whose work it was to root out the ancient Truth under pretence of standing up for it. Rogers retorted with a virulent letter to Fox in December, which upbraided him with bringing forth his imaginations under the notion of night-visions and publishing them for the word of the Lord. Bristol Men's Meeting, in a Minute which shows that the majority inclined against Rogers, forbade the defacing or removal of papers sent to the meeting, though copies might be taken, and desired that Friends, as far as their conscience allowed, should forbear contending about papers that were read; but, if occasion of controversy arose, then a special meeting should be appointed for the discourse thereof.[3] Fox and Penn had been in Holland, in the free air which attends forward spiritual work, and Penn's letter, read at Bristol, had expressed the disgust of a generous spirit at the partisan heat which was diverting Friends from their great mission:

---

[1] *Christian-Quaker*, pt. ii. pp. 72-84 and 85.
[2] The best account is in a Bristol letter, dated 27th Oct. 1677, in Dev. Ho. Penington Colln. iv. 165, which should be compared with Rogers' letter to Fox, dated 3rd Dec., in *Christian-Quaker*, pt. iv. pp. 91–105. The meeting for proving the charges was held 25th Oct. Penn's letter is in *Works*, 1726 edn. i. 94, dated 16th Sept., and in Bristol MSS. i. No. 16; Fox's Vision in *Journ.* ii. 288, and the copy to Vickris in Bristol MSS. v. Nos. 12, 13.
[3] Minute of 19th Nov.

Let us all who have received the gift from God wait in deep humility . . . to eye and prosecute His universal service in the world . . . which noble work, had those that are gone into the separation but laid deeply to heart, they would never have sat at home murmuring, fretting and quarrelling against the comely and godly order and practice of their brethren.

They returned in the autumn, and Fox found his way to Bristol by the beginning of 1678, with the natural result of bringing the *animus* against him to a head. Rogers could not well decline the challenge, and prolonged meetings to go into the matter took place in February. With him were William Ford, a prominent Bristol Friend, and two of the Wiltshire leaders, Arthur Ismeade and John Maltravers. On the other side were Penn, George Whitehead, and William Gibson. Both Fox and Story were present, besides a company of other Friends.[1] Penn and Rogers drew up carefully framed articles of procedure, providing for a joint report, and for notice in writing of the matters to be debated. Rogers and his Friends called their charges "dissatisfactions": they were not satisfied, they said, that Fox in his late proceedings had been guided by the Spirit of Truth, nor that those who looked on him as a man worthy of double honour had had therein a spiritual discerning. They cited in proof a number of passages out of an elaborate paper by Fox, dated November 1676, called "This is An Encouragement to all the Women's Meetings in the World." Fox had marshalled scripture in favour of his favourite thesis, not without straining the text and laying himself open to damaging criticism. The late John S. Rowntree attracted auditors to an able lecture on the Wilkinson-Story controversy by entitling it "Micah's Mother," from the chief instance given of these misapplied passages. Fox had written,[2] "And was not Micah's

---

[1] See the full propositions in Bristol MSS. v. Nos. 87-98, partly in Rogers' handwriting. Accounts of the meeting are in *Anti-Christian Treachery*, pp. 90, 158-174, *Christian-Quaker*, pt. v. 3-12, *An Exalted Diotrephes*, pp. 45, 46. See also letter from Fox to Rogers, Bristol, 4th Jan. 1679, in Bristol MSS. v. Nos. 18, 19.

[2] Reprinted, but without reference to Micah's mother, in Fox, *Epistles*, No. 320. Cf. J. S. Rowntree, *Micah's Mother*, 1893, in his *Life and Work*.

mother a virtuous woman? Read Judges the 17th, and see what she said to her son." On turning to the chapter cited, we find a good-intentioned woman serving Jehovah in a crudely idolatrous fashion, and conclude that Fox might have spared his illustration, and Rogers his anger. The charges on this head, indeed, only showed that the Quaker leader had ransacked the Bible in support of Women's Meetings with undiscriminating diligence, and forgot that one bad argument spoils many good ones. Rogers and his party came nearer to a substantial charge, when they urged that Fox had warned Friends against judging one another behind their backs, but had done it himself; and insinuated that he could only justify himself in this by pleading that he was privileged and was more than a man. But they tried to avoid a clear issue by desiring that Fox and the Friends who had pressed for the meeting should admit that every one who acted contrary to this warning against judging was blameworthy: then only would they elaborate the reasons behind their dissatisfactions. Rogers was urged at least to make good the charges in his December letter, but this he refused and the meetings broke up without result.

No joint report of the proceedings was drawn up as arranged, but Rogers circulated a biased account in manuscript in the West and North, contrary to the spirit of the agreement. The controversy had now degenerated into personalities, to be found in all their venom in a paper written by Rogers, dated 20th September 1678, and read in October at the Bristol Men's Meeting, "at which," he says, "some of the party with G. F. seemed very uneasy."[1] Thomas Camm, writing from Preston Patrick, says of it:[2]

We met with one of the wickedest pieces signed by the great champion W. R. that ever our eyes did see: it is in the preamble directed to your Men's Meeting at Bristol, but the whole bulk of it is poisonous enmity against G. F. We got it by chance; they send it privately up and down amongst their company, who feed

[1] *Christian-Quaker*, pt. v. pp. 25-35, and, for date of reading, *Anti-Christian Treachery*, p. 119.
[2] Letter to Richard Snead of Bristol, 16th Nov., in Bristol MSS. v. No. 83.

upon it as a dainty dish. One that they had showed it to desired to have it overnight, that he might have time to peruse it a little, who brought it to me and I took a copy and sent it to George.

The paper alleged discrepancies between Fox's standards of conduct for himself and for others : in one or two cases he was said to have avoided imprisonment, or to have advised the purchase of impropriate tithes, or the securing of property from Informers ; and, under the stress of the opposition against him, he seems to have made a charge against Story which could not be fully proved.[1] Rogers included in his "smiting queries" a direct attack on Fox's worldly position :[2]

Whether it be fit for one that feeds of the fat of the land and lives in fullness of plenty, attended in many respects like an earthly prince, and that hath twelve or thirteen hundred pounds, with the increase thereof for many years, if any be, well-secured out of the reach of the spoilers and persecutors, to admonish a company of poor, innocent, harmless Friends, that may have three or four cows apiece to feed themselves and children, not to secure them from the spoilers ?

Fox replied that he had not this sum of money secured out of the reach of the spoiler. Something had come to him as his birthright many years before, which he had given to his relations. He was careful not to gratify Rogers' envy and curiosity by disclosing his means, which had nothing to do with the matter in debate. But there is no ground for supposing that he had ever taken any special steps to protect his property.

Meanwhile the spirit of disaffection had come to a head in other places. In Wiltshire in April 1678[3] the

---

[1] See *Christian-Quaker*, pt. v. pp. 11-92, and answers in *An Exalted Diotrephes*, pp. 41-43 (as to fleeing from meetings, cf. *ante*, pp. 219-221), *Anti-Christian Treachery*, pp. 109-157, Ellwood's *Antidote against the Infection of William Rogers' Book*, and *The Accuser of our Brethren cast down*. Rogers put the worst construction on the facts alleged. The papers in Dev. Ho. A.R.B. Colln. Nos. 197-222 mostly relate to these charges. In Bristol MSS. v. Nos. 20, 21 and Swarthm. Colln. transcript v. p. 17 is preserved Fox's letter to Richard Snead and others, dated 7th Jan. 1679, covering his reply to Rogers' "smiting queries." He calls them "charges from his rattle head to please rattle children with."

[2] *Christian-Quaker*, pt. v. pp. 31, 47, and *Anti-Christian Treachery*, pp. 128-130. Joseph Vigors of Manchester spread the charge in the West of England, see Bristol MSS. Nos. 27, 30.

[3] Q.M. Minute, 1st April 1678 (in *J.F.H.S.* x. 182, with Bristol entry of 1680) ;

Wilkinson-Story party "in a very unfriendly manner went away from the [Quarterly] Meeting to an Inn, and ketched up and carried away the Quarterly book from the meeting, and would not send him again nor return themselves," and in August Nathaniel Coleman in like fashion carried off the book of Chippenham Monthly Meeting.[1] The Wiltshire Separatists were zealous for their cause. In the early part of 1679,[2] Coleman and Arthur Ismeade, "a man of large body with a loud strong voice,"[3] paid a visit to Westmorland, and they both proved themselves pertinacious opponents of visiting Friends. There were also difficulties at Hertford[4] and the beginnings of trouble in Reading.[5]

Next to Fox, the two Friends of greatest spiritual insight were Penington and Dewsbury, both of them veteran sufferers for Truth. There can be no doubt of Penington's attitude. He was a man disposed to think the best of others; "the Lord is my witness," he writes, "that I am afraid to wrong any man upon the face of the earth, so much as in a thought, much more any servant or minister of His." Again he says, "The Lord knows I

Wiltshire Friends made two other copies of their Minutes for several years, apparently in fear of another raid. In 1680 Richard Snead had a copy made of the Bristol Men's Meeting Minute Book, lest Rogers should take it away, as had been done in Wiltshire. The Wilts Q.M. testified against the opposing party, 4th Oct. 1680, Ismeade, Coleman, John Jennings, and Maltravers being its leaders, but continued to try to recover them. The question of the possession of meeting-houses was raised 6th Dec. 1681, and it was "unanimously agreed that Friends rather buy and not sell, but all are left to the wisdom of God." A Minute of 30th Oct. 1682 concludes that the Separatists "are not a people worthy to be taken notice of any further, as from the Q.M., but leave them to the Lord, Who is able to deal with them."

[1] See paper in Dev. Ho. Penington Colln. iv. No. 136, and Chippenham M.M. Minutes, 19th Aug. and subsequent dates. In Aug. 1680 we find a beautifully worded Minute agreeing to a special meeting "chiefly and only to sit before the Lord, with our spirits bowed before Him, that He would appear by His Divine arm and living power to preserve from that spirit that hath led some of our brethren to separate from us; and that our spirits might be poured out before Him that so, if it stands good in His Divine wisdom and long-suffering patience, they or any of them might be restored again into unity with the Lord and with us His people."

[2] For Coleman, see *Camb. Journ.* ii. 262, and note, p. 446. For the Westmorland visit, see Fox to Richard Snead, 5th March 1679, in Swarthm. Colln. transcript v. 15, and Bristol MSS. v. No. 16, and Robert Barrow to Snead and others, 15th March 1679, in Swarthm. Colln. transcript v. 21, and Bristol MSS. v. No. 17. [3] This detail is found in Thos. Story's *Life*, p. 121 (1696).

[4] See Dev. Ho. Penington Colln. iv. Nos. 148, 150, and *post*, Chapter XVII.
[5] See *post*, Chapter XVII.

would go along with the sense and sway of life, wherever it is, and not against it by no means." He knew both Fox and Story intimately, and his sensitive nature, feeling their spirits, found Story inwardly hurt and languishing, with a stiff, exalted, selfish wisdom alive in him, while in Fox he had felt the pure glory of life, enabling him to see brightly with the anointed eye over all dark spirits, not desiring to rule over any but to bring every one under the dominion of the everlasting Seed, that it alone might reign in and over all.[1] Dewsbury held a more equivocal position; indeed, there is a letter from Penington warning him and John Crook not to hold aloof from the controversy, for the tender lambs needed the help of the servants of God for their preservation.[2] The thought of strife between brethren was wholly repugnant to Dewsbury's nature, and for many years he laboured his utmost to prevent the printing of papers that tended to quench the love of Friends towards one another.[3] In one case of printing his spirit was so wounded that for many weeks he was not expected to live. He approved men's and women's business meetings, and had a deep sense of the labours of the travelling ministers,[4] but his prayer was that the Lord would

> ... subject all convinced of His truth to throw down their crowns of self-striving before His throne, that in His ancient love all may be buried that is not of His nature, and in Him all bound up in the unity of His spirit; that the Lord may be one, His name one; that all may be restored that hath been in any measure serviceable in the hand of the Lord and not that any be lost that have tasted of His goodness.[5]

By the spring of 1679 Rogers had prepared a historical manuscript detailing the facts from the Wilkinson-Story point of view, and naming some hundreds of Friends on one side or the other. A letter respecting it was sent to

---

[1] See Dev. Ho. Penington Colln. iv. pp. 141-146, containing letters to Story, 21st Sept. 1676 and 26th April 1677, and to Thomas Curtis, 1st, 13th, and 24th Dec. 1677, 25th Feb. 1678, and one undated.
[2] *Ibid.* iv. p. 157, letter from Radway, Warwick, 9th Sept. 1678. I assume that the initials J. C. stand for John Crook.
[3] Dewsbury's *Works*, p. 360 (1682).   [4] *Works*, pp. 339, 341 (1675).
[5] Epistle of April 1678 in Bristol MSS. i. No. 17.

Fox, George Whitehead and Penn, and another, enclosing this, to the Yearly Meeting which met in June. A Committee was appointed to read the two letters, who advised that they should be left to the three Friends to answer "as they find freedom in Truth." Rogers had asked that, before he published his narrative among Friends, a meeting for reading it over might be appointed by the Yearly Meeting before the end of June, either in Wiltshire or at Bristol. Inaction was the natural answer to these veiled threats. But, says Rogers, the noise of printing had this service that several Friends urged the omission of the names of persons reflected upon. Whereupon he prepared a second manuscript, chiefly out of the other, which he directed against one man, George Fox, as "the very chief instrument whereby a biting, devouring spirit is entered in amongst the flock."[1] He professed anxiety to meet Fox, but did not take the opportunities that offered.[2] He informed London Friends in February 1680 that he was going to print his book, and spent the rest of the year in passing it through the press and writing sundry prefaces and postscripts, in the last of which he alleged that printing had begun with a pamphlet on the other side, not, in fact, written till Rogers' book was nearly through the press.[3] The dispute had raged within the Society for five years, and could only be embittered by the course now taken. Dewsbury says that when a supporter of Rogers told him of the intention to print, he replied that he would have his hand cut off before he would assist. He asked the man to tell Rogers that it would prejudice Truth and produce sad consequences. For want of love, he was casting away the power of judgment given to Friends as

---

[1] Preface to *Christian-Quaker*, and 1679 Y.M. Minutes.
[2] See postscript to *Christian-Quaker*, also *Anti-Christian Treachery*, p. 90, two letters of John Raunce to Fox, 30th May and 19th June 1680, in Dev. Ho. A.R.B. Colln. Nos. 135, 136, and *The Accuser of our Brethren cast down*, pp. 254-257.
[3] This was "An Epistle for True Love, Unity, and Order in the Church of Christ, against the Spirit of Discord, Disorder, and Confusion, etc.," by Ann Whitehead and Mary Elson, passed for printing by Morning Meeting, 25th Oct. 1680, and in Rogers' hands by 8th Nov. George Whitehead, *Judgment Fixed*, p. 146, states the facts. See also *The Accuser of our Brethren cast down*, pp. 21-36.

the people of God into the hands of God's enemies, as an inlet for them to come into the midst of Friends to sit as judges and trample upon them.[1]

The *magnum opus* appeared in November under the title of "The Christian-Quaker Distinguished from the Apostate and Innovator, In Five Parts . . . By William Rogers, on behalf of himself and other Friends in Truth concerned." It let loose a flood of polemic, whose turbid waters sullied the stream of Quakerism for many years.[2] Controversy is perhaps the least artistic of all forms of literature, since the combatants as a rule have lost their sense of proportion and of humour. Moreover its cloud of words often darkens knowledge, for the parties are more concerned with scoring points than with facing issues. But some high debate upon the fundamentals of Church government took place, which we shall consider in the next chapter. We may conclude this by completing the narrative so far as it concerns the two leading Separatists, Wilkinson and Story.

Story was a man of weak health, and, in 1677, his death within a year had been presumptuously prophesied by the erratic Solomon Eccles, who afterwards confessed his fault in so doing.[3] In later years, after a sermon, he was usually very sick at night and sometimes ill for days, but continued labouring to the utmost of his strength.[4] In the autumn of 1679 he was in London, and the Morning Meeting procured from him a confirmation of the paper of regret given by him and Wilkinson at Draw-well, which he had afterwards attempted to explain away.[5]

---

[1] *Works*, p. 361 (1682).
[2] Cf. Dewsbury's letter to John Whitehead, 24th July 1682, in Dev. Ho. Portf. 24, No. 57.
[3] *Camb. Journ.* ii. 428, and authorities there cited, also *Christian-Quaker*, pt. v. pp. 31, 50; Steven Crisp, *Works*, pp. 459-461, gives the confession.
[4] 'Testimonies by Sutton [Benger] Friends in Wiltshire, and by Thos. Curtis in *Memory of John Story Revived*.
[5] See *ante*, p. 306. The paper began with the words, "We are sensible that in the hour of temptation." Story had told William Gibson, Burnyeat, and Penn at Bristol that the word temptation meant nothing, for God had tempted Abraham, and James had told us to count it all joy when we fell into divers temptations. This "horrid unplainness," which undid all that had been done at Draw-well, was censured by the Morning Meeting, and Story confessed that he had done amiss in citing the two scripture passages and owned the Draw-well paper according to the common and plain sense of the words. A note was

This was taken as some small sign of a desire to return into unity, and it is clear that London Friends had not abandoned hope of his recovery. Thomas Camm's judgment of him a year earlier is harsh :

> A haughty, scornful, hard man he is grown; but what we laid upon him he will not shake all off in haste. . . . He of late sits down quite amongst his own company, who, being gone from the Father's house where there is living bread enough, are glad of his dry husky stuff.[1]

We must allow for bias in the graphic account given by Camm of Story's last visit to Kendal Meeting, in October 1681.[2] Its perusal is disconcerting to our modern sense of decorum. Camm, without knowing why, was much pressed in spirit to go to Kendal, and accordingly rode in from Preston Patrick.

> And, as soon as I was come to the town, I went directly to the meeting-place, where I found amongst Friends John Story with several others of his companions, who were all surprised and exceedingly troubled at my unexpected appearance, as appeared by their restless behaviour and John Story's standing up to speak as soon or before I was set down upon my seat—whose lifeless, dry and dreaming testimony became a burden to the tender life, so that several sensible ones amongst Friends did sigh and groan under the sense of their present burden and exercise, which did not only grieve but also much confound John Story, so that he cried out because of those sighs and groans, Disorder, Disorder. And the Lord appeared in His glorious power to the joy of the upright; and the exercise of the power [through the sighs and groans], together with several short testimonies against him that sprang through several whose mouths were never opened in meetings before, did so confound him that he lost his matter and fell into reflections against Friends. All which time, which was about a quarter of an hour, I sat still in silence in much peace and contentedness. Several of John Story his party, seeing him so stopped and confounded, begun to be angry, and some of them to mutter, grumble, jangle and propose questions, though John Story was yet speaking. In a little time I was moved to go to prayer, being well satisfied that the Lord would settle

---

taken, and at the Morning Meeting, 2nd Feb. 1680, was ordered to be sent to Westmorland Q.M. at their request, and also to Wiltshire, Bristol, and other places. The Bristol copy is in Bristol MSS. ii. No. 21.

[1] Letter to Richard Snead, 16th Nov. 1678, in Bristol MSS. v. No. 83.
[2] *Anti-Christian Treachery*, pp. 174-177, with some omissions.

Friends' minds in the exercise of His eternal power and confound the spirit of strife and jangling thereby and also make way for that testimony that lived upon my spirit. So, having signified the same to Friends, we kneeled down ; whereupon John Story cried out, It was in vain to think to stop him : he could not be stopped, for he was commissionated by the great God, and went on for a small time while we were praying. But in a little time he was stopped, uttering these or other words to the same effect : I see it's in vain to strive : I may as well be silent as speak. So, when I had cleared my spirit before the Lord in prayer, we all sat down in silence for a considerable time ; and the power of the Lord was over all ; and thereby John Story and his company were all bowed and none of them could then open their mouths. After the time of silence I stood up, being moved to declare— the power of the Lord being upon me. Some time after several of the Separates begun to be filled with wrath, so that they could not give place one to another, but six or eight all at once clamoured against me, with such confusion that but few of their reproachful words and terms could be exactly remembered. Yet over it all the Lord assisted me by His power, carrying me on in testimony-bearing till I was clear, so that they all fell and their mouths were stopped. But one of them, James Moore, stood up, not half of the time of the meeting being expired, and appointed them a meeting on the Fourth-day following ; and then John Story and most of his party went away ; yet, after some time, John Story and several of them came in again ; but most of them was mostwhat silent after, except some muttering words, so that I had a full time of clearing my spirit. But a great part of the time John Story turned himself aside upon the bench he sat upon, and in a scorning, taunting manner muttered many words, some of which were in effect as followeth :—Well said, Tom ;—Finely done, Tom ;—Thou dost notably, Tom ;—Thou binds up thy matter well, Tom. And, when anything hit close upon him, he cried :—Deceit, Deceit, Hypocrisy, Thy tongue is no slander, or the like. So when I had done Brian Lancaster stood up to read an epistle from a Friend, whereat the Separates were again enraged, having an expectation of John Story's declaring again ; whereupon the wife of the said James Moore came rushing over the benches over a great part of the meeting-house and tore the said epistle the most part out of his hands. Upon which John Story was softly spoken to, to see the fruits of his ministry, and, being ashamed with the outrage of the woman, commanded her to give him it again ; so he took and read it as well as he could, it being torn in pieces. After which John Story stood up and spoke a little in a railing, reflecting way ; and before he stood down from off the bench kneeled down to offer his dead sacrifice of prayer, of which none of the faithful took notice. After he had done, I had a few words more that sprung upon my spirit to Friends, but John Story and his company rushed out. So being again moved to go to prayer we had a very sweet, refreshing, overcoming and heart-breaking time, in the blessed springing and flowing of the love and life of God after they of the separation were gone.

It would be interesting, though perhaps as unedifying, to have an equally detailed account from the other side. We are simply told that " on a First-day at a meeting in Kendal [Story] cleared his conscience in testimony to the ancient Truth, in which his doctrine was wonderful weighty and his experience very great."[1]

About a week after this meeting he began to sicken, and on the 22nd November passed away, in much peace and quiet. In 1683 his friends published the tribute of their affection in *The Memory of that Servant of God, John Story, Revived*, but Thomas Camm could not hold his peace and answered it, with the consent of the Morning Meeting, in *The Line of Truth*, written to detect the hypocrisy and deceit of Story's friends in applauding him.

Of Wilkinson's last years little is known. Camm says[2] that he survived Story some years, " and although he was then laboured with and visited by several brethren, and sometimes seemed somewhat softer, yet did not join again in unity." He was a Westmorland " 'statesman," working his own land, amid his labours in the service of the Church, and was to the last loyal to the man who led him into separation and had been his yokefellow in the first publishing of Truth. We may think of him with charity and without bitterness.[3]

[1] John Wilkinson's testimony in *Memory of John Story Revived*.
[2] *F.P.T.* pp. 267, 268.
[3] See *Christian-Quaker*, pt. iv. p. 63. Burnyeat writing to Margt. Fox, 10th Aug. 1678 (Dev. Ho. Gibson Colln. i. pp. 51, 52), describes Wilkinson speaking at Reading, " in a wonderful dead manner, but rather better there than I heard him any time in Bristol, that is, as to get forward with his matter." Later, at Bristol, he was " as dead as an old priest, but, with all the skill he had, driving on his design against or to undervalue the faithful labours of the true servants of the Lord." He spoke of Israel being deceived by them that came with the mouldy bread and old clothes and clouted shoes, and Moses and Aaron taking the honour to themselves when they did not sanctify the Lord.

CHAPTER XII

CONCEPTIONS OF CHURCH GOVERNMENT

[The Church] rests on the conviction that the true Divine order is ever ready to break into the world, if men will only suffer it to break into their hearts. It is the society of those who already realize the blessings of the Kingdom of God in their hearts—pardon, grace, joy—and are so sure that it will come in fulness that they can live as if it actually were come ; and so can disregard the whole question of visible power, organize themselves wholly on the basis of love, and leave all issues with God. The founding of this society took place of itself. . . . Service was to be the only title to authority, and the sole mark of authority was to be yet humbler service. . . . It was a society of souls made one and equal by all being taught of God.—Dr. JOHN OMAN, in Hastings' *Encyclopaedia of Religion and Ethics*, article "Church."

QUAKERISM, like other religious movements, began as a fellowship, thrilling with intense life, with the great purposes of God ringing in its ears and driving it forth to adventurous, if sometimes mistaken service, and later by the necessity for self-realization, the accretions of habit, the stereotyping force of tradition, and the pressure of the outside world, it established a strong organization and lost something of its soul.

Fox's action in strengthening Church government had reanimated Friends, but involved to some extent the subordination of individual guidance to the spiritual leading which came to the meeting. The message, "To your own, to your own," that is, to the Light Within, was now supplemented and sometimes supplanted by the message, "Keep in the unity." And just in so far as the corporate life exercised disciplinary authority there was inevitably some repression of individual freedom and the beginnings of an imposed uniformity.

Stated broadly, the issue was raised of the limits of

spiritual liberty and of Church government, a question having close analogies with our modern problem of the relation of civil liberty to the State. If it was solved imperfectly by the early Friends, it is largely due to the fact that the whole conception of freedom was then far cruder than it is to-day. We live in an atmosphere of free discussion whose potency to advance truth and repress error was unrealized two hundred and fifty years ago. We have developed a type of personality, self-reliant, responsible, self-controlled, which is both root and fruit of our freedom. We are learning that the direction of life by mechanical rules and methods is not the way to foster character. In Church-life discipline accordingly has rightly played a far less important part than formerly, though we have often failed to replace it by methods of group-education and avenues for group-service. We rely, however, more and more, upon the appeal to the conscience made by the living word and the noble life.

The change in atmosphere is so great that it needs a strong effort of historical imagination to do justice to the outlook of the early Friends. They lived in the dawn of freedom, and had not yet garnered its fruits into their lives. But a great sincerity of heart had turned them from all outward authority to an inward experience dominated by the sovereign power of Christ. Through Him they were free by becoming His bondsmen and wearing His yoke, and thenceforth their first duty was faithfulness to the government of His Truth.

Lawrence Steel, the Independent Chaplain who turned Quaker about 1670, before he had any acquaintance with Friends, gives an interesting instance of the way in which loving obedience glorified the common life of Quakerism.[1] Desiring to seek out Friends, he was told of three or four families in the village, who were poor folk, mean in ability; and he learned that, though the men were at

---

[1] *Jacob the Plain Man* (1677), p. 19. When Steel died at Bristol in 1684, shortly after his release from Newgate, he remembered the poor of this Dorset village, and the Q.M. Minutes contain a letter notifying a bequest of £20 for the poor Friends of the County, " where I had a further convincement of the blessed Truth." For Steel, see *Camb. Journ.* ii. 465, and *post*, p. 530.

harvest, their wives were at home. He sent for one of these women, who counselled him to mind the Truth in him, which would bring him further on in spiritual experience as he kept low and obedient to the cross of Christ. He was greatly struck by the gravity and savour of her language and deportment, and by the wisdom of her advice, which he esteemed the more for her outward meanness and plainness. When her husband returned from work he learnt from him that their whole stay and support was in the Spirit of the Lord, Whose teachings they waited for at all times, to guide them out of evil into all truth, in which God alone was worshipped.

Penington, in one of his finest pieces, describes this obedience in words of rare beauty :

What is obedience ? It is the subjection of the soul to the law of the Spirit, which subjection floweth from and is strengthened by love. . . . Everything in the Kingdom, every spiritual thing, refers to Christ and centres in Him. His nature, His virtue, His presence, His power, makes up all. Indeed He is all in all to a believer, only variously manifested and opened in the heart by the Spirit. He is the volume of the whole book, every leaf and line whereof speaks of Him and writes out Him in some or other of His sweet and beautiful lineaments. So that if I should yet speak further of other things . . . I should but speak further of His nature brought up, manifested, and displaying itself in and through the creatures, by His turning the wheel of His life in their hearts. But my spirit hasteneth from words . . . [that it] may sink in spirit into the feeling of the life itself, and may learn what it is to enjoy it there and to be comprehended of it, and cease striving to know or comprehend concerning it.[1]

"Liberty," with him, "is the enlargedness of the heart in the Spirit of the Lord, wherein it hath scope in all that is good, and is shut out of all that is evil."[2]

In these high regions of experience freedom and obedience become one. But side by side with the saints in a religious society are the "saints by calling," who are negligent or unfaithful, and those who make profession without having known the call. The Society of Friends

---
[1] *Works*, 1681 edn. pt. i. p. 420. The piece, printed in 1663, is called "Some of the Mysteries of God's Kingdom glanced at."
[2] *Ibid.* p. 421.

had its share of these, even in the midst of great witness-bearing amid persecution. Penn, in 1681, was urgent for Church order, because it was a time

. . . wherein the cross by too many is not so closely kept to as in days past; and in which there is not only a great convincement but a young generation descended of Friends, who, though they retain the form their education hath led them into, yet many of them adorn not the gospel with that sensible, weighty, and heavenly conversation as becomes the children of the undefiled religion.[1]

Steven Crisp, of Colchester, a year earlier,[2] deplores certain tendencies which were beginning to corrupt the primitive witness. They have their point still.

1. Some were holding the Truth in a bare formality, sitting down at ease in it, and unconcerned whether the noble plant grew, either in themselves or in others. Having become strangers to the actual working of Truth in themselves, they came to question its reality, "for everything that is not experimental is liable to question," and when the time of trial came, they parted with the dry testimony which they had for a long time professed without life, and sold the Truth they had once followed.

2. Others were hurt by a too eager and greedy pursuit after the things of this world. Diligence in their outward callings had been turned into slavery to them; so that their joy and sorrow were pitched upon the transitory things of life.

3. At first the crown of the profession of Friends had been that they were men of their word, but some had let in a false liberty and brought dishonour on the Truth.

4. There was a tendency for those brought up as Friends to rest in a "bare, educable form of the Truth," without inward travail of the soul and growth in the power of godliness. Their bodies and their public profession were amongst Friends, but their minds were in the world, and they were unfitted to suffer for the Truth, because they had not been rooted and grounded in it, through personal experimental warfare.

5. Lastly, there was the constant danger of forgetting the great law of charity, without which all profession was but sounding brass or a tinkling cymbal.

Crisp's searching analysis serves to show how readily experimental truth may be replaced by formalism; and

---

[1] *Works*, 1726 edn. ii. 697, from "Liberty Spiritual."
[2] *Works*, pp. 423-441 summarized.

it may make us pause before we condemn, under the conditions of the age, the setting up of a corporate discipline. While this could be no equivalent for a living first-hand experience, it had power to create among Friends that great and compelling tradition of well-ordered and noble life which in a public school or a regiment we call *esprit de corps*. It was also effectual for dealing with moral lapses.

The vindication of Quakerism, in its newly developed form of a religious Society, established in government and faith, engaged the pen of a young and gifted Scottish convert, the famous Robert Barclay. A systematic Church discipline, more rigid than ever prevailed among Friends, had given Scotland, in Baxter's phrase, godliness without sects.[1] The men who had force to break through the Presbyterian system to Quakerism were necessarily men of power, whose contribution to the Society of Friends would be much greater than their numbers. If we are to understand the nature of this new influence, we must turn for a while to the story of the remarkable Quaker group who about the year 1663 began to trouble the dour Calvinism of Aberdeen.

The central figure is that of Alexander Jaffray. His religious *Diary*[2] gives us the inner life of a leading Scotsman of the time, bailie of Aberdeen, where he was born, and its representative in the Scottish Parliament during the Civil War, one of the commissioners to Charles II. at Breda in 1650, charged with forcing him to take the Covenant, a prisoner at the "crowning mercy" of Dunbar, and afterwards in favour with Cromwell and made by him Director of Chancellary and a member of the Nominated Parliament. He had rendered signal service on more than one occasion to his native town, then a place of some nine thousand inhabitants.[3] Forty-nine at the time of his convincement in 1663, his con-

---

[1] *Reliquiae Baxterianae*, iii. 67 ; Burnet, *History*, i. 271-273 (Airy's edn.) ; cf. *Beginnings of Quakerism*, p. 226.
[2] Published by John Barclay, 1833, from MS. at Ury, with slight verbal revision. My references are to the 2nd edn., 1834.
[3] *Diary of Alexander Jaffray*, note L.

victions were the matured product of a deep religious experience. He regretted his share in pressing the Covenant on the insincere young king in order to secure the triumph of the Presbyterian system over the sectaries. After Dunbar his intercourse with Cromwell, Fleetwood, and Dr. Owen led him to change his views as to a forced uniformity and finally to see the evil of the Solemn League and Covenant. Its object had been to maintain the doctrine, worship, discipline and government of the Scottish Kirk. Jaffray saw that this involved the position that the system was perfect and the only way of Jesus Christ. His study of the subject satisfied him, on the contrary, that episcopacy had in its time been of service to Christianity, and that, though the Presbyterian government might be a step nearer to the true way, yet it was "but a human invention, composed with much prudence and policy of man's wit, fitted for those times when it had its rise in Geneva from that precious and worthy man Calvin." He came to the conclusion that, as the truths of Christ had been for many ages in the hands of antichrist, the Church was only beginning to break through the clouds, which Christ in the brightness of His coming should dispel. His convictions were now moving in the direction of Independency, and in May 1652 he and others in Aberdeen of like mind declared their difficulties in a letter to some Christian friends. They felt that none should be admitted as Church-members but those who to their profession of the Truth joined a blameless and gospel-like behaviour. They also found that "the congregational way comes nearer to the pattern of the word than our classical form." A Church was gathered at Aberdeen, but Jaffray's public life took him to London and to Edinburgh, and he remained for some years without any definite Church-membership, but not without the developing spiritual experience that comes to a man of open mind. His Journal shows how he came to lay the emphasis where Quakerism lays it:

Lord, save me from settling either in a lifeless form of religion without the power thereof, or in any bait or temptation that may arise from the allurements of a present world. . . . So also I pray that the Lord . . . would save me from resisting or refusing to receive light, when it does proceed from Himself Who is the Fountain of light and life, when He is about these glorious manifestations and discoveries of Himself, which shall consume the man of sin, even with the brightness of His coming.—2 Thess. ii. 3, 8.

Humbly make use of what thou hast as the readiest way to come by more. . . . See if the godly may not be afraid that many times their candle be blown out and they left in much darkness, because they have not entertained and walked up to the practice of the light which they had.

The 15th January 1660, after much striving against sin and many vows and promises . . . the Lord gave me in some measure to discern where the fault lies, namely, in not enough diligently watching over my own heart and listening to and receiving the motions of His Spirit, so frequently given by convictions against those evils. . . . That which checks the evil . . . in that is the power, for it comes from the Spirit of power to make way for Him. . . . Listen to and receive this voice of God behind thee, speaking in thy conscience, and the Lord will come in and abide and sup with thee.

Whatever may be of mistake in the way and opinion of the people called Quakers about the Light within them, as to the universality and operation of it, after some inquiry thereabout my resolution is to waive the debatable part thereof and, as I may in the strength of the Lord, to improve and make use of what truth I find in the thing itself. . . . For I do verily find and believe there is light appearing from and holden forth at this time by these despised people in that and some other things, which if prejudice and passion did not hinder might be received with much advantage.

The 14th day of February 1661 I was led to consider more seriously how the Lord is pleased to help and give in strength to the subduing of sin. . . . These two particulars appeared necessary to be taken more heed to :—First, To mind the light as it begins to appear and dawn in the conscience. . . . Secondly, . . . to wait and stand still from self-willing and acting which darken the heart . . . to lie down under and submit to the smitings and judgments of the power of the light, which first wounds and then cures.[1]

---

[1] See *Diary of Alexander Jaffray*, pp. 68, 89, 134, 149, 150.

The Journal breaks off in the middle of 1661 while Jaffray was under a charge of treason, though at liberty in Edinburgh on bail. After his release he went to Aberdeen, and at the end of 1662 professed Quakerism. Dewsbury, some years earlier, had sounded the message in the North of Scotland, casting his bread upon the waters in hope to find it after many days.[1] His visit and also those of John Grave and John Burnyeat were remembered, and it is recorded of Jaffray that "when he first heard of a people that preached and held forth a principle of light and life and revelation of the Spirit of God to be known nowadays within to save the soul, his very heart did leap for joy within him,"[2] but, so far as appears, in the convincement that now took place at

[1] Dewsbury's visit was in Oct. 1658, see *Beginnings of Quakerism*, p. 364, where his companion Watkinson's letter is cited, which states that a merchant and his wife entertained them going and returning. I there say that at Aberdeen "a few years later he was to plant the most important Quaker community in Scotland," following too readily the statements in Besse, *Sufferings*, ii. 496, and *Diary of Alexander Jaffray*, pp. 232, 233. Both are based on a MS. "Record of the Rise of Quakerism about Aberdeen," now in Dev. Ho., written by Alexander Skene, by direction of Aberdeen M.M., 5th March 1672 (see *J.F.H.S.* viii. 41). This says: "The first instruments of proclaiming this everlasting day of glory and salvation, of Christ within the hope of glory, and who sounded the trumpet of Zion in this corner of our nation, were, so far as their names are at present remembered, John Grave, John Burnyeat, and William Dewsbury. William Dewsbury had a meeting in Alexander Harper's house. By whose ministry and labours He Who makes His angels spirits and His ministers a flame of fire soon reached, . . . some in Aberdeen, particularly one Alexander Jaffray. . . . The first beginning of this convincement was about the end of the year 1662. And it was so ordered of the Lord that the said Alexander Jaffray, immediately after his convincement, in the beginning of the year 1663 was drawn to the country to live at Inverurie." The meeting at Alexander Harper's was probably that at the merchant's house referred to in Watkinson's letter, for "Isabel Keillo, wife of Alexander Harper, merchant in Aberdeen," was one of the "first witnesses" in *J.F.H.S.* viii. 41. It is therefore probably the visit in Oct. 1658 that is referred to, a conclusion confirmed by the fact that Dewsbury was still in York prison in March 1663, and the date for Jaffray's profession of Quakerism cannot be altered, because he left Aberdeen at "the beginning of the year 1663." The allusion in Dewsbury's letter of 29th Oct. 1672 in *Diary of Alexander Jaffray*, p. 311, evidently refers to visits which had no immediate results: "The Lord hath a great people in Scotland, for whom I, with many of our brethren, have travailed in jeopardy of our lives in years past, casting our bread upon the waters with hopes to find it after many days." This is exactly what he said, when in Scotland in 1658, "My bread I am casting on the waters, assured I am I shall find it in the time appointed" (Dewsbury to Margt. Fell, 23rd Sept. 1658, in Smith's *Life of Dewsbury*, p. 166, from Swarthm. Colln. iv. 146). See also "Record Book of Ury M.M." in *J.F.H.S.* vii. 92, which refers the convincement at Aberdeen to the visits of Dewsbury and others about 1658. The point may seem small, but nothing is unimportant which throws fresh light on the service of two such men as Dewsbury and Jaffray.

[2] MS. "Record of the Rise of Quakerism about Aberdeen."

Aberdeen among prepared hearts, Jaffray himself was the chief outward instrument. Robert Barclay's account simply says that, about the year 1663, some sober and serious Christians began to weigh the matter more narrowly, and found that Quakerism seemed to have about it the savour of the living Christianity which they had once known. " In these the Lord caused His word to prosper, who were few in number, yet noted as to their sobriety in their former way of profession, and raised them up to own that people and their testimony and to become one with them." [1] This was in spite of the vulgar and familiar language of the pulpits, which described the Quakers

. . . as demented, distracted, bodily possessed of the devil, practising abominations under colour of being led to them by the Spirit; and, as to their principles, blasphemous deniers of the true Christ, of heaven, hell, angels, the resurrection of the body and day of judgment—inconsistent with magistracy, nothing better than John of Leyden and his complices.[2]

The group now gathered included Jaffray himself and some at least of his former religious associates, as, for instance, "that gracious woman," Elspet Goodall, and "that precious woman," Barbara Forbes.[3]

At Inverurie, or Don-side, a meeting was also gathered, much to the chagrin of the parish minister, for it included a weaver and a poor woman, whom he had boasted could defy all the Quakers both for their knowledge and good life. The meetings were kept at the house of the poor woman, Nancy Sim, at Ardiharrald,

. . . and people thereabout began so to flock that her house, not being able to hold them, being but a very mean woman, they were kept without in the field, where Patrick Livingstone, who had come North from other parts, was made a blessed instrument with some others to gather many in that country, where there was an harmless people, but very dark as to any profession, and so, not having any self-righteousness to lose, were the sooner laid

---

[1] Preface to "Truth clear'd of Calumnies" in *Works*, 1692 edn., p. A2.
[2] *Ibid.*
[3] Cf. *Diary of Alexander Jaffray*, pp. 126, 127, with list and other particulars in *J.F.H.S.* viii 40, 41.

hold on by the Truth, which run as a fire in that country till it had reached many.¹

Livingstone and George Keith, another travelling minister who came to labour in and around Aberdeen, claim special mention. Livingstone was from Angus, convinced about 1658, after which with a few others he kept up a meeting for some years in a village below Cheviot, and then lived for a time on the Border with James Halliday, a weaver and Scotsman, who had been long convinced, but had no other Friend near him.² Residing at Edinburgh during the English occupation of Scotland under Cromwell, Livingstone had found all the sects crying out against one another, but all united against what they called the "Quakers' light." He saw, however, that the Quaker preachers did look liker to Christ and His apostles than any of those who preached against them. He found also that when he followed the light in anything, then was the time he had peace, and that as he grew up in the power and virtue of the light the same work was wrought in him which was wrought in holy men of old by the Spirit of Christ. This hard-won first-hand experience made him powerful in ministry and stanch amid all persecution.³

George Keith, the future Separatist, was for twenty-seven years one of the ablest defenders of Quakerism. Born in Scotland about 1638, he graduated at Aberdeen, and was well versed in Oriental tongues and in philosophy and mathematics. After some time as tutor in a rich family, he joined Friends in 1663, apparently in much the same way as Livingstone:

It lay upon me from the Lord to depart from these teachers who could not point me to the living knowledge of God where I could find it: and I came and heard men and women who were taught of God who pointed me to the true principle; and, though

---

¹ MS. "Record of the Rise of Quakerism about Aberdeen."
² "Record Book of Ury M.M." in *J.F.H.S.* vii. 185. The village is called "Emeldoun," perhaps Humbledon, near Wooler.
³ See *Selections from Patrick Livingstone*, 1847, especially the first piece, "Concerning the Heavenly Seed." This book, edited by Lydia M. Barclay, is from a MS., now at Dev. Ho.

some of them could not read a letter, yet I found them wiser than all the teachers I ever formerly had been under.[1]

Keith, after he had left the Society,[2] wrote that though much influenced by the power in Friends and in their meetings, he had not been convinced solely through this, but had had much reasoning with them as to their principles, which he found to be in agreement with fundamental Christianity. As with some other Scottish Friends, who were all well grounded in doctrine, the experience of the Inward Light was accepted in the belief that Fox and the other Quaker leaders were eminent instruments raised up by God to work some further reformation, and was added on to an existing system of religious thought and harmonized with it. It did not dominate the whole experience quite as completely as had been the case with the Seekers who joined Fox in the North of England. We shall see later the important consequences that flowed from this somewhat different way of approach.

In 1664 Keith and Livingstone were imprisoned for some months at Aberdeen, and Jaffray was summoned before the new-fangled episcopal authorities and directed as to his behaviour under heavy penalties. Quakerism, however, had now taken root in the North of Scotland, and could not be extirpated. The movement grew in numbers and strength, especially through the convincement in 1666 of young Robert Barclay.

Barclay's mother[3] was a Gordon and a distant cousin of the King. His father, Colonel David Barclay, was the stout soldier whom Whittier pictures

> Ankle-deep in Lutzen's blood,
> With the brave Gustavus.

Afterwards during the Civil War the Colonel served with great distinction in the Covenanting Army. He sat in two of Cromwell's Parliaments and was one of the Trustees of forfeited lands in Scotland,[4] an entanglement which in

---

[1] *Quakers in the American Colonies*, p. 445, quoting Keith's *Immediate Revelation*.
[2] Keith, *The Standard of the Quakers examined*, 1702, pp. 508-512.
[3] For the Barclays see *Diary of Alexander Jaffray*, pp. 258-273.
[4] Ordinance of 12th April 1654 in Masson's *Life of Milton*, iv. 561, 562.

August 1665 led to his commitment for a time to Edinburgh Castle.¹ He was a man of independent mind, who as far back as 1653 had been ordered by the synod of Moray to be "processed" because he had "professedly declined from the doctrine and discipline of this Kirk, denying it to be a Kirk."² Convinced of Quakerism in London shortly before his imprisonment, he came "to own the Truth openly" through converse with his fellow-prisoner and old acquaintance, John Swinton. Much to the chagrin of the Governor, Robert Barclay, who came to the Castle to visit his father, fell under the same influence and turned Quaker at the end of 1666.³ Though only eighteen, he had already known varied religious experiences.⁴ Bred under the strict Calvinist discipline, he was sent to Paris to be educated at the Scots Theological College, under his uncle and namesake, Robert Barclay. This was an old Roman Catholic foundation, where the young lad, who was a boy of parts, was at the same time well-grounded in French and Latin and in Papist principles. After his mother's death in 1663, his father brought him home by her dying request but against the strongly expressed wishes of his uncle, the Rector of the College. For a time he kept himself free from joining with any religious society, though he took the liberty to hear several. He consorted mainly with men of latitudinarian views, who

... inveigh much against judging, and such kind of severity, seeming to complain greatly for want of this Christian charity among all sects, which latitude may perhaps be esteemed the other extreme opposite to the preciseness of these other sects.⁵

Thus expert in the "notions" of religion, he came into touch with life in the gathered silence of Quaker worship.

Not by strength of arguments, or by a particular disquisition

---

¹ For the commitment order see *J.F.H.S.* v. 199.
² Cited from M. Christabel Cadbury's *Robert Barclay*, 1912, p. 19.
³ "Record Book of Ury M.M." in *J.F.H.S.* vii. 91-92. James Halliday also influenced him.
⁴ The scrap of autobiography at beginning of Barclay's "Universal Love," 1676, *Works*, pp. 677, 678, is our authority here.   ⁵ *Works*, p. 678.

of each doctrine, and convincement of my understanding thereby, came [I] to receive and bear witness of the Truth, but by being secretly reached by this life. For, when I came into the silent assemblies of God's people, I felt a secret power among them, which touched my heart; and as I gave way unto it I found the evil weakening in me and the good raised up; and so I became thus knit and united unto them, hungering more and more after the increase of this power and life, whereby I might feel myself perfectly redeemed.[1]

It is said that some words spoken at the first meeting which he attended had much effect on his mind:[2] " In stillness there is fullness; in fullness there is nothingness; in nothingness there are all things." Such a message may well have been given by John Swinton, the politician turned mystic. According to Bishop Burnet, he was "the man of all Scotland that had been the most trusted and employed by Cromwell.[3] He had been one of the seven Lords Commissioners for the administration of justice, who, under Oliver's regime, replaced the Court of Session; he and another had been the only two Scotsmen on the Council of Scotland, appointed in 1655 with similar functions to the Council already existing in Ireland. He had been "formerly cried up for his piety," but broke with Presbyterianism religiously as well as politically. He had become a Quaker by July 1660, when he was apprehended in London, and at the end of the year was shipped to Scotland with the ill-fated Marquis of

---

[1] *Apology*, Prop. xi. sect. 7.
[2] *Diary of Alexander Jaffray*, p. 271.
[3] For Swinton see Burnet's *History*, i. 194, 229 (Airy's edn.); *Diary of Alexander Jaffray*, pp. 217-219, 565-568, and other references; G. Lyon Turner, *Original Records of Nonconformity*, iii. 758; Firth, *The Last Years of the Protectorate*, ii. 90, 91, 106; references in Masson's *Life of Milton*, Camb. Journ. i. 466, and other places; notice in *Dict. Nat. Biog.*; references in "Aberdeen Y.M. Records" in *J.F.H.S.* viii.; Dev. Ho. Crosse Colln. pp. 16, 31, 33, 52; letters, 21st April 1665, from George Whitehead to Fox in Swarthm. Colln. iv. 98; from Steven Crisp, 25th June 1668, in *Crisp and his Correspondents*, p. 41; letter to Margt. Fox, 8th Dec. 1673, in Dev. Ho. Gibson Colln. ii. 107; reference in *Spirit of the Hat*, p. 34; paper at end of Penn's "The Spirit of Alexander the Coppersmith" (1673); *Extracts from State Papers*, p. 274; John Gratton's *Journal*, 1779 edn., p. 100; *J.F.H.S.* xi. 68. We hear of him in the Eastern Counties in connection with the Perrot difficulty, and he lived for some time at Norton, in Durham, where, according to the "Episcopal Returns, 1669," in G. Lyon Turner, the conventiclers had "one ringleader, a Scotchman, called the Laird Swinton," and "100 persons that frequent conventicles there." In Smith's *Catalogue* nine short pieces, mostly 1663-1666, are attributed to Swinton.

Argyll and lodged in the Tolbooth at Edinburgh. Ten years earlier he had been attainted in the Parliament at Perth for going over to Cromwell, and was now brought up on this old attainder. Burnet says:

> He was then become a Quaker, and did, with a sort of eloquence that moved the whole House, lay out all his own errors and the ill spirit he was in when he committed them, with so tender a sense, that he seemed as one indifferent what they should do with him; and without so much as moving for mercy or even for a delay he did so effectually prevail on them that they recommended him to the King as a fit object of his mercy.

Swinton was evidently possessed of much personal magnetism, but his Quakerism was strongly mystical, and he promoted the Perrot spirit for several years, carrying some of the Scottish Friends with him. He came in time to own his fault, but afterwards his instability of temperament showed itself in a moral lapse, for which Friends held him for a time at "a visible distance and separation . . . as to near converse," though he died in 1679 in unity with the Society, writing at the last that the testimony of the Quakers "as to every part and parcel of it is blessed and may not be foregone, one hoof of it, but is to run and be glorious, even to the ends of the earth." His many-sided life had attracted Burnet[1] and was well calculated to charm young Barclay.

The new convert to Quakerism had less courtliness and wit than Penn, but an equally gracious character. Penn, says George Keith, with a touch of malice, could bow very genteelly when he had occasion to come before persons of honour, and other Friends would incline the head, but Barclay before his superiors "would stand as straight as a post or pillar," though in his natural temper very affable and discreet.[2] Penn describes him as "sound in judgment, strong in argument, cheerful in travels and sufferings, of a pleasant disposition, yet solid, plain and

---

[1] Burnet, *History* (Airy's edn.), ii. 29, speaks of much conversation with him in the winter 1662–3.
[2] Keith, *The Standard of the Quakers examined* (1702), p. 466.

exemplary in his conversation."[1] His even temper joined with a vigorous intellect and unusual advantages of birth and education gave promise of high service as he grew in his experience of spiritual life.

His father's factor was a young Quaker, David Falconer, and he went with him in the summer of 1667 to live at the family seat at Ury, near Stonehaven, where they at once began a meeting,[2] and came into touch with the sturdy Quakerism which had sprung up in and around Aberdeen.

The feud with Calvinism was raging fiercely. Some Friends were in prison; some were excommunicated;[3] some the authorities sought to exile. Jaffray, worn with sickness, was carried thirty miles to Banff gaol for suffering meetings at his house, contrary to the ecclesiastical directions which had been given as to his behaviour.[4]

[1] Testimony at beginning of Barclay's *Works*.
[2] See "Record Book of Ury M.M." in *J.F.H.S.* vii. 92. David Falconer was of good family, and married a sister of Barclay's wife. See particulars in *J.F.H.S.* viii. 41 note, as corrected in *J.F.H.S.* ix. 172.
[3] One case of excommunication has all the dramatic unity which goes to the making of a good short story. The priest of Inverurie, against his own convictions and by order of the presbytery, excommunicated an honest Friend, James Urquhart, and thereafter became so disordered and confused in his preaching that he had to give it up, excusing himself by putting about that he was bewitched and that the pulpit was enchanted by something laid under it. "Yet to see the dreadful effects of the love of money, the root of all evil, and of covetousness, which is idolatry, the same priest, notwithstanding of this clear warning and rebuke from the Lord, some years after, being again put upon excommunicating of his own daughter, Jean Forbes, who had come out to own the holy Truth, rather than lose his place he went on against such manifest light and convictions, entering into a process against her by prayers, etc., at which the Lord was so provoked that he was suddenly pulled away by death immediately before he should [have] given forth that sentence" (MS. "Record of the Rise of Quakerism about Aberdeen"; cf. *J.F.H.S.* i. 52). The story may be matched from the Oxfordshire MS. "Book of Sufferings," under date 1663. Francis Dring, of Brize Norton, was excommunicated in the Bishop's Court: "And this excommunication being sent to the vicar, who was the said Francis his own father, and to be read the next First-day, the father and mother both were troubled in mind and sought to get some one to officiate in his place that day; but none could be got. So the father was forced to go to the steeple-house and read the service appointed for that time and also read the excommunication against his son. His own mother looking on her husband while he read it, observed his countenance to be changed and said that the same countenance that he was struck with at that time continued with him until he departed this life:— mark, he never went to the steeple-house more. His wife spoke these words to Thomas Minchin [of Burford], her son also hearing her, that nothing troubled her more than that the people should tell her that her husband had lived long enough to excommunicate her own son."
[4] *Diary of Alexander Jaffray*, p. 280, from MS. "Record of the Rise of Quakerism about Aberdeen."

There were sermons and papers against the Quakers, which stirred Keith and Barclay to authorship, and there was much preparation for harrying Friends more effectually, when the Declaration of Indulgence of 1672 stopped for a time the intended persecution. Meanwhile the steady growth of the Quaker groups was exciting and confounding the malice of their enemies.

Barclay wedded in 1670, according to the simple Quaker usage, and thereby scandalized the priests, who procured letters summoning him to appear before the Privy Council for an unlawful marriage, "which matter," says the Ury Record, "was so overruled of the Lord that they had never power to put their summons in execution so as to do us any prejudice."[1]

His first piece, *Truth clear'd of Calumnies*, bears date this year. It is a powerful reply to an adverse tract called *A Dialogue between a Quaker and a stable Christian*, and contains a striking passage which shows his view of life:

> Where a man's meat and provision is laid up for him . . . it is an easy thing, in self-will, to take on a demure deportment or to wear haircloth or go barefoot, which by custom becomes familiar. . . . But the matter is, for people to be conversant in this world, to have their occasions and business in it, and to have dealing with the spirit of it, and yet to keep to the meek, lowly, simple appearance, using it as if they were not using it, by keeping out of its spirit and way in all manner of conversation. This is to be like unto Christ, Who did not retire Himself unto an hermit's lodge, but conversed among publicans and sinners.[2]

A little later, in the year 1672, he denied himself and became a fool for Christ's sake by passing in sackcloth and ashes through three of the chief streets of Aberdeen as a Sign from the Lord, calling the people to repentance, some Friends going with him carrying his hat and cloak. The command of the Lord had only come to him in the morning and had greatly burdened him. He had prayed with tears that the cup might pass from him and his

---

[1] *J.F.H.S.* vii. 93. For a letter to his future wife, then Christian Molleson, see *post*, p. 446.   [2] *Works*, p. 27.

whole body had been shaken, until he gave up freely to the Lord's will.[1]

We now hear of Barclay being in England, where the young man of twenty-five would, for the first time, make the acquaintance of the leaders of the Society and become alive to the problems which faced it. He attended the Yearly Meeting of 1673, and signed the important epistle issued by it.[2] He seems also to have been at the Yearly Meeting of Ministers in 1674 with Patrick Livingstone,[3] when Friends had "brave meetings" and "a precious time."[4] The piece on Church government which Barclay now wrote, preface dated from Ury, 17th October 1674,[5] had no relation to the incipient Wilkinson-Story difficulty, of which he states that he then knew nothing.[6] His title laid open his design with the amplitude of the age:

The Anarchy of the Ranters . . . the Hierarchy of the Romanists . . . equally Refused and Refuted in a Two-fold Apology for the . . . Quakers, wherein They are Vindicated from those that Accuse them of Disorder and Confusion on the one hand, and from such as Calumniate them with Tyranny and Imposition on the other, showing that, as the True and Pure Principles of the Gospel are Restored by their Testimony, so is also the Ancient, Apostolick Order of the Church of Christ Re-established among them and setled upon its Right Basis and Foundation.

He lays down clearly enough that "the only proper judge of controversies in the Church is the Spirit of God, and the power of deciding solely lies in it as having the only unerring, infallible and certain judgment belonging to it,"[7] but he promulgates a high doctrine, by no means verified in practice, as to the extent to which the gathered Church will be led by the infallible Spirit. A Church made up of those who hold the truth as it is in Jesus will never, he says, want the certain judgment of truth.[8] Ordinarily this judgment will come from those whom the

---

[1] *Works*, pp. 105-108, and Testimony of Andrew Jaffray, early unnumbered page. Cf. Andrew Jaffray's Sign in 1677 (*Diary of Alexander Jaffray*, p. 401).
[2] *Ante*, p. 293.   [3] John Gratton's *Journal*, p. 99 (1779 edn.).   [4] *Ibid.*
[5] The early Minutes of the Morning Meeting do not show all the business, and contain no reference to the book, but it had their approval (see *Christian-Quaker*, pt. iii. p. 128).
[6] *Works*, p. 238.   [7] *Ibid.* p. 225.   [8] *Ibid.* p. 226.

Lord has made use of in gathering the Church and feeding the flock, though without excluding others.[1]

The following extract sums up his main positions on this part of the question:[2]

(1) That, whereas none truly ought nor can be accounted the Church of Christ, but such as are in a measure sanctified or sanctifying by the grace of God and led by His Spirit; nor yet any made officers in the Church, but by the grace of God and inward revelation of His Spirit, (not by outward ordination or succession), from which none is to be excluded if so called, whether married, or a tradesman, or a servant,

(2) If so be in such a Church there should arise any difference, there will be an infallible judgment from the Spirit of God, which may be in a general assembly yet not limited to it as excluding others; and may prove the judgment of the plurality, yet not to be decided thereby as if the infallibility were placed there excluding the fewer. In which meeting or assembly upon such an account, there is no limitation to be of persons particularly chosen, but that all, that in a true sense may be reckoned of the Church as being sober and weighty, may be present and give their judgment.

(3) And that the infallible judgment of Truth, which cannot be wanting in such a Church, whether it be given through one or more, ought to be submitted to, not because such persons give it but because the Spirit leads so to do, which every one coming to in themselves will willingly and naturally assent to. And, if any through disobedience or unclearness do not, all that the Church ought to do she is to deny them her spiritual fellowship, in case the nature of their disobedience be of that consequence as may deservē such a censure, but by no means for matter of conscience to molest, trouble or persecute any in their outwards.

Barclay's general conception corresponds to a large extent with that which the Society of Friends still holds and practises. In a business meeting of Friends the object in view is not to ascertain the preponderance of opinion but the weight of spiritual judgment; all members may contribute to this and there is no voting. The Clerk records the " sense of the meeting " in a Minute ; and, very frequently, those whose individual judgment was overborne either see that they were mistaken or are content to believe that right guidance has been given. But claims

[1] *Works*, p. 226.   [2] *Ibid.* p. 234.

to corporate or to individual infallibility of judgment are now no longer made. The practice of Friends in their Church meetings, at least on this side of the Atlantic, has been to wait for a fuller consensus of spiritual judgment, where the way does not seem clear. This arrest of judgment has conduced both to the unity of the Society and to the deepening of its experience, where it has been made use of by the Church educationally, for the purpose of re-examining the issue, receiving further spiritual enlightenment upon it and dedicating life to the demands that may be involved in obeying the Truth. But when it has meant that certain members of the Church, perhaps through prejudice or conservatism, have opposed action, without seeking more fully to know or to obey the Light, then it has brought stagnation and decline.

It is by the maintenance of fellowship and the fostering of spiritual life that the Church will avoid disastrous collision between corporate authority and individual freedom. In the theory of Barclay the corporate judgment ought to be submitted to, because the Spirit which gave it forth will lead each rightly convinced member to assent to it.

The foundations and ground thereof is not because they [who gave the judgment] are infallible, but because in these things and at that time they were led by the infallible Spirit. And therefore it will not shelter any in this respect to pretend, I am not bound to obey the dictates of fallible men; is not this Popery, I not being persuaded in myself? Because it is not to be disobedient to them, but to the judgment of Truth through them at such a time; and one or more, their not being persuaded, may as probably proceed from their being hardened and being out of their place, and in an incapacity to hear the requirings, as that the thing is not required of them.[1]

In the opposing theory of Rogers the individual must be convinced by the inward leadings of the Spirit before he can accept with sincerity the judgment of the Church.

No outward order, counsel or advice is sufficient ground for any man to practise this or t'other thing, so as thereby to find acceptance with the Lord, until the conscience of such an one, by the

---

[1] *Anarchy of the Ranters*, in Barclay's *Works*, p. 225.

Light of Christ Jesus, be convinced thereof. For every action, in relation to the things of God, that springs not from an enlightened, convinced conscience is but the fruit of a lifeless form without the power; and seems not to square with this doctrine, " Draw water out of your own wells: let it be your own and not another's"; nor yet with that doctrine which hath often been sounded in our ears, to gather us from the " Lo, heres" and the " Lo, theres."[1]

Barclay's doctrine only held to the full where the Church was filled with the Spirit, and, with every declension of life or infirmity of vision on the part of the leaders, there would be a corresponding lowering of spiritual authority. Rogers' doctrine, in the same way, was only true for individuals who were alive to their responsibilities and were both open to the Light and resolute to obey it. Where the requisites underlying both doctrines prevailed, inspired leadership would reach the life of the individual members and carry forward the Church in a united testimony; but where they were impaired you would have on the one hand some degree of tradition and imitation and imposed obedience, and on the other some abandonment of the living principles to which the Church should be bearing witness. The ideal, which included the two opposite truths, had been finely expressed in the early document on discipline issued at Balby in 1656:[2]

Dearly beloved friends, these things we do not lay upon you as a rule or form to walk by, but that all with the measure of light which is pure and holy may be guided, and so in the light walking and abiding these may be fulfilled in the Spirit—not from the letter, for the letter killeth, but the Spirit giveth life.

In the Church, matters of organization and of discipline have their importance, but should be subordinated to the supreme work of strengthening spiritual life and giving this life free course for the service of the Kingdom of God. This is the pathway to unity and to power.

Barclay's province of Church government is very wide. He begins with outward matters:—the care of the poor and of widows and orphans, the composing of differences,

---

[1] *Christian-Quaker*, pt. i. p. 8.
[2] See *Beginnings of Quakerism*, pp. 311-314.

the care of marriages, and the dealing with cases of moral lapse.[1] With respect to matters spiritual he says :

We being gathered together into the belief of certain principles and doctrines without any constraint or worldly respect but by the mere force of Truth upon our understanding and its power and influence upon our hearts, these principles and doctrines and the practices necessarily depending upon them are, as it were, the terms that have drawn us together and the bond by which we became centred into one body and fellowship and distinguished from others.

Barclay somewhat qualified this statement by an admission in the margin that "this is not so the bond, but that we have also a more inward and invisible, to wit, the life of righteousness," but his conclusions are built on his text and not on his margin. For he proceeds to lay down that if any teach other doctrines, the body may declare, "This is not according to the Truth we profess; and therefore we pronounce such and such doctrines to be wrong, with which we cannot have unity, nor yet any more spiritual fellowship with those as hold them."[2] This, he says, is no more tyranny than for a civil society, based on certain fundamental articles, to exclude from its fellowship those who contradict them.

If a body be gathered into one fellowship by the belief of certain principles, he that comes to believe otherways naturally scattereth himself. . . . Suppose a people really gathered unto the belief of the true and certain principles of the gospel, if any of these people shall arise and contradict any of those fundamental truths, whether has not such as stand good the right to cast such a one out from among them?

Rogers pungently observed that to put the true principle in the margin and to neglect it in the text was like the entertainment of Christ in the manger instead of the inn, and pointed out that principles, doctrines, and practices were the fruit and offspring of the bond, but the bond itself which united the members into one body was the Spirit.[3] Barclay, in reply, explained that he also valued

---
[1] *Anarchy of the Ranters*, sect. v. [2] *Ibid.* sect. vi.
[3] *Christian-Quaker*, pt. iii. p. 55. This pt. iii., though not printed till 1680, was previously circulated in MS. and was answered in Barclay's *Vindication*, dated from Aberdeen prison, 6th March 1679, *Works*, pp. 237-247 ; cf. *post*, p. 347.

the life of righteousness beyond any outward bond, but that those who broke the outward bond manifested thereby that they had broken the inward first.[1] He referred to his treatment of the question in his *Apology*. On turning to the passage [2] we find an unusual classification employed, which distinguishes between the general *ecclesia*, made up of all, whether Christians, Turks, Jews, or heathens, who in fact walk in the light and life of God, and the Church as gathered into a visible fellowship, which is grounded not only on this inward work but also on the outward profession of Christ and on belief in Him and in those holy truths delivered by His Spirit in the scriptures. The members of such a Church,

. . . being united by the same love, and their understanding informed in the same truths, gather, meet and assemble together to wait upon God, to worship Him and to bear a joint testimony for the Truth against error, suffering for the same; and so, becoming through this fellowship as one family and household in certain respects, do each of them watch over, teach, instruct and care for one another, according to their several measures and attainments.

This is a great advance on the statement about terms and fundamental articles in the *Anarchy of the Ranters*, for here Barclay rightly describes the corporate witness which the Church should bear as springing out of a living fellowship and a common service and suffering. A little later he gives the life of the Church its true place of first importance:

It is the life of Christianity taking place in the heart that makes a Christian; and so it is a number of such being alive, joined together in the life of Christianity, that make a Church of Christ. Therefore, where this life ceaseth in one, then that one ceaseth to be a Christian; and all power, virtue and authority which he had as a Christian ceaseth with it. . . . And, as it is of one, so of many, yea, of a whole Church: for seeing nothing makes a man truly a Christian but the life of Christianity inwardly ruling in his heart, so nothing makes a Church but the gathering of several true Christians into one body.

This is used to support an argument against the validity

---

[1] *Vindication, Works*, p. 241. [2] Prop. x.

of an outward apostolical succession derived through men who were often destitute of the life and virtue of Christianity. But it is no less important for a just estimate of the nature and limits of Church discipline. The Church has authority in the Life, and the individual member has liberty in the Life, but not out of it. "As we live by the Spirit, let us be guided by the Spirit: let us have no vanity, no provoking, no envy of one another."[1]

Rogers had his own conception of Church government.[2] He agreed that the Church should look after the needs of the poor and discharge other charitable duties. It should inspect marriages, and should take care that "Truth may not be scandalized through the backslidings of such who have been in fellowship with the Children of Light." He allowed a jurisdiction in cases of differences about outward things, but only with the consent of the parties differing. But, in respect of all matters of conscience, he held

... that the sentence and judgment of any man or men whatsoever ... ought not at this day to be given forth but by way of recommendation to every man's conscience in the sight of God; and that, when the conscience is sensible that God's witness therein doth answer thereto, then the conscience is bound and not before.

He would have those who approved themselves as watchmen over the flock deal with any who ran into looseness of life and yet excused themselves by saying, The light in my conscience condemns me not. They should endeavour to awaken the dulled conscience to God's witness, for nothing merely outward could oblige the evil-doer to forsake his sin and embrace the truth.[3]

In opposing the exaggerations of Church government, the Wilkinson-Story party seem to have disregarded the very real spiritual authority which belongs to a group of disciples gathered in the Life and Light of Christ, and to have allowed little place for leadership in the Church. This was the radical weakness of a position which tended

---

[1] Gal. vi. 1, 2 (Dr. Jas. Moffatt's translation).
[2] *Christian-Quaker*, pt. iii. pp. 19, 21.   [3] *Ibid.* pt. iii. p. 19.

to over-emphasize the individualist side of religion, and to lead not merely to congregational independency, but to an undervaluing of group-fellowship in any form.

Barclay's first doctrine of Church authority, though passed by the Morning Meeting, went beyond the judgment of the Society. The book was written in 1674, but not printed till two years later. Meanwhile the Wilkinson-Story controversy had become acute, and at the Draw-well meeting in April 1676[1] the Friends who were seeking to settle the difference had taken much lower ground and agreed that, with certain reservations, a judgment given forth by a part of the Church could not be a bond upon any other part further than their understandings were illuminated thereby. Rogers naturally enough felt that Barclay's book must be answered, and threw his whole strength into the reply, which he circulated in manuscript. The Yearly Meeting of Ministers in June 1677 provided the occasion for a debate between him and Barclay, which was attended by Fox and others, and arranged by the Morning Meeting.[2] The explanations which Barclay gave, confirmed by the passages in his *Apology* and *Vindication* already referred to, show that he had by this time come to see that the principles and practices of Friends were to be considered as fruits of the spiritual life that united them, and that this life was the real bond of union. Fox himself, as we have abundantly shown, had developed Church government in accordance with the root-idea that the power of God was in His Church for this as for every other necessary function of Church life, and that therefore the arrangements made should allow all, both men and women, who were heirs of this power, to exercise their gift. To him the business meeting was a piece of holy living, a time when life called to life, and all were brought into obedience to the Truth. The other great Quaker leaders took the same position.

[1] *Ante*, p. 305.
[2] See *Christian-Quaker*, pt. iii. pp. 14, 98, 122-140. The date of the meeting was 7th June, see *ibid*. p. 128. Barclay, *Works*, p. 249, quotes same document with date 7th May, but Fox did not reach London till 23rd May (*Journ.* ii. 263). The Explanations are in Rogers' account of the debate, *Christian-Quaker*, pt. iii. pp. 125-127; Barclay, *Works*, pp. 247-249.

"The Light, Spirit and Power in the Church," Penington tells us, "is never contrary to the Light, Spirit and Power in any member; but always one with it and a cherisher and preserver of what God begets and which answers His witness in any. The new Jerusalem, the Church of God's building in His own Spirit and Power, is a city at unity within itself. The greatest degree of Light owns and is at unity with the least: and the least degree of Light hath a sense of that which is in degree and measure above it." [1]

At the height of the controversy, the Yearly Meeting of Ministers that met in 1676 declared, in words which became incorporated in the discipline of the Society: [2]

The Power of God is the authority of the men's and women's meetings and of all the other meetings. All the faithful men and women in every city, county and nation, whose faith stands in the Power of God, the Gospel of Christ, and have received this gospel and are in possession of this gospel, the Power of God, they have all right to the power of the meetings, for they be heirs of the power and the authority of the men's and women's meetings.

Such a declaration is instinct with the vital conceptions of Fox, and expresses the best mind of the Society, though with any ebbing of spiritual life it could easily in practice conform to the more mechanical theory of Church government laid down at first by Barclay.

There is one striking case which shows how the English leaders set themselves against extreme doctrines of Church authority. The Wilkinson-Story controversy had spread to Barbados, where the ill-balanced Robert Rich, who had supported Nayler and Perrot in their extravagances, was now circulating with gusto the papers of disaffected English Friends.[3] The Quarterly Meetings were held at the house of Ralph Frettwell,[4] formerly one of the chief judges of the Court of Common Pleas in the island, who joined Friends at the time of Fox's visit. At the Meeting held 23rd December 1680 an unwise

---

[1] *Works*, 1681 edn., pt. ii. p. 435, "Considerations of Church Government."
[2] MS. "Books of Extracts," title, "Meetings for Discipline."
[3] Letter from Barbados to Curtis and Ismeade, 20th Nov. 1678, in Bristol MSS. i. No. 24, and Richard Snead to John Anderton, Bristol, 5th Nov. 1679, in Bristol MSS. ii. No. 23. Rich died in London, 16th Nov. 1679.
[4] See *Camb. Journ.* ii. 430; *Spiritual Reformers*, pp. 232, 233.

paper was subscribed by thirty-nine men and forty-three women, which seemed to surrender the principle of individual guidance and to recommend implicit faith :

> I desire to give up my whole concern, if required, both spiritual and temporal, unto the judgment of the Spirit of God in the Men and Women's Meetings, as believing it to be more according to the universal wisdom of God than any particular measure, in myself or any particulars [*i.e.* individuals], with which the Men and Women's Meetings have not unity.[1]

This minute disquieted Fox, who, with George Whitehead and Parker, wrote to the Quarterly Meeting asking that it should be called in, for " if this order or judgment should come into the hands of any apostates or opposers they would make ill work with it." They pointed out that the course taken in Barbados, though meant for the best, was the way to weaken the spiritual life of the whole body. " The universal Spirit of God has unity with the least measure now, as it was in the Apostles' days, who kept every one to their own measure—which was both the great rule and line of the new creature in the believers and saints then." Conformity to the Spirit was a question of dedication and not of any outward tie.

The Barbadian Friends accepted the criticism and revised their action, but it had already furnished the Wilkinson-Story party with welcome proof of the pontifical designs of the English leaders. Rogers, for example, in the rhymed doggerel with which he strove to scourge George Whitehead, denounced the Quaker preachers who claimed that the keeping of the flock was committed to their hands, and added, with a hit at the Barbados paper :[2]

> Had but a priest for taking tithes despised
> Compared such doctrine, though with sighs disguised,
> With what's decreed concerning "temporals"

---

[1] The paper and letter are in Thomas Crisp's "The First Part of Babel's-Builders Unmasking Themselves," 1682. See also Rogers, *Seventh Part of Christian-Quaker*, 1682, and reply to same by George Whitehead, called *Judgment fixed*, 1682, pp. 12-15, 90-92, 299-301, also Steven Crisp's reply to Thomas Crisp in *Works*, pp. 451-459. Dev. Ho. Portf. 2, Nos. 1-5, contains the letters sent from Barbados, Jan. 1682, after hearing from English Friends.

[2] "A Second Scourge for George Whitehead, An Apostate Quaker, in A Poem," 1685, p. 16.

And soul-concerns couched under " spirituals,"
He might thus say:—Your Church exceeds our claim :
At sheep and fleece and all we ne'er did aim.

The paper, regretted by its subscribers and disowned in England, served as warning against the aggrandizing of Church authority. Leadership, in the Quaker conception, is amongst the most important functions to be discharged in the Church, but it should be a leadership of inspiration and illumination, and not of outward power.

Barclay, in writing to his friend and distant cousin Elizabeth, Princess Palatine of the Rhine,[1] deals clearly with this question :

What thou says, That the performance of things materially good ought to proceed, not from the persuasion of others or mere opinion, but from the light of faith, is true ; and I agree well to it ; as also it is far from me to require of any, far less of thee, to do anything merely upon my persuasion ; for I am a great enemy to Implicit Faith ; and the end of my labour and ministry is to bring all to the anointing, that they may know that to lead them and be the bottom of their obedience, so as to do what they do in faith: and yet such as come here [*i.e.* to this experience] know that the admonishing and instructing one another and the subjection of the spirits to the prophets is noways inconsistent with it.

Authority in the Life ; and liberty in the Life—this is the phrase which seems best to sum up the Quaker position. It is true that the leaders of the Restoration period believed that this spiritual life was bound to express itself in the Quaker way of conduct ; while we recognize to-day that it may also become the bond of union between persons of widely differing beliefs and practices, who are yet baptized into the one Spirit.[2] But their hold on this fundamental ground of unity, as against the immature suggestions of young Barclay and the individualistic Quakerism of Rogers, shows their sanity of spiritual judgment and helps us to see that even the arid wastes of the Wilkinson-Story controversy were not wholly sterile.

[1] Aberdeen Prison, 5th of the month March 1677, in *Reliquiae Barclaianae*, p. 17.
[2] See *post*, Chap. XXII.

CHAPTER XIII

THE WORK OF THE TRAVELLING MINISTERS

Every one to the ministry yourselves, which is the Seed, Christ; for England is as a family of prophets, which must spread over all the nations; as a garden of plants, and the place where the pearl is found which must enrich all nations with the heavenly treasure, out of which shall the waters of life flow and water all the thirsty ground; and out of which nation and dominion must go the 'spiritually-weaponed and armed men to fight and conquer all nations, and bring them to the nation of God, that the Lord may be known to be the living God of nations, and His Son to reign, and His people [to be] one.—Epistle from Skipton General Meeting, 25th April 1660.

THE health and growth of Quakerism in the first period chiefly depended, so far as human agency was concerned upon the travelling ministers who published abroad their message and animated the Quaker groups by their leadership. Their high missionary zeal at the time of the Restoration is well marked by the quotation which heads this chapter. The Church was conceived to be a family of prophets, spiritually armed for the conquest of the world. No finer conception has ever impregnated a body of Christians, and it remains to-day a challenging ideal to the Society of Friends and to the Church at large. It could not be carried out amid the storm of persecution let loose by the Cavalier Parliament. The ranks of the Publishers of Truth were thinned by imprisonment or untimely death, and for thirty years the energies of Friends were occupied with the defence of their right to live.

Persecution raged most fiercely during the first ten years, and it is significant of the vitality of the movement that even in this time of tempest the Quaker message rooted itself in two new districts. I have already told of its upspringing in the North of Scotland;[1] it remains to give honourable mention to the second case of expansion, in Mid-Wales.

The congregations gathered by Vavasor Powell, the great Baptist itinerant, were the chief source from which the new Quaker groups sprang.[2] Richard Davies, the Welshpool hatter, had separated from Powell and professed Quakerism in 1657, and in the early part of October 1662[3] he and Richard Moore of Shrewsbury held a meeting near Dolobran, the seat of Charles Lloyd, a gentleman of birth, newly married, who had been bred at Oxford with his brother Thomas, where they had been impressed by the bearing of Friends under the rude behaviour of the 'varsity men. Lloyd and his neighbours were much reached at the meeting, and the report soon spread that most of that side of the country were turned Quakers. In December Lord Herbert of Cherbury, great-nephew of the poet, had Lloyd and the others before him and sent them to Welshpool gaol for refusing the Oath of Allegiance. A long discipline of suffering followed hard upon their convincement. The foul prison, still standing,[4] into which they were thrown was made viler by the felons who occupied the chamber overhead. Lloyd himself was put in a little smoky room, with straw to lie on, where his young wife insisted on joining him. The prisoners were praemunired and were only released

---

[1] *Ante*, p. 328.

[2] *Beginnings of Quakerism*, pp. 207-209. *The Broadmead Baptist Records*, pp. 511-518, contain an account of the Welsh Churches and pastors in 1675, which shows how Churches became scattered and "dissipated between the world and the Quakers," upon Powell's imprisonment after the Restoration.

[3] For Davies, see *Beginnings of Quakerism*, pp. 208, 209. The following details are chiefly taken from his *Life* (edn. 1771), pp. 66-81. Davies, however, dates the meeting "ninth-month," *i.e.* Nov. 1662, which must be a mistake, for in a MS. Colln. of Lloyd documents, in my possession, there are several letters, dated in October, written to the "new-born babes," immediately after their convincement. Other letters confirm statement in Besse, *Sufferings*, i. 749, that the imprisonment began about middle of Dec.

[4] A picture of the old "Crib" is in (London) *Friend*, 21st July 1899; and the gaoler's house, where the meetings were held for nearly forty years, "which was a sweet, convenient place near the fields," was also standing, in field at entrance of Powis Park.

XIII WORK OF TRAVELLING MINISTERS 353

under the Pardon of 1672, though, after a time, they had better quarters and the freedom of the town. Davies sums up the matter by saying:

> There was a great convincement in the year 1662 in these two counties, viz., Montgomeryshire and Merionethshire; and, as meetings increased, several Friends came into Welshpool, where our meeting was kept in that house that was their prison. The magistrates and priest were discontented, some saying, That there came as many to the meeting as went to their worship at the church.[1]

Thomas Holme, the chief early Quaker labourer in Wales, visited "the young Friends in prison at Welshpool," and found them "a hopeful people and valiant for Truth."[2]

With the abatement of persecution from 1668 to '70, and again, after the Declaration of Indulgence, in '72, the conditions became more favourable; and remained so for some time after the withdrawal of the Declaration a year later, for, as Baxter says, while some county Justices rigorously executed the laws, most forbore.[3]

Cumberland, in particular, now developed a marked vitality alike in the formation of new Quaker groups and in the raising up of fresh Publishers of Truth. The county had been mainly Royalist in sentiment throughout the troubles; and was in a backward religious state with many of the parsons pluralists or neglectful of their cures. There were, however, some Puritan districts; and the heralds of Quakerism in 1653[4] had gathered meetings in these places out of the Seekers and had brought an

---

[1] Davies, *Life*, p. 101.
[2] Letter of 11th June 1663 (Swarthm. Colln. iv. 245) printed in *J.F.H.S.* Supplmt. No. 6 (John ap John), p. 23.
[3] *Reliquiae Baxterianae*, pt. iii. p. 103. See *ante*, p. 86.
[4] See *Beginnings of Quakerism*, pp. 116-122. Wigton and Abbeyholme, two of the places where Seeker groups developed into Friends' meetings, were among the few Puritan centres, see B. Nightingale, *The Ejected of 1662 in Cumberland and Westmorland*, i. 75. This careful piece of historical research, published too late for use in *Beginnings of Quakerism*, has additional information as to the pre-Quaker careers of John Camm and Gervase Benson. In 1646 they were both proposed for elders in the attempted Presbyterian Classis (see vol. i. p. 109), and Benson was evidently the chief support in Kendal of Henry Masy, who was Presbyterian Minister there during the closing years of the Civil War (see the series of Masy letters in vol. ii. 880-925).

2 A

experience of spiritual life to many other earnest-hearted folk. The Puritan ministers at that time had been greatly alarmed and disconcerted :

Satan . . . disgorgeth from his hateful stomach a swarm of Quakers : these . . . came upon us like a furious torrent; all is on fire on the sudden : many are unsettled, the foundations shaken and some apostatize : here we are beaten off and are forced to lay other things aside that we might more fully bind ourselves to quench these flames.[1]

Friends now, in 1672, some nineteen years later, became the instruments of a new revival of religion in the county. In the Abbeyholme district, by the Solway, where there had been little persecution, we read :

A fresh visitation of the love of God was again renewed to many towns and villages in the said Abbeyholme and amongst the people, insomuch that there was but very few of any rank or sex, of what persuasion of religion soever, but they were awakened in their spirits or had some desires raised in their hearts to seek the Lord by speedy repentance and amendment of their ways, inquiring the way to Sion with their faces thitherward.[2]

In the neighbouring parish of Kirkbride, where the Bishop in 1703 " never yet saw a church and chancel (out of Scotland) in so scandalous and nasty a condition,"[3] there were many convinced and " a holy zeal increased for the promotion of Truth and the spreading abroad the fame thereof."[4] Near the Scottish Border, at Kirklinton, the " general part " of the people was reached, and one of the Cumberland leaders, John Grave, promised the country that when he was next in London he would tell the Earl of Carlisle that he might now take away his gallows, " for Truth had got an entrance in the Borders of England and would make them honest men."[5] According to John Bellers, the Quaker pioneer of social reform,

The Northern Borders are a noted instance of the good effect that our Friends' labour of love had among those robbers called moss-troopers that were there, so far to reform that

---

[1] Nightingale, *op. cit.* i. 98. [2] *F.P.T.* p. 73.
[3] Nightingale, *op. cit.* i. 598. [4] *F.P.T.* p. 59.
[5] *F.P.T.* pp. 61-66, and Christopher Story's *Life*.

WORK OF TRAVELLING MINISTERS

country, where they murdered as well as robbed, that the then Earl of Carlisle told King Charles II. that the Quakers had done more to suppress them than all his troops could do.[1]

In 1703 the Bishop speaks of "the mighty swarms of Quakers in the parish,"[2] and though this was five miles in length, the church was often so deserted that there were only four or five in attendance besides the clerk.[3]

The story of the planting of this Border Quaker community will illustrate the manner of extension work as it was done in the seventeenth century.[4] Cumberland John Wilkinson, as he was often called to distinguish him from the Separatist of the same name, had been a Puritan minister before his convincement,[5] and then "came to know a waiting in deep silence till the Lord opened his mouth."[6] Now, with the Quaker message burning within him, he held a meeting on the Border, followed by another attended by Barclay riding north to Scotland, and a little later by a third at which Thomas Langhorne of Westmorland and Thomas Carleton[7] of Cumberland were present. Christopher Story, who had been at all the meetings, had the Friends to his house, and the neighbours coming in there was another meeting in the long winter evening, and then some queries were written out for the Quakers to answer.

"When the Friends perceived what we aimed at," says Story, "Thomas Carleton, being pretty quick and expert in answering questions, called for a Bible; and did not so much argue with us as endeavour to let us see what the scripture said, putting us gently by for we were much for arguing: we parted pretty well satisfied. Next morning the Friends going to Carlisle, Christopher Taylor and I went with them: and we queried many things which they answered to our satisfaction. In our going along, a heavenly melodious song sounded through Thomas Langhorne and we were affected with it. After we had parted, in our return home, we said one to another, 'If there be saints upon earth, those men are two of them.'"

---

[1] *J.F.H.S.* v. p. 10, from a piece written in 1724.
[2] Nightingale, *op. cit.* i. 312.   [3] *F.P.T.* p. 63.
[4] *F.P.T.* pp. 61-66, and Christopher Story's *Life.*
[5] See *Beginnings of Quakerism*, pp. 117, 374.   [6] *F.P.T.* p. 39.
[7] See *J.F.H.S.* xii. 17, and Rutty, *Hist. of Friends in Ireland*, pp. 138-141.

John Wilkinson now came again and found a group of newly convinced Friends, with whom he stayed a few days; and though there was none to speak words, advised them to settle a meeting for waiting on the Lord. It began in an upper room, and Story says:

> When we sat down together, I may say I was hard beset to keep my mind from running hither and thither after the transitory things of this world; and a great warfare I had for the greatest part of the meeting. Yet near the conclusion those vain thoughts vanished and the Lord was pleased to bring me into my remembrance how that men who had great possessions in this world had their day and were gone; and in a little time I saw clearly my day would soon pass over.

Thus made acquainted in the stillness of all flesh with the eternal order of life that overspreads this transitory world, they kept their silent meetings, and in a few months gathered to the number of thirty or more. "Glorious and heavenly times we had," says Story, "when no words." His description of one such meeting may not be omitted:

> There was much brokenness and tenderness on the spirits of Friends, which spread over the whole meeting, except three or four persons who sat dry—and they proved not well. I, being near the door, saw many in the room filled before the power of the Lord reached me: yet the Lord in His free love and mercy was pleased to give me such a share among my brethren that my heart is always glad when I remember that season of God's love, though now upwards of twenty years ago.

In the above case we see again, as so often before, the value of itinerant ministry. This was now reviving. For example, visits of stranger Friends to Scotland and Ireland were rare up to 1669; but after this date they become frequent.[1] The letter which Fox wrote to Bristol Friends stirring them to faithfulness at the time of the Second Conventicle Act[2] shows the difficulty and urgency of the matter:

---

[1] See the lists, for Scotland in *J.F.H.S.* xii. 82-83 and 137-145, and for South of Ireland in *J.F.H.S.* x. 157-161.
[2] *Epistles*, No. 283, dated 2nd Jan. 1671; cf. *ante*, p. 77.

… Few travel now the countries; it may be well to visit them lest any should faint. Stir up one another in that which is good and to faithfulness in the Truth this day. And let your minds be kept above all visible things.

It was in this spirit that Charles Marshall, who was one of the firstfruits of Camm and Audland's Pentecostal ministry at Bristol in 1654, received the call in 1670 to run through the nation to visit the breathing, bruised birth which God had begotten among His people; and spent some two years in the service, attending about four hundred meetings, without once being stopped or the meeting fined because of his visit. As to results he says:

I believe thousands received the word of life; and many were added to the Church in divers places; and some meetings were settled in some places where there was never a Friend before; and in one place a whole meeting was convinced at one time, and I never heard that any of them turned back, but were faithful unto the Lord.[1]

Friends from the North were specially prominent in such work, as had been the case in the early years of Quakerism.[2] With the help of accounts of moneys disbursed for Friends' horses, we can sometimes estimate the scale on which this inter-visitation of meetings went forward. At Banbury in the year from June 1677 to May 1678 twenty visits were paid by about thirty Friends; and there were no doubt others by ministers who travelled afoot.[3] In Gloucestershire and Bristol the charges for "horse-meat" indicate that the number of visits averaged one a fortnight for many years in succession. A bill brought to Bristol meeting for oats supplied to the horses of ministering Friends amounted to $36\frac{1}{2}$ bushels in a year and a quarter.[4] At York sums representing numerous visits were regularly disbursed and the Quarterly Meeting

---

[1] *Works*, unnumbered pages called "The Journal" with itinerary. Almeley, in Herefordshire, was one of the resulting meetings (*F.P.T.* p. 113).
[2] Richard Davies, *Life*, pp. 135, 136. "Our meetings were pretty much supplied with travelling Friends, especially from the North of England ... I knew there was a great concern upon them to visit the Churches of Christ, wheresoever God sent them."
[3] I have given details in *Friends' Quarterly Examiner*, 1912, pp. 482-488.
[4] Tanner, *Three Lectures*, p. 91.

had to come to the assistance of local Friends.[1] The London plan for distributing the ministry has been already referred to.[2] Many Friends were most assiduous labourers in their own districts. The episcopal return of conventicles, obtained by Archbishop Sheldon, shows this clearly. A column of the return was reserved for the names of the "teachers" at the conventicles; in the Quaker cases it was sometimes left blank or marked "unknown"—the clergy ignoring the spiritual Teacher present even in a silent meeting—but more often names are inserted, now on random rumour, now on reliable information. It is easy to distinguish between these. " A wandering teacher out of the North sometimes," is a fair record against a meeting in Wiltshire,[3] but when you find an entry " one Fox, Dewsbury and Whitehead" in connection with the meeting of which John Whitehead was a member,[4] you recognize that the other two were heard of in the place as prominent Quakers, but you do not infer that they were frequenters of the meeting. In Somerset three Friends were specially active : John Anderdon of Bridgwater, a prisoner at Ilchester from first to last nearly twenty years, but often having liberty to visit meetings in the county,[5] Jasper Batt of Street, who was the special aversion of the Bishop of Bath and Wells,[6] and Christopher Bacon, of Venice Sutton in the Poldens, the Cavalier soldier turned Quaker, "a valiant man for Truth, and freely given up to suffer for it and to spend and be spent for the gathering of people to it."[7] In Bedfordshire and the adjacent counties, we hear much of John Crook, of Beckerings Park ; at Hertford a Baptist meeting of four hundred and upwards was reported and another " of Quakers of as great number, to whom Captain Crook is preacher. He was a Justice of Peace under Cromwell, is of dangerous principles, a subtle fellow and one who hath too much influence upon the people of that town and the country about."[8] He

[1] See Q. M. Accounts and Minutes of York Two Weeks' Meeting, York M. M. and Yorkshire Q. M., 1680. [2] Ante, p. 279.
[3] G. Lyon Turner, Original Records of Nonconformity, i. 109.
[4] Ibid. i. 162. [5] John Whiting, Persecution Exposed, pp. 130-133.
[6] Ibid. p. 108. [7] Ibid. pp. 13-15.
[8] G. Lyon Turner, Original Records of Nonconformity, i. 84. He is spoken

would often preach for three hours at a time, the spring of ministry flowing copiously through him during the fiery trials of persecution with a power which convinced many.[1] Phrases are used of other ministers which imply incessant activity: Oliver Sansom, of Berkshire, "a great seducer";[2] William Smith, of Besthorpe, Nottinghamshire, "who, though a prisoner, is permitted by Robert White, the gaoler, to go all over the country to sow the seeds of schism and faction";[3] Thomas Gilpin, of Warborough, "an Oliverian soldier and a great seducer."[4] The important place of itinerating ministry is shown by such entries as the following: "Itinerant Quakers," "vagrant persons," "itinerants and wanderers," "the teachers of the Anabaptists and Quakers are vagabond, run-about, unknown fellows."[5] There is no perception of the true character of a Friends' meeting, but thumb-nail caricatures occur, as "dumb meetings," "no speaking there, but eating," "they speak by turns in their conventicle," "the Quakers are all speakers."[6]

---

of again (i. 94) as "a grand seducer and disturber of the peace," and I suspect that the entry against St. Albans also refers to him, "one Crock, a subtle fellow and a lace-seller" (i. 92). The "Captain" is probably a malicious embellishment, and the number exaggerated. In the reference to Crook (i. 65) "Guershalt" seems a mistake for Eversholt, near Beckerings Park. Crook's name was sent up from Bedfordshire as a member of the Nominated Parliament of 1653 (see John Brown's *John Bunyan*, p. 101; Smith's *Catalogue*, i. 483) as that of an able man, "loving truth, fearing God and hating covetousness," but it is not in the list of members in Gardiner, *Hist. of the Commth. and Prot.* ii. 308 n.

[1] MS. in Dev. Ho. *ex relatione* John Griffith (1713–1776). The account says that the habit of long preaching continued in quieter times, without the life accompanying it, but after Crook had been spoken to on the subject he realized that he had been speaking only from his natural powers, and for three years after was quite silent as a minister, after which he again broke forth with a few words, as at the beginning of his ministry, and gradually increased in his gift.

[2] G. Lyon Turner, *Original Records of Nonconformity*, i. 111. His *Life*, published in 1710, was reprinted with addition of letters and notes by James Boorne, Jr., in 1848.   [3] G. Lyon Turner, *op. cit.* i. 157.

[4] G. Lyon Turner, *op. cit.* iii. 824. For Gilpin (1622–1703) see *F.P.T.* pp. 215-217, and *Piety Promoted*, pt. iii. The Oxfordshire MS. Sufferings contain a vivid account of his persecution in 1671. The Witney record in *F.P.T.* p. 206, says in oddly spelt phrases: "His ministry was Living & pouerfull, his Labour of Loue afectuell, in prayer fervent & tender ... And may be Cald an apostele of thos parts. He was of good sarvis in ye men & woomens meetings, Zelous for good order in ye Church. ... Ye Lord may be plased to Raise more (in ye plases of thos worthy Antients yt are gon) to suckseed them wth a dubell portion of thair spirit, is ye desire & prayr of we who are as a suckseeding generation." He is called by John Tomkins (*Quaker Post-bag*, p. 188) "an original of the Primitive Quakers, both for purity of doctrine and conversation."

[5] G. Lyon Turner, *op. cit.* i. 117, 46, 104, 137.   [6] *Ibid.* i. 82, 115, 150, 154.

Contributions towards the support of travelling ministers or their families were frequently made, and the subject became one of the issues in the Wilkinson-Story controversy. Friends refused tithes, as being forced payments for the maintenance of a false ministry; but a voluntary provision for the needs of Publishers of Truth whose service prevented them, for the time being, from earning a livelihood was on a very different footing.[1] A general collection for books and service beyond seas was set on foot by the Ministers' Meeting of Christmas 1668, as had been done in the Commonwealth period,[2] and others were requested by the Meetings held in 1672 and '76.[3] Another was directed by the Yearly Meeting in 1679, at the acutest stage of the Wilkinson-Story controversy, with the objects carefully stated. The first was "to accommodate public labourers in the gospel of Truth in their travels in that service into foreign parts beyond the seas." Then came the relief of sufferers at Danzig and Embden, the service of the Meeting for Sufferings, and the circulation of books.[4] Friction arose among Bristol Friends over this collection,[5] and it was debated prior to the Yearly Meeting in their Men's Meeting. In the original Minutes a collection was then ordered in Bristol for the three following local services and no other: the defraying of public debts and house rents and the relief of the poor. In the duplicate Minutes kept by the Friends who were loyal to the Yearly Meeting, a wider collection was ordered among such as were free to contribute which covered the charge of Friends' horses who visited the city, and the charge of the travel of Friends beyond seas; and representatives to the Yearly Meeting were sent up by this section of Friends. After the Yearly Meeting the original

---

[1] See *Beginnings of Quakerism*, p. 136; and Barclay, *Apology*, Prop. x.
[2] *Ante*, p. 217, and MS. Y.M. Minutes.
[3] *Ante*, p. 277; MS. Y.M. Minutes; and *Letters of Early Friends*, p. 327. For 1676 collection see MS. Y.M. Minutes.
[4] See MS. Y.M. Minutes.
[5] See entries in the Bristol Men's Meeting Book: 19th May 1679, original and duplicate book (the duplicate entry is signed by thirty-one Friends, including Thomas Langhorne and Thomas Camm, of Westmorland, who were in the West of England at the time; cf. Bristol MSS. ii. No. 21), 25th Aug. 1679, and 3rd May 1680.

Minutes directed a collection for the poor and local expenses, "and that as large as Friends shall find the Lord to open their hearts to do, to the end we may out of the same answer the request of the Yearly Meeting." In May 1680 a sum of Fifty Pounds was sent up out of this collection: "one part of the meeting was free that it should be used for the general services mentioned in the letter, the other part desiring that it might be wholly employed in relieving distressed Friends at Danzig and Embden, yet all agreed that the money should be sent up." In December a collection for local purposes is ordered, the money "not to be disposed of without the . . . general consent of the Friends of this meeting," presumably because of some jealousy as to paying for the horses of travelling Friends.[1] These Minutes at first sight raise no question of principle; but they are to be read in the light of the disaffection felt by Rogers and his party towards the new central organization and the travelling ministers who were its chief support. During the progress of the Wilkinson-Story controversy the Morning Meeting, which published an answer to the *Christian-Quaker*, over the signature of its Clerk, Ellis Hookes,[2] became anathema to Rogers, and he vented his spleen against it and its chief leader, George Whitehead, in the Sixth, Seventh and Eighth Parts of the *Christian-Quaker*, and in a *Scourge* and a *Second Scourge for George Whitehead*. In this last piece, printed early in 1685, we have an explanation of the motives behind the Bristol Minutes, paraded to the world in all the incongruity of halting verse.

He says of Fox,

> When He had fram'd i' th' Church a Government,
> Preachers approved by Man beyond Seas went,
> Who, when they wanted Moneys to proceed,
> The Church her Cash then did supply their Need,

---

[1] Minute of 13th Dec. 1680. In a Minute, 14th June 1669, Bristol Friends had authorized their Treasurers, with the advice of some other good Friends, "to disburse out of the public stock from time to time unto Friends that travel up and down in the service of Truth according as shall to them seem expedient, without charging the account of public stock otherwise than this, viz.:—to so much disbursed with the assent of A. B. for the service of Truth."

[2] *The Accuser of our Brethren cast down*, 1681.

> If they their Motion freely did Submit
> To th' London Church and do as She thought fit.
> The Spirit's Motion in a home-bred Swain
> Without a City Stamp seem'd but in Vain.
>
> .   .   .   .   .
>
> At length Her Papers like to Briefs did cry
> For Money, Money for the Ministry.
> And, when that Practice was dislik'd by some,
> She frown'd like one whose downfall's near to come.

Further couplets tell us that some Friends, " not fond of new Church Laws," sent no supplies, partly "to prevent the growth of Pride, And Poor Men's running with the Turning Tide," and partly because they thought it a sin to feed travelling ministers who were engaged in wounding their brethren. Ellwood, later in the same year, continued the rhymed battle in *Rogero-Mastix*, which, when transprosed, yields some excellent sense. He cites abundant scripture, perforce in his margin, to show that the Church should supply the needful wants of all her ministry. True it is that Paul did not always use his privilege, and scores of Friends have done the same, and have gone on warfare or crossed the seas at their own charges. But, he adds, with generous warmth :

> May none beyond Seas go but who can spare
> Sufficient of their own the charge to bear?
> Must Christ be so confin'd he may not send
> Any but such as have Estates to spend?
> God bless us from such Doctrine and such Teachers
> As will admit of none but wealthy Preachers.

There is a good deal of evidence in the early Minute Books to show that Ellwood's views were those of Friends in general. A series of extracts from the Yorkshire Quarterly Meeting Records will illustrate the way in which help to approved ministering Friends was given :

> Q.M. 21st December 1671 :—Monthly Meetings to take care out of the public collection that all persons employed in the public service of the Truth have their charges sustained, as may appear to them necessary, rendering account to the Quarterly Meeting.

WORK OF TRAVELLING MINISTERS

Accounts, 14th March 1672.

	£	s	d
Wm. Dewsberry [Dewsbury] by T. Waite ordering [frequently assisted]	5	0	0
Thos. Taylor, by the ordering of Philip Swale	5	0	0
Paid to John Whitehead for his supply	4	0	0
Paid to John Cox for his supply	2	18	4
Paid to John Hall for this quarter sellerage [salary]	2	10	0
Paid more for and towards his necessity by order of this meeting	1	0	0
To be sent to London for service of Truth beyond seas	20	0	0

Q.M. 19th March 1679 :—

	£	s	d
York M.M. for use of Judith Key	3	0	0
To Cuthbert Hayhurst for his charges and necessities' expenses in his travels last winter, four months together, and other travels on Truth's account	5	0	0
To Robert Lodge [frequently assisted] towards his charges in travelling in the public service of Truth, and the loss his family may sustain at home by want of his necessary helpe and charges of his intended journey to London	7	0	0

Epistle at end of Q.M. Book from Joshua Dawson, dated 1673, settling £50 on trusts, with power if necessary to take of the main stock rather than such good Friends and painful labourers in the Lord's vineyard as William Dewsbury, Thomas Taylor, Robert Lodge, Benjamin Brown or others should be in want.

Q.M. 20th June 1683 :—
Malton Friends to be re-imbursed £4 : 10s. for a horse for George Sykes, a public labourer, whose horse died in his journey.

Q.M. 9th March 1687 :—
Agreed that William Dewsbury have £5 given him out of the public stock, as a remembrance of Friends' love and kindness for his former labour and travels amongst us, and considering his old age and weakness coming upon him.

Q.M. 21st September 1687 :—
Agreed that £6 be given to Benjamin Brown as an encouragement to him in his intended journey into Ireland, to visit Friends on Truth's account, with which Friends have good unity.

Q.M. 27th December 1693 :—
George Meggison sends forty-six guineas for £50, to be disposed of by this meeting, £5 to go to John Whitehead, if he had not lately received anything.

Q.M. 21st March 1694 :—
Certificate of unity with Thomas Musgrave in his voyage to visit Friends in America, and £12 towards charge given out of George Meggison's gift, London Friends being asked to see to his further supply.

Q.M. 6th July 1698 :—
Letter from Kelk M.M., as to condition of Thos. Thompson Sr. and Thos. Thompson Jr., of that M.M., they having been and being pretty much concerned in travelling to visit Friends in England, Scotland and Ireland, and thereby have been a-wanting and suffered loss thereby as to the outward; this meeting tenderly weighing their case does agree that £7 be given them as an encouragement to them in their labour and service and towards the supply of their business at home.

These specimen entries, together with other similar ones, show that many of the leading Quaker ministers in Yorkshire received substantial monetary help from the Quarterly Meeting. When at home they earned their livelihood—Robert Lodge was a butcher of Masham; Benjamin Brown, "a deep man of experiences,"[1] "not having much outwardly to live upon, wrought with his hands in several places, when in travels upon Truth's account, that he might not make the gospel chargeable;" John Hall, of York, a future Separatist, had a salary of £10 a year for doing the clerical work of the Quarterly Meeting.[2] But they kept their business within compass

---

[1] *J.F.H.S.* xii. 141.
[2] For Lodge (1636-1690) see *F.P.T.* 315 and *Camb. Journ.* ii. 412. For Benjamin Brown (1634-1704) see *F.P.T.* 288. Of the other Yorkshire ministers mentioned, John Cox, like Hall, became a Separatist; Hayhurst (1632-1683) was an able minister, who emigrated to Pennsylvania in 1682, with other Friends of Settle M.M. (see *F.P.T.* 307 and certificate of M.M. in Bowden, *History of Friends in America*, ii. 15); Musgrave paid a lengthened visit to America, which he reported to the Y.M. of 1697; for Thomas Thompson, Sr. (1631-1704), see *Piety Promoted*, pt. iii.; *Life*, 1708, with title "An encouragement early to Seek the Lord," and references in *Beginnings of Quakerism*. The son (1673-1727) visited America twice (see *J.F.H.S.* x. 124), and wrote several religious pieces. The London Box Meeting Minutes record several gifts to Yorkshire ministers, and also, 14th June 1675, a gift of £5 to Fox, on his journey to the North.

so as to be free to obey the call to itinerant work, and their Friends felt no hesitation in giving them or their families such help as was required. Nothing like a regular stipend was ever paid, so far as I am aware, but the gifts made were often given "in token of Friends' love," rather than for the direct relief of proved necessity. The right relation of the minister to the main body of Friends in this matter depended upon mutual confidence and a certain simplicity of fellowship; and where these were impaired, both the ministry and the Society of Friends suffered loss.

I have given the evidence in some detail; but the misapprehension on the subject is my justification. The principles that governed the question were clear. Ministry was a Divine gift, and not a matter of human ordination or of human learning; and they who had received this gift freely were freely to use it,

> . . . without hire or bargaining, far less to use it as a trade to get money by; yet if God hath called any from their employments or trades, by which they acquire their livelihood, it may be lawful for such, according to the liberty which they feel given them in the Lord, to receive such temporals, to wit, what may be needful for them for meat and clothing, as are given them freely and cordially by those to whom they have communicated spirituals.[1]

The practice, however, depended so entirely upon the willingness of the minister to receive help, and the readiness of Friends to supply it, as to make it inevitable that in periods when the spiritual life of the Society was low the help afforded by the Church should be restricted to certain customary channels, and ministry that involved the giving up of a man's ordinary work should fall largely into the hands of "wealthy preachers." In this, as in some other respects, the Wilkinson-Story point of view prevailed in a later generation of Friends more than is commonly admitted.

But William Rogers and his supporters used the money

---

[1] Barclay, *Apology*, Prop. x. The Latin has "it is lawful," not "it may be lawful."

question mainly as a deadly weapon against the travelling ministers themselves, whom they regarded as the mere puppets of Fox. "Parasites," "prating preachers," "pensioners," "usurpers," "wolves clothed like to sheep," "deceit within a coat that's gray" (a phrase that throws an interesting light on Quaker costume), "mercenary judges," "self-seeking slavish drudges," are some of the choice epithets which Rogers hurls at their heads in his poetic frenzy.[1] Thomas Robertson, of Grayrigg, one of the First Publishers from Westmorland,[2] "an innocent, faithful, patient man, to the adorning the gospel that he preached in holy living,"[3] is thus described in a complaining letter to Fox from Bristol:[4]

. . . an idle, dronish man, who, by his preaching false doctrine, misquoting scriptures and dreaming stories so void of sense, hath caused more dishonour and scandal to our profession, for suffering such preaching amongst us, than he's ever like to repair. . . . Truly we think if thou shouldst give out thy advice or direction for the discouraging of many such dull, senseless, noisy, empty preachers, of which we have had of late too many amongst us, it might prove of more service than several of thy former orders.

To understand this jealousy, we must remember that, in the years of persecution, the Quaker groups had been left largely to their own local resources. The objection to the development of the movement into a Society with strong central organs of influence naturally extended to the travelling ministers who were the most important element of these central bodies and carried their influence into the provinces. If we glance at the work of a few of the leading itinerants, we shall see the variety and importance of their services.

John Burnyeat[5] was a man "whose innocent deportment and blameless conversation preached wherever he came; gravity and patience was with him [and] modera-

[1] *A Second Scourge for George Whitehead* (1685).
[2] See *Beginnings of Quakerism*, pp. 398, etc. He died in May 1695.
[3] *F.P.T.* p. 266. [4] Bristol MSS. v. Nos. 25, 26, dated 1st Sept. 1687.
[5] For Burnyeat (1631–1690) see *Beginnings of Quakerism*, pp. 120, 222, 223, 228 *n.* ; *Quakers in the American Colonies, passim*; *Camb. Journ.* ii. 418. His *Works*, 1691 (also in Barclay's Select Series), contain a brief journal to 1676, and also 1682–1690. Cf. minute of Morning Meeting, 23rd March 1691.

tion in meat, drink and apparel," and "in all his travels, into whose house he entered, he was content with what things were set before him, were they never so mean, which was great satisfaction to many poor, honest Friends amongst whom his lot was cast."[1] His work in America and at the end of his life in Ireland were most important; but he also travelled tirelessly in England during the ten years 1673–1682, and was, as we have seen, one of the Northern leaders who had been called in by the Friends of Westmorland to compose, if possible, the Wilkinson-Story difficulties. An extract from a letter to Fox in January 1677[2] shows the spirit in which he laboured:

Abundance of [disaffected Friends] have I met with in my travels, which doth cost me many hours' discourse to remove things out of the way of the simple-hearted; but light and truth goes over this darkness more and more.

He was "an early comer to meetings, and a diligent waiter therein. Many times he would sit a pretty while in silence, not being forward to speak, reverently waiting upon the opening of the heavenly life, like the good householder spoken of to bring forth of his treasury things both new and old."[3]

John Banks, another Cumberland Friend,[4] was a lad of sixteen, teaching school and taking services at Mosser Chapel near Pardshaw, when Quakerism reached the district in 1653. He was convinced, left his school-work, and took up his father's trade of glover and fellmonger, at which he worked diligently in the intervals of his service. In 1663 he and some other Friends were imprisoned for a time in the common gaol at Carlisle,

. . . where was a Bedlam man, and four with him for theft, and two notorious thieves, called Redhead and Wadelad, two moss-troopers for stealing of cattle, and one woman for murdering of her own child.

---
[1] *Works*, Testimonies, pp. 6, 18.   [2] Dev. Ho. Portf. 31, No. 127.
[3] *Works*, Testimonies, p. 16.
[4] For Banks (1637–1710) see *Camb. Journ.* ii. 466 and *Works*, 1712, containing an interesting Journal, with a Preface by Penn. The last fifteen years of his life were spent in Somerset. The meeting at Street, which he frequented, was held in a low cottage-room, and, as he was a tall man, a portion of the beam of the ceiling was cut away to allow him to stand to preach (Tanner, *Three Lectures*, p. 96).

From 1668 onwards he travelled extensively, his first journey lasting two months and covering twelve hundred and sixty-eight miles. Six times he went across to Ireland; and says :

. . . never at any time was I above two nights together at sea, insomuch that, after some times that I had taken shipping at Whitehaven, the seamen would be very desirous who should have me in their vessel, saying ; I was the happiest man that ever they carried over sea, for they got well along still when they had me.

At Wicklow he was imprisoned ; but held the first Quaker meeting in the town in the gaoler's house ; and on coming there again two years later in 1673 the gaoler said to him, " Oh, Mr. Banks, are you come again ? I think you need not to have come any more, for you did your business the last time you were here ; for I think all the town of Wicklow will be Quakers." In 1677 his arm and hand became numbed and began to wither,

. . . until at last, as I was asleep upon my bed in the night time, I saw in a vision that I was with dear George Fox ; and I thought I said unto him ; George, my faith is such that, if thou seest it thy way to lay thy hand upon my shoulder, my arm and hand shall be whole throughout. . . . At last . . . I was made willing to go to him, he being then at Swarthmore. . . . After the meeting, I called him aside into the Hall, and gave him a relation of my concern as aforesaid, showing him my arm and hand. And, in a little time, we walking together silent, he turned about and looked upon me, lifting up his hand, and laid it upon my shoulder and said ; The Lord strengthen thee both within and without. And so we parted . . . and when I was sat down to supper . . . immediately, before I was aware, my hand was lifted up to do its office . . . which struck me into a great admiration [*i.e.* wonder], and my heart was broken into true tenderness before the Lord. . . . And the next time that G. F. and I met, he readily said ; John, thou mended, thou mended. I answered ; Yes, very well, in a little time. Well, said he, give God the glory.[1]

---

[1] The cases of "Spiritual Healing among the Early Friends" are well summarized by Edward Grubb in two articles in the *Venturer* for April and May 1916, pp. 212-215, 236-239 : cf. *Beginnings of Quakerism*, pp. 247, 253, 256, 391 ; and, as to Fox, xxxi, 107, 247, 341 ; and *Camb. Journ.* i. 140, 141, etc. In Edward Grubb's view, with which I concur, the intense experience which came to the early Friends was attended by an influx of power which enabled them, under certain conditions, to do things beyond the ordinary range of our experience.

John Banks felt that he had a peculiar testimony given to him against the spirit of separation ; and in 1679, in the height of the controversy, laboured much against this spirit in Westmorland and at Hertford, Reading, High Wycombe, and Bristol, and in Wiltshire, especially at Charlcutt, near Calne. He says:

I had little benefit either of meat or sleep, especially in Wiltshire, for they who were of it followed me many of them from meeting to meeting ; so that sometimes in the night season, when I was in sleep, I thought some ugly creatures crawled over my bed, with dreadful sharp claws and teeth and eyes of several colours, with which they looked spitefully upon me, and did bite and scratch me, which to me did bespeak their wicked, envious, hateful, separating, rending spirit.

In 1684 Banks underwent a tedious imprisonment of near seven years at Carlisle for refusing to pay tithes. Here he behaved with indomitable courage, preaching from the gaoler's house to the worshippers at the Cathedral. In the common gaol he was savagely treated ; but at length the rigour of his confinement was abated, and he was even allowed some liberty. But he was much broken in health by his sufferings, though a zealous itinerant for another thirteen years, as a "good, old and valiant soldier and warrior for Truth on earth."[1]

Leonard Fell,[2] of Baycliff, near Swarthmore, was of the same age as Fox, "a man of a truly noble and generous spirit, willing and ready to serve anybody where it laid in his power."[3] He visited Scotland three times

---

What the necessary conditions were deserves careful investigation. But we may agree with Dr. Rufus M. Jones in feeling that "Fox's commanding presence, his piercing eye, and the absolute assurance which his voice gave that he was equal to the occasion, were worth a thousand doctors. Those who understand the psychology of suggestion, and the effect of faith on certain diseases, will hardly question the simple accounts given" (*George Fox*, 1903, p. 113). In some cases, as in this of John Banks, "faith" on the part of the patient is contributory to the cure ; but Edward Grubb considers that "looking at these narratives as a whole, the personality of the 'agent' counts for at least as much as and probably for a great deal more than the personality of the 'patient.'" The bearing of the whole subject on some of the miracles of the Gospels is obvious, especially as suggesting that a "miracle" does not necessarily involve any superseding of the laws of the universe, though it does imply a transcending of the *known* laws.

[1] Thomas Story, *Life*, p. 77.
[2] For Leonard Fell (1624-1699), see *Camb. Journ.* i. 408, etc. ; *Beginnings of Quakerism*, p. 102 ; and MS. particulars in Dev. Ho. Portf. 2, No. 7.
[3] J. J. Green, *Autobiography of Henry Lampe*, p. 59 and note.

and travelled extensively, often as companion to Fox. We hear of him in Cornwall, with Roger Haydock, in 1686, when, owing to the persecution, " few came thus far ; and the company of a ministering Friend was precious in those days."[1] Once, travelling alone, he was robbed by a highwayman of his money and his horse. He warned the robber of his evil ways, who, thereupon, threatened to blow out his brains. Leonard answered him, " Though I would not give my life for my money or my horse, I would give it to save thy soul," which so struck home to the man that he returned all that he had taken.[2] We find him joining in the 1677 paper against Wilkinson and Story ; and he kept his vigour as late as 1695, when he composed a difficult difference between Sedbergh Friends,[3] and " dear, ancient Leonard Fell " paid his last visit to Scotland " in the ancient spring of life."[4]

As a rule, the " public Friends," as the ministers were often called, spent most of their lives in ordinary business and in local service, setting themselves free from time to time for journeys away from home, or attendance at the Yearly Meeting. This was the case with such men as Thomas Salthouse, who settled at St. Austell, but often visited the Western counties, Steven Crisp of Colchester, John Whitehead and others. George Whitehead was now a grocer in Houndsditch, Ambrose Rigge a schoolmaster in Surrey. The conditions had changed, and no longer presented the rare opportunity of earlier days ; and Quakerism itself had lost much of its first ardour and was becoming over-absorbed in Church organization.

There are few books with more of the pith of Quakerism in them than the *Journal* of John Gratton.[5] The readers of my former volume have shared the enthusiasms of the ardent Publishers of Truth whose eager service fell in the intense days of the Common-

---

[1] MS. Journ. of Thomas Gwin, of Falmouth.
[2] Barclay's *Select Anecdotes*.
[3] Westmorland Q.M. Minutes, 4th Jan., 5th April 1695.
[4] *J.F.H.S.* xii. 143.
[5] Edited by John Whiting, and published with Gratton's writings in 1720. I have used the 1779 edition.

wealth, when the flame of their experience ran like a fire through England : how fared it with a man who came to his work in years when Dissent was proscribed and the clergy were in the seat of insolent power? Gratton was the Apostle of Quakerism to " a poor, unworthy and despised people, scattered amongst the rocky mountains and dark valleys of the High Peak country " in Derbyshire.[1] He had been earnest-minded from a boy, and became a Presbyterian ; but when the pastors left their flocks on Black Bartholomew-day, he tried the Episcopal way of worship and found it to consist in ceremony and in outward things without life. Then he associated with a " mixed multitude," made up of Independents, Presbyterians and Baptists, but the Conventicle Act dispersed them, and he consorted for a time with an Independent Church at Chesterfield :

" When we went to meetings," he says, " we were cautioned to go as privately as might be ; so that they went several ways, one under one hedge-side and another under another, that we might not be taken notice of, to meet as we could. Then, when we came to the meeting-places, scouts or watchers were set to see and to give notice, that if a magistrate came we might all run away and break up our meeting."

Leaving these, he " continued alone, like one that had no mate or companion." The young apprentice fell into great distresses of mind ; and body and soul were sick nigh unto death.

" But, after I was pretty well again," he says, " I went to the moor to pull heath, and being alone . . . began to think that that which I had sometimes felt so sweet and precious, and sometimes as a swift witness, a reprover, a just judge, and a condemner of all unrighteousness, was the Holy Spirit of God ; and remembered that I had been often visited by it, and yet did not know it."

He spent a Sunday in talk at a Friend's house ; and a man there who was newly convinced spoke to Gratton's condition and reached the witness of God in him, " a man

---

[1] From opening sentences of the Monyash M.M. Minute Book, Feb. 1673, in Gratton's handwriting. See *J.F.H.S.* iii. 82.

of small appearance and slow utterance, and one that never used to preach in meetings." The same day, as he climbed out of a deep valley through the woods up to the bare hillside, he had a vision; and saw "a people laid close one by another in a very low place, lower than the other parts of the earth, where they lay still and quiet." He knew that they were the Lord's people, and saw them to be the poor, despised Quakers, who were scorned by all. He passed through a village, in a strange frame of mind, his countenance altered, and on the hilltop came to know life's issues clearly, as he rested on a stile.

He saw that if he would be a true follower of the Lamb he must forsake the world, and part with the good name he had among men. It went hard with him to think of losing all for Christ; and the cross was so great that he could not then take it up. By the time he was got home, he had almost persuaded himself that visions and revelations were all ceased, and it was presumption for a man to look for the Spirit of God to be given him. So he flung off the day's experiences and trampled the visitation under his feet.

He now heard of the high claims made by Lodowick Muggleton,[1] who had followers in Derbyshire, and studied his books, thinking in his simplicity that no man would dare to claim a commission from God to bless and to curse, unless it were really true. He found, however, that the Muggletonians had no worship:

... when we met together, those few that were, at one Widow Carter's, we were not for either waiting upon God, or for any other exercise at all of either preaching, praying or reading Holy Scriptures: no, we had no more to do but to believe Muggleton and be saved: so we spent some time in discourse and then parted. ... If he blessed us, we were blessed, live as we would; but, if he cursed us, we were cursed; there was no remedy.

Thrown back on himself, and settling at Monyash, he

---

[1] See *Beginnings of Quakerism*, pp. 19-21, and *ante*, p. 244. Derbyshire, I understand, still contains Muggletonians, who used to hold a Yearly Meeting at the Union Inn, Denby, near Heanor, now the Drury Lowe Arms. Some London Muggletonians came down. Cf. *J.F.H.S.* vii. 62, by my informant Edward Watkins. The Widow Carter was Dorothy Carter, mentioned in Muggleton's *The Neck of the Quakers Broken*. Cf. Gratton's *Journal*, p. 101.

came among a company of earnest Baptists. The meeting was sometimes at his house,[1] and though not dipped, he was allowed on one occasion to speak, which he did so earnestly " that tears ran down." " I was like a bottle uncorked," he says, " and the power of the Spirit flowed in me, and when it stopped I ceased to speak."

The Second Conventicle Act was now out, with its heavy fines, and Gratton found the Baptists shrinking from the penalties, " but there was one that I loved best desired they might meet as they had done formerly." He again became a religious solitary, going sometimes, however, to the house of a woman " who pretended to live without meat," where he met with professors of all sorts. He now remembered his former vision and visitation ; and knew the baptism of the Holy Ghost and fire, until his pride and empty knowledge and notions and opinions, and the faith that he had gained by the wisdom of man, were all burnt up. One day in corn harvest (1670), riding on a journey, illumination came to him :

. . . "so that," he writes, " I was in my inward man full of the power and presence of Almighty God, and His heavenly, glorious light shone in me mightily . . . and I saw that it was the Lord's Holy Spirit that appeared in me ; and I believed and could do no otherwise."

His soul was filled with joy ; and living faith sprang in him, for he felt power and strength to believe. When he came home, he kept his exercise of soul for a time to himself ; and then attended his first Friends' meeting, I think at Eyam,[2] where he was well satisfied, though few words were said.

And there arose a sweet melody, that went through the meeting ; and the presence of the Lord was in the midst of us ; and more true comfort, refreshment and satisfaction did I meet with from the Lord in that meeting than ever I had in any meeting in all my life before.

---

[1] G. Lyon Turner, *Original Records of Nonconformity*, i. 53.
[2] The *Journal* says, " Exton, at one Widow Farnay's house, whose husband had been an honest Friend." I think this may be Eyam, where in 1665 Richard Furnis and Margt. his wife were excommunicated for being Quakers (*J.F.H.S.* iv. 70).

He was now known for a Quaker and ridiculed accordingly; though it was not till a little later that he adopted the plain language and the refusal of hat-honour. He closes this part of his *Journal* with a finely worded prose hymn of praise to God.

The young man of twenty-eight[1] soon became a Publisher of Truth. At his third Quaker meeting he spoke with power out of his own rich and deep experience. A few days later, in a garden at Tideswell, he declared Truth for four hours, his countenance so much changed that there arose a reasoning among the people whether he were John Gratton or no. A woman was convinced whose husband was a Muggletonian; and the prophet thereupon sent him an epistolary curse. Preaching at Matlock on the following First-day, the people, he says, "looked earnestly upon me, at which I marvelled, but perceived it was at a laced band which I had upon my collar," whereupon his wife took off all the rest of his bands; and stripped his dress of all superfluity, a thing which he saw the Holy Spirit did not allow of, "either in apparel or anything else." A time of rapid and extensive itinerant work followed in the North Midlands, and in the High Peak district, where meetings were settled and many of his relations were convinced. "I ran to and fro," he says, "and Truth prospered gloriously." The Monyash Monthly Meeting Minute Book begins with an entry in Gratton's handwriting, which shows that the chief convincement in the district took place in 1672, no doubt as the result of his service.[2]

The story throws a vivid light on the religious condition of the times. We still find, and are perhaps surprised to find, a widespread latent Puritanism; but it maintains itself furtively and is bereft of its leaders; the outward strength is in the hands of its oppressors, and an inward experience able to triumph over every adverse circumstance is known to few. Even some of

---

[1] The *Journal* says in margin "born about 1641 or 1642"; but, as he died in March 1712 in his 69th year, this should be 1643.
[2] *J.F.H.S.* iii. 83.

XIII WORK OF TRAVELLING MINISTERS

the Derbyshire Quakers, in Gratton's Baptist days, are reported as keeping their conventicle on a moor,[1] and there were cases of weakness in Nottinghamshire.[2] " The word of the Lord was precious in those days ; there was no open vision." At such a time the ardent Publisher of Truth found his chief work in a steadfast witness-bearing which strengthened the faith of those who were convinced and made Truth noble in the eyes of the world. The worth of his service could not be judged by the direct results ; for in that evil day it was of priceless value to England that a small remnant of heroic souls, undefeated and undismayed, should play their part in feeding the inward spiritual flame by which alone a nation truly lives.

[1] G. Lyon Turner, *Original Records of Nonconformity*, i. 53.
[2] Notts Q.M. Minutes, 26th Sept. 1670, 27th March 1671.

CHAPTER XIV

FORMULATION OF FAITH

(Cf. the discussion of the subject by Rufus M. Jones, *supra*, Introduction.)

The Faith which is essential to Christianity [is] . . . the response of a man's whole being to the love and grace of God, when this is inwardly revealed to him. It is not only a belief in truth (cognitive), but a surrender to truth (volitional). . . . To think that we have defined our faith, when we have only defined the cognitive side of it, is to treat the definition of the less important part of it as if it were the definition of the whole. If this definition is imposed as an article of faith, we shall only secure a Christianity of notions instead of a Christianity of experience. . . . The essence of Christianity is a personal and collective life in which the experience and character of Jesus Christ are being (in some real measure) reproduced in His disciples. . . . We do not in the least deprecate the attempt, which must be made since man is a rational being, to formulate intellectually the ideas which are implicit in religious experience. . . . But it should always be recognized that all such attempts are provisional, and can never be assumed to possess the finality of ultimate truth. There must always be room for development and progress, and Christian thought and inquiry should never be fettered by theory.—Statement on "The True Basis of Christian Unity," issued with approval of LONDON YEARLY MEETING, 1917.

RELIGION to the first Friends was supremely an intercourse with the Divine, which set them in a place of vision and power and joy, and enabled them to see the things of time in the light of eternity. It was an experience which transformed the whole nature and gave new values to every part of life. As Crisp says in one of his sermons:

There is a people raised by God that feel life in their worship, in their families, in their conversations and in their behaviour towards their relations. They do what they do as to God. Many lads and lasses, men-servants and women-servants, they do their work and service, not barely to please their master and mistress, but to please God: the life they live is by the faith of the Son of God; they live as becomes the members of His body.[1]

---

[1] *Sermons*, 1697, pt. ii. p. 30.

FORMULATION OF FAITH

The Friend had a life within him to wait on and to obey, not chiefly a creed to believe; and it was this life which developed in the Quaker groups a common body of truths to which they sought to bear unflinching witness. Accordingly they accumulated "testimonies" rather than Articles of Faith; and these were put into writing by way of advice to the Church itself, and as a witness to the world; but were not at first thought of apart from the living experience behind them, which was the source of their authority. They represented a particular application of Truth expressed in life, not necessarily the final or perfect Truth.

Much of the counsel which had behind it the united judgment of the Church was issued by the Yearly Meeting in its epistles; but it was not till 1738 that, at the request of Yorkshire Quarterly Meeting, this was digested into a body of practice and discipline, in folio volumes circulated in manuscript, usually called "Books of Extracts."[1] The topics were arranged alphabetically, with some incongruous mixture of subjects:—" Appeals, Arbitrations, Books, Certificates, Children . . . Fighting, Kings and Governors, Law, Love, Marriage, Meeting Houses . . . Negroes, Oaths, Orphans, Parliament . . . Schools, Scriptures, Servants, Singing . . . Tithes, Tombstones, Trading, etc." At one revision of the book in the last century, Friends spent some hours in approving the extracts on Love and desired an adjournment, but Josiah Forster, of Tottenham, pressed them to go on with the next section. Upon this, William Ball, another leading Tottenham Friend, who wrote verses, circulated the following impromptu:[2]

>   Slow coaches all are we
>   Beside Josiah's carriage:
>   Four hours we've spent on "Love";
>   He's ready now for "Marriage."

---

[1] The MS. copy I have used is called, "Christian and Brotherly Advices, Given forth from time to time By the Yearly Meetings in London, Alphabetically Digested under Proper heads." The Yorkshire Minute was passed at the spring Q.M. in 1735; see "Yorkshire Q.M. of Friends, 1650–1900," by John S. Rowntree, pp. 12, 13. The Oxfordshire Q.M. Minutes, 1706–1708, show that Abstracts of the Y.M. Advices were being kept by the M.M.'s from the early years of the century.

[2] *Recollections of Tottenham Friends*, by Theodore Compton, p. 70.

378   SECOND PERIOD OF QUAKERISM   CHAP.

The extracts first took a printed form in 1783, but doctrinal statements, put forth by George Fox, or by the Society, at various dates carefully noted, were only incorporated in 1834 at the time of the Hicksite and "Beacon" controversies. These statements had been originally made to satisfy a suspicious outside world with respect to the general orthodoxy of Friends, and are consequently seriously defective on the side of the distinctive Quaker experience. The earliest we possess was written in 1657 by Christopher Holder and John Copeland, then in prison at Boston in New England,[1] to rebut the charge that Quakers were blasphemers, heretics and deceivers, and is expressed in scripture language, the doctrine of the Inner Light only appearing in the postscript. The famous epistle of Fox to the Governor of Barbados, in 1671, has a similar character. "It deals only slightly and feebly with the distinctive truths of the Quaker message; it is . . . a document written to clear Friends of slander and heresy on points of catholic, *i.e.* universal Christianity."[2]   A formal statement issued by the Morning Meeting on behalf of the Society was printed in 1693 at the time of the Keith division, in order to satisfy others as to the beliefs of Friends with respect to the person and work of Christ.[3]   It was written by George Whitehead, and

---

[1] Printed in Bowden, *Hist. of Friends in America*, i. 90-93, from a MS. brought to light by Goold Brown, of New York, the Quaker grammarian. See also *Quakers in the American Colonies*, pp. 67, 68.

[2] This is given in the main in Doctrinal Part of the London Y.M. Discipline, and is also referred to in the Uniform Discipline adopted by many of the American Y.M.'s as a result of the Indianapolis Conference of 1897. The Uniform Discipline said :—"For more explicit and extended statements of belief reference is made to those officially put forth at various times, especially to the letter of George Fox to the Governor of Barbados, in 1671, and to the Declaration of Faith issued by the Richmond Conference in 1887." At the Indianapolis Five Years' Meeting in 1912, the precise meaning of this reference was considered ; and it was decided that "these documents are historic statements of belief, approved by the Five Years' Meeting . . . but they are not to be regarded as constituting a creed." The letter is usually printed from the *Ellwood Journal*, ii. 155-158. For original form, see *Camb. Journ.* ii. 197-202. Cf. *Quakers in the American Colonies*, pp. 111, 112, from which I quote.

[3] Printed in Sewel, ii. 497-508, and some of it in the present Doctrinal Part of the London Y.M. Discipline, though not the sections as to the Inward Light. The Discipline contains no adequate statement of this fundamental Quaker principle.

submitted in the ordinary way to the Morning Meeting. After being read by a committee it was ordered to be read again "in a pretty full Morning Meeting," and was then approved and signed by Whitehead and six other leading Friends.[1] It is the most adequate of any of the early statements; and is amply authenticated by scripture references.

Doctrinal belief, laying the emphasis in religion on an intellectual assent to Truth, was rightly regarded by the early Friends as a barren substitute for a living inward experience of Christ. As William Penn puts it:

It is not opinion, or speculation, or notions of what is true, or assent to, or the subscription of articles or propositions, though never so soundly worded, that . . . makes a man a true believer or a true Christian; but it is a conformity of mind and practice to the will of God, in all holiness of conversation, according to the dictates of this Divine principle of light and life in the soul, which denotes a person truly a child of God.[2]

"We have undertaken," writes Rufus M. Jones to-day,[3] "to demonstrate and exhibit that true religion is the life of God in the lives of men: to present a gospel, growing, expanding, progressing, with the enlarging life of the race, grounded in the central truth that God is forever humanly revealing Himself, suffering over sin, condemning evil, making hearts burn with His love and sacrifice, and working now as He worked formerly in Galilee and Judaea."

Clear thinking, however, has its important, though subordinate, part to play; for religion, as we are now learning, is a growth out of the whole nature of man, in which intellect, emotions, and will are all concerned. Theological and philosophical statements are accordingly of high value, if so made as to satisfy such conditions as the following. Are they put forward not dogmatically but educationally, so as to bring the soul to its own great moments of discovery? Are they given as final verdicts, or only as provisional statements capable of further

---

[1] Minutes of Morning Meeting, 6th, 7th and 13th Feb. 1693. The postscript was approved 20th Feb.
[2] *A Key*, etc., sect. 2.
[3] Swarthmore Lecture, 1908, *Quakerism a Religion of Life*, p. 17.

expansion? What inspiring experience of the Church lies behind the necessarily imperfect words that are used? Above all, has the definition pressed out the life and wonder of the truth, or does it allow these to be felt?

It is because the utterances of the saintly Isaac Penington satisfy these conditions in a high degree, that his writings, in spite of their unsystematic character and their serious limitations of thought, afford the best clue to the theological explanation that the Quakerism of the seventeenth century had to give of its religious faith. He understood the essentially educational method of his Master, Who withstood again and again the temptation to assert a Divine authority which should force an external acceptance of His kingdom; and chose instead the slow and sure achievement among men of an inward kingdom, which, like His own relation to His Father, should rest on heart allegiance and joyful obedience. Listen to Penington on the right method for evangelists:

> They must not lift up themselves by their gifts; they must not hereupon lord it over others; or hold forth their knowledge or doctrines and think to make others bow thereto; but wait in their service till the Lord make way into men's hearts and plant His Truth there; and upon Him also must they wait for the watering and growth of it.[1]

Accordingly he had a true discerning of the work of a minister:

> The great work of the minister of Christ is to keep the conscience open to Christ; and to preserve men from receiving any truths of Christ as from them, further than the Spirit opens; or to imitate any of their practices further than the Spirit leads, guides and persuades them. For persons are exceeding prone to receive things as truths, from those whom they have an high opinion of; and to imitate their practices; and so hurt their own growth and endanger their souls. For if I receive a truth before the Lord by His Spirit make it manifest to me, I lose my guide and follow but the counsel of the flesh, which is exceeding

---

[1] From "An Examination of the grounds or causes which are said to induce the Court of Boston in New England to make that order or Law of Banishment upon pain of death against the Quakers," in *Works*, 1681 edn. pt. i. p. 238, originally published in 1660.

greedy of receiving truths and running into religious practices without the Spirit.[1]

Penington's own remarkable travel to the Quaker experience has been told in my former book.[2] The son of a "Parliament Grandee," he had been bred in a refined Puritanism; and continued to feel a real unity with the early Puritan state, before it had lost its savour, with later outcomes.[3] He was already a man of forty-two and a practised author when he joined the despised Quakers in 1658. During the twenty-one years of his later life he suffered five imprisonments at Aylesbury and one at Reading, some five years' confinement in all—often in cold, damp, and unhealthy rooms, that nearly cost him his life. These were either without legal warrant or under shameful colour of law, as when he was taken in Amersham street while attending a funeral, or in Reading gaol while visiting the prisoners.[4] Says Robert Jones, one of the Buckinghamshire Friends:[5]

I do not remember that ever I saw him cast down or dejected in his spirit in the time of his close confinement, nor speak hardly of those that persecuted him. . . . O the remembrance of the glory that did often overshadow us in the place of confinement, that indeed the prison was made by the Lord unto us, Who was powerfully with us, as a pleasant palace.

He was much occupied in writing, and in travail of soul, "being," says one of his many private religious letters,[6] "retired in spirit and mourning to my God, for the powerful bringing forth of His pure life yet more perfectly both in myself and others."

Literature is the art of using words and matter so as to express personality. It may be present in a phrase and absent from an encyclopaedia. The writings of

---

[1] *Works*, p. 239. Later in his life Penington had to clear himself from the charge of excluding all government in the Church by this earlier piece (see "Some Misrepresentations," etc., in *Works*, pt. ii. pp. 418-437, published in 1681, after his death).
[2] *Beginnings of Quakerism*, pp. 501-506.
[3] See John Barclay's *Letters of Isaac Penington*, Nos. 4, 55, 66. These are from Dev. Ho. Penington Colln., made by his son John.
[4] An account of his various imprisonments is given in Ellwood's Testimony, at beginning of Penington's *Works*.   [5] Testimony, *Works*.
[6] Barclay's *Letters of Isaac Penington*, No. 18.

Penington, collected in 1681, two years after his death, under the title of *The Works of the Long-Mournful and Sorely-Distressed Isaac Penington*, and written "in the springings of . . . light, life, and holy power," are, in form, unequal, though sometimes strangely beautiful, but as expressions of personality have the pure savour of wafts from the unsullied air of some spiritual Araby. Their cool and healing waters spring from the depths, from regions of being beyond the reach of circumstance and below the cultivated soil of the reason. Vauvenargues has a far-reaching maxim: "Great thoughts come from the heart."[1] Penington's place of study was his heart, where he held converse with the Heart of the universe. When at work here, he excluded, so far as he knew, all intruders, especially the earthly-minded side of his own intellect. I may be allowed to summarize the account which he gives of his method of meditation.[2]

First, he says, "wait for the key of knowledge which is God's gift." This is needed before the true way to the meaning of the scriptures is opened; and the creaturely activity which would search them merely in its own understanding is to be repressed. Nor must the understanding have the handling of the key when it is given. The Divine Hand that gave can alone turn it aright. It is not the understanding that is to be fed by the scriptures but the heart. Nor is any fruit of the tree of life to be grafted upon the tree of knowledge. The life within and not the intellect is the treasury in which knowledge is to be stored, and bread will be provided out of this life for the day's needs. Accordingly, there should be no resting in past openings of truth, although made by the true key. "As for instance, to make it more plain: There may be a knowledge of justification, by the Spirit's opening the words written in scripture concerning justification and the blood of sprinkling; and this is a good knowledge . . . but then there is a knowledge by feeling of the blood of sprinkling in the heart and by seeing with the new eye the way of its justification; and in this knowledge is the power and the cleansing of the life received, which in the other was but spoken of." "Therefore," he adds, "rest not in openings or prophecies, or true meanings

---

[1] Maxim, No. 127.
[2] *Works*, pt. i. pp. 124-126, from "An Axe," etc. Cf. pp. 114, 115, and George Fox, as cited in *Beginnings of Quakerism*, p. 33.

of these things—though this kind of knowledge is very excellent and hath been very rare—but wait to feel the thing itself which the words speak of, and to be united by the living Spirit to that; and then thou hast a knowledge from the nature of the thing itself." Lastly, when this living, inward experience comes, seek its preservation in the spring of its own life. "Learn how to abide in the life, and to keep all that's given thee there; and have nothing which thou mayst call thine own any more, but to be lost in thyself and found in Him. Know the Land of the Living, wherein all the things of life live, and can live nowhere else."

Penington's writings are the fruits of such rigorous meditation. One or two deserve to be widely known, especially the piece entitled "Some of the Mysteries of God's Kingdom glanced at," published in 1663.[1] But he was fettered by the dualistic thought of the age, which put the natural and the Divine in two separate compartments, and accordingly he fails, like others of the early Friends, to reach a unified conception either of human personality or of the person of Christ. "Man," he says, "by nature is dead in trespasses and sins, quite dead and his conscience wholly dark."[2] The Light of the Spirit of Christ which shines into his darkness is another thing than his own nature. It shines upon all, and, if received, begets them into its own life. All that is of the flesh or of the understanding is outside this Divine order of life, though it may become the medium through which the Life works. This conception, with all the splendid truth of its emphasis on life and on vital processes, led Penington to a view of Jesus as a vessel through which the Divine Life worked and of man as such a vessel, if he gave entrance to the Life, which divided rather than unified personality, and, through such division, failed to give either the Historic Christ, possessed of a human mind and body, or the mind and body of man a full place in the purposes of God.[3] No explanation of the mystery of the

---

[1] *Works*, pt. i. pp. 415-426, cited *ante*, p. 326, and *post*, p. 397.
[2] See "The Scattered Sheep Sought after," in *Works*, pt. i. pp. 44-61, published in 1659.
[3] On the whole subject I gratefully acknowledge much help from Edward Grubb's Swarthmore Lecture, 1914, *The Historic and the Inward Christ*, written with the candour, care and spiritual insight which are found in all his books.

Incarnation can satisfy which breaks the unity of our Lord's own self-consciousness. " Separate God and man," said Nayler,[1] " and He is no more Christ." Penington, in his own mind, came to make a sharp distinction [2]

... between that which is called the Christ and the bodily garment which He took. The one was flesh, the other Spirit. ... The body of flesh was but the veil; Heb. x. 20. The eternal life was the substance veiled. The one He did partake of, as the rest of the children did, the other was He which did partake thereof; Heb. ii. 14. The one was the body which was prepared for the life, for it to appear in and be made manifest; Heb. x. 5. The other was the life or light itself, for whom the body was prepared; who took it up; appeared in it to do the will; Ps. xl. 7, 8; and was made manifest to those eyes which were able to see through the veil wherewith it was covered; Jno. i. 14.

The passage relied on in Heb. x. 5 follows the Septuagint of Ps. xl. 6, which reads " a body hast Thou prepared me," instead of the Hebrew, " ears hast Thou digged for me," by which is meant that God has opened the ears of the speaker to hear His voice. We could not to-day rest an argument as to the person of Christ upon a supposed Messianic Psalm, still less upon the adoption in a New Testament book of a Septuagint reading which is probably based on a corruption in the Hebrew or is a corruption in the Greek. But, in the dualistic mental atmosphere of the time, some such theory naturally arose among Friends to explain the co-existence of the Divine and the human in Christ and in human personality; and the verse in Hebrews came as a welcome support to such a theory, and lent it sharp and perilous definition.[3] Pening-

---

[1] *Saul's Errand to Damascus*, 1653, p. 31, also in *Works*, p. 14.

[2] *Works*, pt. i. p. 204, from "An Examination of the Grounds or Causes, etc." Cf. passages cited by Edward Grubb, *op. cit.* p. 35, from " A Question to the Professors of Christianity," published in 1667, and printed in *Works*, pt. ii. pp. 1-35, see pp. 19, 12. In a later piece, " The Flesh and Blood of Christ," published in 1675, and printed in *Works*, pt. ii. pp. 180-196, Penington says of Christ's death (p. 186) : " It was a spotless sacrifice of great value and effectual for the remission of sins ; and I do acknowledge humbly unto the Lord the remission of my sins thereby ; and bless the Lord for it, even for giving up His Son to death for us all ; and giving all that believe in His Name and Power to partake of remission through Him."

[3] Edward Grubb thinks the argument a discovery of Penington, and says : " It is hardly too much to say that some of the greatest troubles and disasters through which the Society of Friends has passed were caused by this theory based

ton himself had no intention of slighting the manhood of Christ. He says in one of his letters:[1]

> We own Christ to be a Saviour; but we lay the main stress upon the life which took upon it the manhood. And that life, wherever it appears, is of a saving nature: and doth save . . . yet none, in the measure of this life, can deny the appearance of the fulness of life in that body of flesh, and what He did therein towards the redemption and salvation of mankind.

Penington's mode of expression is followed by Penn,[2] but Robert Barclay avoids using Heb. x. 5 in his *Apology*; and the Declaration of 1693 is equally cautious and treats the question with great circumspection.

> To preach faith in the same Christ, both as within and without us, cannot be to preach two Christs, but one and the same Lord Jesus Christ (1 Cor. viii. 6), having respect to those degrees of our spiritual knowledge of Christ Jesus in us, and to His own unspeakable fulness and glory as in Himself in His own entire being; wherein Christ Himself and the least measure of His Light or Life (as in us or in mankind) are not divided nor separable, no more than the sun is from its light.[3]

This modest statement is content with affirming the value both of the historic life of Christ in the flesh and of the inward experience of His life, without attempting to explain their relation to one another fully; and, as we shall see, was wiser, in that age of dualistic thought, than an acceptance of the theory of Penington as to the prepared body or of Barclay's conception of a *vehiculum Dei*, which we must now consider.

It is to Barclay that we owe the most systematic formulation of the Quaker faith. I have already pointed

---

on an erroneous Greek text." He finds the earliest use of it in William Bayly's "Short Discovery of the State of Man," dated 24th June 1659 (*Works*, p. 94). See also, more at length, his "Deep calleth unto Deep," 1663 (*ibid.* pp. 299-301). It also occurs in George Fox the younger, *Works*, pp. 153, 195, in a piece published in 1660 and another dated 12th March 1661. The Docetism of the early centuries was, in the same way, due to the attempt to combine Christianity with Greek and Jewish philosophic dualism. (See article on "Docetism" by Adrian Fortescue in Hastings' *Encyclopaedia of Religion and Ethics*.)

[1] John Barclay's *Letters of Isaac Penington*, No. 17, about 1669, which contains the fullest statement of his position that I know. Cf. Nos. 48, 86, and quotation *supra*, p. 384 note.

[2] For Penn's views, see his *Serious Apology* (1671), in *Works*, 1726 edn. ii. 32.   [3] Sewel, ii. 499.

out[1] that in Scotland the men who had force to break through the Presbyterian system to Quakerism were men well-grounded in doctrine, who added their new experience of the Inward Light to an existing scheme of thought, and did not allow it to dominate the whole conception of religion quite as completely as had been the case with the Yorkshire and Westmorland Seekers of 1652. Side by side with their distinctive Quaker convictions they held many of the other great religious conceptions of their day; and found themselves under a necessity of harmonizing the new and the old in their own thought, and of publishing the results for the vindication of Friends from unwarranted aspersions, and for the spread of the Truth. This is the simple account to be given of the origin of Barclay's famous *Apology* and of the reason for its title. The corporate consciousness that had come to Friends with the organization established by Fox was bound to crave for some systematic manual of Quaker principles; and the work fell to the man of the period who was best fitted for the task, by his learning, which was considerable, but still more by his well-balanced judgment.

In 1673 he printed a *Catechism and Confession of Faith*; next, a series of fifteen propositions called *Theses Theologicae*; and lastly, the *Apology*, grounded on these, which appeared in Latin in 1676, and in English two years later. Penn tells us that it came out at the close of a long and sharp engagement between English Friends and a confederacy of adverse critics, and was designed to prevent erroneous charges in the future.[2] Published in Latin at Amsterdam, it does not seem to have been subjected to the censorship of the Morning Meeting, and accordingly lacked any official *imprimatur*, though afterwards in the highest repute among Friends.[3] It was a

[1] *Ante*, p. 334.   [2] Preface to Barclay's *Works*, p. xxi.
[3] See *ante*, p. 184 *n*. John Bellers was foremost in urging the reprinting of the *Apology* in large edns. for circulation to Members of Parliament, etc. (see "An Abstract of George Fox's advice," etc. 1724, pp. 17-19). Up to 1800 there were 8 English, 3 Irish, and 4 American edns.; 2 each in Latin, Dutch, and French, 1 each in Spanish and Danish, and 3 in German (see Smith's *Catalogue*).

great achievement for a young man of twenty-seven to accomplish, even though we allow for much help received from his friend, George Keith, who was ten years his senior and probably a still riper scholar.[1] The *Apology* was a direct challenge to much of the Westminster Confession and the Shorter Catechism (1646–48), which were the maturest and latest formulation of scripture-truth as it appeared to cultured and devout Puritans. Though decked out in abundant learning and often scholastic in its terms and its form of argument, it was the work of a man who cared nothing for School Divinity, and felt that God "hath chosen a few despicable and unlearned instruments, as He did fishermen of old, to publish His pure and naked Truth, and to free it of these mists and fogs wherewith the clergy hath clouded it."[2]

Barclay at the close of the *Apology* claims that the candid reader will find the Christian religion vindicated in all its parts, as a living, inward, spiritual, pure and substantial thing, and not a mere form, show, shadow, notion and opinion. The despised Quakers have been raised up to pull down the corrupt image and shell of Christianity, wherewith antichrist hath deceived the nations. Though they be few in numbers, neither men nor devils shall be able to quench the little spark, but it shall grow to consume all that opposes it. He that hath arisen in them shall go on in His Arm of Power in His spiritual manifestation, until He hath conquered all enemies and the kingdoms of the earth become the Kingdom of Christ Jesus.

---

[1] Keith, when a clergyman of the Church of England, wrote in 1702 a powerful and on the whole temperate criticism of the *Apology*, called *The Standard of the Quakers examined*, in which he claims, as I think correctly, that Barclay followed him in many of his arguments, "as he did in many or most of his distinctions and terms, not to be found in the Quakers' Books that wrote before me . . . and also in his way and method of prosecuting his arguments, both from scripture and authorities of Ancients, most of which last he had by me and by my collection" (p. 22). Cf. Preface and pp. 230, 231, 241, showing that the quotations were in some cases taken at second-hand. Keith's collection, to which Barclay thus had access, was made partly from his own reading and partly from Vossius, Grotius and the Remonstrants in Holland (p. 23). There is an interesting examination of Barclay's indebtedness to Keith, by John Eliot (1771–1830), in *The Yorkshireman* (1834), vol. iii. pp. 4-15.

[2] Address to Clergy in *Theses Theologicae* at beginning of *Apology*.

Barclay's mind, throughout his treatise, is occupied mainly with two convictions—the current conception of the innate depravity of human nature, from which he was not able to escape, and the conviction, grounded in his own living experience, of the inwardness of religion as the power of a universal and saving Divine life incarnated in Jesus, but, in measure, a living gift of God seeking out all men.[1] Owing to the obsession of the first conviction, as Edward Grubb puts it,[2] "the Calvinism of Barclay the Scotchman lay only a little way below the surface. Man, he says, can do absolutely nothing to bring about his own salvation; God must have all the glory. The only thing that man can do is to *wait* for the grace to come—for the moving of the Spirit, the shining of the Light—and not resist it when it works."[3] The permanent value of the *Apology* lies not in the imperfect success which attended Barclay's efforts to press the Quaker experience into these moulds of thought, and thus vindicate it to his own age, but in the sureness of emphasis with which, in spite of them, he is continually asserting that religion is an inward spiritual life received from God and transforming human nature. He accordingly regarded (Prop. iii.) the scriptures as a "declaration of the fountain, and not the fountain itself," though again and again appealing to them as "a secondary rule, subordinate to the Spirit, from which they have all their excellency and certainty."

We now turn to his elaborate doctrine of the Seed, or Divine principle in the hearts of all men. He says:[4]

---

[1] The Latin *Apology* entitles Prop. ii. "Concerning inward and immediate revelation," instead of "Concerning immediate revelation." Any future edn. should include a careful comparison of the Latin and English, which differ in many places.

[2] *Authority and the Light Within*, p. 82. He says: (Preface) "Out of this inconsistency has come division within the Society of Friends itself, and to it we may probably look for one of the chief though hidden causes of its failure to move the world. . . . [Their truth] needs to be restated in modern language, and in the light of modern knowledge."

[3] See in proof, Props. v. vi. sect. 17. It is to be noted that the Hebrew word *qavah*, "wait for," had probably (see the Oxford *Hebrew and English Lexicon* (1906), p. 875) the root idea of twisting and stretching, and so of the tension of enduring and waiting; cf. the noun *qav*, "a line." Accordingly it had by no means a merely passive sense, but was an active stretching out of the soul before God.

[4] Props. v. vi. sect. 13, and following sections. Comparison with the Latin shows that the English form is throughout carefully revised.

By this Seed, Grace and Word of God, and Light, wherewith we say every man is enlightened . . . we understand not the proper essence and nature of God, precisely taken, which is not divisible into parts and measures . . . but we understand a spiritual, heavenly and invisible Principle, in which God, as Father, Son and Spirit, dwells; a measure of which Divine and glorious life is in all men as a Seed, which of its own nature draws, invites and inclines to God; and this we call *vehiculum Dei*,[1] or the Spiritual Body of Christ, the Flesh and Blood of Christ, which came down from Heaven, of which all the saints do feed, and are thereby nourished unto eternal life. And, as every unrighteous action is witnessed against and reproved by this Light and Seed, so by such actions it is hurt, wounded and slain, and resiles or flees from them, even as the flesh of men flees from that which is of a contrary nature to it. Now, because it is never separated from God nor Christ, but, wherever it is, God and Christ are as wrapped up therein, therefore, and in that respect, as it is resisted, God is said to be resisted; and where it is borne down God is said to be pressed as a cart under sheaves, and Christ is said to be slain and crucified. And, on the contrary, as this Seed is received in the heart, and suffered to bring forth its natural and proper effect, Christ comes to be formed and raised, of which the scripture makes so much mention, calling it the new man, Christ within, the hope of glory.

He proceeds to safeguard the doctrine by a number of distinctions. The saints have the eternal Word mediately, through the Seed, not immediately, as Christ had. It is not a property of God, but a real spiritual substance. The doctrine does not derogate from the atonement of Christ; "remission of sins . . . is only in and by virtue of that most satisfactory sacrifice and no otherwise."[2] The Seed is a *vehiculum Dei*, in which God and Christ

---

[1] As Keith points out (*Standard*, pp. 213, 214) the later English editions, though not the first of Barclay's *Works*, change "this we call" into "this some call," as if Friends "were ashamed of the term, or disliked both term and notion." It had, in fact, been adopted by Barclay from Keith (*Standard*, p. 212). In his *Apology Vindicated*, *Works*, p. 855, Barclay explains the phrase, with the help of some marvellous exegesis, from Song of Sol. iii. 9: "King Solomon made himself a *chariot* of the wood of Lebanon." John Norris (*Two Treatises concerning the Divine Light*, 2nd edn. 1727, p. 165) says that several learned men, upon the reading of John vi., had entertained the notion of a *vehiculum Dei*, both before and after the appearance of Quakerism.

[2] Cf. an early piece by Barclay, "Truth Clear'd of Calumnies," in *Works*, p. 19.

dwell, but this does not mean that Christ is in all men by way of union. It is no part of man's own nature, nor any relics of any good which Adam lost by his fall, but something separate from man's soul and faculties. Reason, indeed, has its place, but cannot profit a man to salvation. It is given him for things natural and earthly, a moon that needs itself to be enlightened by the heavenly sun. Nor is the Seed to be identified with conscience, which may be compared to a lantern, and the Light of Christ to the candle shining in it. A man may stir up his own faculties, but the Light and Seed he cannot stir up ; it strives with him as the Lord sees meet. If he resist it not in the day of his visitation, he comes to know salvation by it.[1] No doubt there are some whom God does not suffer to resist. And, on the other hand, those who perish have to confess that there was a time when the door of mercy was open to them. Thus both the justice and mercy of God are established.

This intricate explanation of the nature of the Light Within fails equally with that of Penington to satisfy us to-day, though we admire the skill with which it secured a place for the principle under the conditions of thought of the age. It lays too little emphasis on the Incarnation and its central place in revelation and in the reconciling of man to God. It does not to our mind establish both the justice and the mercy of·God ; for, while an advance on Calvinism, which gave most men no chance of salvation, Barclay allows very unequal chances, often only a brief one in some unheeded day of visitation. It is beset with a dualism of thought which leaves the relation of the Light to the Divine nature vaguely determined as some mysterious *vehiculum Dei*, and denies that it is in any organic relation, either to man's human nature, or his conscience or his mind. It leaves little place in the Divine purpose for the active faith which springs from the human will reaching out to the Divine will. Accord-

---

[1] He goes on to compare the experience with the moving of the "lake of Bethsaida," apparently following the Vulgate reading in John v. 2. "Pool of the new quarter of the town" (Bezetha), seems the probable reading ; see Rendel Harris, *Sidelights on New Testament Research*, pp. 36-78.

ingly, it is not an adequate expression of the living Quaker experience and would become the parent of a spiritual passivity whose negations would react disastrously in later periods of the Society, especially in the low value placed on ministry and on the intellect. It is true that Barclay, even in his statement of the doctrine, escapes at times from some of its tendencies. As we have seen, he formally recognizes, in the terms of the current orthodoxy, the value of the atonement, though to his mind the outward knowledge of this is to be regarded chiefly as a thing "full of comfort to such as are subject to and led by the inward Seed and Light."

Again, in the comparison of reason to the moon, Barclay seems to admit that the mind, though in his view separate in nature from the Light, can do much to explain and verify spiritual perceptions. Indeed, he wrote his *Apology*, not only "according to the Truth manifested to me by the Spirit of God," but also "according to the dispensation of wisdom given me by God,"[1] recognizing in practice the co-operation of the mind and the Light.

The *Apology* was naturally subjected to serious criticism from men who accepted the current scheme of religious thought. Keith seems to have suggested the theory of a *vehiculum Dei*, a vehicle of God, as the clouds are said to be His chariot,[2] and had himself called the Seed, "not the Godhead itself, but a certain middle nature, substance or being, betwixt the Godhead and mankind."[3] It was a Divine influence, outside a man's proper nature, which, if not resisted, would beget in him a new life. If this medium in which Christ was wrapped up was made the

---

[1] Prop. x. sect. 2, from Latin. The English is fuller, and supports the view that the translated English edn. contains the revisions of the author, though the strange mistranslation of "three angles" by "three sides" in Prop. ii. sect. 15, makes it doubtful whether Barclay made the draft of the translation himself. The English runs: "according to the Truth manifested to me, and revealed *in* me by the testimony of the Spirit, according to that proportion of wisdom given me." In his *Apology Vindicated, Works*, pp. 721-891, he speaks (Intro.) of hastening on the English edn. and corrects the Latin in some places (see pp. 794, 852).

[2] *Standard*, pp. 212-214, with a criticism of the theory.

[3] *The Way to the City of God*, written in 1676, p. 130.

sufficient agent in man's salvation, what adequate place remained for the atonement? Neither the theories of Penington nor the carefully chosen position taken by Barclay resolved this fundamental difficulty, which was strongly pressed by Keith in his later days of controversy with Friends.[1]

From a very different standpoint, John Norris (1657–1711), the rector of Bemerton, near Salisbury, was able to show the insufficiency of Barclay's explanation. He was a disciple of Malebranche[2] and was also influenced by Descartes and the Cambridge Platonists, especially Henry More. We are thus introduced to a circle with close affinities to Quakerism, for Descartes, who died in 1650, had been the intimate friend of the Princess Elizabeth, and More was the spiritual adviser of Lady Conway, who became a Friend.[3]

Fox wrote with appreciation of one of Norris's books, and in reply[4] Norris states his own doctrine:

> I think there is nothing in the world more clear and certain than that:
> 1st. There is a light in man; otherwise how can he know or perceive anything?
> 2ndly. That he is not his own light, or a light to himself.
> 3rdly. That God is his Light; and that in and by the Light of God he sees and understands whatever he sees and understands.
> And that therefore:
> 4thly. In order to all further illumination, this Divine Light is to be consulted and its answers carefully attended to. And I know of no other way of attaining knowledge.

He refers Fox for a fuller treatment of the matter to

---

[1] See *Standard, passim* and *post* p. 485.
[2] Voltaire in the second of his *Letters on England* regards Quakerism as "Malebranche's doctrine to a tittle."
[3] See letters in *J.F.H.S.* vii. 7-17, 49-55, and for Henry More (1614–1687), references in J. B. Mullinger, *Univ. of Cambridge*, iii. especially pp. 606-609. Keith held a correspondence with More, and "notwithstanding his mistakes, I would have Friends," he says, "be very loving and tender to him, as indeed I find still a great love to him in my heart" (Letter to Barclay, 12th May 1676, in *Reliquiae Barclaianae*, pp. ix, x).
[4] Letter to Fox, 15th April 1690, in Dev. Ho. Portf. 4, No. 36.

Reason and Religion, published in 1689. Here he says, in words that have a strangely modern ring :[1]

I think that from these considerations, joined with those of Mr. Malebranche, 'tis clear, even to demonstration, that man is not his own light, or a light to himself . . . but that he sees and knows all things in the Divine Logos, or Ideal World, which is that true Light within him so much talked of by enthusiasts ; . . . that all our light and illumination proceeds wholly from Him who at first said, "Let there be light"; that we see so much of Truth as we see of God ; that the ideas which are in God are the very ideas which we see ; and that the Divine Logos is our wisdom, as well as the wisdom of His Father.

Holding this large conception, he criticises Barclay, first, for holding that the light of the intellect is natural and not spiritual ; and secondly, for making the Light within something other than God. He considers that Barclay makes it a creature of God, and a material creature, though this, I think, goes beyond the Apologist's intention. Norris, however, had no place in his scheme of thought for a *vehiculum Dei*, feeling there could be no middle term between the Creator and the created.[2] But he speaks with generous warmth of Barclay's books :

" I know of no Church . . . but might well be proud of the accession of so considerable a writer " ; " Mr. Barclay is a very great man, and, were it not for that common prejudice that lies

---

[1] 7th edn. (1724), p. 145.
[2] Norris's direct criticism of the Quakers begins with the postscript to *Reason and Religion*, to which Richard Vickris, of Bristol and Chew, made an answer in "A Just Reprehension to John Norris" (1691), passed by the Morning Meeting 26th Oct. 1691, and to be prepared for the press by George Whitehead. Vickris asserts that "The Quakers believe this Divine Light to be the quickness of their understandings to know and of their wills to love and practical [*sic*, for 'practise'] Truth ; and that it assists the natural faculties of the soul in the attainments of necessary arts and sciences, as well as capacitate[s] it to know and practise moral and spiritual truths" (p. 10). Norris replied in *Two Treatises concerning the Divine Light* (1692), the first of which answers Vickris point by point. He shows that Barclay makes the Light of Reason distinct from the Light within, as the moon from the sun (2nd edn., 1727, pp. 182-188). The truth is that Barclay's more precise handling of the question was not always the exact explanation that other Friends would have given of the matter. The second Treatise is in the form of a letter to a friend, and gives the best general account of Norris's difference from Barclay's position. At the time of Vickris's reply, Norris was incumbent of Newton St. Loe, near Bath, only a few miles from Chew. Geo. Whitehead, in 1692, replied to the *Two Treatises* in "The Divine Light of Christ in Man," and Vickris in "Truth and Innocency Defended."

against him as being a Quaker, would be as sure not to fail of that character in the world as any of the finest wits this age has produced"; "I had rather engage against an hundred Bellarmins, Hardings or Stapletons than with one Barclay."[1]

There can be little doubt that the failure, however inevitable under the conditions of the age, to reach a Christology and a conception of human personality which covered all the facts was a serious weakness to Quakerism and in its Quietist period led to a disastrous vagueness of experience which tended to reduce Christianity to obedience to an indefinite principle of life in the soul. As Edward Grubb says of the early Friends:[2]

It should be noted that they have hardly a word to say about the *mind* of Jesus, which, if the Incarnation is to be taken seriously, must have been a human mind. They rarely dwell on the growth of His knowledge, on His consciousness of Himself as a man distinct from God and wholly dependent on Him, on His use of prayer, His experience of temptation, His struggle, deep and intense, though always victorious, to know and do the will of His Father in heaven. . . . This absence of insight into the human mind or self-consciousness of Jesus . . . was universal in their day, as indeed it had been since the first century, except among the Nestorians. . . . Their intense insistence on the inward and spiritual nature of "Christ" . . . led them, however unconsciously and unintentionally, to a relative disparagement of the outward and historical facts of the Incarnation.

They knew a great indwelling experience of a life larger than their own. They found it in the fellowship and silence of their worship; they attuned their lives to its guidance; its life wrought a new life within them and gave them power to live by its Divine law. They felt that here was the very Spirit and life of Christ in its regenerating and enabling might. But, as we have seen, they could not place the experience in its right setting with the truth of the Incarnation. Our own age, far beyond anything possible in the seventeenth century, is equipped for this high task, without which the doctrine

---

[1] The second of the *Two Treatises*, 2nd. edn., 1727, pp. 224, 250. Robert Bellarmin (1542-1621), Thomas Harding (1516-1572), and Thomas Stapleton (1535-1598) were leading Roman Catholic controversialists.
[2] Swarthmore Lecture, *The Historic and the Inward Christ*, p. 51.

of the Inner Light and of spiritual guidance, the value of prayer and of silent worship, and the truth that all men have some faculty of response to the Divine, cannot take their full place in Christian thought and experience. The old dualistic conception of the universe is dead or moribund ; we are learning that below the threshold of our separate consciousness lie regions of personality that unite us to one another and to God in a larger self "which is both our very own and yet common or universal, the self of each and yet the self of all."[1] Science and religion are no longer felt to be at work in discordant spheres of truth. Religious thought is finding in the study of the self-consciousness of Jesus an understanding of His person which unifies the truth both of His humanity and Divinity, and reveals through Him the fullness of personality. In the fellowship of silence we are discovering again what George Fox called "the hidden unity in the Eternal Being."[2] There is opening before us a conception of the wholeness of that great process to which we give the name of life, a conception in which the Historic Christ and the Christ of an inward experience are seen to be one ; and we understand that "the spirit which is within us is not other than the Spirit which upholds and maintains the whole universe and works after the same fashion."[3]

Rufus M. Jones, in a companion volume to the present, has shown how closely the Quaker experience corresponds with that of many earlier Spiritual Reformers.

All the Quaker terms for the Principle were used by Sebastian Franck (1499–1542) and by Caspar Schwenckfeld (1489–1561); and all the men who taught the dynamic process of salvation presuppose that something of the Divine nature, as Light or Seed or Spirit, or the resurrected Christ, is directly operative upon or

---

[1] J. A. Smith, chap. on "Progress as an Ideal of Action," in *Progress and History*, essays edited by F. S. Marvin. For the new psychological standpoint see Rufus M. Jones, Introductions to *Studies in Mystical Religion, Beginnings of Quakerism*, and *Spiritual Reformers in the 16th and 17th Centuries*; cf. John William Graham, *William Penn*, pp. 89-91, and Edward Grubb's books, already quoted.

[2] *Ellwood Journ.* i. 29, cited in *Beginnings of Quakerism*, pp. 38, 39. See also *The Fellowship of Silence*, by various writers, edited by Cyril Hepher, and "Swarthmore Lecture," 1919, by L. Violet Hodgkin.

[3] J. A. Smith, *ubi supra*.

within the human soul. That is, salvation is for them more than a moral change, it is a birth-and-life process, initiated and carried through by the real presence of the Divine in the human.[1]

With our fuller conception of personality, our wider historical outlook, and our philosophic sense of an ultimate Reality which includes and explains the whole of life, we formulate the central experience of Friends differently from Barclay or Penington, or even Norris. We no longer hold the Reason at arm's length or feel it necessary to make a sharp division between the human and the Divine. Penington's speculations about a "prepared body" and Barclay's theory of a *vehiculum Dei* are laid aside. We seek expression for the truth in terms of life unified in God, and verify our formulation out of the experience of the saints of all ages and out of a Bible interpreted in the light of a progressive revelation. Above all we relate it vitally to the consciousness of our Lord, Whose personality we find enriching all our conceptions of the nature and powers of man when in fellowship with God. But this re-interpretation leaves the validity of the Quaker experience undimmed, nay, set in an intenser brightness, illuminated on all sides by the light which has come to other souls, the wisdom more mobile than any motion, pervading and penetrating all things by reason of her pureness, the breath of the power of God and clear effluence of the glory of the Almighty, which, from generation to generation, passing into holy souls, maketh men friends of God and prophets.[2]

To us, then, the experience reached by the early Friends is the thing that matters. Below the scholastic surface of Barclay's writings, we shall seek to penetrate to the deep ocean of Divine life in which he found peace and strength, and to know for ourselves the secret power which touched his heart as he came into the silent assemblies of God's people. Or, with Penington, the Quaker mystic,

---

[1] *Spiritual Reformers*, p. 346. He points out that the passage in Barclay about the *vehiculum Dei* could be exactly paralleled in the writings of Schwenckfeld.

[2] Wisdom vii. 24-27. The controversial piece by Vickris, already mentioned, alludes to this passage.

we shall wait for those inwelling tides which carried him forth into the larger life hid with Christ in God. We shall learn with him that Christ "is the immediate offspring of eternal life in Himself, and the fountain or spring of life unto the creation," that Love "is the sweet, tender, melting nature of God, flowing up through His Seed of life into the creature, and of all things making the creature most like unto Himself, both in nature and operation," that Obedience "is the subjection of the soul to the law of the Spirit," that true Peace "is the stillness, the quietness, the satisfiedness of the heart in God," that Prayer "is the breath of the living child to the Father of Life" and Reconciliation "a bringing together the minds and hearts of God and man into one."[1]

Into this larger life we may still come. Most, perhaps all of my readers, can affirm out of their own experience that the hours when it controls their beings are unforgettable, supreme. We think of great days when the spirit of nature embraced us lovingly and made us brothers and sisters of bird and flower and mountain. We recall times of fellowship, when one common life, one common service thrilled us all. We remember hours of worship in which we found ourselves, as Wordsworth says,[2]

> Rapt into still communion, which transcends
> The imperfect offices of prayer and praise.

We dwell again, very near to God, on some wide-viewed hill, the clamour of the world hushed, the peace of the blue sky around us and the grateful green of dewy mountain lawns. Or we revive some dark hour when He walked with us through the valley of the shadow, or spread His table for us in the midst of our foes. Or, sweetest and best, there glows before us the sight of Jesus, as we first saw His face of love. By all these memories, we are able to affirm that the spiritual belongs of right to our natures, is, indeed, however fitfully we may have sought it, the thing most worth living for. The blue

---

[1] I take these from "Some of the Mysteries of God's Kingdom glanced at," Penington's *Works*, 1681 edn. pt. i. pp. 415-426.
[2] *The Excursion*, bk. i.

heaven of the larger life may seem beyond our present reach, yet its very air is on our faces, and we know that we are meant to breathe it into our spiritual lungs from moment to moment, and to incorporate its bracing vigour into our life.

The experience, however, is precarious and fugitive until we come into some sense of vital union with Christ. With us the aim and the achievement lie woefully apart; with Him they came together naturally, inevitably. The great poet finds the right word, the fit rhythm; and the image in his soul leaps into life perfect, like an Athene from the head of Zeus. Jesus had the same fine mastery of a still higher craftsmanship, the Art of Life. Actually, on that Galilean hillside above the shining lake, from one at least of the sons of men, there came the filial cry of understanding love, " Our Father," and in one life there sprang up, as in heaven, the nature and the kingdom and the will of the Highest.

And so, as we see the Father in the face of Jesus Christ, there may come to us, as to the early Friends and to the unnumbered comradeship of His disciples in all ages, some moment of discovery, or perhaps the gradual dawning of a new light, in which we know ourselves defeated and undone, but know also the Divine Love round about us, and open our hearts to its tide of strength.

We say with Penington:[1] " This is He; this is He: there is no other: this is He Whom I have waited for and sought after from my childhood, Who was always near me, and had often begotten life in my heart; but I knew Him not distinctly, nor how to receive Him or dwell with Him." Thenceforth the elements of our personality come together in a new order, under the control of a will that is now seeking to do the will of God. The lower elements of life have not indeed been destroyed, but they are robbed of their mastery; they will serve but they shall no longer rule. We have become Finders of the Truth, disciples of the Christ.

---

[1] Penington's account of his Spiritual Travel, in *Works*, 1681 edn. pt. i. at beginning, in Testimony of Thos. Ellwood.

CHAPTER XV

QUAKER COLONIZATION

> For my country [of Pennsylvania], I eyed the Lord in the obtaining of it; and more was I drawn inward to look to Him and to owe it to His Hand and power than to any other way. I have so obtained it, and desire that I may not be unworthy of His love, but do that which may answer His kind providence, and serve His truth and people, that an example may be set up to the nations: there may be room there, though not here, for such an Holy Experiment.—WM. PENN, Letter to James Harrison, 25th August 1681, in Janney's *Life of Penn*, 6th edn. p. 175.

WE pause here to tell for a few pages, on its English side, the story of the great expansion of Quakerism which took place in America under the guidance of Penn. The American side is well told by Amelia M. Gummere and Isaac Sharpless in the companion volume to the present history.[1] During the proscription of Dissent in the early Stuart period, the Puritans had anticipated Canning's phrase, and "called the New World into existence to redress the balance of the Old."[2] Andrew Marvell recalls the feelings of emigrants to "the remote Bermudas," who praised God for leading them,[3]

> Unto an isle so long unknown,
> And yet far kinder than our own.
>
> . . . . .
>
> He lands us on a grassy stage,
> Safe from the storms, and prelate's rage.
> He gave us this eternal spring,
> Which here enamels everything,

---

[1] *Quakers in the American Colonies*, books iv. and v.
[2] Speech, 12th Dec. 1826, on the recognition by England of the South American Republics.
[3] Probably written about 1657 (*Cambridge Hist. of Engl. Literature*, vii. 180).

And in these rocks for us did frame
A temple where to sound His name.

With Puritan precedents in mind, we naturally ask what were the inducing causes which led to the great emigration of Friends from 1675 onwards, and especially how far it was due to persecution at home. There can be no doubt that with the Quakers, as with the Puritans, the civil disabilities and the restraints on life in England made attractive the congenial conditions that were carefully provided for them in the new colonies. Owen in 1667, and Shaftesbury a year or two later,[1] had pointed out that the persecution of Dissent gave a stimulus to emigration, and Penn, in 1675,[2] held that liberty of conscience would be an open door through which a million people might come into England, for nothing else had preserved Holland from truckling under the Spanish yoke. The larger life offered in the colonies, especially the freedom to worship God, coupled with a fair prospect of material prosperity, was, perhaps generally, the inducing cause both to the Puritan and the Quaker emigrant. But, in both cases, it was the larger life that attracted, rather than any craven purpose of escaping from present sufferings. As early as 1660, and therefore before severe persecution was anticipated, Josiah Coale had been commissioned by English Friends to treat with the Indians of the Susquehanna for the purchase of lands,[3] and wrote to Fox of his ill-success. Quakerism was already firmly planted in America before the Restoration, as the result of the valiant transatlantic missions of Publishers of Truth, who had convinced important groups of colonists along the whole seaboard from Massachusetts Bay to Virginia. Rhode Island, indeed, the "isle of errors" and sanctuary of religious liberty, was now controlled by influential colonists who had become Friends.

[1] Owen, *Indulgence of Toleration considered*, and Shaftesbury, then Lord Ashley, *Memorial to Charles II.*, cited from Seaton, *The Theory of Toleration*, pp. 130, 149.

[2] *Ibid.* p. 177, and Penn, *England's Present Interest Considered* (*Works*, 1726 edn. i. 695).

[3] *Quakers in the American Colonies*, pp. xiv, 358, 418. The letter, from Dev. Ho. A. R. Barclay Colln. No. 53, is given in Bowden, *Hist. of Friends in America*, i. p. 389, note.

The Quaker leaders *expected* to make their type of religion prevail on the Western continent. They believed, in fact, that their "Principle" was universally true and would make its way through the race, and that their experiment was only the beginning of a world-religion of the Spirit. The New World seemed to them a providential field to be won for their truth. It was in the New World alone that favourable opportunities offered in the seventeenth and eighteenth centuries for the application of Quaker ideals to public life, and the opportunities were quickly seized.[1]

The growth of the group-consciousness of Friends had been repressed by bitter blasts of persecution. Fox had made use of the first lull to reanimate Quakerism into a closer and more organic fellowship ; and a fresh corporate sense, surer of itself than in the days before the storm, had spread through the movement. A great period of self-expression began. In the short space of fifteen years, Quakerism grew into an enduring Church organization at the call of Fox ; its faith was formulated into a noble system through the mind of Barclay ; and it set itself to the establishment of an ideal state under the governance of Penn. I have called these developments modes of self-expression, because the fit word is yet uncoined. They were more truly modes through which the Inward Light, which is the artificer of the Church and its bond of fellowship, was finding fresh utterance. Fox, Barclay, and Penn, and in their degree the masses of less-gifted men and women who shared their service, were guiding the Church to new issues, because they were themselves, amid much human waywardness, dedicated to the guidance of the Hand of Life within their souls.

The colonizing movement, then, is no by-product, but a development closely related to the other outgrowths of this vital age of Quakerism. I do not mean that it entered definitely into the policy pursued by Fox, or into the consideration of the Church meetings which he had set up. We find little trace of this. But the knitting together of Friends into a great religious society was the necessary foundation for large enterprises which depended

[1] *Quakers in the American Colonies*, p. xiv.

for their success on the backing that could now be secured from a body drawn into one family life and welcoming proposals designed for the common good. The initiative lay with men of vision, willing to take the risks of colonial ventures, because they could count on this support. The Church organizers prepared the way for the colonizers; and, in settling Quakerism at home, made possible the wonderful expansion by settlement overseas, which replaced the daring missions of the First Publishers of Truth.

The Jerseys were the earliest field of enterprise.[1] The Duke of York had succeeded to the Dutch colonies in America on the fall of New Amsterdam in 1664, and granted the portion that came to be called New Jersey to Lord Berkeley and Sir George Carteret, dividing it between them, as West Jersey and East Jersey, on its permanent acquisition by England ten years later. John Fenwick, a Buckinghamshire Friend, bought West Jersey from Berkeley on behalf of the London Quaker, Edward Byllinge,[2] and the financial embarrassments of Byllinge threw it into the hands of trustees for his creditors, who were three Friends, William Penn, Gawen Laurie a merchant of London, and Nicholas Lucas the Hertford maltster. Penn had already been introduced to the matter as arbitrator between Fenwick and Byllinge at the time of the purchase. His vigorous mind turned this hazardous commercial venture to larger uses. In 1676[3] he framed a democratic charter for the province, containing provisions for full liberty of conscience. "There," the trustees said, "we lay a foundation for after-ages to understand their liberty as men and Christians, that they may not be brought in bondage but by their own consent." They issued a prospectus, or *Description of West New Jersey*, followed by an important cautionary letter, lest any intending settlers, "as is feared by some, should go, out of a curious and unsettled mind, and others to shun the testimony of the blessed cross of Jesus."

---

[1] See *Quakers in the American Colonies*, pp. 362, 363.
[2] I can find no evidence that this purchase was made on behalf of the Society at large.
[3] The papers cited are in Bowden, *Hist. of Friends in America*, i. pp. 394-398.

London Friends approved the Monthly Meetings giving emigrants certificates "concerning their conversation as becoming Truth," to be signed by such Friends as felt free to do so.[1] Between 1677 and '81, it is estimated that at least fourteen hundred persons had found their way to the new province,[2] and in this last year the West Jersey Friends sent a letter to England on the subject of certificates.[3] They were anxious to know if single persons were clear from any engagement to marry. They also desired to be certified of Friends coming over, whose life had been disorderly, "for we are sensible that here are several that left no good savour in their native land . . . and it may be probable that more of that kind may come, thinking to be absconded in this obscure place." They add a wise reference to the moral risks run by young women on the voyage, for "such as are employed in sea-affairs are commonly men of the wildest sort."

In February 1682, William Penn and eleven other Friends purchased East Jersey from the widow of Sir George Carteret.[4] Twelve other persons, including Robert Barclay and other Scotsmen, were associated in the proprietorship, and Barclay was made Governor, directing the project at home, but acting in America through a deputy.

Penn was at this time a man with powerful friends at Court. He belonged, as we have seen, by birth and breeding, to the governing class; and his father, the Admiral, had made it his dying request to the Duke of York, then High Admiral, that he would use his influence with the King to protect his son. It was by the Duke's favour that Penn now obtained, on 4th March 1681, a grant from the Crown of the wide domain to which the King's pleasantry affixed the name of Pennsylvania. Charles and his Council were willing in this way to extinguish a debt of £16,000 owing to the estate of Admiral Penn; the Duke of York was kindly disposed to

---

[1] Six Weeks' Meeting Minutes, 30th Jan. 1677. [2] Bowden, i. 399.
[3] Bowden, i. 403, dated 7th Feb. 1681; for last part of this, which is not in Bowden, see copy of epistle in Kendal Early Record Book.
[4] *Quakers in the American Colonies*, p. 368. The conveyance bears date 1st, 2nd Feb. 1681/2.

his quasi-ward, and not only waived his own claims, but added the gift of Delaware; Penn, then a man of thirty-seven, already saw himself bringing to fruition the great projects ringing in his soul. The Royal Patent declared his objects to be

... a commendable desire to enlarge the British Empire, and promote such useful commodities as may be a benefit to the King and his Dominions; and also to reduce the savage nations, by just and gentle manners, to the love of civil society and the Christian religion.[1]

Within a few weeks of the Grant,[2] Penn wrote:

Many are drawn forth to be concerned with me; and perhaps this way of satisfaction has more of the Hand of God in it than a downright payment. This I can say, that I had an opening of joy as to these parts, in the year 1661, at Oxford, twenty years since; and, as my understanding and inclination have been much directed to observe and reprove mischiefs in government, so it is now put into my power to settle one. For the matters of liberty and privilege, I propose that which is extraordinary, and to leave myself and successors no power of doing mischief, that the will of one man may not hinder the good of an whole country.

This letter was accompanied[3] with his proposals for colonization, in which, after vindicating colonies from the prejudice of those who thought they weakened the mother country, he details his scheme, but cautions settlers against extravagant ideas of an immediate amendment of their conditions.

It is in a letter, four months later, to an intending settler, James Harrison,[4] that he uses the words which stand at the head of this chapter. It is clear that he had in mind the "Holy Experiment" of a community ordered and animated by the Christian spirit, so different from that which was manifesting its fruits in England; he had seized the God-given opportunity, but the achievement

[1] See the full account in Janney's *Life*. It is interesting to find the terms "British Empire" and "Dominions" used as they are to-day.
[2] *Ibid.* p. 172, letter dated 12th April 1681. At Oxford he had been, we may suppose, fired by the political Utopias of the day, such as Harrington's *Oceana*.
[3] *Ibid.* pp. 170-172.
[4] *Ibid.* p. 175. James Harrison was from Kendal (see *F.P.T.* p. 258 and note). He became one of the most trusted of Penn's friends, but died in 1687.

would depend, in part indeed upon a just and liberal frame of government, but, in the main, upon the quality of those who transplanted themselves into the American wilderness.

"Governments," he said a little later, when issuing his constitution,[1] "rather depend upon men than men upon governments. Let men be good, and the government cannot be bad. But, if men be bad, let the government be ever so good, they will endeavour to warp and spoil it to their turn. . . . Good men will never want good laws, nor suffer ill ones. . . . That, therefore, which makes a good constitution must keep it, namely, men of wisdom and virtue."

Penn knew, as King Alfred had known long before,[2] that without the right materials a man is impotent to work out his high designs. It was because the Quaker community provided him with men, strong in sobriety of life, rich in corporate consciousness, devoted with him to ways of justice, that he could commit himself with confidence to the great adventure. The venture would succeed splendidly though with abundant imperfection, for leader and comrades alike would be concerned, beyond all outward government, in giving expression to the inward law of their common spiritual life. Pennsylvania would flourish in so far as it became a transplantation of vital Quakerism.

Fox, in his letters to the American settlements, sees this clearly, and is keenly alive to the responsibility for worthy expression of their Faith that rests on the planters.

To the early settlers in West Jersey, he says: "My desire is that . . . you may have the Lord in your eye, in all your undertakings. For many eyes of other governments or colonies will be upon you; yea, the Indians, to see how you order your lives and conversations."[3] Again, "You know how that Friends in England and other places have admonished the Governors and Rulers to do that which is just and right; and, therefore, now you are come into place, have a care that you do that which is just and right, lest you come under the same reproof by others."[4]

---

[1] Janney's *Life*, pp. 187, 188.
[2] See Alfred's *Boethius*, chap. xvii., the most famous of his many additions to his author.   [3] *Epistles*, No. 340, 4th March 1676/7.
[4] *Ibid*. No. 367, about 1681.

To all planters he writes, " My Friends that are gone and are going over to plant . . . keep your own plantations in your hearts, with the Spirit and power of God, that your own vines and lilies be not hurt." [1]

These settlers, blest with the Divine plantation in their hearts, priceless above all worldly gear, were men of pith and mark. They had been valiant for the Truth in their old homes ; and would carry its wholesome savour with them across the seas, from the wide fells of the North and the bare hills of Wales, from deep-set Derbyshire dales and quiet nooks below the Sussex downs, from the busy hives of trade in London and Bristol, from sea-girt Devon and East Coast Bridlington, the " school of prophets," [2] from old Cromwellian plantations in green Erin and spare homesteads in thrifty Scotland, from the sunny vineyards of the Palatinate and the rich levels of the lower Rhine. The one Spirit whose life they shared had drawn them from the diverse and limited conditions of their past into this larger fellowship, and, like the glad bands of pilgrims going up to Jerusalem or the company of Westmorland Seekers in the first days of Quakerism, they were filled with joy, and their comradeship together became a song of praise. They had no gift of poetic words, but at this creative moment they were poets in their experience, makers together of a new world ; and out of this exalted group-consciousness, which comes to men in the freshness and wonder of a great common life, the early settlers break into rapturous words as they write in fond greeting to their Friends in England.

Blessed be the God of Abraham and of Isaac and of Jacob,
That called us not hither in vain :
This was the testimony of life in our living assembly, through many
    faithful brethren,
That God was with us and is with us,
Yea, He hath made our way for us,
And proved and confirmed to us His word and faithfulness. . . .

---

[1] *Epistles*, No. 379, 22nd Nov. 1682.
[2] Bridlington, locally pronounced Burlington, gave its name to the chief settlement in New Jersey. John Richardson, *Life*, calls it, about 1690, a " school of prophets."

Our God hath engaged us,
Yea, He hath overcome us with His ancient glory;
The desert sounds,
The wilderness rejoices,
A visitation inwardly and outwardly is come to America;
God is Lord of all the earth,
And, at our Setting of the Sun, will His Name be famous. . . .

Oh, remember us, for we cannot forget you:
Many waters cannot quench our love,
Nor distance wear out the deep remembrance of you in the heavenly Truth:
We pray God preserve you in faithfulness,
That, discharging your places and stewardships,
Ye may be honoured and crowned with the reward of them that endure to the end.

And, though the Lord hath been pleased to remove us far away from you,
As to the other end of the earth,
Yet are we present with you,
Your exercises are ours;
Our hearts are dissolved in the remembrance of you,
Dear brethren and sisters in this heavenly love;
And the Lord of heaven and earth,
Who is the Father of our Family,
Keep us in His love and power,
And unite, comfort and build us all,
More and more,
To His eternal praise,
And our rejoicing.[1]

The continuance of this glowing corporate life was a principal object of the immigrants.

" Our first concern," says Richard Townsend,[2] " was to keep up and maintain our religious worship, and, in order thereunto, we had several meetings in the houses of the inhabitants, and one boarded meeting-house was set up where the city [of Philadelphia] was to be, near Delaware; and, as we had nothing but love and goodwill in our hearts one to another, we had very comfortable

---

[1] Epistle from a select meeting of Elders and faithful brethren of Pennsylvania and Jersey, held at Philadelphia 17th March 1683. The letter is signed by Penn and twenty-five others, and is printed in full in Bowden, *Hist. of Friends in America*, ii. 20-23, from a copy in Cotherstone Meeting, Yorkshire. See also Janney's *Life of Penn*, p. 234, using a copy in the MSS. of the Amer. Philosophical Society at Philadelphia. I have set it out rhythmically, as, alas, few Church-letters could be printed.

[2] Narrative in Bowden, *Hist. of Friends in America*, ii. 17-19.

meetings from time to time ; and, after our meeting was over, we assisted each other in building little houses for our shelter."

Within three months of Penn's arrival in October 1682, Monthly and Quarterly Meetings were set up, and a Yearly Meeting, in conjunction with New Jersey, was soon afterwards established.[1]

The migration to the Quaker colonies, which was at its height during the next twenty years, stripped the Society at home of many of its most active and eager spirits, and must be counted among the causes of the decline into Quietism that took place in the eighteenth century. With the rank and file, economic causes, especially the lean years from 1693 to '99, played a chief part. Already in 1685[2] we find an early colonist writing to Fox, " I wish those that have estates of their own, and to leave fullness to their posterity, may not be offended at the Lord's opening a door of mercy to thousands in England, especially in Wales and other nations, who had no estates either for themselves or children." In 1699[3] the Welsh Friends write of "runnings to Pennsylvania having been [the] cause of great weakening, if not total decaying, of some meetings in the Dominion of Wales, so that not only the remnant that is left behind, but likewise the travelling ministering Friends, meeting with discouragement, find cause to complain." About the same time John Gratton of Derbyshire tells us,[4] " The number of Friends multiplied, but many of them went into America ; there was about forty from our Monthly Meeting, and some others, which lessened our meeting pretty much." Thomas Camm, of Westmorland, writes[5] that " a great

---

[1] Narrative in Bowden, *Hist. of Friends in America*, ii. 20, etc. New Jersey began a Y.M. in Aug. 1681.
[2] Thomas Ellis, Letter dated 13th June 1685, in *J.F.H.S.* vi. 173-175, from Dev. Ho. A. R. B. Colln. No. 108. For Ellis, see *F.P.T.* p. 323 *n.*, and *Beginnings of Quakerism*, p. 208. Many Welsh settlers were not Friends.
[3] See the reply to this complaint, from Merion M.M. in the Welsh Tract in Pennsylvania, 11th May 1699, in Dev. Ho. Reynolds Colln. p. 22. In 1688 Welsh Friends had reported one meeting regained " that was lost by Friends going beyond sea, namely in Glamorganshire" (Dev. Ho. Reynolds Colln. p. 17).
[4] *Journ.* (1695) p. 181.
[5] Thos. and Ann Camm to Richard and B. Snead, 21st Jan. 1699, in Bristol MSS. v. No. 84.

deal of the younger sort of Friends are intended for Pennsylvania," a statement confirmed from other sources.[1] East Yorkshire sent a considerable contingent, which reduced the size of the meetings.[2] In 1686 the Friends at Crefeld on the Rhine, and Griesheim in the Palatinate, emigrated in a body. John Claus writes,[3] in the name of Amsterdam Friends:

The meeting of Friends in the Palatinate is in effect dissolved, by reason that most of the Friends of that place have removed themselves from thence to Pennsylvania; and the rest, save one ancient man, are ready, as we hear, to come away too this summer. . . . The meeting at Crefeld is brought into the same condition; for they are likewise all, that were convinced of Truth, gone thither, except one man and his wife.

There was naturally enough some criticism, on which Penn comments:[4]

Truth's authority is raising, I hope, an example to the nations, and they that see not the service of this providence will finally confess that it is of the Lord. All do not, as well as some will not equally see the mind of the Lord therein; but some see it and rejoice; and I believe some shall see it and be ashamed for their hard speeches.

Fox himself expressed his doubt on the subject somewhat brusquely, especially in regard to ministering Friends, some of whom had died after only a short residence in America. This drew from John Blaykling, of Draw-well, a charming letter, which deserves reproduction, if only to show that on occasion the most devoted friends of Fox could question the justice of his actions.[5]

I am sorry for the exercise occasioned through the death of our Friends in Pennsylvania, T[homas] L[anghorne] [and] J[ames]

---

[1] See Minute Books of District, and cf. Wm. Stout, *Autobiography*, pp. 50, 54, 55.
[2] J. W. Rowntree, *Essays and Addresses*, pp. 46, 47.
[3] Letter of 6th May 1686, in *Collectitia*, pp. 253-258. For the Griesheim Friends, see *Beginnings of Quakerism*, p. 414.
[4] Letter to John Blaykling, Thomas Camm, Thomas Langhorne and Robert Barrow, dated Pennsylvania, 16th Sept. 1683, in Dev. Ho. Portf. 31, No. 91.
[5] Dated 29th Jan. 1688, in Dev. Ho. A. R. B. Colln. No. 139. For Langhorne, who died in 1687, see *F.P.T.* pp. 271, 272. Barrow himself died in America in 1697, after some remarkable experiences recorded in *Piety Promoted*, i. 197. Cf. *J.F.H.S.* xii. 33.

H[arrison]. . . . I was something sorry to hear that thou should so often bear upon the matter of Friends' death there, saying that that Province had been a grave for many of the Lord's servants, and in this instancing such as have been taken away there in five or six years' time, and telling Ro[bert] Barrow, under that consideration, that it was well, or that he may be glad, he stayed at home. Dear George, thou may bear me : it's that honourable respect I have for dear W[illiam] Penn, whom God hath honoured with the knowledge of His blessed Truth, and hath preserved him in, and the tender, loving exercise, with many tears, that T[homas] Langhorne was exercised in, touching his going thither, which occasion me to think thou bears too hard up[on] those and other good men, who have lived to God and are laid down in peace. I am exercised under the thoughts of the many worthy men in England, good, able ministers, in a few years that were taken away in the prime of their age :— E[dward] B[urrough], R[ichard] H[ubberthorne], W[illiam] Ca[ton], J[ohn] Aud[land], Jo[hn] Camm, Jos[iah] Coale, G[eorge] Harrison, F[rancis] H[owgill]. And how many dear brethren were taken away in the time of the Great Plague in London in a short time. Great is the wisdom of God and secret His counsels, and submission to Him in all things is the best state. With respect to America and Friends removing from their native countries any way, we are taught by the various dealings of the Lord to be serious, weighty and in abundance of fear to the Lord, that, wherever our lot may fall, our days may be comfortable to us and the refreshing of God's heritage, our latter end peace, and the possession of life and glory our portion for ever. . . . Dear George, I am plain and true—God, He knows—and those respects which in bowedness I owe to thee and the Lord on thy account doth abundantly melt my heart at this time. . . . I am, in due subjection to God and best love to thee, wherein I rest, thy tender and far younger brother.

In an epistle dated 30th July 1685,[1] addressed to American ministers, Fox had urged them to improve their talents and to mind the prosperity of the Truth :

. . . this little time you have to live ; and be not like Adam, *in* the earth, but use this world as though you did not use it . . . and you, being many, and having many of the Friends of the ministry going over into those parts, you may be a hindrance one unto another, if you do not travel in the life of the universal Truth.

---

[1] *Epistles*, No. 405.

If the great Quaker Leader grudged the loss of ministers, it was because he was consumed with eager missionary zeal.

During the bitter attempt to ruin Dissent in the closing years of Charles II. it is probable that many of the authorities would have been glad if all the Quakers had been driven to Pennsylvania.[1] But the cases of actual fleeing from persecution are few. John Moone, of Bristol, one of the signatories to the important letter from Ministers in 1666, had been imprisoned at Bristol in 1682, and seems to have accepted liberty on condition of emigrating. Young John Whiting, then in Ilchester gaol, wrote him a candid remonstrance :[2]

O my ancient Friend, why wilt thou leave us? My heart is sad, with many more, to hear thereof. . . . Why wilt thou go away and leave a clog behind thee to follow thee as a burden? I know thou wast formerly very much against going to New Jersey, and ready to discourage any that were inclined that way; and how is it that thou art now so much for going to Pennsylvania at this time? Not that I am against any's going thither, so they go clearly, but only at such a time as this for any to go to shun persecution, believing the blessing of God will not attend any such therein; whatever pretence any may make people will take it no otherwise, which will strengthen the hands of the evildoers and weaken them that are faithful.

Moone told a Friend that Whiting was a forward lad and he had thrown the letter into the fire, and so went away the next year, "but never prospered after, nor several others that went away to shun persecution, but fell from Truth, and so it was fulfilled on him." I have also come across an Irish certificate of 1683, expressing a godly jealousy that the chief ground for emigration, in the case that was being dealt with, was "fearfulness of suffering here for the testimony of Jesus, or coveting worldly liberty."[3]

Penn only spent two periods of less than two years each in his new province. His service in its interests at

---

[1] *Autobiography of William Stout*, p. 11, and newsletter in Lady Newdigate-Newdegate's *Cavalier and Puritan*, p. 97.
[2] *Persecution Exposed*, pp. 82, 83.
[3] Mountmellick Men's Meeting, 25th Feb. 1683, in *Irish Friend*, i. 27.

Court, where no one else could take his place, and his efforts on behalf of a still greater object, Liberty of Conscience, compelled his reluctant residence in England, at much prejudice in other ways to Pennsylvanian affairs and his own financial position. The difficulties he overcame, as well as those which he could only partly meet, make it evident that, without his unique influence and gifts, the young Colony in spite of the fine human material composing it would have met with disaster. Supported by his influence, both at Court and among Friends, wisely ordered under a generous Frame of Government, and peopled by settlers whose way was guided by an Inward Law, it achieved success from the first. There would, indeed, be much admixture of dross.

[Penn] was to have bitter disappointments; his colonies were to be ungrateful, unappreciative of their great opportunities, haggling over little matters of property, led by demagogues into unreasonable demands; he himself was to lose his splendid patrimony in the enterprise, and go to a debtor's gaol.... [But he] had the opportunity and the wisdom—a combination which comes to scarcely one man in a millennium—to rear in his study a theory of government on the broadest principles of right and justice, and to set it to work in a vast territory with friendly neighbours and a sympathetic population. These principles, by their inherent vitality, went far beyond the bounds of his commonwealth, and a great nation found in them the best expression of its aspirations and needs, and is living on them to-day.[1]

Perhaps only one other Friend deserves to stand with Penn as a colonizer of genius. John Archdale,[2] a Buckinghamshire Quaker squire, became one of the proprietors of the Carolinas in 1680. The Colony had been granted by Charles II. in 1663 to eight English noblemen. It received a constitution from John Locke, by which an hereditary nobility was created, but this ill-fated "Grand Model" only produced friction, though it contained an enlightened provision for liberty of conscience. The early years of the Colony were years of confusion,

---

[1] Sharpless, *Quakers in the American Colonies*, pp. 470, 471.
[2] See *Quakers in the American Colonies*, pp. 340-350, by Rufus M. Jones, for the best account of Archdale.

and towards the close of the century the Governor wrote to England that it was impossible to settle the country, except a Proprietor himself came over with full power to heal their grievances. Archdale was sent in 1695, being no doubt chosen for the success with which he had ruled the Colony ten years earlier in the absence of the Governor Sothell, who was a brother-proprietor and an ambitious, unscrupulous man. During this first term of office, he had written to Fox[1] of his success with the Indians and his hopes soon to have the country at peace with them all and also one with another. On his arrival in 1695, every faction applied itself to him in hopes of relief. He "appeased them with kind and gentle words," and convened an Assembly with a Council, judiciously blended very much after the policy of William III. at home, of "two moderate Churchmen to one High Churchman . . . whereby," he says, "the balance of Government was preserved peaceable and quiet in my time." He was impartial and enlightened in his home affairs, kindly and just in his behaviour to the Indians, friendly with the Catholic Spaniards of Florida, and earnest in his efforts to secure naturalization for immigrant Huguenots. He well deserved the thanks of the settlers when he left: "By your wisdom, patience and labour you have laid a firm foundation for a most glorious superstructure." After his return to England he became, in 1698, the first Quaker chosen a Member of Parliament, but being unable to take the oaths, he was refused his seat.[2] The greater part of Archdale's later life, though

[1] Letter, 25th March 1686, in Dev. Ho. A. R. B. Colln. No. 68, printed in Bowden, *Hist. of Friends in America*, i. 415–417, and read at Morning Meeting, 27th June 1686.
[2] See *e.g.* Luttrell, *Brief Relation*, iv. 467, 469, reprinted in *J.F.H.S.* viii. 5. Chipping Wycombe was the borough which honoured itself by making him its member. The entries in the Journals of the House of Commons are printed in *Yorkshireman*, i. pp. 286, 287, in connection with the election of Joseph Pease, returned for the Southern Division of the County of Durham, in 1833, who was the first Quaker allowed to sit on taking the Affirmation in lieu of the Oaths. (See for this case Joseph Davis, *Digest of Legislative Enactments relating to the Society of Friends*, 1849 edn. pp. 46, 47.) Penn's friend, Henry Gouldney, disapproved the matter, as "it will cause many to imagine that we aim at that post. . . . I think, if we can be quiet, we need not desire any post, as matters now stand." (Letter to Sir John Rodes, 20th Aug. 1698, in *Quaker Post-bag*, pp. 71-73.)

with much further activity in colonial enterprise, was no doubt spent in the ordinary round of his daily duties as a country gentleman. But, when the occasion demanded, he proved himself, in the words of the historian Bryant, "a wise, moderate and far-seeing man." He is, indeed, happy above many who take a more brilliant place upon the page of history; for our memory of him is associated only with words of kindness and deeds of peace.

It remains to sum up the meaning of colonization to the Quaker movement. While essentially due, as we have seen, to the strength of corporate consciousness, it sprang up outside the corporate organization. No Yearly Meeting or Meeting for Sufferings petitioned for the grant of Pennsylvania or planned the building of Philadelphia. No Quaker conference in London as to the right treatment of weaker races preceded the immortal treaty with the Indians at Shackamaxon. Colonial expansion was a spontaneous movement *in* the Society rather than an official movement *by* the Society. Its chief instruments were not the ministers but the men of affairs. Friends were still in the dynamic stage of their history and the plastic stage of their organization; and the new growth could burst forth and blossom, free from the nipping air of established tradition.

This capacity to respond to the leadership of a man of vision and enterprise like Penn marks the vitality of the second generation of Friends. Undefeated by persecution, and grown into disciplined and reliant manhood, they were ready to put their well-tried principles to proof on the largest scale. Quakerism, indeed, would have been to the world an half-uttered thing, if its highest forms of expression had been found in the Church-organization of Fox or the writings of Barclay. It would have produced cloistered saints and a lofty speculative theory of Christianity; it would not have vindicated itself as a Faith able to re-shape the whole of life. In the New World it addressed itself to this high adventure; and, amid much imperfection of execution, supplied the nations with the inspiring precedent of a Christian State. Results were achieved that still bless mankind. The sons of Onas, as the Indians called Penn's people, have taught the white man the just treatment of native races, and the potency of a national policy of goodwill; under the meek leadership of the New Jersey saint, John Woolman, they laid a sure foundation for the overthrow of negro slavery and caught a glimpse of the task that confronts the world to-day—the Christian reconstruction of the social order. America has drawn from Pennsylvania the lineaments of her great democracy. The Quaker message would have been almost inarticulate on these larger issues if Philadelphia, the City of Brotherly Love, had not been born.

But even the noblest enterprise has its limiting conditions. These were found, partly in the tenure upon which the colonies were held, and partly in the limitations of the colonists themselves. The Jerseys and Pennsylvania were grants from the Crown, and could not avoid the entanglements of England's foreign policy and her demands for military establishments. The Quaker way of peace was only fairly tried with regard to the Indians, and, even here, as Fiske shows,[1] its success was partly due to the particular balance of power that happened to prevail among the Indian nations themselves during the seventy years of peace. The limitations of the colonists lay chiefly in their narrow intellectual outlook and imperfect education in the meaning of freedom. Penn himself had some of the defects which belonged to the aristocratic class among whom he had been bred. The Quaker Experiment in Government is a golden page of history in spite of these limiting conditions, because both the Founder of Pennsylvania and his first followers had engaged in the great enterprise in the spirit of his fine letter to Bristol Friends in their sore sufferings: "Oh, great is God's work on earth. Be universal in your spirits; and keep out of all straitness and narrowness: look to God's great and glorious Kingdom and its prosperity."[2]

[1] *The Dutch and Quaker Colonies in America*, ii. 164-167.
[2] *Works*, 1726 edn. i. 230.

CHAPTER XVI

THE PASSING OF THE LEADERS

    They that love beyond the world cannot be separated by it. Death cannot kill what never dies, nor can spirits ever be divided that love and live in the same Divine Principle, the root and record of their friendship. If absence be not death, neither is theirs : death is but crossing the world, as friends do the seas ; they live in one another still. For they must needs be present that love and live in that which is omnipresent. In this Divine Glass they see face to face ; and their converse is free as well as pure.
    This is the comfort of friends, that though they may be said to die, yet their friendship and society are in the best sense ever present, because immortal.
—WM. PENN, *More Fruits of Solitude*, title "Union of Friends."

IT is in the spirit of the ancient Song of Deborah that we now chronicle the closing years of some of the leaders of Quakerism, who survived through its second vital period of expression (1669–1685):

> For that the leaders took the lead in Israel ;
> For that the people offered themselves willingly ;
> Bless ye the Lord.

We find ourselves among the mountains, in the joy and vision of the upper air, where the streams sparkle in their freshness and the turf springs to our tread ; and, braced by converse with these Great Companions, resume the tasks of life with new heart.

    Quakerism, though rich in *acta sanctorum*, has compiled no Calendar of Saints. The witnesses for Truth had left their living memorial in the witness itself :

> Thy monument make thou thy living deeds ;
> No other tomb than that true virtue needs.[1]

---

[1] Bishop Hall, *Satires*, iii. 3.

CH. XVI THE PASSING OF THE LEADERS

Friends indeed, in their rigorous disregard of outward symbols, came to discountenance the use of tombstones, even providing for the removal out of sight of those that had been erected, for, as one Minute quaintly words it, the practice is "of no service to the deceased."[1] But they were careful to preserve the living memorial, especially the words spoken in the hour of death, when the soul, passing from the earthly, sees its retrospect and prospect in the dawn-light of the heavenly.

Among the matters specially directed by the Yearly Meeting of 1676 to be carefully recorded were "the names, travels, faithfulness and unblameable conversations of all the public labourers that are deceased," and "signal living testimonies of dying Friends."[2] The practice still continues,[3] with the caution "that the object is not eulogy, but to preserve a record of the power of Divine grace in the lives of the Lord's faithful servants."

The first collected writings of a Friend are those of George Fox the younger, published in a thin octavo in 1662, the year after his death. The editor is only

---

[1] For instances of early tombstones, see *J.F.H.S.* vi. 2, 25, 26 (with plate of those at Paddock meeting-house, Huddersfield), also the one in Friends' Burial Ground at Budock, near Falmouth, in memory of Thomas Gwin's mother, Margery Gwin, with its admonitory anagram, "Grim warneing," and its halting verses. Others are described in (London) *Friend*, vi. 193, vii. 5, dating from 1662-1704. In 1717 London Y.M., in its desire for a consistent simplicity, directed the removal of existing tombstones and the discontinuance of the practice for the future (see MS. "Books of Extracts," title "Tombstones." Cf. Kendal, M.M. Minute, 2nd Aug. 1717). Bristol Friends, in 1670, for the sake of unity, gave in to those who objected to any at all, some, as we feel more wisely, only objecting to stones that were painted or carved (Men's Two Weeks' Meetings, 12th, 26th Dec. 1670, and 20th Feb. 1671). The phrase in text is from a Minute of Dorset Q.M. 27th June 1705, ordering a gravestone to be put out of sight; and the Budock stone had long lain underground. The *Life of John Roberts* tells how the Bishop of Gloucester, not long before his death in 1672, visited him at Siddington, near Cirencester, and the Bishop's chancellor complimented John on the Burial Ground there, but thought the stones a little superstitious. Roberts replied: "That is what I confess I cannot much plead for; but it was permitted to gratify some who had their relations there interred. We notwithstanding propose to have them taken up ere long and converted to some better use. But I desire thee to take notice we had it from among you; and I have observed in many things wherein we have taken you for our pattern you have led us wrong." At this the Bishop smiled, and said, "John, I think your beer is long a-coming." As late as 1757 and 1765, we find Minutes on the subject in Norwich M.M. Since 1850, plain tombstones have been allowed, of a uniform pattern for the Burial Ground, to avoid distinctions in that place between rich and poor.

[2] MS. "Books of Extracts," title, "Records."

[3] *Friends' Christian Discipline*, 1906 edn. p. 29.

2 E

ambiguously disclosed under the initials J. P., which might denote Perrot or Penington or James Parke or even John Pennyman, the merchant-draper of London, whose extravagances led to his disownment by Friends eight years later.[1] The writer deprecates criticism of his innovation by saying:

Yet not by this do I appear before any clear eye as a person promoting a person in the seat of the hearts of people; for, alas, the dust is already returned to earth again and the spirit to God who gave it; but, though the creature is fallen, flatted and converted to its proper centre . . . since it's now entered into the bosom of the Father, as a life leapt out of a lump of clay, I say I cannot but in a recordance of it and in a concordance with it, even in the selfsame substance, say; "Though the name of the wicked shall rot, yet let the memory of the righteous live. . . ." Surely I need not study a motto, nor dive into invention to fetch up an inscription to be engraven on the tomb, since the names of the faithful are in the book of God, and the glory is in Him for ever.

It was in this spirit that, a year later, Hubberthorne's writings were published, this time in a small quarto, with accompanying testimonies from his friends. Other quartos followed, but the practice of posthumous recognition may be said to have become established with the ample folios that enshrined the memory of Burrough in 1672, William Smith three years later, Howgill in '76, Fisher in '79 and Penington in '81.[2] The freshness of the titles often con-

[1] For Pennyman (1628-1706) see *Beginnings of Quakerism*, p. 456, *Camb. Journ.* ii. 431, 432, and Smith's *Catalogue*.

[2] A few notes as to the printing of Quaker books in the Restoration period may not be out of place, the rather as Arber, *Term Catalogues*, i. p. xii, says: "the history of the Quaker press in London has yet to be written." By the common law it was held to be illegal to print a book or pamphlet without authority; and the Licensing Act of 1662 (St. 13 & 14 Car. II. cap. 33), which was continued till 1679, and again from 1685-95, had confined printing within severe limits, under pain of any punishment short of the capital sentence that the judges might choose to inflict. Penn's first imprisonment in the Tower (see *ante*, p. 61) for writing *The Sandy Foundation Shaken* was no doubt under colour of this law. (See on the whole subject Grant Robertson, *Select Statutes, etc.*, pp. 60-66, 379, 380, and cf. Lodowick Muggleton's case, 1676, in *Acts of the Witnesses of the Spirit*, pp. 154-178.) From 1662-80, and again from 1685-88, Quaker books, because of the possible penalties that attended their unlicensed printing, were almost always published without any printer's name, sometimes with a reference to the difficulty of printing, as in *Works* of Hubberthorne, 1663, and Burrough, 1672. Hubberthorne's *Works*, however, have on the title-page, "Printed, and are to be sold by William Warwick," see for him *Camb. Journ.* ii. 402. For some printers of Friends' books and a list of forty-four Friends in various places

ceals the heavy travelling that awaits the patient reader. William Smith exudes "Balm from Gilead," Howgill's works are "The Dawnings of the Gospel-Day," Richard Samble of Cornwall is preserved to posterity in "A Handful after the Harvest-Man" (1684), and Robert Barclay in "Truth Triumphant" (1692).

There are of course omissions. Farnsworth merited a folio and Alexander Parker at least a quarto, while Nayler's writings, and then in a selection, were only published in 1716. The question of printing his books had been suspended by the Morning Meeting in 1677, but was resumed in 1698 at the instance of Yorkshire Friends. Another eighteen years elapsed before it was judged safe to print.[1]

---

who dispersed them, see *Extracts from State Papers*, pp. 228-230 (about 1664). The following particulars of sufferings in the Restoration period for printing or selling Friends' books may be given—1662 ; Richard Crane was imprisoned for writing "The Cry of Newgate, etc.," and the Friend suspected of printing the pamphlet was also imprisoned (Besse, *Sufferings*, i. 388). Henry Boreman was committed to Newgate for selling Friends' books, and was thrown among the felons, dying there in Oct. (*ibid.* i. 389 and "A Brief Relation . . . Since the beginning of the 7th Month last," pp. 6, 7). Robert Wilson and Giles Calvert also underwent sufferings this year (*Extracts from State Papers*, pp. 148, 155-157, 163). William Warwick suffered imprisonment in 1664 (*Camb. Journ.* ii. 402), and Andrew Sowle (1628-1695) underwent much persecution at various times (see account in *Piety Promoted*, pt. i. 186-192, cf. *J.F.H.S.* iv. 4). On one occasion he was taken at a meeting and carried to Newgate; and Sir Richard Browne, "understanding he was a printer, threatened to send him after his brother twin . . . to whom this meek man replied, 'Thou wilt not live to see it.' And the event justified it, for Browne died soon after." Browne died in 1669, and the allusion is to the savage mutilation and execution of the printer John Twyn, for high treason, in 1663 (*State Trials*, vi. 659). In 1684 John Bringhurst was imprisoned for printing George Fox's *Primer* and sentenced to stand two hours on the pillory (Besse, *Sufferings*, i. 466, note). The Morning Meeting Minutes do not I think refer to the question of licensing, but they order that books directed to the King or Parliament be delivered to them some days before they are published or cried about the city (26th April 1675). They also rebuke a printer, Benjamin Clarke, for printing a book without their authority (20th Dec. 1675). John Bringhurst, who had been apprentice to Andrew Sowle, was dealt with for printing Rogers' *Christian-Quaker*, and, on his writing a paper condemning his proceedings, was directed to send copies to all persons who had employed or encouraged him in so doing (Minutes of Meeting for Sufferings, 15th Oct. 1680, 4th Feb. 1681, cf. Minutes of Six Weeks' Meeting, 25th Oct., 29th Nov. 1681). Francis Bugg charged Friends with having procured an indictment against him in 1693 for printing without licence, which the jury had ignored (*The Great Mystery of the Little Whore*, pt. ii. p. 76). For printing in Commonwealth period, see *Beginnings of Quakerism*, pp. 303-305, and add reference to Giles Calvert in Thurloe, *State Papers*, iii. 94, 116, reprinted in *J.F.H.S.* viii. 148-150. See also "Antiquarian Researches among the Early Printers and Publishers of Friends' Books," 1844.

[1] See Minutes of Morning Meeting, 25th June 1677, Yorkshire Q.M., April 1698, and Morning Meeting from 12th Sept. 1698 onwards.

Penn, in his testimony to Robert Barclay, justifies the practice of Friends in glowing words :

There is an unfading glory in the labours of good men. And, though death is permitted to draw a dark shadow over their persons, they will live in the just reputation of their good works, the lively characters of their undying, pious minds. It cannot wither their fame or obliviate their names. On the contrary, death often silences envy and augments their deserved praise. The author . . . left these to us for his legacy, the better part doubtless of his estate, as befitted the Divine nature of our kindred. Not therefore for ostentation, or to indulge a worldly custom, but to the glory of the invisible God, the edification of His Church, the benefit of all people, and as a testimony of our respect to the deceased author . . . this ensuing volume, reader, is published.

Many shorter accounts and dying sayings were collected in *Piety Promoted*, begun in 1701 by John Tomkins of London, a series whose succession is worthily continued to English Friends of the present day under the title of *The Annual Monitor*.

The sayings are often of great pith :

It's life, it's life, Friends, that overcomes death.[1]
I am so filled with God's love I shall never be emptied again.[2]
I have no more lying upon me that I know of to hinder my journey than a child.[3]
It is a good thing to retire to the Rock : there is safety ; there is good standing, an excellent bottom and room enough.[4]
The Lord comes in upon my spirit : I have heavenly meetings with Him by myself.[5]

Religious Journals also begin to appear, and became the most characteristic form of Quaker literature. With their variety of incident they were attractive to the Society itself, and more readable by the outside public than the heavy doctrinal treatises. Personal passages occur in the writings of most of the Quaker leaders, for a first-hand inward experience was the foundation of their

---
[1] Pt. iii. 20 (Thomas Wresle, of Lincolnshire, died 1704).
[2] Pt. iii. 49 (Mary Johnson, daughter of Samuel Watson, died 1704, aged 34).
[3] Pt. iii. 147 (Hugh Stamper, of Lurgan, Ireland, died 1676).
[4] Pt. iii. 194 (Isaac Alexander, of Sedbergh Meeting, died 1705, aged 25).
[5] Pt. i. 193 (Springett Penn, son of William Penn, died 1696, aged 21).

THE PASSING OF THE LEADERS

faith; and the Divine happenings transcended all others in importance; but I think the first Journal to be printed was that of William Caton, in 1689, with a preface by Fox, soon followed by the one in Burnyeat's *Works* (1691), with a preface by Penn.

The account of his own convincement, says Penn, "is sweet, lively, instructive and persuasive to others to try, as he did, and to embrace the holy Truth. Then follows a relation of his travels and ministry in these nations and beyond the seas, as Luke presented the Churches with the Acts or travels of the apostles in their infancy—a pleasant and seasoning lecture both for the young who love to hear of voyages, to excite them . . . to journey towards . . . Jerusalem; and to quicken those more aged to shake off their dust, the earth, . . . and to lift up their eyes and see the fields, how white they are to harvest, and how few labourers there are to take it in."

Much of the light and shade of my narrative is drawn from these books, which are artless records of Divine guidance, religious diaries rather than autobiographies, filled with a sedate gravity, but often touched into quiet humour by their very simplicity or flashing out into passages of penetrating spiritual insight. You shall find here the true portrait-gallery of Quakerism, and learn that character, inwardly joined to the Divine, has strength and dignity under every assault of circumstance or poverty of outward condition. These homely calf-bound volumes tell of a spiritual travail and an abiding joy in the Lord which thrills this common life of ours with Divine meanings, till it becomes a hymn of praise.[1] One treasured duodecimo, handed down to me through generations of ancestors, revives the civility and courage of Richard Davies, the Welshpool hatter (1635–1708), whose honest face won the love of his neighbours and disarmed the malice of persecutors, a man remembered in old age for "his gravity and grey hairs, his manly presence and lovely countenance, especially when he stood up in meeting."[2] A tiny volume preserves the "Strength in Weakness manifest

---

[1] Cf. Clement of Alexandria, *Protrept.* chap. 10, sect. 107.
[2] *Journal*, published 1710, Rowland Owen's Testimony. I have used the 3rd edn. of 1771.

in the Life . . . of . . . Elizabeth Stirredge" (1634–1706), of Gloucestershire, "a valiant woman for Truth on earth, a mother in Israel, and a worthy faithful elder in the Church of Christ in her time."[1] The *Journal* of John Banks, of Cumberland, has been already mentioned.[2] Better known is the vigorous *Life* of Thomas Ellwood (1639–1713), of Hunger Hill, now Ongar Hill, near Beaconsfield. Loyal in friendship, and of sterling heart and observant eye, he modestly accepted the career that opened before him, and filled its limited opportunities with countless kindly offices and unwearied literary work. The man who was the trusted friend of Fox and Penington, who shared the thoughts of Milton, and was worthy to have mated with Guli Springett, had not Penn come "for whom she was reserved," showed a contented zest in life which fills his book with charm and makes this right true gentleman live on to his readers as their intimate friend.[3] Of a different order is the *Journal* of William Edmondson (1627–1712), the Ironside turned Quaker. We exchange Ellwood's interest in trifles, his romantic affections and his dalliance with poesy, for the intrepid seriousness of a leader of men who walked from day to day in the fear of God. "He was sound in doctrine and in judgment, plain in preaching and free from affectation. In apparel and gesture grave, in his deportment manly, of few words till a just occasion offered, and very exemplary in life and conversation."[4] From Edmondson we turn to John Gratton, of Derbyshire (1643–1712), whose search after truth has already been told, a man to be matched with Richard Davies for his temper of mind and the esteem in which he was held by his neighbours. When fines for preaching threatened

[1] *Journal*, published 1711; Testimony of John Neale. Her bold bearing towards persecutors and stanch opposition to the Wilkinson-Story party are vividly told.
[2] Published in 1712. See *ante*, p. 367.
[3] *The History of the Life of Thomas Ellwood*, by himself, published in 1714, and with careful elucidation by Samuel Graveson in 1906. Two delightful books, Maria Webb's *The Penns and Peningtons* (1867) and W. H. Summers' *Memories of Jordans and the Chalfonts* (1895), are drawn largely from this *History*.
[4] *Journal*, published 1715, Testimony of Munster Province Meeting.

THE PASSING OF THE LEADERS

he was careful to pay off his creditors, so as not to suffer with the money of others,[1] and managed to combine diligence in business with zealous religious service.

The *Christian Progress* of George Whitehead (1636–1723) is a more considerable work than any of the foregoing ; and has special historical value, owing to the central service of the writer and the ample documents with which it is weighted ; but has little of the freshness which makes some of the other pieces of this kind such racy reading.[2] The *Life* of Christopher Story (1648–1720) deserves a passing reference for its faithful account of the rise of Quakerism on the borders of Cumberland.[3] But the gem of the collection is the *Life* of John Roberts, of Siddington, near Cirencester, written by his son Daniel and published in 1746,[4] "good as gold, every word of it," said Oliver Wendell Holmes.

"The readiness of his wit," writes William Howitt,[5] "has perpetuated his memory; and I trust that, even in our day, his words shall produce delight and conviction. There may be some who will charge him with a little fanaticism, and others with a want of courtesy, especially towards the old bishop, who seems to have been a worthy old man struggling helplessly with the limed twigs of his own craft; but let us take John all together, and we shall find his heart in the right place, and his head one of that sort that every man would be thankful to possess. Let us consider the times and the offences given, and we shall even acknowledge that, though he possessed the sharp two-edged sword of a ready wit, he wielded it with the forbearance of a Christian."

It is a long step from this pithy record of the Gloucestershire yeoman to the folio *Life* of Thomas Story, the friend of Penn.[6] Instead of a retired corner of the Cotswold country, we find ourselves with the world before us, sharing the religious travels and conversations of a man of learning and piety whose itinerancy explored

---

[1] *Journal*, published 1720; 1779 edn. pp. 107-109.
[2] Published 1725. [3] Published 1726. See *ante*, p. 355.
[4] Roberts, who had an alternative surname (Hayward), like that other Gloucestershire valiant, William Tindale, died in 1683. The fullest edn., based on the original MS., is by Edmund T. Lawrence, London : Headley Bros. 1898.
[5] Edn. 1834 by William Howitt. [6] Printed in 1747 at Newcastle.

Quakerdom from America to Germany.[1] This minutely detailed diary, which brings in the names, in the British Isles alone, of over five hundred Friends, was designed for his own review, so that he might make a right retrospection into his religious conduct, and was left to be published by his trustees for the serious perusal of others. Smooth in style and abounding in incident and high discourse on religion, it furnishes a photographic presentation of Quakerism in the first half of the eighteenth century. Story, like other Quaker Journalists, gives scant space to the secular interests of his life; but he was a keen student of nature, and "in 1738, sent to James Logan from the Yorkshire coast a forecast of the discovery of stratified geology one hundred years before its time."[2] Like Penn, he was curious in trees, as we see from a reference arising in his journal out of a moral reflection:[3]

On the 20th [Sept. 1736] I went to my farm, called Justice Town [his birthplace, north of Carlisle, now the Lynehow Estate], where I had a large nursery of forest-tree plants, both British and American; from which, having been absent some years, they were in that time grown much out of order, and many of them lost, being overgrown and suppressed by others, very much like the course and way of humankind, among whom the weaker are too often crushed and ruined by the stronger and in vain lament and cry for aid, when none hears, relents or aids, and where the only relief is patient suffering, till kinder death ends the trouble. Here I stayed till the 21st preparing for a further progress in that concern; but the Quarterly Meeting for the County happening to fall at Pardshaw, below Cockermouth, I went thither. . . . On the 27th I went to Justice Town, where, with many hands, I began to plant out several sorts of young trees, as oaks, elms, ashes, acer majors [I suppose sycamores], poplars of several kinds, firs, English walnuts, black walnuts, tulip trees, locust trees, cedars of America, occidental planes, lindels [I suppose limes], chestnuts, horse-chestnuts, divers sorts of willows, beeches, hornbeams, scarlet oaks &c, which I had raised from seeds and cuttings, after their several kinds, at that

---

[1] For Story's early experiences, see *post*, Chap. XVII. He died in 1742.
[2] Joshua Rowntree, Swarthmore Lecture, *Social Service: its Place in the Society of Friends*, p. 17; the original letter is at Dev. Ho. Eighty years would be better, as Wm. Smith's geological map appeared in 1815.
[3] *Life*, pp. 728, 729.

THE PASSING OF THE LEADERS

farm, to furnish that part of the country in time with timber, which is now scarce; and that I might be an example to others in that useful kind of improvement; which several since have begun to follow. In the meantime I visited some meetings in those parts, as Kirklinton, Solport, Carlisle, Scotby and Moorhouse, and the Monthly Meeting consisting of these five.

I have chosen this extract, as it illustrates how a man of Quaker culture, like Story, found it natural to intermix pioneer work of service to the countryside with his religious labours. Out of such a spirit would spring the signal contributions to scientific progress made by later Friends and the fruitful devotion to leisure pursuits which is a fine characteristic of modern Quaker schools. Story's plantations remain to the present day, and his friendship with the Earl of Carlisle, who built Castle Howard in the North Riding, and planted the woods there, makes it probable that he helped in this admirable piece of work.[1]

Other interesting Journals of travel are those of Thomas Chalkley, who died in 1741,[2] and Samuel Bownas (1676-1753),[3] the latter abounding in passages of spiritual insight. Of a more intimate character is the manuscript Journal addressed to his daughters by Thomas Gwin, of Falmouth (1656-1720), which, after two hundred years, might well be published.[4] I pass by the frequent paragraphs of self-examination in favour of the shrewd estimates which mirror the state of Quaker ministry at the turn of the century.

[1709] Two Friends of Westmorland, Thomas Wilson and William Williamson, the former spoke as to people living at ease, and pressed earnestly on the meeting a-putting in practice what

---

[1] See Richard S. Ferguson's *Early Cumberland and Westmorland Friends* (1871), p. 132. He cites, from Wilson Armistead's *Memoirs of James Logan* (1851), some of Story's advanced scientific views. Ferguson states that one or more of the Justice Town tulip-trees still flowered annually. Bulmer's *Cumberland Directory*, 1901, says: "A specimen of every British shrub and tree grows in the carriage-drive, which is half-a-mile long, and several species of foreign trees on the estate have attained a remarkable size."
[2] Published 1749.
[3] Published 1756. For the early experience of Bownas, see *post*, Chap. XVIII.
[4] I have used a copy of the MS. made for the late Nathaniel Fox, kindly placed at my disposal by Arthur E. Fox, of Banbury. For ownership of the MS., see *J.F.H.S.* vii. 90.

they heard, the latter continued the same concern, with more ready expression, but not so great vehemency of spirit.[1]

[1710] The young man John Fallowfield spoke very intelligibly, Henry [Atkinson] was attended with a tone not so intelligible, but had a concern on him, yet many remained unconvinced. . . . Henry Atkinson was with us again, whose service was the less for the tone that attended him. But there was with him Thomas Chalkley, of Philadelphia, an approved minister, who spoke very sweetly and invitingly to all.[2]

[1710. Visit of Lydia Lancaster and Margaret Satterthwaite] They were young women, but was attended with the authority of elders. . . . They were women well-gifted and fitted for the service of Truth, especially Lydia, and, as they keep near the Lord, will be of service in the Church.[3]

[1711] The Sixth-day we had at our meeting two North-country women, the one was called Rebecca Jopson, the other the wife of Robert Turner: the former was a woman pretty intelligible, and had a good concern on her, the latter had an affected singing way, that we could not well understand.[4]

[1711. Visit of Patrick Henderson] A great deal of sweetness, and indeed seemed an approved minister, rightly dividing the word of truth.[5]

[1711. Visit of William Enock and Samuel Overton] Samuel spoke with some sweetness, but the other was sounder.[6]

[1711. Dr. Bettesworth a good deal at Falmouth] Preached

---

[1] This Thomas Wilson came from Cumberland (Caldbeck M.M.), but was at the time settled at Kendal. Williamson was from Windermere. They were liberated for service in the South by Kendal M.M., Nov. 1708.
[2] Fallowfield (1681-1744) was from Hertford, Atkinson from Cumberland.
[3] Lydia Lancaster (1684-1761) was the daughter of Thomas and Dorothy Rawlinson, of Graythwaite, Windermere. A letter from Henry Gouldney to Sir John Rodes, 6th April 1714, in *Quaker Post-bag*, p. 98, calls her "a woman of extraordinary qualifications . . . she may well be accounted of the first rank." For further particulars see Elizabeth J. Satterthwaite, *Records of Colthouse Burial Ground*, pp. 35, 36, and *Piety Promoted*, also Testimony of Lancaster M.M. in (London) *Friend*, vol. i. (1843), p. 236, and Kendal Minutes. She was twice in Ireland and Scotland, and visited America. For Margaret Satterthwaite, afterwards Hoare, see *Records of Colthouse Burial Ground*, pp. 44, 45, and Rutty, *Hist. of Friends in Ireland*, p. 282.
[4] Rebecca Jopson, of Kendal, was liberated for Wales and the South of England by Kendal M.M. in Feb. 1711, and in Nov. reported the visit accomplished to her comfort. She did much itinerant work and died in 1741.
[5] Henderson was an Ulster Friend.
[6] For Samuel Overton, of Warwick (1688-1737), see White, *Friends in Warwickshire*, 3rd edn. pp. 142-145. William Enock, of Harbury, died in 1748.

to them a long, long time, I thought with little effect. . . . Held preaching all the meeting, as I remember.[1]

I have, perforce, left many instructive Journals unnoticed; but suppose that the foregoing may more than suffice the appetite of our own self-absorbed age. We can make to-day more readable books than our forefathers, but not worthier lives.

The printing of Fox's *Journal*, in 1694, edited by Thomas Ellwood, was, beyond question, the most important literary event in the history of Friends. Others of that age could have written, with somewhat less learning, Barclay's *Apology*, or compiled, with somewhat less industry and fairness, Sewel's *History*; but the vital inward experience and the vitalizing service of the Founder of Quakerism were the central spirit and expression of the movement, a treasure much of which would have been lost beyond recall, unless preserved in the artless and sincere record of the *Journal*.

This wonderful book, though largely based on earlier material, took its present shape in the years that followed the return of Fox from America.[2] He landed at Bristol at the end of June 1673, staying through the Fair time, and afterwards going through the meetings to London. He then planned a visit to his aged mother in Leicestershire, who died a few months later,[3] and intended to return again to London; but on his way to Fenny Drayton was taken in mid-December at John Halford's house at Armscott, near Shipston-on-Stour, and thrown into the county gaol at Worcester. At the Quarter Sessions he was tendered the oath and left in prison, but spent some weeks in London on a *habeas corpus*, though finally returned to Worcester. He had a good deal of

[1] Dr. John Bettesworth was a physician of Bath.
[2] See Editor's Intro. to *Camb. Journ.*, my review of *Camb. Journ.* in *British Friend*, Dec. 1911, and *Beginnings of Quakerism*, App. A. Two corrections should be made in the Morning Meeting Minute of April 1692, there cited: "than writing" for "their writing," and "request" for "require."
[3] For her death, hastened by her son's imprisonment, see *Beginnings of Quakerism*, p. 32, citing paper in *J.F.H.S.* vii. 79. She was over seventy years of age (*Camb. Journ.* ii. 294). Charles Marshall's Journal, in his *Works*, shows that he went to see her in Jan. 1672, presumably with news of George, who was then in America.

liberty, even attending the Yearly Meeting in June 1674, but at the sessions in July was praemunired and lay for six months in Worcester gaol. In February 1675, after refusing the offer of a pardon, he was brought to London on a *habeas corpus*, and the indictment was quashed, the Lord Chief Justice, Sir Matthew Hale, refusing to put the oath to him again, saying that though some reported Fox a dangerous man to be at liberty he had heard many more good reports of him.[1] Thomas Lower, his devoted companion during much of his confinement, wrote triumphantly from Swarthmore:[2]

Glory be unto the Lord for ever, Who caused Moses and the Israelites to behold the dead carcasses of their enemies and to rejoice over them and sing the song of deliverance; so hath He caused our Moses and all the true upright Israelites to behold his and Truth's adversaries defeated and slain and to lie as dead carcasses before the feet of our Moses and his people.

After the Yearly Meeting, Fox went north to Swarthmore, reaching it at the end of June and there slowly shaking off the illness into which he had fallen at Worcester. Here he passed a year and three-quarters, the first long spell of rest in his life of incessant labours. The *Journal* proper closes in 1675. There can be little doubt, says T. Edmund Harvey,[3] that the quiet years at Swarthmore "were largely utilized for gathering together scattered manuscripts and for completing up to date this unique religious autobiography, which is supposed to have been begun during his last long imprisonment in Worcester jail." The later years of his life are summarized by Ellwood from less finished material, and are, as the discerning reader soon finds, of inferior interest, both in subject-matter and in execution, wanting "the little vivid touches which light up the earlier pages."

[1] For this imprisonment see *Ellwood Journ.* ii. 204-231, and *Camb. Journ.* ii. 264-310, which gives a number of illustrative documents. Thomas Corbet was the lawyer who succeeded in securing the release of Fox, as shown in Richard Davies, *Life*, pp. 156-161. He is said to have satisfied the judges that they could not imprison on a *praemunire*.
[2] In Elisha Bates, *Appeal to the Society of Friends*, p. 22, dated 4th March 1675, from Spence MSS. iii. No. 171. The Wilkinson-Story party objected to Fox being regarded as the Quaker Moses; see *ante*, p. 308.
[3] Introduction to *Camb. Journ.* pp. x, xi.

We get some human glimpses of the home life during these happy months from Sarah Fell's Account Book and one of her letters. A cask of wine is to be laid down, for they have only some cider and March beer bottled up,[1] a great cheese comes out of Cheshire, the Kendal carrier brings a runlet of wine from Richard Linton, of Newcastle, and three salmon are forwarded from Lancaster. A fat sheep celebrates a visit from Penn; and we even hear of threepence paid for "glue and tobacco pipes for father,"[2] and twopence for a whistle. The glue may have been needed for binding papers together, and the whistle to serve the uses of a call-bell, but there was a time when George had said, "tobacco I did not take,"[3] and we wonder if his practice had changed. Letters are constantly coming, one "with the King's speech in it." Ink and paper, parchment and three sheepskins tell of the literary work that is forward.

At the end of March 1677 he set out on his travels again. His wife writes:[4]

Your father is not altogether so weary as he was; but he cannot endure to ride but very little journeys and lights often; but he is pretty well and hearty, praised be the Lord.

His own joy at resuming itinerating work is shown by a self-revealing touch in a letter to his wife from York:[5]

Dear Heart. . . . The way was many times very bad and deep with snow, that our horses some were down and we were not able to ride; and sometimes we had great storms and rain; but by the power of the Lord I went through all. . . . At York yesterday we had a very large meeting, exceeding throng. . . . Friends are mighty glad, above measure. So I am in my holy element and holy work in the Lord, glory to His Name for ever,

---

[1] Sarah Fell to her mother, Swarthmore, 4th March 1675, in Helen G. Crosfield, *Margaret Fox*, pp. 163, 164, from Spence MSS. iii. No. 171. The other details are from the Swarthmore Account Book, which, we note, uses the "heathen" names of the months.

[2] Entry 17th June 1675; cf. 3rd March 1675, "By money paid for tobacco pipes for father 1d." Also "ink and pipes for him, 8d." (see *J.F.H.S.* xii. 114).

[3] See *Beginnings of Quakerism*, p. 85 (from *Camb. Journ.* i. 44). Cf. pp. 31, 86.

[4] Letter, 31st March 1677, from Draw-well, in *J.F.H.S.* ii. 23.

[5] Letter to wife, 16th April 1677, in *Ellwood Journ.* ii. 258. I follow the original in Fox's hand, in Dev. Ho. Crosfield Colln.; cf. *J.F.H.S.* ii. 123.

though I cannot ride as in days past; but praised be the Lord for ever.

Passing southwards by easy stages to London, he took part in the Yearly Meeting, and then, at the end of July, went over to Holland and Germany with a party of Friends, which included his step-daughter Isabel Yeamans, and the three ablest of the Quakers, Penn, Barclay and Keith. A system of Church government was established, with a Yearly Meeting at Amsterdam, but with Fox another main interest was to complete his visitation of Quakerism by coming into living touch with the continental groups of Friends from Rotterdam to Friedrichstadt in Holstein. The more remote group at Danzig he could only visit by letter. One of the chief services of his later life would be to correspond with Friends overseas, for the whole world was his parish, indeed it was only in a letter brought in sealed to the Morning Meeting after his death and found to be in his own painful and seldom-used hand that he resigns to them this labour of love.[1]

Fox was well qualified for the task, not only by his spiritual judgment but by the sympathy and interest that comes from personal knowledge. He was as deeply read in England as in his Bible. His spirit had savoured the religious soil of Scotland, with its clods of earth above the Seed of Life, and the air of Ireland, corrupt with bloodshed and oppression. He had escaped the Barbary corsairs and the Spanish buccaneers and had traversed the American wilderness, lying at night in the woods or in Indian wigwams. He had ridden in the service of Truth with greater heart and patience than any knight-errant in the service of his lady-love. As he went along his way through Holland and Germany, he was now proclaiming the Day of the Lord from slow canal-boat or straw-strewn wagon-floor with the zest of his old days of footsore vagrancy in Yorkshire. Travel rather than

---

[1] Minute of Morning Meeting (Second Day's Meeting), 19th Jan. 1691. The letter is in *Letters of Early Friends*, p. 353. On 28th Dec. 1690 Fox wrote to Scotland nominating new correspondents (*J.F.H.S.* viii. 64); and a Minute of the Meeting for Sufferings, 23rd Jan. 1691, gives his names for "the north and north-east parts of the world."

XVI THE PASSING OF THE LEADERS 431

books made up his education, not surface-travel amid curious sights, nor inspiring contact with the noble memorials of the past, but that still more intensive travel among men which brought him into their lives and the inner spirit of their lives. Through the wide world of humanity he had wandered and wondered, reading character at a glance and ministering to all the healing wisdom of his own soul's intercourse with God. He was no recluse; his gift of leadership sprang from a heart and memory in which were stored up his pregnant comradeship with hundreds of other lives whom he could picture in all their diverse spiritual and outward surroundings from the forgotten home of his race in Denmark to its latest home in the New World.

One letter, out of scores that could be cited, may serve to give a taste of his correspondence. It is addressed to captive Friends in Algiers, where Fox himself might have lain, had he not escaped the Salee rover.[1]

I understand . . . you have a meeting there in Algiers of about twenty; I am glad to hear you meet; and it is very well that you have so much liberty from your patroons, and my desire is that . . . in your lives and conversations and words you may preach . . . the life of Truth, so that you may answer the Spirit of God, both in the Turks and Moors and the rest of the captives . . . that Christ's ensign may be set up in those parts. . . . Though you remain as captives, yet if ye be Christ's and God's free men . . . be not entangled with any yoke of bondage to bring you out of that heavenly, spiritual liberty. For in this you are free; and they are but small matters to it. And therefore trust in the Arm of the Lord's power, Who can lay the

---

[1] Fox, *Epistles*, No. 366, 17th March 1682. For the Algiers captives see Fox, *Epistles*, Nos. 315, 388, 391, 420. In his *Doctrinals* is a powerful letter to the Great Turk and the King of Algiers (pp. 776-784), 16th July 1680, with an appended letter from Thomas Lurting, recounting how he took some Turks captive by disarming them peaceably, after they had taken the ship, and then succeeded in putting them ashore in their own country. The appended letter is also in Lurting's *The Fighting Sailor turned Peaceable Christian* (1710). In 1679 £800 was raised by Friends for redemption of the captives and another sum a few years later, and Friends also helped in a general collection instituted by the Government. (See Minutes of Meeting for Sufferings and Y.M., and in the Q.M. and Irish Books.) Pepys, *Diary*, 8th Feb. 1661, tells of the manner of life of the slaves at Algiers. Cf. also Dev. Ho. A.R.B. Colln. No. 164, Dix. Colln. sect. C., *J.F.H.S.* i. 66, and note in Fox, *Journal*, Bi-centenary edn. ii. 346.

mountains low and remove the hills out of their places and make His lambs to skip over all. . . . And, though hunger and thirst and cold many times you are in, and many distresses, yet the Lord is able to support you. . . . And, as you do walk in the light, grace, Spirit and gospel, you may turn others to it, that you may have unity with them in it, and that they may come out of the spiritual prison of death, darkness and corruption and captivity into the liberty of the sons of God in Christ Jesus. . . . The Lord preserve you all, tender vines in Him.   Amen.

The Quaker leader, as already narrated,[1] was now the subject of bitter personal attacks by some of the Wilkinson-Story party. These he bore with his usual steadiness and resolvedness of mind ; and they neither deflected his policy nor disturbed his equanimity. He had settled authority in the Church upon a basis which gave scope for the gifts of government of all and knew himself to be no hierarch. The best proof of this lies in the fact that his death made no disturbance in the life of the Church. Indeed, the only succession he had to provide for was that with respect to foreign correspondence, which, as we have seen, he bequeathed to the Morning Meeting. He remained to the last in close touch with affairs, but only as a revered elder among many brethren. After his return from the continent, he continued for a time his itinerating work, and spent another year at Swarthmore in 1679, also visiting Holland a second time five years later, but physical infirmities limited his activities, and he was much in London and the neighbourhood. Here and hereabouts he lived exclusively during the last six years of his life, residing for a few weeks at a time in the city, and then going for long visits to the purer country air of his step-daughter Margaret Rous's house at Kingston, or to Gooses, near Romford, the country house of his step-daughter Sarah Meade. His wife spent some months in London in the winter of 1684 to '5 (19th Nov.–16th March), and again came about half a year before his death (April, I think, to 30th June 1690),[2] finding him

---

[1] *Ante*, Chap. XI.
[2] I take the dates from the "Itinerary Journals."

XVI THE PASSING OF THE LEADERS 433

better in his strength than she had often seen him.[1] We have a glimpse of his health during these last years in a letter from Sarah Meade to her mother:

> Father, I hope, is rather better, though as to his getting strength there is little certainty, for, if he be a little cheery sometimes, then he is presently weak again, for he sleeps but little a-nights which keeps him weak. He was at our meeting last First-day in a coach; he could stay but about three-quarters of an hour in the meeting and was faint and weary when he came home.[2]

Detailed Itinerary Journals, mostly kept by his man, are preserved at Devonshire House, which cover the greater part of the period from August 1681 to his death.[3] The homely record for the last week of his life is a fair specimen of the whole and runs as follows:

The 5th of the 11th month [Jan. 1691] and the 2nd day of the week, he took coach to the Second Day's Meeting, and afterwards went to B[enjamin] A[ntrobus]'s where he stayed that night and the next day.

The day following, being the 7th of the 11th month and the 4th day of the week, towards evening he took coach to the Peel, and was at their Monthly Meeting. He stayed there that night and the next day.

The day following, he took coach to the Meeting for Sufferings, and after went to B. A's where he stayed that night.

The next day, being the 7th day of the week, he took coach towards night to Henry Gouldney's, where he stayed that night and writ an epistle to Friends in Ireland.

The next day, being the 11th of the 11th month, and the 1st day of the week, he was at Gracechurch Street meeting, where he declared a long time very preciously and very audibly, and went to prayer, and the meeting departed, which was very large.

---

[1] Margaret Fox, Testimony to her husband, in his *Journal*.
[2] Letter from Gooses, 6th March 1689, in Helen G. Crosfield, *Margaret Fox*, p. 213, from Spence MSS. iii. fol. 192.
[3] Two of these Journal Books are preserved, both duodecimo volumes. One of them covers the years 1681-87, 1683 being wanting, and seems a transcript from a series of pocket-books of which one is missing. The first six pages are in the first person. The other is an original vellum pocket-book, with clasp, from 1688 to Fox's death, and is throughout in the third person. Ellwood seems to have summarized these for the purpose of the *Journal*. See further C. R. Simpson's article in *Friends' Quarterly Examiner*, Jan. 1918, " George Fox as Home Mission Worker."

2 F

Thence he went to Henry Gouldney's;[1] and he said he thought he felt the cold strike to his heart as he came out of the meeting, but was pretty cheery with Friends that came to him there; and said, He was glad now he was at the meeting, now he was clear. And, after they were gone, he lay down upon the bed, as he was wont to do after a meeting, twice; and at his risings, which were but for a little space, he still complained of cold—the latter time he was worse and groaned much—so that after a very little, being much out of order, he was forced to go to bed; and in about two hours his strength failed him very much; and so he continued spending, till about half-an-hour and half-a-quarter after nine on 3rd day night; and then he departed this life, after the third day's illness, being the 13th of the 11th month 1690 [13th Jan. 1691].

In his illness, he used these words to some Friends that came to see him:—"The Seed of God reigns over all, and over death itself"; and, though he was weak in body, yet that the power of God is over all and reigns over all disorderly spirits.[2]

Such was the death of this "worthy champion," this "prince fallen in Israel," this "fixed star in the firmament of God's glory," as his friends called him.

There was no sign of any great pain upon him, neither did he ever complain. . . . He shut up his eyes and mouth himself, and his chin never fell again, nor needed any binding up, but lay as if he had fallen asleep—one would have thought he had smiled: he was the pleasantest corpse that ever was looked upon, and many hundreds of Friends came to see his face.[3]

On the Wednesday, Friends in the ministry arranged

---

[1] In the same court (Whitehart Court) as the meeting-house.

[2] The passage in the *Journal* seems based on the above, but quotes the words used after the meeting, "Now I am clear, I am fully clear." We have accounts of the illness and funeral in a number of contemporary documents: (*a*) Letters from Penn to Margaret Fox, 13th Jan., in *Fells of Swarthmoor Hall*, p. 362, from Thirnbeck MSS. No. 21, corrections in *J.F.H.S.* ix. 175; and from Penn to Thomas Lloyd, 14th June, in Janney's *Life of Penn*, p. 369; (*b*) Anonymous letter to John Ayrey, of Sedbergh Meeting, 15th Jan., in *Camb. Journ.* ii. 369; (*c*) Letter from Henry Gouldney to Sir John Rodes, 15th Jan., in *J.F.H.S.* i. 55, and *Quaker Post-bag*, p. 51; (*d*) Letter from Robert Barrow, of Kendal, to Lancashire Friends, 16th Jan., from Thirnbeck MSS. No. 22, in (London) *Friend*, 1902, p. 136, and other places. There is also a letter from Barrow to John Vaughton, of London, 28th Jan., giving his testimony at the funeral, copy in Dev. Ho. Reynolds Colln. (*b*) is from the Spence MSS., and seems once to have formed part of a Register Book of Friends at North Shields. See the general note on these documents in *Camb. Journ.* ii. 495.

[3] Barrow's Letter. I have followed a primitive text among my late father's papers.

for the burial at Bunhill Fields on the Friday,[1] one out of each of the six London Monthly Meetings to carry the corpse, and

. . . while we sat together under the deep consideration of the loss of that good man, the wonderful power of God in a miraculous manner fell upon all in the room, insomuch that not one could contain themselves, but was crushed and broken down by the weight of that glory; that for a considerable time there was nothing but deep sighs, groans and tears and roaring to admiration, and, after that all had vented and eased themselves, and grew quiet in their minds, several of them under that great sense gave testimonies concerning him. . . . One Price, a very old man,[2] declared in tears and great tenderness that he had buried his father and mother and many children and, which was nearest to him of all, his dear wife; but was naturally so stronghearted that he could never be overcome to shed a tear; "but now," says he, "I am overcome." . . . Surely I shall never forget that day's work: it was very astonishing to me, and it did appear to me in my eyes that it resembled that day when the apostles were met together and the mighty power of God fell upon them.[3]

After a meeting at Gracechurch Street, the earthly remains were laid in the Quaker Burial Ground at Bunhill Fields, Friends walking behind the bearers, three and three in a rank, on one side the street, "and though the graveyard be a large plat of ground yet it was pitched full, as thick as could stand, only some of the people of the world was not in there."[4]

Though worn in body, the spirit of the veteran had remained unwearied to the last. In November he had addressed a stirring letter to his fellow-ministers.[5]

" All Friends," he wrote, "[that] used to travel up and down in the gift of the ministry, do not hide your talent, nor put your

---

[1] For the reopening of Fox's grave about 1757, see *Fells of Swarthmoor Hall*, p. 369, and for position of grave, Beck and Ball, *London Friends' Meetings*, p. 331.
[2] This would be Peter Price, of Radnorshire (see *Beginnings of Quakerism*, p. 207), a prisoner for tithes many years, "alone, very ancient and low in the world" (see Epistle from Wales to London Y.M., 1688, in Dev. Ho. Reynolds Colln. p. 17). He died two months later about ninety years old.
[3] Letter to John Ayrey. [4] Barrow's Letter.
[5] *Journ.* ii. 500, corrected from copy in Minutes of Morning Meeting, 23rd Feb. 1691.

light under a bushel, nor cumber yourselves nor entangle yourselves with the affairs of this world . . . but be valiant for God's Truth upon the earth and spread it abroad in the daylight of Christ . . . going on in the Spirit, and ploughing with it in the purifying hope, and threshing, with the power and Spirit of God, the wheat out of the chaff of corruption in the same hope. . . . So my desires are that you may be kept out of all the beggarly elements of the world, which is below the spiritual region, to Christ the Head, and hold Him. . . . From him, who is translated into the kingdom of His dear Son with all His saints, a heavenly salutation. And salute you one another with a holy kiss of charity that never faileth."

Another, to ministers in America, glows with his undefeated missionary zeal:[1]

Let your light shine among the Indians, and the Blacks and the Whites, that ye may answer the Truth in them, and bring them to their standard and ensign, that God hath set up, Christ Jesus. . . . All grow in the faith and grace of Christ, that ye may not be like dwarfs, for a dwarf shall not come near to offer upon God's altar; though he may eat of God's bread, that he may grow by it [see Lev. xxi. 17-23]. . . . Keep up your negroes' meetings and your family meetings; and have meetings with the Indian kings and their councils and subjects everywhere, and with others. . . . Take heed of sitting down in the earth and having your minds in the earthly things, coveting and striving for the earth; for . . . covetousness is idolatry. There is too much strife and contention about that idol, which makes too many go out of the sense and fear of God, so that some have lost morality and humanity and the true Christian charity.

A third is addressed to all the "children of God," and superscribed, "not to be opened before the time."[2] It exhorts Friends to keep all their meetings in the name of the Lord, and to be steadfast in Him over all that rebel and oppose. "In Him live and walk, in Whom ye have life eternal, in Whom you will feel me and I you."

It will be noted how much the danger of Friends submerging themselves in the world was urgent with him

[1] *Journ.* ii. 502, 11th Dec. 1690. My friend, A. Neave Brayshaw, suggests that when Fox spoke of old people going into the "earth," see *Beginnings of Quakerism*, p. 31, he probably used the word in the sense he gives it in this letter and elsewhere. Cf. *post*, p. 439, and *ante*, p. 410.

[2] *Camb. Journ.* ii. 367, and sent down with the Y.M. Epistle of 1691. See note in *Camb. Journ.* ii. 494.

during these last months ; his address to the Morning Meeting, eight days before his death, dealt trenchantly with this greatest of all perils to a Society whose very virtues were stifling it with prosperity. He encouraged Friends that had gifts to make use of them,

. . . mentioning many countries beyond the seas that wanted visiting, instancing the labours and hard travels of Friends in the beginning of the spreading of Truth in our days, in breaking up of countries, and of the rough ploughing they had in steeple-houses &c; but now it was more easy ; and he complained of many Demases and Cains, who embrace the present world and encumber themselves with their own businesses and neglect the Lord's and so are good for nothing ; and said They that had wives should be as though they had none, and Who goeth a warfare should not entangle himself with the things of this world.[1]

He saw, with sure insight, that the world was paralysing the mission of Friends and its wealth removing them from their place of service.

Fox had a grave and serious nature,[2] and, as a boy, developed a character of singular purity and sincerity, which made him sensitive, in an unusual degree, to evil and to unreality of life, and open to an inflowing tide of energy that he came to know as the life of Christ within him, the Seed of God reigning over all. Seasons of untempered darkness or of undistracted light came to him, reacting strangely on mind and body and emotions.[3] But the great first-hand experience of Divine life which was continually building him into a man, "all of God Almighty's making,"[4] within a few years overcame the darkness and subdued to itself every region of his personality. The chief psychical crises of his youth and the less frequent later cases, as at Reading in 1659, the Year of Anarchy, and at London in 1670, were induced by a sense of identification with the spiritual needs and sorrows of

[1] John Bowater's Testimony, at beginning of Fox's *Doctrinals*. Bowater was a leading London minister, who travelled in America.
[2] The Friends' Hist. Society has now published, 1918, too late for use here, *The Personality of George Fox*, by A. Neave Brayshaw, which gathers into one portrait the various details of his personal life found in our sources.
[3] See the fine analysis of these psychological transformations by Rufus M. Jones, Introduction to *Beginnings of Quakerism*.
[4] Penn's expression, in preface to *Ellwood Journ.* i. l.

the world around him; and have their parallels in the agonies of spiritual travail that have come to others, notably in Quaker history to John Woolman. He became a princely man, "zealous for the Name of the Lord, . . . valiant for the Truth, bold in asserting it, patient in suffering for it, unwearied in labouring in it, steady in his testimony to it, immovable as a rock."[1] The eager exaltation that we find in Honthorst's impressionist picture of the young prophet in his white slouch hat about 1655 has changed to the collected serenity of white hair, noble eyes, strong features and sensitive mouth, which makes us wish to believe in the supposed portrait attributed to Sir Peter Lely.[2]

Living at the heart of things, in intimacy with the eternal verities, Truth became his second nature, bringing him directness of speech and action, simplicity of behaviour and penetration of insight, and making him sure and dauntless, beyond all birth and breeding.

Deceit and hypocrisy could not stand before him . . . he had a piercing eye,[3] or was wonderfully endued with a spirit of discerning or insight into the inward states and conditions of those he had to do withal.[4]

We have noted the accusations of presumption and pride made against Fox, and the want of tenderness which he showed towards those whom he regarded as hirelings or apostates. We have also marked the apparent vanity that seems to lie behind naïve passages in his *Journal* and made him claim to possess a counterpart for human learning, which he paraded in the *Battle-Door* and else-

---

[1] Ellwood's Testimony in *Ellwood Journ.*
[2] Fine reproductions of these portraits are given at beginning of vols. i., ii. of *Camb. Journ.* The Honthorst face is most unsatisfying. The Lely portrait was purchased in England in 1858, and is now in Swarthmore College, Pennsylvania. When I saw it in 1912, the librarian kindly allowed me to unscrew the canvas from the frame so as to examine the writing on the back, which reads, "Geo. Fox, by Sir Peter Lely." But this is in a comparatively modern hand, and may be a mere guess on the part of the writer. A connoisseur of Lely's work might determine if he is the painter, and, in that case, he may have done a portrait from memory, as it seems out of character for Fox to have sat to him.
[3] See *Beginnings of Quakerism*, p. 68, note 4.
[4] Testimony of Oxfordshire Friends in Q.M. Minutes, 15th Sept. 1691, also in an edited form at beginning of Fox's *Doctrinals*.

where.[1] These evidences of overweening conceit, as his detractors would call them, are, in the main, cases of an overweening confidence in Truth, as he apprehended it, which at times led him, as with other holy men, to forget his charity and meekness while he thought to do God service. Fox was continually comparing and correcting his own subjective experience with that of prophets and apostles, as recorded in scripture, but, as he breathed much of the narrow intellectual and moral atmosphere of the age, his very devotion to an Inner Light, coloured by its medium, sometimes led him seriously astray. These defects in the expression of the life that welled within should keep us from blindly following him, or indeed any other of the Quaker leaders, but only fix attention the more upon the master-quality of his character, his complete reliance on the truth he knew. By that first-hand knowledge he lived, and became one of the world's great religious leaders. No man in England trod the way of heavenly-mindedness with surer steps. "The earth," as he called it, held him lightly. The money that came to him when his parents died he allowed his sister Katherine to use up as long as she lived.[2] On his marriage he engaged not to meddle with his wife's estate, a thing that greatly surprised the judges when it chanced to come under their notice.[3] He speaks of a loss at sea with the utmost composure: "I hear of a ship of Thomas Edmondson [that] is cast away, which I had a part in ; but let it go."[4] At the last he behaved "as if death were hardly worth notice or a mention," thinking not of himself but of Friends and their welfare.[5] Penn describes him as "civil beyond all forms of breeding in his behaviour, very temperate, eating little and sleeping less, though a bulky person."[6] Muggleton, in 1667, had called him "a great

[1] Cf. *Beginnings of Quakerism*, pp. 301, 302 (add reference to *J.F.H.S.* xv. 31-32), 497. The letter to the King of Poland, 13th Nov. 1677 (*Ellwood Journ.* ii. 321-26) is the most learned of his epistles, and must have been written with skilled assistance.
[2] See the testamentary disposition to his relatives in *Camb. Journ.* ii. 352.
[3] *Ellwood Journ.* ii. 357. Cf. advice, *ante*, p. 257.
[4] Letter to wife, Worcester, 8th Feb. 1674, in *J.F.H.S.* xi. 157, from Abraham Colln.   [5] Penn in *Ellwood Journ*. Preface, i. 1.   [6] *Ibid.*

old, fat fox,"[1] and random charges of excess in eating and drinking were made against him in later life by the apostate Quaker Francis Bugg, who said he lived in as much plenty as any knight in England. In reply to these thrusts we have a curious account by Anne Docwra, of Cambridge, which gives the fullest details we possess of Fox's person and habits in the years when the rigour of his imprisonments had left his frame swollen and stiff.[2]

> Some years before his decease, I being at London and understanding where his lodging was, I went about dinner-time. . . . I found him sitting down to dinner, his meat was upon the table; it was only a piece of very salt beef as big as a man's fist—it was cold meat. I sat down by him until he had dined, but did not eat with him, I did like his dinner so well. He had no wine; his beer was said to have wormwood in it; I did not drink with him neither; and this is the whole bill of his fare at that time. I had heard before by one of my brothers that was well acquainted with him that most of his diet was salt beef when he could get it and wormwood stamped and squeezed into his beer. . . . He was pretty tall of stature and a very great-boned man in my judgment; but his face was not so fat as some fat men's faces are by much. His hands were stiff and swelled, so that he could not well write in the latter part of his days. His limbs were stiff; I could perceive that by his rising up and sitting down. It is likely his body was swelled; I have heard him speak to that purpose. He wore loose garments always when I saw him, that I cannot describe his bulk, but I could perceive that he was somewhat burly.

This crudely matter-of-fact description is vivified by the personal touches that abound in the *Journal*, and we picture Fox to ourselves as a man of heavy build, commanding presence, and wonderful eyes, "a goodly person and of an amiable countenance,"[3] who before his body was numbed by hardships could ride as boldly as any of Cromwell's troopers and silence the criers of an assize-court with his voice. His physical prowess, when in his prime, is shown by his behaviour in personal encounters

---

[1] *Answer to William Penn*, p. 141, cited *ante*, p. 245.
[2] *An Apostate Conscience Exposed*, p. 43, etc.
[3] Ambrose Rigge's Testimony in Fox's *Doctrinals*.

with violent men,[1] and by passages of stout horsemanship amid hostile crowds at Cambridge, Warwick and elsewhere.[2]

Fox, to the last, with all his robustness of mind, remained in the narrower sense of the word illiterate. He usually dictated his correspondence and his books, and there is little of his own writing preserved.[3] An interesting bit, undated, on the conduct of a school,[4] may serve to illustrate his handling of the King's English:

> If any mare [mar] ther bovkes, & blot ther bovkes throw carlesnes, lat them sit with ovt the tobel [table] as disorderly children, & if any on torenes [turns] from these things & mendeth & doeeth soe noe more, & then if any doe aqves [accuse] them of ther former action after the[y] be amendd, the same penelaty shall be layd vp on them as vpon them that is mended from his former doinges; & if any be knon to s[t]eale, leat him right with ovt the tabel & say his leson & shew his copy with ovt the bare [bar]: & all mvst be meeke, sober & ientell & qviet & loving & not give one another bad word noe time, in the skovell nor ovt of it, leats [lest] that the[y] be mad to say thr lesen or shew ther copy bovk to the master at the bare: & all is to mind ther lesones & be digelent in ther rightings; & to lay vp ther bovkes when the[y] goe from the skovell, & ther pens & inkonerns, & to keep them sow, eles the[y] mvst be lovk'd vpon as carles [careless] & slovenes: & soe yov mvst keep all things clean, svet, & neat & hanson.

Men were impressed by the outward man, but the influence of this unlettered prophet lay supremely in what may best be called his "over-worldliness." The more ordinary word, "other-worldliness," is chiefly used of a habit of mind concerned only with the future life; Fox, rather, was preoccupied with the life of an overworld, which transcended the material world known to his bodily senses, but was no more separated from it than the light is from the day. By its laws he sought

---
[1] Take the cases at Baldock (1655) in *Camb. Journ.* i. 199, 200, and at Falmouth (1656), *Camb. Journ.* i. 209. In the former he separated two desperate fellows who were fighting, holding them apart; in the second a man tried to throw him down, "but he could not, but I stood stiff and still, and let him strike."
[2] See *Beginnings of Quakerism*, especially chap. ix.
[3] See *J.F.H.S.* i. 6, 61; ii. 2; v. 170.
[4] *J.F.H.S.* v. 2, with a facsimile, and v. 66.

to live ; out of its wisdom he formed his knowledge ; he tested all things in the judgment given by its light; to its heavenly vision he surrendered himself in glad obedience.

This explains both the note of certainty in his bearing and the endless reiteration but perennial freshness of his writings. When John Taylor, afterwards of York, first met him, George took him by the hand and said, "Young man, this is the word of the Lord to thee : there are three scriptures thou must witness to be fulfilled ; first, thou must be turned from darkness to light ; next, thou must come to the knowledge of the glory of God ; and then, thou must be changed from glory to glory." [1]

"Above all," says Penn, "he excelled in prayer. The inwardness and weight of his spirit, the reverence and solemnity of his address and behaviour, and the fewness and fullness of his words, have often struck even strangers with admiration, as they used to reach others with consolation. The most awful, living, reverent frame I ever felt or beheld, I must say, was his in prayer." [2]

But this intimacy with the higher life made him at times a rare humorist, struck with the odd contradictions and confusions of the world about him. At Lancaster, as already narrated, when tendered the oath, he held up the Bible, as the book which forbade swearing, and said he wondered that it was allowed liberty.[3] At Tenby, after he had racily argued the hat question, the governor cried, "Away with these frivolous things," and was met with the retort ; " Why then imprison my friend for frivolous things?"[4] When the Roman Catholic governor groped his way into the smoky room at Scarborough where Fox lay, George says, " I told him that was his purgatory where they had put me into,"[5] and an Anglican dignitary who justified the excommunication of Friends for not coming to church, was told :

"You left us above twenty years ago, when we were but

---

[1] Testimony, at beginning of Fox's *Doctrinals*.
[2] *Ellwood Journal*, preface, vol. i. xlvii. Cf. *Beginnings of Quakerism*, p. 202, from *F.P.T.* p. 276.
[3] *Ante*, p. 36.
[4] *Beginnings of Quakerism*, pp. 347, 348.
[5] *Camb. Journ.* ii. 94.

young lads and lasses, to the Presbyterians, Independents and Baptists, who made spoil of our goods and persecuted us because we would not follow them ; and, as for the old men [whom you left behind] that knew your principles, if you would have kept them alive you should have sent them your epistles and gospels and homilies and evening-songs . . . and not have fled away from us. . . . We might have turned Turks and Jews for any collects or homilies or epistles we had from you all this while. . . . This is madness to put us out before we be brought in."[1]

His humour was drawn from a shrewd English mother-wit which saved him from many extremes. With him extravagances of conduct are dismissed as "mad whimseys," and petty criticisms as "jumbles." He trusted his heart rather than his logic ; and, had he lived, would probably have made short work with the rigours of discipline with respect to dress and behaviour and have guided the Society on the question of oaths with more directness than Whitehead and less scrupulosity than the extreme Friends of the dissatisfied party. His strong practical bent is shown in his wise provisions for marriages and other matters of necessary outward arrangement, and in his statesmanlike ability to mould Quakerism into an enduring organization. His sincerity was never satisfied with mystical exaltations; it demanded outward expression in conduct under the practical conditions of the time. This temper in Fox and other leading Friends more than once saved the Society from disintegration, and inspired his strenuous advocacy of righteousness as the guiding principle for the reformation of the social order.

The work of the Founder of Quakerism is writ large in the history of Friends, and indeed of England and America. He carried the principles of Protestantism to their fullest expression ; but penetrated beyond Protestantism to the Spirit-filled life of the early Church. And it is fortunate for the world that he did this, not by force of argument or strength of learning, but by the untutored wisdom which came from the deeps of his own soul's experience. For, if his name had been associated with schemes or systems, like the names of Luther or of

[1] *Camb. Journ.* ii. 98, 99.

Calvin, much of the inspiration of his life would have passed with changing fashions of thought; as it is, the unlettered Leicestershire countryman, whom his friends loved to call "dear George," taught by the living Spirit of Christ, rooted himself in truths which still satisfy the spiritual yearnings of men and lead them from the clogging world to lives of freedom and joyful service in the City of God on earth.

It has been among the aims of this history, while giving full place to the commanding personality of Fox, to discover both to Friends and others the great company of children of the Light, who contributed to the strength of the Quaker movement. The rare worth of the *Journal* has naturally thrown Fox himself into the foreground and left the other leaders in shadow. He is not to blame for this. He sometimes digresses from his narrative to refer to the spiritual exploits of his companions; and with his sense of historical values made a careful digest, while at Swarthmore, of the service of other Publishers of Truth during the first years of Quakerism.[1] He had in mind a "brave" history based upon these materials, which should record the spreading of Truth after the long night of apostasy since the apostles' days.[2] He could tell the worth of his comrades in homely words: Burrough is a valiant warrior, "who never turned his back on the Truth, nor his back from any out of the Truth"; Hubberthorne, "dear innocent Richard, as innocent a man as liveth on the earth"; Howgill, "one of the Lord's worthies," valiant and bold for His Name; Thomas Taylor, "a faithful, true, upright man in the Lord's Truth to the last, and turned many to the Lord Jesus Christ"; Dewsbury, "a dear friend and brother."[3] His letter to Robert Barclay's widow, written a fortnight before his own death, is filled with tender affection:[4]

[1] For this digest see *Camb. Journ.* ii. 321-338. The Swarthm. Colln. contains many of the letters on which it is based.
[2] See passages in Fox's testamentary papers in *Camb. Journ.* ii., one of which I have chosen as my motto in *Beginnings of Quakerism.*
[3] See Fox's testimonies to the Friends named at beginning of their *Works.*
[4] Letter to Christian Barclay, 28th Dec. 1690, in *Reliquiae Barclaianae*, p. 71, and Barclay's *Diary of Alexander Jaffray*, p. 449.

THE PASSING OF THE LEADERS

Do not look at the outward presence of thy husband, but look at the Lord, Whose he was, and in Whom he died; and enjoy him in the Spirit; for the Church of the living God written in heaven are come to the spirits of just men made perfect; and so, enjoy him in the Spirit and be cheerful in the Lord. . . . From him that had a great love and respect for thy dear husband for his work and service in the Lord, who is content in the will of God in all things that He doth, and so must thou be.

Barclay had died of a fever in October 1690 in his forty-second year. The loss was keenly felt. Though his *Apology* challenged the theological scholarship of Europe,[1] still riper fruits of his learning and spiritual experience might have been expected. "He had not left his fellow in Scotland," said a gentleman of his acquaintance eighteen years later.[2] When he came to die, though in great bodily weakness, he could say, "God is good still . . . my peace flows."[3] In that last hour he was carried forth into the larger life on a tide of inward peace:

> such a tide as moving seems asleep,
> Too full for sound and foam,
> When that which drew from out the boundless deep
> Turns again home.

A broad, unhurrying stream of life flowed within him and had made him notable for a rare equanimity. Says his kinsman, Patrick Livingstone, "I never knew him at any time to be in passion or anger: he was a man of a sweet, pleasant and cheerful temper, and above many for evenness of spirit"; "of such a bearing, contented mind," says his intimate, Andrew Jaffray, and "kept in such a dominion over anything that would have disordered his own spirit, that I can truly say I never saw him in any peevish, angry, brittle or disordered temper."[4] This inward peace had given a breadth and calm strength to his writings which separates them from the impetuous efforts of many other Quaker controversialists. It had

---

[1] I take the phrase from T. E. Harvey, *Rise of the Quakers*, p. 131.
[2] Thomas Chalkley, *Journal*, p. 62, *sub anno* 1708.
[3] *Piety Promoted*, pt. iii. 164.
[4] Testimonies at beginning of *Works*.

given ripeness to his learning and clarity to his style. The collectedness of mind which comes from waiting on the Lord made him the trusted spiritual counsellor of women of quality such as his distant cousin, Elizabeth, the Princess Palatine of the Rhine, and Lady Conway, of Ragley in Worcestershire. It gives a quaint finality to the letter with which he won the daughter of Gilbert Molleson, the Aberdeen bailie, for his bride, whose motherly devotion to her family and to Friends would make of Ury a second Swarthmore.

"The love of thy converse," he wrote, "the desire of thy friendship, the sympathy of thy way and meekness of thy spirit has often, as thou mayst have observed, occasioned me to take frequent opportunity to have the benefit of thy company, in which I can truly say I have often been refreshed, and the life in me touched with a sweet unity. . . . Many things, in the natural will, concur to strengthen and encourage my affection towards thee and make thee acceptable unto me; but that which is before all and beyond all is that I can say in the fear of the Lord that I have received a charge from Him to love thee, and for that I know His love is much towards thee, and His blessing and goodness is and shall be unto thee, so long as thou abidest in a true sense of it."[1]

It brought him the inflexible resolution, when under suffering with other Friends in 1677, in the Chapel Prison at Aberdeen, never to renounce the Truth nor the public profession of it, though "pursued to death itself," "which," says he, "by the grace of God, we hope cheerfully to undergo for the same; and we doubt not but God would out of our ashes raise witnesses who should outlive all the violence and cruelty of man."[2] It showed again in his calm behaviour when he found himself on a journey looking down the barrel of a highwayman's pistol. He took the fellow by the arm and asked him, How he came to be so rude? The man, trembling, dropped the pistol in great surprise, and did not so much as rifle his pockets.[3] With life-work

---

[1] Letter, 28th March 1669, in *Diary of Alexander Jaffray*, p. 295.
[2] *Ibid.* p. 392, letter to James Sharpe, Archbishop of St. Andrews, 26th March 1677.   [3] *Ibid.* p. 442.

seemingly unfinished, this tide of inward peace carried him from quiet Ury with its belts of pine and stretches of gorse and shining sea, away from his stricken wife and houseful of young children, into the peace of God.

"The Lord," wrote Fox to Christian Barclay, "will be a Husband to thee and a Father to thy children."[1] And so it proved. Notably impressed as our annals are by the Hand of God, no case of spiritual guidance exists clearer than the mission on which Peter Gardner was sent to Ury a few years later.[2] He was an Essex Friend, of humble condition, with a concern in 1694 to visit Scotland. His Monthly Meeting would have provided him a horse, but he said, "Nay, my Master has promised to give me hinds' feet." Going by the East Coast, he came to Bridlington, where and at Scarborough he gave remarkable evidence of his insight into the states of Friends whom he visited. "I cannot stay in this house," he said, "here is light and darkness, good and bad." The hostess's husband, it afterwards appeared, was at the time lying drunk on his bed upstairs. John Richardson and another Friend went with him to Scarborough, they on horseback, he afoot.

He kept before them full as fast as they chose to ride, and when they had got about half way he gained ground upon them. John was filled with admiration, for he seemed to go with more sleight and ease, he thought, than ever he had seen any man before. And, riding fast to overtake him and going over a field for a nearer cut, he appeared to be surrounded by glory, and his feet seemed not to touch the ground.[3] When he overtook him, John said, "Thou dost travel very fast." Peter replied, "My Master told me before I left home that He would give me hinds' feet, and He hath performed His promise to me."

Peter told John he was satisfied he was to die of smallpox and had only a short time for the service that lay before him. His money was but two half-crowns, yet, he said, "I have enough; my Master told me I should not want; and now a bit of bread and some water from

[1] Letter cited *ante*, p. 445.
[2] The documents are given in *Diary of Alexander Jaffray*, pp. 454-468 and 585-589.   [3] We are reminded of Mark x. 32.

a brook refreshes me as much as a set meal at a table." Richardson pressed some small pieces of silver on him and thus they parted.

Gardner reached Ury in January 1695, having already been used in bringing forth Andrew Jaffray's eldest surviving daughter Margaret in a public testimony. At his first meeting he felt the life stopped in some who would not give up to the Lord's requirings. The same night, after supper, he had a meeting attended by three of the young Barclays, Robert, then twenty-two, Patience, who was nineteen, and David, a boy of twelve. "We were all so mightily overcome that we were made to cry out," says the record, and Robert prayed and said a few words confessing that he should have spoken in the meeting where the life had been stopped. Next day Peter met with the children, when Christian, a girl of fourteen, prayed. At a public meeting on the First-day, Robert preached, saying that the Lord had now raised up the third generation to witness for His Truth at Ury. Here the aunt Jane Molleson spoke for the first time, and, at another meeting the same day, David, Catherine a girl of sixteen, and Christian all took part, and the Ury gardener, John White, had a few words.[1] "Yet, notwithstanding all this, Peter Gardner could not obtain ease, but felt the life stopped in one there, and at last named the person and desired him to clear himself; and so John Chalmers their schoolmaster"—a young man of nineteen and afterwards an acceptable minister at Dublin—"stood up and said a few words by way of testimony. Then Peter ended the meeting in prayer and came away easy." After further service in the district, he passed on to the West of Scotland, writing to Robert from Edinburgh, "Eternity will be little enough to admire the great love of God. . . . Let nothing be nearer unto thee than the glory of God and the good of poor souls."[2] He reached

[1] This last detail is from a variant copy among my late father's papers of account in *Diary of Alexander Jaffray*.
[2] Letter, 28th Jan. 1695 in *Reliquiae Barclaianae*, p. 83. There is a letter of same date to the mother, *ibid.* p. 84, and another from Edinburgh, 8th Feb. to Robert, *ibid.* p. 93. Letters from other Friends show that Robert Barclay was a young Friend of promise, before Gardner's visit.

Carlisle about April, and was there stricken with smallpox, dying after a twelve-days' illness and showing his singular power of spiritual discernment to the last. His money had proved just sufficient for his needs and the expenses of his burial. His last words are in curious harmony both with Robert Barclay's dying utterance and with Tennyson's poem. " I have sweet peace with Him that is the Redeemer of Israel, and am now waiting for my Pilot to conduct me to my long home."[1]

Rather more than two years before the death of Barclay, William Dewsbury had passed away, on 17th June 1688. After his release from Warwick under the Pardon of 1672, he had liberty for some years and travelled in the West and North, having much upon him while the door was open.[2] At the time of the Popish plot, he was accused as a Jesuit, being taken up at Leicester, and, though cleared by Titus Oates, seems to have continued a prisoner at Warwick until the general pardon under James II.[3] He helped to maintain himself by making laces, and a letter is extant soliciting the custom of a Friend near Darlington, if it would not prejudice his taking laces from the prisoners at York.[4] In 1680, he was living comfortably with his granddaughter, Mary Sam, in the Sergeant's Ward in Warwick; and tells us of her dying words, one April day, when the chimes were going four, and of his promising to follow her " as fast as the Lord orders my way."[5] His health was much broken by his long confinement; " being nineteen years a prisoner in this town of Warwick, and four of them being kept close prisoner, it hath pleased God to suffer my health to be impaired, that many times I am forced to rest two or three times in going to the meeting in the town, not being of ability of body to travel as in years past."[6] He came

---

[1] For his death see *Diary of Alexander Jaffray*, pp. 464-467, and pp. 588-589, and letter from Alexander Seaton to Robert Barclay, Glasgow, 29th April 1695, in *Reliquiae Barclaianae*, pp. 100, 101.
[2] See letters in *Works*, pp. 328-330.
[3] John Whiting's account in *Persecution Exposed*, p. 182, and certificate of Oates in Dewsbury's *Works*, p. 343.
[4] Letter, 30th Jan. 1683, in *J.F.H.S.* iv. 151.
[5] Account in *Works*, pp. 348-352.
[6] Postscript to letter, 4th Dec. 1686, in *Works*, p. 376.

to London for the Yearly Meeting of 1688, being restless till he could come to the great city to preach the everlasting gospel there, but after visiting most of the meetings, was forced to leave before the Yearly Meeting by a violent attack of the "ancient distemper" which had accompanied him for many years in prison.[1] He reached Wellingborough, where he had founded a Quaker Church in 1654.[2]

And, as Friends were tenderly concerned by him seeing his great weakness, he with ardency revived himself and earnestly spake and said, "If anyone has received any good or benefit thorough this vessel, called William Dewsbury, give God the glory; I'll have none, I'll have none," and again, "I'll have none." So desiring to go to Warwick, he grew weaker and weaker, and, being brought thither, soon changed, and, after a little while, fell asleep in Christ.

Some of his last words rank with those of James Nayler for their rare beauty. He recalled a sign which had been given him in the first days of his service; and bore triumphant witness:

For this I can say; I never since played the coward, but joyfully entered prisons as palaces, telling mine enemies to hold me there as long as they could: and in the prison-house I sung praises to my God; and esteemed the bolts and locks put upon me as jewels; and in the Name of the eternal God I alway got the victory; for they could keep me no longer than the determined time of my God.[3]

We possess a shorthand report of one of his last sermons in London, which gives a taste of the earnestness and power of his ministry.[4]

---

[1] Letter to the Y.M., London, 30th May 1688, in *Works*, p. 401.
[2] Account in *F.P.T.* pp. 197-199; cf. *Beginnings of Quakerism*, p. 174.
[3] *Works*, early unnumbered page; cf. *ante*, p. 221.
[4] Sermon preached at Gracechurch Street, 16th May 1688, in Sewel, ii. 456-465, from *The Concurrence & Unanimity Of the People Called Quakers*, 1694, pp. 11-37. The book contains a sermon by each of the following: Barclay, Dewsbury, George Whitehead, Francis Camfield (1628-1708), a London Friend who in 1706 created a Trust for poor Friends "whom God hath endued with His power to preach the gospel," which is still in existence; John Bowater (1629-1704), another London Friend, whose "Christian Epistles, Travels and Sufferings" were printed in 1705; Penn (two sermons); Charles Marshall; Richard Ashby (1663-1731), of London and afterwards of Norfolk, see his writings in Smith's *Catalogue*; William Bingley (1651-1715), see *Camb. Journ.* ii. 496; Samuel Waldenfield (1652-1715), see *Camb. Journ.* ii. 497; John Butcher (1666-1721), see *Camb. Journ.* ii. 497; John Vaughton (1644-1712), see *Camb.*

XVI THE PASSING OF THE LEADERS 451

The subject is the need of a new birth. "A new world," he says, "comes by regeneration. A man is not lifted up in his own mind, but laid low in his own eyes. He waits for the wisdom of God to govern him; and he is as a steward of the grace of God to give to them that stand in need. When a man is regenerated and born again, he is as contented with bread and water as with all the enjoyments of this world. What is the matter? His own will is gone and put down under his feet. . . . There is a harmony of all within a man, praising of God and blessing His holy Name. There are no entanglements shall draw away his heart from serving of God and seeking His glory. . . . Will you live as the Quakers? Then you must live contemptibly: the mistress and maid are hail-fellow well met. . . . Here is now a new world; and the fashions of the old world are gone, all pride, haughtiness, grossness and trampling upon one another are gone; all slain, through the operation of Christ."

Such words express the spirit of Dewsbury's own life. Without either the practical genius of Fox or the finely-tempered mind of Barclay, he excelled the former in tenderness and the second in depth. "His speech was plain and powerful, reaching to the tendering and breaking of many hearts, his discerning clear and piercing, whereby many had their conditions plainly demonstrated and laid open before them, whom before he never saw."[1] Above all, he spent himself in travail for the souls of his friends. His letters in times of persecution gave heart to the Church militant like the songs of angel-choirs. We have seen how a blessed ministry of reconciliation was given to him in the case of James Nayler; and how he yearned for the recovery of John Perrot. The bitterness of the Wilkinson-Story controversy "hath been," he wrote, "a greater exercise and trouble to me than all the sharp persecutions and imprisonments I have endured for the word of God."[2] The sweetness of his spirit had made the soldiers' hearts fail them at Northampton and the magistrates weep at Torrington.[3] To those who look below the surface of early Quaker history to its hidden

---
Journ. ii. 487; James Parke, died 1696, for writings see Smith's *Catalogue*; and Francis Stamper, died 1698, see *Camb. Journ.* ii. 496. These last were all London Friends.
 [1] *F.P.T.* p. 197.   [2] *Works*, p. 374; cf. *ante*, p. 319.
 [3] *Beginnings of Quakerism*, pp. 361, 362.

springs of strength, the great heart held fast at Warwick, whose unconfinable love streamed its spiritual life through the whole fellowship, beats at the very heart of the movement for it drew an infinite warmth and tenderness from the heart of God.

One other name may perhaps be ranked with Fox, Barclay and Dewsbury, that of Steven Crisp of Colchester, who died at the end of August 1692, some twenty months after Fox. Convinced by young James Parnell, he had devoted himself through a long life to the welfare of the Church, and at his death he and George Whitehead were its acknowledged leaders.[1] Colchester had close trading relations with Holland; and Crisp learnt the language and visited the groups of Friends there no less than thirteen times, proving a worthy successor to Ames and Caton, the founders of Dutch Quakerism. Several of his writings were translated into Dutch and many were only printed in that language, though always written first in English.[2] Dutch Friends loved him as a father, for his heart was always with them and their concerns, and he was continually assisting them, whether present or absent.[3] He travelled much in England and was often in London, and shorthand reports of thirty of his sermons[4] enable us to judge the character of his ministry more fully than is possible with other Friends.

There is the root of Quakerism in them all, simply and straightforwardly expressed, without flourishes or show of learning, but with many pointed questions reaching home to the condition of his hearers and much directing of them away from the preacher and his words to the inward source of living faith. They are profoundly

---

[1] In proof see postscript by him and Whitehead to the Y.M. Epistle of 1692, and letter from Robert Barrow, of Kendal, Aberdeen, 15th Jan. 1692 (*Steven Crisp and his Correspondents*, p. 51, from Colchester Colln.), which is addressed to Whitehead and Crisp and says that he used formerly to write to Fox, but now writes to them of affairs in Scotland, believing they have a universal eye over all the Churches in Europe and America.
[2] See Smith's *Catalogue* and letter from John Claus, 1st Dec. 1693, in *Steven Crisp and his Correspondents*, p. 18, from Colchester Colln.
[3] Testimony from Amsterdam Y.M. in Crisp's *Works*.
[4] Published in three parts by Nathaniel Crouch, not a Friend, in 1693, 1694. The 1707 English and 1787 Philadelphia editions contain two additional sermons.

evangelical in their temper, designed to produce repentance and a change of heart; but lay the stress not on doctrine but on a life of loving obedience to the will of God. The reader may care to sample the collection, which was several times reprinted:

Christian words will not make the Christian religion, there must be a Christian life (pt. i. 48).

The soul hath eyes and ears as well as the body; it can hear and see as the body . . . [it] can see things that are invisible and heavenly . . . you may hear the voice of Christ inwardly (pt. i. 50).

Men think by reading, and learning, and hearing this and the other men's notions and opinions, they may be edified and profited and come to the true knowledge of God. But, while they are waiting upon God . . . they may receive knowledge from Christ and be more certain and infallible in what they do know than by consulting all the wise men and learned doctors in the world. For no man knows all at once; and no man knows all things neither. It is not a thing necessary that man should know all things in relation to God; for, as He is in Himself, He is incomprehensible. . . . Yet that which he knows of God, he may know it as certain and infallible (pt. i. 123, 124).

If professors [of religion] were resolved to answer the principles of Truth in their own hearts and go through-stitch in their profession, they might live courageously; Truth will crown them with victory. . . . If you will give them a world, they will not give away an hair's breadth of the Truth which they have professed. When Truth thus comes to have dominion, then Truth shall overspread the earth (pt. i. 145, 146).

The great thing that I would have ushered into the hearts of men is that they may believe the Truth for Truth's sake (pt. iii. 34).

We know when our Friends are in captivity, in Turkey or elsewhere, we pay down our money for their redemption; but we will not pay our money if they be kept in their fetters still. . . . This is for bodies, but now I am speaking of souls. Christ must be made to me redemption, and rescue me from captivity. . . . There is one come that hath paid a price for me. That is well; that is good news; then I hope I shall come out of my captivity. . . . No, say they, you must abide in sin as long as you live. What benefit then have I by my redemption? . . . I must wear my shackles and fetters still, and be subject to my old master and patroon ; and when he will have me be drunk I must be drunk ; and when he will have me unclean I must be unclean. . . . What sort of redemption is this? (pt. iii. 123, 124).

The cry of the poor and the sighing of the needy and the effectual fervent prayer of the righteous hath availed much for the saving of this nation many years (pt. iii. 207).

With the death of Fox, Dewsbury and Crisp, Whitehead remained the chief of the leaders whose convincement dated back to the first days of the Quaker movement. Alexander Parker had died in 1689, John Burnyeat in the following year, and Thomas Salthouse within a few days of Fox ; Miles Halhead, Thomas Taylor, and John Stubbs were gone ;[1] Thomas Goodaire only survived Crisp a few months ; John Whitehead passed away in 1696, and John Crook in 1699. Ambrose Rigge, James Lancaster, and Stephen Hubbersty lived a few years longer ; with Ann Camm and Margaret Fox.[2] The first leaders were one by one joining the ranks of the Church triumphant ; would the new generations that followed stand as they had stood in the life of Jesus Christ, the same yesterday, to-day, and for ever ? The inspiration of a great past would henceforth always remain with the Society of Friends ; but, as we shall see in the following chapters, the noble witness and service of the Founders would establish a great tradition, and the new generation, while following the example of the fathers, would not always imitate their faith. It would often walk with reverted eye, instead of pressing forward to the glad service into which the Truth would be leading it.[3] To-day, the lives of these heroes of our past shall no longer be a tradition that numbs, but an immortal memory that braces, challenging our worldliness and insincerity, and calling us to a loyalty, as true as theirs, to the Great Leader, whose Life is ever giving the Church heart for new ventures of faith.

---

[1] Stubbs died in 1674, Taylor in 1682, Halhead prior to 1690.
[2] Ann Camm, formerly Audland, died in 1705 ; Margaret Fox, formerly Fell, in 1702.
[3] Cf. quotation from Durham letter of 1st Oct. 1659 in *Beginnings of Quakerism*, p. 329.

BOOK III

POSITION AND OUTLOOK AT CLOSE OF THE CENTURY

CHAPTER XVII

THE CLOSING YEARS OF THE CENTURY

> We cannot without resentment take notice of the great growth and daily increase of the Quakers, and the mischiefs and dangers from thence threatening this nation. 'Tis observable with what restless zeal their deluding teachers, and, as we suspect, many Romish emissaries under their disguise, ramble into all parts of these kingdoms, and boldly spread their venomous doctrines everywhere, attempting to infect and shake the minds of weak Protestants, and assuming rules of discipline, powers in matters of religion and forms of government, repugnant to the established laws of this kingdom, contrary to the very Acts of Toleration and not allowed to any other Dissenters; vouching all their actions by Divine inspiration for their warrant, and the indulgence of the Government for their indemnity. — Norfolk Petition of Justices and Grand Jurors, to the House of Commons, about 1699, printed in George Whitehead, *Christian Progress*, p. 675.

IN the years that followed the death of Fox, the Society of Friends was at the height of its numbers and organization. Judging by all external signs it was rapidly growing in power and in worldly prosperity, reaping the immediate fruits of toleration in abundant measure. We may survey its outward position, so far as materials allow, before examining the state of its inward life.

It is by no means easy to ascertain the numerical strength of Friends in England at the close of the century. With the help of the statistics of the Fifth Monarchy imprisonments, I was able in my former book[1] to reckon their number in 1660 at from 30,000 to 40,000 men, women, and children, out of a population of about five millions. The Episcopal Returns of 1669[2] provide a tempting but unreliable basis for a further estimate. They

---

[1] *Beginnings of Quakerism*, p. 512.
[2] Given in G. Lyon Turner, *Original Records of Early Nonconformity*, i. 3-191, iii. 823-836.

were Black Lists of Conventicles, procured as damning proof of the need for the Second Conventicle Act, and are both imperfect and prejudiced. Moreover the entries, reflecting the fears and virulence of the clergy, often treat the occasional large gatherings at some general or business meeting as though they showed the normal attendance at the place named. These precarious data suggest a total of at least 25,000 Quakers in 1669.[1] A more reliable basis of calculation is at first sight furnished by the Statistics of the Births, Marriages, and Deaths recorded in the Monthly Meeting books according to the system of registration set on foot by Fox.[2] The figures are probably too imperfect to serve for our present purpose until the decade after the organization of Monthly Meetings. For this and the following periods they are as under:[3]

	Births.	Marriages.	Deaths.
1670-79	9753	2820	10,142
1680-89	9211	2598	11,245
1690-99	9130	2193	10,657
1700-09	9074	2221	11,274
1710-19	8358	1930	10,876

There are no reliable general vital statistics for the country at this time, but the birth-rate and death-rate would both be much higher than is the case to-day. The

[1] Herbert G. Wood, *George Fox*, pp. 76-78, gives this as the result of his examination.
[2] *Beginnings of Quakerism*, p. 144.
[3] John S. Rowntree, *The Friends' Registers of Births, Deaths, and Marriages, 1650-1900*, p. 14. The figures were compiled from the Register Books surrendered to the Government in 1840. Others, afterwards found, were handed over in 1857; many were duplicate entries, but a considerable number were new. Some books have been lost or are still in private hands. Josiah Newman, article on "The Quaker Records" in *Some Special Studies of Genealogy*, 1908, gives the dates of the earliest entries for the county districts, ranging from 1578-1653 for births, 1642-1662 for marriages, 1570-1670 for deaths, the pre-Quaker entries being of course only sporadic. There must be a large number of omissions, especially perhaps in deaths of Friends buried in private grounds. See, *e.g.*, Elizabeth J. Satterthwaite, *Records of Colthouse Burial Ground*, pp. 55-57. J. S. Rowntree, paper cited, p. 10 *n.*, says no entry has been found of the second marriage of Wm. Dewsbury; and I know of other cases. With respect to marriages the entries could often be supplemented from Monthly and Preparative Meeting Minute Books.

marriage rate was perhaps somewhat higher than its present yearly figure of about fifteen persons per thousand, but is probably the best guide to the total number of Friends. On this footing the 1670–1679 figures show a total of 37,600, to which an addition, bringing the figure, say, to 40,000 or at most 50,000, must be made for imperfections in the record, and for the many persons who were already married when they became Friends. There was no formal membership till 1737, and then only as a by-product of poor relief.[1] The population in 1680 was about five and a half millions.

The figures do not support the idea that the Society increased in size after the Toleration Act. The extensive emigration to America, where there were many thousands of Friends by the close of the century,[2] is alone a sufficient ground for caution. The building of meeting-houses, the open allowance of all Friends' meetings, their crowded gatherings on special occasions, their growing singularities of dress, and their outward prosperity may easily have led many persons to recognize their numbers and influence in a new way, and to suppose that there had been a great increase. So Francis Bugg[3] talks of them as "multiplied to 100,000 men in England, Scotland, Ireland, and the plantations, besides women and children"; Charles Leslie,

---

[1] J. S. Rowntree, paper cited, pp. 6, 7, shows how formal membership was only introduced through the necessities attaching to the administration of relief to poor Friends: There "grew up a body of legislation and of practice, determined sometimes by appeals to superior Meetings. The often-quoted Minute of 1737 was largely a consolidation of previously existing law. . . . The opening sentence shows its connection with the system of poor relief. Edmund Gurney presented the report or Draft Minute, which declared 'that all Friends shall be deemed members of the Quarterly, Monthly, or Two Weeks' Meeting within the compass of which they inhabited or dwelt the 1st day of 4th mo. 1737, except such who are settled pensioners to or have within one year last past been relieved by any other such Meeting. In that case, he, she, or they shall be deemed a member or members of the Meeting to which they are a pensioner, or by whom they have been so relieved.'" The Rules are in the MS. "Books of Extracts," title, "Removals and Settlements," and amongst other things provide that the children of a Friend are to be deemed members of the meeting to which the father belonged. This assumes the existence of Birthright Membership and gives it formal recognition.

[2] See *Quakers in the American Colonies*, pp. 522-524, which quotes an estimate of 20,000 in Pennsylvania alone as "doubtless too large a figure." There were also strong bodies in New Jersey and Rhode Island, and contingents in other plantations, though many were old colonists convinced in America or were the children of immigrants.   [3] *Vox Populi*, 1702, p. 2.

author of the venomous *Snake in the Grass*, on the footing of a thousand meetings, and a hundred to a meeting, wildly computes a body of Quakers 100,000 strong in England alone.[1] It was no small sign of their virility and energy that they should maintain their numbers, in spite of emigration.

The social condition of Friends has been a matter of some uncertainty. They were originally " drawn principally from the trading and yeoman classes, though there were also some artisans and labourers, a fair number of merchants, and a few gentry."[2] During the Second Period of Quakerism, until the Toleration Act, the proportion of manual workers probably increased. It is true that the Quaker way of life tended to prosperity; and many were rising in the social scale, up to the degree of merchant, beyond which, as a rule, neither their principles nor their political disabilities allowed them to go without ceasing to be Friends. But there was a constant accession of new adherents from the middle and lower classes, and the Quaker meetings made a powerful appeal to an England which was still Puritan at heart. The care given to the poor, both by direct assistance and by setting them in a way of living, was also an attractive force, though it would finally, while eliminating extreme poverty, discourage admissions into the Society. Accordingly, in this Second Period, the number of poor Friends was great. The returns made to Archbishop Sheldon are no doubt coloured on this as on other points.[3] They abound in depreciating epithets. " Meanest mechanics," " some rich, some very poor," " very mean, and most women," " all of very poor condition, scarce a yeoman amongst them," " ordinary sort," " inconsiderable fellows," " vulgar sort," " middle sort," " inferior people," " all mean people, only [two] abettors are rich farmers," " mean people and ignorant," " farmers, tradesmen and husbandmen," " some of them have

---

[1] I take this from *Some Seasonable Reflections upon the Quakers' Solemn Protestation*, 1697, p. 13, which, though anonymous, is by Leslie. Cf. *Snake in the Grass*, 3rd edn. p. 249. Joseph Wyeth, in his *Switch for the Snake*, 1699, p. 372, cautiously says : " I wish he may speak true."
[2] *Beginnings of Quakerism*, p. 512.
[3] G. Lyon Turner, *Original Records of Early Nonconformity*.

considerable estates," " mean and ordinary persons," " tailors, shoemakers, weavers," " some of them are masters of vessels, and well to pass, others tradesmen and the rest mechanics " (this is at Whitby), " mechanics," " middle sort of people," " of the inferior gang, though some of them have considerable estates," " many people of good estates," " tradesmen and mostly women " (this at Manchester), " poorer sort of people," " the principal frequenters and promoters . . . are such as were officers and soldiers in the Parliament army " (this at Henley)—such are some of the flowers of speech, culléd almost at random, mainly from country meetings. After every allowance for bias, the phrases used suggest a large number of persons in very moderate or in humble circumstances. The returns give little help as to the large towns, but we know that in London the charge for the poor was very heavy at the end of the century,[1] and an analysis of 250 marriages about 1680 shows a proportion of some 60 per cent of manual workers, against 20 per cent for the same number of marriages a century later.[2] We have seen[3] that almost all the extant Middlesex convictions under the First Conventicle Act relate to Quaker meetings. Deducting persons of unknown occupation, or only described as spinsters or widows, we are left with 570 names, who may be classed as follows, though exact figures are out of the question, for in some cases the descriptions given may cover either masters or men :[4]

Class of gentry	29
Tradesmen, Masters, etc.	169
Artisans and Seamen	341
Unskilled labourers	31
	570

The figures, it will be seen, give a very similar percentage to that afforded by the marriages about 1680.

The results show that the Quaker movement was at

[1] See Beck and Ball, *London Friends' Meetings*, p. 101.
[2] *Ibid.*, with Table, p. 90.   [3] *Ante*, p. 41.
[4] My notes, "London Friends sentenced to Transportation, 1664-1665," at Dev. Ho.

this time in far more vital touch with the people than at some later periods. Its despised meetings did not suffer from an oppressive respectability, and resembled in composition one of our modern Quaker Adult Schools.

At the Yearly Meetings, reports were given from each county as to the " prosperity of Truth " ; and from these we get a picture of the state of the Society, though no doubt somewhat over-coloured as such accounts commonly are. This verbal reporting was something of an ordeal to country representatives. Says Thomas Gwin, of Falmouth, then a young man of twenty-nine :[1]

> In the year 1685, I went to London, being the only Friend . . . from this county. . . . When I was to answer as to the condition of our county meetings, I had great dread, being bashful, and not used to speak in such large assemblies ; but the Lord gave me mouth and wisdom ; and I did deliver a sensible, short account . . . to the satisfaction of the Yearly Meeting.

The Toleration Act for a time evidently brought a great flocking to meetings. The 1690 reports contain such phrases as the following : " Things very well and a great increase of people," " great comings-in," " a great openness and gathering," " Truth spreads, meetings added," " several meetings set up, many convinced of late," " things well and meetings increase greatly." There was much building or enlarging of meeting-houses and a considerable breaking of new ground. In 1693, Yorkshire reports over seventy meetings and a great coming in.[2] The general tone is hopeful and even sanguine. It is clear that there was much openness towards Friends ; and, where the harvest was not gathered, it was due to lack of missionary zeal or of labourers able to give worthy utterance to the Quaker message.

An adverse tract by an anonymous parish priest, printed in 1700 under the title of " Remarks upon the Quakers, wherein the Plain-Dealers are Plainly Dealt

---

[1] MS. Journal.
[2] J. W. Rowntree, *Essays and Addresses*, p. 38, makes up a total of 279 places in the county where Friends worshipped. But a meeting kept in private houses was often held in rotation at three or four places, so that the places registered for meeting are no safe guide to the number of Quaker congregations.

with," has a lively caricature of the Quaker methods of stealing sheep from the Anglican fold. They pitch, he says, on some large village, previously free from Dissent, "getting into some odd house or other, that hath little or no neighbourhood, and at a distance from the minister, and so they prevail with some and make them converts before he is aware." In other words their country meetings were often remote from the parish church, where they naturally enough served the religious needs of outlying and neglected parishioners.[1] They begin, he suggests, with small game, mean and needy persons, "who are presently put in hopes of a better trade or livelihood by turning Quakers." Afterwards they cultivate men of more standing who have fallen out with the clergyman. Or perhaps they get at the men by leading captive some silly women. Moreover, they always have an eye to the men of bad character, who are persuaded that the best way to clear their credit is to close with such as pretend to so much godliness. The demure Quaker visits his chosen victim, and, after long silence, addresses him in a prophetic tone ; " Friend, at my first coming under thy roof, I did not know that I had anything to say unto thee ; but, since my being here, I have received a word from the Lord, Who I perceive hath a great kindness for thee and thine ; and thus saith the Lord ; 'Come out of darkness and be enlightened, that thou mayest be saved and all thine house.'" This may pass muster as a description of the Quaker way of approach, and of the zeal with which Friends carried their message to others, often reforming persons of ill-life ; but we must strip the account of its sinister suggestions, for the work was done with pure motives, at a time when morals and religion were declining. Of the meetings we are told in the same vein :

---

[1] Many old country meetings were in outlying parts of a parish, as, for example, Frenchay, Sidcot, Sibford, Colthouse, Jordans ; and the account of the Peak district in Derbyshire by the correspondent of the S.P.C.K. in April 1701 must have been true of other parts, "that the Quakers, as well as other Dissenters, do rather increase amongst them, and make many proselytes among the poor people of the Peak, who live remote from churches, which for want of tithes cannot be supplied as they ought" (*Hist. of S.P.C.K. 1698–1898*, p. 68).

The company meets and the speaker, having stayed some
time for the Spirit, starts up, being that day secure of his office.
. . . I shall not here make sport with their way of preaching . . . but yet I think we may safely expose that dullness,
grunting and groaning in the people . . . with those postures,
and grimaces, spitting in their hands and pulling off their coats, so
unworthy in a Christian preacher. However, the man, you may
be sure, showeth his best; and the hearers return with full cry of
his parts and their own improvement, being wonderfully edified
by the sermon. . . . Above all, care is taken to invite the best
of the parish; no importunity nor impudence is spared in order
to get my landlord or my landlady thither. And thus the whole
neighbourhood is set a-longing; and all Jerusalem alarmed and
for going, as if John Baptist was come again. But, if you'll take
their word, a greater than John is here. So that the meeting is
sure to be thronged the next time; and 'tis hard if the Quakers
miss of gaining some amongst so many, who are apt to be
affected either with zeal of the new teacher, or the novelty of the
doctrine. . . . And 'tis very remarkable, when the wonder is a
little over, and the meeting not thronged so much as it used to
be, what a subtle art the Quakers have to regain the company
and fill the house afresh; for then 'tis given out, as the mounte-
banks never show the best tricks till last, that a woman is to
speak the next time, which sets the people a-madding and makes
them all for coming again; and, if they are not edified, yet, it
may be, they are more diverted than they were before. . . .

Not otherwise did many of the clergy inveigh against
Wesley and his followers for the odious crime of being
Methodists. Religious earnestness is always anathema to
the Sadducee.

The statistical returns are some guide as to the parts
of the country where Quakerism was growing or declining. The petition cited at the head of the chapter shows
that Norfolk was a centre of life, and this is borne out by
the figures and by the reports to the Yearly Meeting.
Lincolnshire again has an increase, with five Monthly
Meetings and about twenty-two meetings in 1693, compared with four and eighteen twenty-five years before.
Here, in the Isle of Axholme, where the people were "so
extreme ignorant that not one in twenty can say the
Lord's prayer right," Samuel Wesley, the rector of
Epworth, and father of the founder of Methodism, was

XVII CLOSING YEARS OF THE CENTURY 465

troubled with about forty Quakers who insulted him everywhere.[1] Sturdy John Whitehead, now of Fiskerton, near Lincoln, was a pillar of the Church; and the death in 1696 of "so tender a father, and furnished a minister, . . . love-worthy, because the love of God dwelt in him wonderfully,"[2] was a great loss.

Yorkshire, after declining between 1670 and '89, shows a strong recovery during the next ten years. The Minute Books give the impression of much vigorous life. The June Quarterly Meeting, or Yearly Meeting as it was often called, was an important time, of which John Rous, Margaret Fox's son-in-law, gives a clear account in 1689.[3] He comes the evening before the Meeting; and the next day visits the Men's and Women's Meetings, both very large. In the Women's Yearly Meeting, the chief in the country, which issued a series of important epistles,[4] "there was a very heavenly and blessed appearance of the Lord, it being taken notice of by some of the elder women that divers young women were getting into new-fangled fashions, concerning which they spoke to several, who received their reproof in love, and altered their dress before they went out of town."[5] Friends in the ministry were early risers, gathering at 6 A.M. on the second day of the Yearly Meeting, when some thirty attended; and, at the request of Rous, meeting again the following morning at 5 A.M., when they arranged to meet quarterly for the supervision of the ministry. The great

[1] Letter of 16th June 1701, in *Hist. of S.P.C.K. 1698-1898*, p. 88.
[2] Testimony of North Lincolnshire M.M. in *Works*.
[3] Letter to Fox, from Sunderland, 27th June 1689, in Dev. Ho. A.R.B. Colln. No. 137.
[4] The 1688 epistle was printed—the folio edn. with a wrong date 1668 (see *J.F.H.S.* ii. 42)—with its curious mention of "those holy ancients, . . . as Lydia, open-hearted to God and to one another, as Dorcas, careful to do one another good, as Deborah, concerned in the commonwealth of Israel, and as Jael, zealous for the Truth, who was praised above women." Sisera, by fleeing into Jael's sleeping tent, committed a gross breach of desert law which forfeited the rights of sanctuary: see *Expository Times*, July 1917. The epistle had great currency, and was copied into some Women's Meeting Books. This is the case in the Oxfordshire Women's Q.M. Book; and the opening paragraph of the letter supplies many phrases, used with almost liturgical monotony, in subsequent minutes which record the exercise of the Meetings. Other epistles were printed in 1686, 1690, 1692, 1696, 1698, and 1700. I infer that it was the most important Women's Meeting in the country. [5] Cf. *post*, p. 511.

2 H

time for worship was on the second day "a very blessed and heavenly meeting, wherein near twenty Friends spoke and Friends generally were very much comforted and refreshed one in another."

Cumberland grew considerably towards the end of the century, especially along the Border;[1] and showed more missionary zeal than most counties. We hear of "great comings-in of people and many convinced," of "several men and women this year brought forth in a public testimony," of "a great openness . . . and many added, and people that are not Friends offer them houses for to meet in," of "several lately convinced in the lower parts of the county," of "a great openness in several parts especially on the Border," of "pretty great additions in the Borders and meetings large," and, through it all, of a great love and unity.[2] Of the Border meeting at Sikeside, or Kirklinton, Christopher Story says in 1699:

Now the number of Friends increasing, many being convinced, and Friends growing up, . . . it being about twenty-seven years since our meeting was first settled, we enlarged the meeting-house, which it is supposed will contain about three hundred and is generally well-filled, many of our children growing up in the Truth and being zealous for the God of their fathers.[3]

With good reason Cumberland was at this time "counted the nurse of England,"[4] and the accounts in the *First Publishers of Truth*, more ample than for any other county, show the maintenance of a strong evangelistic spirit for many years. Thomas Story, of Justice Town, in the parish of Kirklinton, now Lynehow Estate, whose brother became Dean of Limerick, gives us the wholesome Cumbrian stock at its best. A man of finely sensitive

[1] For the beginnings of this evangelizing of the Border see *ante*, p. 354.
[2] See reports to Y.M. 1691-1700.
[3] Christopher Story's *Life*, under date 1699.
[4] Letter of Elizabeth Jacob to Richard Jacob, 30th June 1712, in *J.F.H.S.* xiii. 63. In 1712, however, it had "become the hardest country to travel through; it would be too tedious to let thee know the particulars, but this I may say that never such a wicked spirit rose since Friends were a people." This was owing to the virulent hostility of a group of apostates at Wigton, who had come under the discipline of Friends, and disturbed meetings in the most intemperate manner. They were led by Job, Lot, and Isaac Pearson and William and John Robinson. See Thomas Story, *Life*, pp. 467, 590-593; *Quaker Post-bag*, p. 100; James Dickinson's *Life*, *sub anno* 1717.

CLOSING YEARS OF THE CENTURY

temperament, his unmetrical religious rhapsodies in pre-Quaker days deserve reading for their beauty of mystical expression. Some wizardry of glad North Country air, some radiant sanity of simple North Country life, cherished this forgotten poet, for whose sake we may stray awhile from the beaten track of our story. Well might Lord Brougham charm away a tedious Assize Sunday at Lancaster over the buried treasure in Story's ponderous journal.[1]

From a " Song of Praise to the Saints in Zion," I take the following :

Come sing with me, O ye valleys, and flowers of the plain :
Let us clap our hands with joy :
For the King of the East hath visited us and smiled on our beauty :
For He sees His holy Name on every flower,
And glorious image on every lovely plain. . . .

Come, ye ragged ones, come sit down before the King :
For He is meek and lowly and loveth the humble.
Though you be naked, He will clothe you with righteousness ;
Though you be hungry, He will feed you with the bread of eternal life. . . .

Smite Thy people with great thirst, O Lord God of Mercy,
That they may drink abundantly of the waters of Thy salvation. . . .

Call them from the husks of outward shadows ;
And feed them with Thy hidden manna and Tree of Life. . . .

Bereave Thy people, O most faithful and true, of the waters which they have polluted ;
And wash them in the laver of regeneration by Thy Holy Spirit ;
And cleanse them by Thy righteous judgments ;
That they may retain Thy glowing Love. . . .

I was silent before the Lord, as a child not yet weaned ;
He put words in my mouth ;
And I sang forth His praise with an audible voice.

I called unto my God out of the great deep ;
He put on bowels of mercy, and had compassion on me ;
Because His Love was infinite,
And His Power without measure.

He called for my life, and I offered it at His footstool ;
But He gave it me as a prey,
With unspeakable addition.

---

[1] Richard S. Ferguson, *Early Cumberland and Westmorland Friends*, p. 118.

He called for my will, and I resigned it at His call ;
But He returned me His own,
In token of His love.

He called for the world, and I laid it at His feet,
With the crowns thereof ;
I withheld them not at the beckoning of His Hand.

But mark the benefit of exchange :
For He gave me, instead of earth, a Kingdom of eternal peace,
And, in lieu of the crowns of vanity,
A crown of glory.

My God called me from my father, and I went apace :
He called me His son,
And clothed me with His garments. . . .

What moved Thee to this, O life of my soul, O glory of Thy saints ?
For I was become vile with the blackness of Egypt.

Was it not Thine infinite love and mercy,
Thine unalterable patience and wonderful condescension,
That brought Thee from Thy throne,
Below Thy footstool,
In the likeness of vanity,
That Thou mightest exalt me above the high heavens,
In Thy Kingdom of everlasting rest ? . . .[1]

This piece, he tells us, was composed in some eight hours ; and the next day, observing in it things writ in the first person, which did not belong to his own spiritual state, he was ready to destroy it. But, since the matter had been set down as it came, and with undoubted evidence of the Divine presence, he preserved it, concluding it given by dictation from the Mind of Truth. It was true in itself, and might answer the states of many, and be his own experience in time, if faithful. Such a passage shows us the inspiration of poet and prophet actually at work.

These songs of Story, worth, with one or two of Ellwood's pieces, all the rest of early Quaker poetry, have something of the spirit of the recently-discovered Christian Psalter, known as the *Odes of Solomon*, and spring across the span of sixteen centuries, from a like spiritual experience and meditation on the scriptures.

Story had the education of a gentleman and a legal

[1] *Life*, pp. 17-24.

XVII CLOSING YEARS OF THE CENTURY 469

training. Bred as an Anglican, he became a Quaker by conviction before he attended the worship of Friends. A meeting at Broughton in 1691, favoured by "a sweet abounding shower of celestial rain," brought him into the religious fellowship which his soul craved, and, at the following Carlisle Assizes, he became the laughing-stock of his acquaintance. The great Dr. Richard Gilpin, whose son had taught him law, tried without avail to reason him out of his Quakerism, and the young man soon began visiting meetings, speaking a few words for the first time at one in Fife. At several places he and his older companion John Bowstead, a Cumberland minister, supported Thomas Rudd in his difficult service of declaring Truth through the streets.[1] He laid the foundation of a lifelong intimacy with Penn at the Yearly Meeting of 1693, and soon after spoke in his home meeting at Kirklinton, " with a voice just so audible as that the meeting generally heard," breaking down in tears, " and the meeting in general was immediately affected the same way." And so, as the Lord led him on, this fresh young life added its dedicated service to the Quaker movement.

We may now resume the highway of our discourse. The remaining Northern counties have a fairly steady membership; but the only other districts with increasing figures are London-and-Middlesex, Devonshire and Dorset-and-Hants. Bristol-and-Somerset and Essex show substantial declines. It is, however, probable that the increasing efficiency of the discipline was reducing the number of loosely-attached Friends ; and we can well believe that, judged by the external standard of a consistent Quaker way of life, the Society was never stronger than at the close of the century.

The development of organization had, as we have seen, led to internal controversy and the secession of many from the main body. We proceed to trace the dreary fortunes of these Separatist movements. Westmorland and Wiltshire were the prime areas of disturbance. But the infection spread to some other counties, particularly to Berkshire, Buckingham and Hertford, and, a little later,

[1] See *post*, Chap. XXI.

to York and the East Riding. Bristol and London were also affected. The organization of the Society always triumphed; and the dissentients showed little power of maintaining a separate Church and ultimately relapsed into the world or into other Churches or rejoined Friends. The Society, however, overcame the opposers not without dissipation of energy and spiritual damage to itself.

The case of Reading is typical of others. The dust of a confused controversy dimmed the lustre of the great testimony which Friends had borne during the persecution that fell upon them at the time of the Conventicle Acts.[1] Men who had refused all compromise with the world did not find it easy, on any acute issue, to come to an accommodation with one another. The heightening of personality which had attended their heroic witness sprang from deep inward communion with the Divine and from close group-fellowship. When these were weakened, the superman shrivelled, alas, into a prejudiced and often contentious mortal. Obstruct the issues of the Lord's love and the manifestation of His presence, and the great air we breathe, the larger life we live, pass away.

After the condemnation of Wilkinson and Story at the London meeting in 1677,[2] many leading Reading Friends, including Thomas and Ann Curtis, stoutly espoused their cause. When the *Christian-Quaker* came out three years later, and was diligently spread through the county, the discord came to a head; and John Buy was called to account for a letter to London reflecting on Curtis.[3] The meeting-house[4] had been built in 1671, in the heat of

---

[1] *Ante*, p. 226.
[2] See *ante*, p. 309. The history, from the anti-Curtis point of view, is told in the paper from Q.M. to Curtis and others, 1st Jan. 1694, in Dev. Ho. Portf. 23, No. 169.
[3] M.M. Minutes, 26th Nov. 1680, 28th Jan., 25th March 1681.
[4] In Sun Lane, a narrow lane formed by the division of the present King Street into two. *Per* Howard R. Smith, whose excellent paper on "The Wilkinson-Story Controversy in Reading," in *J.F.H.S.* i. 57-61, has greatly assisted me. The M.M. Books of both sections, with their sharply contrasted statements, are in the Q.M. Safe at Reading, and the story I am telling, if fully supplied with documents, could be easily elaborated into a volume. H. R. Smith (*J.F.H.S.* i. 60, 61) gives a list of eleven pamphlets, 1685-1693, and there are some later pieces mentioned in Smith's *Catalogue*. The meeting-house was held on a 41 years' lease.

XVII CLOSING YEARS OF THE CENTURY 471

persecution, and the dominant party now placed the trust in the name of the chief subscriber, Curtis, alone, thus gaining vantage-ground for their later proceedings.[1] They also insisted on an afternoon meeting on the First-day, with the design of "thrusting down" the one in the evening previously held.[2] In their dislike of Women's Meetings, they refused the premises to the Women's Quarterly Meeting, locking the doors and forcing them to gather in an adjoining malt-house. Curtis declared against women gadding about the county away from their household duties.[3] Benjamin Coale, one of the party, was clerk both to the Quarterly and Monthly Meetings, and, after a disorderly scene, was displaced in the former, and two Quarterly Meetings resulted, held on the first occasion at the same time and place, each with its own clerk.[4] In the Monthly Meeting, each party kept a record of the business, the Friends opposed to Curtis showing much dissatisfaction with the laxity of proceedings as to marriages and the disregard of the advices from superior meetings.[5]

In August 1684, however, according to the Curtis Minute, "William Lamboll, Oliver Sansom and the rest of their company, did make a separation by turning their backs upon Friends and had a writer to take account of things by themselves in the same room." To stop this, the Curtis party in October met early in a lower room, and when the others came and found the usual upper room shut, they were asked, says the Minute, "to sit down with Friends, but, after some discourse, they all went away and left us." All Friends met together for worship, so far as persecution allowed, for another year, when, after

[1] M.M., 26th May 1682, in the anti-Curtis Book. The other Book does not refer to the matter, but calls to account William Lamboll, the dissenting Trustee, for speaking against Friends by saying they would pass anything at their M.M.'s. It also rebukes the anti-Curtis Friends for keeping on their hats in time of prayer, a practice indulged when no unity was felt with the offerings.

[2] M.M. Minutes of Curtis party, 24th Feb., 31st March 1682, and opposite account in other M.M. Book.

[3] H. R. Smith's paper and M.M. Minute of Curtis party, 24th Aug. 1682.

[4] H. R. Smith's paper: this was in April 1682, twenty-nine men Friends signing a paper removing Coale and ordering him to be paid what was due.

[5] A marriage of first cousins had been allowed in July 1679, and there were other frequent departures from settled procedure.

fruitless attempts at an accommodation, the Curtis party arranged to meet elsewhere, and high-handedly decided to "shut up the doors, seeing that it is the house only that keeps us together, for which Thomas Curtis is liable to be fined, if the magistrate should be strict upon us." Later on, they "made a wall with bricks before it ; for, having stopped up the witness in themselves, they would fain stop it up without, the door being a witness against them."[1] For seven years the meeting-house remained unused, but the other party of Friends persistently met in the yard outside, wind and rain, frost and sunshine alike, in protest against their eviction.[2] Curtis, says Thomas Robertson, writing to Fox, was "like Aesop's dog that would not let the ox eat hay, nor ate none himself."[3] At last, in 1693, his party proposed "Expedients for true Reconciliation," offering to open the doors if the others would put off their hats in time of prayer, and not to deem them apostates if the others would not deem them bad spirits and opposers of Truth. Some accommodation was under consideration, but was stopped by a letter from John Blaykling and Thomas Camm "till repentance be wrought and satisfaction be made in some measure sincerely."[4] The Quarterly Meeting answered on these lines, and the Curtis party, who had now reopened the house, replied through their leading minister, Leonard Key, that it had been closed for the sake of peace, and they were never better satisfied of anything in their lives. The other Friends, accordingly, leased new rooms for their meeting. The original Curtis Monthly Meeting, always held by men and women jointly, was continued till May 1716, but the entries become very meagre towards the close. Ann Curtis died about 1703, and her husband married again, but died some nine years later, and Benjamin Coale soon afterwards. William Soundy was now their chief preacher, and promoted a reconciliation with help from Thomas Story and others, which was

[1] M.M. Minute, 26th March 1689. [2] H. R. Smith's paper.
[3] Bristol, 2nd Feb. 1685, in Dev. Ho. A. R.B. Colln. No. 151.
[4] Camsgill, 14th Oct. 1693, in Dev. Ho. Gibson Colln. iii. 37, with Key's reply.

XVII CLOSING YEARS OF THE CENTURY

effected in the summer of 1716, and the Curtis meeting was laid down.[1] Friends re-united in a new house on the site of the present meeting-house in Church Street.[2] The Curtis Friends at Newbury had built a house in 1698,[3] but by 1716 most had either joined the Church of England or become loose and irreligious:[4] the rest followed the example of Reading and returned.[5]

At Reading the Friends who sided with the main body were technically the seceders. The others had only asked to be let alone, retaining Quakerish ways and principles, though somewhat laxly. The division had been due, chiefly, to loyalty to Story, who had stayed in the town for long periods, and had often worshipped with Friends in prison, while Fox was loath to do this, preferring rather to be taken in a public meeting.[6] But the Curtis party also disliked the new Church order, especially the separate Women's Meetings. Their practice had been to meet together, as indeed has again become the rule among Friends in modern days. Penington felt that they had given entrance to a wrong spirit;[7] and the breach of fellowship, with its pitiful developments, must have been damaging to the spiritual life of both parties. We may wish that Curtis had seen his way to subordinate his judgment to that of the main body; but I do not think we need lose our respect for a man whose service to Quakerism had been great, and whose sincerity is unquestioned.

There is a letter to him from Penn which shows the affection in which he had been held by Friends:[8]

---

[1] See Curtis M.M. Minutes and Thomas Story, *Life*, pp. 525, 526, 530, 531.
[2] H. R. Smith's paper.   [3] Curtis M.M. Minute, 26th April 1698.
[4] Thomas Story, *Life*, p. 526.
[5] *Ibid.* p. 607: see also James Dickinson's *Journal*, *sub anno* 1717, *quaere* 1716.
[6] *Camb. Journ.* ii. 163 (1670). For Story see Testimony of Benjamin Coale in *The Memory of John Story Revived*.
[7] Letters to Curtis and to Reading Friends in Dev. Ho. Penington Colln. iv.
[8] The letter is dated 14th Nov. 1706, and is in a little MS. Book made by Thomas Speakman of Reading in 1818. It looks as though it must be 1677: but asks for a reply directed to Henry Gouldney (of London). The Henry Gouldney whose letters are preserved in the *Quaker Post-bag* was then only twenty. The date must be left under suspicion, but the letter, in any case, deserves insertion.

What is the matter that my old friend is under temptation to desert us? What I have heard from originals was so great a surprise that my love questioned the integrity of those that related the sad story to me. Has not thy soul felt immortality brought to light among us, and, with all our weaknesses, that Urim and Thummim are with us beyond what thou ever felt among any other sort of people? What strange eclipse is this? 'Tis like an apoplectic on the mind. What, doubt our foundation, or go from the pattern brought us down by our spiritual Moses from the Mount? Dear Thomas, look back, look forward, and remember the days wherein we took sweet fellowship together in the Heavenly Power that has often filled the gospel temple with its holy smoke and been an agreeable odour amongst us. . . . Our fear, our grief, our love weighs us down on thy account. Dear Thomas, return at the door at which thou wentest out and be again a fool and a little child, delighting thy soul in simplicity, meekness, and humility, which the feeling of Divine life brings into, wherein all doubtings are resolved, all fears dissipated, and an entire sweetness and content reposing the soul. . . . Hear, fear, and answer; and by this stumble thou wilt at last get ground to help others. Yea, the godly sorrow that may follow this hour and power of darkness, in which thou art rather tried than overcome, may break up a deeper sense and travail than ever, and both restore and augment thy gift and service.

The trouble in Hertfordshire, another centre of persecution, need only be briefly referred to. It seems to have arisen on the question of Women's Meetings, and was accompanied by personal bitterness against Fox.[1] In 1684 it was reported to the Yearly Meeting that through the Lord's mercy a remnant was preserved. By 1700, however, Friends could say that the separation at Hertford, Ware, and Hitchin was much laid aside. John Crook, who had something of the spirit of Dewsbury, was the Friend of most weight in the district. He died in April 1699; and had not felt himself concerned in some of the new methods of Church government; but his passiveness on these questions and his tenderness to those who differed from the leaders of the Society were accom-

---

[1] See two letters from Penington to Hertford Friends, 22nd March and 27th April 1678, in Dev. Ho. Penington Colln. iv. Nos. 148, 150, *Christian-Quaker*, pt. v. pp. 83, etc., and Dev. Ho. A.R.B. Colln. Nos. 199*a*-208. Fox visited Hertford several times in his later years, and refers to the spirit of division: see *Journ.* ii. 331, 347, 456, 499.

XVII CLOSING YEARS OF THE CENTURY 475

panied by much zeal against disorderly living or any factious spirit of division.[1] His experience was summed up in a note he found in the margin of an old Bible: "When the mind thinketh nothing, when the soul coveteth nothing, and when the body acteth nothing contrary to the will of God, this is perfect sanctification."[2]

In Buckinghamshire separation centred round John Raunce, a physician of High Wycombe, and his son-in-law, Charles Harris, both of whom, in 1676, as we shall remember, had supported Wilkinson and Story, under cover of disinterestedness.[3] Harris visited meetings in London and other places, and in 1687[4] was reported as of loose behaviour and turbulent spirit, and "joined to the separate meetings his father Raunce hath set up in this country, and is an encourager of them; so that we do not look upon him as a Friend." By 1703 he had compounded with his creditors and was supposed to be still a prisoner in the Fleet, because when at home he kept himself private except on First-days. Even then he did not go to his own separate meeting, "his flock there being so much disgusted with him that they are not willing he should preach amongst them.[5]

The chief disaffection in Yorkshire was somewhat later and arose over the question of re-marriage within a year of the husband's or wife's death.[6] It came to a head in 1682, when York Monthly Meeting refused to approve the second marriage of John Hall, the Clerk to the Quarterly Meeting.[7] A hot debate ensued in the Quarterly

---

[1] Testimony of George Whitehead at beginning of Crook's *Works* (1701).
[2] Intro. to *Works*.   [3] See *ante*, p. 307.
[4] Minutes of Morning Meeting, 12th Sept. 1687, and of Upperside M.M., 3rd Oct. 1687, in Bristol MSS. v. No. 125.
[5] Letter from Wycombe Friends in Bristol MSS. v. No. 123. For the Wycombe separation see Fox, *Journ.* ii. 315, 316 (1677); Richard Davies, *Life*, pp. 189-191 (1682); and the controversial pieces by Raunce, Harris, and Ellwood, noted in Smith's *Catalogue*.
[6] There had been some apostasy in Thirsk M.M., at Craike and Ampleforth, in 1672, and the moneys subscribed by the apostates to burial-grounds were returned (see Letter in Q.M. Minutes, 19th Sept. 1672). John Hogg, a minister of Howden, in Elloughton M.M., was already prejudiced against Friends in 1674 (see Morning Meeting Minute, 11th Jan. 1675).
[7] York M.M., 2nd Nov. 1682. In Dev. Ho. A.R.B. Colln. No. 107 is a letter from Fox to Christopher Holder, then in Rhode Island, dated 15th June 1677, condemning re-marriages within a year. Cf. Fox, *Epistles*, No. 383, to Yorkshire Q.M. in 1683.

Meeting, which had decided against such marriages two years earlier,[1] and now agreed to refer the question to the Yearly Meeting but later was content to endorse its previous judgment.[2] Owstwick Monthly Meeting, covering the Holderness district, objected to the Quarterly Meeting giving more than a caution. The reply to this was lovingly worded, but reiterated the judgment, except where, "through the weakness of any," the prohibiting of re-marriage until the year "is likely to produce more blemish to Truth than passively to suffer" it, in which cases the Monthly Meetings were to use their discretion.[3] John Cox, a minister formerly of Holderness but now of York, led the opposition, which developed on Wilkinson-Story lines, and resulted in a separate meeting at York in 1684,[4] under the patronage of Edward Nightingale, a merchant in Ousegate, and one of the founders of the meeting. As at Reading, the second meeting on First-days became one of the irritant causes. Two meetings had been held for some years, as in other large towns. For several First-days in succession, Cox and his friends came late to the morning meeting and continued holding it into the time of that in the afternoon.[5] As their design for forcing a single meeting did not succeed, they set up a private one of their own, "in a time when there were above two hundred prisoners for the testimony of Truth belonging to the city and castle of York, . . . letting fall the standard of [their] nobility in the Truth and

[1] York M.M., 5th Aug. 1680, and Q.M., Dec. 1680.
[2] Q.M., Dec. 1682. "John Cox, in a boisterous kind of an uncomely manner," insisted on reading a paper on the subject. See "Truth Exalted and the Peaceable Fellowship and Exercise thereof Vindicated against the abusive clamours of a dividing false spirit," printed 1685, which gives the history of the separation from the "orthodox" point of view. This and other papers relating to the separation are in York Records. At the second Q.M., March 1683, a letter from Joshua Middleton, I suppose of Darlington, is also given.
[3] Q.M. Minutes, Oct. 1683. The Bristol Two Weeks' Meeting more than once passed these marriages, though disliking such hasty proceedings (Minutes of 24th Aug. 1691 and 28th Nov. 1692). Disaffection smouldered in Owstwick and the neighbouring Elloughton M.M. for some years, and two Friends who represented them, John Lyth of Hull and John Hogg, gave trouble (see especially answers to the two M.M.'s in Q.M. Minutes, Dec. 1685); but ten years later the feeling had a good deal abated.
[4] See paper by Cox party, 7th Dec. [1683], in York Records. The grounds of separation, on Wilkinson-Story lines, are given in "Truth Exalted, etc." p. 12.
[5] *Ibid.* p. 9.

the public testimony thereof."[1] A tenderly worded letter from Dewsbury to his "ancient friend, Edward Nightingale,"[2] says :

It is very much to me how you let the enemy get over you, as to cause you to separate from Friends, which, if you had kept your places in meeting with Friends, you in time might have seen a service in meeting twice a day, as well as they. For you may be sure that separation neither restores any to love the Truth, neither gathers any to God, but rather scattereth and driveth away some that was gathered in love to Truth by the painful and faithful labourers that was truly sent of the Lord.

In May 1684 the Monthly Meeting admonished them to return, but they replied with a protest against all imposed forms, saying "we see no end of the methods you would have us proceed in traditionally."[3] The ensuing Quarterly Meeting sent out a Committee to admonish them personally, and on its return issued a paper of disownment with seventy-five names to it, which for greater expedition in sending down to the fourteen Monthly Meetings was to be transcribed by Friends in prison at the public charge.[4] The Separatists made answer in a printed pamphlet[5] and traversed the right of the Church to make new rules, binding on the conscience of dissenting Friends ;

... for the unity of the Spirit, which should be kept in the bond of peace, standeth not always in an outward conformity, as some evilly prosecute and others as weakly condescend ... and, if we conform for fear of the judgment, is it not blind obedience, implicit faith, or worse ; and are not all those things exploded as antichristian ? ... If you have a mind to stay a year or more before you marry, we shall be content ; nay, if you should judge it your duty to advise or caution others so to do, we should not be offended, provided you kept in the true charity ; ... nay, further, if you judge your reason for it better than ours against it, we should be willing that they should be fairly

---

[1] *Ibid.* pp. 10, 11.
[2] Letter dated Warwick, 21st Jan. 1685, in *Works*, pp. 365-368.
[3] The letter and reply are in M.M. Minutes.
[4] See Minutes of June 1684. The Minute is printed in "A paper of condemnation ... Whereby in part may be seen the difference between the Conforming and Dissenting parties." [5] *Ibid.*, see pp. 9, 11.

stated together, and so left to the witness of God to decide the controversy, and in the interim ... the greater number's conclusion against Truth are no more concluding than the lesser.

After the separation, in fact, and too late to undo its mischief, the Quarterly Meeting somewhat receded from its position of authority over the component Monthly Meetings, passing a Minute in July 1685, which was confined to a caution on the subject of re-marriages, and, in a general paper six years later, simply recommending a period of considerable forbearance.[1]

Cox became a Baptist in London in 1691, and Steven Crisp wrote that he was in a forlorn condition and like a vagabond in the earth. The Baptists were shy of him and bade him go gather a Church in his own country where he was known, and the London Separatist Friends had held a solemn meeting and suspended him from preaching. Crisp says that he had never taken him for a religious man and had counselled him thirty years before to sell his horse and boots and follow his employ.[2] In 1708 he wrote a letter condemning his actions, but does not seem fully to have cleared himself.[3] Nightingale had died, I think, about the beginning of 1693.[4]

At York, as elsewhere, the faults were not all on one side. John Taylor (1637–1708), who had spent much of his life in the West Indies, and settled in the city in 1676, was evidently an irritable man, though devoted to the service of Friends.[5] It is probable that the clash of temperaments in the local group at York made it impossible for the Quarterly Meeting, with all its strength, to moderate the differences in time to avoid mischief.

I have already sufficiently traced the separation in Wiltshire.[6] As early as 1684, the Quarterly Meeting

---

[1] Q.M. Minutes, July 1685 and March 1691.
[2] Letter, 4th July 1691, in York Records, and Minutes, no doubt based on this, of York M.M. 4th Sept. and Q.M. Sept. 1691.
[3] See this and other papers of about same date in York Records.
[4] The meeting-house in Water Lane was leased from him, and the Two Weeks' meeting of 26th April 1693 made an appointment to ascertain if Emmanuel Nightingale could give a receipt for the rent, which looks as though the father had recently died.
[5] See *Camb. Journ.* ii. 496, *Account of* ... *John Taylor*, 1710, reprinted 1830, and York M.M. Minutes.   [6] *Ante*, pp. 316, 317.

XVII CLOSING YEARS OF THE CENTURY 479

reported that the opposite spirit was blasted and gone, and many came back again.[1] Ismeade, however, troubled London and Bristol meetings as late as 1696.[2]

At Bristol there is, I think, evidence that no separate meetings were set up,[3] but there was often much disturbance in the regular ones; and in 1692 a special Two Weeks' meeting recognized that many Friends were burdened with some out of unity who imposed preaching upon them, but strongly discouraged public opposition "by open testimony against them and striving to silence or to outspeak them, to the great hurt and dishonour of our religion."[4] A year earlier Friends had reported to the Yearly Meeting that Truth bore dominion over the contrary, and meetings were large and peaceable, except sometimes when Separatists came. There was a great desire after unity, as is shown in the establishment of the Yearly Meeting for the Western Counties in 1695.[5] The letter of invitation [6] says:

Dear Friends, you cannot be ignorant . . . of that cloud of darkness that have been over this city for some years past, what with . . . cruel persecutors, and what with those troubles and divisions that have happened amongst ourselves. . . . But now . . . the one is wholly extinct and the other so much abated that we hope the footsteps thereof in a little time will be rarely seen. And, because we are right sensible that the true and ancient love begins again to spring up after so long a winterly time, we cannot but in a sense thereof call to you to come and rejoice with us. Blessed be His Name for ever, the time as of old of the ingathering is known.

There were still occasional difficulties, especially at the big meetings at Fair times. Samuel Bownas tells of one such case about 1696 at the winter Fair. Ismeade stood up to speak. In his sermon he asked, "Do I bring my

---

[1] Report to Y.M. Later reports speak several times of the separation declining. [2] Thomas Story, *Life*, p. 121.
[3] Thomas Robertson, writing to Fox, 2nd Feb. 1686 (Dev. Ho. A.R.B. Colln. No. 151), says: "they are not like to have a separation here, for anything that I can see."
[4] Minutes of 12th, 13th Dec. 1692.
[5] For this Y.M. see A. Neave Brayshaw, in *Handbook to Birmingham Y.M. 1908*, pp. 56-60, and *post*, p. 546.
[6] Letter, 20th Aug. 1694, to Gloucester Q.M. in Bristol Records.

deeds to the light?" and Charles Harford replied, "If thou didst, thou wouldst not do as thou dost." Whereupon Bownas, regardless or ignorant of the Minute of 1692, began to preach in a strong voice, Ismeade crying out that he had not done: "but," says Bownas, "I took no account of that, but went on, and he soon sat down and fell asleep; and we had a blessed, edifying meeting that day and Truth was exalted above error."

The moderate policy which became established at Bristol is illustrated in a striking way by what we may call an ultra-orthodox separation which took place at Frenchay as late as 1718. A separate meeting was set up, under pretence that Bristol Friends had shown partiality and injustice and gone into the grossest evils. Sarah Dixon seems to have been the leader of the women who governed this group, and they spoke most bitterly of Bristol Friends, because the Men's Meeting, as I understand it, discouraged a separate Women's Meeting in the city.[1] The young people there, says Thomas Story,[2]

... are not apt to relish the harsh and unwary discourses of ... Sarah Dixon and her disciples and accomplices, who very unwarrantably and falsely apply unto them and even to the Men's Meeting there all the woes and judgments against old Israel in their most degenerate state; of which these young people ... are greatly offended and hurt, judging the prating of such to arise from no other ground than their own ill-nature, heightened by some private offences taken at some particulars [*i.e.* particular individuals] against whom they cannot have their revenges in their own way.

Rogers, the champion of the Wilkinson-Story party in the West of England, "though a rich man in the world, became very poor, grew dark, and lost almost all sense of religion."[3] He was alive in 1708, when he published *Quakers, a divided People, distinguished*, and Thomas Gwin saw him at Chippenham:[4]

---

[1] *Life*, p. 615. For the Bristol policy as to Women's Meetings see *ante*, p. 312. [2] *Life*, p. 627.
[3] Joseph Pike, *Life, sub anno* 1677. [4] MS. Journal, June 1708.

CLOSING YEARS OF THE CENTURY

There it was William Rogers came to me and still would justify his ancient, abusive scribbling. I was plain in my advice to him, though unwilling to go into many words, he being wise in his own eyes; so he left us in a little time and we were easier amongst ourselves.

In Westmorland the separation lingered on into the new century. In 1691 Friends reported:[1]

The Lord's power is come over the spirit of division. Most of its adherents come to nothing: many [have] returned to Friends. . . . A new meeting-house at Preston [Patrick]. Things better than formerly: meeting books that had been taken away by the Separatists are recovered, but defaced, and Friends do meet again in their meeting-houses which the Separatists had shut them out of, and are quiet, save when some of the Separatist preachers come.

In 1698 they report "the spirit of separation totally subdued," and in 1709[2] we are told:

Those that continue yet in that separation are grown very few and small in number, loose in their lives, has lost their ancient testimony against tithes, and several running out to be married by priests, etc.

It was inevitable that these scattered groups of dissenting Friends, often gathered round some minister who had lost touch with the main body, should disturb the London meetings and seek to make a centre for themselves in the metropolis. Thomas Kent, of London, but afterwards of Tenby in Wales, was one of the troublers of Israel, and with Cox and some others set up a separate meeting about 1686,[3] which we find held at Harp Lane near Tower Street a few years later. In 1689 we are told that "the separate meeting continues in London, and such as fly the cross of Christ resort to them; and disorderly marriages of persons with top-knots and such-like that resort to them are admitted."[4] Ten years later we

---

[1] Report in Y.M. Minutes.　　[2] *F.P.T.* p. 256.
[3] The letter, 24th Jan. 1687, to the London M.M.'s is in York Records and Dev. Ho. Portf. 2, No. 38. See also Morning Meeting Minutes, 28th Feb. 1687, 18th, 25th July 1687, the paper these two last refer to being in Dev. Ho. Portf. 23, No. 182. Cf. Six Weeks' Meeting Minutes, 1st Feb., 7th June, 19th July 1687.
[4] Report in Y.M. Minutes.

hear of opposition by apostates, but there are no separate meetings,[1] so that the effort, probably involving more cost than could be well afforded, proved short-lived. Opposition is often ready to strengthen itself from strange quarters. A common grievance may unite men who differ widely on other questions. We need not be surprised, therefore, that Harp Lane was a cave of Adullam for all discontented spirits, even for a time for George Keith and his followers, who were seeking to bring the Society into a strict membership and an orthodox uniformity alien to the lax views on Church government of the Wilkinson-Story party. Keith, indeed, soon left the Separatists, and the Friends of Harp Lane became as violent opposers of him as those of Gracechurch Street.[2]

I need only refer briefly to the early history of this new schism.

Keith[3] had shared to the full the sufferings of Scottish Friends, and his learning made him one of the most powerful of Quaker controversialists. He emigrated to New Jersey in 1684, and as Surveyor-General, for he was a skilled mathematician, did important work in running the boundary-line between East and West Jersey. Five years later he became for a short time Headmaster of the newly-founded Friends' Public School at Philadelphia. A man of commanding intellectual ability, and a Scottish theologian in spite of his Quakerism, he now assumed a censorious attitude towards all that he considered lax or unsound in the current discipline and preaching of American Friends, and behaved with a temper and pugnacity which fomented bitterness. An upheaval ensued which for a time "shook the Society of Friends in the Middle Colonies and also in England to its foundations."[4] He organized his body, " The Christian-Quakers," with a discipline of its own, adopting the name but not the

[1] Report in Y.M. Minutes.
[2] In Leslie's "Satan Disrob'd from his Disguise of Light," 2nd edn. 1698, p. 97, after an account of a Keithian dispute with Thos. Curtis in Berkshire.
[3] See *Quakers in the American Colonies*, pp. 369, 370 and pp. 446-452; Thomas, *Hist. of Friends in America*, 4th edn. pp. 95-98; Bowden, *Hist. of Friends in America*, ii. 75-104.
[4] Thomas, *op. cit.* p. 97.

XVII CLOSING YEARS OF THE CENTURY 483

principles of the followers of Rogers.[1] His system contained developments, parts of which have been since adopted or might in the opinion of some Friends be followed with benefit to-day.[2] Membership was to be confined to those who made open confession of their faith; and children reaching years of discretion were to be received in the same way, these convincements being properly registered. The business meetings were to consist of all such members, and to be regularly attended by them, and were to exercise a strict discipline. Elders and Deacons were to be appointed, the first for oversight and inspection of the membership, the second for money matters and the poor. Ministers and Elders were to prevent disorder from raw and unseasoned persons taking part in meetings; and to that end ministers should "give some proof of their sound knowledge, experience and spiritual ability to their elder brethren and to the Church before they presume that liberty to preach and pray in open assembly."

Had Keith been a *persona grata* and shown a more loving spirit, he might have joined hands with the zealous Friends in Ireland and the North of England who were pressing a close discipline on the Church, and have affected their policy with advantage in certain directions. As it was, he was disowned by the Pennsylvania Yearly Meeting, and set up meetings at several places, developing a strong attack against Friends for their alleged denial of the outward Christ.

Early in 1694, in company with Thomas Budd, his chief supporter,[3] he carried the controversy to England. The Yearly Meeting of this year lasted for fourteen days and went fully into the whole matter,[4] reaching a conclusion adverse to Keith. The following letters show the im-

[1] "The Gospel Order and Discipline in Men and Women's Meetings of faithful Friends of Truth for the effecting a more perfect separation from the world" is printed, from MS. in possession of late George Vaux of Philadelphia, in *J.F.H.S.* x. 70-76, and takes the form of twelve queries. It is endorsed, evidently by an anti-Keithian hand, "Articles of George Keith for his proselytes to sign before they receive admittance into his Church-fellowship."
[2] Cf. *Quakers in the American Colonies*, p. 450.
[3] A son, I think, of the Thomas Budd of Martock, near Yeovil, mentioned in *Beginnings of Quakerism*, pp. 386, 387, who died in 1670.
[4] Bowden, ii. 95-99, gives a full account of the proceedings from the Y.M. Minutes.

pression he made better than any formal account of the proceedings would do.

Henry Gouldney, writing prior to the Yearly Meeting, says :[1]

I have little to give thee account of; the most considerable is G.K.'s being here. He is not a man governed with that meekness that becomes his doctrine, who puts a great value upon the outward coming of our blessed Lord, which I hope all honest Friends finds it their duty to do ; yet himself far from making him a lively example in meekness and humility. Friends have had many private meetings with him, and by them all I don't find great hopes of his coming more near us in spirit. His doctrines in the general are I think owned by all sound Friends ; but he seems to lay down about seven points which he calls fundamentals, in any of whom, if we disagree in, he cannot hold fellowship ; though, upon the whole, was not his spirit wrong, that would easily be accommodated. He takes commonly large time in meetings, but mostly flat : he has a tone sometimes, especially when on one of his particular points that he hugs more than ordinary, that he carries off more lively. . . . He speaks of appealing to the Yearly Meeting, and will submit to their judgment so far as it agrees with his and not otherwise.

John Banks writes :[2]

We have had a long and tedious time with that contentious man, George Keith, for several days together ; he is of a very turbulent and troublesome spirit, vexatious to the Church of Christ ; but the power of God, for all his quarrelling, is over him, and the life of our meeting run in one channel, to set the judgment of Truth upon his head ; for it was clearly made manifest to us, in the Light of the Lord Jesus Christ, that he was not only gone into and entertained the spirit of division and separation, but of envy and deep deceit ; by which he warred strongly, to prove Friends in the ministry to preach false doctrine and himself the true, chiefly about the body of Christ and the Light within. But, by the unruliness of his spirit and the darkness that he is gone into, he hath so manifested himself that all his enticing words could take no place with us.[3]

---

[1] Letter to Sir John Rodes, 27th April 1694, in *Quaker Post-bag*, pp. 56-59.
[2] *Journ*, sub anno 1694. The letter is dated 8th June.
[3] Whiting, *Persecution Exposed*, p. 232, also gives an account of the Y.M., and see "A True Account of The Proceedings, &c.," with a preface by Robert Hannay. This scandalized the Morning Meeting, see Minutes of 25th June, but in the Quaker note at the end of Croese's *History*, Engl. edn. 1696, App. p. 30, it is referred to with approval. A pamphlet controversy ensued with Ellwood as the chief antagonist of Keith (see Smith's *Catalogue*).

Keith, for a time, frequented the London meetings, but in the autumn resorted to Harp Lane, whither but few followed him.[1] A small volume of Christian-Quaker sermons preached between 17th June and 4th November of this year[2] contains six by Keith, three by Thomas Budd, and one each by John Raunce and Charles Harris. Keith's sermons are powerful and well-balanced: they lay stress on the atonement, but insist " that true saving faith respects Christ both inwardly and outwardly. . . . Whoever hath the faith of Christ without them, and hath not, at the same time, the faith of Christ within, it is but a hearsay and traditional faith." [3]

In February 1695 there was a painful meeting at Ratcliff, which shows the tension of feeling.[4] Penn, John Vaughton, and Keith were present. Vaughton, who was a leading London minister, had offered prayer, and the meeting was about to close, when Keith stood up, and after reflecting on the prayer, charged Friends in their printed books with misinterpreting the verse in 1 John i. 7, which says: " If we walk in the light, as He is in the light, we have fellowship one with another, and the blood of Jesus Christ, His Son, cleanseth us from all sin." The blood, they said, was the life, and the life was the light of men, and the light was within ; and so they shut out any benefit by the blood of Christ ; whereas Keith, though speaking nothing to the derogation of the Light within, pointed out that the plain meaning of the text was the blood that was shed in the outward body of the man

---

[1] Tomkins, writing to Sir John Rodes, 20th Dec. (*Quaker Post-bag*, pp. 116-121), says that for about six weeks past Keith had quite left Friends' Meetings and resorted to Harp Lane.

[2] *The Great Doctrines, &c.*, printed for Nathaniel Crouch, 1694. One of Budd's sermons is of earlier date, 11th April.

[3] *Ibid.* p. 114.

[4] For this meeting see Henry Gouldney to Robert Barclay, 28th Feb. 1695, in *Reliquiae Barclaianae*, pp. 95-97, and MS. account among my late father's papers, in handwriting of Josiah Forster, endorsed, " copied at Kendal, 10th mo. 1833." In one of Keith's sermons, in *The Great Doctrines, &c.*, p. 115, there is the same charge about 1 John i. 7, and passages in some Quaker books gave colour to it. When Penn was asked by Keith at the Y.M. of 1695 to make good the charge of apostasy, he said that at Ratcliff he was in no passion, but was so transported by the glorious power of God, that he knew not whether he was standing, sitting, or kneeling (Keith's " Narrative of Turner's Hall Meeting, 11th June 1696," p. 14).

Christ Jesus. It was a great and mixed meeting, and, after a quarter of an hour of Keith's criticism, Penn pulled off his hat and interrupted him, saying:

In the name and fear of the great God, I have a testimony to bear and sound among you over the head of this apostate and false accuser and common opposer, who makes it his business to go from meeting to meeting to carp, catch, accuse and raise disturbances and troubles, and to sow enmity, animosities and divisions amongst us; and would, under the pretence of order, by sly insinuations and open reflections, falsely accuse us, as if we were not sound in the faith, though he himself once thought otherwise of us, but now is gone into division and separation from us.

He protested against Keith making meetings for worshipping God a stage of contention, and testified that it was always the Quakers' faith that they were saved by no other than Jesus, Who shed His precious blood for man, a measure of Whose spirit is communicated to every one, "and they who come to walk up unto it are thereby instituted to the benefit of His precious blood, shed for an atonement and a propitiation for the sins of the whole world." Friends, he said, had not so often been found preaching the outward appearance of Christ as the first apostles, because it was a truth historically believed by all Christians, "but the spiritual appearance of Christ in the soul, which is so requisite to salvation, is little regarded and has been much opposed." Keith exclaimed against being called an apostate: he was never so called in any meeting in his life before and desired to be heard in his own vindication. But the meeting cried out, the world as well as Friends, "Let us be going and not stay to hear him rail"; on which they dispersed, leaving him "in a great anger and quarrel." One man of the world said: "Why do they suffer him to disturb their meetings thus, to spoil a good sermon and a good prayer thus? I wonder at Mr. Penn's patience, that he did not fling him over the gallery."

At the Yearly Meeting of 1695 he had a further hearing and another Minute against his spirit and works of division was passed, on hearing which he broke out in great anger and left the meeting, which then passed a Minute disowning him.[1] "His behaviour," says Jasper Batt, "was very proud, arrogant and uncivil."[2] After this he visited Reading, High Wycombe and Marlborough,[3] but became dissatisfied with the Quaker Separatists at Harp Lane, and set up his own meeting at Turner's Hall, in Philpot Lane, Fenchurch Street. Here he challenged leading Friends to public disputes, which they refused, but he attended at the times announced and printed the proceedings.[4] In this way, and through pamphlets written by Keith or by other opposers, Friends, though sheltered from persecution by the Toleration Act, found themselves beset by a storm of controversy, which laid bare their weaknesses and attacked their principles without stint. Francis Bugg, of Mildenhall in Suffolk, the bitterest and most persistent of all the relapsed Quakers, poured forth a stream of abusive books and pamphlets—over sixty in all—between 1680, when he became disaffected to Friends, and his death more than forty years later, an old man of eighty-four.[5] I have examined several, which are stuffed full of scavengings of unguarded passages in Quaker writings, stories to the discredit of individuals, and venomous hostility to Fox and George Whitehead, the same insipid hotch-potch being served up again and again with fresh seasonings of malice. There is a pillory of twelve perjured Quakers, and a cage of unclean birds, both of which appeared first, I think, in *New Rome Arraigned*, 1693;[6] a Quaker on crutches illustrates *Quakerism Withering* in 1694,[7] and in *The Pilgrim's Progress from Quakerism to Christianity*, 1698,

[1] See Bowden, *Hist. of Friends in America*, ii. 99-100, from Y.M. Minutes.
[2] Letter to Matthew Perrin, 18th May 1695, in Swarthm. Colln. v. 75.
[3] Tomkins to Sir John Rodes, 24th Sept. 1695, *Quaker Post-bag*, pp. 124-126.
[4] These meetings were held 11th June 1696, 29th April 1697, 21st April 1698, 11th, 18th, 23rd Jan. 1700; see Smith's *Catalogue, sub nomine* George Keith, and other pieces noted in Smith.
[5] For Bugg, see *Dict. Natl. Biography, Camb. Journ.* ii. 499, and Smith's *Catalogue*.
[6] Friends had called the Church of England a cage of unclean birds, and this was his *tu quoque!*
[7] The woodcut is given from *Quakerism Drooping*, in *J.F.H.S.* x. 41.

besides the cage, the reader is presented with Bugg's portrait and with a plate of "The Quakers' Synod."[1] This shows a meeting of some eighty Quakers, all wearing their low broad-brimmed hats, except the president, George Whitehead, gathered about a large cloth-covered table, on which lie "the Journal of G. Fox" and an open volume of "Church Canons." At one end sits the "scribe," Benjamin Bealing; and in the gallery above the table are five Friends, Whitehead in the middle, with Penn on his right and William Bingley at the end seat on the left. Penn is saying, "Call over the list: are none of Truth's enemies here?" Whitehead asks, "Are the doors shut?" and Bingley replies, "Yea, the doors are locked." In *Quakerism Drooping*, 1703, he reproduced George Fox's Will in all its vagaries of spelling and grammar,[2] and seems, first and last, to have printed some 50,000 copies of this.[3] Bugg's general picture of Quakerism is a gross distortion, the work of a pen filled with envy and all uncharitableness; but his industrious raking together of garbage, and his inside knowledge of the Society and the extravagances to be found in its history, enabled him to make out an *ex parte* case, which was readily accepted by those in other Churches who were glad to think ill of Quakerism, or by worldlings who were glad to think ill of Christianity.

In 1696 an abler opponent of the Quakers appeared in the anonymous author of *The Snake in the Grass*. This was Charles Leslie, a non-juring divine of Irish extraction, who followed the profession of a pamphleteer,[4] "smooth-

---

[1] Also appears, though from a worn plate, in the VIth pt. of Bugg's folio, 1712, which he called *A Finishing Stroke*, p. 530.

[2] This first appeared in Bugg's "Seasonable Caveat," 1701, pp. 88-96, "as it is of his own handwriting in the Prerogative Office, both for spelling and pointing as near as I can." He afterwards printed it as a Broadside (see *Camb. Journ.* ii. 491).

[3] According to Smith's *Catalogue*, there are eight impressions or edns. of this Will, and it appears in several of Bugg's larger books. Bugg tried to hold disputes with Friends at Banbury, Bristol, and other places, but they usually declined to meet him (see Smith's *Catalogue*, and Thos. Gwin's MS. Journal.)

[4] For Leslie (1650-1722), see *Dict. Natl. Biography*, Rev. R. J. Leslie's *Life and Writings of Charles Leslie, M.A.*, 1885, and notice of this in *J.F.H.S.* xix. 123-126. My father immured books like *The Snake* in a dark dungeon of his library, which he called "hard-cap."

tongued, witty and sly,"[1] with "an indifferent glib style."[2] He professes himself sick of the dirty job in hand.

> I am abundantly surfeited with raking the dung-hill of their writings; and nothing should oblige me to undergo that drudgery but the hopes of doing them good by it. . . . For whose sakes I grudge not the office of a scavenger, and the Herculean labour of cleansing so foul a stable, a sink and complication of the vilest heresies that ever have been broached in the Christian Church, even all of [16]41 blended and improved.[3]

The book is fairly enough described as

> . . . much of it . . . made up of old stories, with great mixtures of falsehood, many of which . . . are answered. And those which have any part of truth in them, as the wickedness and falsehood of any professing Truth among us, our adversaries knows that we disown such things. Only *The Snake* has new-licked them over and jumbled them together, to render Truth and Friends odious.[4]

It had a considerable vogue, being "largely spread, and especially among divers great men and many sober professing people,"[5] and it was difficult to give the same currency to George Whitehead's less lively *Antidote* and to Joseph Wyeth's *Switch for the Snake*, which appeared in answer.[6] *The Snake* was a readable compendium of the adverse literature printed against Friends during the previous forty years, and was well calculated to cast odium on Quakers, though its author confesses:[7]

---

[1] Letter from London Friends to Robert Barclay, 22nd Dec. 1696, in *Reliquiae Barclaianae*, pp. 104-106.
[2] Tomkins to Sir John Rodes, 14th April 1698, *Quaker Post-bag*, pp. 135-139.
[3] Preface to Leslie's further attack on Friends, called "Satan Disrob'd from his Disguise of Light," 2nd edn. 1698.
[4] Letter as above in *Quaker Post-bag*, p. 137.
[5] Minute of Morning Meeting, 7th June 1697. Five pounds' worth of the *Antidote* were to go to Penn and to others for distribution in likely quarters.'
[6] The *Antidote* came out in 1697, the *Switch* in 1699, after second and third edns. of *The Snake* much improved in arrangement. For proofs of the influence of Leslie's books, see *J.F.H.S.* xiv. 123-126.
[7] *The Snake*, 3rd edn. pp. 2, 3. As Leslie was a strong Jacobite, he lets Penn off more lightly than other Quakers. *The Snake* is almost entirely drawn from Bugg, Thomas Crisp, Keith and other adverse writers, Leslie admitting in the Account of the Second Edn. that he had only spent a little time on the subject and was gradually learning the language of Quakerism more perfectly.

Many of them have really gone off from that height of blasphemy and madness, which was professed among them at their first setting-up, ... especially of late some of them have made nearer advances towards Christianity than ever before. And among them the ingenious Mr. Penn has of late refined some of their gross notions and brought them into some form [and] has made them speak sense and English.

The piece, in fact, harked back to all the extravagances of language and writing which attended the rise of Quakerism, and set out these and some later material of the same sort in the most prejudiced light, without any appreciation of the great truths for which Friends stood or of the nobility and constancy of the Quaker witness.

In illustration of the animus aroused against Friends, we may take the Norfolk Petition, an extract from which heads the present chapter. At Bugg's instigation, some of the Norfolk clergy had appointed a dispute with Friends in West Dereham church on Friday 8th December 1698, which local Friends and five from London attended.[1] Two stages were erected, and the proceedings were opened with Church prayers and one from Samuel Waldenfield. The day was largely spent in debates as to procedure, each side claiming that the other was the challenger, but the "priests" got in a good many of their charges, and Friends bore full witness to their Faith. "Judas, that is Francis Bugg," we are told, "stood at the priests' elbows and was their agent to look out places, quotations &c."[2] After this, the petition was prepared for Parliament, with a similar one from Bury St. Edmunds, but the county members did not see fit to present them.[3] Of the West Dereham debate John Tomkins says:[4]

[1] There is a lively account of the proceedings in a letter from Tomkins to Sir John Rodes, 3rd Jan. 1699, in *Quaker Post-bag*, pp. 148-159. For the clergymen's report and the sequel of controversial pieces, see Smith, *Bibliotheca Anti-Quakeriana*, pp. 66-69, under name of Edward Beckham, rector of Gaytonthorpe.
[2] *Quaker Post-bag*, p. 151.
[3] For these petitions, see Whitehead, *Christian Progress*, pp. 672-681.
[4] *Quaker Post-bag*, pp. 152, 156. Friends distributed a paper of their Christian belief, of which 1000 copies had been specially reprinted by order of the Morning Meeting, 27th Nov. Bugg tried to continue the dispute the next day, and, says Tomkins, "had but a small company, a hundred people ... and Friends ... did so manage the matter that [he] was much confounded in his work, and making no earnings of it; for they spoiled his drollery and sport

More rudeness and confusion, especially from men so high in profession of religion, was hardly ever seen, and Francis Bugg with them, hooting and hallooing and laughing, and a few [of the people] joined with them, about twenty or thirty as near as I could compute, who was ready at their beck and notice to laugh, bawl or hiss. Such ugly laughter as I saw in the priests I never beheld except on a mountebank's stage. . . . But, while the people was departing, the priests and Friends had very friendly conference, as they stood on the opposite stages; and they wished us well and did declare, as they had done two or three hours before, that they did believe that the Quakers of this present generation were orthodox.

Keith's congregation at Turner's Hall was styled by Leslie "the poor Church of the Quakers," in contrast with the rich Gracechurch Street Meeting.[1] It published in April 1696 a "Seasonable Testimony," containing a confession of its Christian Faith, signed by George White, "an old Separate."[2] There is no evidence that the Turner's Hall company had any strength.[3] Keith's own position was changing. His attempts at reforming, from his point of view, the Quaker Church had failed, and he had grown more and more suspicious of the central experience of the Inward Light. His views on Church organization and on theology were approximating to those of a moderate Anglican, and, after his final breach with English Friends, Turner's Hall became for him only a halting-place on the road to the English Church. He must have joined this before March 1699, when he became the first travelling agent of the newly-established Society for Propagating Christian Knowledge.[4] He was

---

that he intended amongst the mob, and he shut up his books and broke off a considerable time before the people expected." Cf. also letter from Daniel Phillips, 9th Dec., in Dev. Ho. Portf. 24, No. 10.
[1] *Snake in the Grass*, 3rd edn. p. 362.
[2] Smith's *Catalogue*, ii. 31. White had already written a pamphlet against Friends, in 1694, answered by Henry Gouldney (see Smith, i. 858), and, in referring to this answer, Tomkins calls him "an old Separate" in letter to Sir John Rodes, 20th Dec. 1694 (*Quaker Post-bag*, p. 119).
[3] See reports to Y.M. 1697, 1699, Penn's letter of 26th Dec. 1696 (*Quakers in the American Colonies*, p. 454), which says "not five people in the unity, before he came over here, adhere to him," and London Friends to Robert Barclay, 22nd Dec. 1696, in *Reliquiae Barclaianae*, p. 105, which says, "Last Fifth-day, George Keith had but about ten or twelve at his meeting; his show is much over."
[4] *Hist. of S.P.C.K. 1698–1898*, p. 25.

ordained in 1700, preaching his farewell sermon at Turner's Hall on 5th May and a week later his first sermons after ordination at St. George's, Botolph Lane.[1] John Tomkins writes maliciously: [2]

> They make a tool of him: he preaches every First-day at a new place, but generally even[ing]. Such as are of the Church have him in derision: he serves for a jest. Even whilst he is in the pulpit, there is such a murmur with the secret talking and observation of his hearers, together with their dumb notices and laughter, that many could not hear him.

His American followers became mostly Baptists or Episcopalians, though a few returned to Friends.[3] Outside London, the only district seriously affected had been Huntingdonshire. Here James Dickinson had great exercise with Keithians at the end of 1699,[4] and the reports to the Yearly Meeting speak of some Friends having received hurt.[5] After Keith joined the Church of England, we are told:[6]

> As to those Quakers the public prints speak of being baptized, they are of the old shattered Separates; and, even in Huntingdonshire that G. K. boasts of the great conversion, John Everard says but four who was in unity with Friends have gone to steeplehouse, his wife [Margaret] and R[obert] B[ridgman] two of them. The other poor people who flocked after him was of the weak sort who leaned to the old separation, but G. K. has outrun them, and they will not follow, but returns to Friends' meetings, though it cannot be denied but he has muddled the minds of many weak persons, which time will help to reduce as well as Truth.

The S.P.C.K., out of which branched the Society for the Propagation of the Gospel in 1701, was from the first zealous in promoting Keith's efforts for instructing and converting the Quakers, "in order to redeem that misguided people to the knowledge and belief of Christ,"[7] and Dr. Thomas Bray, its devoted founder, included in his plan for the plantations the object of reducing "the

---

[1] These sermons were printed, see Smith's *Catalogue*.
[2] Letter to Sir John Rodes, 4th June 1700, in *Quaker Post-bag*, pp. 162-164.
[3] *Quakers in the American Colonies*, p. 454.
[4] *Journal, sub hoc anno*.   [5] Reports to Y.M. 1699, 1700.
[6] Letter of Tomkins as above: cf. letter 18th Nov. 1698, in *Quaker Post-bag*, pp. 145, 146.   [7] *Hist. of S.P.C.K. 1698-1898*, p. 25.

CLOSING YEARS OF THE CENTURY

Quakers, who are so numerous in those parts, to the Christian Faith, from which they are totally apostatized and so may be looked upon as a heathen nation."[1] At its second meeting it resolved to disperse two of Keith's books "up and down the kingdom among the Quakers for their better conviction and instruction,"[2] and the earnest-minded Churchmen who were its correspondents were hot against Friends.[3] Keith was at Bristol for some weeks in the summer of 1700, where he challenged a debate, which was declined.[4] His ill-success in making converts was accounted for because he had not been seconded, and because the Quakers had circulated some of their best literature and had been sedulous in "helping new converts to good matches."[5] He was at Colchester in the following year,[6] and in 1702 went over to America for the S.P.G.[7] On his return after two years of labour he did some further itinerating work, but in 1706 became rector of Edburton, near Steyning in Sussex, a remote and miry parish with a meagre living, where he died ten years later.[8] Keith was the most formidable of all the antagonists of Quakerism, alike from his knowledge of the Society, his learning, his sincerity, and the general moderation of his writings. He no doubt lost his temper under provocation, and probably never understood sympathetically the spiritual side of Quakerism; but in confronting the Society of Friends with the claims of historic Christianity much of his criticism was salutary medicine, which did not altogether fail of effect.

---

[1] *Hist. of S.P.C.K. 1698 1898*, p. 24.
[2] *Ibid.* pp. 26, 28. [3] *Ibid.* pp. 61-107.
[4] See "Narrative" of debate, described in Smith's *Catalogue*, and Gouldney to John Gratton, 29th Aug. 1700, in *Quaker Post-bag*, pp. 85-86.
[5] *Hist. of S.P.C.K. 1698–1898*, p. 79, from letter of Bristol Correspondent, Mr. Bedford, 3rd May 1701.
[6] For Colchester visit, see Smith's *Catalogue*, ii. 38, 39, 838.
[7] See *Quakerism in the American Colonies*, pp. 454-458.
[8] For the close of his life see extracts in Smith's *Catalogue*, ii. 42, 43, to which it would be unsafe to attach much credit. He was about 77 at his death. Thomas Story, *Life*, p. 259, says "all sorts of people [in America] becoming weary of him and his work, and slighting him, he became as the salt which had lost its savour, and returning by way of Virginia for England, he became a parish priest and died very poor and miserable." He made a progress in the West of England in 1706, but had a poor reception and soon returned. (Cornwall report to Y.M. 1707, and Thos. Gwin's MS. Journal, Sept. 1706.)

I may have surfeited my readers with these accounts of separations and controversies, which make unpalatable and sometimes nauseous reading; but they form an important part of any honestly-drawn picture of seventeenth-century Quakerism, and I have compressed into a few pages subjects whose involutions might easily have occupied volumes. The contemporary literature and the private letters of the time are full of them; and they reacted powerfully on the behaviour of the Society. We do not find much direct admission of this; for men say little of changes produced by hostile and unwelcome criticism from without, and often persuade themselves into thinking that the resulting alterations in their conduct spring from their own initiative or go on asserting and believing that they have not changed at all. It is our business, however, to go behind the face values to the unacknowledged motives.

I sum up my conclusions as follows :

(1) The Wilkinson-Story controversy, as already shown,[1] undoubtedly checked the high conception of corporate authority which had been mooted by Barclay in his *Anarchy of the Ranters*.

(2) It was also, by its discouragement of strong leadership, one of the causes which would gradually produce a change in the position and service of the travelling Publishers of Truth.

(3) The serious breach of unity that resulted from the separation presented Quakers to the world as a divided people, whose inward law led them into opposing camps. Discredit was therefore thrown on the validity of this inward law; just as discredit is thrown on the validity of Christianity by its divisions to-day. Under the urgent stress of the world-situation, we are at last beginning to see some light on this question, but the Church catholic has still to reach a true conception of Christian unity. The contribution that Quakerism has to make will be dealt with in my final chapter.

(4) The unscrupulous criticism of Quaker extravagances by such men as Bugg and Leslie and Thomas Crisp added its weight to the other influences which were pressing the Society into a rut of eminent respectability and robbing it of ill-regulated enthusiasms.

---

[1] *Vide supra*, Chap. XII.

(5) The severe doctrinal handling of Quakerism especially by Leslie and Keith obliged Friends to reconsider their message and affected their manner of expressing it. They were now a body of Protestant Dissenters, tolerated by the State on the footing that their views were substantially in line with those of other orthodox Christians. This assumption was well-grounded, for Quakerism had always, at its best, been in the closest touch with primitive Christianity and with the Spirit of Christ. But, as we have seen, the relation of the inward law by which the Quaker sought to live to the great body of conviction which had grown up through the centuries as to the historic life and work of Christ had only been made imperfectly, and could only be made imperfectly in the mental climate of the age. The criticism had laid bare undoubted weakness, but in trying to give safer expression to their message Friends often lost their old vigour without gaining any new clearness; and in the Quietist period developed a diction of their own, scarcely intelligible to the outside public and scarcely readable to-day.

At the beginning of the Keith controversy, Friends defended themselves from the attacks of the orthodox by the carefully written statement from the Morning Meeting in 1693, already referred to,[1] and in November 1696 the Morning Meeting[2] took in hand the inspection of the books of twenty-eight "ancient Friends" with respect to—

The scriptures and their being given by Divine inspiration,
Jesus Christ, as God and as man,
His sufferings, death, blessed sacrifice, propitiation, resurrection, ascension into glory, mediation and intercession,
Repentance, Faith in Christ,
Sanctification and justification,
Perfection and infallibility,
Resurrection and future state,
General judgment, rewards and punishments,
How Christ is in heaven and in the hearts of His people,
How [He is] in all as a Divine Light and Seed,
Measure of the Spirit given to all, or universal grace and its sufficiency to salvation,
The Word nigh in the heart and Truth in the inward parts,
Baptism and the Supper.

It was agreed that the several doctrines should be

[1] See *ante*, p. 378. Printed in Sewel, ii. 497-508. Cf. Edward Grubb, *The Historic and the Inward Christ*, pp. 44, 45.
[2] Minutes of 30th Nov. and 3rd Dec. 1696. Keith's older books were also to be perused.

collected into distinct sheets, and that in reading a treatise all the places should be noted, the most material passages being written out, with memoranda of the other references. Elaborate appointments were made for doing the work. This inspection must have proved of great service to the Morning Meeting in dealing with adverse literature and would powerfully promote a cautious handling of new Quaker books or old books proposed for reprinting.

Richard Claridge came into favour as an answerer of hostile pamphlets. His extensive knowledge of Anglican books allowed him to use a new and effective method of reply, by supporting the distinctive Quaker tenets from the writings of Church divines.[1]

The growth of religious societies within the Church of England during the closing years of the century and the reign of Anne is good evidence of vitality and earnestness among certain Anglican circles in the period preceding the Latitudinarian ascendancy and placidity of her Hanoverian days. It is equally cogent proof of the strength of Quakerism at home and in the colonies that the efforts of the two chief societies, the S.P.C.K. and the S.P.G., should have been largely directed against the Quakers, and that this campaign should have enlisted the pen amongst others of Leslie, whom Dr. Johnson regarded as the ablest of the Non-jurors, "a reasoner, and a reasoner who was not to be reasoned against."[2] When Quakerism failed to arouse controversy it would be a sign that it had ceased for the time to have a live message for the needs of England, and could be left alone as a harmless survival of the past.

---

[1] Claridge's controversial pieces date from 1701 to 1710, and there were others printed in his posthumous *Works*, 1726. Bugg, in the preface to "Quakerism Anatomized," 1709, one of the parts of his folio *Finishing Stroke*, complains that the Quakers have got Claridge to assist them with books, and that this is why John Whiting, in his *Rector Corrected*, 1708, says, "If ever I am concerned with quotations again, I intend to answer them with quotations out of the priests' books, being now stored with books to that purpose." Claridge, in the preface to his *Melius Inquirendum*, 1708, says he uses these quotations as confessions of men who oppose Quakers for asserting the same doctrines as they themselves had done.

[2] Boswell's *Life*, under date 9th June 1784, note.

CHAPTER XVIII

THE QUAKER WAY OF LIFE

> They are a people that have . . . mourned after God and waited for a Deliverer. . . . In spirit they are fervent; in mind staid and fixed; in their purpose to cleave unto the Lord resolute; in sufferings for His Name's sake joyful and patient; in trials constant; in the visitations of the Father's love and openings of His life they fear, and their hearts bow before Him. In discourse they are solid, in gesture grave; in speaking in the Name of the Lord reverent. . . . Being leavened through with love and mercy, it is against their very nature to revenge themselves or use carnal weapons to kill, hurt or destroy mankind. . . . Their dealings are just, their behaviour good, . . . their Yea, Yea, and their Nay, Nay, in all things. They cannot swear at all in any case whatsoever, but by a perpetual covenant are bound to speak truth to their neighbour and keep their word, though to their hurt. Covetousness they deny as idolatry; cruelty, oppression and uncleanness they abandon as destructive to the innocent life. . . . And, being sensible that the earth is the Lord's and the fullness thereof, and that they are but stewards of the portion He hath given them, they do not use things superfluous, which are destructive to the creation and hurtful to their neighbours. But in apparel they are modest, in meats and drinks temperate; that they may have wherewith to give a portion to the afflicted, feed the hungry and cover the naked with a garment. . . . Unwholesome words they are not free to use; nor to men will they give flattering titles, because the fear of God is in them; neither can they bow to the spirit of pride in men, nor stand uncovered before them, as they do when they approach unto God in prayer, because His honour ought not to be given to another. The customs of the world which are foolish and vain, wherein there is no true service to God nor man, they cannot countenance, nor uphold its invented worships by a conformity thereto. . . . They are willing to give up all that they may follow the leadings of the Life of Christ Jesus their Lord. . . . And they do all these things in the integrity and simplicity of their hearts towards God, not thinking thereby to merit life or engage His love and favour by what they can do. But, being beloved of the Father and having received life freely, by it they are bound faithfully to serve Him.—JOHN WHITEHEAD, *A Small Treatise* (1661) in *Life* by Thomas Chalk, 1852, pp. 80-101.

THE Inward Law by which the Quaker lived had from the first fashioned for him a way of life which marked him off from his neighbours.[1] It was not adopted as a badge of distinction, though it became one; and, what is of more consequence, it was not in its origin an outward rule impressed, but an inner life expressed. When George Fox, with his passion for sincerity, set out to make his behaviour conform with his spiritual experience, his way of life was largely determined, unconsciously to himself, by his own Puritan outlook and the limited mental horizons of the age. Moreover, definite external guidance came from the religious movements round him and from the authoritative precedents of prophets and of primitive Christianity. But it is important to note that the "notions" of others and even the experience of prophets and apostles did not become a principle of action with him until they had been transmuted within his own soul into "openings" of Divine Light and Life. As Hubberthorne said, in conversation with Charles II., in 1660,[2] "I have believed the scriptures from a child to be a declaration of truth, when I had but a literal knowledge, natural education and tradition, but now I know the scriptures to be true by the manifestation and operation of the Spirit of God fulfilling them in me."

The unification of the members of the Quaker groups into a common witness and way of life had been achieved at first through a fellowship and leadership and worship in the Life. But, as years passed, a great tradition began to impose itself; and, with the growth of organization, the acceptance on the authority of the Church of rules of conduct became in many cases a substitute for living principles of truth in the heart. The Church came to contain Quakers by birth and tradition, and by outward profession, as well as by convincement. We have seen in a previous chapter[3] the importance of the issues that are involved when a spiritual movement begins, often without definite intention, to rely on tradition and organization. We reached the conclusion that there is

---

[1] I must refer the reader to *Beginnings of Quakerism*, chaps. xix., vii., especially pp. 137-140, and for Fox, pp 33-42.
[2] *Works*, p. 27.   [3] *Ante*, Chap. XII.

room for both corporate authority and individual liberty in the Life but not out of it. It is from this standpoint that we proceed to examine the methods which the Society of Friends pursued for maintaining its group-testimony to Truth and fostering the witness of its members.

There is no doubt that prosperity was clogging the spiritual life of many Friends. Fox, as we have seen, was keenly alive to this and made it the main theme of his last letters and addresses.[1] Leslie had said that the Gracechurch Street Meeting was made up of "the richest trading-men in London,[2] and Keith remarks that Friends "seem to be of late years as much busied in thoughts how to increase in wealth and riches as any."[3] Another adverse writer suggests[4] that one of their ways of gaining converts was to claim that they were always rich and never in such want as others. "When Quakerism was poor," he goes on, "and walked in rags, they railed at riches; and the reason was because they had none. But . . . the case is altered; and now they are reconciled to the riches and gaieties of the world, being apt to purchase estates, to ride in leather, and to eat and drink as well as any of the unconverted." He explains this increase in wealth by the industry and application to business of Friends, their thrift, their habit of trading with one another, and their method of setting-up again those who had failed in trade. Their care over apprenticeship and their character for integrity might have been added; indeed, the reasons for prosperity were highly creditable, and made them a most useful section of the community.

So Benjamin Holme writes of Irish Friends in 1725:[5]

Many . . . do very much covet to have Friends for their tenants, for many of our Friends have been so diligent and industrious and have made such fine improvements upon the farms that they have taken, and have also been so punctual in paying their rents, that they are very much respected by their

---

[1] *Ante*, p. 436. [2] *Snake in the Grass*, 3rd edn. (1698), p. 362.
[3] *The Magick of Quakerism* (1707), p. 24.
[4] "Remarks upon the Quakers, Wherein the Plain-Dealers are Plainly Dealt with" (1700), pp. 9, 10.
[5] Letter to Daniel Bell, of Tottenham, in *Works*, pp. 45, 46.

landlords. And many Friends . . . that are very considerable traders, by their fair and just dealing, have gained great reputation in the minds of many that are not of our Society. . . . Many, by their fair and just dealing, have got abundantly the more trade; so that some from small beginnings have got very considerable estates . . . but some . . . have launched out so far beyond their stocks, that they have failed in keeping their words and promises, and so have greatly stained their credit, and several by such doings have come to ruin. But there is great care amongst Friends here to advise against such doings.

Yet the attendant dangers of wealth were a serious menace to the deeper life of the Church. Others, besides Fox, were alive to this. John Banks, for example, writes:[1]

The Spirit of Truth not being minded, to lead and guide, the spirit of the world gets in, and draws and leads into the earth and earthly things; and instead of labouring to be rich in faith and good works towards God such labour chiefly how to grow rich in the world, that they may have great substance to leave to they know not who.

Cautions against over-trading were frequent. Take the following advice as found in the "Books of Extracts":

1675 :—Advised that none trade beyond their ability, nor stretch beyond their compass; and that they use few words in dealings, and keep their word in all things, lest they bring, through their forwardness, dishonour to the precious Truth of God.

Fifty years later further counsel is given, after the bursting of the South Sea Bubble, but the setting is now Quietist.

'Tis earnestly desired that all Friends everywhere be very careful to avoid all inordinate pursuit after the things of this world, by such ways and means as depend too much on the uncertain probabilities of hazardous enterprises, but rather labour to content themselves with such a plain way and manner of living as is most agreeable to the self-denying principle of Truth, and which is most conducive to that tranquillity of mind that is requisite to a religious conduct through this troublesome world.

A Query in use in Westmorland at the end of the century shows this class of advice at its best:[2]

---

[1] Epistle, 8th Sept. 1687, in *Journal*.
[2] At beginning of Q.M. Book, 1691-1743. Cf. the Hardshaw Minute of 1703, in Barclay, *Inner Life*, p. 495.

[Are Friends] careful not to concern themselves in things of this world more than is necessary, and to satisfy themselves therewith, lest by launching too far into things that may seem lawful in themselves they thereby loose or hurt themselves as with respect to their growth in the Truth?

Friends then were alive to the dangers of their prosperity. The case of Joseph Pike of Cork, one of the zealous Irish leaders,[1] son of the Cromwellian soldier Richard Pike, well illustrates the standard set by the more earnest-minded. He began business at eighteen, with a small portion left by his father, mostly in shop-goods, which he sold off for about three pounds. He traded in wool, bargaining for a bag of short fell-wool, by which he made twenty shillings. Then he bought two bags and made another fifty shillings. He went for a time to Minehead and gradually made way in his trade, being always careful to keep his word and not to venture more in one ship than he could bear, if lost. He lived frugally, and was never much straitened for money, so as to be dunned for his payments. He married at twenty-four, with a pretty good stock of his own and his wife's portion in addition, and, after a time, joined his brother in opening the first linen-draper's shop in Cork. On his brother's marriage he took up the serge trade, till war stopped it; and then bought yarns for export to England, " trading moderately," without encumbering himself in business, so that he might spare time to travel to meetings and serve Truth in his station. Somewhat later he declined buying much, although his stock and credit would have well afforded it, that he might give an example to others, who ran headlong into great dealings. He never had a lawsuit, and but two or three arbitrations, and believed he had never wronged or cheated any one in his life.

"And," he adds, "I can say in the sincerity of my heart, that I never inclined or strove to be rich, or to make my children great or high in the world, seeing the ill effects of it in others; but what I have always desired for them is that they may grow and increase in the Truth and in the fear of the Lord, and then,

---

[1] See his *Life*, first published in 1837, by John Barclay.

whether I had little or much to leave them, they would have enough, if they had His blessing."

Such a case could be multiplied by the score throughout the Society, but the one instance may suffice. Prudence, industry and integrity were the natural fruits of the serious Quaker way of life ; and led on to well-deserved worldly success : it was less easy then as now to keep to the bounds of a moderation which should preserve freedom for the soul's growth and for service to the Church and the Kingdom of God.

Here lay the problem which confronted Friends. The Society in Ireland attempted to solve it by the institution of a close discipline, on lines which were afterwards largely adopted in England, though never I think with the same completeness. Irish Friends had escaped serious persecution ; for they formed an important part of the Protestant community, whose ascendancy it was the main object of the Government to maintain. Group-consciousness, accordingly, had developed in a natural way, with a free circulation of spiritual life which allowed little room for the growth of the Perrot spirit or of the excessive individualism of the Wilkinson-Story party. National Half-Year's Meetings held at Dublin in May and November from 1670 onwards had quickly followed the setting-up of Provincial and Monthly Meetings by Fox and Edmondson.[1] These National and Provincial Meetings were often times of glowing fellowship, which fostered a holy zeal and a readiness to bow to the requirings of Truth. Oliver Sansom, of Berkshire,[2] says of the one in November 1676 that it began with a time of worship for four hours. Then business was to have been taken ; " but the power of the Lord brake forth so mightily amongst Friends in many testimonies, prayers and praising the Lord " that there was no time for it that day. The next morning there was a six-hours' meeting—" a precious heavenly time "—and again, in the evening, " the Lord's power mightily appeared, whereby many mouths were opened, so

---

[1] *Ante*, p. 260.   [2] *Life*, edited by James Boorne, 1848, p. 200.

that little business could be done. Church affairs occupied the following two days, and on the First-day two public meetings were held, "which were very large and lasted almost all the day."

Under the influence of such meetings as these, great efforts were made to check the growth of worldliness in the Society. In the early days, says Edmondson,[1] Friends were given up to a spiritual warfare, under the discipline of the daily cross and self-denial of Christ, and the Lord's truth outbalanced all the world. Then great trading was a burden, and great concerns a great trouble—all needless things, fine houses, rich furniture and gaudy apparel were an eyesore. But another spirit came to gain entrance:

. . . and this began to look back into the world, and traded with the credit which was not of its own purchasing, and [was] striving to be great in the riches and possessions of this world; and then [appeared] great fair buildings in city and country, fine and fashionable furniture and apparel equivalent, with dainty and voluptuous provision, with rich matches in marriage, with excessive customary uncomely smoking of tobacco under colour of lawful and serviceable, far wide from the footsteps of the . . . elders . . . and far short of the example our Lord . . . left us.

This tendency had been interrupted by the heavy privations and losses suffered during the time of war (1689–91),[2] but the prophetic words of John Burnyeat to a Province Meeting in 1690[3] soon came true: "It is now a time of great trial upon you in losing what you have; but the time will come when you will be as greatly tried with getting wealth."

An important pronouncement on the subject, as pertinent to the needs of the Church as when first penned, was made by the Leinster Meeting, held at Castledermot, in County Kildare, in September 1698.[4] The concern

---

[1] Postscript to Epistle from Leinster Province Meeting, Sept. 1698, printed in Rutty, *Hist. of Friends in Ireland*, pp. 172-184.
[2] *Post*, end of Chap. XXI.   [3] Rutty's *History*, p. 160.
[4] Rutty's *History*, pp. 172-184; Minutes of Leinster Province Meeting, Sept. 1698; and Edmondson's *Journal*, *sub anno* 1698. The extract I give is from the Epistle, of which 2000 copies were printed, with a preface by Thomas Trafford of Wicklow and a postscript by Edmondson. Some Friends from England and Munster were also present.

laid deep hold of Friends, and, at the instance of Edmondson, was considered at a special adjourned sitting of men and women :

. . . and many heavenly things were opened in the testimony of Jesus, concerning the bounds and right use of the lawful things of this world, and . . . unanimously it was agreed and adjudged :
> That a competency of the lawful things of this world is sufficient for every one, and is the right bounds, with a due consideration of every one's charge, station, place and service ;
> And that mind which will not be content with this bears the character of covetousness, and renders such unfit to rule in the Church of Christ ; [1]

And there was an unanimous consent, one by one, to offer up ourselves to the judgment of the Province Meeting, or other approved elders, as the Province Meeting shall think fit, if in anything we do exceed those bounds. . . . Not that we intend to deprive any of the moderate and lawful use of the things of this world, or to take from any man his possessions or to invade and take away property ; but to bring all things into right bounds and set them in their right places.

In his heavenly possession in the Lord, the epistle continued, the rich man will not glory in his riches, but see the danger of them, nor lay hold of opportunities to heap up more, to make himself and his posterity great in the world ; but will rather endeavour to lessen them, and be rich in good works, considering he is a steward and accountable to God for all things he possesses under Him.

The method of discipline, already established in Ireland at the time of this Minute, deserves notice, as it would also spring up in England and give rise to the appointment of the Church-officers, called "Overseers." [2] As early as 1677 we find the Half-Year's Meeting directing

---

[1] See Exod. xviii. 21 (A.V.), and *post*, p. 506.
[2] Yorkshire Q.M. March 1691, directed the appointment of two Friends in each meeting to inspect Friends' faithfulness in the Truth. In June 1694 Oxfordshire Q.M. made a similar appointment. The Minutes of the Dec. Q.M. contain the names, and a letter of instructions was issued. London Y.M. in 1698 advised such an appointment generally (see MS. "Books of Extracts," title "Discipline"). In July 1701 the Minute of Oxfordshire Q.M. calls the appointed Friends "Overseers." In 1697 Chesterfield Friends speak of "Overseers" (Barclay, *Inner Life*, pp. 386, 387).

inquiry by faithful Friends in each particular meeting, with reports to the Province Meetings.[1] In 1692 the foundation for a more searching inspection was laid.[2]

A weighty concern took hold of the Meeting "that Friends might keep out of running into any extreme and excess of the world, either seeking to get great farms, or running into extravagancy of trading or dealing of any kind, and also from airiness in deportment and multiplicity of words in bargaining, buying or selling, or superfluity in apparel, furniture or household stuff"; and Friends in each Province were directed to appoint "clean, honest and faithful Friends" to inspect into matters in every meeting and family and report to the Half-Year's Meeting.

In Leinster the six Friends appointed met prior to the Province Meetings to receive written reports from two Friends in each meeting,[3] and a visitation of families was arranged in 1694. In Munster each family was visited. Pike describes the method followed:

We first sat down with them together, and, as we found a concern to come upon our minds, suitable to their respective states and conditions, we gave them advice and counsel, &c., and particularly to keep close to the witness of God in themselves, . . . whereby the inside would be made clean and then the outside would be made clean also. . . . We then proceeded to other things relating to conversation and behaviour, &c., as occasion offered. Then we read sundry rules of superior meetings, and spake the needful to those rules and advices, without partiality to any. . . . We had very melting seasons in many places . . . and I do not know that we met with any opposition or stubbornness in all the places we visited, but a general condescension in all to put away superfluities.[4]

In May 1699 the Half-Year's Meeting directed a general visit on the Munster lines, and the visitors reported "a general condescension, some few excepted, in the

---

[1] Minutes of Nov. 1677 and 1687. Cf. Minute of Leinster Province Meeting, Sept. 1691.
[2] Minutes of Nov. 1692, May 1693 (directing the continuance of the concern in each Province from meeting to meeting), Nov. 1693 (directing that the eighteen Friends on the appointment, six from each Province, should be at the Half-Year's Meetings). Edmondson was the prime mover in the matter. Cf. Minute of May 1696.
[3] Minutes of Province Meeting, Dec. 1692, March, July and Nov. 1693, and July 1694. In June 1695 the inspectors were authorized to call for information from any Friend in a meeting. [4] Pike's *Life*, *sub anno* 1692.

parting with and putting away those things that the testimony of Truth has appeared against."[1] These domiciliary visits became characteristic of Irish Quakerism.[2]

Cases of disownment are comparatively rare, though in November 1697 the Half-Year's Meeting encouraged a more speedy disowning of wilful transgressors, "without needless or indulgent delay, yet with desire and endeavours for their repentance." The usual disciplinary action, after admonition had proved ineffectual, was exclusion from business meetings.[3] Great care came to be taken as to the membership of these, especially of the Half-Year's Meeting. By a Minute of May 1709, this was confined to Friends included in lists locally prepared of those "whose lives and conversations answers Truth and have some concern on their spirits for the promotion thereof." There was at this time no formal membership; a person was known as a Quaker, through professing with Friends, but the authority of the Church meetings only belonged to fit persons, especially, according to Mosaic precedent, "able men, such as fear God, men of truth, hating covetousness" (Exod. xviii. 21). A Leinster Minute of January 1700 well expresses the spirit that prevailed during the years of reforming zeal: "it being a glorious day of great discovery, so that none can hide; and the zeal of the Lord is in Friends' hearts as a fire against all unrighteousness." Next to Edmondson, who died in 1712, Joseph Pike was one of the Friends most earnest for a searching discipline.[4] When a young man of twenty, he was invited to be a member of the Men's Meeting at Cork, a practice which I suspect came into general use throughout the Society.[5] At the time of the action taken in 1692, he

[1] Minutes of Half-Year's Meeting, May and Nov. 1699, and of Leinster Province Meeting, Aug. and Nov. 1699. Cf. Rutty, *History*, p. 171.
[2] We hear of them in Ulster, 1702, 1705, 1706; in Leinster, 1707, 1711; in Munster, 1708, and so on. Rutty gives a list, *History*, p. 330.
[3] The earliest Minute of this kind that I have found is one of Leinster Province, Sept. 1679: cf. Minutes of Aug. 1682, July 1693, Nov. 1696, Feb. 1698, Oct. 1700, &c., and Half-Year's Meeting Minutes of May and Nov. 1696, May 1701, &c. The subject is discussed, though in too categorical a way, by Barclay, *Inner Life*, pp. 361-372. [4] See his *Life*.
[5] In 1704 London Y.M. (see printed Epistle of this year) recommended Friends to encourage "such young men and women" to take part "as they are

became greatly concerned for strict gospel-order and a constant attender at the Half-Year's Meetings. He says that many of the wives of Friends were then in the habit of wearing silk, though of a plain colour, and there was much fine furniture and household stuff, but not to the extent common in some parts of England. When he and his cousin Samuel Randall were on the Munster appointment for inspection, they determined to begin reformation with their own households :

> As to our own clothing, we had but little to alter, having both of us been pretty plain in our garb, yet some things we did change to greater simplicity. But my dear cousin, being naturally of a very exact and nice fancy, had things in more curious order as regards household furniture than I had; and therefore, as a testimony against such superfluities and that spirit which led into it, he altered or exchanged, as I did, several articles that were too fine. . . . Our fine veneered and garnished cases of drawers, tables, stands, cabinets, escritoires, &c., we put away, or exchanged for decent plain ones of solid wood, without superfluous garnishing or ornamental work ; our wainscots or woodwork we had painted of one plain colour ; our large mouldings or finishings of panelling, &c., our swelling chimney-pieces, curiously twisted banisters, we took down and replaced with useful plain woodwork, &c. ; our curtains, with valences, drapery and fringes that we thought too fine, we put away or cut off ; our large looking-glasses with decorated frames we sold, or made them into smaller ones ; and our closets that were laid out with many little curious or nice things were done away.[1]

---

sensible are qualified . . . that they may come up and stand in the life of righteousness, to be serviceable in the Church, helpful to the ancient Friends and fitted to supply their places, as such shall be removed." Admissions to take part in business meetings are sometimes noted in the Preparative Meeting Books, *e.g.* at Banbury.

[1] See *Life*. The Half-Year's Meeting of May 1694 went into the subject of furniture carefully, discouraging large looking-glasses and all hangings as much as possible, and approving the sumptuary advice prepared for the meeting by such Friends as were joiners, ship-carpenters and metal-founders. This curious specification of truly plain furniture may deserve the attention of couples setting up housekeeping to-day.

"As to chests of drawers, they ought to be plain and of one colour, without swelling works,

"As to tables and chairs, they ought to be all made plain, without carving, keeping out of all new fashions as they come up, and to keep to the fashion that is serviceable [a good phrase],

"And, as to making great mouldings one above another about press-beds and clock-cases, &c., [they] ought to be avoided, only what is decent according to Truth,

He showed equal sincerity, as already recorded, on the business side of the testimony against worldliness. A few years earlier he and his cousin had refused great profit through buying tobacco imported under a low duty that would be shortly raised, considering that people would justly say : " Here are Samuel Randall and Joseph Pike, rich Quakers ; they are grasping and covetous ; they cannot be content without turning monopolizers."

Pike continued a pillar of discipline to the end. By the close of his life he found the libertine spirit increased again above what it had been prior to the reformation of 1692 ; which he attributed to too much ease, indifferency and want of zeal in many elders, and to laxity in allowing unqualified members to sit in meetings for discipline, " some of whom . . . have . . . pleaded for liberty and wrong things, and by their numbers, noise and clamours have brought a cloud over a meeting and kept down the power of Truth from arising." None, he felt, should sit in business meetings unless they were orderly in life, consistent in apparel and one with Friends in their spirits in the discipline.[1] He greatly feared that the Wilkinson-Story leaven was at work, though in a different form, " not by opposing all discipline, as they did, but by the breaking of Minutes and the weakening of the hands of the faithful."[2]

Meanwhile, Irish Friends were an example to the rest of the Society. Christopher Story, of Cumberland, visited them in 1687, and again fourteen years later, and notes " a great reformation " in the interval.[3] Gratton, Penn and Thomas Chalkley all speak in high terms of their good order and government ;[4] and, in 1716, Thomas Story, after attending a Half-Year's Meeting where affairs were carried on in " great ease and unity and much sweetness,"

" So that all furniture and wainscoting should be all plain, and of one colour." The advice was repeated in Nov. 1698, with a warning against " running into high, lofty fabrics, to gratify a high, proud and curious mind."
[1] Letter to Henry Jackson, 9th Nov. 1723, in *Life*.
[2] Epistle to the Half-Year's Meeting, 2nd May 1726. Pike died 7th Jan. 1730.
[3] *Life*, *sub anno* 1701.
[4] Gratton's *Journal*, *sub anno* 1696 ; Penn's Epistle to London Y.M. 2nd June 1698, in Rutty's *History*, pp. 166-168 ; Chalkley's *Journal*, *sub anno* 1707.

observes,[1] with the heat in London over the Affirmation question in mind:

> It were happy, and greatly to the benefit and growth of the Church, if the affairs of the Yearly Meeting at London could be so unanimous and peaceable, which could not well be expected till some men are removed and others regulated, who have crept in unawares under the wings of others, who were never true members of the living body or ever qualified for the stations they have assumed by the connivance of such as ought to have been more vigilant and kept them at a due distance.

Story himself, a few years later, came under the admonition of his good friend Joseph Pike for going "a little too fine and modish," particularly as to his hat and long hair, which encouraged others to exceed in a greater degree. Some "libertines" had used his name as a cloak to their own pride and vanity "in their long curled and powdered hair, flourishing wigs, long cravats, many unnecessary folds in their coats, fashionable sleeves and cuts of several kinds, cocks and strings in their hats, with other such-like things after the modes of the world."[2]

Often the Irish Minutes, and corresponding ones in Great Britain, pursue the spirit of worldliness with odd phrases. We are told[3] that several Friends "who have hair enough on their heads do without any real necessity cut it off, and get great ruffling periwigs, and others who have some necessity for want of hair, or some other infirmity, do get such periwigs as are superfluous in length or otherwise." We find Friends warned against admitting unsuitable persons to business meetings,[4] "particularly guzzling drinkers and company-keeping smokers." "Proud-like, unsettled girls or lasses" are not to accompany

---

[1] *Life*, p. 543. [2] Letter in *Life*, dated 22nd Nov. 1723.
[3] Epistle from Half-Year's Meeting, Nov. 1684. A later Minute advises Friends who design to cut off their hair and get wigs to consult their M.M. first; cf. a M.M. Minute of 1718 in *J.F.H.S.* xi. 116, and the similar practice in Westmorland (Q.M. Minute 6th July 1705; Sedbergh M.M. 27th May 1712). In 1715 London Y.M. deplored the fact "that some have cut off good heads of hair and put on long, extravagant and gay wigs." (See *J.F.H.S.* xii. 36, from MS. "Books of Extracts," title "Plainness.") I may refer the curious reader to *J.F.H.S.* vi. 187, and references there noted which could easily be added to.
[4] Leinster Province Meeting, Feb. 1698.

travelling Women Ministers,[1] and inquiry is to be made what Friends' sons keep "greyhounds or hunting dogs."[2] Friends are reminded, in a Minute of rich Irish flavour that there may be a great superfluity and too great nicety in gardens. "It is therefore desired that all Friends in planting gardens do it in a lowly mind and keep to plainness and the serviceable part, rather admiring the wonderful hand of Providence in causing such variety of unnecessary things to grow for the use of man than [seeking] to please a curious mind."[3] We hear of meetings of tailors, who declare against making men's coats with too great compass in the skirts, or too large sleeves or cuffs, or with "very large buttons or long button-holes, or signs of holes that are not holes," and against riding-coats for women Friends with great plaits laid towards the shoulder; and, they add, "we also think it more plain to have the pocket-holes cut lengthway than cross."[4] Women's dress gave great scope for sumptuary rules. I have not seen the books of Women's Meetings in Ireland, but those in the North of England are diffuse on this head. At the time of the foundation of Monthly Meetings,[5] a letter from Fox says:

---
[1] *Ibid.* Sept. 1698 : Irish Friends showed their zeal in this as in other matters. John Banks, in 1694, speaks of ten or twenty or more Friends accompanying him twenty-five miles from one meeting to another, even in harvest-time (*Journal*, p. 137). Throughout the Society careful arrangements were made for providing guides. Penrith Preparative Meeting, in March 1709, establishes a rota of seven Friends to go by turns, and, "for the better keeping it in every one's remembrance, it is agreed a paper be drawn up, and signed by themselves, and, as one doth his office therein, to deliver it to the next named." Cf. Selby Preparative Meeting, Minutes 6th Feb. 1701, 25th April 1717, directing that the list should be on parchment, " and, if he that went last neglect so to deliver the copy in due time, then he ought to go again, because his succeeding Friend had not timely notice." See also Aberdeen Q.M. Minute of 1700 in *J.F.H.S.* viii. 80.

[2] Leinster Province Meeting, Sept. 1702 : the matter came before the Half-Year's Meeting in 1704, and the three Province Meetings report, in Leinster that all occasion of offence is taken away, in Ulster that few are guilty thereof, in Munster that those thought likely have been admonished and are inclined to take the advice given.

[3] Leinster Province Meeting, Oct. 1705, and Half-Year's Meeting, Nov. 1705, objecting to artificial knots and other needless things, "only to satisfy a vain, curious mind, that so the work of God may be admired above men's inventions." Upon this, Munster Friends reported that certain Friends had agreed to have their gardens altered in the season of the year.

[4] Half-Year's Meeting, May 1703, and cf. May 1687 and 1688. In May 1695 a meeting of tailors in each province was directed to be held twice a year. For London Tailors see their Epistle, 25th March 1672, in *Life of Gilbert Latey*, pp. 81-88, and another approved by the Morning Meeting, 5th May 1690.

[5] In Bristol MSS. ii. No. 10, dated 5th May 1668, and see No. 11, the disciplinary paper issued by Somerset Q.M. 8th March 1669.

Away with your skimming-dish hats, and your unnecessary buttons on the top of your sleeves, shoulders, backs, and behind on your coats and cloaks. And away with your long slit yokes on the skirts of your waistcoat; and short sleeves, and pinching your shoulders so as you cannot make use of your arms, and your short black aprons and some having none. And away with your visors, whereby you are not distinguished from bad women, and bare necks, and needless flying scarves like rollers on your back.

Women Friends in the North went into curious detail in their advice. Take the following from Yorkshire :

Several things remains amongst us, which are very burdensome to the honest-hearted . . . viz., the imitating the fashions of the world in their headcloths, some having four long pinner ends hanging down &c., and handkerchiefs being too thin, some having 'em hollowed out and put on far off their necks, also their gown sleeves and short laps, with a great deal to pin up in the skirt; also their quilted petticoats, set out in imitation of hoops, some wearing two together; also cloth shoes of light colour, bound with a differing colour, and heels white or red, with white rands, and fine coloured clogs and strings; also scarlet or purple stockings and petticoats made short to expose 'em. Friends are also desired to keep out of the fashion of wearing black hats or shaving or straw ones, with crowns too little or too large, with what else the judgment of Truth is gone out against.[1]

The desire was[2] that Friends "should come to a stability, and be satisfied in the shape and compass that Truth leads into without changing as the world changes." One Monthly Meeting directed that young women intending to go to the Quarterly Meeting should appear before their own meeting "in those clothes that they intend to have on at York."[3] There is a delightful Minute against display of china and waste of time in tea-drinking :[4]

---

[1] Yorkshire Women's Y.M. June 1720. Women, especially women of rank, often wore a coif, or close-fitting cap, with long flaps on either side, pinned on and hanging down. The flaps were called "pinners." A "rand" is the strip of leather above the heel of a shoe. For other Minutes of the Yorkshire Women's Meeting see July 1694, March 1708, April 1710, June 1712 (printed in J. W. Rowntree, *Essays and Addresses*, p. 60), Sept 1716, Testimony concerning Barbara Jackson of Skipton-in-Craven, March 1718, telling how after recovery from smallpox, when a girl of eighteen, "her first work was to cut her headcloths and bring 'em into as much plainness as possibly she could," March 1721, March 1724, and, at end of Minute Book, June 1706.

[2] See 1712 Minute.   [3] Barclay's *Inner Life*, p. 491.
[4] Minute of Sept. 1714. Cf. Cork Minute of 1724 in *J.F.H.S.* xiii. 19.

It is the judgment of Friends that we should . . . refrain from having fine tea-tables set with fine china, being it is more for sight than service ; and that Friends keep clear of the superfluous part in drinking tea, we thinking that some of the time and money that's spent thus might be made better use of. It's advised that Friends should not have so much china or earthenware on their mantelpieces or on their chests of drawers, but rather set them in their closets until they have occasion to use them ; and likewise to keep from wearing painted calicoes &c.

In Westmorland the Women's Meeting has similar concerns, and declares itself against :

. . . many superfluous fashions of the world, as wide-sleeved mantles, cross-laces, knotting handkerchiefs in a superfluous manner —they are desired to pin them down and to be plain in their head-dresses and short head-tabs, and not to have short-lapped mantles with long trains; with all the rest of their apparel of a modest colour becoming Truth, not looking after the many changes that are among the world's people, but, having good and serviceable fashions, to keep in them.[1]

A dislike of wearing bonnets is expressed, which indicates that the " Friends' bonnet," known to later days in its well-known " coal-scuttle " form, was not then evolved. The advice given is to wear either little bonnets or none ; and a later Minute advises " that all our women Friends do cover their hair with their linen, and that their linen be plain, without so many needless nips and pinches."[2] One delicate question is left for further consideration : whether light-coloured silk handkerchiefs, as red or orange, might be allowed.[3]

From Scotland, in 1698, we have an elaborate Minute, directly resulting from a visit of two Irish Friends.[4] It furnishes a complete guide to the approved Quaker garb for men and women.

---

[1] Women's Q.M. 4th Oct. 1706.
[2] Ibid. 3rd Oct. 1707, 5th Oct. 1711, 7th Oct. 1715.
[3] Ibid. 7th July 1710, on a Minute from the Kendal Women's M.M. 30th June 1710.
[4] Aberdeen Q.M. 28th July 1698, in J.F.H.S. viii. pp. 77-80. It was issued "in joint unity of both Men and Women's Meetings," and Overseers were appointed to see that the directions were carried out. The argument was used, that "the right mind will rather abridge itself, even in its lawful liberty, if it were in the eating of flesh, than to offend one weak brother, much more so many well-wishers to Sion's peace and prosperity."

THE QUAKER WAY OF LIFE

First, among the men, we condemn all shooting with guns of any sort for game or recreation; all shooting with bows and arrows, all playing at dams [*i.e.* draughts], golf, billiards, or any other foolish game so-called; and are sorry and ashamed any of our youth should need any caution as to such things. Also we condemn all hunting with dogs and hawking, as altogether unsuitable to that weighty testimony God hath called us unto.

Also in their apparel, we condemn:
    all broad ribbons for hatbands,
    all cocking up the side of their hats,
    all vain powdering of wigs or their own hair;
as also,
    all their bushy and long cravats, fringed or speckled;
we condemn,
    their false shoulder-pieces, like necks of shirts, called by several "cheats," and desires they may put comely necks to their coats;
we condemn their hand-bands of cuffs like shirt-sleeves;
we desire their coats may be buttoned to the top,
and not some buttons kept loose to make a show with their cravats.
Let all their big cuffs and flapping sleeves be cut off and made meet with the rest of their sleeve.
Let all superfluous buttons and blindholes be put away,
and the buttons further down than needs for fastening their coats.
Let the pockets of their coats be in the inside, and so needless slits, and shows of ranges of buttons, be prevented on the outer side of their coats:
and [let] all needless lips and superfluous cloth be forborne in their coats,
and all rows of heads of stockings at their knees be altogether forborne:
and let plain buckles be in their shoes.

Having thus adjusted the man's dress from top to toe, the Meeting turns to the women, "either younger or elder."

    We jointly do desire:
they forbear vain cutting or shedding their hair to set it out in their faces or foreheads; but that it be put straight back;
and that they wear on their heads a plain coif, without any ruffling or needless lips in the front of it;
and their hood above it, without any wire or paste-board to keep it high; but let it be tied straight and low, and not waving loose about their faces.
And let no long laps nor "maseimd" [*sic*] laps be on their hoods

or headcloths—an ell and an half being judged to be fully sufficient for their hoods about their faces, laps and all.
Let none wear ruffled neckcloths, but either plain bands or plain napkins.
Let their mantles or other gowns be made plain, without broad or ruffled lips on the shoulders of them, and without lead or great rows on the sleeves of them, but only a plain uplay thereon ;
and without short tails or lying-over lips in the pinning of them to make them sit out big behind.
Let them be pinned straight that they may lie plain and broad behind.
Let there be no side or low trains, neither at gowns nor coats.
Let the long scarves be cut, it being judged that two ells and an half is fully sufficient for a scarf.
Let no " stamenger " [stomacher] be of any other colour but the same with their gowns.
Let no coloured plaids be used any more, but either mantles or long hoods ; and the poor that cannot reach to that, let them wear white plaids, without fine-coloured sprayings in them.
Let none want aprons at all (and that either of green or blue or other grave cloth colours and not white) upon the streets or in public at all ; nor of any spangled or speckled silk or cloth, nor any silk aprons at all.

We further find, both in Ireland and Great Britain, a number of cautions on other matters of domestic concern ; especially against feastings at births, marriages, and burials, and like extravagances.[1] York Friends, in 1677, decided that the practice of giving gloves, rosemary or the like at funerals was a relic of Popish superstition.[2] At this time it was the habit of people in the North of England to provide large quantities of cheese at burials, from 30 to 100 lbs. weight, according to their means, which was shaved into two or three slices to the pound, and given with a penny manchet-loaf to all who came. At Lancaster they gave round one or two long Naples biscuits, from 20 to 100 lbs. weight in all, at a cost of about a shilling a pound.[3] West-

---
[1] There is a Query to this effect, added in 1701, at the beginning of the Westmorland Q.M. Book, 1691–1743.
[2] York Two Weeks' Meeting, 14th Feb. 1677. Cf. case in *J.F.H.S.* v. 142.
[3] William Stout, *Autobiography*, p. 35.

morland Friends declared against these practices in 1699,[1] directing that where some refreshment was needed it should be done in a plain way, not above a loaf to a person, and that Quakers attending the funerals of neighbours should behave accordingly. Cumberland Friends, says Christopher Story, "could see no real service in making such doles, when people were met together on such a weighty occasion, but, on the contrary, great disorders often happened."[2]

Restrictions, naturally enough, came to be placed on the making or selling of superfluous things; Gilbert Latey, we shall remember, had given up his court-tailoring,[3] Roger Hebden, the Malton draper, had burnt his ribbons and silks,[4] Humphrey Bache had ceased to sell rings and toys to proud and vain people,[5] and now tailors, shoemakers, and joiners held their meetings and retrenched their occupations. Many Minutes could be cited, on the lines of that passed in 1688 at a meeting of Irish Friends who were merchant-clothiers and tailors:[6]

We, being met . . . together to consider whether it be convenient for Friends to make draught, figured or striped work, or to sell such or make them up into cloth, upon the whole debate and resolve, we do believe it is according to Truth . . . for Friends to wear plain apparel and to make plain stuffs and to sell plain things . . . and that Friends would do well to employ Friends that are tailors for the encouragement of Friends of that trade who cannot answer the world's fashions.

One case is that of the selling or making of bone-lace, lace made by knitting with bone-bobbins on a pattern marked by pins. The craft flourished in Buckinghamshire, established, it is supposed, by immigrants from Flanders,

[1] Paper from Q.M. 5th Jan. 1699, in Dev. Ho. Gibson MSS. iii. p. 107. In 1704 the Q.M. repeated the advice, at the instance of Kendal M.M., which in turn acted on the motion of Kendal Preparative Meeting. Sedbergh M.M., 28th June 1709, deals with a widow, who at her husband's funeral, after providing sufficient for the guests, did, notwithstanding, "give cakes over and above to pretty many." The *Swarthmoor Account Book*, 22nd Aug. 1677, shows that for their Uncle Richardson's funeral the Fell family spent 4s. 6d. at Lancaster for biscuits and 5s. for 30¾ lbs. of cheese, a moderate provision, according to Wm. Stout's standards.

[2] *Life*, edn. 1820, pp. 50-52.   [3] *Beginnings of Quakerism*, p. 378.
[4] *Ibid.* pp. 71, 72.   [5] *Ibid.* p. 519.   [6] Half-Year's Meeting, May 1688.

and the Friends of the county, including Penington and Ellwood, testified against it in 1669,[1] "as a thing wholly useless in the creation," and in 1671 we find Oxfordshire Friends dealing with a culprit and recommending him to throw it over and take to malting.[2] To-day Friends discountenance malting, but have done their best to keep alive the craft of Belgian lace-makers who are victims of the Great War.

It is often assumed that the uniformity of dress which came to prevail among Friends goes back to the early days of the movement ; and that Quakerism was born in a plain coat and a broad-brimmed hat. But it is evident to the careful student that at first the stress was laid on simplicity rather than uniformity. The Quaker dressed according to his station in life, but without superfluity or ostentation.[3] The disciplinary Minutes aim at securing this by outward rules, descending to minute particulars, and are the best proof that a wide variety of dress was in vogue. The new instrument of Church government was a ready means for retrenching extravagances which gave insidious entrance to the spirit of the world ; and zealous Friends did not see that they were substituting legalism for liberty, the control of the form for the control of the Spirit. Nor did they perceive that every legalism that fenced in the Jew would bar out the proselyte, till Quakerism would become a self-contained, introspective sect, out of touch with the world that it should be conquering for the Kingdom of God. But, however radically imperfect was the method adopted, they were right in seeking to preserve a vital Church by waging a crusade against the worldly spirit that threatened to

---

[1] Meeting 31st March 1669, in Dev. Ho. Gibson MSS. iii. p. 5 : cf. paper of 29th June 1687 in Dev. Ho. Gibson MSS. following the former. According to G. Lyon Turner, *Original Records of Nonconformity*, "Episcopal Returns 1669," i. 92, one "Crock," who I suspect is to be identified with John Crook, was at one time a lace-seller.

[2] Oxfordshire Q.M. Minutes, 27th Sept., 27th Dec. 1671, 10th July, 25th Sept. 1672.

[3] Joseph Phipps, of Norwich (1700–1787), in his *Observations*, 1767, p. 108, says : "'The present form of dress amongst the plainer Quakers was pretty much the common dress of sober people in middling stations of ife, when and amongst whom the Society was first raised."

overwhelm it; and it is significant that Ireland and the Quarterly Meetings in the North of England and Scotland which followed the Irish lead were the districts which refused the compromise of the Affirmation of 1696 and possessed at the time the greatest spiritual life.

Margaret Fox, in her old age, uttered the necessary words of prophetic criticism. Her writings, as a rule, have little force: it is as a mother in her home, and as a mother in Israel, that she holds her unique place in Quaker story; but here was a theme for which fit words sprang forth out of her own past. Her convincement dated back to those words of Fox in Ulverston church, " He is not a Jew that is one outward, neither is that circumcision which is outward; but he is a Jew that is one inward, and that is circumcision which is of the heart."[1] How could she be silent when she saw Friends turning again to the pit out of which they had been digged? The paper she wrote is one of those rare documents in which a whole life's rich experience flames out in passionate wisdom.[2]

Friends, she says, are the people of the living God, Who has shined from the throne of His glory into their hearts, in His spiritual Light, and has given them knowledge of Himself in the face of Jesus Christ. Let them beware of limiting the Holy One of Israel and meddling with the things of God otherwise than His Spirit leads and guides. Christ always testified against the Jews' manner of making and prescribing outward rules; for His testimony is in every heart to work inwardly and make clean the inside. He testified against the Pharisees that said, " I am holier than thou." Let us then beware of looking upon ourselves to be holier than in deed and truth we are; " for what are we, but what we have received from God? And God is all-sufficient to bring in thousands into the same spirit and light, to lead and guide them as He doth us."

[1] *Beginnings of Quakerism*, p. 101.
[2] Paper dated April 1700, in Dev. Ho. Portf. 25, No. 66. Cf. the epistle dated June 1698, in her *Works*, p. 534, and extracts from the two papers in Helen G. Crosfield, *Margaret Fox*, p. 198. It seems addressed primarily to Friends of her own county.

Paul tells us (1 Cor. x. 27) that if an unbeliever ask us to a feast and we are disposed to go, we may eat what is set before us, asking no questions for conscience' sake. Away with the whimsical narrow imaginations that would forbid us from going to a birth or a burial of the people of the world.

For it is now gone forty-seven years since we owned the Truth, and all things has gone well and peaceably, till now of late that this narrowness and strictness is entering in, that many cannot tell what to do or not do. Our Monthly and Quarterly Meetings were set up for reproving and looking into suspicious and disorderly walking . . . and not [for] private persons to take upon them to make orders and say, This must be done and the other must be done. And can Friends think that those who are taught and guided of God can be subject and follow such low, mean orders? . . . We are now coming into Jewism, into that which Christ cried Woe against, minding altogether outward things, neglecting the inward work of Almighty God in our hearts . . . insomuch that poor Friends is mangled in their minds, that they know not what to do. For one Friend says one way and another another.

She had loved the bright flowers and the changing lights on Furness Fell and distant mountain and adds:

But Christ Jesus saith, That we must take no thought what we shall eat or what we shall drink or what we shall put on; but bids us consider the lilies, how they grow in more royalty than Solomon. But, contrary to this, we must not look at no colours, nor make anything that is changeable colours, as the hills are, nor sell them, nor wear them. But we must be all in one dress and one colour.

This is a silly, poor gospel. It is more fit for us to be covered with God's eternal Spirit and clothed with His eternal Light, which leads us and guides us into righteousness; and to live righteously and justly and holily in this present evil world. This is the clothing that God puts on us, and likes, and will bless. This will make our light to shine forth before men . . . for we have God for our Teacher; and we have His promise and His doctrine; and we have the apostles' practice in their day and generation; and we have God's Holy Spirit to lead us and guide us; and we have the blessed Truth that we are made partakers of to be our practice. . . .

Friends, we have one God, and one mediator betwixt God

and man—the man Christ Jesus. Let us keep to Him or we are undone.

This is not delightful to me, that I have this occasion to write to you; for wheresoever I saw it appear I have stood against it several years; and now I dare neglect it no longer. For I see that our blessed, precious, holy Truth, that has visited [us] from the beginning, is kept under; and these silly, outside, imaginary practices is coming up, and practised with great zeal, which hath often grieved my heart.

Now I have set before you Life and Death; and desire you to choose Life and God and His Truth.

In another letter, she writes:[1]

Legal ceremonies are far from gospel-freedom. . . . It's a dangerous thing to lead young Friends much into the observation of outward things, which may be easily done; for they can soon get into an outward garb, to be all alike outwardly; but this will not make them true Christians. It's the Spirit that gives life.

Margaret Fox had always lived and dressed according to her station, though no doubt in simpler fashion than the quality of the neighbourhood;[2] and it is to be feared that her zealous friends, who disliked her practice, were disabled from receiving her wise counsel with unprejudiced minds. But the danger of a discipline that emphasized the outward at the expense of the inward, and continually tended to become mechanically rather than spiritually administered, was apparent to other Friends of penetration. The judgment of honest Samuel Bownas, a man at the other end of the social scale, whose widowed mother had a subsistence of less than Five Pounds a year for herself and her two children, is of special value, when we remember the nature of his own convincement. The visitor to the grey meeting-house at Brigflatts, near Sedbergh, set mid ancient trees above the Rawthey, under

---

[1] Letter of June 1698, in *Works*, p. 535.
[2] See the biased account quoted in *Beginnings of Quakerism*, p. 364, and cf. the letter from Sarah Meade to Rachel Abraham, dated 19th Dec. 1683, in Helen G. Crosfield, *Margaret Fox*, p. 203, and Fox's letter to his wife with the present of a piece of scarlet cloth for a mantle. (This is to be dated April 1678, and is referred to in *Fells of Swarthmoor Hall*, p. 294. The original text is in Sotheby's "Catalogue of autograph letters to be sold March 1st, 1917": "At Bristol I did buy as much scarlet as would make thee a mantle, which thou may line it. I had it of Richard Smith of Nailsworth, and it is fine," *per* A. Neave Brayshaw.)

the shoulders of the Yorkshire fells, can still picture for himself the incident which reached the life of the young Westmorland apprentice, who had been used to spend the greater part of meeting in sleep. A young woman-preacher, Ann Wilson,[1] was there one day, and, fixing her eye on Sam, and with a great zeal pointing her finger at him, uttered these words with much power in the course of her sermon: "A traditional Quaker! Thou comest to meeting as thou went from it, and goes from it as thou came to it, but art no better for thy coming; what wilt thou do in the end?"[2] "This," says Bownas, "was so pat to my then condition, that, like Saul, I was smitten to the ground . . . but, turning my thoughts inward . . . a voice as it were spoke in my heart, saying, Look unto me and I will help thee, and I found much comfort, that made me shed abundance of tears." The scriptures and the sermons he heard were now so living to him that he wondered anybody remained unconvinced, and we find him, in 1698, at the close of his apprenticeship, a young man of twenty-two, penniless save for his harvest-work at hay and corn, travelling on foot in the ministry with a still younger comrade out of Sedbergh Meeting, Isaac Alexander, who had been convinced at fourteen, and had become a preacher at seventeen.[3] Ten years later Bownas visited Ireland, after service in England, Scotland and America, now become a man of matured inward experience and unusual spiritual power. He found the work in the Irish meetings hard, but meeting with "that worthy Friend, and heavenly-minded, meek and Divine preacher," Gilbert Thompson, the schoolmaster of Penketh, conversed with him about it:[4]

. . . and, as he was in experience and age much my superior, I requested what he thought might be the reason why it seemed

---

[1] Perhaps the same Ann Wilson who was cautioned by the Morning Meeting in July 1699 for reflecting on Friends.
[2] See *Life*, published 1756, and frequently reprinted, one of the best of Quaker spiritual biographies.
[3] Notice in *Piety Promoted*, iii. 192; cf. *F.P.T.* pp. 272, 273. He died in Jan. 1706, after a visit to the Westmorland M.M.'s.
[4] For this and next extract see Bownas's *Life*.

more dead amongst Friends in this nation now than in some other places. He gave this as a reason; That the professors of Truth in that nation were very strict and exact in some things, and placed much in outward appearance; but too much neglected the reformation and change of the mind, and having the inside thoroughly cleansed from pride and iniquity. "For thou knowest," said he, "the leaven of the Pharisees was always hurtful to the life of religion in all shapes."

Herein, as we understand to-day, lay the danger of this strong emphasis on rules of discipline. In the time of Christ, the Rabbis, in their desire to secure the observance of the Law, had multiplied rules of conduct, many of them as "a fence to the Thorah,"[1] designed to keep the pious at a safe distance from forbidden ground, until it became almost impossible for the ordinary man to keep all the precepts, and the Pharisees could say, "But this multitude, which knoweth not the law, is accursed" (Jno. vii. 49). The teaching of Jesus was a profound criticism of this legalism. With Him the inward disposition, the filial relation to the Father, was the essential thing, and, as it was maintained, would express itself in right conduct. Bownas, in 1740, had the same concern on his mind :

I found in that nation a brave, zealous and living people in the root of true religion and discipline . . . but there were also some who seemed very perfect in the form . . . but for all that the inside was not right, so that I found very close exercise amongst them, in warning them against the leaven of the Pharisees, which was equally if not more hurtful to religion than that of the publicans . . . setting forth that a form without life . . . would not avail.

This had been emphatically the witness borne by the first age of Quakerism against the "notional" and formal religion which had invaded the current Puritanism. The same danger of substituting the outward for the inward was now besetting the Quaker movement. The maintenance of a standard, itself an essentially "static" conception, became the main object of the Society, when its chief

[1] The three "Words" of the men of the Great Synagogue, which arose after the return from the Captivity, were "Be deliberate in judgment; and raise up many disciples; and make a fence to the Thorah" (*Pirqe Aboth*, i. 1.)

strength should have been given to cherishing a rich spiritual life. It was not without reason that Charles Marshall, who had been one of the firstfruits of Camm and Audland's wonderful service at Bristol,[1] was concerned during his last illness in 1698 [2] to direct Friends "to the living, Divine power and life of Truth, that thereby they might be kept a people fresh and green, and living to God, that so formality might not prevail over them." In like manner, Dewsbury, in his last days in 1688, would often say to Friends that a holy conversation worthy of the Truth could not be attained "by largeness of knowledge and strength of comprehension, but by a real dying to their wills and affections, by virtue of the daily cross."[3] Here lay the authentic Quaker discipline with which to combat the invasion of wealth and worldliness:

"Friends," said Priscilla Cotton, the day she died,[4] "the cross is the power of God. When you flee the cross, you lose the power. That which pleaseth self is above the cross; and that which pleaseth man is above the cross; and that which shuns the cross yields to the carnal part and loses its dominion. Though the cross seems foolishness, stand in it: though it seems weak, stand in it: though it be a stumbling-block to the wise, stand in it: there the dominion, authority and crown is received. And this is not for you to be exercised in only for a time, as at your first convincement; but daily, even to the death, as long as a desire, will or thought remaineth in you contrary to God's pure Light; and judge by it, and, as you wait in the Light, you will come to know a cross in the use of meat, drink and apparel; and keep to the cross when alone or in company; what the pure Mind of God stands against in you that the cross is against."

The crusade against worldliness should have devoted itself, not to the multiplication of rules of outward conduct, but to the fostering of this inward discipline by vital methods. Living ministry and leadership, the maintenance of warm and open-hearted fellowship, and a generous method of education were all needed, and could they have been secured would have kept the tradition of

---

[1] See *Beginnings of Quakerism*, pp. 166, 167.
[2] *Piety Promoted*, pt. ii. pp. 150-157.   [3] *Ibid.* pt. ii. p. 4.
[4] *Ibid.* pt. ii. p. 12. She was one of the first to receive Friends at Plymouth in 1654, and died ten years later.

the fathers and the authority of the elders from narrowing the outlook and service of the Church. A Quaker way of life would have been assured by the power of first-hand conviction renewed in each generation and continually drawing into the Society others of all ranks who were reached by the Quaker message—a way of life growing out of the rich inheritance of the past but not limited by it.

CHAPTER XIX

PROBLEMS OF EDUCATION AND THE MINISTRY

If there is to be a strong ministry in our Church, a rich soil must be provided for its growth. . . . As a Church, we have yet to learn that a minister is both born and made. . . . Our first preparation for the ministry must be as wide as the Church. In accepting the sacred burden of a free ministry, we lay it upon every member of the Society of Friends. We must so shape our life that we may bear that burden worthily. We demand more of our members than almost any other Church ; and we must adopt special measures to qualify them.—JOHN WILHELM ROWNTREE, "The Problem of a Free Ministry," in *Essays and Addresses*, pp. 124, 125.

IT must be confessed that the tendency of Friends to combat worldliness by a legalism that laid stress on outward rules was turning the Church aside from its mission and from the deeper way of inward discipline which the First Publishers of Truth had known. The inward way of taking up the cross was dynamic, and could not have failed to be progressive and adventurous, in spite of any temporary limitations of outlook ; the outward was a rule which held in bondage the free activities of the soul.

But we must always beware of the anachronism which censures the past by the standards of the present ; and shall be disposed to accept the Quaker way of life, described in the last chapter, with its fine simplicity and carefulness of conduct, and its drab intellectual and artistic standpoint, as in the main the natural expression, as things were, of the Quaker experience. The first leaders had been mostly men of yeoman birth, with the Puritan outlook of their day, whose fresh spiritual awakening filled life with deeper meanings, but left them yeomen and Puritans still. Indeed, a certain gravity of behaviour and seriousness of spirit would survive among Friends after it had decayed in the rest of the country.

A far wider conception of life has, however, opened before us. We are beginning to see, as Rufus M. Jones puts it,[1] that "the entire universe from material husk to spiritual core" is to "be unified and comprehended as an organic whole," so that the spiritual man is man "raised to his highest and best by co-operation with the Divine Spirit in Whom his finite life is rooted." One of our modern poets has well described the type of life that should flourish in the free air of the Spirit:[2]

Let me walk in the Light of the Lord; let me live in His power;
And ready for instant service, equipped for the hour,
To speak to the few or the many whate'er He may send,
Or to sit in silence and wait, and His power attend.
Let me live with my heart ever open to God and to man,
Living in human love, as I only through God's Spirit can,
And knowing my strength is as nought, that the smile of His face,
Which evermore lives in my heart, is the proof that His grace,
Which answers my need as a man, is to reach all the race.

We shall desire, on these lines, to develop, by methods of illuminating and inspiring fellowship and by the provision of fit avenues for action, lives nobly equipped for the service of the hour, hearts ever open to God and to man, souls thrilled in the power of the Spirit with a gospel to reach all the race.

With these thoughts in mind, we may consider, in more detail, the place of education in the Quaker Church.

Fox, as we have noted,[3] as early as 1668, had set on foot two schools, one for children at Waltham Abbey, and one for girls at Shacklewell. Christopher Taylor, brother of Thomas Taylor, the minister to the Westmorland Seekers, had kept a Latin school for Friends' children at

---

[1] *Quakers in the American Colonies*, pp. xxiv, xxv.
[2] Dr. R. H. Thomas, of Baltimore (1854–1904), "The Prophet," in *Echoes and Pictures*, p. 110. See also his *Life*, by Anna B. Thomas, p. 288, a book which gives an attractive picture of a modern Quaker minister.
[3] *Ante*, p. 254. In 1662 Friends who were prisoners in the Friary at Ilchester carried on a school for a time as a piece of social service, see account in *J.F.H.S.* viii. 16-19. For Thomas Lawson's school at Newby Stones, in Westmorland, see *Beginnings of Quakerism*, p. 370.

Hertford,[1] and became the first master at Waltham Abbey.[2] Eleven years later the school was moved to Edmonton; and, in 1682, Taylor emigrated to America, and was succeeded for a time by George Keith.

Taylor obtained the assistance of a learned and devoted German Friend, John Matern[3]; and, at the instance of the Six Weeks' Meeting, who desired "a book for teaching children at the schools Court hands, Lawyer's Latin, etc., the better to enable them to read a writ and other Law process,"[4] published in 1676 *Institutiones Pietatis*, to which the chief principles of Latin were added.[5] With Matern's help he also produced *Compendium Trium Linguarum*, an abridgment of Latin, Greek and Hebrew, "in a short and easy method for the use of the studious and Christian youth."[6] The book lays aside "all the old, corrupt, heathenish books and grammars thence educed," and illustrates the languages from scripture. A remarkable visitation came to the school at Waltham Abbey on 4th June 1679:[7]

> At a meeting . . . where was present about forty or fifty young boys and maidens, God's heavenly power brake forth in some maids and young girls. It begun with three or four at first, broke them into tears and melting of heart, continued so a small time, then it reached two or three of the younger boys, which melted them into tears; and in a very small time reached all the boys and young girls, many of them being but about eight or nine years old . . . and at last it reached unto the elder people, so that all in the meeting was broken by the power into tears and melting, which did continue for about one hour until the meeting ended.

Matern was so overcome that he shook and trembled

---

[1] *Extracts from State Papers*, p. 193, about 1664.
[2] He and Richard Richardson were brought before the Quarter Sessions at Chelmsford in 1670 for teaching school without licence, Besse, *Sufferings*, i. 204.
[3] There is an account of Matern (*c*. 1640–1680) in *J.F.H.S.* x. 149-152. A Minute of the Six Weeks' Meeting, 30th March 1675, says: "The matter relating to the Silesian [is] referred to the M.M. of Devonshire House, in which quarter he dwells, and to the six Friends, overseers of the schools." His father-in-law was Hilarius Prache, for whom see *Steven Crisp and his Correspondents*, pp. 15, 16. The Hebrew part of the *Compendium* (see Matern's preface "To the Reader") is mainly the work of Prache. See also *J.F.H.S.* x. 114.
[4] Minute of 11th May 1675.   [5] Smith's *Catalogue*.   [6] *Ibid*.
[7] *A Testimony to the Lord's Power* . . . *amongst Children*, 1679, p. 7.

before the Lord.[1] At the school were two sons of Penington and a grand-daughter of Margaret Fox.[2]

In 1674 London Friends took in hand a school at Devonshire House for the children of poor Friends.[3] The learned Richard Richardson was chosen master, to be paid by a salary of £20 per annum and fees where they could be afforded; and was to teach gratis all children sent by the Monthly Meetings. He succeeded Ellis Hookes as Clerk to Friends in 1681, and served up to a few weeks of his death eight years later.[4]

About this time several Friends were teaching Latin in and near London, including Richardson and Taylor, Edward Plumstead, Ambrose Rigge, at Gatton in Surrey,[5] and John Field, who kept school at the Bull and Mouth meeting-house.[6] In 1681 Richard Scoryer had a school in Southwark, held afterwards at Wandsworth where he offered to train Friends who wished to become teachers.[7] Samuel Crisp, a young curate whom Leslie castigated for his "relapse to Quakerism," was for a time his usher;[8] and Scoryer had to rebut the charge that in the Quakers' "great school at Wandsworth" Fox's "odious *Journal*

[1] *A Testimony to the Lord's Power* . . . *amongst Children*, 1679, p. 17. This account was approved by the Morning Meeting, 2nd Feb. 1680. Keith, in his Church of England days, cited it as an instance of the seizing by the power which attended Quakerism (*The Magick of Quakerism*, p. 51). His explanation of this phenomenon, for which see *Beginnings of Quakerism*, pp. 57, 73, 74, 76, 124, is worth giving, and may be referred to psychologists for further examination : "The whole matter may be resolved into a natural enthusiasm, or a sort of natural magic or magnetism, by a certain efflux or effluvium of certain animal volatile spirits, mightily invigorated by exalted imagination, in Quakers, that flow from their bodies by the command of their will into the bodies of these new proselytes, that produce the like imagination in their credulous admirers ; as like in most cases produceth its like in fit disposed subjects, and as fire kindleth fire by application in dry wood." He works out this theory at length and with much ingenuity.

[2] *The Testimony of John Matern* . . . *with several Testimonies of Sensible Children who had been under his tuition*, 1680.

[3] Six Weeks' Meeting, 28th April, 13th Oct. 1674, and 5th Jan. 1675.

[4] For Richardson see above Minutes and article in *J.F.H.S.* i. 62-68.

[5] See account in Marsh, *Early Friends in Surrey and Sussex*, p. 68. The parish priest says he "thinks to roost here and impudently presumes to board and teach youth in his house, and hath at this time twelve or fourteen."

[6] Beck and Ball, *London Friends' Meetings*, pp. 142, 143. The reference to Friends teaching Latin is from Minutes of Six Weeks' Meeting, 20th March 1678.

[7] *J.F.H.S.* vii. 46. Thomas Chalkley was one of his pupils, and went two miles through the streets, sometimes beaten and stoned because of his plain dress (*Journal*, p. 2).

[8] Memoirs in Thomas Chalk's *Autobiographical Narrations*, 1848. He died in 1704, aged 34.

is daily read, where the Holy Bible is suffered to mould."[1] Non-Friends of the place, however, certified that the Bible was in daily use, beginning at Genesis, and so on through the Old and New Testaments.[2]

In 1677 the Shacklewell school for girls, in Hackney, was in the hands of Jane Bullock, but in a poor way. Money was lent her, and women Friends were directed to consider how to procure more scholars.[3]

Fox cherished some large educational views. Shacklewell was to teach "whatsoever things was civil and useful in the creation,"[4] and he proposed that William Tomlinson should set up a school to teach languages, "together with the nature of herbs, roots, plants and trees."[5] Thomas Lawson, Quaker schoolmaster and botanist, has a reference to this or a similar project:[6]

Some years ago, George Fox, William Penn and others, were concerned to purchase a piece of land near London for the use of a garden school-house and a dwelling-house for the master, in which garden one or two or more of each sort of our English plants were to be planted, as also many outlandish plants. My purpose was to write a book on these in Latin, so, as a boy had the description of these in book-lessons and their virtues, he might see these growing in the garden or plantation, to gain the knowledge of them: but persecutions and troubles obstructed the prosecution hereof, which the Master of Christ's College in Cambridge [Ralph Cudworth, who was keenly alive to the advantages of a study of nature] hearing of, told me was a noble and honourable undertaking and would fill the nation with philosophers. Adam and his posterity, if the primitive original station had been kept, had had no book to mind, but God Himself, the book of life and the book of the creation; and they that grow up in the knowledge of the Lord and of His creation, they are the true philosophers. . . . His work within

---

[1] See *Satan Disrob'd*, p. 94; cf. *Snake in the Grass*, 3rd edn. p. 148.
[2] *Switch for the Snake*, pp. 226, 227.
[3] Minutes of Six Weeks' Meeting, 28th Nov. 1677, 12th Feb. 1678.
[4] *Camb. Journ.* ii. 119, *ante*, p. 254.
[5] Minute of Six Weeks' Meeting, 11th May 1675. At his death Fox desired that a part of the Philadelphia property given to him by Penn should be enclosed "for a garden, and to be planted with all sorts of physical plants, for lads and lasses to learn simples there, and the uses to convert them to—distilled waters, oils, ointments, &c." (*Fells of Swarthmoor Hall*, pp. 366-369; and *Camb. Journ.* ii. 494 note).
[6] Letter to Sir John Rodes, 18th Jan. 1691, in *Quaker Post-bag*, pp. 20-23.

EDUCATION AND MINISTRY

and His works without, even the least of plants, preaches forth the power and the wisdom of the Creator; and, eyed in the spark of eternity, humbles man.

Penn held enlightened opinions on education, as is shown by his efforts in Pennsylvania.[1] His letter to his wife and children, on leaving England in 1682,[2] says:

For their learning be liberal . . . but let it be useful knowledge, such as is consistent with Truth and godliness, not cherishing a vain conversation or idle mind, but ingenuity mixed with industry is good for the body and mind too. I recommend the useful parts of mathematics, as building houses or ships, measuring, surveying, dialling, navigation; but agriculture is especially in my eye: let my children be husbandmen and housewives; it is industrious, healthy, honest and of good example, like Abraham and the holy ancients, who pleased God and obtained a good report. This leads to consider the works of God and nature, of things that are good, and diverts the mind from being taken up with the vain arts and inventions of a luxurious world. It is commendable in the princes of Germany and the nobles of that empire that they have all their children instructed in some useful occupation. . . . Be sure to observe their genius and do not cross it as to learning: let them not dwell too long on one thing, but let their change be agreeable, and all their diversions have some little bodily labour in them.

In his *Fruits of Solitude* he gives the robust workings of his mind on the subject.[3] Men he would make, not scholars, and begin not by pressing the memory of children with words and rules but by appealing to their senses and their love for making things, shaping, drawing, framing and building, studying and following nature, and so not missing of making them good naturalists. It was in this sense that he described Fox as "a divine and a naturalist, and all of God Almighty's making."[4]

It would go a great way to caution and direct people in their use of the world, that they were better studied and known in the creation of it. . . . It is pity therefore that books [such as Lawson wished to write] have not been composed for youth,

---
[1] *Quakers in the American Colonies*, pp. 527-528.
[2] Janney's *Life*, p. 199.   [3] Section on Education.
[4] Preface to *Ellwood Journal*, p. l.

by some curious and careful naturalists and also mechanics, in the Latin tongue, to be used in schools, that they might learn things with words, things obvious and familiar to them, and which would make the tongue easier to be obtained by them.

Then, he goes on, we should raise gardeners, husbandmen and artificers who would know the reason of their callings and be masters of them. To learn ourselves and the nature around us is to read as in a glass the characters of the power that made us, which can best tell us what we are and should be.

It is possible that, if circumstances had allowed, Friends might have developed a great system of "natural" education, which would have been of wide service to the country. It is in this direction, joined with a strong spiritual atmosphere, that in recent times the Society of Friends has done its most characteristic educational work in England, and in the last two centuries a number of its members have been distinguished for their scientific attainments.[1]

At Bristol there was an attempt to get a school as early as February 1669,[2] and Lawrence Steel began one five years later, when the room over the Friars meeting-house was granted him.[3] He published a system of shorthand,[4] and was a man of sweet, even temper and disposition.[5] In 1690, six years after his death, a Scotsman, Patrick Logan, who had been teaching Latin in Ireland, became the schoolmaster,[6] though at first he received little encouragement and wrote, "all the Friends that have put any children to me at present are but twelve."[7] Four years later the school was in the hands of his son [8] James Logan, who went in 1699 to Philadelphia

---

[1] For a list of Quaker members of Royal Society, see *J.F.H.S.* vii. 30-33, 45.
[2] See Minutes of Two Weeks' Meeting, 12th Feb., 22nd March 1669, 17th Jan. 1670, 22nd Jan. 1671. John Toppin, the Friend in treaty for the place, was, I think, from Westmorland.
[3] Minute of 27th April 1674. For Steel, see *ante*, p. 325 ; *Camb. Journ.* ii. 465 ; and Knight, *Sidcot School*, pp. 4, 5.
[4] Arber, *Term Catalogues*, Hilary, 1679.
[5] See account in Whiting, *Persecution Exposed*, pp. 115-119.
[6] Minutes of 30th June, 14th July, 20th Oct. 1690 ; and Minute of Dublin Half-Year's Meeting, May 1681.
[7] Letter in Knight, *Sidcot School*, pp. 5, 6. [8] *J.F.H.S.* vii. 47.

and became Penn's right-hand man in the colony.[1] He was followed by another University scholar, Alexander Arscott, the leading Bristol Friend in the early years of the new century.[2] Logan was only a young man, and in 1696 Bristol Friends were seeking the services of William Sewel of Amsterdam, who would become the first Quaker historian, and was then a man of forty-two.[3] The proposal was attractive both financially and as promising wider scope for his talents. But the love of his country, and still more the sense that he was needed in Holland for the cause of Truth and to strengthen the little Quaker Church, outbalanced these considerations, and he declined the post in a charming Latin letter to Penn. He was already at work on his *History* ; and I fancy that the Church is richer for his generous choice, as Bristol Friends would have left him scant leisure for research work.

From 1699 to 1728 William Jenkins, of Hertford, taught a successful boarding-school at Sidcot in Somerset, at first with help from the Quarterly Meeting. One of his pupils tells the gains of a boy's five years' schooling : " I have learned in grammar, Latin Testament, Corderius, Castalion, Textor, and Tully, and am got through Arithmetic, except one rule, and also have learned merchants' accounts."[4]

[1] *J.F.H.S.* vii. 6 ; and *Quakers in the American Colonies*, especially pp. 483, 484.
[2] For Arscott (1677-1737), see Tanner, *Three Lectures*, pp. 125, 126 ; and Gough, *Hist. of the Quakers*, iv. 307-311. Henry Gouldney, writing 5th Sept. 1699 to Sir John Rodes (*Quaker Post-bag*, pp. 75, 76), says : "From Bristol . . . came an Oxford scholar, not long since convinced. His grave and wise deportment gave me great hopes of his usefulness. At Bristol they have provided him a school." For his writings see Smith's *Catalogue.*
[3] Sewel's letter to Penn, in Latin, is in Bristol MSS. v. No. 85, and in a translation in Dev. Ho. Portf. 31, No. 133.
[4] Knight, *Sidcot School*, pp. 9-17, the letter, dated 1714, is on pp. 12, 13. For the probable books referred to see Arber's *Term Catalogues.* Sebastian Castellio's Latin Testament was current in editions for the use of schools ; the reference to J. Ravisius Textor and to Cicero may relate to Charles Hoole's "Century of Epistles, English and Latin, selected out of the most-used School authors, viz. Tully, Pliny, and Textor. By imitating of which children may readily get a proper style for writing letters," a book published in 1677. Care was no doubt taken, as advised by the Yearly Meeting in 1690, to see that the boys were not corrupted " by learning heathen authors and the names of their gods, but to . . . train them up in the language of Truth." Cf. *J.F.H.S.* xii. 149.

The Irish records show[1] that by 1675 the project for a school was on foot. This was settled at Cork. A few years later London Friends were consulted as to their methods of teaching languages, and it was found by five Irish Friends who taught Latin that the rules in Taylor and Matern's *Compendium* were too short. By 1687 some of these had given up their schools, " alleging that some Friends take their children from them and so discourage them, and they making conscience of teaching many vain Latin books usually taught by the world's people get few scholars but Friends' children." The disturbed state of the country added to the difficulty. In Scotland a flourishing school was begun at Kinmuck in 1681 under John Robertson " for the Latin tongue and other commendable learning ; and several considerable people of the world have sent their children thereto, highly commending their profiting therein beyond their own schools."[2]

The provision of higher education was at this time one of the unjust perquisites of the Church of England. Several Acts contained clauses penalizing schoolmasters who taught without licence from the bishop.[3] These Acts were suspended as to Protestant Dissenters by the Toleration Act, but prosecutions continued until the matter came to an issue in the case of Richard Claridge, who in 1707 was a schoolmaster at Tottenham. He legalized his position by subscribing the declarations under the Toleration Act,[4] and Chief Justice Holt gave it as his opinion that this exempted him, but he left it to the

---

[1] *Per* Edith Webb, and see *Education in the Society of Friends*, 2nd edn., 1871, pp. 114-117, by Joseph Bewly, of Dublin. For a purging out of doubtful Latin books in 1705, see Barclay, *Inner Life*, p. 496. Robert Barclay's *Catechism* and *Apology* were put on the approved list.

[2] See article on "Early Schools in Scotland," by W. F. Miller, in *J.F.H.S.* vii. 105-113. Robertson died in 1714, aged 77.

[3] 23 Eliz. cap. 1, sections 6, 7 ; 8 Jac. I. cap. 4, sect. 9 ; 13 & 14 Car. II. cap. 4 (the Act of Uniformity), sections 8, 11 ; 17 Car. II. cap. 2, sect. 4. A. Neave Brayshaw says (*J.F.H.S.* viii. 107 n.) that after the Toleration Act, at least twelve Friends were prosecuted for keeping school without licence. See details supplied by him in Knight, *Sidcot School*, pp. 13-15. He only knew of two cases before 1689 ; see *ante*, pp. 216 n., 526 n. There is a useful note on the subject in *Camb. Journ.* ii. 409.

[4] See *ante*, p. 180 n. David Hall (1683–1754) opened a boarding-school at Skipton in 1703, and for this was "rigidly prosecuted" by the priest of the town. (See his *Works*, 1758.)

jury to bring in a special verdict stating the facts that had been proved. The prosecution then discontinued the proceedings.[1] During the High Church reaction at the end of Anne's reign, the Schism Act of 1714 was passed, which required schoolmasters to be licensed and to be communicants, but the Whigs who succeeded to power did not enforce it and it was repealed in 1718.[2]

The foregoing particulars show that advanced teaching, including Latin, was within the policy of Friends, and that a number of men of University learning who joined the Society were encouraged to establish schools of this kind. Such men could no longer receive money for preaching, but they could use their talents as teachers to the great advantage of the Quaker community, and could often eke out their modest gains in this calling by clerical work provided them by Friends.

The encouragement of Latin schools did not mean any abatement of the Quaker scorn of University learning as a qualification for the ministry. Barclay explains the position clearly.[3] He refers to the darkness of the ages when the whole worship and prayers of the people were in Latin and the Bible was a sealed book. The first Reformers, he says, naturally set a high value on a knowledge of languages, Greek, Latin, and Hebrew, which enabled them to read and translate the scriptures. For such a purpose, and for other good reasons, such as promoting intercourse between nations through the use of a common tongue,[4] a study of languages is commendable. But this knowledge cannot, even in the most learned and eloquent, make up for the want of the Spirit. He has a story of a poor Quaker shoemaker[5] who could not read a word, and yet, by the certain evidence of the Spirit in himself, set right a professor of Divinity who assaulted him with a false citation of scripture, and when

---

[1] Gough, *Hist. of the Quakers*, iv. 213-216, gives full particulars.
[2] See *ante*, p. 191. The Act contained an exception limiting it to higher education. [3] *Apology*, Prop. x. sect. 19.
[4] Cf. the Y.M. advice of 1737, encouraging the teaching of French, High and Low Dutch, Danish, etc. for purposes of trade and for the service of the Church.
[5] Supposed by John Barclay, *Diary of Alexander Jaffray*, p. 381, to be Richard Rae, of Edinburgh.

the Bible was brought it was found as the poor shoemaker had said.

The conception of the age that inspiration possessed man without the help of human personality, and the undue emphasis placed by some of the other Churches on human learning, were the chief causes which led to its neglect by Friends. They found that the inward way of meditation and waiting on the Lord had developed men and women of deep experience and of wonderful insight and power. They were perhaps hardly conscious of the extent to which many of their own leaders had already received a wide training in religious things before they joined Friends. These men preached out of a rich past and from well-furnished minds, but the succeeding generation, born and bred in the Society, had little of this adequate equipment. There was an urgent need for the Church to promote Bible study and a teaching ministry. The family reading of the scriptures was, however, encouraged, including the instruction of children "in the great love of God through Jesus Christ, and the work of salvation by Him and of sanctification through His blessed Spirit,"[1] and Barclay's *Catechism and Confession of Faith*, with its 237 questions, its answers expressed in scripture language, and its twenty-three articles of faith, went through eight editions between 1673 and 1740.[2] I have failed to trace the direct catechetical use of this or any similar work; but it was widely distributed to young people.[3] There were few books published by Friends which could rank as aids to Bible study. Perhaps the most important were Ellwood's folios, in 1705 and 1709, called *Sacred History*, which digested the historical parts of the Old and New Testaments.[4] They were designed as profitable and

---

[1] The MS. "Books of Extracts," under title "Scriptures," give this from the Y.M. of 1706, and others, dated 1709, 1720, 1731, etc.

[2] See Smith's *Catalogue*, and Barclay's *Works*, 1692 edn. pp. 109-179. The 1690 and later editions were "corrected and very much amended."

[3] In 1712 Longford M.M. (Middlesex) purchased a supply of the Catechism and of Fox's and Crisp's Primers for their young people, and renewed their stock a few years later; and in 1706 the boys at the Friends' Workhouse and School at Clerkenwell were each given a Catechism (Beck and Ball, *London Friends' Meetings*, pp. 292, 364).

[4] Smith's *Catalogue*, and account in Ellwood's *Life*, 1714 edn. pp. 455-459 and 466-470. The book was reprinted both in folio and 8vo in 1720.

entertaining reading for young people in their leisure time, and were written with such help from other writers as was then available.

By the close of the century the policy of sending children to Quaker day- or boarding-schools was well established. From 1690 onwards London Yearly Meeting issued Minutes advising against children being trained in the world's ways, and urging the provision of Quaker schoolmasters and mistresses.[1] Irish Friends were concerned with the same question,[2] and a Minute of 1701 shows the guarded and utilitarian training that came into vogue.

It warns against:

(1) Pride and idleness, with too much of the hurtful conversation of the world;
(2) Schooling children with non-Friends and in company with other children, whose example occasions their losing the plain language and excites them to pride and vanity;
(3) Too much fullness and choiceness in eating and drinking, especially having the opportunity too frequently to drink strong liquors;
(4) Giving children money to spend at their own will, both before and when they are apprentices;
(5) Keeping children too long at schools without labour;[3]
(6) Finery in apparel and liberty of too much of the world's conversation;
(7) Keeping children unemployed at home and exposed to the roving vanities for which idleness makes way.

The Minute accordingly recommends:

(1) That children be taught at Friends' schools or by their own parents;
(2) That concerned Friends show themselves examples in plainness and moderation, and in keeping their children to necessary labour;

---

[1] See Minutes of 1690, 1695, 1696, in MS. "Books of Extracts," titles, "Schools," "Children."

[2] Half-Year's Meetings, May 1691, Nov. 1693.

[3] Leinster Province Meeting, March 1701, had a concern against keeping children longer at school than will answer the vocation they are to follow, which led to this Half-Year's Meeting Minute of May 1701. Cf. the educational views of John Bellers, *post*, p. 579.

(3) If employed at home, they should be bound apprentices that they may be kept under subjection as servants;

(4) Rich Friends are advised, so as to afford a powerful example, to bring up their children to labour and in plainness out of costly apparel;

(5) Children are to be kept to meetings and not left to stay at home by themselves.

There is much that is excellent in this advice; but the stress throughout is laid on the efficacy of outward regulation; and there is no vision of the higher meaning of true education as we understand it to-day. Irish Friends, however, were alive to the need of inward spiritual discipline; and their counsel on this head is needed to complete the picture. In 1693[1] parents are advised:

. . . often to examine their children and servants after meetings for worship, what benefit they have reaped . . . as to their inward comfort and refreshment, and what they have felt of the tendering power and love of God . . . that so our children and youth may not only be educated in the sound sense of Truth, but be made living witnesses and partakers of the inward and spiritual life and power thereof.

The above Minutes are typical of the prevailing Quaker point of view at the end of the century. It will be seen that reliance is placed on a sedulously guarded education and on a religious atmosphere. The guarded education meant protection from evil influences, which during the period of immaturity is as salutary for young human life as for plants. But it meant also the careful inculcation of prescribed ideas and an approved way of life; and this training, however excellent, confined the mental and moral outlook and pruned luxuriance and vigorous growth to its own trim patterns. It was not education at all, in the higher sense of the word. Life is continued by reproduction and grows by absorbing into its substance that which ministers to its fuller life. It is itself the begetter of the new life: *omne vivum ex vivo*. Accordingly vital processes are the supreme need in education; and the continuance of a living Church comes on the human side by fostering

[1] Half-Year's Meeting, Nov. 1693.

these processes, not by laying the emphasis on the form of Truth. Outward profession is the husk of religion, a change of heart its kernel; the garb of discipleship is nothing, loyalty to Christ everything; the mere ritual of worship vain, its sincerity effectual; a leadership of authority sterilizing, a leadership of inspiration and illumination and personal friendship fruitful; an outward membership mechanical, an inward comradeship of heart with heart dynamic; service is the free activity of a soul that loves the will of God, and growth a continuous nourishment with larger life. But the Quaker was now given a fixed mental and moral environment, to which he was to accommodate himself; he was not taught to make his own life. The vital experience of the early Friends had not been so learned. They had discovered and appropriated Truth for themselves; and thereby had come into a world of new joy and power. I have tried faithfully to record the extravagances which attended the first years of unrestrained fervour; and to note the disintegration that threatened the movement from the negative mysticism of Perrot and the extreme individualism of the Wilkinson-Story party. But it is equally necessary to perceive the evils that followed the over-assertion of corporate authority. It rooted itself, as we already see in the epistle of 1666, in the pattern-conduct of the elders, and thus became the parent of an imposed tradition, and betrayed Friends into the fallacy of thinking that walking in the footsteps of men who walked with God was the same thing as walking with God. It provided the Society with ready-made ways of life and thought and thus weakened personal initiative and responsibility. And, in checking aberrations from the standard conduct, it limited the large guidance which had been the glory of the first Quaker adventure to guidance within a confined area of action.

As the individual became stereotyped in conduct and outlook, at the bidding of the corporate life, so the corporate life itself became dulled, for it was made up of these individuals. The remedy might have been found in fearless education and aggressive service. But the mental boundaries of the age prevented the one, and worldly prosperity and the grateful ease of toleration benumbed the other. The central Quaker principle, writes Rufus M. Jones : [1]

. . . called for a fearless education, for there is no safety in individualism, in personal responsibility, or in democracy, whether in civil or religious matters, unless every individual is given a chance to correct his narrow individualism in the light of the experience of larger groups of men. If a man is to be called upon to follow "his Light," he must be helped to correct his *subjective seemings* by the gathered objective wisdom of the race, as expressed in scientific truth, in historical knowledge, in established institutions and in the sifted literature of the world. The Quaker ideal of ministry, too, calls for a broad and expansive education even more than does that of any other religious body. If the particular sermon is not to be definitely prepared, then the person who is to minister must himself be prepared. If he is to avoid the repetition of his own petty notions and commonplace thoughts, he must form a richer and more comprehensive experience from which to draw.

As events fell out there was no proper cultivation of a soil suited for the growing of leaders, and it followed that the human harvest was poor. The large-hearted Publishers of Truth, rich in knowledge and experience, died ; and authority passed into the hands of smaller men, who permeated the Society with pettier conceptions. The world-shattering truths for which Fox stood needed to be lived according to Emerson's fine sentence, " Everything great must be done in the spirit of greatness." [2] The young people were there, but no adequate appeal was made to their minds, no career of high venture and sacrifice was opened before them. They were trained in a prescribed way to a contracted service, and the walls and windows of their Church began to shut them out from the wider world and the full sunshine.

The need of enlisting the service of the young was indeed recognized.

---

[1] *Quakers in the American Colonies*, p. xxvi.
[2] Essay on "War," Riverside edn., *Miscellanies*, p. 197.

EDUCATION AND MINISTRY

In 1704 the Yearly Meeting [1] encouraged action to secure the attendance of young Friends "worthy to be esteemed members of [business] meetings . . . that they may come up and stand in the life of righteousness, to be serviceable in the Church, helpful to the ancient Friends, and fitted to supply their places as such shall be removed." Middlesex the same year [2] reported that several of the Monthly Meetings "invite their youth once a quarter to wait upon the Lord, when the several advices of [the Yearly] Meeting are read, and many Friends are frequently drawn forth in good counsel to exhort and encourage them to walk in plainness of speech and apparel and in all other respects as Truth requires."

Here again the over-emphasis on outward conformity is apparent.

Thomas Story describes the sterile consequences of this formalism. In 1716 he says of one English meeting : [3]

We had a large meeting . . . but not very open, there being many young people in it, not yet arrived at a sufficient sense of Truth. And, though under a profession of it, many of them have little desire after it, but think themselves safe, having had their education in the form; [so] think all is well and want nothing. And so it is in many other places.

In 1733 he attended a large Circular Yearly Meeting at Kendal [4] consisting mostly of young people, and remarks that they were like the Samaritans in Acts viii. 16, who accepted Jesus as the Messiah but had not received the Holy Ghost. They believed in Christ and in the doctrine of His Light, grace or Holy Spirit, "yet the Spirit Himself is not fallen upon many of them, as a sensible and experimental dispensation of life and power ; which is properly the Gospel, and the former is rather previous and introductory." Some years later, in 1751, Bownas summed up the situation in a candid letter of great historical significance : [5]

The young generation of this age don't seem to come up so

---

[1] Printed Epistle of 1704.
[2] Longford M.M. established these meetings in 1698 (Beck and Ball, *London Friends' Meetings*, p. 292). Barking M.M. had them in 1703 (*London Friends' Meetings*, p. 280). [3] *Life*, p. 536.
[4] *Life*, p. 689. [5] Letter in *J.F.H.S.* i. 121.

well as could be desired. The Church seems very barren of young ministers to what it was in our youth; nor is there but very little convincement to what was then. It seems to me—and I have been a minister fifty-four years—that I had more service, and better success in my ministry, the first twenty years than I have since had for a long time. I do not find any fruit or good effect of what I do that way; and yet what I am con cerned in seems to be very acceptable and well-received by others; but they don't to my observation have that good effect as I could desire they should. I have closely examined where the fault is, but don't find it out.

It must not of course be inferred that there was no continuance of spiritual life. The over-emphasis on the outward could not, so long as the Friends' meeting was maintained, altogether supersede the inward way of direct access to God. Side by side with prosy speaking and drowsy silence there was much true waiting upon the Lord, and the fountain of prophetic ministry was not wholly quenched. The inward way could strengthen and illuminate the earnest soul apart from outward helps. Had it been otherwise the state of the Society, in its Quietist days, would have been destitute indeed. But here was a power that made for growth, in spite of the most adverse environment. Take the following from Dewsbury, in which I have used italics for the phrases which show the essentially progressive character of this deeper education that was open to all Friends.

All you young and tender people . . . do not rest in an outward profession of the Truth, by what you have received by education, but all watch to the heart-searching Light of Christ in you, which will let you see you must be regenerated and born again; and so be made real and faithful Friends by the heavenly inspiration of the powerful Spirit of God in you. Which, if you be careful upon your watch, you will see judgment upon all in you that is not obedient to the Light of Christ, *in whose Light you will see more light.* . . . And, until you enjoy it . . . you will pour forth your supplications . . . as the blessed and heavenly travellers and companions did and doth, who could not find the Kingdom of God in outward observations. . . . But, the Kingdom of God not consisting in outward observations, *you in the Light press forward* . . . weeping and seeking the Lord your

God, asking the way to Sion, *with your faces thitherward*, that you may enjoy His salvation for walls and bulwarks.[1]

The fountain of prophetic ministry was not wholly quenched, but the channels were partly choked. It is characteristic of the time that the twenty "Cautions and Counsels to Ministers," issued by the Yearly Meeting of Ministers in 1702,[2] are almost entirely negative, as the following summary will show:

1. Against restless behaviour while another is speaking,
2. Against unnecessary preambles,
3. Against pretending to a few words and then discoursing at length,
4. Against misquoting scripture, "for preventing whereof it's desired that all those concerned to be conversant in reading the Holy Scriptures,"
5. Against falling upon disputable points or "dialoguing" in their testimonies,
6. Against hurting meetings by speaking at the close when the meeting was left well before,
7. Against tones, sounds and gestures, courting popularity,
8. Against running into employments for which they are not fitted; also against idling. Importance of applying themselves to some lawful employment, yet so as not to overcharge themselves in business to the hindrance of their service,
9. Against sowing discord,
10. Importance of an unspotted and consistent life,
11. Importance of business integrity and moderation,
12. Importance of simplicity in dress, furniture and food,
13. Against men and women travelling together,
14. Against women ministers hindering their brethren or the brethren discouraging the women in their service,
15. Against too much familiarity, tending to draw out the affections,
16. Against disturbance, in the minister's own will, of the worship of others,
17. Against laying too great stress on authority of message,

---

[1] Epistle dated 4th Dec. 1686, in *Works*, pp. 369-376. Cf. Crook's "Epistle to young people," dated 16th Aug. 1686, in *Works*, pp. 336-344, and Steven Crisp's "Epistle" (1680) in *Works*, pp. 423-441 (referred to *supra*, p. 327), especially pp. 435-438.

[2] From a copy at beginning of Kendal Book of Half-Year's Meetings of Ministers, 1702-1743.

18. Against presumptuous prophesying against a nation, town or person,
19. Against exposing writings before approval by Morning Meeting,
20. Against paying burdensome visits.

Irish Friends had already issued similar though less comprehensive advice, against local ministers interfering with the service of travelling ministers or speaking too often in long testimonies, against young ministers exceeding the measure of their gift, and against ancient ministers speaking tediously and unseasonably or falling into a strain of tuning or singing.[1]

This kind of counsel reached its height in the Yearly Meeting's advice of 1738, that ministers in preaching, writing, and conversing about the things of God, should keep to sound words and scripture terms, and none should pretend to be wise above what was there written, or go about to explain the things of God in the words that man's wisdom teaches. They were encouraged, however, to give their own experiences.

Amidst this plethora of cautions, many of them salutary while others are cramping or obscurantist, we look in vain for words of hearty encouragement such as Fox and the first leaders again and again used; and there is no perception of the need for a richly varied service, or a well-furnished mind. The institution of Eldership throws further light on this attitude towards the ministry. In Ireland, as early as 1692, it was directed that in each Province one or two Friends from each meeting should meet apart to inquire into the condition of worship and ministry;[2] and a year later quarterly meetings of ministers in each Province were set up, which these Friends were to attend.[3] Elders not in the ministry were appointed in Westmorland and Yorkshire, and probably in other districts, about the turn of the century, and these met with the ministers at their meetings.[4] It was not till

[1] Half-Year's Meeting, Nov. 1693. As to tones, see *ante*, pp. 426, 484, 541, and Samuel Bownas in *J.F.H.S.* xiv. 42. Cf. *ibid.* xiii. 124, xiv. 94, xv. 125.
[2] Half-Year's Meeting, Nov. 1692. [3] *Ibid.* Nov. 1693.
[4] Kendal Book already cited, and Yorkshire Minister's Book, 1689–1798, also similar book of Brighouse M.M.

EDUCATION AND MINISTRY

1727, however, that London Yearly Meeting advised the appointment of such elders to encourage and advise young ministers, and directed that they should sit in local meetings of ministers. In Ireland we hear of the elders being told to stir up ministers to be diligent in extension work;[1] but their influence was on the whole repressive and accentuated the decline in the ministry that was now taking place.

This official eldership by Friends not in the ministry was a late development of the system of Church government. The organization as set up by Fox had relied mainly on the Publishers of Truth. It was their annual meeting which had prepared the way for the representative Yearly Meeting, and continued side by side with it, nor did elders form part of this till 1754. Ministers had the right of attendance at the representative Yearly Meeting, the Meeting for Sufferings and the Six Weeks' Meeting; while the Morning Meeting, with its important functions, was for many years entirely in their hands. Only slowly and almost imperceptibly did the spiritual government of the Church pass to the main body of Friends. The late Robert Barclay was the first to give prominence to the question in his *Inner Life of the Religious Societies of the Commonwealth*, published in 1876, after his death, a book of great originality, though faulty and ill-balanced. He cites the important letter written to the Morning Meeting in 1765 by John Fry, of Sutton Benger near Chippenham. He had found no minister present at the meeting on First-day morning for distributing the ministry to the London meetings, and writes:

> I went away disappointed and sorrowful, reflecting on the flourishing state of that meeting, when I first attended it nearly forty years since, when it consisted of ministers only, who met together with hearts full of concern for the edification of each other; and, when any Friend found drawings of mind, or even a freedom to go and sit in any meeting in the City or near it, it was their frequent practice to call upon a younger minister to bear him company. Thus they were helped and encouraged to

---

[1] Half-Year's Meeting, Nov. 1701.

faithfulness . . . to their great advantage and improvement and to the great comfort and joy of each other; and then the least slight or mean esteem for each other was scarce known among them; but, alas, since elders have been added as members of that meeting to assist, the end hath not been fully answered, perhaps from their being inexperienced in the various exercises and conflicts which young ministers pass through in their first engaging in that solemn work, and therefore not capable of sympathizing with them.[1]

The change effected was a reversal of the policy of Fox, who was far from supposing that the ministers would be relegated to a secondary place. The loss of leaders during the period of persecution seems to have weakened the aggressive spiritual forces in the Church to an extent that was never recovered; and the jealousy of their influence, fomented by the Wilkinson-Story party, affected the temper of the whole Society, till the less spiritual part of the Quaker body gained full control. If there could have been a rich supply of men and women, furnished with the power of the First Publishers of Truth, the course of events would have been different. As it was the Society failed to foster an inspiring leadership and this root-question has still to be faced, if the Quaker Church is to go forward with power.[2]

It is a far cry from the ardent energy of the early years of missionary zeal to the circumscribed labours of "public Friends" of the eighteenth century. Within their contracted sphere, however, they continued to do fine work, and were still the most living force in the Church. As early as 1670 they had met each week to distribute themselves over the London meetings, and sixty years later the practice was also set up at Bristol.[3] Entry in the London lists was for many years a chief

---

[1] *Inner Life*, pp. 532, 533.
[2] See *post*, Chap. XXII. The training of preachers among the Independent Methodists, who arose at the end of the eighteenth century, in South Lancashire, as a blend of Quakerism and Methodism, deserves examination, as their position with regard to the ministry is the same as that taken by Friends.
[3] *Ante*, p. 279, and Morning Meeting Minutes, 17th May 1675 and 16th May 1681. The London lists are extant from 1699 to 1793, and there is one earlier volume, 1682–1684. For Bristol, see Two Weeks' Meeting Minute, 20th Jan. 1729: the books, which dealt with the two meetings at the Friars and Temple Street, and with neighbouring country meetings, run from 1729 to 1770.

EDUCATION AND MINISTRY

form of acknowledging a minister, though certificates granted for service by the Monthly Meetings had the same effect. Recognition was not entirely taken out of the hands of the ministers till 1723.[1] In London, "the plan," as the Methodists now call it, was made at the previous Second-day's Morning Meeting, and at the one referred to in John Fry's letter held on the First-day morning itself,[2] when saddled horses were provided for Friends going to the more distant places. The lists, at the times of Yearly Meetings, often assign as many as six or eight to one place. At the meetings for worship then held the ministry was sometimes almost continuous, as has happened in our own days. Thomas Story says in 1717, "It was a crowding time . . . there not being for the most part one minute's time between the end of one testimony and the beginning of another, an indecency I have ever disliked."[3] At Bristol, in 1678, a proposal for a retired meeting on First-day afternoons was made, in order "to wait upon the Lord in the pure silence of all flesh," and Friends, "in a sense of the benefit of such meetings in the time of our first gathering," allowed them as an experiment for three months, the meeting to be dissolved if persecution should arise;[4] and at the end of this time their further continuance was arranged.[5] I presume they were dropped at the time of the great persecution a little later, but the matter was revived at the end of the century.[6] In 1688 George Fox proposed the appointment or restoration of retired meetings in London; and this I think was done.[7] Four such meetings were being held ten years later.[8] These

[1] See paper, with facsimile page, in *J.F.H.S.* i. 22-26, on the case of William Gibson (1674-1734), which led to the action of the Y.M. of 1723.
[2] John S. Rowntree, in a paper in *Friends' Quarterly Examiner*, 1897, pp. 254-259, reprinted separately, gives the lists for 4th June 1699 and 28th May 1710. See also (London) *Friend*, 1901, pp. 442, 719. [3] *Life*, p. 578.
[4] Two Weeks' Meeting Minute, 21st Oct. 1678.
[5] Minute of Meeting for cases of Discipline, 10th Jan. 1679, recommending their continuance to the Two Weeks' Meeting, Lawrence Steel to bring the matter forward. There is no confirming Minute of this meeting.
[6] Tanner's *Three Lectures*, p. 90.
[7] Morning Meeting Minute, 15th Oct. 1688, and action of Six Weeks' Meeting, as stated in Beck and Ball, *London Friends' Meetings*, p. 125.
[8] *London Friends' Meetings*, p. 125.

arrangements suggest that in some of the larger centres there was a plethora of ministry.

A channel for service to Friends and the wider public was made in the setting-up, with the consent of London, of a number of provincial "Circular" Yearly Meetings, as they were called from their circulating round the Quarterly Meetings associated in their establishment.[1] They became important agencies in stimulating the spiritual life of Friends and spreading the Quaker message, though seldom followed up in an efficient way.

The earliest was that for Wales, which met from 1682 to 1797, about a month before the Yearly Meeting in London. In 1694 Friends of the West of England were authorized to have one for worship at Bristol, which began in the following year.[2] Four years later another for Cumberland, Westmorland, Lancashire and Cheshire was approved, which lasted from 1699 to 1798. In 1699 London Yearly Meeting declared that all such meetings should be for worship only, and should continue only from year to year, entirely subject to its control. The one at Bristol, however, presumably through always being held in one place, which was a chief centre of Quakerism, usurped disciplinary powers, and adopted Queries, the answering of which caused dissatisfaction in the Quarterly Meetings. Dorset objected in 1699, and again fifteen years later, and set up an annual meeting for worship at Ringwood or Poole with Hampshire Friends from 1708 to 1796.[3] Somerset and Wilts also objected, and in 1721 the answers ceased to be recorded.[4] They were, however,

---

[1] See the Y.M. Minutes, 1681 (Wales), 1694 (Bristol), 1698 (Four Northern Counties), 1699 (asserting control of London Y.M.), 1720 (Circular Y.M. for Western Counties). For Wales see *J.F.H.S.*, *John ap John Supplement*, pp. 29-32, and references. For Bristol and the Western Counties Circular Y.M. see Tanner, *Three Lectures*, pp. 132, 133, 141; Alfred W. Brown, *Evesham Friends in the Olden Time*, pp. 149-168 (with notes also on those for Wales and the Four Northern Counties); A. Neave Brayshaw, *Handbook to Y.M. at Birmingham 1908*, pp. 56-60; Bristol Y.M. Minutes, at Bristol, and references in the Journals of Ministering Friends of visits to the various Yearly Meetings. For the Four Northern Counties see *J.F.H.S.* ix. 147-151, xv. 126.

[2] See *ante*, p. 479.

[3] Dorset Q.M. Minutes, 12th April 1699, 12th June 1699, 23rd June 1714, 5th Oct. 1715, and (as to the Dorset-Hampshire Meeting) 6th Oct. 1708, *per* A. Neave Brayshaw.   [4] *Per* A. Neave Brayshaw.

received for another fifty years, when the Bristol Yearly Meeting was laid down for discipline, but continued for worship till 1798.

In 1720 leave was obtained for another Yearly Meeting in the West, which circulated through a district including seven counties.[1] This was held at various places from Truro to Rugby till 1786. Of these meetings the late Alfred W. Brown says:[2]

[They] were sometimes held in a meeting-house, as at Worcester in 1723, and occasionally in a large barn or a town-hall; but they more frequently took place in great wooden booths, erected for the purpose at considerable expense. . . . Almost every description of these meetings contains some special reference to the vast crowds that attended them. Besides many Friends, amongst whom were a good proportion of "our beloved youth," there were sometimes present "those called the quality and gentry and several national priests," as well as "high professors of religion," and "a mixed multitude of all sorts and notions." Overflow meetings had often to be held. At Rugby in 1735 the crowd was so great "that scarce half of them" could get into the booth; and some of the ministers addressed them "in a large court behind an inn." . . . They constituted a bond of union between the seven counties, and served to stimulate the religious life of the Society itself. They were the means of influencing large masses of people who could have been reached at no other time; and [when discontinued] there is no evidence to show that their popularity or usefulness had materially decreased.

In the Four Northern Counties, the system consolidated the Quakerism of the area, for it was arranged in 1704 that Friends should stay over the local Quarterly Meeting, with the right of proposing whatever might concern the prosperity of Truth.[3] The method in use was for ministers and elders to meet on the first afternoon: two gatherings for worship occupied the next day, and a third was given to a conference on the state of the

---

[1] The counties were Devon, Cornwall, Somerset, Gloucester, Hereford, Worcester, and Wilts till 1734 when Warwickshire took its place.
[2] *Evesham Friends in the Olden Time*, 1885, pp. 158, etc. At Rugby a collection for the poor of the town was made among Friends at the inns (Thomas Story, *Life*, p. 718).
[3] Westmorland Q.M. Minutes, 7th April 1704, with copy of Lancaster Q.M.

Society, followed by the local Quarterly Meeting.[1] At Chester in 1717,[2] on the Sunday afternoon a public meeting was held in the Tennis Court, the place where Penn had preached during the royal progress in 1687. Ministers met on the following day, and public meetings occupied the Tuesday. Both in the forenoon and afternoon the great Tennis Court was crowded, as well as two specially erected galleries; and a large room overlooking the Court was filled with officers and others, who did not care to come into the meeting itself. On the Wednesday morning Friends conferred as to the affairs of Truth, and met with the public in the afternoon, " where was supposed to be near 4000 people, and things were well, and Truth over all." The meetings had increased "both in number and openness, the people being more and more ready to hear; and several were convinced, so as to come to meetings and own Truth openly."

We hear of other Yearly Meetings for worship in various places, as at Colchester,[3] Norwich,[4] Woodbridge in Suffolk,[5] York,[6] Banbury,[7] and in Scotland,[8] which brought together Friends of the districts concerned. There was also a large number of General Meetings, held at longer or shorter intervals. Westmorland Friends,[9] for instance, arranged a rota of these covering seven-month periods— Preston Patrick, Kendal, Crook, Sedbergh, Windermere, Grayrigg, Sedbergh, then Preston Patrick again, and so on. In 1722[10] there is an illuminating Minute which tells how the Friends from the dales—Dent, Garsdale, and Ravenstonedale—found a hardship in going to these

---

[1] The Westmorland Q.M. Minutes give the arrangements for each year and short reports of the Y.M.'s.

[2] Thos. Story, *Life*, pp. 569, 570. Story attended many of the Y.M.'s up and down the country.

[3] Held shortly after the London Y.M. It was attended by Thomas Story, 1715, 1718, 1722 (see *Life*, pp. 477, 606, 634).

[4] Attended by Story, 1715 (see *Life*, p. 477).

[5] Attended by Story, 1722 (see *Life*, p. 635).   [6] See *ante*, p. 465.

[7] Attended by Benjamin Holme, 1728, whose *Works*, 1753, contain frequent references to the various Y.M.'s. The Oxfordshire Q.M. Minutes show that in 1728 there was a proposal to establish a general circular meeting with adjacent counties, which was not proceeded with.

[8] Attended in 1729 at Edinburgh by Benjamin Holme.

[9] Q.M. Minutes, 6th Oct. 1704.   [10] Minute of 4th Jan. 1723.

EDUCATION AND MINISTRY

General Meetings, considering their remoteness, "the storms that frequently fall amongst 'em, and the inability of a great many of them as to horses, &c.," and desired leave to hold their week-day meetings in the General Meeting week, except when at Sedbergh. These dales' Friends preserved a finely conservative type of Quakerism, so that it became proverbial to "do as they do in Dent."[1]

Ministers, when travelling, often arranged for invitations to the public, and men of spiritual insight, like Thomas Story, laid special stress on this. In 1717, for example,[2] he visited Whitby, where was a fine body of Friends. He attended their two week-day meetings and that on the First-day morning, all "open and comfortable" times.

The afternoon meeting was put off till five in the evening, and notice given, which fully answered the intent; for there was such a crowd as the Friends there had never seen in that place; and many things opened to them in the wisdom and authority of Truth, to general satisfaction. I do not see, but at this day, in all places where Friends are diligent to draw people to meetings, the Truth appears most freely and things are most lively; but, where Friends themselves are set down contented without any such concern, things are cold and heavy to themselves also, and little appearance of Truth but in reproof and dislike.

At Yearly, General and Quarterly Meetings, as well as at meetings for worship held in ordinary course or specially appointed, it is evident that travelling ministers continued to find much scope for service. Itinerancy and intervisitation by local Friends flourished. From 1700 to '19 inclusive, about a hundred English ministers visited Cork,[3] and in 1698, though the number is more than ordinary, twenty came to Aberdeen,[4] including young Jonathan Ostell from Cumberland, "two sweet young

---

[1] I had this from my father, who was Westmorland born and bred. Dent Meeting was set up, as a regular meeting, in 1681, on a petition from thirty-three Dent Friends, there having been several lately convinced. (See Sedbergh M.M. Minutes, June, Aug. and Sept. 1681, and Q.M. Minute, 6th Oct. 1681.) For the earlier work see *F.P.T.* pp. 329-334. The new meeting had a speedy baptism of suffering (see Christopher Story's Life, *sub anno* 1682).
[2] *Life*, p. 598. For Whitby in 1668, see *ante*, p. 461.
[3] See the Record of Friends visiting Cork 1656–1765 in *J.F.H.S.* x. 157-180, 212-262.
[4] See "Records of Aberdeen Y.M. 1672–1786" in *J.F.H.S.* viii. 76, 77.

lads on foot" and "two Yorkshire young men." It is not easy to estimate fairly the quality of the ministry. There was little learning, and all rhetorical flourishes were discouraged; but both preacher and sermon were often instinct with spiritual power for all their plainness. There is a story told of Bownas at a Western Counties circular Yearly Meeting.[1] His preaching was "slow in the uptake," and a lady interrupted him, on which he remarked, "Have patience, woman, 'twill be better by and by." He preached a most powerful sermon, and she was profuse in her apologies. A like experience came to Thomas Wilson[2] at a meeting in London,

. . . where was a great concourse of people, and amongst them two persons of high rank in the world, who sat very attentively while a Friend was speaking, and seemed to like what was delivered; but, when Thomas stood up, being old, bald and of mean appearance, they despised him; and one said to the other, "Come, my lord, let us go, for what can this old fool say?" "No," said the other, "let us stay; for this is Jeremiah the prophet: let us hear him." So, as Thomas went on, the life arose and the power got into dominion, which tendered one of them in a very remarkable manner: the tears flowed in great plenty from his eyes, which he strove in vain to hide. After Thomas had sat down, this person stood up and desired he might be forgiven of the Almighty for despising the greatest of His instruments under heaven or in His creation.

The ministry was often evangelical in the best sense of the word. Thomas Story,[3] at the close of the Welsh Yearly Meeting at Shrewsbury in 1718, which lasted six days, was speaking of the Crucifixion, and became so affected under a sense of Christ's suffering for the sins of men that he broke down in tears, and the "whole auditory was bowed and many surprised, and generally broken and melted; so that many confessed the Truth and that they had never known the like." The object of the great

---

[1] Tanner's *Three Lectures*, p. 133, *ex relatione* Young Sturge.
[2] *Life* of Samuel Neale, *sub anno* 1758, *ex relatione* James Wilson of Kendal, then in his 83rd year. Thomas Wilson is, I suppose, the leading minister of that name, 1654-1725, of Cumberland and Ireland, whose *Life and Travels* were printed in 1728.
[3] *Life*, pp. 603, 604.

Quaker preachers of the period—men like Story, Thomas Wilson, James Dickinson, Bownas, and Aaron Atkinson—was to lead their hearers to an inward experience of Christ's cleansing and renewing life. Story calls Thomas Wilson "to me the most able and powerful minister of the Word of life in the age,"[1] and tells of his spiritual authority in a meeting at Oxford, whither were come many 'varsity men to make sport. His "voice was as thunder from the clouds, and with words penetrating as lightning," he said; "It is the pride, luxury and whoredoms of the priests now, as in the days of Eli the highpriest, which deprives them of the open vision of heaven." Dickinson, another Cumberland man (1659–1741), and Wilson's usual companion, visited Ireland twelve times, America thrice, Holland and Germany once, besides much travel in Great Britain.[2] Aaron Atkinson (1665–1740) was also from Cumberland and intimate with Story.

There was a special fervour about the ministers from the North, who were homely in speech and dress, and simple in their circumstances of life compared with those from the South. They seem to have been scarcely touched by the worldly spirit that showed itself in prosperous trading centres such as Bristol and London.

Luke Cock (1657–1740),[3] who had been a butcher in the fishing village of Staithes on the North Riding coast, may serve as a type of the quaint sincerity of these north-country preachers. Having lost his temper in folding a flock of sheep, he punished himself by letting them all out, and penning them a second time. Once, finding his thoughts in meeting wandering to his horse tethered outside, he rose and said, "Friends, if I don't turn my horse out of this gallery, my Master will turn me out." His sermon at York, 2nd November 1721,[4] with all its

[1] *Life*, p. 78.
[2] See his *Journal*, edited with that of Thomas Wilson, by Thomas Chalk, 1847.
[3] See George Baker, *Unhistoric Acts*, pp. 22-24.
[4] Printed in *Irish Friend*, iv. 159. I supply date and some verbal corrections from MS. copy in my possession. George Baker gives the wife's remonstrance in pure Yorkshire: "We'se all be ruined. What! Is tha ganging stark mad to follow t' silly Qua-akers?" The Weeping Cross is a couple of miles on the London side of Shrewsbury. Luke Cock is buried in Danby dale.

oddity, lets us into the experience of inward guidance known by plain honest-hearted Friends better than any piece I have met with.

Necessity, Friends, outstrips the law : necessity has made many people go by the Weeping Cross. . . . I remember I was travelling through Shrewsbury, and my guide said to me: " I'll show thee the Weeping Cross." " Nay," said I, " thou need not ; I have seen it a great while." Now this place that he showed me was four lane ends.

I remember when I first met with my Guide, He led me into a very large and cross one, where I was to speak the truth from my heart—and before I used to swear and lie too for gain. " Nay, then," said I to my Guide, " I mun leave Thee here : if Thou leads me up that lane, I can never follow ; I'se be ruined of this butchering trade, if I mun not lie for gain." Here I left my Guide, and was filled with sorrow, and brought to the Weeping Cross : and I said, if I could find my Guide again, I'll follow Him, lead me whither He will. So here I found my Guide again, and began to follow Him up this lane and tell the truth from my heart. I had been nought but beggary and poverty before ; and now I began to thrive at my trade, and got to the end of this lane, though with some difficulty.

But now my Guide began to lead me up another lane, harder than the first, which was to bear my testimony in using the plain language. This was very hard ; yet I said to my Guide, " Take my feeble pace, and I'll follow Thee as fast as I can. Don't outstretch me, I pray Thee." So by degrees I got up here.

But now I was led up the third lane : it was harder still, to bear my testimony against tithes—my wife being not convinced. I said to my Guide, " Nay, I doubt I never can follow up here : but don't leave me : take my pace, I pray Thee, for I mun rest me." So I tarried here a great while, till my wife cried, " We'se all be ruined : what, art thou going stark mad to follow these silly Quakers ? " Here I struggled and cried, and begged of my Guide to stay and take my pace : and presently my wife was convinced. " Well," says she, " now follow thy Guide, let come what will. The Lord has done abundance for us : we will trust in Him." Nay, now, I thought, I'll to my Guide again, now go on, I'll follow Thee truly ; so I got to the end of this lane cheerfully. . . .

But I mun read you a little more out of my journal. Bide my din a little, I pray, you'se not be troubled with it long ; and you'se have it for nought : I'll be content with a little buttermilk and a bit of bread when the meeting is over, if you will but bide my din a little. Now to my journal again: my Guide led me up another lane, more difficult than any of the former, which was to bear testimony to that Hand that had done all this for me. This was a hard one: I thought I must never have seen the end of it. I was eleven years all but one month in it. Here I began to go on my knees and to creep under the hedges, a trade I never forgot since, nor I hope never shall. I would fain think it is almost impossible for me to fall now, but let him that thinks he stands take heed lest he fall.

I thought to have had a watering; but ye struggle so I cannot get you together. We mun have no watering to-night, I mun leave you every one to his own Guide.

It was this close following of a Divine Guide which gave strength to the life and speech of many a homely and unlettered Quaker minister. Travelling afoot or on horseback, two and two, we picture these men and women giving themselves to their service in the love of Christ and by their sincerity and simplicity, in spite of all limiting conditions, bringing people everywhere into the very presence of their Lord.

CHAPTER XX

THE CHURCH AND SOCIAL QUESTIONS

> Learned men have learnedly thought, that where once reason hath so much overmastered passion as that the mind hath a free desire to do well, the inward light each mind hath in itself is as good as a philosopher's book; seeing in nature we know it is well to do well, and what is well and what is evil, although not in the words of art which philosophers bestow upon us, for out of natural conceit the philosophers drew it. But to be moved to do that which we know, or to be moved with desire to know, *Hoc opus, hic labor est.*—Sir PHILIP SIDNEY, *An Apologie for Poetrie*, written about 1581.

THE message that came to Fox in the fresh morning of his service was universal rather than sectarian, social as well as religious, the programme not of the founder of a sect, but of the prophet of a new age.[1] The Light within gave a new illumination and interpretation to all the facts of life, and compelled the Quaker to seek first the Kingdom of heaven and its righteousness. In the great words which sum up the spirit of Hebrew prophecy, he could say : "Justice, justice, shalt thou pursue, that thou may'st live" (Deut. xvi. 20). The social impulse of Quakerism was thus essentially religious rather than political : it sprang from an inward law of equity in the heart ; and made its appeal to conscience. Like another John the Baptist, Fox began his mission with an alarum call to repentance, for the Day of the Lord was at hand ; and, in his first ardour, he expected a response from people generally and especially from county magistrates and others in authority. The Inward Light had made his own spirit keenly alive to injustice. He was burdened

---

[1] See *Beginnings of Quakerism*, pp. 48-50.

CH. XX CHURCH AND SOCIAL QUESTIONS 555

with the callous brutality of the criminal law which hung a man for a trifling theft: he visited the Justices to urge the fixing of fair wages for farm labourers: he addressed papers to the merchants and magistrates of London in favour of the poor.[1]

How are you in the pure religion . . . when both blind and sick and halt and lame lie up and down, cry up and down, in every corner of the city; and men and women are so decked with gold and silver in their delicate state, that they cannot tell how to go? Surely, surely you know that you are all of one mould and blood that dwell upon the face of the earth. Would not a little out of your abundance and superfluity maintain these poor children, halt, lame and blind, or set them at work that can work; and they that cannot, find a place of relief for them; would not that be a grace to you?

In his days of fervent itinerancy, he placarded market-place and church-door with stirring appeals for practical righteousness, manuscript "tracts for the times," written in a passion of social sincerity. Take the following example:[2]

To you all this is the word of the Lord . . . fishermen, boatmen, watermen and carpenters, and all tradesmen and professors whatsoever, who swear, take God's Name in vain, and drink until you be drunk; and fights and quarrels, and are full of vain speeches without the fear of God, and cozening and cheating one another, and lying and dissembling, and are not Yea and Nay in your com[munications]; there is that in all your consciences knows that these things before-mentioned are contrary [to Truth] and Christ; and He hath given you a light, every one of you, which doth let you see these things before-mentioned to be evil deeds, and you that follow such things hate the light. . . . And this is to be stuck up; and thou that takes it down I charge thee in the presence of the living God of life, as thou wilt answer it to the living God, to read this amongst the people; for it is the word of God, which the light of God in every conscience shall witness.   GEORGE FOX.

While the seed sown broadcast by Fox often fell

[1] Fox, *Doctrinals*, to magistrates, 1657, pp. 105, 106, quoted above, and to merchants, 1659, pp. 127-130, quoted in *Beginnings of Quakerism*, p. 523, where the note needs correction, as it was the paper to magistrates and not that to merchants which Bellers reprinted in part in 1724.

[2] Dev. Ho. Samuel Watson Colln., p. 25. For similar papers, see *Beginnings of Quakerism*, pp. 49, 50.

among thorns, it had sprung into rich harvest in the hearts of thousands who were seekers after Truth; and these "children of the Light," like Fox himself, set the inward law of the Spirit beyond and above the outward law and customs of society. Through them a way of life found expression, which, if it could have prevailed in England, would have transformed the social order. Some of its characteristics may be briefly recalled :

1. The treatment of all life as a sacred thing, thus making social service a religious duty.[1]
2. Sensitiveness to oppression and injustice, due to the habit of following the Light.
3. A sincerity of behaviour, which, in courts of justice, refused oaths, in civil life rejected all servilities and flattering titles and compelled simplicity of dress and address, and, in business, obliged men to plain and straightforward dealing, at fixed prices.
4. An inwardly-controlled temperance, which retrenched luxuries, frivolities and excesses in food or drink, as pampering the lower self and contrary to the service of God.
5. A Puritan outlook on Art and recreations.
6. A recognition of the Divine worth of every human being, which overthrew the dominance of racial and class distinctions and gave woman her place of equal comradeship with man.

We need not be surprised that the Quakers were charged with holding "levelling" principles[2]; it is indeed one of their titles to honour. But they were religious reformers, seeking to change the spirit of life, rather than political levellers; though John Lilburne and some others of less pronounced views, such as George Bishop of Bristol and Anthony Pearson, found their spiritual home in Quakerism without altogether ceasing their political activities.[3] Friends had a nearer affinity to the social levellers. The remarkable leader of this group, Gerrard Winstanley, was fifteen years the senior of Fox, and developed views which at many points closely resembled those of the Quaker

---

[1] As regards civil government, however, Friends seem at times to have treated it as belonging to a special order of life (see next chapter).
[2] See *Beginnings of Quakerism*, pp. 171, 520.
[3] For Lilburne, see *Beginnings of Quakerism*, pp. 186, 366, for Bishop and Pearson, pp. 175 *note*, 161, 461-463.

leader. But the two men seem to be independent products of the peculiar social and spiritual climate of the age; and it is doubtful if Winstanley ever influenced Fox or associated with Friends.[1] The sincerity of conduct by which he sought to live out his inward experience puts him, however, by the side of Fox as a practical mystic, and he was led into a noble form of communism.

No man shall have any more land than he can labour himself, or have others to labour with him in love, working together and eating bread together, as one of the tribes or families of Israel, neither giving hire nor taking hire.[2]

He and a few followers asserted their principles in the spring of 1649 by digging up a piece of common on St. George's Hill, near Cobham in Surrey, "on that side the hill next to Camp Close," and sowing the ground with parsnips, carrots and beans. The "Diggers" failed to reach the conscience of Puritan England by their valiant but poverty-stricken experiment, though their voice crying in the wilderness has, after long forgetfulness, been reawakened into life. "The visionaries of the world are not too numerous. They aspire, they suffer, and they pass, while the world scarcely casts upon them a careless eye."[3]

Fox was no "Digger," but he could express himself trenchantly on the land question:[4]

O ye earthly-minded men, give over oppressing the poor: exalt not yourselves above your fellow-creatures; for ye are all of one mould and blood: you that set your nests on high, join house to house, field to field, till there be no place for the poor, woe is your portion. The earth is the Lord's and the fullness thereof. And you that have not so much of the earth, give over your murmuring and reasoning, fretting and grudging, for all your want is the want of God. The righteous God is coming to give to every one of you according to your works.

---

[1] Lewis H. Berens, in his able book, *The Digger Movement in the Days of the Commonwealth* (1906), gives the best available account of Winstanley, but goes too far in asserting (p. 40) that his writings were the source from which Friends drew their doctrines. Cf. account of Winstanley in *Studies in Mystical Religion*, pp. 493-500.
[2] Cited from Berens, *op. cit.* p. 74.
[3] Review of Berens in *Athenaeum*, 26th Jan. 1907.
[4] "The Vials of Wrath, &c." (1654), in *Doctrinals*, p. 12.

Friends shared in the disillusionment that attended the closing years of the Commonwealth and predisposed men's minds to escape from "sword-government" by restoring the monarchy. They felt a hardening taking place in the temper of the dominant Puritanism, which gave their witness for righteousness less and less chance of acceptance by the nation, except during some precarious months of the "Year of Anarchy." Their protests addressed to the ruling powers lay bare the heart of the situation with prophetic insight. Fox, Nayler, Howgill, Burrough, Hubberthorne strike the same insistent note. They see men who ten years before had been earnest for godliness and liberty now corrupted by power and turned into self-seekers, neglectful of the public good—rulers greedy for the spoils and authority of office, judges blinded with gifts and rewards, lawyers prostituting justice for fees; and, worst of all, Churches, endowed under the Commonwealth regime, forgetting their testimonies for the sake of their tithes.[1]

Fox, at the end of the Commonwealth period, had far-reaching social reforms in his mind. I have referred in my first chapter[2] to his trenchant letter to Parliament in 1660, on the savage criminal law and kindred matters. In the previous year he had issued similar proposals under fifty-nine heads.[3] Many of these are aimed at money-loving priests, and he takes a strongly Puritan position against games and music, crosses, bells, images, and pictures; others denounce the persecution of Friends for refusing oaths, using the plain language, and the like; but he touches general social grievances in several of the clauses. The prolixity of legal processes, the unknown tongues made use of, the exactions of lawyers, the corruption of justice, the disgraceful conditions of prison life, the death punishment for petty felonies, the need for houses for the blind, cripples, orphans, widows, and beggars, all

[1] For the views of Fox, see *Beginnings of Quakerism*, p. 355, of Nayler, p. 481, of Howgill, p. 357, of Burrough, pp. 466, 467, of Hubberthorne, *Works*, pp. 217-224 and p. 235.
[2] *Ante*, p. 16.
[3] "To the Parliament of the Comon-wealth of England. Fifty-nine Particulars, &c.," 1659.

come under notice. He would have all fines belonging to Lords of manors given to the poor, "for Lords have enough"; and would let none wear sword, dagger, or pistol but those in office or service: he would abolish tithes, give abbey-lands and glebe-lands to the poor, and turn the great houses, abbeys, churches, and Whitehall itself into almshouses, and he would have all fines and amercements, and great gifts given to great men, devoted to the relief of poverty. This outspoken piece was not reprinted in Fox's *Works*.

The most specific social proposals made by Friends at this time were those of Thomas Lawson, the Quaker schoolmaster and botanist of Westmorland. In 1660 he addressed "An Appeal to the Parliament, concerning the Poor, that there may not be a Beggar in England."[1] He planned that each parish should employ competent undertakers to relieve those who could not work, and to arrange with manufacturers and tradesmen for the employment of others. He urged that all persons should have free access to inform the magistrates of any neglect of the poor, and that at Assizes and Quarter Sessions the law should be explained and its administration supervised. The poor should not be denied their liberty till good means had been used to supply their wants. So far there is nothing strikingly original; but he also suggested a labour bureau or "poor man's office," a thing now generally accepted as one of the best means for reducing unemployment. It was to be in the charge of the parish "undertakers," and was to bring together employers and workmen wanting work, boys seeking apprenticeships, and servants needing places, "but none to be put to service until they be first taught to spin, knit, sew, [or] learn some trade or way of livelihood."

The Restoration and the sore persecution that followed

---

[1] This phrase was frequently used by Friends, and is an interesting instance of the influence of the old translations, long after the Authorized Version had come into use. It is taken from Deut. xv. 4, which is rendered in Wyclif (1382), and similarly in other versions, "Needy and beggar there shall not be among you." Cf. the vivid use of "groat" in the extract from Howgill in *Beginnings of Quakerism*, p. 97, taken from Luke xv. 8, as in Tindale, Great Bible, and Rheims versions.

left Friends little scope for social reform except within their own community. In my former book I have shown how closely the beginnings of Quaker organization were bound up, as in the early Church, with the needs of the poor and of travelling ministers.[1] Already, in 1659, Hubberthorne could say that there was no beggar among Friends, and they needed no maintenance from any people or profession in the nation.[2] Even in the thick of sufferings the prisoners and the poor were cared for. The attention always given to these matters was greatly quickened by the strong organization created by Fox; and led to notable developments at the close of the century. Before entering upon the story of these, it will be convenient to refer to the way in which the social conscience of the Society worked upon matters of conduct towards those outside the Quaker fellowship.

Commercial integrity and plain dealing were insisted on; and we seem to owe to the practice of Friends the introduction of fixed prices in retail trade.[3] Insolvencies were carefully inquired into and supervised.[4] We find numerous advices against the guilt of absconding from creditors[5] and against overtrading.[6] We have already

---

[1] *Beginnings of Quakerism*, chap. xiii., especially pp. 320, 321.
[2] *Works*, p. 219.
[3] See *Beginnings of Quakerism*, pp. 152, 211, 523. Cf. Charles Marshall, *Works*, p. 14, George Fox the younger, *Works*, pp. 41, 42. William Stout, the Lancaster ironmonger, says in his *Autobiography*, p. 22: "I always detested that [which] is common; to ask more for goods than the market-price, or what they may be afforded for; but usually set the price at one word, which seemed offensive to many, who think they never buy cheap except they get abatement of the first price set upon them; and it's common for the buyer to ask the lowest price, which if answered they will still insist of abatement: to whom I answered they should not tempt any to break their words. And I observed that such plain-dealing obliged worthy customers and made business go forward with few words." In the South of Ireland a customer will, even now, say to a shopkeeper who refuses to reduce his price: "Why, you might be a Quaker!"
[4] See, for example, a full Minute of Stockton M.M. 12th Feb. 1689, in *J.F.H.S.* xi. 53, 54, and for a further reference to the case the letter of John Rous to Fox, 12th March 1689, in Dev. Ho. A.R.B. Colln. No. 80.
[5] See Minutes of Six Weeks' Meeting, 30th March, 22nd June 1675, and the pathetic letter of Dorothy Hutchinson to her absconding husband, 26th May 1680, in *Collectita*, pp. 245-252, from Colchester Colln. Further particulars of the case are found in the Yorkshire Q.M. Minutes. Cf. *J.F.H.S.* v. 98, 101, and *Steven Crisp and his Correspondents*, p. 29. As to fleeing to the Mint and other privileged places, see Minute of Six Weeks' Meeting, 3rd Oct. 1693, in *J.F.H.S.* i. 92, and cf. *J.F.H.S.* ii. 5.
[6] On this and some of the other points see title "Trading" in the MS.

referred to the care taken by Friends exposed to fines to reduce their liabilities so as to avoid involving others in their losses.[1] They were also advised against the smuggling of goods and other customary frauds on the revenue.[2]

They were to use measures " exactly agreeing with the market-measures to which they do belong " ;[3] and were to

. . . be careful to make and sell such goods as may be honest, good and substantial, according to the several sorts and uses designed for, that so buyer and wearer may not be disappointed of his or her expectation, either as to goodness, weight or measure.[4]

The teaching of Fox on the matter is summed up in a paper[5] printed in 1661, called "The Line of Righteousness and Justice stretched forth over all Merchants, etc.," which was reprinted in 1674 and again, in part, in 1710, when the Yearly Meeting advised that it be read in Quarterly and Monthly Meetings at least once a year. The paper, with its strong emphasis on strict integrity, became the standard for generations of Quaker conduct.

I have touched these points of business rectitude lightly, because to-day they seem commonplaces, however frequently they may be violated in practice. But they lie at the foundation of credit and are among the chief causes of national prosperity. In helping, side by side with others, to establish them as fundamental conceptions

---

"Books of Extracts," and cautions issued by Q.M.'s. Yorkshire Q.M. addressed a letter in Sept. 1673 to their M.M.'s, taking notice how of late years several Friends had run into great debts, contracted by undertaking greater things than they were well able to manage, or by wasteful courses in living beyond their degree. Such Friends were not to suppose that the Q.M. or M.M. would help. Friends should not take in hand great things, nor desert their proper vocations to run into others but by advice of Friends. Westmorland Friends had a query on the subject (see also *ante*, Chap. XVIII.).

[1] See *ante*, pp. 109, 110, 422, 423.
[2] See *post*, p. 602, and a striking letter from Roger Hebden to Hull Friends in Minutes of Yorkshire Q.M. March 1677.
[3] Leinster Province Meeting, Feb. 1695. Cf. Minutes of Horslydown M.M. in 1670 as to measurement of casks (Beck & Ball, *London Friends' Meetings*, pp. 231, 232).
[4] Dublin Half-Year's Meeting, May 1702, at instance of Leinster.
[5] Printed in Fox, *Epistles*, No. 200, and summarized in *Beginnings of Quakerism*, pp. 516, 517. The Q.M. Minutes, *e.g.* Westmorland Q.M. 6th Aug. 1710, 4th Jan. 1712, show that the advice was followed.

2 O

of commercial life, Friends, as is generally recognized, were performing no mean service to the body politic.

We now pass to industrial relations, including agriculture, the greatest industry in those days. Machinery was still in its infancy; and manufactures were mostly conducted on the "domestic system," in which the master was himself a workman, and gave out work to be done in the homes of his workpeople. Among Friends, there were serge makers at Plymouth who kept above five hundred poor people at work, and one in Suffolk who employed at least two hundred in the woollen manufacture.[1] There were cloth makers in Somerset, and in 1691 the Quarterly Meeting passed a Minute which anticipated the legislation against the abuse of the system of "truck" or paying wages in kind.[2]

It being proposed to this meeting that several tradesmen do impose cloth or other goods on their working-people for their wages, more than the value, which is a great oppression, it is the advice and warning of this meeting that none which profess Truth for the future be found in such position, that so our testimony may stand firm against all oppression whatsoever.

Cork Friends had already taken similar action in 1678, appointing some in each meeting[3]

. . . to speak with the Friends of the clothing or spinning trade that they take care in all their dealings with spinners and other work-folks to pay either money for their work or such goods as they shall fully agree for beforehand; and to desire, if they pay goods, it may not be valued above the current price.

Apprenticeship was the established law of the country in all trades, and came under the direct care of the Men's and Women's Meetings, who thus secured a start in life for many of their poor. Cases of ill-usage were inquired into;[4] and Irish Friends declared that the practice of

---

[1] See petition in Sewel ii. 409, and *ante*, p. 109.
[2] Minute of 24th Dec. 1691, *per* A. Neave Brayshaw.   [3] *J.F.H.S.* xii. 52.
[4] See *e.g.* Minutes of Somerset Q.M., 17th June 1669; Six Weeks' Meeting, 27th May 1673; Kendal Preparative Meeting, 21st June 1702, etc.; Kendal Monthly Meeting, 4th Sept. 1702, etc. (the apprentice, George Braithwaite, was an ancestor of mine); Dublin Half-Year's Meeting, May 1682. The treatment of maidservants was in the same way under the care of Women Friends. See *e.g.* Epistle from London Women Friends, 4th Jan. 1675, in *Letters of Early Friends*, pp. 343-346; *ante*, p. 272.

binding an apprentice not to "follow the same trade in the same place or near the said master when his time is out" was "contrary to liberty and freedom of Truth" and had the "appearance of covetousness in it."[1]

Other disputes between master and workmen came occasionally under notice. A difference between Robert Allen, a leading Friend of Southwark, and other coopers who were Friends, claimed the long-continued attention of the Six Weeks' Meeting in 1673. In 1689, Margaret Fox's son-in-law, John Rous, tells of a Monthly Meeting at Newcastle, "where a long difference among the glass-makers was referred to Friends that were strangers, which was made an end of after near two days spent in hearing all parties; and I hope they will have a care of falling into the like for the future."[2]

George Fox the younger gives a good summary of the treatment of workmen as approved by early Friends:[3]

> Lay no more upon your servants than ye would be willing should be laid upon you, if ye were in their places and conditions. Mark that. And forbear threatening them; and be not hasty to turn them away, if they be willing to abide with you; but in patience and meekness show them their place and service, and therein teach them, if they know it not. And let them have for their service that which is convenient, just and reasonable, that they may have no just cause to murmur or complain. And keep out of covetousness, lest that hinder you from giving them sufficient liberty, who desire it, for going to the meetings of the people of the Lord. And if in the wisdom of God ye see freedom to turn them away, give them sufficient warning, that they may provide themselves other ways, for this is just and reasonable.

Many Friends were sea captains or sailors, or, like Fox himself, had shares in vessels, and Irish Friends advised those who were owners or undertakers of ships bound to foreign parts, "not to undertake such voyages without being well provided with suitable provisions, nor

---

[1] Half-Year's Meeting, Nov. 1705.
[2] Letter, 12th March 1689, in Dev. Ho. A.R.B. Colln., No. 80.
[3] *Works*, pp. 39, 40. Cf. the advice in the Balby epistle of 1656 (*Beginnings of Quakerism*, p. 313).

to overcrowd their vessels with goods and passengers to endanger the lives and healths of the passengers."[1]

It is also from Ireland, with its close discipline, in a land where Friends formed part of the dominant Protestant population, that we get the best guidance as to the duties of landlords and tenant-farmers. Friends were warned against setting their lands at rack-rents, "to the oppressing and grinding the faces of the poor and bringing reproach upon the precious Truth."[2] It was declared that if a Friend took a large tract of land and set part of it at too dear a rate, or refused to let part of it to Friends in need of land at a moderate rent, such conduct should be inquired into as bearing "a broad character of covetousness."[3] The holding up of corn to raise the market was condemned as oppressive to the poor,[4] and a Minute was passed against the buying of plundered cattle.[5] In England, Steven Crisp, of Colchester, wrote a powerful piece against evil and dissolute customs at harvest time; and said:[6]

In the time of harvest . . . remember that the portion of the poor be not gathered; . . . Lev. xix. 9; "And when thou reapest the harvest of thy land, thou shalt not wholly reap the corners of thy field," (mark) "neither shalt thou gather the gleaning of thy harvest: it is for the poor and for the stranger." . . . And all you that have much of the earth in your hands, and many hired servants, see that ye stand in the power and wisdom of God . . . giving that which is due for their encouragement, not oppressing them in work nor in wages; but all mind the Truth of God, the equal witness between you, which secretly calls for righteousness towards all men and equity, as ye would have from all men.

Some miscellaneous advices may be added. Sedbergh

---

[1] Half-Year's Meeting, May 1700.
[2] *Ibid.* May 1695, cf. *ibid.* Nov. 1695, and Leinster Province Meeting, 13th March 1697, 10th Sept. 1698, Feb. 1702.
[3] Leinster Province Meeting, 10th Sept. 1698. Cf. *ibid.* 13th March 1697.
[4] Half-Year's Meeting, May 1709, Leinster Province Meeting, 8th June 1698; *ibid.* Nov. 1708. In 1756, three Warwickshire meeting-houses at Baddesley, Atherstone, and Hartshill were damaged by rioters owing to alleged holding up of corn by Quaker millers, some of whom cleared themselves by affirmations. The riots were directed against others besides Friends and led to a number of executions (*per* Chas. R. Simpson).
[5] Half-Year's Meeting, May 1700.
[6] "A Word in due Season, or Some Harvest Meditations" (1666) in *Works*, pp. 147-153.

Monthly Meeting considered the question of killing salmon or trout in breeding time, and advised Friends against the practice, that they might "lay down a good example by their forbearance, though there may appear something of profit or pleasure in it."[1] They also discouraged Friends from following or hunting the hare with packs of hounds "by reason it's in danger to hurt youth and provoke them to such levity and lightness of mind as is not becoming the professors of Truth."[2] The cruelty as well as the wantonness of many of the customary sports was much on the mind of the Westmorland Seeker, Thomas Taylor, imprisoned at Stafford, and he wrote against those who pleased themselves

... with beholding one creature hurt and torment another, yea, sometimes even to death, as at bull-baitings, bear-baitings, cock-fightings and the like. Oh, what minds have ye; and how contrary are ye herein to the tender nature of Christ and all Christians, truly so-called, who could never rejoice in any such things, by reason of their tender, pitiful and merciful nature.[3]

An Oxfordshire Minute of 1727 condemns as a clandestine practice, opposite to the testimony of Truth, "all gratuities either in money or other ways received by any elector" voting for members of Parliament.[4]

The measures taken by Friends for the relief of poverty within their own community were, however, their most systematic attempt in the seventeenth century to deal with social questions, and were the inspiration for the far-reaching projects associated with the name of John Bellers.[5] The care of the poor had from the first been

---

[1] M.M. 25th Sept. 1705.
[2] Ibid. ; cf. Irish Minutes, *ante*, p. 510, and Aberdeen Minute, *ante*, p. 513.
[3] *Works*, pp. 128, 129 (1661); cf. *ibid.* pp. 62, 159.
[4] Minute of 26th Sept. 1727; cf. *post*, p. 589.
[5] German investigators have brought out the importance and the consequences of this system of poor-relief; in particular, Eduard Bernstein, in *Die Geschichte des Sozialismus*, "Die Vorläufer des Neueren Sozialismus" ("The Pioneers of latter-day Socialism"), vol. i. pt. ii. pp. 507-718, Stuttgart, 1895 ; Dr. Auguste Jorns, *Studien über die Sozialpolitik der Quäker*, Karlsruhe, 1912, pp. 22-54 ; Dietrich von Dobbeler, *Sozialpolitik der Nächstenliebe, dargestellt am Beispiel der "Gesellschaft der Freunde,"* Goslar, 1912, pp. 25-47. All these writers quarried much of their material from the Dev. Ho. Reference Library. Bernstein's investigation is a fine piece of work, but he suspects an underlying motive of communism in early Quakerism of which I have found little trace. Cf. Joshua Rowntree, *Social Service: its Place in the Society of Friends*, pp. 91-93.

accepted, on apostolic precedent, as an obvious duty of the Church ; and the Skipton General Meeting of October 1659 endorsed proposals from Durham, which laid it upon each group of Friends to provide for their own poor. When overburdened, a meeting was to be helped by the County Monthly Meeting.[1]

Friends took the matter in hand so completely that they often objected to their poor applying to the parish or to the world. We find York Meeting refusing relief to a Friend who had gone for help to the Lord Mayor,[2] and a series of Minutes forbids poor Friends going abroad to beg.[3] The London Six Weeks' Meeting decided in 1680 that they would not receive relief offered from the parish.[4] This maintenance by Friends of their own poor won the admiration of Eden, the historian of the Poor Laws.[5]

Steven Crisp, at the end of his life, gave wise advice on the subject which agreed with the best Quaker practice.[6]

A man, he wrote, should keep a liberal mind, feeling that his means were given him as much for charity as for personal ends. There were three kinds of poor : the sick, lame, aged and impotent, who were poor through the hand of providence, those that had made themselves poor, by sloth and carelessness or headiness and wilfulness, and those whom others had made poor by oppression and cruelty. The first should be the peculiar care of the Church, and the true Christians would "find out the poor's part in the corners and gleanings of the profits of their trades and merchandizings, as well as the old Israelite did the corners and gleanings of his field." The second class should be

---

[1] *Letters of Early Friends*, p. 290, and *Beginnings of Quakerism*, pp. 328-332. When the later M.M. system was established by Fox, his so-called "Canons and Institutions" contained similar advice.

[2] Two Weeks' Meeting, 1st Aug. 1677.

[3] See *e.g.* Six Weeks' Meeting, 10th Sept. 1678, cautioning Friends to be careful how they set their hands to begging papers ; York M.M. 7th Mar. 1690 ; Sedbergh M.M. 27th April 1696, directing that no poor who profess themselves Friends go abroad to beg or " to penny doles " at funerals.

[4] Minute of 9th March 1680. There was some variety of practice. William Tanner says, *Three Lectures*, p. 85, "Numerous cases occurred in which . . . temporary aid was given, and application directed to be made to the parish officers . . . One Minute states that as Friends paid the poor-rates they thought they had a right to such assistance ; and another advises a Friend to make such application, 'she having no scruple against it.'"

[5] Eden, *State of the Poor*, i. 588, 589.

[6] *Works*, pp. 536-540, from Epistle " to all the Churches of Christ throughout the world," *i.e.* " to Friends everywhere," London, 15th Sept. 1690.

advised, and, if willing to amend, should be helped into a way to support themselves; but, if they would not be advised, Friends need not feel responsible further. As to the third class: "These oppressed poor cries loud in the ears of the Almighty, and He will in His own time avenge their case; but in the meantime there is a tenderness to be extended to them, not knowing how soon it may be our turn; and, if there be need of counsel and advice, or if any applications can be made to any that are able to deliver them from the oppressors in such cases, let all that are capable be ready and willing to advise, relieve and help the distressed."

In administering relief the intimate knowledge which Friends had of one another greatly aided. "Help to self-help" was the principle followed.[1]

Two women Friends are recommended to the Monthly Meeting for 1s. a week apiece, instead of 9d.; "they being weakly and aged, and can do but very little; and work being scarce for that little they can do."[2]

The weak and poor condition of a man and his wife is carried to the Monthly Meeting, "they desire one to be assistant to 'em to make their bed and sweep their house and wash their dishes, the old woman being incapable of performing the same."[3]

Money is distributed to a number of Friends, in part "for procuring of working tools and other necessaries taken from several by distresses upon the late [Conventicle] Act."[4]

The Monthly Meeting considers the condition of the widow of a captain lost at sea, who was left with three children, and had always been ready to assist Friends in prison. They grant her 10s. and ask the Quarterly Meeting to help her son to a trade, "being somewhat decrepit and not for hard labour."[5]

A widow, not a Friend, left very poor with four young children, whose husband had been an honest Friend, is given 40s. to apprentice her eldest son to the trade of a linen-webster.[6]

A Friend is given 15s. towards clothes for a daughter and helping the girl to go to a relative who had promised to educate and maintain her till she could keep herself.[7]

After repeatedly trying to get a Friend to work and "to keep him from running up and down idling," Friends apply to the mayor of the town to suffer him "to be had to the House of Correction and there moderately used, if thereby he could be got to work, and to keep him from rambling up and down." This

---

[1] Dr. Auguste Jorns, *op. cit.* p. 37.
[2] Banbury Preparative Meeting, 31st March 1708. [3] *Ibid.* 1st June 1715.
[4] York Two Weeks' Meeting, 12th Dec. 1670. [5] York M.M. 6th July 1676.
[6] Kendal M.M. 5th Dec. 1673. [7] *Ibid.* 5th Feb. 1675.

solution does not prove agreeable to the mayor and the case continues a care to the meeting.[1]

A poor blind Friend from Ireland is given 10s. and is afterwards provided with a lodging and other necessaries, being "unable to take in hand any employment by reason of his infirmity."[2]

A loan of ten cows is made to a Friend, he to take the benefit of the milk and of the calves.[3]

The earliest systematic arrangements for providing work took place in connection with Friends in prison, who needed employment not only for their maintenance but also as an occupation for mind and hand—a reason which recently led Friends' Committees to find work for Belgian refugees in Holland and for German prisoners in internment camps. We have noted how young Penn in 1669 found the Quaker prisoners at Cork busily employed,[4] and Ellwood says the same of Bridewell in 1662.

The chief thing I wanted was employment, which scarce any wanted but myself; for the rest of my company were generally tradesmen, of such trades as could set themselves on work. Of these divers were tailors, some masters, some journeymen; and with these I most inclined to settle. But, because I was too much a novice in their art to be trusted with their work, lest I should spoil the garment, I got work from an hosier in Cheapside, which was to make night-waistcoats, of red and yellow flannel, for women and children. And with this I entered myself among the tailors, sitting cross-legged as they did; and so spent those leisure hours, with innocency and pleasure, which want of business would have made tedious.[5]

So, when imprisoned at Aylesbury in 1665, he says:

I betook myself for an employment to making of nets for kitchen-service, to boil herbs, &c. in, which trade I learned of Morgan Watkins; and, selling some and giving others, I pretty well stocked the Friends of that country with them.[6]

At Reading, after the Second Conventicle Act, almost the whole meeting was in prison.[7] They seem to have pooled their resources to some extent; for the Monthly

---

[1] Kendal M.M. 7th May, 4th June 1686, 1st July 1687.
[2] *Ibid.* 5th Oct. 1688, 5th July 1689.
[3] *J.F.H.S.* xv. 80 (Co. Tipperary M.M.). For other similar Minutes, see Tanner, *Three Lectures*, pp. 84-86.
[4] *Ante*, p. 64.   [5] *Life*, 1714 edn. pp. 152, 153.
[6] *Ibid.* p. 239. For Morgan Watkins, see *Camb. Journ.* i. 448, and *Beginnings of Quakerism*, pp. 348, 389.   [7] See *ante*, p. 227.

Meeting (held in gaol) deals with a Friend "concerning his making of silk-laces and not acquainting his fellow-prisoners of it," and orders the treasurer of the stock to take 8000 shoemaker's pegs every week off Christopher Cheesman, that he may not want employment.[1] In January 1673, after Friends had been released, it was directed that the balance of the stock go towards the cost of the meeting-house, built in the height of persecution ;[2] and when sufferings again befell two years later it was agreed that the pegs made by poor Friends be paid for out of the stock as before, and it was thought that those that had no other employment would "make most upon shoemakers' pegs, because Friends judge those may sell best, and they encouraged to work."[3]

For many years there was a constant flow of Quaker prisoners to York Castle. Good relations were maintained with the gaolers, and the Quarterly Meeting, where necessary, paid "chamber-rent" and "deputation-money" for such Friends as were allowed liberty to go home or into the city and look after their business.[4]

[1] M.M. Minutes, 7th July 1671, 3rd May 1672. For Cheesman see *ante*, p. 50 *n.* He became one of the opponents of the Curtis party. The M.M.'s were held in prison, *e.g.* 4th Aug. 1671, two Friends are passed for marriage. "The parties desires Friends' advice whether it be judged meet to be married here in prison or not. It is agreed and thought convenient, seeing it cannot well be otherwise, the generality of Friends being kept close prisoners, that they finish their marriage here ; and they were accordingly joined in marriage the 7th of this instant month." Surely the strangest of all Quaker weddings, fit subject for artist or story-teller. They were two Reading Friends, William Yeet and Hannah Wrenn. Yeet had been praemunired in 1665 for refusing the oath. The Judge asked him, "What say you ? Will you swear ?" His reply was, "The day of the Lord is come ; therefore I rather choose to obey God than man." He was not released till the Pardon of 1672. The gaol was the Grey Friars Church, turned into a prison in 1613 and so used for over 200 years. The roof of the Nave was removed and the Nave used as a yard, the cells being formed by blocking up the arcades between the nave and aisles (*per* Howard R. Smith). Yeet was again in prison in 1675 when a further spell of suffering beset the Church. The Q.M. during this year made Minutes such as the following :—2nd April 1675. "Ordered that the next Q.M. shall be at Blewbury . . . but, if Friends at Reading shall happen to be generally in prison at that time, then it is ordered to be here at Reading." The Church had been in prison for eight years, and, if it so fell out again, it was all in the day's work and in the Lord's ordering.
[2] Minute, 6th Jan. 1673.   [3] *Ibid.* 6th Dec. 1675.
[4] William Crouch, in London, on one occasion "had some liberty to be at home to look after my business . . . paying only my chamber-rent, which was threepence a night" (*Posthuma Christiana*, chap. iii.). When York Castle was crowded with prisoners in 1684-5, it was agreed by Friends that threepence a

John Taylor, of Barbados, a man of energy, settled in York as a sugar-refiner in 1676; and at the end of the following year the Quarterly Meeting decided to raise a stock for prisoners "whereby they might be employed in some labour to their subsistence; and this will be a refreshment to them and a good savour to Truth."[1] A sum of £160 was collected throughout the county and placed in the charge of Taylor and two other Friends. The prisoners were employed in cutting corks and picking oakum, and by the end of 1680 the accounts showed a stock of £176, so that the venture had paid its way. In the following year, the Friends in charge were encouraged to set up linen-weaving, "or any other thing that may tend to the advantage and employment of prisoners." This was no doubt done, for we hear of looms being mended; but in 1693 stockings and laces were also being made; and it was agreed that the laces could not be sold by the prisoners to the stock at a cheaper rate than 8s. 6d. a gross, there "being eighteen threads in a lace." By 1696 the stock was down to £114, and the Quarterly Meeting decided that it should be kept at £100, "standing stock for the use of prisoners which suffers ... for Truth-sake; and the residue ... shall be ... for the future service of the Quarterly Meeting." There had been at times over two hundred Friends in the Castle.

After the Reading undertaking, but earlier than the arrangements made at York, the Six Weeks' Meeting initiated a scheme of wider scope, to furnish work for any poor London Quakers.[2] In 1669,[3] Fox had advised

---

week was enough to pay to the gaoler "for all such as have rooms in the Castle, and only have but liberty to go into the city and not home" (Q.M. March 1685). The Q.M. bore the cost, or a great part of it, of defending gaolers who were proceeded against for granting liberty.

[1] See, *inter alia*, Q.M. Minutes Dec. 1677, March and June 1678 (this last in *J.F.H.S.* x. 189), June and Dec. 1679, Dec. 1680, Sept. 1681, March 1684, Dec. 1692, Sept. and Dec. 1693, Dec. 1696. I have not examined the minutes beyond Dec. 1698. For making laces cf. Dewsbury, *ante*, p. 449.

[2] Minutes of Six Weeks' Meeting, 19th Dec. 1676, 30th Jan., 12th June 1677, 3rd Dec. 1678, 1st July 1679, 27th Jan. 1680, 4th Feb., 14th Oct. 1684. Most of these are printed in the careful paper by Charles R. Simpson on "John Bellers in Official Minutes," in *J.F.H.S.* xii. 120-127. I infer that the decision in the spring of 1684, when the stock seems to have stood at £62, that £50 should be paid to the "poor's money keepers," *i.e.* the Six Weeks' Meeting Committee of Twelve, and the balance to Women Friends, who also distributed poor relief, means that the experiment was then wound up. [3] *Epistles*, p. 287.

Friends to provide "a house for them that be distempered,"[1] also to have an Almshouse, "for all poor Friends that are past work" and "a house or houses where an hundred may have rooms to work in, and shops of all sorts of things to sell, and where widows and young women might work and live." It was now decided (in January 1677) to use £100 as a stock for buying flax to employ poor Friends in spinning; and William Meade undertook the management for a year, buying the flax, supplying it in due proportions to persons appointed for each Monthly Meeting, paying the spinners, delivering the yarn to the weaver, and keeping an account. The work was evidently to be done at home. It was not till later in the year that the scheme was carried out; and in December 1678 a woman Friend, Margery Browne, was appointed "to sort the flax, and deliver it to the spinners and to oversee the spinners and to direct them in their work." A year later, in January 1680, John Bellers took over the financial management from Meade, and during the remaining four years of the experiment must have gained much of that sympathy with the poor which inspired the great projects of his later life.

Bellers in 1680 was a young man of twenty-six, in business as a cloth merchant, the son of Francis Bellers, a well-to-do grocer and prominent Friend, who had lately died.[2] Karl Marx describes him as "a veritable phenomenon in the history of political economy,"[3] and we should be glad of more light than we have on the growth of his noble mind and heart, for he became the first of the long line of great Quaker philanthropists, and the pioneer of modern Christian Socialism. Little remains to us, apart from his published pamphlets, which, for the

[1] In 1673, the Six Weeks' Meeting directed a house to be hired where "discomposed persons" should have their necessities supplied, and, at a later meeting, encouraged John Goodson, chirurgeon, to take a house on his own responsibility, the meeting paying him for any use they made of it. Rent for a house was paid by the Six Weeks' Meeting to Andrew Sowle, the Quaker printer, in May 1685.

[2] C. R. Simpson's paper and its sequel in *J.F.H.S.* xii. 165-171 contain most of the outside facts known about Bellers. Cf. Joshua Rowntree, Swarthmore Lecture, *Social Service: its Place in the Society of Friends.*

[3] *Das Kapital*, 2nd edn. i. 515.

most part, are only extant in rare first editions, and still await publication in the collected form that their contents merit. His Will indeed directs : [1]

. . . that all my printed books and papers . . . shall be reprinted in one volume, . . . and one of them to be presented to the Envoy of every Sovereign Prince and State in Europe . . . for their respective Masters' perusal, and one to every public library in London and Westminster, and to the two public libraries of Oxford and Cambridge. . . . As for my books, instruments, maps, drafts and letters, both those that are at London as well as those which are at Cowne Allins [Coln St. Aldwyn] in the county of Gloucester, I appoint that they shall be kept in one place for the use of all my children and their posterity.

Alas, for the care of testators and the negligence of their heirs.[2] The mid-Georgian age had little use for philanthropic enthusiasms; and time, the devourer, consumed the memorials of the prophet of a new social order.

Nevertheless the lineaments of the man stand out from his writings. Bellers was no preacher and of few words and dry humour.

"Some," he says,[3] "may think me too short in expression. I desire such, if they are at leisure, to read this tract twice ; and it will be then more intelligible unto them ; and, if they have not time for that, I conceive they would not have read a larger comment half through. And, though short sentences are most liable to be mistaken, yet they are best to be remembered. And,

---

[1] Made, with codicil, in year of his death, 1725, and printed in *J.F.H.S.* xii. 103-108. His remains lie in Bunhill Fields.

[2] Rules for the use of the books are carefully laid down. The son, Fettiplace Bellers, of the Inner Temple, F.R.S., wrote a play and a philosophy of law ; and was something of a geologist. He was 38, unmarried, at his father's death. The elder daughter, Mary, married a son of William Ingram, of London, by his first wife (his second wife was Susanna, the sixth of the Fell daughters, see *Camb. Journ.* ii. 451). About the beginning of the last century there was an Ingram of somewhat feeble character, who never married, in residence at Coln St. Aldwyn, and presumably the owner of its archives. The property was sold some fifty years later to Sir Michael Beach, and gave the title to Viscount St. Aldwyn. The younger daughter, Theophila, became the second wife of John Eliot, of Falmouth, and afterwards a London merchant, whose descendant, Eliot Howard, would have rescued from oblivion any papers preserved in the Eliot records. (*J.F.H.S.* xii. 103-108, and article by W. C. B[owly] in (London) *Friend*, July 1861.)

[3] "Essays about the Poor, Manufactures, Trade, Plantations, and Immorality, etc." (1699), Preface to the Reader.

if I can strike them sparks from whence others may set up bigger lights for the good of mankind, I shall not think my time ill-bestowed. My brevity may make me seem too positive with some; but I doing of it to prevent being tedious, and desiring no more credit than as I demonstrate what I writ, I hope my reader, for my good intention, will excuse me in that seeming fault."

The depth of his own religious experience is seen in a paper called "Watch unto Prayer," published in 1703, and in paragraphs added to "An Epistle to the Quarterly Meeting of London and Middlesex," printed in 1718. The former piece was reprinted in England and America a century later—a note on the copy I have used shows the stimulating force of Bellers' writing:[1]

Is this John Bellers an ancient or modern Friend? This was brought from England by Elizabeth Coggeshall, when she returned the first time:—it was so grateful to my state of mind that I then gave every cent I had to the printer to strike of[f] 200 in this form: it was in the year 1802, just after my apprenticeship expired.

Bellers tells us that watching is as needful to the soul as breathing is to the body: it is the mark of life, and its absence means the dominion of the sensual and earthly, which tends to death. It is the preparation for bringing every thought into captivity to the obedience of Christ, "and he that thinks no evil will be sure to act none":

... He that keeps not a watch upon the thoughts of his heart is much out of his way; for, though he should imitate the best of forms, he is but of the outward court; it being impossible to worship God in the beauty of holiness with an irregular mind.

Watchfulness out of meetings is the best preparation for worship within; neither hearing the best preachers, nor a bare turning the thoughts inward when one comes into a meeting, is the true spiritual worship, for the heart within may be but a den of darkness, but he that watches

---

[1] Copy in Dev. Ho. Reference Library. This American reprint followed an English reprint, which added some extracts from Penington. Elizabeth Coggeshall, of Rhode Island, paid a religious visit to the British Isles in 1798, returning in 1801, and a second, which included the continent, in 1814-1815. Her companion on part of her first visit was Hannah Barnard, who developed views that were strongly condemned by Friends, and the two separated.

in the light will be led into the new Jerusalem, where God and the Lamb are both the light and the temple to worship in, and nothing that defiles can enter.

The religious paragraphs in the second piece begin with an " excellent discourse," ascribed to Tauler, taken by Bellers from the works of John Everard.[1] This is the story of the Learned Divine and the Beggar, the subject of Whittier's fine poem " Tauler." The Divine, seeking the way of Truth, is told to go forth to the church doors, and there he shall find a man that can teach him.

And, going forth, he found there a certain beggar, with patched and torn apparel and filthy-dirty feet, all whose apparel was scarce worth three-halfpence, to whom, by way of salutation, he thus spake.

Divine. God give thee a good morning.
Beggar. Sir, I do not remember that ever I had an evil one.
Divine. God make thee fortunate and prosperous ; why dost thou speak in this manner?
Beggar. Neither was I ever unfortunate or unprosperous.
[He explains that when pinched with hunger, he praises God ; whatever befalls, he gladly receives it at His Hands as the best, and is therefore never unfortunate ; his one resolve is to cleave to the will of God, into which he has so fully poured his own will, that, whatever God wills, he wills also.]
Divine. This is very strange. But what, I pray thee, wouldst thou say, if the Lord of Majesty would drown thee in the bottomless pit? Couldst thou then be content with His will?
Beggar. Drown me in the bottomless pit? Why, certainly if He should, I have two arms, by which I would still embrace Him and clasp fast about Him. One is true humility, and that I lay under Him, and by him I am united to His most sacred humanity. The other, and that is the right arm, which is love, which is united to His divinity. And, by this love given to me from Himself, I hold Him so fast that He would be forced to go down to hell with me. And it were much more to be wished by me to be in hell with God than to be in heaven without Him.

---

[1] For Everard (1575-1650), see Rufus M. Jones, *Spiritual Reformers*, pp. 239-252, and Chas. R. Simpson, *Friends' Quarterly Examiner*, 1913, pp. 493-502. Vaughan, *Hours with the Mystics*, i. 379, says the story is to be found in an Appendix to Tauler's *Medulla animae*, and attributes it to Eckhart.

By this, that Divine learned, that the most compendious way to God is a true resignation with profound humility. Hereupon the Divine spake again to the beggar and asked him:

Divine. Whence camest thou?
Beggar. From God.
Divine. Where foundest thou God?
Beggar. Even there, where I left all the creatures.
Divine. But where didst thou leave Him?
Beggar. In humble and clean hearts, and in men of goodwill, which is His temple and dwelling-place.
Divine. I pray thee, Friend, who art thou?
Beggar. Who am I? Truly, I am a king, and Jesus Himself hath crowned me with peace, power, and rest.
Divine. Art thou a king? But where is thy kingdom?
Beggar. Sir, the Kingdom of Heaven is within me, in my soul; and I can now and do, by His power in me, so govern and command all my inward and outward senses, that all the affections and powers of the old man in my soul are conquered, and are in subjection to the new man in me; which kingdom no man can doubt but it is better than all the kingdoms, sceptres, crowns, and glories of this world.
Divine. What brought thee to this perfection?
Beggar. My silence, sublime meditation, and, above all, my union with the ever-blessed God of peace and rest which is my kingdom. And, to say the truth, I could rest in nothing which was less than God; and now, having found my God, I have forsaken the unquiet world, and in Him I have found Everlasting Peace and Rest.

Bellers adds something on the two words " silence " and " resignation."

"The silence of a religious and spiritual worship," he says, " is not a drowsy, unthinking state of the mind, but a sequestering or withdrawing of it from all visible objects and vain imaginations unto a fervent praying to or praising the invisible, omnipresent God, in His light and love: His light gives wisdom and knowledge and His love gives power and strength to run the ways of His commandments with delight. But, except all excesses of the body and passions of the mind are avoided, through watchfulness, the soul doth not attain true silence."

Resignation he regards as an essential part of true religion, there being in heaven no will but God's. " True resignation preserves men from all evil, when they come to prefer His will before their own." He closes with a beautiful prayer :

... Do Thou enable us, O Lord, to prostrate ourselves in deep humility before Thee, with our wills subjected and resigned unto Thy holy will in all things. ... Make us, O Lord, what is right in Thy sight, suitable to the beings which Thou hast made us and the stations which Thou hast placed us in, that our tables nor nothing that we enjoy may become a snare unto us; but that the use and strength of all that we receive from Thy bountiful hand may be returned unto Thee. ...

To a man of this spirit the condition of the people made a loud appeal. It is generally agreed that manual workers fared ill in the second half of the seventeenth century. The rise in wages did not keep pace with the rise in the prices of necessaries. Much of the social legislation was oppressive in effect if not in intention. An Act of 1662 allowed a parish, which was the unit of poor relief, to remove any stranger back to his own parish, within forty days of his arrival, unless he could give security that he would not become chargeable.[1] Thus began a new era of serfdom for the agricultural labourer. Eight years later the killing of game was forbidden except by wealthy freeholders and leaseholders.[2] In 1677 the Statute of Frauds, not inaptly named, reduced all interests in land, except short leases, to tenancies at will unless evidenced in writing.[3] Moreover, enclosures and improvements were continually restricting the user of woods, marshes, heaths, and commons. Then came the seven lean years (1693–99) which with foreign war forced down the purchasing power of wages to an extraordinarily low point. The rising poor-rates, which naturally resulted, led to much discussion of the subject and especially to schemes for improved workhouses. Bellers, in the famous " Proposals for raising A Colledge of Industry," which he

---

[1] St. 13 & 14 Car. II. cap. 12. Friends gave this security for their poor, where necessary. See Yorkshire Q.M., Dec. 1667, York M.M., 2nd April 1674.
[2] St. 22 & 23 Car. II. cap. 25.
[3] St. 29 Car. II. cap. 3, "An Act for Prevention of Frauds and Perjuries," commonly called "the Statute of Frauds."

published in 1695,[1] approached the matter from a radical point of view. · The excellent statistician Gregory King had argued that nearly half the nation actually diminished the wealth of the community because its expenditure was greater than its income, and the difference had to be made up by the poor-rates, a conclusion that would only be valid if the wages earned by the labourer were a full remuneration for his work. Bellers held, on the other hand, that it was " Industry brings plenty ":

> I believe the present idle hands of the poor of this nation are able to raise provision and manufactures that would bring England as much treasure as the mines do Spain, . . . [whenever sending such treasure abroad] can be thought the nation's interest more than breeding up people with it among ourselves, which I think would be the greatest improvement of the lands of England that can be—it being the multitude of people that makes land in Europe more valuable than land in America, or in Holland than Ireland, regular people, of all visible creatures, being the life and perfection of treasure, the strength of nations and glory of princes.[2]

In other words, the end of wealth was the making of life; and so, in opposition to the settlement-laws, he says :

> I think it the interest of the rich to encourage the honest labourers marrying at full age; but, by the want of it, it seems to me the world is out of frame, and not understanding its own interest, the labour of the poor being the mines of the rich.[3]

He proposed the foundation, by voluntary subscription, of a college of say three hundred persons, of all sorts of useful trades, who would work for one another, without other relief. He calculated that the labour of 200 would find the rents and necessaries for all, and that the other 100 would make £1000 profit a year for the Founders. Preferably, £18,000 should be raised, which would buy the land and provide £8000 for stock, plant, and rebuilding. The objection that he should have given the poor all the profit brings out a satirical plea for the classes who did no manual work :

[1] Republished in 1696 with enlargements. I quote from reprint of the 2nd edn. in 1916 (Headley Bros.) of the *Proposals*.
[2] *Proposals*, p. 22. Not in first edn.   [3] p. 8.

The rich have no other way of living but by the labour of others, as the landlord by the labour of his tenants, and the merchants and tradesmen by the labour of the mechanics, except they turn levellers and set the rich to work with the poor.[1]

He therefore confines his design to a profitable employment for the capital of the rich in a useful way to the country, but so that the maintenance of the workers shall be a first charge on it :

. . . a comfortable living in the college to the industrious labourer being the rich man's debt and not their charity to them ; labour giving the labourer as good a right to a living there as the rich men's estates do them.[2]

The scheme is one for a mixture of industries and agriculture, all the mechanics helping at harvest-time.[3] With a due variety of trades, the community would eliminate middlemen and be self-sufficing, with little need of money :

This college-fellowship will make labour and not money the standard to value all necessaries by ; and though money hath its conveniences, in the common way of living, it being a pledge among men for want of credit, yet not without its mischiefs, and called by our Saviour the mammon of unrighteousness. Most cheats and robberies would go but slowly on, if it were not for money. And, when people have their whole dependence of trading by money, if that fails or is corrupted [as in the currency crisis which had recently taken place] they are next door to ruin : and the poor stand still, because the rich have no money to employ them, though they have the same land and hands to provide victuals and clothes as ever they had ; which is the true riches of a nation and not the money in it, except we may reckon beads and pin-dust so, because we may have gold at Guinea for them. "Money," he says, with a final thrust at the prevalent mercantile theory, "is what a crutch is to the natural body crippled ; but when the body is sound the crutch is but troublesome. So, when the particular interest is made a public interest, in such a college money will be of little use there."[4]

Bellers contemplates a regulated work-colony, and accordingly plans an institution, with four wards for young men and boys, for married persons, for young women and girls, and for sick and lame, the men and women having

---

[1] p. 24.   [2] p. 24.   [3] p. 12.   [4] pp. 8, 9.

distinct work-rooms, as far as possible.¹ The children would have an English education, with manual training from four or five years old, and careful moral supervision throughout. Those of pregnant understanding it may be worth encouraging to the furthest degree, but for most "it's labour sustains, maintains, and upholds, though learning gives a useful varnish." "There may be a library of books, a physic-garden for understanding of herbs, and a laboratory for preparing of medicines." "The hand employed brings profit, the reason used in it makes wise, and the will subdued makes them good."² Young men should be apprenticed in the institution till 24, and young women till 21 or marriage.³ The older people must keep the rules, the restraints of which will not be more, if so much, as the best-governed 'prentices are under in London.⁴ The elder men are to do less work, and, if suitable, to be made overseers.⁵ By a curious lapse from wisdom, Bellers proposes to allow Founders to keep a nominee at the College, either without working, or only doing partial work, though he may be expelled "in case of exorbitancy."⁶ He seeks to justify the institutional character of his proposals as follows :

The variety of tempers, and the idle expectations of some of the first workmen, may make the undertaking difficult, and therefore the more excellent will be the accomplishment : and, if the poor at first prove brittle, let the rich keep patience, seven or fourteen years may bring up young ones that life will be more natural to. And, if the attaining such a method would be a blessing to the people, certainly it's worth more than a little labour to accomplish it. When by the good rules thereof may be removed in great measure the profaneness of swearing, drunkenness, &c., with the idleness and penury of many in the nation, which evil qualities of the poor are an objection with some against this undertaking, though with others a great reason for it. For the worse they are, the more need of endeavouring to mend them, and why not by this method, till a better is offered ?⁷

He further points out that such a college will be attractive to many because of the great abatement of worldly cares to its inmates.⁸

¹ p. 18.   ² pp. 18-21.   ³ p. 18.   ⁴ p. 26.
⁵ p. 17.   ⁶ p. 15.   ⁷ p. 9.   ⁸ p. 17.

On the side of management the scheme was defective. Bellers, like others of his age, shows little perception of the unusual combination of qualities needed for the control of a great business. He seems to have supposed that efficient managers would be readily found, and lays down that neither the governors nor under-officers are to have any salary, but only all the reasonable conveniences the College can afford.[1] The final control is to be in the hands of the Founders, according to their shares, no one to have more than five votes.[2] There is no provision for self-government by the inmates.

In a second piece, four years later,[3] addressed like the former to Parliament, Bellers greatly enlarges the scale of his proposals, but limits their institutional character by wisely separating off the sick, crippled and disabled poor, who he thinks can best be kept at the public charge and so under the public care, and by confining his colleges to "such poor who are thrown into want by an idle education, or such as being supernumerary in the trade they were bred in, who are now accounted burdensome." He claims to demonstrate :

First, that in such collections of people there may be all conveniences for instruction and oversight, both in virtue and industry;
Secondly, they cannot there want work any time of the year, they having all the conveniencies of life to raise for themselves and their founders;
Thirdly, they cannot there want vent for what they raise more than they spend, because the founders will gladly receive it, it being all profit to them;
Fourthly, and, as a proportionable part of them are employed upon the land in husbandry, they will raise food sufficient for the whole society. . . .

Such colleges and colonies will be an excellent expedient to people the Northern Counties and the waste lands of the kingdom, and greatly increase the value of the lands of the nobility and gentry of England . . . and will prevent the loss of thousands of people that by going to London drop there, now, as untimely

---

[1] p. 17.   [2] p. 13.
[3] "Essays About the Poor, Manufactures, Trade, Plantations & Immorality, &c."

fruit—this city, being one-tenth of the people of England, it is too numerous in proportion to the rest of the kingdom ; for what it hath more than its proportion, they must live either by sharping or begging, or starve ; because the nation can maintain but a number of tradesmen and gentry, in proportion to the number of labourers that are in the nation to work for them.[1]

He reiterates his fundamental position that the increase of regular labouring people is the country's greatest treasure : " land, cattle, houses, goods and money are but the carcass of riches ; they are dead without people, men being the life and soul of them."[2] In a later piece he concludes that every man, regularly and usefully employed,

. . . adds £200 or more to the value of the kingdom, land without people being of no worth. And this treasure are the poor ; but the polishing of these rough diamonds, that their lustre and value may appear, is a subject worth the consideration and endeavour of our greatest statesmen and senators.[3]

Bellers revised his calculations,[4] but pushed his scheme to the close of his life.[5] As late as 1723 he addressed Parliament upon it,[6] estimating that the nation lost five millions sterling a year for want of a good method for employing the poor. His fertile brain supported his main theme with many shrewd observations on kindred matters. He sees that the caprice of fashions, by making seasonal industries, increases the necessitous poor,[7] and that dear bread will make dear manufactures and ruin trade, especially foreign trade ; " for whatever strangers can supply us withal cheaper than we can supply ourselves, to be sure they will much easier supplant us with

---

[1] "Essays About the Poor, &c.," pp. 4, 5.   [2] p. 7.
[3] "An Essay Towards the Improvement of Physick. . . . With an Essay for Imploying the Able Poor," 1714, p. 37. The second sentence is quoted with approval in Eden, *State of the Poor*, i. 264.
[4] In the "Essays about the Poor, &c.," he underestimated, according to his own data, that 500,000 would earn above two million a year beyond their keep, see pp. 5-7. In the "Essay Towards the Improvement of Physick, &c.," he raised this figure, including the saving in poor-rates, to above five million, pp. 40, 41.
[5] He urged the City of London to reform their workhouses on these lines, in an Address printed in "An Essay Towards the Improvement of Physick, &c.," pp. 29-34.
[6] "An Essay for Imploying the Poor to Profit," 1723.
[7] "Essays about the Poor, &c.," p. 9.

them manufactures in any foreign market."[1] He claims that the Plantations are a great strength to the mother-country.[2] He deprecates the import of luxuries,[3] and opposes all laws against shortening labour (that is, against labour-saving machinery or methods).

If encouragement were given by the legislature for any new discovery in the mechanics and husbandry, it would produce great effects, possibly to double the conveniencies they have with the same labour, and therefore to double the people that have them now. The suppressing of Saw-mills I account a great loss to the nation, by which many of the boards we use are sawed in foreign countries, and our building of houses and shipping are the more chargeable, to the poor as well as the rich. Laws against shortening of labour are as unreasonable as to make a law that every labouring man should tie one hand behind him, that two men might be employed in one body's work; which would be to make the rich poor by doubling their charge, and the poor miserable for the same reason, whilst they would earn less or must pay double what is usual for all their necessaries of life.[4]

He insists, however, that " to increase our manufactures, without increasing our husbandry, we shall come to short allowance, as they do at sea when they set five or six men to four men's mess, by placing more men to table, without putting any more food there."[5]

Through it all there runs a dislike of trade restrictions, a concern for the improvement of conditions by voluntary effort, and a passion of sympathy with the lot of the workers as contrasted with the ease of the rich. He makes out that the wealth of the country works out at about £40 a head, and everything beyond this imposes on the possessor an imperative duty of stewardship.[6] His " Essays about the Poor " begin with a strong address to the Lords and Commons, occasioned by the riotous petitions of the starving Spitalfields weavers in the winter of 1696–7 against the silk importation of the East India Company.

[1] "Essays About the Poor, &c.," p. 10.　　[2] *Ibid.* p. 14.
[3] *Ibid.* p. 11; cf. "Essay for Imploying the Poor to Profit," pp. 6, 7.
[4] "Essay for Imploying the Poor to Profit," p. 8.
[5] *Ibid.* p. 5; cf. "Essays about the Poor, &c.," p. 10.
[6] "Essays about the Poor, &c.," pp. 14, 15.

It was lamentable and frightful to behold the tumult of weavers that in a late sessions attended your doors; and when the scarcity of corn hath pinched the poor how fearless have they appeared to plunder against all law in many parts of this kingdom. Now, if the needy of but one trade of a city shall through penury dare to brave you that are as the vitals to move and heads to govern the nation and that have the strength of it to support you, how much more dismal would it be to have a poor starved crowd attack single gentlemen at their own home, and what advantage may restless spirits take to disturb the public peace with such opportunities? Foreign wars wastes our treasure, but tumults at home are a convulsion upon our nerves, and . . . if provision fail, what can awe the misery of starving?[1]

And, again, writing to London Friends, he says, with his beautiful tenderness of heart:[2]

How many distressed souls and helpless orphans lie in our streets as the dry bones in the valley wanting to be gathered together by others' assistance before they can be united. And they must be united before sinews and flesh will come and skin cover them; and then may their own labour make them happy in this world; and good instructions, through the blessing of God, may prepare them for the happiness of the next. The children called "The Black-Guard"[3] are a considerable part of these dry bones: they are our neighbours, our flesh and blood, our relations, our children, however mean and contemptible they may now appear. They are capable of being saints on earth, and as angels in heaven. How much is owing to birth and education that hath made the difference between them and us? Was it our virtue or their vice that made that difference? Had we any capacity before we were born? Hath not God made the difference, and given us the opportunity, if we use it well, to be able to give rather than receive, and put us into a capacity of receiving the blessing of feeding the hungry and clothing the naked? But what an aggravation will it be to any man's account, when he shall be charged with being an unfaithful steward with such a trust? Is not this a little sister that hath no breast? What shall we do for our sister in the day when she shall be spoken for? If she be a wall, may we not build upon her a palace of silver—by their own industry, if we put them in

---

[1] "Essays About the Poor, &c.," A2. For the petitions and riots, see Luttrell's *Brief Relation*, vol. iv., entries from 24th Nov. 1696 to 23rd March 1697, when the Bill restraining the trade was lost.
[2] "Epistle to the Q.M. of London and Middlesex," 1718, pp. 7-9.
[3] The "city Arabs" of the day; see *Oxford English Dictionary*. Cf. "An Essay Towards the Improvement of Physick, &c.," p. 30.

the way of it? The labour of the poor being the mines of the rich. And, when a good education may have made them of the nature of the good ground, and any of them come to be seamen or travel, they will be as so many missionaries or ministers; and though not in a ministry, yet their regular lives will greatly strengthen the testimony of such as shall have a ministry, whilst the profane and vicious lives of our present seamen, &c., is one of the greatest scandals and strongest obstacles to the Indians' conversion.

Should we not therefore endeavour to reform our people at home? . . . Our people . . . hurried with their vicious inclinations and passions, and many distressed with necessities through a mean birth and vicious education. . . . It is not he that dwells nearest that is only our neighbour, but he that wants our help also claims that name and our love.

Such words are instinct with the spirit of Lord Shaftesbury and Dr. Barnardo, of Peter Bedford and Elizabeth Fry.

Bellers' first proposals contained an appeal to Friends, as a well-organized body, with the requisite readiness and ability for such an undertaking.[1] In 1697 the Yearly Meeting appointed a Committee of eight to examine the scheme. They recommended its reference to the Monthly and Quarterly Meetings, and this was done in a letter dated 2nd July.[2] An Epistle from Bellers was printed with a postscript signed by forty-five leading Friends, Penn, Marshall, and Leonard Fell at their head, advising that it would be of use "if one house, or college, for a beginning, were set on foot, with a joint-stock, by the Friends of estates through the nation." Cornwall looked on the design as reasonable and charitable, but distance would prevent them from doing much. The London City Meeting desired its encouragement and it was approved by Gloucestershire.[3] The Meeting for Sufferings examined the legal difficulties, and prepared a Bill

---

[1] Omitted from 2nd edn., 1696. The proposals had been before the Morning Meeting in 1695 (see Minutes of 2nd July, 26th Aug., and 2nd Sept. 1695) when they were "left to him to do with as he sees meet"; and on 21st Oct. they were referred to the Meeting for Sufferings for consideration. Cf. C. R. Simpson in *J.F.H.S.* xii. 165, 166.

[2] *Ibid.* pp. 166-168, with letter to counties *in extenso*.

[3] *Ibid.* p. 168. In several Q.M.'s the letter helped the setting-up of Quaker day-schools.

enabling Friends to employ their own poor, which failed to pass. After other fruitless efforts for legislative sanction, opinions of Counsel were at last obtained in June 1701, which satisfied Friends that they could embark on a scheme without an Act if it was restricted to their own poor.[1]

On these lines, Bristol Friends had already established a Workhouse in 1696.[2] There was great distress in the city, and the Meeting agreed "to set the poor to work in the weaving trade," raising a stock of £420 for the purpose. In the following year a large building was erected as a house "for the willing Friends to work in and the aged and feeble to live in." Boys were afterwards admitted, who received school instruction and were taught the weaving trade. This trade was carried on till about 1721, chiefly in the sort of woollen stuffs, called "cantaloons." Orders for these goods from various places are extant, usually with patterns attached.[3] For some time the scheme answered and the stock was reported as "whole, with some advantage," but afterwards loss ensued and the place became an asylum for aged and infirm Friends.[4]

London Friends raised money for their project in 1701, and took over a Workhouse at Clerkenwell that had been erected for certain London parishes in 1663, and after the plan had failed, had been converted by Sir Thomas Rowe into a "College" for the Protestant education of poor infants. On his death the children had been removed to Hornsey, and the "College" became available for the new experiment.[5] Thirty inmates were found at

[1] *J.F.H.S.* pp. 168-170. Bellers, see "Proposals" and "Essays about the Poor, &c.," was fully alive to the difficulty, and urged Parliament to incorporate any persons that would raise a stock for employing the poor. Parliament about this time passed an Act for Bristol, and afterwards for Exeter and a number of other towns, see Eden, *State of the Poor*, i. 253, and a Company called the Royal Fishery Company designed to have workhouses for employing the poor in the making of nets, see Luttrell's *Brief Relation*, iv. 466 (29th Dec. 1698). The city workhouse at Bristol in 1697, due to the exertions of John Carey, economized the rates by being used as a test of destitution, and its example was followed in other towns.

[2] Tanner, *Three Lectures*, pp. 86-87; and Barclay, *Inner Life*, pp. 324, 325.
[3] In Dev. Ho. Dix. Colln.
[4] The premises are now used by Friends for Mission and Adult School work.
[5] See W. J. Hardy, *Middlesex County Records*, Sessions Books, 1689-1709, preface, pp. ix, x and references.

once, and children were introduced a year or two later.[1] Work was done by the able poor, and the Monthly Meetings made certain payments on a scale considerably less than if the poor had been looked after at home. Southwark, for example, understood that thirty infirm persons in the workhouse would cost them £130 a year, against £300 in their own homes, not reckoning expenditure for coal and rent.[2] For many years the place succeeded, amid much petty internal friction, and finally became on its educational side the parent of the Islington Road School, from which the present Friends' Boarding School at Saffron Walden derives descent. One chief source of trouble lay in the adoption of Bellers' proposal that pensioners should be admitted.[3]

In 1686 Bellers had married Frances, the daughter of Giles Fettiplace, a Gloucestershire Friend belonging to one of the county families, who had his seat at Coln St. Aldwyn,[4] and used to drive in to Cirencester meeting in a coach and six.[5] Thither Bellers removed about 1701, and mooted his proposal for a workhouse to the Gloucestershire Quarterly Meeting.[6] The project fell through; had it been proceeded with, we might have had a scheme which combined manual trades with agriculture and would have given his ideas a fairer trial than was possible in London or Bristol.

As it was, the full proposals were never tested and lay dormant for a hundred years. Then came a curious repetition of the circumstances which caused the reprinting of "Watch unto Prayer." The radical reformer, Francis Place (1771–1854), chanced upon them as he was rearranging his library, and took them with glee to his friend Robert Owen, saying, " I have made a great discovery, of a work advocating your social views a century

---

[1] The best account of the Workhouse is in Beck and Ball, *London Friends' Meetings*, pp. 361-380.
[2] 6th Nov. 1706, cited from Dr. Auguste Jorns, *op. cit.* p. 44; cf. Beck and Ball, *op. cit.* p. 365.
[3] In leaving £100 to the Workhouse, Bellers gave two of his daughters the power of nominating a child.
[4] *J.F.H.S.* xii. 123. , [5] Article in (London) *Friend*, Jan. 1861, cited above.
[6] *J.F.H.S.* xii. 125.

and a half ago." Owen (1771–1858) thereupon circulated, in 1818, 1000 copies of the piece.[1] The proposals were in line with his own communistic experiment at New Harmony, which, though unsuccessful, prepared the way for many of the more scientific efforts of our own day after a municipalized Socialism not segregated but in touch with the whole organism of society.

It is to Marx, and after him to Eduard Bernstein and other German social students, that Bellers owes the enduring recognition he has now won as a great social pioneer, a recognition based not only on the "Proposals" but on the trenchant criticism of the social order found in his other writings.

To these we may now turn. They show the breadth of his interests and his unbounded faith in the renovation of the world by the bold and public-spirited application of sanctified reason. We take first his further writings on social questions at home. He published in 1714 a far-sighted scheme for the care of the sick and the improvement of medicine.[2] There should be hospitals in London for the poor, preferably for each class of disease, with registration of each patient and a record of the case; one certainly for the blind, and another for incurables at which hitherto unknown cures might be tried; a public laboratory for the preparation of drugs and a physical observatory for research purposes; hospitals at each university, parish doctors paid by the overseers, examination and publication of new medicines, commissions of inquiry after medicines to the East and West Indies, a Queen's hospital specially concerned with maladies to which the sovereign was subject, advice to practitioners from time to time from the College of Physicians and Company of Chirurgeons, a Royal Society for the promotion of medicine, and regular reports to Parliament from the College of Physicians. The proposals involved a large State endowment of medicine and were supported

[1] *Life* of Robert Owen, by himself (1857), i. 240, cited in *J.F.H.S.* xi. 93. Also printed by Owen in his *New Vision of Society*, 1835.
[2] "An Essay Towards the Improvement of Physick, In Twelve Proposals, &c.," 1714.

by the sage and pithy comments of which Bellers was master.

The sending of ambassadors abroad in time of peace, or spies in time of war, or the supporting of any foreign trade, are not more necessary, nor of greater advantage to a prince or State than it is for them to procure all the knowledge of the art of healing that the universe can possibly supply them withal. . . . When a disease comes with a summons to the grave, a white staff or a star and garter are made of no value. It is too great a burden to be left upon the shoulders or to the care of the physicians alone . . . the State should bear a good part of the expense of it.[1]

Another matter that stirred his heart was the state of the criminal law.[2] It seemed to him a mockery to pray, "Forgive us our trespasses as we forgive them which trespass against us," and then prosecute a man to death for the loss of a possible twenty shillings. The life of a man was of greater value with God than many pounds; and it was a great defect in the Law to make no difference between the punishment of theft and of murder. Transportation or imprisonment with proper employment might turn felons into honest folk of use to the State. He also wrote a letter to Friends (his last piece) urging them to visit gaols, that some of those dry bones might be raised to life; and suggested that the Yearly Meeting each year should treat the poor prisoners in London "with a dinner of baked legs and shins of beef and ox-cheeks, which is a rich and yet cheap dish, with which they may be treated plentifully for 4d. a head or less," and should help them to suitable work in prison, and hang up broadsheets of good advice.[3] We think of Peter Bedford a century later and his queer friendships with thieves. In a letter to his friend and physician, Sir Hans Sloane, in August 1724, Bellers alludes to his plan, and records with gusto that on the marriage of his man and chambermaid he had enter-

---

[1] "An Essay Towards the Improvement of Physick, &c.," 1714, pp. 3, 4.
[2] "Some reasons against puting of Fellons to death," in "Essays About the Poor, &c.," pp. 17-19.
[3] "An Epistle . . . concerning the Prisoners, &c.," 1724. He printed a broadside "To the Criminals in Prison," in about twenty paragraphs of exhortation arranged in two columns.

tained fifty-eight of his poorer neighbours with baked beef, " much [to] their satisfaction, and but about 3d. [a] head cost."[1]

Public affairs also claimed his courageous thought, especially during the time of embittered politics at the end of Anne's reign, when the distractions of Low and High Church and of Whig and Tory seemed to portend civil war. He urged the Convocation of Canterbury to call a convention of all religious persuasions " not to quarrel about what they differ in, but to find wherein they agree, in order to settle an amicable society among all parties . . . though they may differ in religious forms."[2] He addressed statesmen on the need for abating party strife:[3]

Extremes are never good; neither do they hold long; one side must fall without some condescension. All extremes have a medium, and virtue lies there. Can there be a greater obligation upon any body of men in the world, than there is upon our nobility, gentry and clergy, to seek after and find out such a medium as will prevent any such direful effects among us? Have not they the estates, the offices and the benefices of the kingdom? Can they have more or can the rest of the people have less? . . . As dominion and territory hath been the dispute among the Powers of Europe, so profit and honour is the difference between the Old and New Ministry.

He sought to purify and improve the method of Parliamentary elections.[4] He would disfranchise any new seller of liquor and impose a fivefold penalty on a voter receiving a bribe; but his chief remedy lay in the registration of freeholders, in substitution for the practice of the voter swearing that he was qualified, a reform that would allow any county Poll to be subject to scrutiny.

Bellers, it will be noted, is no mere visionary: his ideas are turned into plans, drawn to scale. Several of them have been realized since his day; others are only now

[1] Cited from *Dict. Natl. Biography*, and *J.F.H.S.* xii. 127 (original in Brit. Mus., Sloane MSS. 4047, fol. 208).
[2] "To the Archbishop, &c." (1712).
[3] "Some Considerations As an Essay towards Reconciling the Old and New Ministry" (1712).
[4] "An Essay towards the Ease of Elections" (1712).

winning a public support adequate to give them effect. This is especially the case with two of his widest aspirations—one for a world-wide basis of Christian unity, the other for the federation of Europe.[1] These proposals were put forward together in 1710 under the influence of those made by Henry IV. of France and by William Penn.

Henry IVth's "Great Design" of 1603 [2] was to bring about a re-settlement of the Continent by reducing the possessions of the House of Austria, and to place all States under a "General Council of Europe," on which the ten principal would have four commissioners apiece and the others two. Bellers notes that he excluded the Muscovites and Ottomans, which he took to be out of "compliment to the see of Rome."[3] This he thought a serious blemish, for the Muscovites were Christians, and the Mohammedans men possessed of reason, "but to beat their brains out to put sense into them is a great mistake, and should leave Europe too much in a state of war."

Penn, in 1693, during his retirement from public life, wrote anonymously his "Essay towards the Present and Future Peace of Europe,"[4] based on his conviction that the means of peace is to be found in justice rather than war, which men wage not for the sake of peace but that they may have their own will. All government amounts in practice to a surrender by the individual of a part of his freedom in return for security given to him freely to exercise the remainder. "He is not now his own judge nor avenger, neither is his antagonist, but the Law, in indifferent hands, between both." In the same way, the sovereign Princes of Europe, including the Muscovite and the Turk, should agree to meet by stated deputies in a General Diet, and there establish international rules of justice, afterwards meeting at intervals to adjust all differ-

---

[1] "Some Reasons for an European State, &c.," 1710.
[2] Sully's *Mémoires* (1822 edn.), vi. pp. 129, &c., reprinted in W. Evans Darby, *International Tribunals*, 3rd edn. pp. 10-15.
[3] "Some Reasons, &c.," *ad fin.*
[4] *Works*, 1726 edn. ii. 838-848, reprinted by John Bellows, Gloucester, 1914, with Foreword by J. B. Braithwaite.

ences that could not be made up by diplomacy. If any constituent sovereignty refused to submit its claims or abide by the judgment of the Court, the others, united in one strength, should compel submission. It will be seen how definite are Penn's views. He constitutes his High Court, its first duty is to codify International Law: it is afterwards to apply the code to differences as they arise: its sanction is to be the united force of the Powers. Some period, he thinks, should be agreed upon beyond which no title to territory could be disputed. The representation in the High Court should be on a basis of wealth; the office of president circulating, the room round, with divers doors for entrance and exit to avoid quarrels for precedency, the voting by ballot and a three-fourths majority, the language Latin or French. Sovereigns, it may be objected, will not brook this interference with their authority. But the only restraints will be that the great fish can no longer eat up the little, and that each will be equally defended from injuries and disabled from committing them. Alas, for Penn's sanguine hopes; autocracies do not readily renounce their pike-like habits.

Bellers proposed that the Powers then in alliance against France should at once take the matter in hand, extending it to neutrals and enemies at the next general peace. The object should be to settle

... an universal guarantee and an annual congress, senate, diet or Parliament by all the Princes and States of Europe, as well enemies as neutrals, joined as one State, with a renouncing of all claims upon each other, with such other articles of agreement as may be needful for a standing European Law, the more amicably to debate and the better to explain any obscure articles in the Peace and to prevent any disputes that might otherwise raise a new war in this age or in the ages to come.

He had an ingenious scheme by which Europe would be treated as divided into a hundred equal cantons, for each of which its sovereign Prince or State would have one member in the Senate and would raise a thousand men for enforcing its decrees. The Senate so constituted would go by arguments and not by scimitars, reason ruling because the majority would not be interested in the matter in dispute. Europe being thus considered as one government, there should be a strict limitation of each State's military and naval armaments :

... "for without it," as he wisely said, "the Peace may be little better than a truce, if than a cessation of arms; for, besides the hazards of sudden surprises, the multitude of troops that every State will keep up . . . will leave them the third year of the peace . . . under little less expense than they were at the first year of the war, considering the charges . . . added to the interest . . . for the vast debts this war will leave them in. . . . The unlimited will of monarchs to invade their neighbours is no more a privilege for them than it would be for their subjects to have liberty to destroy each other, which is to reduce the earth to a desert."

He is aware that War is often followed by civil strife at home, which, in his day, seemed most likely to arise on religious grounds, and accordingly supplements his main proposals by a broad-minded plea for full toleration. " Truth is strongest and will prevail, let it be fairly heard, for a falsehood can never be proved to be true. . . . There is no need of a rack to force a mathematical demonstration, nor to make a mechanic a good workman." He proposes a new sort of General Council of all the several Christian persuasions in Europe. It should first take account of the things in which all agree. The eternal articles of loving God and their neighbours will be two of these things, which alone would put an end to all wars and bloodshed for religion. Then they should state their differences in words which do not bear ambiguous meanings, and the differences would soon be found less than they seem. He closes with his own simple basis of unity : belief in a God that made and preserves all beings, Who is a Spirit omnipresent and filling all places, and is to be worshipped with an humble, sincere and clean heart : belief in Jesus as the Messiah, sent by God as Saviour : belief in the duty of virtuous living according to the will of God, and in the duty of men doing good to one another as they would have others do to them. In a later piece,[1] he

[1] "Essay Towards the Improvement of Physick, &c." (1714), p. 47.

criticizes the *Projet de Paix perpétuelle* of the Abbé de Saint Pierre, which first appeared in 1713,[1] as defective for making no suggestion of this kind.

Viewing these proposals in the lurid light of war-stricken Europe to-day we feel that both Penn and Bellers saw the great problem too exclusively as one of statics rather than of dynamics, accepting the existing frameworks of the European States as fixed for all time, and too little regarding the fresh life, springing from the peoples themselves, which would mould new nations and dethrone outworn tyrannies. They accordingly failed to anticipate the basis for peace laid down in Immanuel Kant's immortal Essay (1795)[2] that the States themselves must be democratic in their constitution. Bellers, however, reaches perhaps a still more fundamental basis in his vision of a catholic spiritual unity for Christians, still, alas, unachieved, binding them together, amid much healthy diversity of forms, in common spiritual worship and common offices of goodwill to all men.

The reader may be disposed to belittle Bellers' faith in sanctified reason and in his fellow-man. He may not agree with the *dictum* of Sir Arthur Helps:[3]

The first of all things in a great cause is to reason it out well. When it is securely reasoned, it is gained. There remains much to be done by the head and by the hand, with the tongue and with the pen; and there may be many partial issues of success and defeat, but superior intelligences, if such regard mortal affairs, would know that the work was, spiritually speaking, done.

Nor may he think of mankind, after the Quaker fashion, as impregnated with the seed of a Divine life. Bellers knew well enough that he was speaking to a stubborn age, not perhaps prepared as former centuries had been to count Fust a conjurer for inventing printing, or Galileo a heretic for his conviction of the earth's motion, but ready to banter any novelty instead of examining it.[4] Yet the prophet-fire burned within him and he could not be silent.

---

[1] Printed in Darby, *International Tribunals*, pp. 20-46.
[2] *Ibid.* pp. 84-89, and in full in English edn. of Kant's *Zum ewigen Frieden*.
[3] *Friends in Council*, First Series, 1872 edn. ii. 96.
[4] From "Essay Towards the Improvement of Physick, &c.," pp. 15, 16.

He that doth not write whilst he is alive can't speak when he is dead. And, if a man shall not be heard in the age and country he lives in, if what he writes is for the general good of mankind, he may be more minded in other countries or in succeeding generations.[1]

He must utter himself, even if it were left to the nineteenth century and to German writers to do justice to his thoughts. He must speak, because he knew the reality of converse with the Divine, and felt that "the inspirations of the Almighty are inexhaustible."[2] When the brave pioneer of enlightened philanthropy passed away, unnoticed and unhonoured, in 1725, England lost "one of the best men of his time."[3]

He was no mere theorist. . . . He forms not only chronologically but also in his ideas the boundary-stone between the communism of the seventeenth and the efforts for reform of the eighteenth centuries. . . . We find in him the most daring and clearest thoughts of the religious and social revolutionaries of the age.[4]

John Bellers was by far the greatest of the early Quaker social reformers, and it has been right to give prominence to his work, so that he may become known in his own land, but some reference must be added to other Quaker service in kindred fields.

Friends, naturally enough, opened their hearts and purses to cases of distress outside their own Society, the transportation to America of German Pietists,[5] the relief of French Protestant refugees after the Revocation of the Edict of Nantes,[6] the appeals for distressed Palatines and other suffering Protestants abroad,[7] collections on Fire-

---

[1] "Essay Towards the Improvement of Physick, &c.," p. 51. The story of Fust being arrested at Paris for printing his Bible by magic is now generally admitted to be fabulous, but in any case was an apt illustration of the temper of the time.
[2] *Ibid.* p. 54.   [3] Bernstein, *op. cit.* p. 697.   [4] *Ibid.* pp. 716, 717.
[5] See *J.F.H.S.* vii. 136-139, and references there given. Also Meeting for Sufferings Minutes, Dec. 1693, Jan. 1694. The Pietists originated in a movement begun at Frankfurt about 1670 by Philipp Jakob Spener, and had affinities with Quakerism.
[6] See Tanner, *Three Lectures*, p. 82, Bristol Two Weeks' Meeting Minute, 9th April 1688, and particulars in Bristol "Collection Lists," 1686-1793, *per* A. Neave Brayshaw.
[7] Tanner, *Three Lectures*, p. 83, and *J.F.H.S.* vii. 46. Bellers, in 1709, wrote a piece, not in Dev. Ho. Library, to the "Commissioners appointed to take care of the poor Palatines." There is a copy in the Rylands' Library, Manchester.

briefs,[1] and much miscellaneous charity. One seafaring Friend, Michael Yoakley, of Margate, founded almshouses for the poor at Drapers, under Quaker Trustees, who, in recent years, have purchased land at Aylesford, including the famous cromlech, overlooking the Medway valley, known as Kit's Coty House.[2]

Temperance claimed a good deal of attention. Excessive drinking was the subject of frequent action in the Monthly Meetings, the delinquent Friends being sometimes directed to condemn their miscarriage in the public-houses they had frequented.[3] Gin-drinking, which about 1724 infected the masses of the population and spread with the violence of an epidemic, was not yet the master-curse of English life.[4] But the Government, while prohibiting the importation of foreign spirits in 1689, had thrown open the home distilling trade, and the time was approaching when you could get drunk for a penny, dead-drunk for twopence, and have straw for nothing on which to sleep off your debauch. Fox had written an outspoken epistle on the subject in 1682, approved by many Friends engaged in the trade,[5] warning vintners and innkeepers never to let any have "any more . . . strong liquors than what is for their health and their good ; in that they may praise God for His good creatures, for every creature of God is good and ought to be received with thanksgiving." He instituted a meeting of

---

[1] These Briefs, or authorized collections for loss by fire, were constantly circulating, and open to great abuses. See *J.F.H.S.* iii. 106–112. William Stout, *Autobiography*, p. 47, speaks of the great charge of collecting, and forgeries were rife, see *Cal. State Papers, Dom.*, 1670, p. 472. They were not abolished till 1828. The method of Fire Insurance was just beginning, and Bellers seems to have been one of its founders. See Edward Baumer, *The Early Days of the Sun Fire Office*, 1910, p. 8. Friends collected large sums for their own members' losses by fire.

[2] Robert H. Marsh, in *J.F.H.S.* xiv. 146-156, with illustrations.

[3] *E.g.* Bristol "Book of Condemnations," *per* A. Neave Brayshaw (1668): "It is the expectation of Friends that the party concerned shall call to mind all the places and houses where he hath thus transgressed, and bring a list . . . to the end that a copy of this his testimony may be sent to each and every of those places where Truth by him hath been dishonoured, for the clearing thereof." At Bristol Two Weeks' Meeting, 6th April 1691, a Friend is advised "to go to the public-house where the offence was given and condemn himself before all that may be there present, which he seems [inclined] unto."

[4] Lecky, *Hist. of England in the Eighteenth Century*, 1913 edn. ii. 97-105.

[5] *Epistles*, No. 381.

Friends in the trade, and issued a broadsheet, which they stuck on the walls of their most public rooms. Two others, by John Kelsall of London, himself in the trade, and by George Whitehead, were used in the same way. These posters proved of great service in enabling them "to withstand all disorder in their houses and families, as people drinking to excess, singing, rioting and gaming, or keeping unreasonable hours, and other disorders and debaucheries," and the meeting was continued for many years.[1] It will be seen that conviction as to the evil of drink was only in an immature stage among Friends in the seventeenth century. The same may be said of another great question, that of negro slavery. Fox, indeed, when he visited Barbados in 1671, had advised Friends to deal mildly and gently with their negroes and to make them free after thirty years' servitude,[2] and urged the holding of family meetings with them,[3] while in 1688 the German Friends who had migrated to Pennsylvania[4] addressed the Yearly Meeting there against the buying and keeping of slaves. But it was reserved, as we know, for John Woolman fully to awaken the conscience of Friends on this matter.[5] Evils, which have struck their roots deep in the fabric of human society, are often accepted, even by the best minds, as part of the providential ordering of life. They lurk unsuspected in the system of things until men of keen vision and heroic heart drag them into the light, or until their insolent power visibly threatens human welfare.

It is here that the Quakers have made their greatest contribution to social reform. Seeking to live at all times in a Divine order of life, they have always counted social service part of Christianity. In fidelity to the genius of their inward experience, they have set themselves the task of developing their own spiritual

---

[1] For the foregoing, see Paper (1701) in Dev. Ho. Gibson MSS. iii. No. 191.
[2] *Camb. Journ.* ii. 195, in a letter of John Hull. The *Ellwood Journal*, ii. 149, softens this into "certain years of servitude." Cf. *Beginnings of Quakerism*, p. 495.
[3] *Epistles*, No. 293 (1673).
[4] See *Beginnings of Quakerism*, pp. 414, 415.
[5] For the whole subject see *Quakers in the American Colonies, passim*.

sensitiveness to the light of truth; and have then resolutely confronted the unawakened conscience of the world with the demands of the new light, and have borne witness to it with undaunted patience. This has resulted in progressive enlightenment for themselves, and in the slow but sure triumph of many of the causes of which they have become champions. The reform of the criminal law, the improvement of prisons, the suppression of the slave-trade and of the institution of slavery, the abolition of the opium traffic, the protection of native races, the repeal of the state regulation of vice, the emancipation of women, have all been powerfully helped to victory—however incomplete—by Quaker action on these lines, side by side with that of other noble-hearted reformers. Other great ills, patent or latent in our civilization, have yet to be overcome, perhaps have yet to be perceived; the old philanthropy has to deepen into something more vital if the full demands made by the teaching of Christ are to be obeyed;[1] but the faithful following of the Light that illumines the alert conscience still seems to many of us the truest way for securing this deeper experience and for recognizing and combating the evils that menace social and international life. The Church may thus discharge her redemptive duty towards mankind along lines in harmony with the mind and methods of the Great Redeemer.

[1] See Lucy F. Morland, Swarthmore Lecture, 1918, *The New Social Outlook.*

CHAPTER XXI

THE CHURCH AND THE STATE

Christians are not distinguished from the rest of mankind either in locality or in speech or in customs. For they dwell not somewhere in cities of their own, neither do they use some different language, nor practise an extraordinary kind of life. . . . But, while they dwell in cities of Greeks and barbarians as the lot of each is cast . . . yet the constitution of their own citizenship which they set forth is marvellous and confessedly contradicts expectation. . . . They find themselves in the flesh, and yet they live not after the flesh. Their existence is on earth, but their citizenship is in heaven. They obey the established laws, and they surpass the laws in their own lives. . . . In a word, what the soul is in a body, this the Christians are in the world. . . . The soul is enclosed in the body, and yet itself holdeth the body together; so Christians are kept in the world, as in a prison-house, and yet they themselves hold the world together. The soul though itself immortal dwelleth in a mortal tabernacle; so Christians sojourn amidst perishable things, while they look for the imperishability which is in the heavens. . . . So great is the office for which God hath appointed them, and which it is not lawful for them to decline.—THE EPISTLE TO DIOGNETUS.

THE Church catholic on earth consists, as I understand it, of all sincere disciples of Christ, together with the living Spirit of their Master. Its relation to the State-systems of which these disciples are also members affects profoundly both its own welfare and the welfare of the State. The Christian has his paramount duty as a servant of the Kingdom of God, and has also his position as a member of the State. The first binds him to the threefold aspiration of the Lord's prayer, the hallowing of the Divine nature, the advancing of the Kingdom, and the doing of the will of God. The second has also its rightful duties, which are as sacred in their place as those flowing from other forms of *status*, such as that of husband and wife or parent and child. A spiritual

CH. XXI   THE CHURCH AND THE STATE   599

Church, under the headship of Christ, cannot leave it to any outward authority to determine these duties ; it must itself seek to see, in the light of the Spirit, what are the provinces and functions of the Church and the State in the Divine order.

I propose to summarize the contributions made by early Friends to this great discussion, pointing out the changed conditions in which a spiritual Church finds itself in the democratic nations of to-day, and illustrating the adequacy of the early Quaker contribution by an examination of the testimony borne on the question of war. The inward Christ-life in which Quakerism was rooted was the source and strength of true witness on this as on all other questions, but its promptings were verified to the Church by the teaching of Jesus and the experience of the primitive disciples. Friends, during the period comprised in the present volume, developed not so much a theory of Church and State as an interpretation in practice of Christian citizenship. Their noblest contribution lay in the constancy and character of their protest against the invasion by the State of the conscience of the Christian, a witness already recorded in these pages. Its character is as notable as its constancy. When the law could not be obeyed, the Quaker suffered its consequences without evasion or resistance. He stood clear of all plots against the constituted authorities, and could be no party to revolution by violence.[1] In this way, Friends, as Masson says,[2] "by their peculiar method of open violation of the law and passive resistance only . . . rendered a service to the common cause of all the Nonconformist sects which has never been sufficiently acknowledged."

Beginning with the Toleration Act, the State at last found room for the Quakers and their way of life within its own system. It tolerated their worship, with that of other Nonconformists, and protected their meetings from disturbance : it tacitly allowed their marriages and burials; it accepted their Affirmation for many purposes instead of an oath. In other cases, as in tithes and military

[1] See *ante*, Chap. I. [2] Cited in full, *supra*, p. 21.

service, the claim of the State Church or of the State was accommodated to the policy of toleration by using the legal process of Distress, which forcibly took the goods of the Quaker, without compromising consent on his part.[1]

Side by side with this witness against the invasion of conscience, Quakerism developed an equally clear law-abiding conscience. It held that all true authority was from God; and, where rightly used, was derived from Him. "In all just and good commands of the King and the good laws of the land relating to our outward man," says Burrough,[2] "we must be obedient by doing." "Those who are Christ's subjects," writes Penington,[3] "are more faithful to men, and more subject to any just law of government than others can be, for their fidelity and subjection is out of love and for conscience' sake."

This position was frequently stated to the authorities. After the Rye House Plot, for example, the Petition presented by George Whitehead[4] declared "that God Almighty hath taught and engaged us to acknowledge and actually to obey magistracy, as His ordinance, in all things not repugnant to His Law and Light in our consciences."

While seeking to govern their own lives by a higher law, Friends, in accordance with Pauline teaching, thus accepted civil government as a Divine institution in its place and time; and, so far as I am aware, show no trace of anarchical opinions. In this matter they made the example of Christ their guide, especially His famous answer to the ensnaring question about the tribute-money (Mark xii. 13-17; Matt. xxii. 15-22; Luke xx. 19-26), "Render unto Caesar the things that are Caesar's, and unto God the things that are God's."

---

[1] There are references in *F.P.T.* 308, 314, to sufferings undergone by Richard Robinson, of Countersett, for failing to find a man for the militia, presumably under the Militia Act, 14 Car. II. cap. 3. Cf. Besse, ii. 109, 157. John Furly, the Colchester merchant, was distrained on in 1659 for not sending a horse and man for the militia (Besse, i. 194). For the special clauses in later Acts, especially 42 Geo. III. cap. 90, see Joseph Davis, *Digest*, 1849 edn., pp. 82-103. A substitute was provided, the expense being recovered by Distress.
[2] Cited *supra*, p. 17.
[3] Cited *supra*, p. 18.
[4] *Christian Progress*, p. 538.

THE CHURCH AND THE STATE

Penn paints, in vigorous language, our Lord's standpoint, as he conceives it:[1]

I am Caesar's friend: I seek none of these kingdoms from him; nor will I sow sedition, plot or conspire his ruin: no, let all men render unto Caesar the things that are Caesar's: that is My doctrine; for I am come to erect a kingdom of another nature than that of this world, to wit, a spiritual kingdom, to be set up in the heart; and conscience is My throne; upon that will I sit and rule the children of men in righteousness. . . . I never imposed My help, or forced any to receive Me; for I take not My kingdom by violence but by suffering.

The payment of taxes to the civil authority was explicitly covered by Christ's words. Fox, during the Commonwealth period,[2] had advised payment, and wrote as follows about one of the Poll Acts of Charles II.:[3]

To the earthly we give the earthly: that is, to Caesar we give unto him his things, and to God we give unto Him His things. And so in the other Power's days we did not forget on our parts, though they did fail on their's . . . Which, if Friends should not do and had not done—give Caesar his due, and custom and tribute to them that look for it, which are for the punishment of evil-doers—then might they say and plead against us; How can we defend you against foreign enemies and protect everyone in their estates and keep down thieves and murderers?

In 1697, in conversation with Peter the Great, Thomas Story said:[4]

Though we are prohibited arms and fighting in person, as inconsistent we think with the rules of the gospel of Christ, yet we can and do by His example readily and cheerfully pay unto every Government, in every form, where we happen to be subjects, such sums and assessments as are required of us by the respective laws under which we live. . . . We, by so great an example, do freely pay our taxes to Caesar, who of right hath the direction and application of them, to the various ends of government, to peace

---

[1] *Address to Protestants*, in *Works*, 1726 edn. i. 800, etc.
[2] Fox, *Epistles*, No. 177, cited *Beginnings of Quakerism*, p. 462.
[3] Swarthm. Colln. vii. No. 165. *The Swarthmoor Account Book* shows £1:2s. paid for George and Margaret Fox in 1678. For the Poll Acts, see note in *J.F.H.S.* xii. 111.
[4] *Life*, p. 124. A Morning Meeting Minute of 2nd July 1695 rebukes Elizabeth Redford for speaking against the Act for Duties on Marriages, &c. (6 & 7 W. & M. cap. 6). The Minute said that tribute was to be paid, without disputing or questioning the use to which the Government put it.

or to war, as it pleaseth him or as need may be, according to the constitution or laws of his kingdom, and in which we as subjects have no direction or share : for it is Caesar's part to rule in justice and in truth, but ours to be subject and mind our own business and not to meddle with his.

By this time the Quietist position, which pushed the division between the provinces of State and Church to an extreme, was already beginning to be taken by the Society of Friends in England, and a long series of Yearly Meeting utterances [1] enforces the duty of faithful subjection to the Government in all godliness, and of clearness from defrauding the King in his revenue.

In a third direction early Friends had taken a course of great value, however mingled at times with extravagance. Quakerism belongs to the prophetic and "charismatic" type of Christianity, by contrast with the priestly and institutional types.[2] It has consequently understood something of the "prophetic" function of the Church towards the State.

The living Church has a prophetic function—the duty of using its faculty of spiritual vision so as to penetrate below the surface of life to its inner meaning. Its insight should lay bare the issues of good and evil that underlie the conventional morality and the current conduct of the time. Its faith should give it the courage to judge these issues from the standpoint of righteousness, not by worldly policy, or the promptings of self-interest. The ideals of the Master are often regarded as impracticable in our unbrotherly world. But the Church is their natural guardian and has the mission of vindicating and realizing them.[3]

This "prophetic" function was zealously discharged during the first eager years of Quakerism. The emphatic form of testifying by signs and through the streets continued in the Restoration period, though on a reduced scale.[4] The Friend whose service most continuously took

---

[1] The MS. "Books of Extracts," under the head "Kings and Governors," contain extracts dated 1698, 1703, 1709, 1715, 1719, etc. A Query on the subject was adopted in 1723.
[2] Cf. *Beginnings of Quakerism*, pp. 523-529.
[3] My *Spiritual Guidance in Quaker Experience*, p. 103.
[4] See, *e.g.*, *Beginnings of Quakerism*, p. 372 ; and cases *ante*, p. 25 (Solomon Eccles, &c.) ; pp. 339, 340 (Barclay and Andrew Jaffray) ; p. 216 (Elizabeth Adams) ; p. 238 (John Browne). Abiah Darby, as late as 1766, proclaimed

this form was Thomas Rudd of Yorkshire, who in 1692 and subsequent years went through the towns of England, Scotland and Ireland with messages such as the following: "Woe from God, Woe from God, Oh, all be warned, Oh, to fear God." These words he cried through the streets of Bristol, with a loud and distinct voice, with great zeal and weight of spirit, lifting up his hands as he went. Thomas Story says: "He had a voice suited to the measure of his words, with an innocent boldness in his countenance, frequently lifting his right hand towards heaven as he passed along, which was with a slow and grave pace." He and Friends who accompanied him suffered many short imprisonments and much rude behaviour from the crowd; but a deep impression was often made.[1] Personal remonstrance, of the prophetic type, also in some degree continued, though its dangers were recognized; and we find the Yearly Meeting of Ministers in 1702[2] advising:

Against anyone's running headily in their own wills to disturb or interrupt any people in their worship. . . .

That none follow their own spirits and presume to prophesy therein against any nation, town, city, people or person.

The larger appeal to the conscience of the nation which we now feel may properly be made by the Church continued to be given by individuals, and, on the question of relief from violations of conscience, came from the Society as a whole. The utterances by individuals were sometimes nobly spoken on great subjects. I may instance Barclay's "Epistle of Love and Friendly Advice" addressed in 1678 to the Ambassadors of the Powers, who

---

repentance through the streets of Shrewsbury (*J.F.H.S.* x. 295). There were other interesting cases, especially those of Thomas Ibbott, of Hemingford, Hunts, in connection with the Fire of London (see *Camb. Journ.* ii. 90, and references in ii. 397), and of Margaret Brewster in Barbados in 1673 (Besse, *Sufferings*, ii. 319-322).

[1] A good many materials for an account of Rudd (1643-1719) exist. See papers in Dev. Ho. Box C; accounts of his Scottish experiences in Thomas Story's *Life*, pp. 54-76; "Ury Book of Record" in *J.F.H.S.* vii. 97, 98; Dublin account in Dev. Ho. Portf. 32, No. 113; Bristol account in Bristol Men's Meeting Minutes, 14th May 1694; Smith's *Catalogue of Friends' Books*, etc. He came from Wharfe, near Settle, and was by trade a miller. His severest treatment seems to have been at Liverpool, where he was whipped through the streets, and he also suffered at Chester.

[2] From a copy in Kendal Book of Half-Year's Meeting of Ministers.

negotiated the treaties known as the Peace of Nymegen, Penn's " Summons or Call to Christendom," written from Amsterdam, 20th October 1677, and Steven Crisp's " To the Rulers and Inhabitants in Holland." Almost all the writings of Friends addressed to the general public or to other professing Christians are written in something of the vein of the Hebrew prophets.

In these ways, alike by conscientious disobedience and obedience to the law, and by a bold witness which confronted the State with the ethics of Christianity, Quakerism took a definite relation to the world-order round it. The position taken requires, however, much re-verification and enlargement before it can be accepted as adequate by the Church to-day, under greatly altered conditions, and with our wider mental horizons. It was taken at a time, when, even after the Toleration Act, Friends in England were disabled from giving direct service to the State, and in the dawn of free institutions of government, as we understand them. We have responsibilities of public service and of membership in a self-governing democracy which did not come to Friends in the seventeenth and eighteenth centuries, and have to consider not only how the Christian should bear himself towards the State, but how he should behave as part of the State.

Quakers often voted at elections but they were excluded from public posts, for they could not take the oaths of office, since the Affirmation Acts did not extend to service on juries, nor to any place of profit in the Government. We are therefore almost without materials for judging how the Society in Great Britain would have acted if its members had been able to take their natural part in the affairs of the country.

In 1687, when a number of Friends in Dublin, Cork, and Limerick were made aldermen and burgesses, the Irish Half-Year's Meeting[1] advised them to humility and watchfulness on all occasions, considering how weightily the whole body of Friends was concerned in their behaviour in this unexpected exercise. They must be willing to

---

[1] Paper signed by John Burnyeat and John Watson, in Minutes of Nov. 1687.

take up the cross in keeping out of such words, customs, gestures, and garbs as were not agreeable to the simplicity of Truth. Fox wrote to Edmondson to the same effect:[1]

If they keep to Truth, they can neither take any oaths nor put any oaths to anyone; neither can they put on their gowns and strange kind of habits—as Friends have considered it here [in London] when they talk of putting them in such places, and, again, when they have the aldermen or mayor's or common-council feasts, Friends here cannot join them in such things, but, if they will make the poor a feast that cannot feast you again, Friends have proferred themselves to join with them; but to feast them that will feast you again, and to join with them in their strange kind of habits and formalities, is not like Truth, that denies the pomps and fashions of this world: but, in their places they should do justice to all men, and be a terror to them that do evil and a praise to them that do well; and preserve every man both in his natural rights and properties and in his Divine rights and liberty, according to the righteous law of God.

The difficulty in accepting public offices was evidently one of practice and not of principle. Accordingly, where a fair field offered, Friends felt little hesitation in taking their full share in the work of government. A number of the leading colonists of Rhode Island became Quakers, and they controlled the affairs of the colony for many years.[2] For seventy years Friends were in power in Pennsylvania. These chapters of Quaker experience in government are of high importance, alike in their record of success and of failure. The question of administering oaths caused Pennsylvanian Friends gradually to withdraw from judicial functions,[3] but it was only in 1756, in the face of adverse conditions felt to be intolerable from the standpoint of their testimony against war, that they adopted the policy of abdicating their political responsibilities.[4] The line of action thus taken belongs to a Quakerism differing widely in spirit from the virile years of eager expression which attended the first period of Penn's Holy Experiment.

[1] Rutty, *Hist. of Friends in Ireland*, p. 144.
[2] The authorities on this important American side of the subject are *Quakers in the American Colonies*, and two books by Isaac Sharpless, *A Quaker Experiment in Government* and *The Quakers in the Revolution*.
[3] See *ante*, p. 190.   [4] See *post*, p. 621.

In those early days, there was room in the Society of Friends, as is happily again the case to-day, for varied types of temperament and service, for Penington and Dewsbury and Crook, for Penn and Barclay, as well as for Fox, Crisp, and George Whitehead. Tradition and Church-authority had not yet pressed the Society into one mould. Quakerism had kept the Faith in the place of scorn and suffering, and ventured to challenge the world from the more perilous seat of power. It had pith and robustness to take the risks that belong to action ; and sought freedom to express itself. In the New World it believed that it could live out its Faith in every department of life ; and would have scorned to confess its principles unequal to the task.

A letter from Steven Crisp to Penn well describes the spiritual difficulties which attend government, and shows how heavenly wisdom lies behind true statesmanship and heavenly power behind true authority.

I have had a sense of the various spirits and intricate cares and multiplicity of affairs, and these of various kinds, which daily attend thee—enough to drink up thy spirit and tire thy soul—and which, if it be not kept to the inexhaustible fountain, may be dried up. And this I must tell thee, which also thou knowest, that the highest capacity of natural wit and parts will not and cannot perform what thou hast to do : viz. to propagate and advance the interest and profit of the government and plantations; and, at the same time, to give the interest of Truth and testimony of the Holy Name of God its due preference in all things : for to make the wilderness sing forth the praise of God is a skill beyond the wisdom of this world.

It is greatly in man's power to make a wilderness into fruitful fields, according to the common course of God's providence, who gives wisdom and strength to be industrious ; but then, how He, Who is the Creator, may have His due honour and service thereby, is only taught by His Spirit in them who singly wait upon Him.

There is a wisdom in government that hath respect to its own preservation, by setting up what is profitable to it and suppressing what may be a detriment, and this is the image of the true wisdom. But the substance [of wisdom in government] is the birth that is heavenly, which reigns in the Father's Kingdom till all is subdued, and then gives it up to Him Whose it is.

There is a power on earth that is of God, by which princes

decree justice : this is the image : and there is a power which is heavenly, in which the Prince of Peace, the Lord of Lords, doth reign in an everlasting Kingdom, and this is the substance. By this power is the spiritual wickedness in high places brought down; he that is the true delegate in this power can do great things for God's glory, and shall have his reward; and shall be a judge of the tribes; and whosoever else pretend to judgment will seek themselves; beware of them; the times are perilous.[1]

The growth of English freedom since the days of the Stuarts has altered the atmosphere, even from that prevailing in the democratic air of the American colonies. A type of national character has been formed, which is perhaps the greatest fruit of a climate of liberty. In his preface to Penn's *Life* by Clarkson,[2] William Edward Forster says suggestively :

Individual self-government, that alone is the [ultimate] cause of national freedom—the source and guarantee of the liberty of the subject—for that alone makes liberty compatible with social order; and of this power of self-control, the force whereof gauges the freedom of all governments, and without which all constitutions, yes, even the "glorious constitution of 1688," are mere waste-paper, of this power the highest possible ideal is a strong sense of religious duty.

To the creation and maintenance of this serious-minded spirit of self-control, which underlies democratic self-government, as developed in English-speaking communities, many influences have no doubt contributed; but not the least, I believe, has been the life in the nation of generation after generation of Friends, conscious of their individual responsibility and ordered by an inward law. A conception of public spirit has been slowly formed, which makes possible in many directions a service to the Kingdom of God through the service of the State, that could only be seldom given, and then very imperfectly, in the more self-willed climate of the seventeenth century. The growth of this spirit, moreover, has been accompanied by a diffusion of self-government

[1] Janney, *Life of Penn*, 6th edn. p. 258, original copy in Colchester Collection (*Steven Crisp and his Correspondents*, No. 24). The letter is dated London, 4th May 1684.
[2] Clarkson's *Life*, edn. 1849, p. lix.

which spreads sovereign power and political responsibility over the mass of the nation and implicates us all in public affairs at home and abroad. Any compartment-theory of the relation of Church and State, such as the early Friends held, has therefore only an *interim* value,; and now that the higher law of the Kingdom of God is beginning to shape much of the action and ideals of government, the political duties and problems of the Christian have to be faced in a new light—with full recognition of the fact that he is part of the State, contributing by his spirit and service the finest and in many ways the most essential elements to the great unity that we call the life of the nation. It was in this temper that the Balby letter had faced the question in the Commonwealth days.[1]

The foregoing summary will help us to understand the position taken by seventeenth-century Friends on the question of war, before the testimony was developed on its humanitarian side in the later philanthropic age of Quakerism. We shall find much faithful obedience to the commands of Christ and a living experience of His peaceable Spirit, notable both on its own account and as the foundation for a great historic witness. We shall expect the position to be expressed in terms which put the duty of Church and State further apart than we should do to-day. We shall look for intimations of the deep spiritual and social implications of the question, but shall not think to find these thoroughly explored in an age which was without our methods of historical and scientific criticism, and when the subject was not a living issue to Friends in England at all comparable with the general question of worldliness and with the issues raised by such matters as religious liberty and oaths and the claims of the State Church. We shall not suppose that all the early Friends saw alike on the question nor that any of them is likely to have uttered the last word. We shall be inspired by the vitality of their experience and the tenacity of their faithfulness ; but shall not

[1] *Beginnings of Quakerism*, p. 313.

suffer ourselves to be limited by the mind-mark of their age.

The first-hand spiritual experience of the Quaker Publishers of Truth had brought them seasons when they knew themselves, in the profound phrase of Fox, partakers of a "life and power that took away the occasion of all wars."[1] Its quintessence of expression is found in Nayler's dying sentences:[2] "There is a spirit which I feel that delights to do no evil nor to revenge any wrong, but delights to endure all things, in hope to enjoy its own in the end. . . . Its crown is meekness, its life is everlasting love unfeigned ; and [it] takes its kingdom with entreaty and not with contention, and keeps it by lowliness of mind." Whittier calls these words "solemn as eternity, and beautiful as the love which fills it."[3] In times when this heavenly order of life was known, as perhaps most often when retired into the cloistral calm of gathered worship, the Quaker, as Ruskin says of Fra Angelico,[4] lived in perpetual peace. Not seclusion from the world. No shutting out of the world was needful to him. There was nothing to shut out. Envy, lust, contention, discourtesy were to him as though they were not ; and the quiet meeting a possessed land of tender blessing, guarded from the entrance of all but holiest sorrow. To men who had known this uplifting from the spirit of the world into the Spirit of Christ, the use of carnal weapons either for His Kingdom or for worldly ends was unthinkable ; and we have seen how consistently Friends abhorred all plots and violence against a persecuting State. But all the more were they vowed to a nobler warfare, with weapons,

---

[1] *Beginnings of Quakerism*, p. 54 ; cf. p. 180.
[2] *Ibid.* p. 275. As there cited, from Nayler's *Works*, p. 696, the concluding words are omitted, which deserve to be supplied, from Robert Rich, *Hidden Things brought to Light*, pp. 21, 22. "Thou wast with me when I fled from the face of mine enemies ; then didst Thou warn me in the night : Thou carriedst me in Thy power into the hiding-place Thou hadst prepared for me ; there thou coveredst me with Thy Hand, that in time Thou mightst bring me forth a rock before all the world. When I was weak Thou stayedst me with Thy Hand, that in Thy time thou mightst present me to the world in Thy strength in which I stand, and cannot be moved. Praise the Lord, O my soul. Let this be written for those that come after. Praise the Lord. J. N."
[3] Article in (London) *Friend*, iv. 120 (1846).
[4] *Modern Painters*, pt. iv. chap. 6.

as Cyprian puts it,[1] that knew no defeat—the breastplate of unbreakable justice, the sword of the invulnerable Spirit. The higher life was dynamic with its own forces, calling its servants not to a passive and negative witness but to a spiritual crusade, in which its kingdom might prevail through the energy of righteousness and love and the strength of dedication to the cross.

It is true that neither in the first days nor at any period since was this high experience the habitual possession of more than a limited number of Friends. The Church rightly includes disciples in every stage of growth, united in their quest but not uniform in their attainment. Yet the Inward Light, as its guidance was obeyed, was continually bringing moments of insight, which revealed the beauty of this life and pointed it out as the ultimate order for the whole world. The problems arising from the existence of the world-order by the side of this higher kingdom began to claim attention. Penington, who inhabited its climate, dealt with the question in a treatise, published in 1661 and called after his tentative, educational manner, "Somewhat spoken to a Weighty Question concerning the Magistrates' Protection of the Innocent."[2] Magistracy, he says, was intended by God for the defence of the people, both those who can fight and those who cannot. Women and children, the sick and aged, and the priests have the benefit and protection of the law without fighting in its defence. The same protection should be given to those whom the Lord of Lords has redeemed out of the fighting nature. The time when nation shall not lift up sword against nation must begin with individuals, who are not thereby prejudicial to the world, but emblems of that blessed state that is to be set up. Their witness is in reality a great service to their country," for, if righteousness be the strength of a nation, and the Seed of God the support of the earth,[3] then, where righteousness is brought forth and where the

---

[1] *Epist.* 31, cap. 5.
[2] *Works*, 1681 edn. pt. i. pp. 320-324.
[3] Cf. quotation from *Epistle to Diognetus* at head of Chapter.

Seed of God springs up and flourisheth, that nation grows strong; and, instead of the arms and strength of man, the eternal strength overspreads that nation; and that wisdom springs up in the spirits of men which is better than weapons of war." But, it will be said: If all a nation were of this mind, and should be invaded, would it not be of necessity ruined? Penington answers that such a nation would wait on the Lord for preservation, and proceeds:

> I speak not this against any magistrates or peoples defending themselves against foreign invasions; or making use of the sword to suppress the violent and evil-doers within their borders—for this the present estate of things may and doth require, and a great blessing will attend the sword where it is borne uprightly to that end and its use will be honourable; and, while there is need of a sword, the Lord will not suffer that government or those governors to want fitting instruments under them for the managing thereof, who wait on Him in His fear to have the edge of it rightly directed—but yet there is a better state, which the Lord hath already brought some into, and which nations are to expect and travel towards. Yea, it is far better to know the Lord to be the Defender, and to wait on Him daily, and see the need of His strength, wisdom and preservation, than to be never so strong and skilful in weapons of war.

God's deliverances of Israel, he adds, suggest that He will preserve and defend the first nation whom He teaches to leave off war, so that they shall not be preyed upon while He is teaching others the same lesson.

Barclay approached the subject with a keener intellect and almost equal spiritual depth. He says [1] that the refusal to defend self is the hardest and most perfect part of Christianity, because it requires the most complete denial of self and the most entire confidence in God. He was thinking perhaps of his father, the gallant old soldier who calmly bore the indignities of the Aberdeen mob, and found more satisfaction in bearing insult for his faith than in his former entertainment by the magistrates of the town, when they had feasted him and attended him on his way in order to improve their favour with the laird

[1] *Apology*, prop. xv. sect. 15.

of Ury.[1] Christ, and His apostles, says Barclay, afford the most perfect example of patience, but the present magistrates of the Christian world, though professedly Christian, are far from any such perfection, not having come to the pure dispensation of the Gospel :

... and therefore, while they are in that condition, we shall not say that war, undertaken upon a just occasion, is altogether unlawful to them. For, even as circumcision and the other ceremonies were for a season permitted to the Jews ... because that spirit was not yet raised up in them whereby they could be delivered from such rudiments ; so the present confessors of the Christian name, who are yet in the mixture and not in the patient, suffering spirit, are not yet fitted for this form of Christianity and therefore cannot be undefending themselves, until they attain that perfection. But, for such whom Christ has brought hither, it is not lawful to defend themselves by arms, but they ought over all to trust to the Lord.[2]

Thomas Story, with his Pennsylvanian experience, put the same position in a still broader way, when talking to the Earl of Carlisle in 1718 :[3]

God, by Whom kings reign and princes decree justice, having ordained government and rule, entrusts it with whom He pleases ; and the temporal sword, as well of civil magistracy as military force, being in the hands of kings and rulers to exercise as need shall be, they and not the disciples of Christ must apply and minister accordingly, till, by degrees, the Kingdom of Christ, the Prince of Divine Peace, have the ascendant over all kingdoms ; not by violence, for His servants can offer none, not by might nor by power, but by My Spirit, saith the Lord. It will not be by human force or policy, but by conviction ; not by violence but consent, that the kingdoms of this world will become the kingdoms of God and of His Christ. Nor will the kingdoms and powers in this world ever cease, being God's ordinance in natural and civil affairs, till the reason of them cease, and evil-doing come to an end, by the advancement of truth, righteousness, love and peace over all nations.

It is evident from the foregoing that the witness

---

[1] Barclay, *Diary of Alexander Jaffray*, pp. 267, 268. Cf. Whittier's "Barclay of Ury."

[2] The Latin (1676) has "pure, patient, suffering spirit," and at the end, "*per omnia*," "in all things" for "over all."

[3] *Life*, pp. 618, 619.

against war must not be dissociated from the experience behind it, which lifted Friends above the spirit of the world. War was unlawful to the Christian who was redeemed out of the world : but it was not necessarily unlawful to others who had not reached this great experience. Indeed, only as a nation came into something of this temper, could it forgo the use of carnal weapons for its defence. Its policy would determine its armaments; and, until justice and goodwill supplanted greed and animosities and fears, its armoury of defence would contain a mixture of spiritual and carnal weapons.

There is a vigorous paper by John Crook, after the Peace of Ryswick in 1697,[1] called "The Way to a Lasting Peace," directed to showing that now the outward war was at an end there must be another war to destroy men's corruptions and lusts, out of which outward wars commonly proceed. The Catholics must cease persecuting and learn catholic love and goodwill towards their enemies; the Protestants and Nonconformists must protest by their practice against all ungodliness and against nonconformity to the Divine will.

For the end of the bloody or Lion's war must be the beginning of the Lamb's, who shall have the victory, not by garments rolled in blood—for He wars not to destroy men's lives, but their corruptions and lusts, and to save their souls . . . and of the increase of His government and peace there shall be no end; for the stability of His times shall be righteousness and peace. When this comes to be fulfilled, times will be settled in good earnest; and there will be no doubt of a firm, lasting and perpetual peace; for the Lion and the Lamb shall lie down together.

Who knows, he goes on, in prophetic anticipation of Foreign Missions, but that the King of Kings may send forth His ambassadors of peace to the nations yet afar off, that they also may be partakers of a saving and lasting peace through Jesus Christ ? Who knows but that God in the day of His power may bow the strong-willed and stout-hearted ones of this world to yield up unto Christ

[1] *Works*, pp. 345-350, dated 1st Oct. 1697.

the old power of wickedness that ruled over them? For now "there is no whole, entire nation that is the people of God; but they only that fear God and work righteousness, in every nation, are accepted of Him." Let princes purge themselves and their courts from unrighteousness, nobles their families from the workers of iniquity, and peoples their consciences from dead works to serve the Living God. "Reform from the highest to the lowest, both great and small, then may you expect a firm and lasting peace."

William Smith of Besthorpe, in 1661, had stated the dynamic positive of the Quaker witness in fervent words:

The Lord God [hath] gathered a remnant and orders them under His banner, by which they are encouraged to make war in righteousness, and in love to overcome their enemies, and in patience to silence the foolish and gainsayers . . . and their weapons are love and patience by which they overcome . . . and they seek to save men's lives and not to destroy them. Their weapon is stretched forth to cut down the proud, lustful nature, from whence all wars arise, and so to bring people to the meek and quiet spirit and to live peaceably with all men. . . . The aliens' army draw their swords and kill one another; the royal army have put up their swords and would have all men saved; and who needs to fear such an army, whose banner is love and their weapons goodwill? There need no horsemen and strong armies to oppose them, nor prisons to quiet them; for they are marching under the banner of love, and in love meet their enemies and quench their fury. . . . For there is nothing stronger than love; it makes an easy passage and drives that back which stands in the way . . . for in the strength of love one chases a thousand and the army of royalty marches forward and takes possession. . . . For the Lamb makes the way and His royal army follows Him . . . and in His royal army doth His purity shine; and His meekness, patience and gentleness is the garment of their praise; and with His virtuous life are they beautified; and their strength is in Him; . . . and His lovely banner covers them; and with it He preserves them; and He bears the affliction with them; and so upholds them in it, and makes way through it, and works deliverance from it. . . . Stand still, ye aliens, and see the salvation of God. Go on, ye free-born children, for great is your reward.[1]

---

[1] "The Banner of Love, &c.," in *Works*, p. 1.

THE CHURCH AND THE STATE

The only official document of first-rate importance issued by Friends on the subject of war in the Restoration period is the declaration against plots prepared by Fox and Hubberthorne at the time of the Fifth Monarchy rising, and republished by the Morning Meeting in 1684.[1] This is deeply grounded on the fact that fighting proceeds from the lusts of men, out of which Friends are redeemed, and so out of the occasion of war. It is amply worded to cover the refusal of the body of Friends to use arms for any ends; but naturally does not deal with the lawfulness of their use by a partially Christianized State. But at a much later date, when Quietism was setting in, the Address to the Crown in 1716, after the First Pretender's rebellion, speaks of the Lord of Hosts having most signally appeared to the confounding of that Black Conspiracy,[2] which implies that the measures taken by the Whig Government were Divinely aided. The central testimony, like the rest of the Quaker witness, was simply the living out, in a particular field of action, of the indwelling life of Christ, and derived its authority from this inward source, though verified abundantly to Friends out of the teaching and conduct of Christ. In the life of this experience the witness could be nobly borne, as with Thomas Lurting,[3] and in the still more vivid case of Richard Seller, "who would not take life but was swift to save it."[4] He was a long-shore fisherman of Kilnsea, pressed at Scarborough Piers for the naval campaign against the Dutch in 1665. At the Nore he was put on the *Royal Prince*, the flagship of Admiral Sir Edward Spragge. He refused to serve or to eat the king's victuals, for, said he, "my warfare was spiritual, therefore I durst not fight with carnal weapons." He was beaten mercilessly and brutally punished in other ways; and

---

[1] Cited *ante*, p. 12; see also *ante*, p. 113. Cf. p. 29, *n.* 1.
[2] See *ante*, p. 199. The 1746 Address, after the Second Pretender's rebellion, was still more strongly worded. (See Gough, *History*, iv. 336.)
[3] *Beginnings of Quakerism*, pp. 521, 522, and account of behaviour to Turks, *ante*, p. 431 *n*.
[4] See account in Besse, *Sufferings*, ii. 112-119, taken down, says the anonymous writer, in Seller's very words, "who sat before me weeping." The phrase in quotation marks is from an edn. by J[oshua] R[owntree].

finally lay in irons for a fortnight. Then a Council of War condemned him to death, and ordered him out to be hung at the yard-arm before the captains of the fleet. The judge of the Council was a Papist, and said, "Sir Edward is a merciful man, that puts that heretic to no worse death than hanging." On this Sir Edward, who had formed his own opinion of the case, flared out, "He is more a Christian than thyself, for I do believe thou wouldst hang me, if it were in thy power." He called for the evidence against the Quaker; but no one offered any, whereupon Seller was set free, and "the men heaved up their hats, and with a loud voice cried, 'God bless Sir Edward; he is a merciful man.' The shrouds and tops and decks being full of men, several of their hats flew overboard and were lost." After this, the honest sailor, lying on deck one night, believed the ship would be in action such a day of the month, with the wind at south-east, and had a vision of a shoal endangering its safety. He managed to acquaint the pilot, and, when the great fight with the Dutch came off, sure enough the two espied the shoal water and saved the vessel. Seller's employ was to carry down the wounded men[1] and look out for fireships, and his fine service in both these ways earned him a free discharge when the *Royal Prince* returned to the Nore. He seems to have settled at Scarborough, suffering a distress of £4 : 2 : 6 in 1684 for attendance at a meeting.[2] It was through being pressed for the Navy that English Friends suffered most; and in 1678 and '79 the Yearly Meeting appointed Daniel Lobdy of Deal, on hearing of any cases, to apply for their discharge at the expense of Friends.[3]

In 1675 we find the Morning Meeting directing that "in the several counties they that find arms, etc. [for the militia] be tenderly admonished about it, according to the ancient testimony of Christ Jesus,"[4] and in the same

---

[1] Cf. Thomas Story's readiness to help in this way had they fought a privateer (*Life*, p. 441). Thomas Lurting, on the other hand, when pressed on a man-of-war, refused such service, "for it is all an assistance" (*Fighting Sailor turned Peaceable Christian*, 1710).
[2] Besse, *Sufferings*, ii. 159.
[3] Y.M. Minutes. (The 1678 Minutes are in Meeting for Sufferings Minutes.)
[4] Minute of 31st May 1675.

year Bristol Friends complained of excessive distress levied by the marshals for fines upon Friends for not appearing in arms.[1] The Meeting for Sufferings decided that all distresses on such accounts should be recorded as sufferings "for the Lord and His Truth."[2] In 1690 it had under notice a Liverpool shipmaster who carried guns on his vessel, and wrote to Friends of the town "to let them know that our weapons are not carnal but spiritual; and that it hath not been the practice of Friends to use or carry carnal weapons; and Friends at London have suffered much for refusing."[3] In the Society Discipline contained in the old manuscript "Books of Extracts," the first entry under the head of "Fighting" is taken from the Yearly Meeting's epistle of 1693, and deals with this question of carrying guns. The shipmasters are to be dealt with in tender love, "that they may seriously consider how they injure their own souls in so doing" and bring discredit on the Society, "placing their security in that which is altogether insecure and dangerous; which we are really sorry for, and sincerely desire their recovery and safety from destruction, that their faith and confidence may be in the Arm and Power of God." The advice urges, amongst other things, that the practice gives occasion for more severe hardships to be inflicted on Friends pressed into ships of war, "who for conscience' sake cannot fight nor destroy men's lives." It was only in 1744, however, that the Yearly Meeting directed disownment in the special case of Friends concerned in privateering or as owners of ships going with Letters of Marque.[4]

The Queries as first sent down to the counties by the Yearly Meeting in 1682, and in revised forms up to 1700,

[1] Minute of Men's Meeting, 19th July 1675.
[2] Minute of 6th March 1679; cf. Besse, *Sufferings*, i. 443. There are several pages of such sufferings in a Kent Q.M. Book of papers at Dev. Ho. Cf. Besse, *Sufferings*, i. 296 : Daniel Lopdall is no doubt the Daniel Lobdy referred to in text.
[3] Minutes of 13th and 20th June 1690.
[4] See MS. "Books of Extracts." Friends in the South of France, now almost extirpated by conscription, were originally a spiritual group sprung from the "French Prophets" and ultimately from the Camisards, who came into touch with Friends in 1785 through an advertisement in the Paris papers respecting the restitution of some prize-money by Edward L. Fox. (See Martha Braithwaite, *Memorials of Christine Majolier Alsop*, pp. 1-5 ; *Yorkshireman*, ii. 328-330 ; *Irish Friend*, i. 97, 98, ii. 1, 2 ; and *J.F.H.S.* ii. 83.)

contained no request for information as to the faithfulness of Friends in their several testimonies. In 1700 it was asked how the advices as to education had been practised, three years later how the advices generally had been attended to, and in 1721–23 additions were made as to tithes and as to defrauding the public revenue; but it was not until 1742 that a Query, including a reference to war, was framed: "Do you bear a faithful and Christian testimony against the receiving and paying tithes, and against bearing arms; and do you admonish such as are unfaithful therein?"[1]

A severe and long-continued test came to the Quakers in Barbados; and redeems their otherwise chequered history. The island, blessed with a wind-tempered climate that allowed the settlement of Europeans, and at this time the mart of American trade, was in the full tide of prosperity. It contained an influential body of Friends, including Thomas Rous, formerly a Lieutenant-Colonel, whose son, John Rous, married a daughter of Margaret Fell; Lewis Morris, formerly a Colonel and member of Council; and Ralph Frettwell, who before his convincement held one of the chief judicial posts in the island.[2] Though scarcely larger than the Isle of Wight it had five meetings and several hundred Friends.[3] At this time the population was about 60,000, two-thirds of them negro slaves in a dangerous state of insubordination, and, as an outpost of British rule, Barbados was also exposed to foreign enemies. Its legislature consisted mainly of sugar planters, who instituted a compulsory and universal militia service, under fines which increased in severity with successive Acts.[4] There were trainings and patrollings every few weeks, besides work at the fortifications and other services; and at last, in 1692, an Act was passed requiring every

---

[1] MS. "Book of Extracts," under title "Questions," and for the development of the Queries, Beck and Ball, *London Friends' Meetings*, pp. 54-56. The present form of the Query dates from 1875. It now reads, "Are you faithful in maintaining our Christian testimony against all War, as inconsistent with the precepts and spirit of the gospel?" and is considered in all the meetings at least once in the year.

[2] For notices of these Friends see *Camb. Journ.* ii. 429, 430.

[3] See article in *J.F.H.S.* v. 43-46, with useful bibliographical note.

[4] The Acts and consequent sufferings are minutely detailed in Besse, *Sufferings*, ii. 278-351, which is my authority for the account following.

man who kept a horse to ride "armed with sword and pistols well-fixed and [with] powder and ball suitable about him." There were imprisonings and finings for refusing oaths and church dues, but in the main the long record of sufferings consists of fines for refusing militia duties, assessed in the Barbadian standard of value—pounds of muscovado or unrefined sugar. From 1658 to '85 the fines amounted for all offences to 1,423,164 lbs., or reduced into sterling at the rate of 12s. 6d. for 100 lbs., £8894 : 15 : 6. It should be added that these exactions were out of all proportion to the wage value of the service which Friends had refused to render.

There is one case of brutal treatment, resulting in death. A youth of nineteen, Richard Andrews, was forced from his master's shop to the training ground; but steadfastly refused to bear arms, saying he durst not break Christ's command. After one such refusal he was taken to a fort, tied neck and heels for an hour, and savagely struck by the captain. They kept him a week, lodging mostly on the cold stones. A little later they fetched him again; tying him up till he could hardly speak. Within a few days he was taken with dysentery and died, expressing great satisfaction of mind for having stood faithful.

Several remonstrances were addressed to the authorities, which show the position taken by Friends. They stated their diligence and readiness in watching, and warding, and patrolling in their own persons and horses, but without weapons, which for some time had been accepted; and that they were ready to serve as jurymen, surveyors of the highways, constables and officers of the poor, if they could do it without an oath. But their consciences would not allow them to bear arms or to swear.

Friends of position suffered equally with others. The account for the four years up to August 1678 includes a hundred and ten Friends, amongst others the following:

Thomas Rous, for default of an horse and a man in the troop, 600 lbs., and for repairing the church and for priest's wages, 1428 lbs.

Lewis Morris, for the like, 9220 lbs., and 973 lbs.
Ralph Frettwell, for the like, 14,865 lbs., and 917 lbs.
Joseph Borden, in whose shop Richard Andrews had served, for not bearing arms, though, upon summons to ride on the patrol, he went with his horses several times and rode with the rest, 6880 lbs., and for opening his shop on holy-days, so-called, 2000 lbs., and eleven weeks' imprisonment for refusing the oath, when summoned on a jury.

The joining without arms in patrol work had been expressly approved by English Friends in a letter prepared by Fox, primarily addressed to Friends in Nevis, but also directed to the other Caribbean islands, which included the Windward Isles, whose centre of government was Barbados.[1] It congratulates the Friends of Nevis upon having a governor who allows them to watch in their own way, without carrying arms, a thing that Friends in Jamaica and elsewhere would willingly have done :

For, if any should come to burn your house, or rob you, or come to ravish your wives or daughters, or a company should come to fire a city or town, or come to kill people, don't you watch against all such actions? And won't you watch against such evil things in the power of God in your own way? You cannot but discover such things to the magistrates, who are to punish such things, and therefore the watch is kept and set to discover such to the magistrate, that they may be punished ; and, if he does it not, he bears his sword in vain. . . . So, where Friends has the government, as in Rhode Island and that province, Friends was willing to watch in their own way; and they made a law that none should be compelled to take arms. So Friends have always proferred [to] the magistrates, though they could not join with them in carrying arms, swords and pistols, yet to watch in their own way against the evil-doer. And this

---

[1] *Epistles*, No. 319, from Swarthmore, 5th Nov. 1675, approved by the Six Weeks' Meeting, 7th Dec. 1675. The Minute shows that nineteen Friends signed it as having unity with its contents. M. E. Hirst has supplied me with particulars of a similar question in Antigua. "In 1708 Friends liable for service in Antigua were assigned by the authorities not to the militia but to subsidiary work. Older Friends agreed with the compromise, but some of the young men affected thought the work 'all one' with military service and 'not bearing a faithful testimony.' The London Meeting for Sufferings, when appealed to, upheld the older Friends, and even went beyond them by instancing 'digging trenches' as a form of work open to Friends (London Y.M. Epistles received, ii. pp. 65, etc. ; Epistles sent, ii. p. 122). The young men added, 'We are very willing to dig ponds, repair highways and build bridges . . . when they are done for the general service of the island, and other people at work therein equal with us, and not to balance those things which for conscience' sake we cannot do.'"

they have proferred in Barbados, as I have heard, to discover if negroes should rise up to burn plantations or steal, or do any hurt, or other Indians invading the land. And so, if the foreign Indians should come to steal your goods or to kill, for you to be left to your freedom to watch in your own way, and to discover to the magistrate such as would destroy your lives or plantations or steal—let them come from at home or come from abroad—such evil-doers the magistrate is to punish, who is for the praise of them that do well.

The declension of Friends in Barbados, already very evident by the time of Thomas Story's visits in 1709 and '14,[1] was attended by a compliance with the militia law, but had many causes, especially, perhaps, the laxity of morals in the island, the contaminating effects of slave-holding, and the poverty of ministry in the meetings.

The testimony against war, being essentially the outcome of an inward spirit of life, was borne with less consistency when Friends themselves were in the seat of power. The plantations, though the government might be in Quaker hands, were held under grant from the Crown, and were involved in the foreign policy of England, while, in addition, the Rhode Island Indian policy was compromised by that of the surrounding colonies. Moreover, they contained, or came to contain, many persons who had no principle against war.

In Rhode Island,[2] Friends in the government were in every instance devoted to the maintenance of peace. "But they seem to have settled it as their policy to stay in office, when they were put there by the people, even though they found themselves compelled, by unavoidable conditions and circumstances, to perform public acts of a warlike nature."

There has always been in the Society of Friends a group of persons pledged unswervingly to the ideal. To those who form this inner group compromise is under no circumstance allowable. . . . But there has always been as well another group who have held it to be equally imperative to work out their principles of life

---
[1] *Life*, pp. 437, 459. When Edmund Peckover visited the island in 1744, there were scarce a hundred Friends left, including children, and there was no ministering Friend (*J.F.H.S.* i. 108). By the end of the century Quakerism had practically disappeared (*ibid.* v. 43-46).
[2] I follow and cite *Quakers in the American Colonies*, p. 175.

in the complex affairs of the community and the State, where to gain an end one must yield something; where to get on one must submit to existing conditions; and where to achieve ultimate triumph one must risk his ideals to the tender mercies of a world not yet ripe for them. John Woolman, the consummate flower of American Quakerism in the eighteenth century, is the shining type of the former principle, and the Rhode Island Governors are good types of the other course.

In Pennsylvania, the policy of justice and goodwill towards the Indians secured the internal peace of the colony. " This I will say," wrote Penn to the Indians,[1] " that the people who come with me are a just, plain and honest people, that neither make war upon others, nor fear war from others, because they will be just." As regards foreign enemies, Penn, as we have seen,[2] accepted the regrant in 1694 under stringent conditions as to military affairs, and accordingly appointed Deputy-Governors who were not Friends. Under this regime, chief difficulty arose with respect to the voting by a Quaker legislature of supplies for military purposes. In 1693 money had been given on an undertaking that it should not be converted into the uses of war and " dipped in blood." In 1709 a grant was made, after the Quaker members had consulted with other Friends, who advised that " notwithstanding their profession and principles would not by any means allow them to bear arms, yet it was their duty to support the government of their sovereign the Queen, and to contribute out of their estates according to the exigencies of her public affairs, and therefore they might and ought to present the Queen with a proper sum of money." In 1711, £2000 was voted. " We did not see it," says Isaac Norris, " to be inconsistent with our principles to give the Queen money, notwithstanding any uses she might put it to, that not being our part but hers." The long thirty years' peace followed, but in 1745 the question again became pressing. A grant was made for

---

[1] Letter 21st June 1682 in Janney's *Life of Penn*, p. 195.
[2] *Ante*, p. 171. For the following see Sharpless, *A Quaker Experiment in Government*, pp. 185-225. John Woolman, in the adjacent colony of New Jersey, shared the burden of spirit that rested upon Pennsylvanian Friends in the years preceding 1756; see his *Journal*, 1900 edn. pp. 108-111.

"bread, beef, pork, flour, wheat or other grain," which the Governor cynically accepted, saying that "other grain" meant gunpowder. For the following ten years appropriations were made "for the King's use," in response to calls for military assistance. In 1754 a militia law was adopted for those "willing and desirous" of joining, prefaced with a preamble, used in other like cases, "Whereas this province was settled and the majority of the Assembly have ever since been of the people called Quakers, who, though they do not, as the world is now circumstanced, condemn the use of arms in others, yet are principled against bearing arms themselves." In the same year £55,000 was voted, for the relief of friendly Indians and distressed frontiersmen, and "other purposes." In spite of the precedent of 1711, many Friends refused to pay and were distrained on.

It is not surprising to find that the position had now become an intolerable one, and in 1756, when an Indian war had at last broken out, a number of Friends resigned their seats, this being judged the best course by the Meeting for Sufferings in England, who had been consulted owing to the agitation against Friends leading to proposals in London threatening the Frame of Government. The Society thus dissociated itself from the direct responsibilities of rule, with results, both good and ill, to itself and to the State which deserve close attention but cannot be pursued in these pages.[1]

It will be seen that the early Quaker witness against plottings and war reached its point of permanent value and inspiration to the Church, where it was borne by individuals or groups as the natural outcome of a heavenly-minded order of life to which they were dedicated. It was valid, for all time, to the extent of this dedicated experience. In other directions, the limitations of thought and circum-

[1] For an estimate of these results see *A Quaker Experiment in Government*, pp. 260-263, 270-272 ; also the companion volume of President Sharpless, *The Quakers in the Revolution*, and his chapters on "The Quakers in Pennsylvania" in *The Quakers in the American Colonies*. He suggests a third course which Friends might have taken : "They might have stood rigidly by their principles, so long as their constituents would have returned them." This deserves close attention if translated into the terms of our current politics.

stance, which attended its various forms of expression preclude us from accepting it as more than a contribution, often indeed daring and suggestive, to the fresh examination and experience which are needed under the changed conditions of thought and circumstance to-day. Especially has the Church to consider three great questions: the function of the democratic State in the Divine order, and the functions of the Church and of the individual Christian in the democratic State. Meanwhile, and always, let us find room both for our Penns and our Woolmans.

In concluding this chapter, we turn from the perplexed problems which entangled the wider applications of the peace testimony to record the dauntless courage born of inward calm with which Friends could remain at their posts and serve their neighbours in time of war.

Under Charles II. the Protestant ascendancy established by Cromwell in Ireland had remained unimpaired; and the old Catholic population, numbering three-quarters of the whole, was excluded from power and only retained a sixth of the profitable land. James, on the other hand, pursued a policy which was continually inflaming the hopes of the Irish and alarming the Protestant settlers. Under the guidance of the Earl of Tyrconnel, who was finally made Viceroy in 1687, the Army and the Government became predominantly Catholic, and when James abdicated he sought to retrieve his flight by challenging the Revolution from Ireland, aided by Louis XIV., ambitious as ever to overthrow William and secure French domination in Europe.

Friends in Ireland were part of the English plantation; who were withdrawn, however, from the distracted world around them into their own fellowship. In 1683, during the years of the second Stuart tyranny, the Government ordered Dissenters to cease from meeting in public; and the Quakers alone refused compliance.[1] A few of their leaders in Dublin were imprisoned for a time; but the chief effect was to crowd the meetings with people, much

---

[1] See Burnyeat's letters in *Works*, pp. 78-81; and Rutty, *Hist. of Friends in Ireland*, pp. 133-138.

to the chagrin of Dissenting ministers, who, we are told, " envy Friends' good, and are offended that we do not fly into holes as they do."[1] When the Catholic policy of James began to declare itself, there was a great disturbance in men's minds, and many Protestants fled the country. Burnyeat, then resident in Dublin, writes:[2]

Though the world be full of tumults, disquietness and amazements, yet blessed be the God of our salvation, Who hath brought us into a degree of that rest, which the distresses that are from below cannot reach. So that there is something known to retire unto for a sanctuary that the world knows not, neither can the destroyer come into it. Therefore, our safety is always to keep our interest therein, that we may have our privilege unto our mansion there, and so rest in the time of trouble.

Inhabiting this higher order of life, Friends were lifted above the material anxieties that harassed their Protestant neighbours. They were in favour with Tyrconnel as with James, and we have seen that public offices were pressed on them. The corporations were remodelled, and it was natural for the Government to leaven its Catholic nominations with Quakers and other Protestants well-affected to James.[3] Anthony Sharpe, a Gloucestershire woollen manufacturer, who settled in Dublin to buy wool in 1669, and was known through Ireland for "a wise, honest and just dealer,"[4] lent money to the Crown and was Master of the Weavers' Guild, to which he secured the admission of freemen on a declaration instead of an oath.[5] But the downfall of the Protestant ascendancy, accompanied by the arming though not the punctual payment of newly-raised Irish troops, jeopardized the position of all non-Catholics. William

[1] Burnyeat, *Works*, p. 87.
[2] Letter from Dublin, 29th June 1686, in *Works*, p. 90.
[3] Thos. Davis, *The Patriot Parliament of 1689*, pp. 21, 30. See *ante*, p. 143.
[4] He had been convinced by Dewsbury, when on a visit to Warwick gaol. My information as to Sharpe is from a paper by Isabel Grubb, in *Friends' Quarterly Examiner*, 1916, pp. 169-187, called "Irish Friends' Experience of War, 1689-92," which is the best modern account of the matter, and is based on MS. sources.
[5] See Isabel Grubb's paper and Anthony Sharpe's statement, recorded in London Y.M. Minutes, 1688, that the Baron of the Exchequer in Dublin had indulged Friends from taking the Oath and had accepted their affirmation as in the presence of God.

Edmondson, the apostle of Irish Quakerism,[1] an old Cromwellian soldier, saw a time approaching of great exercise and trial and "that the Lord would spread the carcasses of men on the earth as dung." He went through the meetings advising Friends to lessen their concerns in the world, and be ready to receive the Lord in His judgments that were at hand, and to flee unto Him for succour and safety. Anthony Sharpe says:

The Irish, having gotten arms from the English and no pay, fell to plundering the Protestants by day and by night, driving sheep and black cattle by hundreds on open places, and sold them cheap at 1d. per lb. to their relations and neighbours of the Roman faith, who had public notice of such plunder to be sold. Some of the English therefore went into strong houses and castles to secure themselves, which was judged rebellion to their land and all taken from them, and some put to death; yet those that lived privately, as our Friends and others, were in the night-time robbed, their houses broken up [and] their cattle driven away to the ruining many thousand families.

Edmondson lived at Rosenallis, near Mountmellick, fifty miles inland from Dublin, and, as early as May 1687, had to complain of the oppressive conduct of the dragoons quartered in the district.[2] In January 1689, in the months of acute unrest that preceded the arrival of James, he was shamefully abused by the troops and reported to have been killed, whereupon the Protestants concluded a massacre was intended. To stay the panic he went to Dublin, at hazard of life, and confronted the Viceroy with the gross abuses done to himself and his neighbours. He came back convinced that no project was afoot for massacring the Protestants, but the design was to affright the rest of them out of Ireland. During this dark year calamities increased, both from soldiers and the Irish freebooters, who were armed for the most part only with a scythe or half-pike, from which they got the name of "rapparees." Both sorts took what they pleased, treating the English as their servants; and there was so much

---

[1] For Edmondson see *Beginnings of Quakerism*, p. 210, and *ante*, pp. 260, 268, 422. His *Journal* vividly narrates his sufferings, but with few dates.

[2] See Isabel Grubb's paper. She dates the next incident Jan. 1688, that is, 1689 N.S. The following account is from Edmondson's *Journal*.

wholesale and wanton destruction that a sudden famine seemed imminent. Edmondson's Protestant neighbours thronged his house and brought the remnant of their cattle on to his land, thinking themselves and their goods safest there. After the battle of the Boyne (1st July 1690) the fleeing Irish plundered him several times, but the stanch old soldier kept his post, urging his Irish neighbours to keep their men from spoiling the English of the little they had left, and promising to do the like by them when the English came. He was as good as his word, venturing his life among the rude soldiers to save the Irish, but when the troops had withdrawn to winter quarters the ravages from the rapparees were resumed. Friends, however, kept meetings constantly and enjoyed them peaceably, being wonderfully preserved, "so that," says Edmondson, " I do not know of above four Friends in this whole nation that were killed by violent hands all the time of this great calamity."[1] He went to the Half-Year's meeting at Dublin in November as usual ; "we had an heavenly, blessed, powerful meeting ; and Friends were more than ordinary glad one of another in the Lord Jesus, Who had preserved us alive through so many dangers to see one another's faces again." Spoiling and cruelty increased, but, he says, " I durst not remove, for I knew it would discourage Friends and the English about us . . . for they took notice of me, and many of them thought they were safer for my staying in my place. I also believed that one hair of my head should not fall without God's providence." His house was now burned and his cattle taken, and he and his two sons were hurried off through the winter night as prisoners, bare-legged and bare-headed and not much better than naked, though he was lent one of his own old blankets to lap himself in. A council was held in a wood next morning, and it was concluded to hang the two sons and shoot Edmondson. He challenged them to prove that he had wronged any of their folk one farthing during the times of trouble.

[1] Three Bandon Friends were dealt with for taking up arms and acting "scandalous to the principles of Truth by us professed." (See Isabel Grubb's paper.)

"They wondered," he says, "at my boldness; and, indeed, my life was little to me, for I desired to die, if it were the will of God. Then they hoodwinked my sons to hang them, and prepared two firelocks to shoot me. They came to hoodwink me also, but I told them they need not, for I could look them in the faces and was not afraid to die."

He was, however, taken to Athlone, where he came before the officers at the castle still lapped in his old blanket, and was asked his name. Quoth he, "I am old William Edmondson," whereupon the Governor, who had been at his house, stood up with tears in his eyes and said he was sorry to see him there in that condition. He durst not release him for there were many eyes over him, because he was kind to the English; but he left him in custody, with some victuals and a bare floor to lie on and twenty shillings of the token gun-money which James had made current for lack of silver. After a day or two, a neighbouring Friend, John Clibborn, was allowed to have him to his home, engaging life and body to produce him if called on, and a little later he was set free.

Prior to the troubles, John Burnyeat, having lost his wife, was thinking of settling in England; but he gave himself up to stay with Irish Friends and share their dangers. He died, however, in the autumn of 1690, travelling among Friends to the last. It is difficult to describe adequately the suffering and service of these three years of war—1689-91. The losses of Friends came to about £100,000, the equivalent of a much larger sum to-day. "From the English army and its mercenaries, and from the Irish army, they suffered chiefly by having to provide free quarters, but the farmers lost most of their stock and household goods, through the depredations of the robbers who followed the armies."[1] Many were driven from their homes, especially in the zone of military operations. In Cork, during the siege, when other Protestants were interned, the Irish left Friends free, fearing no danger from them.[2] At Limerick, which was in Irish hands, they did good work in relieving starving

---

[1] Isabel Grubb's paper. [2] *Life* of Joseph Pike, 1837.

English soldiers who were held prisoners, when other Protestants were fearful to attempt it, and at Dublin and other places Friends did the like, so that many afterwards said that, but for the Quakers, they would have starved to death.[1] Their houses, as those of John Clibborn, at Moate near Athlone, of James Hutchinson, at Knockballymagher, and of Gershon Boate, at Borrisoleigh in County Tipperary, often became centres of refuge and succour to the Protestants.[2] A Friend, Francis Randall, of Randall's Mills near Enniscorthy, assisted James II. in his flight to France after the battle of the Boyne.[3] Supported by inward spiritual strength, they did much to save their neighbours from despair, and were kept, even when stripped of goods and cattle, from falling a prey to the depression under which many of the plundered English languished and died. Their hearts were "open one to another, so that those who had something left were willing to communicate to those that were in want; and Friends that were driven from their dwellings did generally return to their places; and the National Men's Meeting took care that in every quarter Friends should be supplied with such necessaries as time and their abilities did afford,"[4] aided by generous help from English Friends, and even from Barbados. Truth gained ground, and in Dublin the meeting-house at Eustace Street, where Friends still meet, was built, as many thronged to their meetings in the year after the war.[5] The English and Irish had been fighting each other for power and outward possessions, because of deep-seated bitterness and rankling memories of oppression; it was the part of the Friends to be redeemed from these things into a spirit of life which enabled them to minister to the soul of Ireland with unwearied hands of mercy and hearts of undefeated faith.

[1] Isabel Grubb's paper.
[2] Rutty's *Hist. of Friends in Ireland*, pp. 148-151.
[3] Note to Joseph Pike's *Life, sub anno* 1718. A seaman, Richd. Carver, who became a Friend, had helped Charles across to France after Worcester fight and carried him ashore (*Extracts from State Papers*, p. 158, and *Letters of Early Friends*, 169-173). For another interesting Quaker link with the Stuart family, see account of Jane Stuart in M. R. Brailsford, *Quaker Women*, pp. 304-323.
[4] Rutty's *Hist. of Friends in Ireland*, pp. 151, 152.
[5] Isabel Grubb's paper.

CHAPTER XXII

THE CHURCH AND THE KINGDOM OF GOD

> There is room yet for a fellowship, all-inclusive in its tender sympathy, drawn close in the loving bondage of sincerity and truth; for a noble simplicity of life and manners, rich in true culture and the taste born of knowledge; for a freedom that scorns the flummeries of rank, the perquisites of pride, because it knows the worth of manhood and loves the privilege of friendship; for a simple worship, homely and informal, because intimate and real.
>
> Climb Pendle Hill with Fox and see once more his vision—"a great people to be gathered"—enter in spirit the dungeons of the past and learn why they were palaces, and the bolts precious jewels; repeat again with Nayler his tender words, and in the spirit of his message face the future that lies before you. "Its crown is meekness; its life is everlasting love unfeigned; it takes its kingdom with entreaty and not with contention, and keeps it by lowliness of mind."—JOHN WILHELM ROWNTREE, *Essays and Addresses*, pp. 75, 76.

MAN himself, as Biology and History show, belongs to the past, the present, and the future, and his progress depends upon the living elements of all three co-operating in his growth. Some survive from the rich inheritance left him by former generations, others are the dominant forces of the hour, others again are new births, nascent with the promise of the days yet to be. Or, to illustrate this conception of progress from the fountain-heads of our Western Civilization, we may say that the conserving genius of Rome, the humanism of Athens, the forward-reaching faith of the Hebrew race, which, separately pursued, would mean stagnation, or a brief hour of fevered brilliance, or an unpractical idealism, are all needed, in their due combination, for the upward growth of man. They flourish best in an atmosphere of self-

CHURCH AND KINGDOM OF GOD

controlled freedom, since this allows a great variety of temperaments and capacities to serve the Commonwealth.[1]

The same truth may be stated in the terms of its religious equivalent. Three great purposes, as Christ teaches, are to be pursued by His disciples. There is the doing of the Father's will, and here the revelation and experience of the past have their high place; there is the fresh delight of hallowing His nature wherever we find it in the life of to-day:

> Earth's crammed with heaven,
> And every common bush afire with God;
> But only he who sees, takes off his shoes.[2]

There is the vision of the Kingdom "ever ready to break into the world, if men will only suffer it to break into their hearts."[3] And the climate in which these purposes flourish and make earth new is the Spirit of Jesus, the same yesterday, to-day, and for ever.

It is from this standpoint that we may estimate the forces at work in the Society of Friends during the opening years of the eighteenth century, when it had become fully organized as a Church and had reached in the British Isles its highest numbers in proportion to the population. Behind us lies its vigorous Second Period of expression, inspired by the tremendous sincerity of Fox, by Dewsbury's tenderness and Penington's rare spiritual sensitiveness, by Penn's adventurous heart and Barclay's nobly-tempered mind. We ask ourselves, How far are we still in the vision splendid, and how far is it beginning to fade into the light of common day?

It must be confessed that the Quaker movement, after two generations of vitality, was resting on its past, accommodating itself to the ease of the present, and losing its vision. Similar changes have often blighted the early promise of other great religious awakenings, and the historian cannot too carefully examine the causes of

---

[1] For a further treatment of this theme, see my paper on "Controlling factors of Progress" in *Friends' Quarterly Examiner*, Oct. 1916.
[2] Elizabeth Barrett Browning, *Aurora Leigh*, bk. vii.
[3] See quotation from Dr. John Oman, *supra*, head of Chap. VIII.

these declensions. I have already dealt with many of them as occasion served, but it is worth while, having regard to the importance of the subject, to present them here in a general view.

The words in which Thomas Story describes the position of the Dutch Mennonites in 1715 can be transferred, almost without change, to the condition of the Society of Friends :[1]

> I inquired more particularly into the state of the Menists in those parts, and found that all along their ministers had preached freely, till of late some here and there had begun to receive hire, but were moderate therein ; and, though they still keep up their old testimony against fighting and swearing, yet they are not so lively in their worship, nor so near the Truth as they were in their first appearance ; and I was informed that their ministers are for the most but weak and dry in their ministry ; and sometimes their hearers had rather some of them would be silent than preach, though gratis. If thus it be, it hath fared with them as with many others, who, having had a day of visitation from the Lord, and obtained a reputation through His goodness among them and by that holy and innocent conversation they have had through His grace ; yet, some becoming more loose and not keeping in the grace of God and the virtue and power of it, have ended in mere formalists ; and then, in a generation or two, little has appeared but the outside and form of godliness . . . and yet, in the main, they are preserved from the gross evils of the world ; and I hope the Lord hath a visitation of life and power yet in store for them.

A religious movement, beginning in the first-hand convincement of all its adherents, inevitably alters its character as new generations succeed. The mechanism of organization begins to replace the free activity of the living organism. Some remain associated with the movement who have lost their first love ; the men who had spiritual force to found the Church grow old and pass away in the course of nature, or fall before their time through the ardour of their service or the stroke of persecution ; and the membership consists largely of those born and bred within the Church and accepting its great

---

[1] *Life*, pp. 520, 521. There were, of course, no paid Quaker ministers.

traditions and well-ordered way of life from their elders, rather than as their own vital discovery. The problem of rekindling a living love to God in each generation is as old as the great Phylactery passage in Deuteronomy,[1] and was not adequately solved by the guarded methods of Quaker discipline, which threw the emphasis on outward conduct and failed to nourish a first-hand experience. There were undoubted limitations in the Quaker outlook which prevented the development of a rich type of education. But, in rejecting a professional clergy and throwing the burden for living ministry and evangelism and teaching upon the whole body, it was imperative for the Society to prepare a fertile soil out of which an abundant harvest of service could spring. The failure to provide this was due to potent causes which I have already detailed in a previous chapter; and seriously weakened the Church both for intensive and extensive work. The First Publishers of Truth, usually equipped with Biblical and theological knowledge prior to their convincement, in most cases retained their zest; but much of the later ministry sprang from an impoverished ground. This, together with the growing power of corporate authority and of elders who were not ministers, gradually resulted in a dearth of fresh, vital leadership. The Society in more recent days has outgrown the confined mental outlook which hampered its life; and there is now probably no religious body in which freedom is less fettered or learning less suspect. But it has not yet, either in England or America, fully solved the problem of preserving the spiritual spontaneity which lies at the heart of Quakerism while fostering an inspired leadership. The solution does not depend only upon the prevalence of a rich type of education such as we enjoy to-day: it depends also upon a warm fellowship of sympathy, a widespread dedication to Christ, and the provision within the Church of avenues for service which shall allow full scope for the varied spiritual gifts possessed by its members.

The rejection of sacerdotalism means that all living

[1] Deut. vi. 4-9.

members of the body, men and women, have the right and the duty of offering their own *charismata*—their own spiritual gifts—in the service of the brotherhood and of the Kingdom of God. In the letters of Paul we see the Church at its moment of impact on the Pagan world. He gives us, in two great passages, a list of the gifts bestowed for its need. Apostles and prophets come first in both cases; and he names, besides these, evangelists, pastors, and teachers, in Ephes. iv. 11; and teachers, powers, helps, guidances, and tongues in 1 Cor. xii. 28. Clearly, all these are regarded as belonging to the service of the Church, though all subordinate to the possession of the more excellent spirit of love.

First in Paul's lists come the apostles, the men who were able at first-hand to witness to Jesus and the Resurrection, and had in consequence been called to go forth and disciple the nations—the men, in modern language, with an experience and a mission. Then follow the prophets, to whom came fresh visions of truth to be revealed to the Church under the influence of the Spirit, the power of whose gift, as known at Corinth, has been repeated again and again in Quaker story:

If all prophesy, and some unbeliever or outsider come in, he is convicted by all, he is judged by all; the secrets of his heart are made manifest; and so he will fall down on his face and worship God, declaring "God is indeed among you." [1]

But Paul recognizes, and the Church must always recognize, other right gifts of ministry, those belonging to teachers, pastors, and evangelists, gifts equally proceeding from the one self-same Spirit, but into the use of which human study and thought and reflection more largely enter. The teacher meditates on the things of God, and then declares them to the Church; a pastoral ministry of exhortation comes from those with experience to comfort and admonish the flock; while the evangelist will have full place in a body of disciples that is engaged in the Master's work of seeking and saving the lost.

---

[1] 1 Cor. xiv. 24, 25: for a reference to the work of the itinerant apostles and prophets of the early Church, see *Beginnings of Quakerism*, p. 527.

Meetings that will allow all these varied gifts to be used should form part of the arrangements of any Church which seeks service for the Kingdom of God from all its members. In the first fervour of the Quaker movement, it is clear that in addition to the quiet times of worship, glowing with the presence of the Spirit and the fellowship of the saints, groups of Friends did much of their best work in meetings for "threshing" the heathenish nature, and in public discussion by speech and writing. They were not content to hide their light from the world, nor supposed that the guidance of the Spirit could only be given in a silent meeting. Friends will always, it may be hoped, seek to maintain the unique place and power of their times of gathered worship; but they will more and more develop meetings and study-groups of other kinds, fitted for the varying religious needs of their own members and of the wide circles of seekers after Truth to whom their message appeals. They need a courageous use of new ways of expression, not copied from others, but developed according to the genius of Quakerism, if they are to fulfil their mission to the world, or release the stores of unused energy which should be called out for the Church and the Kingdom of God. Especially do they need a fostering of spiritual gifts, by an atmosphere of generous and open-hearted fellowship in the Church, and by the promotion of associated service in active work. The mutual help of such association is great—two and two, as with the first Quaker Publishers, or in small groups— under conditions which allow practical training and guidance to be given, through the vitalizing contact with one another of disciples united in a comradeship of service.

We now pass to another cause for the declension into Quietism. The vision of the Society was undoubtedly dimmed by the failure even of men like Penington and Barclay to relate the experience of the Inward Light to the Historic Life of Christ, in a way which gave each its true value. We have seen that this failure was almost inevitable in the state of thought and knowledge of the age; and that it does not render invalid the great fact of the indwelling life of Christ out of which Quakerism sprang and in which it has always been rooted. But it led to much vagueness of thought and was a chief sterilizing influence in later days. The fuller intellectual outlook of our day is carrying the question to a solution which will enable spiritual Christianity to make a new appeal to the mind of mankind.

There was a third cause of decline due to altered conditions. A change of environment was subduing the Society to its own tone. Nothing but a re-baptism of power, issuing in a vigorous growth of fresh spiritual life and a daring spirit of new adventure under clear-sighted leadership, such as came to the Moravians at Herrnhut in 1727, could, so far as we can judge, have overcome the perils around and within the Church. Many men of enterprise were finding scope for their energies in the Quaker colonies of the New World. The clogging growth of wealth and worldly prosperity was producing its natural consequence of spiritual lethargy. The tremendous change from an era of harassing persecution to the privileged ease of toleration disinclined the Church to aggressive work which might affront the authorities and endanger the position, and practically condemned it to a narrow sectarian life, as the price to be paid for the ease granted it. What this meant, in the early Georgian days, may be seen in an extract from the Diary of John Kelsall, of Dolobran in Montgomeryshire, in 1731.[1]

> The Government and better sort of people are very kind and civil to Friends; and they have respect and interest with them, yea the very priests in divers places are seemingly at least loving to Friends. Now I greatly fear that too many Friends, being unwilling to give them offence, as they call it, are too easy towards them in respect to religious matters; ... so pass smoothly on; and the common people, knowing the favour that is showed us by their superiors, behave themselves more civilly. But I do not see that this adds little or anything to the increase and prosperity of Truth; and had Friends commission ... to testify openly against the reigning wicked practices in

---

[1] MS. Diary (copy at Dev. Ho.), vi. 248, cited from *J.F.H.S.* x. 281.

the great, and the lifeless superstitious ministry of the priests, both of which in my thought are as visible and flagrant as ever, there would be more converted to God in a little time; for it is in vain to be lopping at the branches when the root remains strong and spreading. And it is my belief God will raise in due time a people out of Friends or others, who will be commissioned to strike at the root and branch of antichrist, without regard to the frowns and favours of High or Low clergy or others; and then and not till then I greatly fear it will be that we shall have any considerable addition to the Church.

Religion as a whole was suffering from the lassitude of Dissent and the devastations of Deism. "Men," as Lecky says,[1] "became half-believers. Strong religious passions of all kinds died away. The more superstitious elements of religious systems were toned down, unrealized, silently dropped. There was a tendency to dwell exclusively upon the moral aspects of the Faith." Enthusiasm, appealing to the emotional side of religion, was out of favour. But, even while Kelsall was writing, the Oxford Methodists arose, who would take up the mission that had passed for a time out of the ken of Quakerism.[2]

The story of Friends in England reminds us of the rivers of Damascus, rising fresh and pure in the great mountains, tumbling turbulent among the hills, flowing cool and grateful through the thirsting city, and then sucked up by the parching desert and the burning sun. But the figure fails us here; for though the stream became retracted and tepid its glad springs of life never wholly ceased. The inward strength known in the gathered power of Quaker worship had preserved the fellowship through the heat of persecution, and would carry it through the days when it seemed to the world a spent force. The sequel lies beyond the confines of this volume, but will be found eloquent with proof that the stream whose fountain-head was the first-hand experience of the early Friends

[1] *Hist. of England in the Eighteenth Century*, iii. 310.
[2] The experience of some of the early Methodists closely resembled that of the early Publishers of Truth. See *e.g.* that of John Nelson, the Yorkshire stonemason (1707-1774), as told in *A New History of Methodism* (1909), i. 312-315. His *Journal*, under date 1744, gives his persecution for refusing to fight, showing the same spirit and the same effect of his witness upon his hearers, as we find in such a man as Dewsbury.

may be perennially renewed from fresh tributaries of like living water.

Throughout the seventy-five years of Quakerism which have been the subject of my study, the master-clue through the labyrinth of problems has been found in the gleaming thread of this inward life. The Society of Friends, from the first, has been a "Holy Experiment" in spiritual guidance, abundant in evidence of its reality and rich in material for judging of the conditions under which it can be known. In one of the most glorious illuminations of the Book of Kells, mutilated alas by the binder, is the portrait of the Fourth Evangelist within a border beyond which extend the head and hands and feet of another Diviner figure. So, behind the Church, always stands the outstretched form of her living Lord. Creeds become obsolete and institutions decrepit, but He abides, gathering into the holy communion of His Spirit the goodly fellowship of prophets and apostles, of martyrs and confessors, of saints and servants of God, through all the ages.

It is by the vital recognition of this truth that Quakerism makes its greatest contribution to catholic Christianity. We are seeking to-day a basis of Christian unity. Confronted with the pagan saturnalia of European war, we are becoming aware that the State has triumphed over the Church by engulfing it in its own spirit of division and envy. We see beyond the Governments of men a Kingdom of God waiting to come on earth; and we know that the recovery of catholicity is an urgent need of the day, if the divided fragments of the Church are to declare the Kingdom with power. The world is eager for the triumph of righteousness. "All creation is expectant, waiting for the revealing of the sons of God."[1] The divisions of Christendom have indeed shown that sincere followers of Jesus are found under widely-varied formulæ of faith and forms of Church order; and that therefore it is not in these that we shall reach the true principle of unity in the body of Christ. Christianity, like Freedom, is greater than the institutions that diversely manifest it,

[1] Rom. viii. 19, W. G. Rutherford's translation.

or the definitions that imperfectly express it. It is a spirit of life drawn from the life of the Spirit. Here, in this larger air, the Church is one and universal.

A fellowship in spirit is accordingly the real and sufficient basis for the unity of the Church catholic which embraces all the groups of Christ's disciples under whatever name, throughout the world. The many families, in many houses, must gain a new consciousness—the larger consciousness of their community of life in the one City of God.

The first Friends, as I have shown in my former book,[1] called themselves by such universal names as "Children of the Light," and "Friends in the Truth." They held that in all men there was some germ of Divine life. There was nothing sectarian in their outlook. They declared an evangel, which they believed would spread through the world,[2] and spoke of themselves as reviving primitive Christianity after a long and dark night of apostasy. Their bond of union was unity in the Life. They rejected sacerdotalism, and reached a deep spiritual conception of the nature of the Church, which, under the conditions of the time, threw them into violent opposition to the other Puritan Churches,[3] and to the persecuting Anglicanism of the Restoration. Their special ways of behaviour also put a barrier between them and their fellow-Christians. But the essentially catholic character of their standpoint showed itself from the first in their broad advocacy of religious liberty for all men and their teaching as to the universality of grace. Burrough says, though with too high a notion of the uniformity into which a unity of spirit would lead:[4]

To all ye that are of divers judgments in matters of faith and worship in religion . . . though ye be divided in the belief and practice of spiritual things, yet live in peace and unity with all men, in all outward relations, and do not envy nor hurt one another's persons, though you are in difference about religion . . .

---

[1] *Beginnings of Quakerism*, pp. 131, 132.
[2] See extract from Skipton epistle, *supra*, p. 351. Cf. *supra*, p. 401.
[3] See *Beginnings of Quakerism*, pp. 280-282.
[4] *Works*, p. 837, "A discovery of Divine Mysteries," 1661.

but seek to inform one another . . . and persuade one another out of that which is evil to that which is good. . . . The means and way to be reconciled and to come out of all division . . . into peace with God and one with another about faith and Church government is by the Spirit of God . . . that it may work in every one of your hearts true faith, and teach every one of you the true worship of God and the way of doctrine and true Church government . . . for it is that which is the bond of peace and love among true Christians, and it is that which reconciles people's hearts into oneness. And, if you receive that Spirit, every particular person of you, it will bring you to be of one faith, of one worship, and then your doctrine and Church government will agree.

Penington, as we should expect, had a true insight into the nature of Christian unity : [1]

He that keeps not a day may unite in the same Spirit, in the same life, in the same love, with him that keeps a day : and he who keeps a day may unite in heart and soul with the same Spirit and life in him who keeps not a day ; but he that judgeth the other because of either of these errs from the Spirit, from the love, from the life, and so breaks the bond of unity. . . . And here is the true unity, in the Spirit, in the inward life, and not in an outward uniformity. . . . Men keeping close to God, the Lord will lead them on fast enough ; and give them light fast enough ; for He taketh care of such, and knoweth what light and what practices are most proper for them. . . . And oh, how sweet and pleasant is it to the truly spiritual eye to see several sorts of believers, several forms of Christians in the school of Christ, every one learning their own lesson, performing their own peculiar service, and knowing, owning and loving one another in their several places and different performances to their Master. . . . The great error of the ages of the apostasy hath been to set up an outward order and uniformity and to make men's consciences bend thereto, either by arguments of wisdom or by force ; but the property of the true Church government is to leave the conscience to its full liberty in the Lord, to preserve it single and entire for the Lord to exercise, and to seek unity in the Light and in the Spirit, walking sweetly and harmoniously together in the midst of different practices.

Penn, with his universal spirit, in the best-known passage in his *Some Fruits of Solitude* (1693) wrote : [2]

[1] *Works*, 1681 edn. pt. i. pp. 240, 241, "An Examination of the Grounds or Causes," &c., 1660.
[2] Edmund Gosse's edn., 1900, pp. 99, 100 ; *Works*, 1726 edn. i. 842.

CHURCH AND KINGDOM OF GOD

The humble, meek, merciful, just, pious and devout souls are everywhere of one religion; and, when death has taken off the mask, they will know one another, though the divers liveries they wear here makes them strangers.

John Bellers, as we have seen,[1] desired general councils of all Christian persuasions to consider a basis of unity both at home and in Europe, and to put an end to all wars and bloodshed for religion.

Quakerism, indeed, has always found the bond of union for itself and for the wider fellowship of the Church catholic in inward experience—the experience of the one Divine Life that is reproducing in men the character of Jesus Christ.[2] It has refused to lay the emphasis on creed or ritual or in its days of vigour on institutions. Where Christ is, there is His Church, made up of all who seek to live in His spirit, whatever the words by which they try to find expression for their faith, or the practices which have become means of grace to their souls. We are learning to-day that a rich variety of expression and of practice is to be expected as the Life streams through disciples of every race and clime and condition. It cannot be confined to any one vessel, however nobly fashioned, but would fill all cups to overflowing. It does not press men into a rigid mould of thought or action; rather would it pour its own joy into every mould of humanity. We have sought unity through agreement in doctrines and in institutions; and the track of Church history, like some road through the desert, is strewn with the parched skeletons of our failures. The time is come for finding that the Divine Light rejoices to paint the world with manifold hues, and that, amid all our differences, in that Light we may be one. The time is come for the feet of a new band of Publishers of Truth to be shod with the preparation of this gospel of peace, that it may be carried not only into midnight lands, but through a Christendom often made impotent by its divisions and its worldliness,

---

[1] *Supra*, pp. 589, 592.
[2] See an important paper, cited *supra*, p. 376, in the *Proceedings of London Yearly Meeting*, 1917, pp. 153-159, under the title of "The True Basis of Christian Unity."

and a civilization that is waiting for the free air of Christ's Spirit to save it from death. There is room for the growth, in a rich diversity of outward form and expression corresponding with the varied gifts of humanity, of an all-embracing fellowship of "children of the light," catholic as the spirit of Freedom itself, but unified amid all its manifold manifestations by the central Divine heart which pulses through the whole. This Kingdom of God, for which the Seekers after Truth in every land are waiting, would gather into its "beloved community" all true hearts within the Churches, and unnumbered multitudes in wider circles without, who have turned from a Christianity dominated by institutions and forms, but are eager for a fellowship of righteousness and peace and joy in the Spirit of Christ.

A company of disciples that knows its true life to be here has still a place of power and service for the world, if it has vision and dedication enough to use the strength and the joy fostered by its own fellowship in a universal spirit. The late Bishop Lightfoot opens his famous Dissertation on the Christian Ministry [1] with an ideal picture :

The Kingdom of Christ, not being a kingdom of this world, is not limited by the restrictions which fetter other societies, political or religious. It is in the fullest sense free, comprehensive, universal. It displays this character, not only in the acceptance of all comers who seek admission, irrespective of race or caste or sex, but also in the instruction and treatment of those who are already its members. It has no sacred days or seasons, no special sanctuaries, because every time and every place alike are holy. Above all it has no sacerdotal system. It interposes no sacrificial tribe or class between God and man, by whose intervention alone God is reconciled and man forgiven. Each individual member holds personal communion with the Divine Head. To Him immediately he is responsible, and from Him directly he obtains pardon and draws strength.

He goes on to point out that the conception is strictly an ideal, always to be kept in mind, but not to be applied without regard to the necessary wants of human society.

---

[1] Lightfoot, *Philippians*, Dissertation No. i.

CHURCH AND KINGDOM OF GOD

The early Quakers in the exhilaration of their great experience realized it for a time with singular completeness; and Friends to-day have the task, side by side with others who share the ideal, of building fellowships within the one Kingdom of God, which shall be worthy of the dream. The story I have told in these volumes shows abundantly that

> Spirits are not finely touched
> But to fine issues.[1]

The vision that came to Fox on Pendle Hill of a great people to be gathered was fulfilled; and the Publishers of Truth thrilled England with their re-discovery of Christ and the high adventure of their service. Their ardour carried them into the lions' den of Boston and the seat of cruelty at Rome; they bore their witness at Jerusalem and before the Sultan, and sought to reach the Emperor of China and that most elusive of potentates, Prester John. At home the stocks were often their Mount of Transfiguration and the dungeon their palace and pulpit. Then, when the red dragon of persecution herded Quakers by the thousand into noisome gaols, or set their estates at the mercy of hungry Informers, out of the fierce travail-pangs our country's religious liberty was born. Neither bonds nor fines could fetter the Life within. It still had force for new tasks of Church government at home and for fresh ventures of faith in the American wilderness. The life only ebbed when the day of outward prosperity and ease dawned; and the Church became pre-occupied with its tradition and its own narrow interests and forgot its mission. Yet a temper of mind and a type of character had been established, which, as they were continually nourished by Divine guidance, would still make the Quaker dauntless in witness, strong in practical philanthropy, and sensitive in his social conscience.

The two generations of heroic energy had, as we have noted, their large intermixture of weakness. The new experience was conceived under the serious mental limitations of the age, and was at times marred and compromised

---

[1] Shakespeare, *Measure for Measure*, Act i. Scene 1.

by extravagance. The clash of individual and corporate guidance led to desolating divisions. The Society often failed to overcome the usurping spirit of the world; and its young life was stunted by an education of authority rather than of inspiration and courageous experiment. To-day, while the spirit of the world still sadly clogs the Quaker Church, many of these limiting conditions have given place to a wider knowledge and vision. If our hearts were open to the pulsating Life which filled the First Publishers of Truth with ardour and dedication, we who share the priceless heritage and know something of the inward experience of Quakerism could go forth with joy to the new era of service and sacrifice that awaits the disciples of Christ.

Bishop Westcott attempted a sketch of the Christian fellowships of the future in his sermons on *The Social Aspects of Christianity*. Their object, he said, must not be perfection for a select few, but a healthy type of living for all. They must proclaim that God is not to be found more easily in the wilderness and the solitary place than in the study, or in the market, or in the workshop, or by the fireside. They must welcome light from every quarter, knowing that it comes finally from one Divine source, and must make it clear that they strive not for victory but for truth. The fellowship must be open, bearing frank witness to its ideals, as, for example, by a measured and unostentatious simplicity in dress, in life and establishment. Above all, it must have two dominant notes—its social aim and its spiritual inspiration. Its members must be given to personal service, making themselves one with humanity and using their endowments of character or intellect, position or wealth, as a trust for the general good; and the voice and vision of God must be continually restoring their souls. Dr. Westcott finds in the history of the Franciscans, the Moravians, and the Quakers the best instances of such fellowships.

We recall the *De Adventu Minorum* of Thomas of Eccleston, with its picture of the Friars settling in the low, swampy purlieus of the large towns, cheek by jowl with crowded poverty and loathsome disease, living by the gaol at Cambridge with the same entrance as the prisoners, and afterwards in a hovel built in one day out of a score or two of planks, or at Cornhill, their cells made of wattles like sheepcotes, or in a mere barn-like structure with walls of mud at Shrewsbury; and yet filled with gladness at the sight of one another, zealous in studying Divine things and knowing the joy of the Lord to be their strength. We think of the Moravian villagers of Herrnhut in Saxony, with their emphasis on unity, personal religion and personal service, with their educational outlook and that flaming missionary zeal which is their praise in all the Churches. We revive our own Quaker beginnings, when the Lord daily appeared to those plain North-country ploughmen, and they often said one to another, "What? Is the Kingdom of God come to be with men?"[1]—those years of exulting strength when the Quaker fellowship was "as a family of prophets, which must spread over all the nations; as a garden of plants, and the place where the pearl is found which must enrich all nations with the heavenly treasure."[2] And as the wonder and the joy of such experiences come home, we say, as did Wordsworth in the presence of God's perfect day:[3]

> I made no vows, but vows
> Were then made for me; bond unknown to me
> Was given, that I should be, else sinning greatly,
> A dedicated Spirit.

Days of fresh daring and dedication are before us, in which, with Dewsbury, we may glad our hearts in the unlimited power of God; and, with Fox, know all things new; and the creation giving us another smell than before, beyond what words can utter.[4] Then will walls of partition crumble down and no longer hold us from wider fellowships and our rekindled mission. We shall welcome poverty and the scorn of the world, if they bring us nearer to our fellow-men and the heart of the Divine purpose.

---

[1] *Beginnings of Quakerism*, pp. 95, 96.
[2] Skipton Epistle, 1660, *supra*, p. 351.
[3] *The Prelude*, bk. iv.
[4] *Ante*, p. 11; and *Beginnings of Quakerism*, p. 38.

Our social service will be given alongside the needs of humanity; and we shall think first not of self nor of our Society but of the Kingdom and its righteousness. We shall find in every face some feature of the Divine love, and in the lowliest service some sacrament of grace. The radiant joy of our worship will overflow into the manifold tasks of the day's work and will turn each fresh duty laid upon us into a glad adventure. Our Captain will take us through uncharted seas in the service of His Kingdom; but as the Church trusts her helm to Him she will hold a true course and outride every storm.

This is the message that comes across the two hundred and fifty years that separate us from the blithe morning of Quakerism. It is the message that would have been uttered in ringing words by my friend, John Wilhelm Rowntree, who planned this History but received the wages of going on, not to death but into higher service, when the task was scarce begun. He breathed the brave air of the Divine Life and knew its bliss. As the shadows of blindness dimmed the dappled lights of earth to him, the windows of his heart were open towards the sunrising. He has ridden forth into the fuller day, as it seemed to us before his time, like Burrough and Audland, Caton and Barclay, but the members of the Church he loved may make his experience and prayer their own:[1] "Good men do not die ... Love bridges death. We are comrades of those who are gone; though death separate us, their work, their fortitude, their love, shall be ours; and we will adventure with hope, and in the spirit and strength of our great Comrade of Galilee, who was acquainted with grief and knew the shadows of Gethsemane, to fight the good fight of faith.

"Glory of warrior, glory of orator, glory of song,
    Paid with a voice flying by to be lost on an endless sea?

"No! Give me

    "The wages of going on, and not to die." [2]

---

[1] J. W. Rowntree, *Essays and Addresses*, pp. 417, 418, xlvii.
[2] Tennyson, "Wages."

"Thou, O Christ, convince us by Thy Spirit; thrill us with Thy Divine passion; drown our selfishness in Thy invading Love; lay on us the burden of the world's suffering; drive us forth with the apostolic fervour of the early Church! So only can our message be delivered. Speak to the children of Israel that they go forward!"

INDEX

(The figures in black type indicate the main entries.)

Abbé de Saint Pierre, 593
Abbeyholme, 353, 354
Aberdeen, xliii, 118, 134, 198, 204, **328**, 331, 334, 339, **446**, 510, 512, 549, 611
"Abhorrers," 93
Accuser of our Brethren cast down, 361
Acklam, Peter, 146
Acton, 221
Adams, Elizabeth, 216
Address to Protestants, 96
Adventure, Spirit of, *see* Spirit of Adventure
Affirmation question, **chap. vii.**, 509, 599
Agricultural labourers, 555, 559, 562, 564, 576, 577, 578
Alexander, Isaac, 420, 520
Alfred, King, 405
Algiers, 431
Allen, Robert, 563
Almeley, 357
Almshouses, 595
Ambulance work, 616
American Colonies, 167, 171, 190, 208, 216, 235-240, **267**, 268, 348, 367, **399-415**, 430, 436, 459, 482, 483, 492, 493, 582, 605, 618-623, *see also under the several Colonies*
Amersham, 381
Ames, William, 452
Ampleforth, 475
Amsterdam, *see* Holland, *also* 47, 48
Amyraut, Moyse, 57, 147
Anarchism, 600
Anarchy of the Ranters, chap. xii., 494
Anderdon, John, 93, 358
Andrews, Richd., 619, 620
Anger, cautions against, 205
Anne, Queen, 191
Antigua, 620
Antrobus, Benjamin, 433
Apocryphal Gospels, 147

Apollonius, 15
Apology of Barclay, *see* Barclay
Apostolic Christianity, xxiv
Appleby, 30, 33, 37, 219
Apprenticeship, 499, 536, 562
Arbitration, 257, 402
Archdale, John, 412-414
Ardiharrald, 332
Argyll, Marquis of, 334
Arlington, Lord, 64, 65
Armaments, limitation of, 592
Armorer, Sir Wm., 84, **226**, 227, 228
Armscott, 427
Arran, Lord, 57
Arscott, Alex., 531
Asceticism, 339
Ashby, Richd., 201, 450
Atherstone, 564
Athlone, 628
Atkinson, Aaron, 551
Atkinson, Christopher, 297
Atkinson, Henry, 426
Atkinson, John, 39
Atkinson, Capt. Robt., 30, 31
Atterbury, Bishop of Rochester, 202
Audland, Ann, *see* Camm
Audland, John, 219, 410
Austria, 216
Authority, Church, **chap. xii.**, 301, 305, 310, 312, 432, 537
Authority of State, 600
Axholme, Isle of, 464
Aylesbury, 10, 108, 381, 568
Aylesford, 595
Ayrey, John, 434
Ayrey, Thos., 250

Bache, Humphrey, 515
Bacon, Christopher, 358
Bacon, Roger, 120
Baddesley, 58, 564
Bailey, *see* Bayly
Bailey, Dr. Thos., 139

Baker, Daniel, 217
Balby, epistle of 1656, 17, 343, 563, 607
Baldock, 441
Ball, William, 377
Banbury, 198, 222, 253, 357, 488, 507, 548
Bandon, 627
Banff, 338
Bangs, Benjamin, 76
Banishment, see Transportation
Banks, John, 54, **367-369**, 422, 484, 500, 510
Baptism, 495
Baptists, 7-9, 25, 26, 51, 77, 99, 102, **108**, 133, 259, 294, 300, 352, 371, 373, 478, 492
Barbados, 43, 44, 46, 216, 235, 237, 240, 348, 349, 378, 603, **618**, 621, 629
Barclay, Christian (formerly Molleson), xliii, 339, 444, 446, 447
Barclay, Colonel David, 334, 335, 611
Barclay, Robert (the Apologist), early life and convincement, 328, 334-339; goes thro' Aberdeen as a sign, xliii, 339; *Anarchy of the Ranters* and conceptions of Church Government, 340-350; *Apology* and his Christology, xxxi-xlv, 184 n., 385-394, 396; interest in colonization, 403, relations with James II., 118, 134, 149-150; death, 444, 445; character, 445 - 447. Quotations from and references to writings, 88, 94, 168, 184, 186, 332, 365, 419, 450, 533, 534, 603, 611, 612; other references, 246, 306, 355, 396, 403, 420, 430, 606, 631, 635
Barclay, Robert, son, 188, 198, 204, 448
Barclay, Robert, uncle, 335
Barclay, Robert, *Inner Life*, 543
Barclay family, 448
Barking, 207, 539
Barnard, Hannah, 573
Barrow, Robt., 311, **409**, 410, 434
Batt, Jasper, 313, 358, 487
Baxter, Richd., 41, 52, 53, 65, 73, 82, 217
Bayly, Chas., 216, 237, 238
Bayly, Mary, see Fisher
Bayly, William, 12, 29, 235
Bealing, Benjamin, 488
Beane, Wm., 42
Beckham, Edward, 490
Bedford, Peter, 588
Bedfordshire, 358
Beginnings of Quakerism, corrections and additions, 8, 18, 229, 250, 271,

272, 331, 353, 419, 427, 436, 439, 555, 559, 560, 609
Bellers, Fettiplace, 572
Bellers, Francis, 571
Bellers, John, 27, **205**, 354, 386, 535, 565, **571-594**, 640
Bellers, Mary, see Ingram
Bellers, Theophila, see Eliot
Benson, Gervase, 304, 353
Bergen, 48
Berkeley, Lord, 402
Berkshire, *see* Reading, *also* 50, 274, 469, 482
Bermudas, 216
Bernstein, Eduard, 565, 587
Besse, Joseph, *Sufferings*, 160, 285
Bettesworth, Dr. John, 427
Bezae, Codex, 61
Bible, the, *see* Scriptures
Bibles, use of, by Friends, 220, 249, 315, 355, 528, 534
Billing, Edward, see Byllinge
Bingley, William, 105, 450, 488
Birmingham, 52
Birthright membership, **459**, 483, 498
Births, registration of, 258, **458**; feasting at, 514
Bishop, George, 29, 46, 51, 312, 556
"Black Bartholomew," 5
Blackbury, Sarah, 25
Blaikling, *see* Blaykling
Blaykling, John, 295, **304**, 409, 472
Blewbury, 569
"Bloody Assizes," 123
Boate, Gershon, 629
Bond, Nicholas, 18
Bone-lace, 515
Bonnets, 512
Book of Meetings, materials for, 1670, 256
Books, *see* Literature
"Books of Extracts," **377**
Booth, Mary, 241
Borden, Joseph, 620
Borders of Cumberland, **354**, **355**, 466
Boreman, Henry, 419
Borrisoleigh, 629
Bourn, Edward, 222, 245
Bowater, John, 437, 450
Bownas, Samuel, 425, 479, 480, **519**, 521, 539, 550, 551
Bowstead, John, 469
"Box" meeting, **272**, 286, 364
Boys, disturbance of meetings by, 259
Bradford (Yorks), 54
Braithwaite, George, 562
Bramber, 96
Bray, Dr. Thos., 492
Breda, Declaration of, 6, 29
Brewster, Margaret, 603

INDEX

Bribery at elections, 565, 589
Bridgeman, Sir Orlando, 42, 84
Bridgman, Robt., 492
Bridlington, 405, 447
Brigflatts, 519
Briggins, Peter, 192
Briggs, Thos., 248, 260
Bringhurst, John, 419
Bristol, Persecutions, 9, 46, 50, 51, 68, 77-78, 99-107, 109, 123; Wilkinson-Story controversy, 303, 304, 312-316, 319, 323, 360-366, 369, 470, 479-481; Bristol Workhouse, 585; other references, 8, 18, 26, 54, 59, 133, 137, 177, 180, 195, 219, 234, 238, 254, 259, 262-264, 273, 275, 276, 357, 415, 417, 427, 469, 488, 493, 530, 544, 545, 546, 547, 551, 595, 603, 617
Brize Norton, 338
Broughton (Cumberland), 469
Brown, Benjamin, 363
Browne, John, 238
Browne, Margery, 571
Browne, Sir Richd. (Major-General), 24, 27, 235, 419
Brush, Edward, 45, 46, 47, 241
Buckingham, Dukes of, 53, 65, 169, 216
Buckinghamshire, 274, 469, 475, 515
Budd, Thos., 483, 485
Budock burial-ground, 417
Bugg, Francis, 146, 263, 419, 440, 459, 487, 488, 489, 490, 491, 494, 496
Buildings, plainness in, 508
Bull and Mouth meeting-house, 24, 25, 41, 42, 45, 49, 53, 172, 178, 208, 234, 235, 238, 527
Bullock, Jane, 528
Bunhill Fields, 27, 435, 572
Bunyan, John, 85
Burial-grounds, 132, 257, 417
Burials, registration of, 258, 458; feasting at, 514, 515
Burlington, 405
Burnet, Gilbert (Bishop), 55, 128, 157
Burnyeat, John, 168, 267, 268, 302, 313, 331, 366, 421, 454, 503, 604, 625, 628
Burr, Thos., 108, 111
Burrough, Edward, xxvi, 12, 17, 22, 26, 29, 132, 186, 222, 234, 235, 288, 311, 410, 418, 444, 558, 600, 639
Burton (near Barnsley), 50
Burton, Philip, 125
Bury St. Edmunds, 490
Busby, Thos., 198
Bushell, Edward, 71

Bushell's Case, 45, 70-73
Business integrity, 497, 499, 508, 560, 561
Business - meetings, *see* Meetings for Church Affairs
Butcher, John, 450
Butterfield, Rebecca, 209
Buy, John, 470
Byllinge, Edward, 28, 402

Caesar-cult, 15
Callowhill, Hannah, *see* Penn
Callowhill, Thos., 209
Calvert, Giles, 419
Calvin, John, xxxii, 329
Calvinism, xxxii-xxxvi, xxxix, 390
Cambridge, 10, 138
Cambridge Platonists, xxxiii, 392
Cambridgeshire, 100, 256
Camfield, Francis, 450
Camisards, 617
Camm, Ann (formerly Audland), 286, 311, 454
Camm, John, 219, 353, 410
Camm, Thos., 311, 315, 321, 323, 360, 408, 472
Canterbury, 216
Capital punishment, *see* Criminal Law
Captivity, redemption of Friends in, 431, 453
Carey, John, 585
Carleton, Thos., 37, 355
Carlisle, Earls of, 354, 355, 425, 612
Carlisle, 367, 369, 425, 449
Carolinas, 412
Carrickfergus, 57
Carter, Dorothy, 372
Carteret, Sir George, 402, 403
Cartwright, Bishop Thomas, 138
Carver, Richard, 629
Castle Dermot, 503
Castle Howard, 425
Catechisms, Quaker, 386, 534
Cater, Samuel, 250
Caton, William, 19, 49, 219, 410, 421, 452
Certificates to emigrants, 403
Chadlington, 14
Chalkley, Thos., 425, 426, 508, 527
Chalmers, John, 448
"Chamber-rent," 569
Charleutt, 369
Charles II., 4, 6, 22, 29, 39, 53, 65, 81, 83, 85, 86-93, 99, 100, 106, 107, 108, 112, 113, 117, 238 *n.*, 403, 629
Chauncey, Dr. Ichabod, 107
Cheesman, Christopher, 50, 569
Chelmsford, 84
Chester, 138, 548, 603

Chesterfield, 371, 504
Chew, 137
Chigwell, 56
Children, *see* Education
Children, Meetings kept up by, 102, 226; membership, *see* Birthright membership
Chippenham, 317, 480
Christ indwelling, *see* Light within
Christian-Quaker, **318-320**, *and see* William Rogers
Christian-Quakers, **482, 485**, *and see* Wilkinson-Story controversy, *and* Geo. Keith
Christian Unity, 293, 350, 494, 589, 592, **638-642**;
Christmas Day, observance of, 207, 223
Christology, of Isaac Penington, 383-385
——, of Declaration of 1693, 385
——, of Early Friends generally, 394-395, 495
——, of Early Spiritual Reformers, 395
——, of Jas. Nayler, 384
——, of Robert Barclay, 388-394
——, of Wm. Penn, 385
Church and State, xxv, xlvi, **chap. xxi.**, 97, 179
Church, claims of State, *see* Church of England, Tithes, *also* xxv, 608
Church, definition of, xxiv, xxv, xxvi, xxvii, **chap. xii.**, 159, 351, 598, 641
Church Authority, *see* Authority, Church
Church Government, chaps. ix.-xii., *see* Organization
Church of England, 5-6, **65-68, 68-69**, 78, 86, 89, 99, 113-115, 131, 133, 136, 138-141, 144, 153, 154-157, 158, 190-191, 193, 202, 207, 462-464, 488-493, **496, 532, 533**, 608, 641, 642, 644, see also *Tithes*
Circular Yearly Meetings, 539, **546-551**
Cirencester, 586
Clarendon, Earl of, 4, 23, 53
Clarendon Code, 7, *see* Corporation Act, Uniformity (Act of), Conventicle Act (First), and Five Mile Act
Clarges, Sir Thos., 156
Claridge, Richard, 180, 185, 197, 496, 532
Clarke, Benjn., 419
Claus, John, 48, 409
Claypole, James, 255
Clerkenwell Workhouse, 534, 585
Clerks to Friends, *see* Recording Clerks
Clibborn, John, 628, 629
Coale, Benjamin, 471, 472
Coale, Joseph, 228

Coale, Josiah, 59, 244, 246, 248, 400, 410
Cock, Luke, **551-553**
Coggeshall, Elizth., 573
Colchester, 80, **225**, 234, 276, 452, 493, 548
Coleman, Nathl., 317
College of Industry, *see* John Bellers
Coln St. Aldwyn, 572, 586
Colonization, Quaker, **chap. xv.**
Colthouse, 463
Communism, 557, 565, 587
"Comprehension," 5, 6, 53, 153, 156
Compton, Bishop Henry, 138
Conceptions of Church Government, chap. xii.
Condemnations, papers of, 297, 301
Congregational singing, *see* Singing
Conscience, Liberty of, *see* Liberty of conscience
Conscientious scruples, *see* Affirmation question *and* 283, 284, 616, 620
Conscription, 617
Controversy, *see* Perrot division, Wilkinson-Story controversy, George Keith, Affirmation question, *also* 386, 469-478
Conventicle Act, First, 7, **40-52**
Conventicle Act, Second, 7, **64-81**, 227, 265, 294, 356, 373, 568
Convincement, cases of, 55-61, 325, 326, 328-337, 352-356, 367, 370-374, 381, 448, 462-464, 466-469, 517, 520, 550-553, 571-576
Conway, Lady, 392, 446
Coole, Benjamin, 192, 200
Cooper, Anthony Ashley, *see* Shaftesbury, Earl of
Cooper, Samuel, 109
Copeland, John, 378
Corbet, Counsellor Thomas, 108, 428
Cork, 56, 58, 64, 261, 501, 506, 532, 549, 562, 568, 604, 628, *see* Joseph Pike
Cork-cutting, 570
Cornish, Henry, 124
Cornwall, 234, 369, 493, 547, 583, *see* Thos. Gwin
Corporate consciousness, 401
Corporation Act of 1661, 7
Cotton, Priscilla, 522
Cox, John, 363, 476, 478, 481
Crab, Robert, 250
Craike, 475
Cranbrook, 8
Crane, Richard, 25, 45, 419
Creech, Thos., 139
Crefeld, 409
Criminal Law, Reform of, 16, 558, 588

INDEX

Crisp, Samuel, 527
Crisp, Steven, 27, 110, 111, 143-145, 179, 216, 226, 248, 290, 327, 370, 376, **452-454**, 478, 564, 566, 604, 606
Crisp, Thos., 312, 349, 489, 494
Cromwell, Oliver, 329
Crook, 312, 548
Crook, John, **24**, 235, 236, 255, 318, **358, 359**, 454, **474**, 516, 606, 613
Cross, Mary, *see* Fisher
Crosse, Edmund, 234
Crouch, Judith, 250
Crouch, Mildred, 250
Crouch, Nathaniel, 452, 485
Crouch, William, 569
Cudworth, Ralph, 528
Cumberland, 353, 424, 466, 515
Curtis, Ann (formerly Yeamans), 296, 470, 472
Curtis, Thos., 227, 296, **470-474**, 482

Danby, Sir Thos. Osborne, Earl of, 89, 91
Danzig, 360, 430
Darby, Abiah, 602
Davies, Richard, of Welshpool, 80, 224, 236, 352, 353, **421**, 422
. Davis, Richard, of London, 18
Dawson, Joshua, 363
Deacons, 483
Deal, 616
Deaths, *see* Burials
Declaration of Faith, 1693, **378, 379, 385**
Declarations of Faith, 378
Declarations of Indulgence, *see* Indulgence
Defrauding the revenue, 561, 602
Deism, 637
Delaware, 404
Dent, 548, 549
" Deputation money," 569
Derbyshire, 371, 408, 463
Derwentdale, Plot of, 1663, 29
Descartes, René, xxxi, xxxviii, xl, 392
Devizes, 137
Devonshire, 109, 123, 469, 547
Devonshire House, 253, 527
Dewsbury, Alice, formerly Meades, 223
Dewsbury, Wm., imprisonments, 11, 85, 125, 221-223; treatment of Perrot question, 242, 243, of Wilkinson-Story controversy, 304, 318-320, of York separation, 477 ; close of life and his character, **449-452**. Quotations from writings, 522, 541, 645 ; other references, 248, 284, 331, 358, 363, 444, 458, 606, 625, 631, 637

Dickinson, James, 285, 492, 551
" Diggers," 557
Diognetus, Epistle to, 598
Dirtcar, 222
Discipline, Quaker, chap. xviii., *and* 253, **256**, 259, 299, 325, 328, 483, *also under special headings*
Disownment, 30, 198, 253, 259, 487, 506
Dixon, Sarah, 480
Docetism, 385
Doctrinal Statements, xxx-xlv, 156, chap. xiv., 490, 592
Docwra, Anne, 440
Doily Bray, 144
Dolobran, 352, 636
Don-side, 332
Dorset, 121, 123, 189, 256, 325, 417, 469, 546
Dover, 11, 238
Dowell, Widow, 102
Draw-well, 301, 304, 347
Dress, plainness in, chap. xviii., 366, 374, 465, 556
Dring, Francis, 338
Drunkenness, 253, 595
Dry, Elizth., 266
Dublin, 261, 502, 603, 604, 627, 629
Duncon, Ann, 234
Duncon, Robert, 234
Durham, 12, 39, 50
Dutch War, 46, 53, 57, 89, 615

East Indies, 217
East Riding, 218, 409, 470 .
Eastern Counties, 234, 237, 254
Eccles, Solomon, 25, 246, 320
Eccleston, John, 201, 202
Eckhart, Meister Johann, 574
Edburton, 493
Edinburgh, 335, 548
Edmondson, Thos., 439
Edmondson, William, 260, 268, **422**, 503, 505, 506, 605, **626-628**
Edmonton, 266, 526
Education, **chap. xix.**, 191, 254, 257, 579, *see also* Latin, teaching of, Schoolmasters, Schools
Edwards, Cadwallader, 237
Elders, 483, 542-544
Elections, 413, 565, 589, 604
Eliot, John, 572
Eliot, Theophila, formerly Bellers, 572
Elizabeth, Princess, xxxi, xliii, 58, 62, 350, 392, 446
Ellis, George, 50
Ellis, Thos., 408
Elloughton, 476
Ellwood, Thos., **27**, 79, 173, 186, 192,

654 SECOND PERIOD OF QUAKERISM

235, 236, 293, **362, 422,** 427, 484, 516, 534, 568
Elson, John, 42
Elson, Mary, 272, 319
Ely, 256
Ely, Bishop of, 164
Embden, 360
Emigration, 459, *see also* chap. xv.
Enfield, 266
Enniscorthy, 629
Enock, William, 426
Epistle of 1666, 247
Europe, Peace of, 590-593, 613
Essex, 220, 469, *see* Colchester
Evans, Katherine, 271
Everard, John, 574
Everard, John (Hunts), 492
Everard, Margaret, 492
Eversholt, 359
Ewins, Thos., 51
Excommunication, 338, 373, 442
Exeter, 585
Expenses of Society of Friends, 285
Eyam, 373

Faith, Formulation of, xxx-xlv, chap. xiv.
Falconer, David, 338
Fallowfield, John, 426
Falmouth, *see* Thos. Gwin, 441
"Fanatics," **4,** 7, 112
Farnley Wood Plot, 39, 44
Farnsworth (Farnworth), Richard, treatment of Perrot question, 243-244, 247; controversy with Muggletonians, 244-246 ; share in Letter of May 1666, 247, 248 ; death, 244, 246, 247. Quotations from and references to writings, 43, 185, 419
Fawcett, Reginald, 30
Federation of Europe, 590-593
Fell, Bridget (afterwards Draper), 10, 263
Fell, Henry, 217
Fell, Isabel, *see* Yeamans
Fell, Leonard, 369, 370, 583
Fell, Margaret (formerly Askew, afterwards Fox), efforts for Friends imprisoned after Fifth Monarchy Rising, 9, 13 ; imprisonment at Lancaster, 33-37 ; marriage to Fox, 262-264 ; married life, 262-264, 428-429, 432, 439 ; later sufferings, 265, 267 ; attitude to Wilkinson and Story, 295, 298 ; her Whig antipathy to Penn, 172, 174, 189, 208 ; her protest against excessive discipline, 517-519 ; other references, 221, 250, 271, 454, 527, 601
Fell, Margaret, Jr., *see* Rous

Fell, Sarah (afterwards Meade), 70, 207, 286, 429, 432, 433
Fell, Susanna, *see* Ingram
Fellowship, xxvii, xxix, 249, 256, 365, 397, 406, 470, 633, 635, 639, 643, 645
Fenwick, John, 402
Fettiplace, Giles, 586
Fidelity, Declaration of, 183, 203
Field, John, 527
Fife, 469
Fifth Monarchy Men, 7, 9, 13, 221, 223, 230
Fire-briefs, 594
Fire Insurance, 595
Fire of London, 51, 53, 75, 251, 603
Fish, killing in breeding time, 565
Fisher, John, 185
Fisher, Mary (afterwards Bayly and Cross), 271
Fisher, Samuel, 4, 186, 288, 418
Fiskerton, 465
Five-Mile (Oxford) Act, 7, 52, 74
Fixed prices, 556, 560
Fleetwood, General Charles, 329
Fleming, Daniel, **31,** 32, 33, 37, 39, 82
Fletcher, Col. Benjamin, 165, 171
Fletcher, Richard, 34
Florida, 413
Forbes, Barbara, 332
Forbes, Jean, 338
Forbes, Roderick, 192
Ford, Philip, 208
Ford, William, 314
Foreign Missions, 215-217, 267, 613
Forgiveness of persecutors, 11, 27
Formalism, xxv, 327, 524, 539
Formulation of Faith, xxx-xlv, chap. xiv.
Forster, Josiah, 377
Foster, John, 259
Fox, Edward L., 617
Fox, George, escapes Fifth Monarchy imprisonment, 9, 12 ; service after Restoration, 219-221 ; imprisonment at Lancaster and Scarborough, 32-39 ; work in setting-up Monthly Meetings, 251-260, 292, 294 ; visit to Ireland, 260-262 ; marriage to Margaret Fell, 262-264 ; illness in winter of 1670, 265-267 ; work in setting-up Women's Meetings, 273-274 ; visit to America, 267, 268, 378 ; imprisonment at Worcester, 296, 297, 427-428 ; rest at Swarthmore, 428-429 ; service in closing years of life, 429-433 ; death and burial, 27, 163, 433-435 ; last advice to Friends, 435-437 ; character and personal appearance, 262, 437-444 ; will, 488 ; advices to ministers, 261,

INDEX

264, 410, 435, 436, 542; social questions, 554-559, 595, 596; attitude to Perrot question, 233, 234, 241, **242**; attitude to Wilkinson and Story, 296, 299, 301, 302, 303, 306, 313-316, 319, 347, 349, 474; other quotations and references to writings, xxvi, 16, 18, 19, 36, 75, 168, 173, 185, 216, 218, 222, 248, 265, 280, 288, **308**, 356, **378**, 405, 419, 421, **427**, 433, 441, 605, 645; other references, xxvii-xxxi, 60, 77, 78, 145, **245**, 248, 249, 265, 270, 275, 284, 291, 316, 358, **364**, **368**, 392, **409**, 422, 473, 475, 487, 488, 498, **519**, 525, 528, 529, 545, 601, 606, 615, 630, 631
Fox, George, the younger, 417, 563
Fox, Katherine, 439
Fox, Margaret, *see* Fell
Fox, Mary, 427
France, 217, 617
Francis, Alban, 138
Franciscans, 644
Franck, Sebastian, xxvi, 395
Frauds, Statute of, 576
Free Trade, 581
Freedom, growth and conception of, 205, 325, 326, 415, **607**, 642
Freemen in corporations, 132
Frenchay, 463, 480
Frettwell, Ralph, 348, 618, 620
Friedrichstadt, 430
Friends, Society of, *see* Quakerism
Friends' Reference Library, 281
Fry, John, 543
Fuce, Joseph, 11
Fullove, Lawrence, 47
Funerals, *see* Burials, 27, 102
Furly, Benjamin, **166**, 234, 237, 255
Furly, John, 600
Furnis, Richard and Margaret, 373
Furniture, plainness in, 507

Games, testimony against frivolous or cruel, 223, 224, 253, 513, 558, 565
Gardens, plainness in, 510
Gardner, Peter, 447-449
Garsdale, 548
Gatton, 527
Gaunt, Elizabeth, 125
Gee, Joshua, 202
Geology, Thos., Story's observations on, 424
George I., 194, 199
Germany, 216, 430, 551
Gibson, Thos., 46
Gibson, William, 303, 314
Gibson, William (1674-1734), 545
Gilburne, Christopher, 300

Gilpin, Dr. Richard, 469
Gilpin, Thos., 359
Glamorganshire, 408
Gloucester, Bishop of, 417
Gloucestershire, 109, 357, 547, 583
Godden v. *Hales*, 127
Godfrey, Sir Edmund Berry, 91
Goodaire, Thos., 14, 223, 454
Goodall, Elspet, 332
Goodson, John, 571
Gooses, near Romford, 207, 432
Gosnell, Wm., '84, 255
Gouldney, Henry, 197, 199, 202, 413, 433, 434, 473, 484, 491
Government, Church, chaps. ix.-xii.
Gower, Sir Thos., 39
Gracechurch Street, 69, 75, 111, 192, 253, 256, 433, 450, 491, 499
Graham, Richd. (see Preston)
Gratton, John, 80, 208, 246, 247, 370-375, 408, 422, 508
Grave, John, 302, 331, 354
Grayrigg, 548
Great Case of Liberty of Conscience, 74
Great Fire, *see* Fire of London
Great Pardon of 1672, *see* Pardon
Great Plague, *see* Plague
Green, Thos., 248
Griesheim, 409
Griffith, John, 359
Groom, Daniel, 109
Grotius, Hugo, 387
Group-consciousness, 401
Guidance, *see* Spiritual Guidance
Guides for travelling ministers, 509, 510
Guildford, 79, 95
Gurney, John, jr., 200, 202
Gwin, Margery, 417
Gwin, Thos., 174, 192, 208, 417, **425**, 462, 480

Habeas Corpus, 92, 427, 428
Hale, Sir Matthew, 43, 428
Hales, Sir Edward, 127
Half-Year's Meeting, *see* Ireland, Half-Year's Meeting
Halford, John, 427
Halhead, Miles, 312, 454
Halifax, Marquis of, 93
Hall, David, 532
Hall, John (York), 363, 475
Halliday, James, 333, 335
Hampshire, 85, 469, 546
Hannay, Robert, 484
Harding, James, 45, 46, 241
Harford, Charles, 103, 480
Harley, Sir Edward, 107
Harp Lane, 481, 482, 485, 487
Harper, Alex., 331

SECOND PERIOD OF QUAKERISM

Harris, Chas., 307, 475, 485
Harrison, George, 410
Harrison, James, 404, 409
Hart, Stephen, 18
Hartshill, 564
Harvest customs, 564
Hat-honour, 62
Hat in prayer, see Perrot division, 233, 253, 257, 292
Haydock, Robert, 192
Haydock, Roger, 370
Hayhurst, Cuthbert, 363
Healing, cases of, 358
Heathcote, Dr. Gilbert, 201
Hebden, Roger, 515
Hebrew, see Languages, and 36
Hellier, John, 123
Helling, Joseph, 39
Henchman, Humphrey, see London, Bishop of
Henderson, Patrick, 426
Henley-on-Thames, 461
Henry IV. (of France), 590
Herbert, Edward, Baron of Cherbury, 352
Hereford, 547
Herrnhut, 636
Hertford, 42, 241, 317, 369, 474, 526
Hertfordshire, 44, 469, 474
High Church party, 191, 193, 202, 207
High Commission Court, 138, 149
High Wycombe, 307, 369, 413, 475, 487
Highwaymen, robbery by, 370, 446
Hilton, Captain John, 126
Hitchin, 474
Hoare, Margaret, see Satterthwaite
Hogg, John, 475, 476
Holder, Christopher, 120, 378
Holderness, 8, 476
Holland, 19, 48, 55, 96, 128, 216, 313, 386, 430, 432, 452, 531, 551
Hollister, Dennis, 220
Holker Hall, 32
Holme, Benjamin, 499, 548
Holme, Thomas, 353
Honthorst, Gerard, 438
Hookes, Ellis, 48, 83, 282, 288, 527
Hooton, Elizabeth, 46, 246, 271
Hooton, Samuel, 245
Horn, 48
Horses, payments for Friends', 357
Horsham, 224
Horslydown, 42, 75, 253, see also Southwark
Hoskins, James, 198
Hospitals, 587
Hough, Dr. John, 138

Howard, John, 222
Howden, 475
Howell, Sir John, 70
Howgill, Francis, 12, 27, 30, 31, 34, 37, 38, 186, 215, 219, 222, 234, 235, 248, 288, 410, 418, 419, 444, 558
Howitt, William, 423
Hubbersty, Miles, 312
Hubbersty, Stephen, 454
Hubberthorne, Richard, 12, 22, 25, 27, 186, 222, 234, 410, 418, 444, 498, 558, 615
Huddersfield, 417
Huguenots, 413, 594
Hull, 476
Humbledon, 333
Humility of God, Perrot's doctrine of, 231, 232
Hunting with dogs, etc., 513, 565
Huntingdonshire, 256, 492
Hurd, Sarah (afterwards Whiting), 121, 122
Hutchinson, Dorothy, 560
Hutchinson, James, 629
Hutton, 295, 311

Ibbott, Thomas, 603
Ilchester (Ivelchester), 10, 92, 119, 121, 525
Implicit obedience, 349, 350
Imprisonments, see Sufferings
Independent Methodists, 544
Independents, 7, 65, 99, 217, 224, 329, 371
Indians, American, 210, 413, 414, 415, 436, 621, 622, 623
Individual responsibility, 259, 269
Indulgence, Declaration of 1662, 29
——, Declaration of 1672, 81, 353
——, Declaration of 1687, 130
Informers, 55, 67, 78-79, 102, 106, 109, 113, 125, 160, 294
Ingram, Mary (formerly Bellers), 572
Ingram, Susanna (formerly Fell), 572
Ingram, William, 572
Innkeepers, 16, 595, 596
Innocency with her open face, 61
Inquisition, 216, 229
Insane, care of, 571
Insolvencies, 560
Inspection of families in Ireland, 505
Inspiration, 468
Integrity, see Business Integrity
International questions, see under Armaments (Limitation of), Europe (Peace of), Native races, Negro slavery, War
Inverurie, 331, 332, 338
Inward Light, see Light within

INDEX

Ireland, condition of Quakerism in early Restoration period, 260, visit of Fox, 260-262, condition under Charles II. and James II., 502, 604, 624; sufferings of Friends during War, 624-629; strict discipline established by Irish Friends, 502-510, 483; attitude on Affirmation Question, 180, 185, 187, 188, 189, 199, 202; Half-year's meeting, 188, 261, 502; other references, 12, 133, 201, 234, 287, 302, 356, 363, 364, 367, 368, 426, 430, 433, 499, 520, 532, 535, 542, 551, 564
Islington Road School, 586
Ismeade, Arthur, 314, 317, 479
Itinerating Work, see Travelling Ministers

Jackson, Barbara, 511
Jackson, Henry, 222
Jacob, Elizabeth, 466
Jacobites (Jemmites), 179, 189
Jaffray, Alexr., 328-332, 334
Jaffray, Andrew, 340, 445
Jaffray, Margaret, 448
Jamaica, 43, 45, 217, 238-240
James II. (Duke of York), 81, 89, 91, 92, chap. v., 151, 173, 402, 403, 624, 629
Jeffreys, George (Judge), 107, 123, 125, 140, 151
Jenkins, Sir Lionel, 112
Jenkins, Wm., 531
Jennings, John, 317
Jerseys, East and West, see New Jersey
John of Leyden, 332
Johnson, Mary, 420
Jones, Robert, 381
Jones, Rufus M., quoted, 369, 379, 395, 525, 538
Jopson, Rebecca, 426
Jordans, 209, 463
Journals of Friends, 420-427
Judgment of God on persecutors, 46, 282
Justice Town (Lynchow estate), 424, 425, 466

Kaber Rigg, plot of 1663, 29, 30, 224
Kant, Immanuel, 593
Keillo, Isabel, 331
Keith, George, 333-334, 339, 378, 387, 389, 391, 430, 482-487, 491, 493, 495, 499, 526, 527
Kelk, 364
Kells, Book of, 638
Kelsall, John (of Dolobran), 636

Kelsall, John (of London), 596
Kelyng, Sir John, 44
Kendal, 30, 31, 32, 300, 321, 515, 539, 548
Kent, Thos., 481
Kent, 617
Key, Judith, 363
Key, Leonard, 472
Kiffin, Wm., 108, 137
Kilnsea, 615
Kingston-on-Thames, 432
Kinmuck, 532
Kirkbride, 354
Kirkby, Col. Richard, 37, 38
Kirkby, William, 37
Kirkby Moorside, 218
Kirklinton, 354, 425, 466, 469
Kit's Coty House, 595
Knight, Sir John (Sheriff of Bristol), 100, 102
Knockballymagher, 629

La Bruyère, Jean de, 169
La Chaise, Père, 91
La Rochefoucauld, Duke of, 169
Labadists, 56
Labour bureau, 559
Labour-saving machinery, 582
Lamb, John, 198
Lamboll, Wm., 471
Lancashire, 9, 10, 100, 109
Lancaster, 32, 33, 36, 224, 262, 442, 514
Lancaster, Brian, 322
Lancaster, James, 260, 268, 454
Lancaster, Lydia, 209, 426
Land question, 557, 559, 564
Langdale, 224
Langhorne, Thos., 37, 355, 360, 409, 410
Languages, teaching of, see Latin and 268, 533
Latey, Gilbert, 42, 47, 77, 150, 510, 515
Latin, teaching of, 525-532, 533
Latitudinarians, 157, 191, 335
Lauderdale, Duke of, 65
Laundy, Lewis, 44
Laurie, Gawen, 402
Law, codification of, 16
Law-abiding conscience, 17, 18, 112, 600, 610
Lawrence, John, 42
Lawson, Thos., 525, 528, 559
Lawton, Charlwood, 135
Laythes, Thos., 302
Leadership among Friends, 278, 350, 351, 416, 544, 633, see Barclay, Burrough, Crisp, Crook, Dewsbury, Farnsworth, Fox, Howgill, Hubber-

2 U

thorne, Penington, Penn, Story, Whitehead
Lecky, W. E. H., quoted, 116, 151, 637
Leicester, 220
Lely, Sir Peter, 438
Leslie, Charles, 459, **488**, 489, 494, 495, 496, 499, 527
"Levelling" principles, 556, 578
Liberty, *see* Freedom (growth and conception of)
Liberty of conscience, *see* Book I., *especially* 18, 94, 97, 131, 157, 158, *also* Toleration Act, Toleration, religious, Affirmation question, *and* 399-402, 412, 599, 603
Liberty of the Press, *see* Literature (Quaker)
Licensing Act of 1662, 418
Light within, xxvi, xxx, xxxvii-xli, 18, **249**, 325, 326, **330**, 334, 378, 383, 386, 401, 495, **497**, 540, 554, **596**, 599, 610, 635, **637-638**, 640, *see also* "Seed"
Lightfoot, J. B., Bishop, 642
Lilburne, John, 556
Limerick, 604, 628
Lincoln, 254, 256
Lincolnshire, 464
Linton, Richard, 429
Literature, Quaker:
  Censorship by Friends, etc., *see* Morning Meeting, *also* **280-281**, **496**
  Controversial pamphlets, *see* Controversy
  Cost of printing, 286
  Distribution of, 12, 146, 286, 419
  Printers of, **418-419**
  See also under separate titles of books and names of authors
Littleport, 250
Liverpool, 603, 617
Livingstone, Patrick, 246, 332, 333, 334, 340, 445
Lloyd, Charles, 236, 352
Lloyd, Elizabeth (formerly Lort), 352
Lloyd, Thos., 165, 352
Lobdy, Daniel, 616, 617
Locke, John, 158, 159, 166, 167, 412
Lodge, John, 255
Lodge, Robert, 260, 302, 363
Loe, Thomas, 56, 58, 59, **60**, 245, 246, 248
Logan, James, 424, **530**, **531**
Logan, Patrick, 530
London, Bishops of, *see* Compton, Sheldon, *and below*
London, Bishop of, Humphrey Henchman, 64, 68, 82

London, *passim*, especially, **9**, **22-29**, **44-51**, **68-77**, **110-111**, **125-126**, **253**, 292, 461-462, 469, 481, 491, 580, 581, 585, *also* 53, 109, 189, 195
London Six Weeks' Meeting, *see* Six Weeks' Meeting
London Two Weeks' Meeting, 253, 258, 292
London Yearly Meeting, *see* Yearly Meeting
Long Sutton, 121
Longford, 534, 539
Looe, 294
Lords of Manors, 559
Lothersdale, 181
Lotteries, 223
Low Church, 191
Lower, Dr. Richard, 37
Lower, Thos., 37, 172, 173, 174, 208, **296**, 297, 428
Lowther, Anthony, 62, 124, 164
Lowther, Sir John, 50
Lowther, Margaret (formerly Penn), 62, 124, 130, 141
Lucas, Nicholas, 402
Luffe, John, 229
Lurting, Thos., 431, 615, 616
Luther, Martin, xxiv
Luxury, 62, *see* Plainness
Lynehow, *see* Justice Town
Lyth, John, 476

Macaulay, Lord, charges against Penn, 124, 125, 137, 139, 152, 167, 170, *also* 128, 154, 163
Magdalen College Case, 138-141, 149
Magistracy, 112, 600, 610
Maids of Taunton, 124
Maidservants, 563
Maidstone, 216
Malebranche, Nicolas, 392, 393
Malins, Robert, 217
Malting trade, 516
Maltravers, John, 314, 317
Man, Edward, 84
Man, Isle of, 216
Manchester, 52, 461
Maning, Edwd., 44
Mansfield, 245
Marche, Richard, 38
Market-measures, 253, 561
Markham, Col. William, 171
Marlborough, 137, 487
Marriage, securing wife's property for her children of a previous marriage, 257, 264
Marriage of first cousins, 471
Marriage shortly after wife's death, **475-478**

INDEX

Marriages, 253, **254**, 257, 258, **262**, 297, **458**, 481, 514, **569**
Marsh (Esquire), see Marche
Marshall, Chas., 27, **357**, 427, 450, 522, 583
Marshall, Degory, 47
Martindale, Adam, 51, 82
Marvell, Andrew, 399
Marx, Karl, 571
Maryland, 216, 238
Masham, 364
Mason, Martin, 10
Massachusetts, 266
Masson, David, quoted, 21
Master and workmen, 555, 563-564
Masy, Henry, 353
Matern, John, 526
Matlock, 374
Meade, Sarah, see Fell
Meade, Sir Nathaniel, 207
Meade, William, **69-74**, 172, 173, 174, 189, **207**, 208, 571
"Meadites," 175
Medicine, improvement of, 587
Meditation, 382
Meeting for Sufferings, see Sufferings, Meeting for
Meeting-houses, see *under* places; protecting against persecutors, 77, 110; keeping Friends out of, in times of persecution, 21, **68-69**, 77, 89, 101-104, 110, 471, 472; destruction of, 21, **75-77**, 89, 101, 194; building of, 226, 459, 462, 463, 466, 470, 473, 629; registration of, 180, 462
Meetings, disturbance of, 21, 24-26, 27, 55, 101, 106, 219; holding through times of persecution, 9, 10, 21, 23, **26**, 32, 33, **41-43**, 49, 54, 55, 68, 69, **75**, 89, 110, 111, 225-228, 265, **300**, 624; weakness in holding, 77, 103-104, 294, 298, 375; children and women maintaining, 10, 102, 226, 227; sleeping in, 259; singing in, 261, 298, 300
Meetings for Church Affairs, see chaps. ix.-xii., *also* Yearly Meetings, Quarterly Meetings, Monthly Meetings, Preparative Meetings, Women's Meetings, Morning Meeting, Six Weeks' Meeting, Sufferings (Meeting for); basis of membership, 260, 298, 483, 506, 508, 509
Meetings for worship, nature of, 56, 58, 192, 225, 321, 336, **355-356**, 359, 479, 485, 545, 569, 573, 609, 635, see Retired Meetings, Silence in Meetings
Meggison, George, 364

Membership, see Birthright Membership *and* 483, 506
Mendlesham, 234
Mennonites, 183, 632
Merioneth, 353
Methodists, 464, 637
"Micah's Mother," 314
Middlesex, see Longford, *also* 41, 42, 189, 461
Middleton, Joshua, 476
Mildenhall, 487
Mile-end, 42
Militia, 101, **600**, 616, 618, 620
Militia, Commissioners for, 18
Milnthorpe, 302
Minchin, Thos., **338**
Minehead, 254, 501
Ministers, see Travelling Ministers, Geo. Fox, advices to Ministers, Sermons, *also* **278**, 483, 541, 542; advice as to tones in preaching, 426, 484, 541, 542; status of, 543, 545
Ministers, General and Yearly Meetings for, see Yearly Meeting
Ministers, maintenance of, 268, **360-365**, 450
Ministers, plans for distributing, 279, 358, 543, 544, 545
Ministry, nature of, see Sermons, *also* xxviii, **380**, 464, 541, 545, 550-553, 642
Ministry, Quaker, problems of, **chap. xix., 633-635**
Miracles, 368
Moate, 629
Modyford, Sir Thos., 239
Mohammedans, 590
Molleson, Christian, see Barclay
Molleson, Gilbert, 446
Molleson, Jane, 448
Monmouth, Duke of, 91, **117**, **119**, **122**
Monopolizers, 508, 564
Montgomeryshire, 353
Monthly Meetings, establishment of, chap. ix., 269, 291, see *also* Discipline (Quaker)
Monyash, 374
Moone, John, 235, 248, **411**
Moore, James, 322
Moore, Richd., 352
Moore, Thos., 13, 82
Moore, Wm., 216
Moorhouse, 425
Moravians, 636, 644
More, Henry, 392
Morning Meeting, **279-281**, 303, 320, 386, 419, 430, 432, **495**, 545
Morris, Lewis, 618, 620
Moss-troopers, 367, see Borders
Mucklow, Wm., 293

SECOND PERIOD OF QUAKERISM

Muggleswick, 29
Muggletonians, and Lodowick Muggleton, **244-247**, 372, 374, 418, 439
Musgrave, Sir Philip, 34
Musgrave, Thomas, 364
Mysticism, negative, of John Perrot, 232, 249, 336

Nailsea, 121
Nailsworth, 519
Native races, just treatment, *see* Indians
Nayler, James, 156, 219, 242, 243, 250, **419**, 558, **609**, 630
Negro slavery, 415, 436, 596, 618, 621
Nelson, John, 637
Nepho, Jeremiah, 124
Nevis, 46, 100, 620
New England, 216, 266
New Jersey, 402, 403, 415, 482
Newbury, 473
Newby Stones, 525
Newcastle, 563
Newgate, London, 24, 26, **27**, 41, 49, 51
Newton, Sir Isaac, 62
Nightingale, Edward, 476-478
Nightingale, Emmanuel, 478
No Cross, No Crown, **61-63**
"Nobility of Truth," 26, 301, 476
Nominated Parliament, 328, 359
Nonconformists, difficulties in meeting during persecutions, 41, 51, 53, 55, 102, 371, 373
Nonconformists, *see under* Baptists, Independents, *also* 6, **86**, 191
Non-jurors, 157, 488, 496
Norfolk, 50, 100, 109, 457, 464, 490
Norris, Isaac, 208, 622
Norris, John, 389, 392
North of England, 357, 483, 580
North of Scotland, *see* Aberdeen, *also* 188, 192, 195, **328-340**, 356, 512
Northamptonshire, 50, 109
Northern Counties Yearly Meeting, **546**
Northern Plot of 1663, 6, **29-40**, 221
Northumberland, 189
Norton, 336
Norway, 48
Norwich, 11, 111, 112, 417, 548
Notional Religion, xxxii, 335, 373, 376, 379, 453, 498
Nottingham, 35, 245
Nottingham, Daniel Finch, Earl of, 153
Nottinghamshire, 79, 375

Oates, Titus, 90, 449

Oath of Allegiance, 9, 14, 24, 111, 221, 227, 352
Oaths, *see* Affirmation question *and* **15**, 23, 36, 40, 181, **182**, 185, 197, 203, **413**, 497, 558, 605, 625
Occasional Conformity, 191, 201
Oman, Dr. John, quoted, 324
Organization of Quakerism, xxiii-xxx, **217, 250, chaps. ix., x., xii., xviii., 541-546**, *see also under* Yearly Meetings, Quarterly Meetings, Monthly Meetings, Preparative Meetings, London Two Weeks' Meeting, Six Weeks' Meeting, Morning Meeting, Sufferings (Meeting for), Women's Meetings, Discipline, Meetings for Church Affairs (basis of membership)
Ormonde, Duke of, 57
Orrery, Roger Boyle, Earl of, 59
Osborne, Elias, 122
Osgood, John, 255
Ostell, Jonathan, 549
Overseers, 504
Overton, Samuel, 426
Owen, Dr. John, 4, 56, 329, 400
Owen, Robert, 586, 587
Owstwick, 476
Oxford, Samuel Parker, Bishop of, 138
Oxford, 14, 56, 138, **194**, 404, 551
Oxford Act, *see* Five Mile Act
Oxfordshire, 65, 465, 504, 516, 548, 565

Palatines, 594
Pardon of 1672, 44, 50, 51, **82-85**, 119, 123, 222, 353, 569
Pardon of 1686, 125, 449
Pardshaw, 367, 424
Paris, 57
Parke, James, 224, 248, 418, 451
Parker, Alexander, 27, 248, 296, 299, 303, 349, 419, 454
Parliaments, *see* chaps. i.-vii. *and* Elections
Parnell, James, 25, 452
Parsons, Thomas, 78
Party Politics, 589
Pascal, Blaise, 169
Passive obedience, Anglican doctrine of, 113, 136
Passive resistance, 17, 18, 47, 599
Patrol work, 620
Peace of Nymegen, 604
Peace of Ryswick, 613
Peace Testimony, *see* War
Peachey, John, 51
Pearson, Anthony, 556
Pearson, Job, Lot, and Isaac, 466

INDEX   661

Pease, Joseph, 413
Peckover, Edmund, 621
Peel, 42, 253, 433
Penington, Isaac, imprisonment at Aylesbury, 10; other imprisonments, 381; writings and quotations from, 11, 15, 186, 326, 348, **380-382**, 418, 600, **610**, 611, **640**; Christology of, **383-385**, 635; attitude to Perrot division, 230, 234, 235, 236, 238, 255, 293; attitude to Wilkinson-Story separation, 295, 308, 317, 473; other references, 418, 422, 516, 527, 606, 631
Penketh, 520
Penn, Gulielma (formerly Springett), 75, 169, 422
Penn, Hannah (formerly Callowhill), 209
Penn, Springett, 420
Penn, Admiral Sir William, 55, 59, 73, 239, 403
Penn, William, early life and convincement, 55-60; imprisonment in Tower, 61-64, 418; *No Cross, No Crown*, 60-63; imprisonment and trial for speaking in Gracechurch Street, 69-74; imprisonment under Five-mile Act, 74; marriage, 74, 75; political activity, 1678-79, 94-97, 112; grant of Pennsylvania, 167, 171, **chap. xv.**; first stay in Pennsylvania, 99; service at close of Charles II.'s reign, 99; position and service during reign of James II., chap. v.; arrests and confinements after the Revolution of 1688, 151-152, 161-172; charges against, by Lord Macaulay, *see* Macaulay; disaffection towards, by Whig Quakers, 172-176, 208; second stay in Pennsylvania, 208; attitude towards Affirmation question, 190, 192; closing years of life, 208-210; estimates of character and career, 129, 210, 211, 246, 337; attitude on Hat-question, 293; attitude to Wilkinson-Story controversy, 299, 307, 313, 319; attitude to Keith controversy, **485**, 486; quality as a writer, his *Fruits of Solitude*, 168-169; other quotations from, and references to writings, 63, 74, 95, 97, 173, 185, 186, 196, 262, 269, 327, 379, **399**, 405, **416**, 420, 421, 439, 442, 450, 473, **529, 590**, 601, 604, **640**; miscellaneous references, 101, 246, 261, 284, 403, 429, 430, 469, 488, 489, 490, 508, 528, 568, 583, **606, 622**

Penne, George, 124
"Pennites," 175
Pennsylvania, 148, 165, 167, 170, 171, 172, **190**, 208, **chap. xv.**, 459, 482, 528, 530, 596, **605**, **622**
Pennyman, John, 255, 418
Penrith, 510
Pepys, Samuel, 22, 59, 61
Perfection, doctrine of, 495
Perrot, John, and Perrot division, 217, **228-250**, 251, 253, 255, 260, 337, 418, 502
Persecution, fleeing, *see* Meetings, weakness in holding, *and* 235, 298, 402, 403, 411
Persecution, *see* Sufferings of Friends
Persecution Exposed, 120, 160
Perswasive to Moderation, 128
Peter the Great, 601
"Petitioners," 93
Petre, Father Edward, 128, 151
Pharisaism, 521
Philadelphia, *see* Pennsylvania
Philanthropy, Quaker, *see* John Bellers, *also* 596, 597, 608
Philley, John, 216
Phillips, Daniel, 491
Phillips, Sir Edward, 120, 122
Phipps, Joseph, 516
Pietists, 594
Piety Promoted, 420
Pike, Joseph, 192, 199, **501-502**, 505, 506, 508, 509
Pike, Richard, 501
Pinder, Richard, 37
Pinney, Azariah, 124
Pitman, Henry, 124
Pitt, Andrew, 202
Place, Francis, 586
Plague, The Great, 47, 48, **49**, 52, 57, 410
Plaice, Thos., 123
Plain language, 62
Plainness, *see* Simplicity of life
Plans for distributing ministers, *see* Ministers, plans for distributing
Plots and fightings, testimony against, **12**, 29, 32, 112, 113, **615**
Plumstead, Edward, 527
Plymouth, 10, 48, 562
Poetry, Quaker, 467
Poland, 439, *see* Danzig
Politics, Quaker action in, 90, 94, 95, 98, 144
Poll Acts, 601
Polycarp, 15
Pontefract, 218, 279
Poolbank, 298, 301
Poole, 546
Poorer classes, relief of, 47, **49**, 50,

662 SECOND PERIOD OF QUAKERISM

360, 459, 460, 461, 547, 555, 558, 559, 560, **565-571, 576-587**, 588
Pope, Blanche, 39
Popple, William, 146, 159
Population, 459
Poulner, 220
Powel, Mary, 250
Powell, Vavasor, 352
Power, workings of the, 439, 527
Prache, Hilarius, 526
Praemunire, **14, 24**, 34, 109, 112, 160, 185, 223, 224, 265, 428, 569
Preparative Meetings, 458, 507, 510, 515, 562
Presbyterians, 7, 51, 61, 65, 99, 328, 329, 353, 371
Press, Quaker, 418-419
Preston, Patrick, 294, 295, 298, 301, 311, 481, 548
Preston, Richard Graham, Viscount, 125, 162, 166
Pretenders' (First and Second) Rebellions, 199, 200, 615
Price, Peter, 435
Prison Reform, 16, 558
Prisons, *see* Sufferings, as palaces, 11, 221, 228, 381, 450; employment in, 64, 220, **568-570**; preaching from, 224, 369; meetings in, 569; marriage in, 569
Prize-money, 617
Progress, elements of, 630
Prophesying in own will, 603
Prosperity, Quaker, *see* Worldliness
" Public Friends," 544, *see* Travelling Ministers
Public offices, 17, 132, 143, 401, **604-605**, 625
Publishers of Truth, *see* Travelling Ministers
Puritanism and Puritan outlook of Friends, **3**, 7, 8, 29, 53, 354, **374**, 460, 498, 524, 556, 558, 639
Pyott, Edward, 23

Quaker Act, 1662, **22**, 23, 112, 220, 226, 227, 235
Quakerism, antecedents of, xxiv-xxvi ; its universal outlook, xxvii, 215, 351, 401, 414, 415, 494, **chap. xxii.** ; legislation concerning, *see* Quaker Act, Toleration Act, Affirmation question, Tithes, Militia ; narrows into a religious Society, 248 ; relation to historic Christianity, 249 ; extravagances of early, 271, 488, 489, 490, 494 ; period of self-expression, 401, Book II. ; way of life, chap. xviii., *see also* Discipline, Quaker, Traditionalism, Worldliness ; causes for decline of, **631-638** ; position and outlook at close of century, Book III. ; caricatures of, 245-246, 463-464, 487-490. *See also* Affirmation question, Authority (Church), Christology, Church and State, Education, Emigration, Faith, formulation of, Individual responsibility, Leadership, Light within, Ministry, Organization, Quietism, Separatist movement, Spirit of adventure, Social Reform, Spiritual guidance, Sufferings, Testimonies, Traditionalism, Worldliness
Quarterly Meetings, 291
Queries, 500, 514, 617
Quietism and Quietist tendencies, xli-xlvi, 160, 177, 179, 391, 408, 495, 540, 602, 615, 635, 636

Rae, Richard, 533
Randall, Francis, 629
Randall, Samuel, 507, 508
Ranelagh, Richard Jones, Viscount, 169, 170
Ranters, 39, 242, 340
Ratcliff, 68, **76**, 253, 274, **485**
Raunce, John (High Wycombe), 46, 307, 475, 485
Raunce, John (Horslydown), 46
Ravenstonedale, 20, 125, 548
Rawlinson, Thomas, 426
Reading (Berks), 9, 84, **210**, **225-228**, 317, 323, 369, 381, **470-474**, 487, **568**
Recording clerks, *see* Ellis Hookes, Richard Richardson, Benj. Bealing
Recusancy, Acts against, 100, 103, 119, 131
Redford, Elizabeth, 601
Reeve, John, 244
Registration of births, marriages, and burials, 258, **458**
Registration of meeting-houses, 180, 462
Remonstrants, 387
Reresby, Sir John, 86
Resignation, 575
Restoration, The, 3-8
Retired meetings, 545
Rex v. Wagstaffe, 45, 73
Rhode Island, 400, 605, 620, 621, 622
Rich, Robert, 241, 348
Richardson, John, 447
Richardson, Richard, 267, 526, **527**
Richardson, William, 201
Richmond (Yorks), 79, 218
Richmond (U.S.A.), Conference, 378
Rigge, Ambrose, 85, 224, 370, 454, 527
Ringwood, 220, 546

Roberts, Daniel, 423
Roberts, Gerrard, 233, 266, 279
Roberts, John, 417, 423
Robertson, John, 532
Robertson, Thomas, 366, 472
Robinson, Sir John, 76
Robinson, Richard, 39, 302, 600
Robinson, Wm. and John, 466
Rochester, Lord, 170
Rodes, Sir John, 201; letters to him, *passim*, chap. vii.
Rogers, William, 103, 220, 293, 295, 298, **304**, 307, 308, **318, 342, 343, 344, 346, 347**, 349, 350, 361, 365, 419, **480**, 481
Roman Catholics, 4, 5, 14, 20, 53, 54, 65, 78, 81, 82, 86, 89, **90-91**, 93, 97, 100, 101, 113, **116-150**, 159, 160, 216, 229, 335, 394, 413, 442, 449, 616
Rome, 216, 229
Romney, Earl of, *see* Sidney, Henry, Viscount
Rosenallis, 626
Rous, John, 69, 255, 465, 563, 618
Rous, Margaret (formerly Fell), 175, 266, 432
Rous, Thos., 618, 619
Rowe, Sir Thos., 585
Rowntree, John Stephenson, quoted, 251, 314
Rowntree, John Wilhelm, quoted, 524, 630, 645, 646
Rudd, Thomas, 469, **603**
Rugby, 547
Ruscombe, 209
Russell, Lord William, 99
Russians, 590
Rye House Plot, 99, 112, 600

Sacerdotalism, 633
Sacheverell, Dr. Henry, 191
Saffron Walden school, 586
St. Austell, 370
St. Omer, 147
Salisbury, 14
Salt, William, 237
Salthouse, Thos., 54, 370, 454
Sam, Mary, 449
Samble, Richard, 419
San Domingo, 239, 240
Sancroft, William, Archbishop, 78
Sandy Foundation Shaken, 61
Sansom, Oliver, 359, 471, 502
"Satisfied" and "Dissatisfied" Friends, 192, *see* Affirmation question
Satterthwaite, Margaret (afterwards Hoare), 426
Saumur, 57, 147
Savoy Conference, 5

Scarborough, 38, 442, 447, 615
Schism Act of 1714, 191, 194, 201, 533
Schoolmasters, 7, 52, 448, 482, 520, 525, 526, **527**, 528, 530, 531, 532
Schools, 441, **525-532**, 583, 586; teaching without licence, 216, 526, 532
Schwenkfeld, Caspar, 395
Scientific researches, 424, 425, 530
Scoryer, Richard, 527
Scotby, 424
Scotland, *see* North of Scotland, Aberdeen, *and* 133, 430, 520, 532, 548
Scott, Francis, 122
Scriptures, *see* Bibles, use of, *and* **155, 156**, 315, 388, 396, 495
Sea Captains, 563
Seasonal Industries, 581
Second Conventicle Act, *see* Conventicle Act, Second
Sedbergh, 298, 370, 515, 519, 548, 549, 564
"Seed," Quaker principle of the, *see* Light within, *and* xxvii, xxxvii-xli, 27, 35, 388, 389, 495
Seekers and Seeking spirit, 57, 328, 353, 370, 642
Selby, 510
Seller, Richard, 615
Separatist movements, *see* Perrot division, Wilkinson-Story division, George Keith, William Rogers, Sarah Dixon
Sermons, Quaker, 58, **450**, 452, **550, 551, 552**
Settle, 603
Seven Bishops, 144, 157
Sewel, William, **531**
Shacklewell, 254, 528
Shaftesbury, Earl of (Anthony Ashley Cooper and Lord Ashley), 64, 65, 81, 90, 93, 98, 400
Sharpe, Anthony, 625, 626
Sheldon, Gilbert, Bishop of London, afterwards Archbishop, 4, 52, 65, 82, 358
Shepherd, Fleetwood, 62
Shrewsbury, 550, 603
Sibford, 463
Sidcot, 463, 531
Siddington, *see* John Roberts
Sidney, Algernon, 62, 95, 99, 101
Sidney, Henry, Viscount (afterwards Earl of Romney), 62, 163-166, 170
Sidney, Sir Philip, quoted, 554
Sidon, Henry, 58
Signs, testifying by, xliii-xliv, 25, 216, 238, 339, 340, 469, **602**
Sikeside, *see* Kirklinton

Silence in worship, 41-43, 225, 356, 575
Silesia, 526
Sim, Nancy, 332
Simplicity of life, see Buildings, Dress, Furniture, Burials, Gardens, Plain language, Tombstones, also 62, 501, 504
Sincerity in religion, 97, 437, 537, 555
Singing, see Meetings, singing in, also 355
"Sirrah," a word of abuse, 34
Six Weeks' Meeting, 275, 570
Skene, Alexander, 331
Skidmore, Joseph, 196-198
Skipton, 218, 351, 532
Sloane, Sir Hans, 588
Smith, John (Cambridge Platonist), xxxiii
Smith, Richard, 519
Smith, William (Notts.), 186, 245, 288, 359, 418, 419, 614
Smith, William (geologist), 424
Smoking, 429, 503, 509
Snake in the Grass, 488
Snead, Richard, 293, 317
Social justice, 63, **chap. xx.**, *see also under* Social Reform
Social position of Friends, 460-462
Social Reform, 63, 415, **chap. xx.**, **596, 597**, *also separate headings*, Agricultural labourers, Bellers (John), Bribery, Business integrity, Criminal Law, Defrauding the revenue, Free Trade, Freedom, Fixed prices, Games, Innkeepers, Labour bureau, Labour-saving machinery, Land question, Law-abiding conscience, Law (codification of), Liberty of conscience, Lotteries, Market-measures, Master and workmen, Medicine, Monopolizers, Oaths, Party Politics, Plots, Poorer classes, Prison Reform, Simplicity of Life, Smoking, Socialism, Temperance, Trade, Truck-system, Women (position of), Worldliness
Socialism, 571-594
Society of Friends, *see* Quakerism
Soldiers who became Friends, 224, 334, 358, 359, 422, 461, 501
Solport, 425
Somers, Lord, 169
Somerset, 10, 52, 54, 79, **119**, 121, 123, 189, 217, 218, 221, 256, 258, 358, 469, 546, 547, 562
Somerton, 121
Sothell, Governor Seth, 413
Soundy, William, 472
South Sea Bubble, 500

Southwark, *see* Horslydown, *also* 10, 253, 527, 563, 586
Sowle, Andrew, 419, 571
S.P.C.K., 491, 492, 496
S.P.G., 492, 493, 496
Speakman, Thos., 473
Spener, Phillip Jakob, 594
Spirit of Adventure, 211, 215, 351, 402, 405, 414, 454, 645-647, *see also* George Fox, advices to ministers
Spirit of the Hat, 292
Spiritual freedom, 642
Spiritual gifts, 634-635
Spiritual guidance, xxix, 291, 324, **447**, 533, 552, 638, 643
Spiritual healing, 368
Spiritual Reformers, early, xxiv-xxvi, 395
Spiritual religion, 537
Spitalfields, 42, 77, 582
Sports, *see* Games
Spragge, Sir Edward, 615
Springett, Gulielma, *see* Penn
Stafford, 85, 223, 565
Staithes, 551
Stamper, Francis, 137, 451
Stamper, Hugh, 420
Staples, Benjamin, 14
Starling, Sir Samuel, 55, 70
State and Church, xxv, xlvi, **chap. xxi.**, 97, 179
State of Society of Friends, Reports on, 462
Statistics, of sufferings, 98, 109, **114, 115**; of Society of Friends, **457-460**; of Persecution and sentences of transportation, 1664-65, 41, 42, 50, 51, 461
St. 29 Chas. II. cap. 9, 108
St. 35 Eliz. cap. 1, 34, 40, **106**
Steel, Lawrence, **325**, 530, 545
Steele, John, 306
Stevenson, Robert Louis, quoted, 169
Stillingfleet, Dr. Edward, Bishop of Worcester, 61, 64
Stirredge, Elizabeth, 422
Stoddart, Amor, 18, 266
Stoke St. Gregory, 121
Stokes, Jane, 237, 238
Stonehaven, 338
Story, Christopher, 355, 356, 423, 466, 508, 515
Story, John, *see* Wilkinson-Story controversy *and* xxviii, 14, 247, **295-297**, 298, 301, 303, 304-307, 308, 310, 311, 314, 318, **320-323**, 473
Story, Thomas, early life and convincement, **466-469**; *Life*, **423-425**; position on Affirmation question, 195, 200, 201, 202; other refer-

INDEX

ences, 174, 209, 472, 473, 480, 493, 508, 509, **539**, 545, 548, 549, **550**, 551, 601, 603, 612, 616, 621, 632
Stout, William (Hertford), 44
Stout, William (Lancaster), 193, 560
Stratford, 266
Street, 367
Strickland Head, 298, 525 (Newby Stones)
Stuart, Jane, 629
Stubbs, John, 33, 217, 260, 266, 267, 268, 454
Substituted imprisonment, offer of, 24
Sufferings of Friends, Records of, *see* Sufferings, Meeting for, *and* 8, 218, 257, **281**, **282**; behaviour under, **21**, **55**, **88**, 131, 132, 158; statistics of, 98, 109, **114**, **115**; effects of, on Quakerism, 225; judgment of God on persecutors, 282; sufferings during war in Ireland, 624-629. *See also passim,* **chaps. i.-iv., viii.**
Sufferings, Meeting for, 196, 197, **281-286**
Suffolk, 79, 109, 562
Sunderland, Robert Spencer, Earl of, 124
Superfluities, *see* Simplicity of life
Sussex, 256
Sutton Benger, 320, 543
Swale, Philip, 363
Swannington, 220
Swarthmore, 10, 32, 33, 34, 271, 309, 428, 432
Swearing, *see* Oaths
Swinton, John, 335, **336-337**
Sykes, George, 363

Tailors, 510, 515
Tanner, William, *Three Lectures,* 205
Tauler, John, 574
Taunton, 120, 122, 124
Taxes, payment of, 601, *see also* Defrauding the revenue
Taylor, Christopher, 355, 525
Taylor, John (York), 240, 442, 478, 570
Taylor, Thomas, 3, **85**, 223, 248, 363, 444, 454, 525, 565
Teachers, training, 527
Tea-drinking, 511, 512
Temperance, *see* Drunkenness, *also* 497, 509, 556, **595**
Tenby, 442, 481
Tenterden, 220
Test Acts, 89, 91, 201
Testimonies held by Friends, **377**. *See under* Arbitration, Baptism, Bribery at elections, Business integrity, Capital punishment, Christian unity, Church

(claims of State), Defrauding the revenue, Fixed prices, Games, Harvest customs, Hat-honour, Individual responsibility, Insolvencies, Land question, Law-abiding conscience, Liberty of conscience, Market measures, Master and workmen, Ministry, Monopolizers, Native races, Negro slavery, Oaths, Party Politics, Passive resistance, Plots, Poorer classes, relief of, Scriptures, Silence in worship, Simplicity of life, Social justice, Spiritual guidance, Temperance, Taxes, payment of, Tombstones, Trade, University learning, War, Worldliness
Tests under Corporation Act, 7, 123
Tests, 127, 153, 190
Thirsk, 475
Thomas, Margaret, 219
Thomas, Dr. Richard Henry, quoted, 525
Thompson, Gilbert, 520
Thompson, Thomas, Senior, 364
Thompson, Thomas, Junior, 364
Thornaby, William, 79
Tickell, Hugh, 302
Tideswell, 374
Tiffin, John, 302
Tillotson, Dr. John (Archbishop), 146, 157, 165, 184
Tindale, William, 423
Tithes, 16, **180**, 181, 257, **283**, 297, 300, 360, 369, 481, 559, 599
Toleration Act, xlvi, **153-158**, 180, 206, 462, 599
Toleration Act for Ireland, 201
Toleration, Religious, *see* Liberty of conscience, *also* xlvi, 6, **19**, 53, 65, 86, 97, 157, 201
Tombstones, 417
Tomkins, John, 174, 420, 490, 492
Tomlinson, William, 528
Toppin, John, 530
Tories, 89, 179
Tottenham, 532
Townsend, Richard, 407
Trade, *see* Business integrity, Fixed prices, Market measures, Master and workmen, Monopolizers, *also* 499, 500, 501, 515, 560
Traditionalism, 327, 454, 498, **520**, 537, 539
Trafford, Thomas, 503
Transportation, 23, **40-52**, 223
Transportation, Friends sentenced to, 50, 51
Travelling Ministers, 218, 225, 233, 269, 278, **351-374**, 494, **549-553**, 633

Trees, planting of, 424
Trenchard, Sir John, 169, 170, 171
Truck-system and fair wages, 555, 562
Truro, 547
Tuke, Samuel, 206
Turin, 57
Turks, 19, 431, 590
Turner, Robert, 426
Turner's Hall, 487, 491, 492
Twisden, Sir Thomas, 33
Twyn, John, 419
Tyrconnel, Earl of, 624

Ulverston, 180
Underbarrow, 298, 311
Uniformity, Act of, 5, 52, 532
Unitarians, 159, 160
University learning, 387, 533
Unlicensed printing, 418
Urquhart, James, 338
Ury, 338, 447, 448

Vaughan, Sir John, Lord Chief Justice, 73
Vaughan, Sir John (Earl of Carbery), 73
Vaughton, John, 450, 485
Vauvenargues, 382
Venice, 216
Venner, Thomas, 9
Vickris, Richard, 107, 137, 313, 393
Vigors, Joseph, 316
Vincent, Nathaniel, 108
Vincent, Thomas, 61
Virginia, 46, 216, 238, 239, 493
Visitation of families, 505
Voltaire, François, 202, 392
Vossius, 387

Waite, Thos., 363
Waiting, 388
Walden, Mr., 124
Waldenfield, Samuel, 450, 490
Wales, 236, 352-353, 408, 546, 550
Walker, George, 30, 31
Walpole, Sir Robert, 181
Walter, Sir William, 14
Waltham Abbey, 254, 525, 526
Wandsworth, 527
War, Testimony against. *See* chap. xxi. *and* Plots and fightings, *also* 60, 121, 168, 171-172, 415, 497, 503, 559, 604
Ware, 111, 474
Warre, Sir Francis, 124
Warwick, 125, 222-223, 449-450, 625
Warwick, William, 418, 419
Warwickshire, 9, 547
Watchfulness of spirit, 573
Waterford, 234

Watson, John, 604
Watson, Samuel, 420
Wellingborough, 450
Welshpool, 80, 224, 352-353
Wesley, Samuel, 464
West Dereham, 490
Westcott, B. F., Bishop, quoted, 644
Westminster, 18, 68, 253, 408
Westmorland rising of 1663, *see* Kaber Rigg
Westmorland, 10, 100, 180, 187, 188, 200, 203, 218, 294-312, 317, 369, 425, 469, 481, 542
Weston Zoyland, 122
Wharton, Robert, 30
Whichcote, Benjamin, xxxiii, xxxvi
Whigs, 89, 179, 189, 194
Whitby, 461, 549
White, George, 491
White, Jeremy, 114
White, Robert, 359
Whitehart Court, 68, 69. *See* Gracechurch Street
Whitehaven, 368
Whitehead, Ann (formerly Goddard), 319
Whitehead, George, efforts for suffering Friends, 22, 82-85, 207; imprisonments, 11, 108, 111; leadership after death of Fox, 452, 454, 488; attitude to Wilkinson - Story controversy, 296, 299, 303, 304, 309, 314, 319, 349, 361; attitude on Affirmation question, 183-185, 188, 191, 192, 193, 198-200; estimate of character, xlvi, 177, 178; death and burial, 27, 178; references to and quotations from writings, 43, 179, 186, 293, 393, 423, 450, 489, 596, 600; his *Christian Progress*, 423; other references, 34, 42, 69, 89, 110, 123, 126, 156, 174, 175, 208, 234, 246, 248, 370, 378, 487, 606
Whitehead, John, 11, 17, 38, 236, 248, 255, 303, 358, 363, 364, 370, 454, 465, 497
Whitehouse, John, 237
Whithart, Margaret, 227
Whiting, John, 92, 102, 105, 120, 121, 221, 235, 411, 496
Wicklow, 368
Widders, Robert, 268
Wigs, 58, 207, 509
Wigton, 353, 466
Wilkinson, John (Cumberland), xxviii, 355, 356
Wilkinson, John (Separatist), 295, 307, 323

INDEX

Wilkinson-Story controversy, 220, 255, **290-323**, **360-366**, 422, 428, 432, 451, **469-482**, **494**, 502, 508, 544
William III., 89, 128, 143, 151-153, 170, 183
Williamites (Billites), 179
Williamson, Wm., 425
Wilson, Ann, 520
Wilson, James, 550
Wilson, Robert, 419
Wilson, Thos. (Cumberland and Ireland), 550, 551
Wilson, Thos. (Cumberland and Kendal), 425
Wilson, William, 33, 224
Wiltshire, 180, 185, 295, 313, **316-317**, 369, 469, 478, 546, 547
Winchester, Marquis of, 170
Winchester, 221
Windermere, 548
Winstanley, Gerrard, 556, 557
Witney, 359
Women, position of, **270-271**
Women's Meetings, *see* Box meeting and **272-274**, **286-288**, 297, 312, 464, **465**, 471, 473, 474, 480, 556
Woodbridge, 548
Woodcock, William, 18
Wooldale, 222
Woolman, John, 63, 415, 438, 596, 622
Worcester, **296-297**, 427, 547
Worcestershire, 187
Worldliness, 327, 436, 437, 499, 500, 503, 508, 509, 522, 636
Workhouses, 571
Worminghurst, 96
Wren, Sir Christopher, 75
Wresle, Thos., 420
Wrexham, 224
Wrington, 121
Wyeth, Joseph, 192, 201, 489

Yeamans, Isabel (formerly Fell, afterwards Morrice), 430
Yearly Meeting, 1668-69 (Ministers), 217, 276
——, 1670 (Ministers), 276
——, 1671 (Ministers), 276
——, 1672 (Ministers and others), 276, 280, 282
——, 1673, 277, 293, 294, 340
——, 1674 (Ministers), 277, 340, 428
——, 1675 (Ministers), 277, 283, 300-301, 500
——, 1676 (Ministers), 277, 284, 285, 348, 417
——, 1677 (Ministers), 277, 307, 309, 347, 430; *see also* 307, **309**, 313, 370, 470 for additional meeting

Yearly Meeting, 1678, 277, 616
——, 1679, 285, 319, 360, 431, 616
——, 1680, 286
——, 1681, 546
——, 1682, 109, 617
——, 1683, 110
——, 1684, 474
——, 1685, 462
——, 1686, *nil*
——, 1687, 133
——, 1688, 132, 144, 145, 146, 435, 450, 625
——, 1689, 160, 161, 481
——, 1690, 161, 462, 535
——, 1691, 167, 436, 466, 479, 481
——, 1692, 179, 183, 193, 452
——, 1693, 462, 464, 469, 617
——, 1694, 483, 484, 546
——, 1695, 486, 487, 535
——, 1696, 187, 535
——, 1697, 187, 188, 287, 491, 584
——, 1698, 174, 208, 481, 504, 508, 546, 602
——, 1699, 481, 482, 491, 492, 546
——, 1700, 466, 474, 492, 617, 618
——, 1701, *nil*
——, 1702, 541, 603
——, 1703, 602
——, 1704, 506, 539
——, 1705, *nil*
——, 1706, 534
——, 1707, *nil*
——, 1708, 620
——, 1709, 481, 534, 602
——, 1710, 1711, *nil*
——, 1712, 192, 193
——, 1713, 193, 194, 198
——, 1714, 189, 193, 194
——, 1715, 194, 195, 602
——, 1716, 199, 200, 615
——, 1717, 200, 201, 545
——, 1718, *nil*
——, 1719, 602
——, 1720, 534, 546, 547
——, 1721, 201, 618
——, 1722, 203, 204
——, 1723, 545, 602, 618
——, 1724, *nil*
——, 1725, 198, 500
——, later references, 206, 376, 377, 378, 459, 533, 534, 542, 543, 615, 617, 618, 641
Yearly and Half-Yearly Meetings, America, Amsterdam, Dublin, establishment of, 261, 408, 430
Yearly Meetings for business at London, establishment of, **275-278**; other references, *see* below *and* 217, 488, 509. *See also* Books of Extracts, Recording clerks, Queries

Yearly Meetings for worship, 465, 479, 539, 546-551
Yearly Meetings of Ministers, 255, *see* below (in 1678, etc., held at time of Y.M. for business); elders' part of it after 1754, 543
Yeat, Wm. and Hannah (formerly Wrenn), 569
Yoakley, Michael, 595

York, 11, 29, 221, 222, 357, 429, **465**, 470, **475-478**, 548, 551, **569-570**
York, Duke of, *see* James II.
Yorkshire, 9, 39, 50, 79, 84, 85, 109, 112, 146, 180, 218, 256, 258, 278, **362-364**, 419, 462, 465, **475-478**, 504, 511, 542

Zachary, Thomas, 79, 95

THE END

Printed by R. & R. CLARK, LIMITED, *Edinburgh*.

www.ingramcontent.com/pod-product-compliance
Lightning Source LLC
Chambersburg PA
CBHW071229300426
44116CB00008B/970